Domjan and Burkhard's

The Principles of
Learning and Behavior

3_{RD}
EDITION

Domjan and Burkhard's

The Principles of
Learning and Behavior

3**RD**
EDITION

Revised by Michael Domjan

University of Texas at Austin

Brooks/Cole Publishing Company
Pacific Grove, California

ITP ™ The trademark ITP is used under license.

Brooks/Cole Publishing Company
A Division of Wadsworth, Inc.

Printed in the United States of America

10 9 8 7 6 5 4 3

Library of Congress Cataloging in Publication Data
Domjan, Michael, [date]
   The principles of learning and behavior / Michael Domjan.—3rd ed.
      p. cm.
   Includes bibliographical references and index.
   ISBN 0-534-18912-1
   1. Learning, Psychology of.   2. Conditioned response.
3. Behaviorism (Psychology)   I. Title.
BF319.D65 1992
150.19'43—dc20   92-10828
                                                   CIP

Sponsoring Editor: *Vicki Knight*
Editorial Assistant: *Heather Graeve*
Production Editor: *Linda Loba*
Manuscript Editor: *Ann Mirels*
Permissions Editor: *Karen Wootten*
Interior Design: *E. Kelly Shoemaker*
Cover Design: *Katherine Minerva*
Art Coordinator: *Lisa Torri*
Photo Researcher: *Gail Meese*
Photo Coordinator: *Larry Molmud*
Typesetting: *Graphic World*
Cover printing: *Phoenix Color Corporation*
Printing and Binding: *R.R. Donnelley and Sons, Crawfordsville*

To Alice, Katherine, and Paul

Preface

Investigations of learning and behavior have been an integral part of the study of psychology throughout much of the twentieth century. In addition to providing important insights into the ways in which experience can lead to long-lasting changes in behavior, investigations of learning and behavior provide the behavioral technology for many allied fields, including behavioral neuroscience, developmental psychobiology, psychopharmacology, behavioral medicine, and behavioral toxicology. Studies of basic associative learning phenomena also provide the building blocks for some prominent theories of cognitive function. Thus, the study of learning is at the crossroads of many different approaches to investigating behavior.

The aim of the third edition of this book is the same as the aim of previous editions—to provide a lucid introduction to contemporary phenomena and theories about learning and behavior. The book strives to present a balanced perspective of the contemporary state of the field, rather than advocating a particular point of view. We attempt to point out the strengths and weaknesses of ideas in an even-handed fashion. As before, we have tried to emphasize the development of ideas instead of simply listing major findings. Although some contemporary ideas and phenomena cannot yet be fully integrated with previous findings, we have tried to provide an integrated approach wherever possible.

The order of chapters in the third edition is the same as it was in the second edition. Information is presented in increasing order of complexity, both within chapters and across chapters. The basic ideas presented at the beginning of each chapter serve as a foundation for material presented in subsequent chapters, with critical concepts repeated as they are needed. Technical terms are identified by bold-faced type the first time they appear, and definitions for them are provided in the Glossary.

Much has happened in the field of learning and behavior since 1985, when the previous edition of this book was prepared. The third edition presents new perspectives on old phenomena, as well as new phenomena and ideas that have become important in recent years. Numerous new examples of learning are provided in the revised text, many involving human subjects. In addition, we made a greater effort to use actual rather than hypothetical data in the illustrations.

Chapter 1 has been largely rewritten to include discussion of the roots of learning studies in questions dealing with comparative cognition, functional neurology, and animal models of human behavior. Chapter 1 also includes a more detailed discussion of methodological issues in the study of learning, as well as discussions of the use of animals in research and alternatives to animal research. Chapter 2 introduces the concept of a "modal action pattern" in place of "fixed action pattern" and includes numerous new human examples of habituation and sensitization. Chapter 3 includes new information about the origins of classical conditioning and a revised discussion of control procedures in classical conditioning. In Chapter 4, the discussion of the Rescorla/Wagner model has been expanded and its shortcomings better described. In addition, a number of new theories have been added to the chapter, including scalar expectancy theory, the comparator hypothesis, SOP, and AESOP. Chapter 5 includes an expanded discussion of response shaping and an expanded discussion of reinterpretations of the learned helplessness effect in terms other than learned helplessness theory. In Chapter 6, discussions of the matching law and of concurrent-chain schedules have been updated and expanded. Chapter 7 now includes a critical appraisal of the behavioral bliss point approach and an expanded discussion of optimal foraging within the context of behavioral regulation. In Chapter 8, much new information has been added about configural conditioning, contextual conditioning, and control of behavior by hierarchical relations among stimuli. In Chapter 9, the concept of predatory imminence, and related ideas, has been added. Chapter 10 includes a new section on contemporary studies of the associative structure of instrumental conditioning. In Chapter 11, the discussion of memory mechanisms is now organized around the concepts of acquisition and stimulus coding, retention and rehearsal, retrieval, and forgetting. In Chapter 12, new information has been added on serial pattern learning in simultaneous chains, perceptual concept learning, and language learning by nonhuman animals.[*]

I am grateful for the assistance of a number of individuals including Dr. Robert H. I. Dale, Butler University; Dr. Michael S. Fanselow, University of California, Los Angeles; Dr. Robert Ferguson, Buena Vista College; Dr. Nelson Freedman, Queen's University; Dr. Lewis R. Gollub, University of Maryland at College Park; Dr. Harry Strub, University of

[*]As before, the book is accompanied by a test bank.

Winnipeg; and Dr. Michael Zeiler, Emory University, who provided thoughtful reviews of the revision, and numerous others who also provided information and suggestions. I am also grateful to Vicki Knight for her editorial guidance and to Linda Loba for coordinating the production of the book.

Michael Domjan

Brief Contents

Contents

3 | *Classical Conditioning: Foundations* 53

7   *Reinforcement: Theories and Experimental Analysis*   *192*

8   *Stimulus Control of Behavior*   *221*

Domjan and Burkhard's

The Principles of
Learning and Behavior

3_{RD}
EDITION

1 *Introduction*

The goal of this chapter is to introduce the reader to the study of learning and behavior. We begin by discussing key concepts in the study of learning from a historical standpoint, including a description of the origins of experimental research in the area. These origins lie in studies of the evolution of intelligence, functional neurology, and animal models of human behavior. The defining characteristics of learning will be described next, followed by a discussion of methodological approaches to the study of learning. Because numerous experiments on learning have been performed with animal subjects, we will conclude the chapter by considering the pros and cons of using animals in research.

People have always been interested in understanding behavior, be it their own or the behavior of others. This interest is more than idle curiosity. How we live our lives is largely governed by our own actions and the actions of others. Whether you were admitted to the college of your choice depended mainly on your prior scholastic record and the decisions of an admissions officer. Whether you get along well with your roommates depends on how accommodating you are and on what they do that you find irritating. Whether you get to school on time depends on how crowded the roads are and how well you manage to navigate the traffic.

Any systematic effort to understand behavior must include consideration of what we learn and how we learn it. Numerous aspects of both human and animal behavior are the products of learning. We learn to read, to write, and to count. We learn how to walk down stairs without falling, how to open doors, how to ride bicycles, and how to swim. We also learn when to relax and when to become anxious. We learn what foods are good for us and what will make us sick. We learn who will be fun to visit with and whose company to avoid. We learn how to tell when someone is unhappy and when that person feels fine. We learn when to carry an umbrella and when to take an extra scarf. Life is filled with activities and experiences that are shaped by what we have learned.

Learning is one of the biological processes that are crucial for the survival of many forms of animal life. The integrity of life depends on a variety of biological functions. Animals have to take in nutrients, eliminate metabolic wastes, and otherwise maintain proper balance in internal functions. Through evolution, a variety of biological systems have emerged to accomplish these tasks. Many of these systems are primarily physiological, such as the respiratory, digestive, and excretory systems. However, finely tuned internal physiological processes are often not enough to maintain the integrity of life. Animals and

people live in environments that are constantly changing because of climatic changes, changes in food resources, the coming and going of predators, and other external factors. Adverse effects of environmental change often have to be minimized by behavioral adjustments. Animals have to know, for example, how to find and obtain food as food sources change, avoid predators as new ones enter their territory, and find new shelter when storms destroy their old homes. Accomplishing these tasks obviously requires motor movements, such as walking and manipulating objects. These tasks also require the ability to predict important events in the environment, such as the availability of food in a particular location and at a particular time. Acquisition of new motor behavior and new anticipatory reactions involves learning. Thus, animals learn to go to a new water hole when the old one dries up and learn new anticipatory reactions when new sources of danger appear. These learned adjustments to the environment are no less important for survival than internal physiological processes such as respiration and digestion.

Most people automatically associate learning with the acquisition of new behavior. That is, they identify learning by the gradual appearance of a new response in the organism's repertoire. This is the case when people learn to read, ride a bicycle, or play a musical instrument. However, the behavior change involved in learning can just as well consist of the decrease or loss of some behavior in the organism's repertoire. A child, for example, may learn not to cross the street when the traffic light is red, not to grab food from someone else's plate, and not to yell and scream when someone is trying to take a nap. Learning to withhold responses is just as important as learning to make responses, if not more so.

When considering learning, people commonly focus on the kinds of learning that require special training—the kinds of learning that take place in public schools and colleges, for example. Learning calculus, physics, or the skill of making a triple somersault when diving does require special instruction. However, we also learn all kinds of things without an expert teacher or coach during the course of interacting routinely with other people and upon encountering events in the environment. Children, for example, learn how to open doors and windows, how to respond to a ringing telephone, when to avoid a hot stove, and when to duck so as not to get hit by a thrown ball. College students learn how to find their way around campus, how to avoid heartburn from cafeteria food, and how to predict when a roommate will stay out late at night, all without instruction.

In the coming chapters, we will survey research on basic principles of learning and behavior. We will deal with the types of learning and behavior fundamental to life that, like breathing, they are often ignored. Our focus will be on pervasive and basic forms of learning that are a normal part of living, even though we rarely think about them. We will consider the learning of simple relationships between events in the environment, the learning of simple motor movements, and the learning of emotional reactions to stimuli. These forms of learning are investigated in experiments that involve "training" procedures of various sorts. However, these forms of learning occur in the lives of people and animals without explicit or organized instruction or schooling.

Historical Antecedents

Theoretical approaches to the study of learning have their roots in the philosophy of René Descartes (see Figure 1.1). Before Descartes, the common belief was that human behavior was entirely determined by conscious intent and free will. People's actions were not thought to be controlled by external stimuli or mechanistic natural laws. What someone did was presumed to be the result of

Figure 1.1 René Descartes (1596–1650). *(Bettman Archive.)*

his or her will or deliberate intention. Descartes took exception to this view of human nature because he recognized that many things people do are automatic reactions to external stimuli. However, he was not prepared to totally abandon the idea of free will and conscious control of one's actions. He therefore formulated a dualistic view of human behavior known as Cartesian **dualism.** According to this view, there are two classes of human behavior: involuntary and voluntary. Some actions are involuntary and occur in response to external stimuli. These actions are called **reflexes.** Another aspect of human behavior involves voluntary actions that do not have to be triggered by external stimuli; rather, they occur because of the person's conscious choice to act in a certain way.

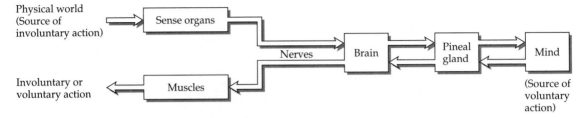

Figure 1.2 Diagram of Cartesian dualism. Events in the physical world are detected by sense organs. From here the information is passed along to the brain. The brain is connected to the mind by way of the pineal gland. Involuntary action is produced by a reflex arc that involves messages sent first from the sense organs to the brain and then from the brain to the muscles. Voluntary action is initiated by the mind, with messages sent to the brain and then the muscles.

The details of Descartes' dualistic view of human behavior are diagramed in Figure 1.2. Let us first consider the mechanisms of involuntary, or reflexive, behavior. Stimuli in the environment are detected by the person's sense organs. The sensory information is then relayed to the brain through nerves. From the brain, the impetus for action is sent through nerves to the muscles that create the involuntary response. Thus, involuntary behavior involves the reflection by the brain of stimulus input into response output.

Several aspects of this system are noteworthy. Stimuli in the external environment are seen as the cause of all involuntary behavior. These stimuli produce involuntary responses by way of a neural circuit that includes the brain. However, only one set of nerves is involved. Descartes assumed that the same nerves transmitted information from the sense organs to the brain and from the brain down to the muscles. This circuit, he believed, permitted rapid reactions to external stimuli; for example, quick withdrawal of one's finger from a hot stove.

Descartes assumed that the involuntary mechanism of behavior was the only one available to animals other than humans. According to this view, all of nonhuman animal behavior occurs as reflex responses to external stimuli. Thus, Descartes did not believe that nonhuman animals had free will or that they were capable of voluntary, conscious actions. He considered free will and voluntary behav-

ior to be uniquely human attributes. This superiority of humans over other animals existed because only human beings were thought to have a mind, or soul. The mind was assumed to be a nonphysical entity. But if the mind is not physical, how can it generate the physical movements involved in voluntary behavior? Descartes believed that the mind was connected to the physical body by way of the pineal gland, near the brain. Because of its connection to the brain, the mind could be aware of and keep track of involuntary behavior. Through this mechanism, the mind could also initiate voluntary actions. Because voluntary behavior was initiated in the mind, it could occur independently of external stimulation.

From the mind–body dualism introduced by Descartes, two intellectual traditions emerged. One was concerned with the contents and workings of the mind; the other, with the mechanisms of reflexive behavior.

Historical Developments in the Study of the Mind

As we noted, one set of issues that concerned philosophers involved questions about what is in the mind and how the mind works. Descartes had some things to say about both these questions. Because Descartes thought the mind was connected to the brain by way of the pineal gland, he believed that some of what is in the mind came from sense experiences. However, he also believed that some of the contents of the mind were innate — that they existed in all human beings independent of worldly experience. He believed that all humans were born with certain ideas, including the concept of God, the concept of self, and certain fundamental axioms of geometry (such as the fact that the shortest distance between two points is a straight line). The philosophical approach that assumes we are born with innate ideas about certain things is called **nativism.**

Some philosophers after Descartes took issue with the nativist position. The British philosopher John Locke (1632–1704), for example, believed that all the ideas people had were acquired directly or indirectly through experiences after birth. He believed that human beings were born totally innocent of any preconceptions about the world. The mind was considered to start out as a clean slate (*tabula rasa,* in Latin), to be gradually filled with ideas and information as the person had various sense experiences. This philosophical approach to the question of what the mind contains is called **empiricism.** Empiricism was accepted by a group of British philosophers who lived from the seventeenth to the nineteenth century and who came to be known as the British empiricists.

The nativist and empiricist philosophies differed not only on what the mind was assumed to contain but also on how the mind was assumed to operate. Descartes believed that the mind did not function in a predictable and orderly manner according to discoverable rules or laws. One of the first to propose an alternative to this view was the British philosopher Thomas Hobbes (1588–1679). Hobbes accepted the distinction between voluntary and involuntary behavior stated by Descartes and also accepted the notion that voluntary behavior was controlled by the mind. However, unlike Descartes, he believed that the mind operated just as predictably and lawfully as reflex mechanisms. More specifically, he proposed that voluntary behavior was

governed by the pursuit of pleasure and the avoidance of pain. Thus, functions of the mind were not determined by reason but by a principle of **hedonism.** Whether or not the pursuit of pleasure and the avoidance of pain were laudable or desirable was not an issue for Hobbes. Hedonism was simply a fact of life. As we will see, this conception of behavior has remained with us in one form or another to the present day.

According to the British empiricists, another important aspect of how the mind works involved the concept of **association.** Recall that empiricism assumes that all ideas originate from sense experiences. But how do our experiences of various colors, shapes, odors, and sounds allow us to arrive at more complex ideas? Consider, for example, the concept of a car. If someone says the word *car,* you have an idea of what the thing may look like, what it is used for, and how you might feel if you sat in it. Where do all these ideas come from just given the sound of the letters *c, a,* and *r*? The British empiricists proposed that simple sensations were combined into more complex ideas by associations. Because you have heard the word *car* when you saw a car, considered using one to get to work, or sat in one, associations may have become established between the word *car* and various aspects of cars. The British empiricists considered such associations very important in their explanation of how the mind works; hence, they devoted considerable effort to detailing the rules of associations.

The British empiricists accepted two sets of rules for the establishment of associations, one primary and the other secondary. The primary rules were originally set forth by the ancient Greek philosopher Aristotle. He proposed three principles for the establishment of associations — contiguity, similarity, and contrast. Of these, the contiguity principle has been the most prominent in considerations of associations. It states that if two events repeatedly occur together, they will become associated. Once this association has been established, the occurrence of one of the events will evoke a memory of the other event. The similarity and contrast principles state that two things will become associated if they are similar in some respect or have some contrasting characteristics (one might be strikingly tall and the other strikingly short, for example).

The various secondary laws of associations were set forth by a number of empiricist philosophers—among them, Thomas Brown (1778–1820). Brown proposed that a number of factors influence the formation of associations, including the intensity of sensations and the frequency and recency of their pairing. In addition, the likelihood of one event becoming associated with another was considered by the empiricists to depend on the number of other associations in which each event was already involved and the similarity of these past associations to the current one being formed.

The British empiricists discussed rules of associations as a part of their philosophical discourse. They did not perform experiments to determine whether or not the rules were valid. Nor did they attempt to determine the circumstances in which one rule was more important than another. Empirical investigation of the mechanisms of associations did not begin until the pioneering work of the nineteenth-century German psychologist Hermann Ebbinghaus (1850–1909). Ebbinghaus invented **nonsense syllables,** three-letter combinations (two consonants separated by a vowel), devoid of any meaning that might influence how they were learned. With himself as subject, Ebbinghaus studied lists of these nonsense syllables and measured his ability to remember the syllables under various experimental conditions. This general method enabled him to answer such questions as how the strength of an association improved with increased training, whether syllables that appeared close together in a list were associated more strongly with one another than syllables that were farther apart, and whether a syllable became more strongly

associated with the next one on the list than with the preceding one.

Historical Developments in the Study of Reflexes

The concept of reflex action, introduced by Descartes, greatly advanced our understanding of behavior. However, Descartes was mistaken in his assumptions about how reflexes were produced. He believed that sensory messages going to the brain and motor messages going to the muscles traveled along the same nerves. The nerves were thought to be hollow tubes. The pineal gland was thought to release so-called animal spirits that flowed down the tubes and entered the muscles, causing them to swell and create a movement. Finally, Descartes considered all reflexive movements to be innate and to be fixed by the anatomy of the organism.

Later experimental observations showed that Descartes was wrong about both the anatomy of the reflex arc and the mechanism of neural conduction. Furthermore, it was shown that not all reflex responses are innate. The anatomy of the reflex arc was established in experiments performed by Charles Bell (1774–1842) in England and Francois Magendie (1783–1855) in France. They discovered that separate nerves are used to transmit sensory information from sense organs to the central nervous system and motor information from the central nervous system to muscles. If a sensory nerve is cut, the animal remains capable of muscle movements; if a motor nerve is cut, the animal remains capable of registering sensory information.

Establishing the mechanisms of neural conduction involved much more extensive experimentation. The idea that animal spirits were involved in neural transmission was disproved soon after the death of Descartes. In 1669 John Swammerdam (1637–1680) showed that mechanical irritation of a nerve was sufficient to produce a muscle contraction. Thus, infusion of animal spirits from the pineal gland was not necessary. In other studies, Francis Glisson (1597–1677) demonstrated that muscle contractions were not produced by swelling due to the infusion of some fluid, as Descartes had postulated. Glisson had people submerge one arm in water and observed that the water level did not change when he had them contract a muscle. Such experiments indicated that neural conduction did not occur by the mechanisms Descartes had proposed. However, positive evidence of what was involved in neural conduction had to await the great advances in the understanding of electricity and chemistry that occurred in the nineteenth century. According to contemporary thinking, neural conduction involves a combination of chemical and electrical events.

Descartes and most philosophers after him assumed that reflexes were responsible only for simple reactions to stimuli. The energy in a stimulus was thought to be translated directly (reflected) into the energy of the elicited response by the neural connections. The more intense the stimulus, the more vigorous the resulting response. This view of reflexes is consistent with many casual observations. If you touch a stove, for example, the hotter the stove, the more quickly you withdraw your finger. However, reflexes can also be more complicated.

When the physiological processes responsible for reflex behavior became better understood in the nineteenth century, the role of reflexes in the explanation of behavior was expanded. Two Russian physiologists, I.M. Sechenov (1829–1905) and Ivan Pavlov (1849–1936), were primarily responsible for extending the concept of reflexes to explain more complex behaviors. Sechenov proposed that in some cases a stimulus did not elicit a reflex response directly. Rather, a stimulus could release a response from inhibition.

If the intensity of a stimulus does not determine the vigor of the elicited behavior, it is possible for a very faint stimulus to produce a large response. Small pieces of dust in the nose, for example, may cause a vigorous sneeze. Sechenov took advantage of this type

of mechanism to provide a reflex analysis of voluntary behavior. He suggested that complex forms of behavior (actions or thoughts) that occurred in the absence of an obvious eliciting stimulus were in fact reflexive responses. It is simply that in these cases the eliciting stimuli are so faint that we do not notice them. Thus, according to Sechenov, voluntary behavior and thoughts were actually elicited by inconspicuous, faint stimuli.

Sechenov's ideas about voluntary behavior represent a major extension of the use of reflex mechanisms to explain a variety of aspects of behavior. However, his proposition was a philosophical extrapolation from the actual research results he obtained. In addition, Sechenov did not address the question of how reflex mechanisms can account for the fact that the behavior of organisms is constantly changing, depending on their experiences. From the time of Descartes, reflex responses always had been considered innate—fixed by the anatomy of the organism's nervous system. They were thought to depend on a prewired neural circuit connecting the sense organs to the relevant muscles. According to this view, a given stimulus could be expected to elicit the same response throughout the organism's life. Although this is true in some cases, there are also many examples in which the response to a stimulus changes. Explanation of such cases by reflex processes had to await the experimental and theoretical work of Ivan Pavlov. Pavlov showed experimentally that not all reflexes are innate. New reflexes to stimuli could be established through mechanisms of association. Pavlov's role in the history of the study of reflexes is comparable to the role of Ebbinghaus in the study of the mind. Both were concerned with establishing the laws of associations through empirical research.

The Dawn of the Modern Era

Experimental studies of basic principles of learning often are conducted with animal subjects, in the tradition of reflexology. Research in animal learning came to be pursued with great vigor starting a little more than a hundred years ago. Impetus for the research came from several sources (see Domjan, 1987). Some investigators became interested in comparative cognition and the evolution of the mind. Others viewed studies of learning as providing important insights into how the nervous system works. Still others pursued research on animal learning in an effort to better understand human behavior. As we will see in the ensuing chapters, these three areas of concern continue to dominate contemporary research in learning processes.

Comparative Cognition and the Evolution of Intelligence

Interest in comparative cognition and the evolution of the mind was sparked by the writings of Charles Darwin (see Figure 1.3) who took Cartesian arguments about human nature one step further. As we saw earlier, Descartes started chipping away at the age-old idea that human beings have a unique and privileged position in the animal kingdom by proposing that at least some aspects of human behavior (their reflexes) were animal-like. However, Descartes preserved some privilege for human beings by assuming that humans (and only humans) have a mind.

Darwin attacked this last vestige of privilege. In his second major work, *The Descent of Man and Selection in Relation to Sex*, first published in 1871, Darwin argued that "man is descended from some lower form, notwithstanding that connecting-links have not hitherto been discovered" (Darwin, 1897, p. 146). In claiming a continuity from animals to humans, Darwin attempted to characterize not only the evolution of physical traits but also the evolution of psychological or mental abilities. Thus, he suggested that the human mind is a product of evolution. In making this claim, Darwin did not deny that human beings had such special mental abilities as the

Figure 1.3 Charles Darwin (1809–1882). *(Bettman Archive.)*

capacity for wonder, curiosity, imitation, attention, memory, reasoning, and aesthetic sensibility. Rather, he suggested that nonhuman animals also had these abilities. Moreover, he maintained that nonhuman animals were capable even of belief in spiritual agencies (Darwin, 1897, p. 95).

Darwin collected anecdotal evidence of various forms of intelligent behavior in animals in an effort to support his claim of the evolution of human mental abilities. Although the evidence was not compelling, the research question was. Investigators ever since have been captivated by the possibility of tracing the evolution of intelligence by studying the abilities of various species of animals.

In order to investigate the evolution of intelligence in a systematic fashion, one must first provide a criterion for identifying intelligent behavior in animals. A highly influential proposal was made by George Romanes, in his book *Animal Intelligence,* published in 1884. Romanes suggested that intelligence can be identified by determining whether the animal learns "to make new adjustments, or to modify old ones, in accordance with the results of its own individual experience" (p. 4). Thus, Romanes defined intelligence in terms of the ability to learn. This definition was widely accepted by comparative psychologists at the end of the nineteenth and the start of the twentieth century and served to make the study of animal learning the key to obtaining information about the evolution of intelligence.

As we will see in the upcoming chapters, much research on mechanisms of animal learning has not been concerned with trying to obtain evidence of the evolution of intelligence. Nevertheless, this issue remains of considerable contemporary interest. About 20 years ago a major resurgence of interest in cognitive processes in animals began. We will describe the fruits of this contemporary research on animal cognition in Chapters 11 and 12.

Functional Neurology

As previously mentioned, the modern era in the study of learning processes was also greatly stimulated by efforts to use studies of animal learning to gain insights into how the nervous system works. This line of research was led by the Russian physiologist Ivan Pavlov, quite independently of the work of Darwin, Romanes, and others interested in evolution.

While still a medical student, Pavlov became committed to the principle of **nervism,** according to which all key physiological functions are governed by the nervous system. Armed with this principle, Pavlov devoted his life to documenting how the nervous system controlled various aspects of physiology.

Much of his work was devoted to identifying the neural controls of digestion.

For a time, Pavlov's research progressed according to plan. Then, in 1902, two British investigators (Bayliss and Starling) published results showing that the pancreas, an important digestive organ, was partially under hormonal rather than neural control. Writing some time later, Pavlov's friend and biographer noted that these novel findings "produced almost a sensation in our laboratory.... [They] shook the very foundation of the teachings of the exclusive nervous regulation of the secretory activity of the digestive glands" (Babkin, 1949, p. 228).

The findings of hormonal control of the pancreas presented Pavlov with a dilemma. He could continue his investigations of digestion, but if he did that he would have to abandon his interest in the nervous system. Alternatively, he could maintain his commitment to nervism, but if he did that he would have to stop studying digestive physiology. Nervism won out. Pavlov changed his course from studying digestive physiology to studying the conditioning of reflexes as a way to maintain his interests in the nervous system. Thus, Pavlov regarded his studies of conditioning (which is a form of learning) as a way to obtain information about the functions of the nervous system — how the nervous system works. (For further discussion of Pavlov's work, see Chapter 3 on classical conditioning.)

The rationale for using behavioral studies of learning to obtain information about how the nervous system works was stated forcefully by Babkin (1949) who characterized Pavlov's work on conditioning in the following terms:

[It is] certainly neurophysiology and not psychology in any form or under any name. Actually, [the conditioned reflex] is a more physiological method than those used by the neurophysiologist, which require anesthesia, the breaking of the skull, the implanting of electrodes into the tender mass of the brain, the application of drugs like strychnine, and so on.

Yet the aim of these crude methods is to explain the normal functions of the cerebral hemispheres, which is precisely the purpose for which the method of conditioned reflexes is employed! (p. 323)

Babkin's sentiments overstate the value of studies of learning in efforts to gain information about neurophysiology. Behavioral studies of learning cannot tell us how the nervous system accomplishes the tasks of registering experience and altering future behavior in accordance with that experience. The neurophysiological processes involved in various aspects of learning can only be discovered by direct neurophysiological investigations (see Thompson, Donegan, & Lavond, 1988). Because contemporary neurophysiological procedures are considerably more sophisticated than they were in Pavlov's time, many of Babkin's reservations about these procedures would be unfounded today.

While Babkin may have overestimated the scope of the information studies of learning can provide, he (and Pavlov) were nevertheless correct in assuming that such studies are extremely useful in determining what the nervous system can accomplish. Thus, studies of learning tell us about the functions of the nervous system. This is well accepted by contemporary neuroscientists. Kandel, for example, has commented that "the central tenet of modern neural science is that all behavior is a reflection of brain function" (Kandel, Schwartz, & Jessell, 1991, p. 3).

The behavioral psychologist can be compared to a driver who tries to find out about an experimental car by immediately taking it out for a test drive instead of first looking at how the car was put together. By driving a car, we can learn a great deal about how it functions. We can discover its acceleration, its top speed, the quality of its ride, its turning radius, and the speed with which it comes to a stop. Driving the car will not tell us *how* these various functions are accomplished. But it will reveal the major functional characteristics of the internal machinery of the car.

Knowledge of the functional characteristics of a car helps us discover features of its internal machinery in the following ways:

1. Functional characteristics provide clues about the internal machinery. For example, if the car accelerates sluggishly and never reaches high speeds, chances are it does not have a powerful rocket engine.

2. Studies of function can tell us what aspects of the machinery we should look for to understand how the car works. For example, if the car being tested only goes forward when facing downhill, there is no point in looking for an engine that propels the car forward. On the other hand, if the car cannot be made to come to a stop quickly, there is no point in looking for brakes.

3. Studies of function can also help us decide which aspects of the internal machinery are important. The configuration of a car engine (number and size of cylinders, and so forth) is much more important, for example, than its color.

In a similar manner, behavioral studies of learning provide important information about the machinery of the nervous system. Such studies tell us about the kinds of plasticity the nervous system can exhibit, the conditions under which information is acquired, the length of time the nervous system retains information, and the circumstances under which learned information is accessible or inaccessible. By detailing the functions of the nervous system, behavioral studies of learning define the features or functions that have to be explained in efforts to understand how the nervous system accomplishes the tasks of learning.

Animal Models of Human Behavior

The third major impetus for the modern era in the study of animal learning was the suggestion that animal research could be used to provide information in solving problems about human behavior. The model system approach to the study of animal learning is more recent in origin than comparative cognition and functional neurology. The approach was systematized by Dollard and Miller and their collaborators (Dollard, Miller, Doob, Mowrer, & Sears, 1939; Miller & Dollard, 1941) and developed further by B.F. Skinner (1953).

Drawing inferences about human behavior on the basis of research with animal subjects can be hazardous and controversial. The inferences drawn are hazardous if they are unwarranted; they are controversial if the rationale for the model system approach is poorly understood. Although animal models of human behavior have been developed based on research with a variety of species, rats and pigeons most frequently serve as subjects.

In generalizing from research with rats and pigeons to human behavior, one does not make the assumption that rats and pigeons are like people (or that people are like rats and pigeons). Animal models of human behavior are like other types of models. Architects, pharmacologists, medical scientists, and designers of automobiles all rely on models. Architects, for example, often make small-scale models of a building they are designing. Obviously, such models are not the same as the real building. They are much smaller, made of cardboard and small pieces of wood instead of mortar and bricks, and they are hollow inside.

Models are commonly used because they permit investigation of certain aspects of what they represent under simpler, more easily controlled, and less expensive circumstances. With the use of a model, an architect can study the design of the exterior of a planned building without the expense of actual construction. The model can be used to determine what the building will look like from various

vantage points and how it will appear relative to other nearby buildings. Studying a model in a design studio is much simpler than studying an actual building on a busy street corner. Factors that may get in the way of getting a good view (for example, other buildings, traffic, power lines) can be controlled and minimized.

In a comparable fashion, a car designer can study the wind resistance of various design features of a new automobile with the use of a model in the form of a computer program. In the program, spoilers can be added or the shape of hood of the car changed to see how these alterations affect calculations of wind resistance. The computer model used in this case bears not even visual resemblance to a real car. It has no tires or engine and cannot be driven. However, the model permits testing the wind resistance of a car design under conditions that are much simpler, better controlled, and less expensive than if the actual car were built and driven down the highway under various conditions to measure wind resistance.

What makes models valid for studying something given all the differences between the model and the real thing? For a model to be valid, it must be comparable to the real thing in terms of the feature under study. This is called the *relevant feature*. For a model of a building to be valid for learning about the planned building's exterior appearance, the model must be proportional to the planned building in all of its exterior dimensions. Since the model is being used only for studying the visual appearance of the exterior design, other features of the model are irrelevant. If, instead, the model was intended to show how well the building would withstand an earthquake, then structural elements (for example, the beams and how they are connected) would be much more important than visual appearance.

In a similar manner, the only thing relevant in a computer model of car wind resistance is that the computer program provide calculations for wind resistance that match the results obtained with real cars driving through real air. No other feature is relevant; therefore, the fact that the computer program lacks an engine or rubber tires is of no consequence.

The rationale and strategies associated with animal models of human behavior are similar to those pertaining to models in other areas of inquiry. Animal models permit investigation of problems that are often difficult, if not impossible, to investigate with human subjects directly. The model permits the investigation to be carried out under circumstances that are simpler, better controlled, and less expensive. Furthermore, the validity of animal models is based on the same criterion as the validity of other types of models. The important thing is similarity between the animal model and human behavior in *features relevant to the problem at hand.* For example, similarities between rats and humans in the way they learn to avoid dangerous foods makes a rat model valid for the investigation of human food-aversion learning. The fact that rats have long tails and are smaller and more furry than humans is entirely irrelevant.

The critical task in constructing a successful animal model is to identify a relevant similarity between the animal model and the human behavior of interest. Because animal models are often used to push back the frontiers of knowledge, the correspondence between the animal findings and human behavior always must be carefully checked.

The rationale and strategy for the development of animal models of human behavior was stated succinctly by Dollard and Miller (1950):

> In using the results from [research with rats] we are working on the hypothesis that people have all the learning capacities of rats. . . . Even though the facts must be verified at the human level, it is often easier to notice the operation of principles after they have been studied and isolated in simpler situations so that one knows exactly what to look for. Furthermore, in those cases in which it is impossible to use as rigorous experimental controls at the human level, our faith in what evidence can be gathered at that level will be increased if it is in line with the results of more carefully controlled experiments on other mammals. (p. 63)

Dollard and Miller advocated an interplay between animal and human research in which laboratory studies with animals are used to isolate and identify phenomena that can then be investigated in human subjects more successfully. The animal research is also used to increase confidence in human data obtained with weaker research methods.

Animal models have been developed for a wide range of human problems and behaviors (for example, Bond, 1984; Keehn, 1986; Maser & Seligman, 1977; Serban & Kling, 1976). In the upcoming chapters we will discuss animal models of love and attachment, drug tolerance and addiction, food-aversion learning, learning of fears and phobias, and stress and coping, among others. Animal models have also led to the development of numerous procedures now commonly employed with human subjects, such as biofeedback, programmed instruction, systematic desensitization, token economies, and other techniques of behavior modification. We will provide examples of such applications throughout the text at relevant points.

The Definition of Learning

Learning is such a common human experience that we hardly ever reflect on exactly what we mean when we say that something has been learned. A universally accepted definition of learning does not exist. However, many critical aspects of the concept are captured in the following statement:

Learning is an enduring change in the mechanisms of behavior involving specific stimuli and/or responses that results from prior experience with those stimuli and responses.

We will now consider several aspects of this definition.

The Learning–Performance Distinction

Whenever we see evidence of learning, we see the emergence of some new behavior — the performance of a new response or the suppression of a response that occurred previously. A child learns to snap the buckles of her sandals or learns to wait to eat dinner until everyone is seated at the table. Such changes in behavior are the only way we can tell whether or not learning has occurred. However, notice that the preceding definition attributes learning to a change in the mechanisms of behavior, not to a change in behavior directly.

By *mechanisms of behavior* we mean the underlying machinery that makes behavior happen. As Pavlov assumed, the physical machinery of learning resides in the nervous system. However, it is not necessary to observe the neural mechanisms of behavior directly to identify learning. Most investigators are satisfied with studying learning in terms of behavioral mechanisms or theoretical constructs. These theoretical constructs constitute a conceptual or hypothetical machinery that is assumed to be responsible for behavior. We have already mentioned one such theoretical concept — the concept of an association — which is used to explain certain changes in behavior that result from experience. We will encounter numerous other theoretical concepts or components of the hypothetical machinery that is used to summarize data about learning.

Why should we define learning in terms of a change in the mechanisms of behavior (be these conceptual or physical mechanisms) rather than focus on changes in behavior directly? The main reason is that behavior is determined by many factors in addition to learning. Consider, for example, eating. Whether you eat something depends on how hungry you are, how much effort you have to expend to get to the food, how much you like the food, and whether you know where the food is. Of all these factors, only the last one necessarily involves learning. This example illustrates the importance of the distinction between learning and performance.

Performance refers to an organism's actions at a particular time. Whether an organism does something or not (its performance) depends on many things. Even the occurrence of such a simple response as jumping into a swimming pool is multiply determined. Whether you jump depends on the availability, depth, and temperature of the water, motivation to jump, physical ability to spring away from the side of the pool, and so forth. Performance is determined by opportunity, motivation, and sensory and motor abilities, in addition to learning. Therefore, a change in performance cannot be automatically considered to reflect learning.

The definition stated earlier identifies learning as a change in the mechanisms of behavior to emphasize the distinction between learning and performance. The behavior of an organism (its performance) is used to provide evidence of learning. However, because performance is determined by many factors in addition to learning, one must be very careful in deciding whether a particular aspect of performance does or does not reflect learning. Sometimes evidence of learning cannot be obtained until special test procedures are set up. Children, for example, learn a great deal about driving a car just by watching others drive, but this learning is not apparent until they are permitted behind the steering wheel. In other cases (next to be discussed), a change in behavior is readily observed but cannot be attributed to learning, either because it is not sufficiently long-lasting or because it does not result from experience with specific environmental events.

Distinction Between Learning and Other Sources of Behavior Change

Evaluating various situations in terms of the abstract definition of learning we have stated may be difficult because some aspects of the definition are somewhat vague. For example, it is not specified exactly how long behavioral changes have to last to be considered instances of learning. It is also sometimes hard to decide what constitutes sufficient experience with environmental events to classify something as an instance of learning. Therefore, it is useful to distinguish learning from other known mechanisms that can produce changes in behavior.

Several mechanisms produce changes in behavior that are too short-lasting to be considered instances of learning. One such process is **fatigue.** Physical exertion may result in a gradual weakening in the vigor of a response because the subject becomes tired or fatigued. This type of change is produced by experience. However, it is not considered an instance of learning, because the decline in responding disappears if the subject is allowed to rest and recover. Behavior also may be temporarily altered by a *change in stimulus conditions.* If birds that have been housed in a small cage are suddenly set free, for example, their behavior will change dramatically. However, this is not an instance of learning, because the birds are likely to return to their old style of responding when returned to their cage. Another source of temporary change in behavior that is not considered learning is *alteration in the physiological or motivational state* of the organism. Hunger and thirst induce responses that are not observed at other times. Changes in the level of sex hormones will cause temporary changes in responsiveness to sexual stimuli. Short-lasting behavioral effects

may also accompany the administration of psychoactive drugs.

Other mechanisms produce persistent changes in behavior, but without the type of experience with environmental events that satisfies the definition of learning. The most obvious process of this type is **maturation.** A child will be unable to reach a high shelf until he grows tall enough. However, the change in behavior in this case would not be considered an instance of learning because it occurs with the mere passage of time. One does not have to be trained to reach high places as one becomes taller. Maturation can also result in disappearance of certain responses. For example, shortly after birth, touching an infant's feet results in foot movements that resemble walking, and stroking the bottom of the foot causes the toes to fan out. Both these reflex reactions disappear as the infant gets older.

Generally, the distinction between learning and maturation is based on the importance of special experiences in producing the change in behavior. However, the distinction has become blurred in instances in which exposure to stimuli has been found to be necessary for developmental changes that originally were thought to involve experience-independent maturation. Experiments with cats have shown that their visual system will not develop sufficiently for them to be able to see horizontal lines unless they are exposed to such stimuli early in life (for example, Blakemore & Cooper, 1970). The appearance of sexual behavior at puberty also was originally thought to depend on maturation. However, experiments suggest that successful sexual behavior may require social interactions early in life (for example, Harlow, 1969).

So far we have discussed mechanisms that create changes in behavior during the lifetime of the organism. Changes in behavior may also occur across generations through **evolutionary adaptation.** Individuals possessing genetic characteristics that promote their reproduction are more likely to pass these characteristics on to future generations. Adaptation and evolutionary change produced by differential reproductive success can lead to changes in behavior just as they lead to changes in the physical characteristics of species. Evolutionary changes are similar to learning in that they are also related to environmental influences. The characteristics of individuals that promote their reproductive success depend on the environment in which they live. However, evolutionary changes occur only across generations and are therefore distinguished from learning. (For a discussion of the relation between learning and evolution, see Plotkin & Odling-Smee, 1979.)

Although learning can be distinguished from maturation and evolution, it is not independent of these other sources of behavioral change. Whether a particular learning process occurs or how it operates depends on the subject's maturational level and evolutionary history. The dependence of learning on maturation is obvious in certain aspects of childrearing. For example, no amount of toilet training will be effective in a child until the nerves and muscles have developed sufficiently to make bladder control possible. The dependence of learning on evolutionary history can be seen by comparing learning processes in various types of animals. For example, fish and turtles appear to learn differently than rats and monkeys in instrumental conditioning situations (Bitterman, 1975). We will have more to say about the interaction of evolutionary history and learning processes in later chapters.

Methodological Aspects of the Study of Learning

There are two prominent methodological features of investigations of learning processes. One of these is the exclusive use of *experimental* as contrasted with *observational* research methods. The second is reliance on a general-process approach. The exclusive use of experimental research methods is an inev-

itable consequence of the nature of learning. The phenomena of learning simply cannot be studied any other way. By contrast, reliance on a general-process approach is more a matter of preference than of necessity.

Learning as an Experimental Science

To review for a moment, we have argued that learning is identified by changes in behavior that result from prior experience with specific stimuli and/or responses, provided those changes are sufficiently long-lasting to rule out other possible factors such as fatigue, temporary shifts in motivation, and the like. The fact that our definition restricts learning to aspects of behavior that result from prior experience has some important implications. When we say that a change in behavior results from prior experience, we are attributing the behavior to something the subject encountered previously. In other words, we are making a claim about the causes of the behavior change. Therefore, *the study of learning is a study of certain types of causes of behavior*—causes that alter behavior through prior experience. Prior experience may be thought of as a "training procedure" that causes a long-lasting change in behavior.

The fact that learning involves certain types of causes of behavior sets tight limits on the kinds of evidence we can use to make claims about learning. To study learning we are limited to the investigative methods that are used to identify causes. The basic problem with studying causes is that they cannot be observed directly. *Causes can only be inferred from the results of experimental manipulations.*

Consider the following example. Mary opens the door to a dark room. She quickly turns on a switch near the door and the lights in the room go on. Can you conclude that turning on the wall switch "caused" the lights to go on? Not from the information provided. Perhaps the lights were on an automatic timer and would have gone on anyway just at the time Mary entered the room. Alternatively, the door may have had a built-in switch that turned on the lights after a slight delay each time someone opened the door. Or there may have been a pressure switch in the floor that activated the lights. The wall switch might not have been connected to any electrical circuit.

How could we determine that manipulation of the wall switch caused the lights to go on? We would have to see what would happen under other circumstances. More specifically, we would have to instruct someone to enter the room in exactly the same manner as Mary had, but ask this person not to turn on the wall switch. If the lights did not go on under these circumstances, we could conclude that the wall switch "caused" the lights to go on. Thus, to determine whether something "causes" something else to happen, we have to conduct an experiment in which the "cause" is removed. We would then compare the results obtained with and without the presumed cause. The conclusion that something causes another event to occur is based on this comparison.

In studying learning, we are interested in the behavior of people and animals—not in the behavior of lights. However, we proceed in a similar fashion to identify causes. We have to conduct experiments in which behavior is observed with and without the presumed cause. In studies of learning, the "cause" we are interested in has to do with the prior experience of the subjects (the "training" experience). Studies of learning require comparisons between subjects who previously received the "training" experience in question and subjects who did not have that experience. The only conclusive way to prove that the "training" experience is causing the behavior change of interest is to experimentally vary the presence and absence of that experience. It is for this reason that *learning can be investigated only with experimental techniques.* Thus, the study of learning is exclusively a laboratory science.

The need to use experimental techniques to investigate learning is not always appreciated. Certainly, many aspects of behavior can be studied with observational procedures that do not involve experimental manipulations of behavioral causes. For example, observational studies can provide a great deal of information about whether and how certain animals set up territories, the manner in which they defend those territories, the activities involved in the animals' courtship and sexual behavior, the ways in which they raise their offspring, and the change in activities of the offspring as they mature. Many aspects of animal behavior are open to observational study, and much fascinating information has been obtained with observational techniques that involve minimal, if any, disruption of the ongoing activities of the animals.

Unfortunately, learning cannot be observed directly in the same manner as activities such as territoriality, aggression, or parental behavior. We can form hypotheses about what animals may be learning by observing their behavior unobtrusively in nature. However, to be sure that the changes in behavior are not due to changes in motivation, sensory development, hormonal fluctuations, or other possible nonlearning mechanisms, it is necessary to conduct experiments in which the presumed "training" experiences of the subjects are systematically varied.

The General-Process Approach to the Study of Learning

The second prominent methodological feature of studies of learning is the use of a general-process approach. This is more a matter of preference than of necessity. However, in adopting a general-process approach, investigators of animal learning are following a strategy employed in many areas of science.

Elements of the general-process approach. The most obvious feature of nature is its diversity. Consider, for example, the splendid variety of minerals. Some are soft, some are hard, some are brilliant, others are dull in appearance, and so on. Plants and animals occur in a similar array of shapes and sizes. Dynamic properties of objects are also diverse. Some things tend to float up, whereas others rapidly drop to the ground; some tend to remain still, others tend to remain in motion. In studying nature, one can either focus on these differences or ignore the differences and search for commonalities.

Scientists ranging from physicists to chemists to biologists to psychologists have all elected to follow the latter strategy. Rather than being overwhelmed by the tremendous diversity in nature, scientists have opted to focus on the commonalities. They have attempted to formulate *general laws* by which to organize and explain the diversity of events in nature. Investigators of animal learning also have taken this approach.

Whether or not general laws are discovered often depends on the level of analysis that is pursued. The diversity of the phenomena scientists try to understand and organize often makes it difficult to formulate general laws at the level of the observed phenomena. It is difficult, for example, to discover general laws that govern chemical reactions by focusing simply on the nature of the chemicals involved in various reactions. Similarly, it is difficult to explain the diversity of species on Earth by simply cataloging the features of various animals. Major progress in science has often come from analyzing phenomena at a more elemental or molecular level. For example, by the nineteenth century, chemists knew many specific facts about what would happen when various chemicals were combined. However, a general account of chemical reactions had to await the development of the periodic table of the elements, which describes and organizes chemical elements in terms of their constituent atomic components.

A fundamental assumption of the general-process approach is that the phenomena of interest are the products of more elemental processes. Furthermore, those elemental processes are assumed to operate in pretty much the same manner no matter where they are found. Thus, generality is assumed to exist at the level of basic or elemental processes.

Investigators of conditioning and learning have been committed to the general-process approach from the inception of this field of psychology. They have focused on the commonalities of various instances of learning and have assumed that learning phenomena are products of elemental processes that operate consistently across learning situations.

This commitment to a general-process approach guided Pavlov's work on functional neurology. In his study of conditioning, Pavlov adopted the general-process approach that he had followed in his previous research on digestive physiology. Commitment to a general-process approach to the study of learning is also evident in the writings of early comparative psychologists. For example, Darwin (1897) emphasized commonalities among species in cognitive functions: "My object . . . is to show that there is no fundamental difference between man and the higher mammals in their mental faculties" (p. 66). Jacques Loeb (1900) pointed out that commonalities occur at the level of elemental processes: "Psychic phenomena . . . appear, invariably, as a function of an elemental process, namely the activity of associative memory" (p. 213). Another prominent comparative psychologist of the time, C. Lloyd Morgan, stated in 1903 that elementary laws of association "are, we believe, universal laws" (p. 219).

The assumption that "universal" elemental laws of association are responsible for learning phenomena does not deny the diversity of stimuli different animals may learn about, the diversity of responses they may learn to perform, and species differences in rates of learning. The generality is assumed to exist in the rules or processes of learning—not in the contents or speed of learning. This idea was clearly expressed nearly a century ago by Edward Thorndike:

> Formally, the crab, fish, turtle, dog, cat, monkey, and baby have very similar intellects and characters. All are systems of connections subject to change by the laws of exercise and effect. The differences are: first, in the concrete particular

connections, in what stimulates the animal to response, what responses it makes, which stimulus connects with what response, and second, in the degree of ability to learn. (Thorndike, 1911, p. 280)

According to Thorndike, what an animal can learn about (the stimuli, responses, and stimulus–response connections it learns about) may vary from one species to another. Animals may also differ in how fast they learn ("in the degree of ability to learn"). However, Thorndike assumed that the rules of learning were universal. We no longer share Thorndike's view that these universal rules of learning are the "laws of exercise and effect." However, contemporary scientists continue to adhere to the idea that universal rules of learning exist. The job of the learning psychologist is to discover those universal laws. (More about the work of Thorndike will follow in Chapter 5.)

Evidence of the generality of learning phenomena. The available evidence suggests that elementary principles of learning of the sort that will be described in this text have considerable generality. Most research on animal learning has been performed with pigeons, rats, and (to a lesser extent) rabbits. Similar forms of learning have been found with hamsters, cats, dogs, human beings, dolphins, and sea lions. In addition, some of the principles of learning observed with these vertebrate species also have been demonstrated in newts (Ellins, Cramer, & Martin, 1982); fruit flies (Holliday & Hirsch, 1986; Platt, Holliday, & Drudge, 1980); honeybees (for example, Couvillon & Bitterman, 1980, 1982, 1988, 1989; Menzel, 1983); terrestrial mollusks (Sahley, Rudy, & Gelperin, 1981); and various marine mollusks (Carew, Hawkins, & Kandel, 1983; Farley & Alkon, 1980; Susswein & Schwarz, 1983). These examples of learning in diverse species provide support for the general-process approach. However, the evidence should be interpreted cautiously. With

the exception of the extensive program of research on learning in honeybees conducted by Bitterman and his colleagues, the various invertebrate species in the studies we have cited have been tested on a limited range of learning phenomena, and we do not know whether their learning was mediated by the same type of processes responsible for analogous instances of learning observed in vertebrate species.

Methodological implications of the general-process approach. If we assume that universal rules of learning exist, then we should be able to discover those rules in any situation in which learning occurs. Thus, an important methodological implication of the general-process approach is that general rules of learning may be discovered by studying any species or response system that exhibits learning.

If it does not matter which species or response system we select for investigation, then the obvious thing to do is to select situations based on convenience. Another consequence of this line of reasoning is that we can limit our study of learning processes to a small number of experimental situations. If the processes of learning are in fact universal, then there is no need to study learning in a great number of situations.

Although the total list of species and situations in which learning has been investigated is rather long, the general-process approach has encouraged investigators to develop a few "standard" or conventional experimental paradigms. Most studies of learning are conducted in one of these paradigms. Figure 1.4 shows an example of a pigeon in a standard Skinner box. We will encounter other examples of standard experimental paradigms as we discuss various learning phenomena in future chapters.

Proof of the generality of learning phenomena. The general-process approach has dominated studies of animal learning throughout the

Figure 1.4 Pigeon pecking a response key in a Skinner box. *(Omikron/Photo Researchers, Inc.)*

cannot be empirically verified by investigating learning in just a few standard experimental paradigms. The generality of learning processes has to be proven by studying learning in many different species and situations.

The Use of Animals in Research on Learning

Many of the experiments we will be considering in subsequent chapters have been conducted with animal subjects. Numerous types of animals have been used, including rats, mice, rabbits, fish, pigeons, and monkeys. Animals are used in the research for both theoretical and methodological reasons.

Rationale for the Use of Animals in Research on Learning

Given the critical role of learning in both human and animal behavior, no one can deny the importance of better understanding learning processes. To understand learning completely, we have to know what kinds of things are learned and how they are learned. We have to know the evolutionary origins of learning, and we have to know its physiology. All of these kinds of questions about learning require the use of animals in research.

As we have argued, experimental methods are needed to investigate learning phenomena. Experimental methods enable us to attribute the acquisition of new behaviors to particular previous experiences of the subjects. Such experimental control of past experience cannot be achieved to the same degree of precision in studies with human subjects as in laboratory studies with animal subjects. For example, it is difficult, if not impossible, to study biologically important forms of learning with human subjects. With animal subjects, we can study learning involved in acquiring food, in avoiding pain or distress, and in finding potential sexual partners. With animal subjects, we can study how strong emotional

twentieth century. As we will see in the chapters that follow, the approach has provided an extensive and sophisticated body of knowledge. Given the successes of the general-process approach, it is tempting to conclude that learning processes are indeed universal. However, it is important to keep in mind that the generality of learning processes is not proven by adopting a general-process approach. Assuming the existence of common elemental learning processes is not the same as empirically demonstrating those commonalities.

Direct empirical verification of the existence of common learning processes in a variety of situations remains necessary in efforts to build a truly general account of how learning occurs. A general theory of learning

responses are learned. With human subjects, we are limited to trying to modify maladaptive emotional responses after such responses have appeared. However, even the development of successful therapeutic procedures for the treatment of maladaptive emotional responses has required knowledge of how strong emotional responses are acquired in the first place—knowledge that could only have been obtained with the study of animal subjects.

Knowledge of the evolution and physiology of learning also cannot be obtained without the use of animals in research. The question of the evolution of cognition and intelligence, first formulated by Darwin, is one of the fundamental questions about human nature. The answer to this question will shape our view of human nature, just as knowledge of the solar system has changed our view of the role of the Earth in the universe. As we have seen, investigation of the evolution of cognition and intelligence rests heavily on studies of learning in animal subjects.

Knowledge of the physiology of learning is not likely to change our views of human nature, but it is apt to yield important dividends in the treatment of learning and memory disorders. Such knowledge also rests heavily on research with animals. The kind of detailed physiological investigations that are necessary to unravel the mysteries of the physiology of learning simply cannot be conducted with human subjects. As we have argued, a search for the physiology of learning first requires documenting the nature of learning processes at the behavioral level. We cannot begin to study the physiology of something unless we know what that thing is. Therefore, behavioral studies of learning in animals are an inescapable prerequisite to any investigations of the physiology of learning employing animal subjects.

Animal subjects provide important conceptual advantages over human subjects in studies of learning processes. There is the hope that processes of learning may be simpler in animals reared in controlled laboratory situations than in people, whose backgrounds are much more varied. Although all the respects in which learning in animals is simpler than in humans are not yet clear, it is agreed that most animal behavior is not complicated by the linguistic processes that have a prominent role in certain kinds of human behavior. One of the most exciting contemporary areas of research is the study of linguistic abilities in primates (see Chapter 12). However, there is no evidence that learning processes of the sort we will discuss in most of this text involve linguistic functions.

Another important advantage of using animals is that demand characteristics of the experiment do not come into play. In many forms of research with people, it is necessary to ensure that the actions of the subjects are not governed by their efforts to please (or displease) the experimenter. People serving in experiments often try to "figure out" what the purpose of the study is and what they are "supposed" to do. Whether or not they identify the purpose of the experiment correctly, their actions may be motivated by their wish to "do well" rather than by the experimental conditions that were set up. Consequently, a person may react to circumstances in the laboratory very differently than he or she would respond to the same circumstances outside the laboratory. Such problems are not likely to arise in research with rats and pigeons. There is no reason to suspect that the actions of rats and pigeons in the laboratory are determined by their desire to please the experimenter or to do well in the experiment to avoid embarrassment.

Laboratory Animals and Normal Behavior

Some have suggested that domesticated laboratory strains of animals may not provide useful information because such animals have degenerated as a result of many generations of inbreeding and long periods of captivity (for example, Lockard, 1968). However, this notion is probably mistaken. In an interesting test, Boice (1977) took five male and five female albino rats of a highly inbred laboratory stock and housed them in an outdoor pen in Missouri without artificial shelters. All ten rats survived the first winter with temperatures as low as −22 °F. The animals reproduced normally and reached a stable population of about 50 members. Only three of the rats died before showing signs of old age during the 2-year period. Given the extreme climatic conditions, this level of success in living outdoors is remarkable. Furthermore, the behavior of these domesticated rats in the outdoors was very similar to the behavior of wild rats observed in similar circumstances.

The vigor of inbred laboratory rats in outdoor living conditions indicates that they are not inferior to their wild counterparts. Domesticated rats act similarly to wild rats in other tests as well, and there is some indication that they perform better than wild rats in learning experiments (see, for example, Boice, 1973, 1981; Kaufman & Collier, 1983). Therefore, the results we will be describing in this text should not be discounted simply because many of the experiments were conducted with domesticated animals. In fact, it may be suggested that laboratory animals are preferable in research to their wild counterparts. Human beings in civilized society are raised and live in somewhat contrived environments. Therefore, research with animals may prove most relevant to the human case if the animals are domesticated and live in artificial laboratory situations. As Boice (1973) commented, "The domesticated rat may be a good model for domestic man" (p. 227).

Public Debate About Animal Research

There has been much public debate in the past 15 years about the pros and cons of animal research. Part of the debate has centered on the humane treatment of animals. Other aspects of the debate have centered on questions of what constitutes ethical treatment of animals, whether human beings have the right to benefit at the expense of animals, and on possible alternatives to research with animals.

The humane treatment of animals. Concern for the welfare of laboratory animals has resulted in the adoption of very strict federal standards for animal housing and for the supervision of animal research. Many of these changes were necessary and desirable. D.E. Koshland, editor of the prestigious journal *Science,* commented in 1989 that "ten years ago, before the current wave of legislation, it could fairly be said that some animal experiments were done improperly, in inadequate facilities, or with inappropriate supervision. These days are largely past. The current protocols for care and treatment of animals are so stringent that most modern animal facilities are models for responsible and considerate treatment" (p. 1253).

Federal regulations concerning housing of animals for research are now more stringent than standards for human habitation. At the University of Texas, for example, two animal laboratories were recently moved to newly renovated facilities in order to comply with federal regulations concerning the housing of laboratory animals. The old laboratory rooms failed to meet federal regulations in several respects. For example, air exchange was deemed inadequate and the ceiling tiles and light fixtures were considered to be inappropriate. Ironically, once the animals were moved out, the same rooms were put to use as graduate student offices, without any inspections, changes in the air-circulation system, or changes in the ceiling tiles or lights.

Sometimes scientists involved in animal research are portrayed as being so intent on completing their experiments that they disregard the welfare of their research animals in the process. Every scientist must be concerned about the welfare of research subjects. This is particularly relevant for investigators committed to the study of animal learning. We use the behavior of organisms to obtain information about learning as it occurs under ordinary circumstances. Information about normal learning and behavior cannot be obtained in diseased and terrorized animals. Investigators of animal learning must ensure the welfare of their animal subjects if they are to obtain useful scientific data.

Laboratory rats, common subjects of animal learning research, cower in a corner if they are sick and upset. No useful information about their learning and behavior can be obtained under such circumstances. Investigators have to take great pains to make sure their subjects are not upset by serving in an experiment. The animals must be healthy and adapted to handling; the experimental chambers must be suitable for the species; and the animals must be comfortable being in the chamber.

Learning experiments sometimes do involve discomfort. However, every effort is made to minimize the degree of discomfort. In studies of food reinforcement, for example, subjects are made hungry before each experimental session to ensure their interest in food. However, the hunger imposed is no more severe than the hunger animals are likely to encounter in the wild, and often it is less severe (Poling, Nickel, & Alling, 1990).

The investigation of certain forms of learning and behavior require the administration of aversive stimulation. Important topics, such as punishment or the learning of fear and anxiety, cannot be studied without some discomfort to the subjects. However, even in such cases, efforts are made to keep the discomfort to a minimum. Electric shock is often used as a source of aversive stimulation. The term *electric shock* is likely to conjure up images of electric chairs used to impose the death penalty. Or it may bring to mind the pain children suffer when they accidentally put their fingers in an electrical outlet. However, electric shock is used in studies of learning not because it can be made horrendously painful; rather, shock is used because it can produce low but effective levels of discomfort. Unlike other sources of aversive stimulation, electric shock can be precisely regulated, permitting its administration at controlled low levels. The shock levels employed in studies of animal learning are far removed from the levels experienced from a wall outlet or an electric chair. In addition, in many procedures the animals are permitted to control their exposure by making escape or avoidance responses.

What constitutes the ethical treatment of animals?   Although treating laboratory animals as humanely as possible is in the best interests of the animals as well as the research, formulating general ethical principles is difficult. This is illustrated by the fact that animals seem to have different "rights" under different circumstances. Currently, every effort is made to house laboratory animals in conditions that promote their health and comfort. However, a laboratory mouse or rat loses the protection afforded by federal standards when it escapes from the laboratory and takes up residence in the walls of the building (Herzog, 1988). The trapping and extermination of rodents in buildings is a common practice that has not been the subject of either public debate or restrictive federal regulation. Why should a mouse that lives in the walls of a building have fewer "rights" than one that lives in a laboratory? How about the "rights" of mice that are fed to boa constrictors kept in homes, zoos, or laboratories (Herzog, 1988)? Boa constrictors depend on such food, but what gives them more "rights" than mice have?

There are no easy answers to such questions. We can all agree on the inappropriateness of willful neglect and abuse of animals in certain situations. By contrast, in other situations, many people agree that extermination is the proper course of conduct. Mites, fleas, and ticks are animals, but we do not tolerate them in our hair or on our pets. Which species have inalienable rights to life? And under what circumstances do they have these rights? Such questions defy simple answers.

TABLE 1.1 *Numbers of animals used annually in the United States*

Type of Use [a]	Number Used	% of Total
Food	6,086,000,000	96.5%
Hunting	165,000,000	2.6%
Killed in animal shelters	27,000,000	.4%
Fur garments	11,000,000	.2%
All teaching and research	20,000,000	.3%
Grand Total	6,309,000,000	100.0%
Graduate Departments of Psychology[b]	198,019	.003%

[a]From "Analysis of Animal Rights Literature Reveals the Underlying Motives of the Movement: Ammunition for Counter Offensive by Scientists," by C.S. Nicoll and S.M. Russell, 1990, *Endicronology, 127,* pp. 985–989. Copyright © 1990 by Williams & Wilkins. Reprinted by permission.
[b]From *Animal Research Survey,* 1985 by the American Psychological Association.

Should human beings benefit from the use of animals? Part of the public debate about animal rights has been fueled by the argument that human beings have no right to benefit at the expense of animals; humans have no right to "exploit" animals. This argument goes far beyond issues concerning the use of animals in research. Therefore we will not discuss the argument in detail here, except to try to put its implications for animal research in perspective.

The number of animals used in research is a small fraction of the number of animals used to human advantage in other ways. Table 1.1 summarizes estimates of the number of animals used each year in all forms of teaching and research as compared to the numbers of unwanted animals killed in animal shelters annually or sacrificed for food, for clothing, and in hunting. By far, the greatest numbers of animals are used for food and in hunting. The number of animals used in all forms of teaching and research is substantial (about 20 million), but this is just .3% of the total usage. Moreover, with respect to psychological research in particular, only about 200,000 animals are used each year. This is but .003% of the total number of animals used for various purposes in the United States each year. Then, too, studies of animal learning account for less than half of all animals used in psychological research. Thus, if animal research represents

the "exploitation" of animals, it is far less extensive than that represented by other forms of human uses of animals.

In addition to the explicit human uses of animals for such things as food, clothing, and recreation, a comprehensive account of human "exploitation" of animals has to include disruptions of habitats that occur whenever we build roads, housing developments, and factories. We should also add the millions of animals that are killed by insecticides and other pest-control efforts. (About a decade ago, about 9 million pounds of rat poison were used each year by professional exterminators [Miller, 1985].) In this context, the contributions of animal research to the total "exploitation" of animal life takes on even more trivial dimensions.

In a recent survey, 85% of animal rights advocates questioned agreed with the statement, "If it were up to me, I would eliminate all research using animals" (Plous, 1991). When asked what should be the top priority of the animal rights movement, only 4% of them said that they should work to eliminate the use of animals in sports or entertainment, 12% said that they should work to eliminate the use of animals in clothing or fashion, and 24% considered it most important to try to discourage the use of animals for food (see also Nicoll & Russell, 1990). The focus of animal rights advocates on curbing animal research efforts is puzzling given the far greater numbers of animals used in other ways. This antiresearch focus is also puzzling when we consider that alternatives to the use of animals are much more readily available when it comes to foods, clothing or fashion, and sports and entertainment.

Alternatives to research with animal subjects. As pointed out by Gallup and Suarez (1985), good research on learning processes cannot be conducted without experiments on live organisms, be they animal or human. Nevertheless, public debate on the pros and cons of animal research has focused interest in possible alternatives to testing animal subjects. Some of these alternatives are considered in the following list.

1. *Observational techniques.* As we discussed earlier, learning processes cannot be investigated with unobtrusive observational techniques. Experimental manipulations of past experience are necessary in studies of learning. Field observations of undisturbed animals cannot yield the kind of information about learning mechanisms that we will be describing in upcoming chapters.

2. *Plants.* Learning also cannot be investigated in plants because plants lack a nervous system, which is where learning occurs.

3. *Tissue cultures.* Although tissue cultures may reveal the operation of cellular processes, how these cellular processes operate in an intact organism can be discovered only by studying the intact organism. Furthermore, as we pointed out earlier, a search for cellular mechanisms of learning first requires knowledge of the characteristics of learning at the behavioral level.

4. *Computer simulations.* Unfortunately, before we can write a computer program to simulate a natural phenomenon, we must know a great deal about that phenomenon. In the case of learning, we would have to have precise and detailed information about the nature of learning phenomena and the mechanisms and factors that determine learning. The absence of such knowledge necessitates experimental research with live organisms. Thus, experimental research with live organisms is a prerequisite for effective computer simulations of learning. For that reason, computer simulations cannot be used in place of experimental research.

Computer simulations can serve many useful functions in science. They are effective in showing us the implications of the experimental observations we have already made. Computer simulations are often used in studies of behavior to show us the implications of various theoretical assumptions. They can be used to identify gaps in knowledge, and they can be used to suggest important future lines of research. However, they cannot be used to generate new, previously unknown observations about behavior. That can only be done by studying live organisms.

Earlier in this chapter, we used the example of a computer simulation to measure the wind resistance of various automobile designs. Why is it possible to construct a computer program to study wind resistance when it is not possible to construct one to study learning processes? The critical difference is that we know a lot more about wind resistance than we know about learning. Wind resistance is determined by the laws of mechanics—laws that have been thoroughly explored since the days of Sir Isaac Newton. Application of those laws to wind resistance has received special attention in recent years, as the wind resistance of automobile designs has become an important factor in increasing gas mileage.

Designing automobiles with low wind resistance is an engineering task. It involves the application of existing knowledge, rather than the discovery of new knowledge and new principles. Research on animal learning involves the discovery of new facts and new principles. It is science, not engineering.

2 *Elicited Behavior, Habituation, and Sensitization*

We begin our discussion of the principles of learning and behavior in the present chapter by describing elicited behavior—behavior that occurs in reaction to events in the environment. Numerous aspects of behavior are elicited by environmental events, and some of the most extensively investigated response systems involve elicited behavior. Our discussion will progress from a description of the simplest form of elicited behavior, reflexive behavior, to a discussion of complex emotional responses elicited by stimuli. Along the way we will describe two of the simplest and most common forms of behavioral change: habituation and sensitization. Habituation and sensitization occur in a wide variety of response systems and are therefore fundamental properties of behavior.

The Nature of Elicited Behavior

All animals, whether they be single-celled organisms such as paramecia or complex human beings, react to events in their environment. The calls of an intruder elicit territorial defensive responses in white-crowned sparrows. The odor of a sexually receptive female dog or cat elicits approach and sexual behaviors in male dogs and cats. If something moves in the periphery of your vision, you are likely to turn your head in that direction. A particle of food in the mouth elicits salivation. Exposure to a bright light causes the pupils of the eyes to constrict. The pain of touching a hot surface elicits a quick withdrawal response. Irritation of the respiratory passages causes sneezing and coughing. These and numerous similar examples illustrate that much of behavior occurs in response to stimuli—it is elicited.

Elicited behavior has been the subject of extensive investigation. Many of the chapters of this text deal, in one way or another, with elicited behavior. We begin our discussion of elicited behavior by describing its simplest form, reflexive behavior.

The Concept of the Reflex

A light puff of air directed at the cornea makes the eye blink. A tap on a certain part of the knee causes the leg to kick. A loud noise causes a startle reaction. These are all examples of reflexes. A reflex involves two closely related events, an *eliciting stimulus* and a *specific response*. The stimulus and response are linked. Presentation of the stimulus usually is soon followed by the occurrence of the response; moreover, the response will rarely occur in the absence of the stimulus. For example, dust in the nasal passages will elicit a sneeze, which does not occur in the absence of nasal irritation.

The specificity of the relation between a particular stimulus and its associated reflex response is a consequence of the organization of the nervous system. In vertebrates (including humans), simple reflexes are typically mediated by three neurons, as illustrated in Figure 2.1. The environmental stimulus for a reflex activates a **sensory,** or **afferent, neuron,** which transmits the sensory message to the spinal cord. Here, the neural impulses are relayed to the **motor,** or **efferent, neuron,**

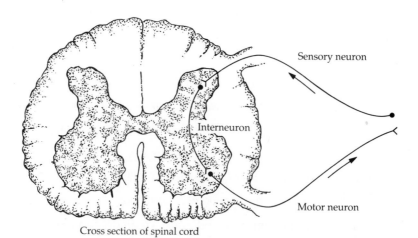

Cross section of spinal cord

Sensory neuron

Interneuron

Motor neuron

Figure 2.1 Neural organization of simple reflexes. The environmental stimulus for a reflex activates a sensory neuron, which transmits the sensory message to the spinal cord. Here, the neural impulses are relayed to an interneuron, which in turn relays the impulses to the motor neuron. The motor neuron activates muscles involved in movement.

which activates the muscles involved in the reflex response. However, sensory and motor neurons rarely communicate directly. Rather, the impulses from one to the other are relayed through an **interneuron.** The neural circuitry ensures that one set of sensory neurons is connected to a corresponding set of motor neurons. Because of the limited connections between particular sensory and motor neurons, a particular reflex response is elicited only by a restricted set of stimuli. The afferent neuron, interneuron, and efferent neuron together constitute the **reflex arc.**

The reflex arc in vertebrates represents the fewest neural connections necessary for reflex action. Frequently, additional neural structures are also involved in the elicitation of reflexes. For example, the sensory messages may be relayed to the brain, through which the reflex reaction may be modified in various ways. Arousal mechanisms, for example, may increase reflex responsivity. A tap on the shoulder may startle you more easily if you are engrossed in watching a horror movie as opposed to eating lunch in a cafeteria. We will discuss this type of effect in greater detail later in the chapter. For now, it is sufficient to keep in mind that the occurrence of even simple reflexes can be influenced by higher nervous system functions.

Most reflexes promote the well-being of the organism in obvious ways. For example, in many animals painful stimulation of one limb causes withdrawal, or flexion, of that limb and extension of the opposite limb (Hart, 1973). Thus, if a dog stubs a toe while walking, it will automatically withdraw that leg and simultaneously extend the opposite leg. This combination of responses removes the first leg from the source of pain and at the same time allows the animal to maintain balance. The same sequence of reflex responses, however, would not benefit the two-toed sloth, a mammal that spends much of its time hanging upside down on branches. Consider what would happen if it responded to pain in the same way as the dog. If it flexed the injured limb and extended the opposite limb, it would end up putting

most of its weight on the injured foot. As you might suspect, the sloth has evolved with a different sequence of responses. It extends the injured foot, thereby removing that foot from the branch it is on, and flexes the opposite limb, thereby putting more of its weight on that limb, as shown in Figure 2.2 (Esplin & Woodbury, 1961).

Reflexes constitute much of the behavioral repertoire of newborn infants. Some of these reflexes can be a source of enjoyment for the parents; for example, when newborn babies

Figure 2.2   Painful stimulation of one limb of a dog causes withdrawal (flexion) of that limb and extension of the opposite limb. By contrast, painful stimulation of one limb of a sloth causes extension of that limb and flexion of the opposite limb. *(From "Reflexive Behavior" by B.L. Hart in G. Bermant (Ed.), 1973, Perspectives in Animal Behavior. Copyright © 1973 by Scott, Foresman. Reprinted by permission.)*

Figure 2.3   Sucking is one of the prominent reflexes in infants. *(Photo courtesy of Allen Zak.)*

reflexively clench their fingers around anything placed in their hand. Another prominent reflex probably evolved to facilitate finding the nipple. If you touch an infant's cheek with your finger, the baby will reflexively turn her head in that direction, with the result that your finger will probably fall in the baby's mouth. When an object is in the infant's mouth, she will reflexively suck. The more closely the object resembles a nipple, the more vigorous the elicited sucking behavior.

Although reflex responses are usually beneficial to the organism, the organization of reflex behavior can also lead to unexpected difficulties. The head-turning and sucking reflexes make it easy for newborn babies to get fed. However, sometimes another important reflex, the respiratory occlusion reflex, gets in the way. The respiratory occlusion reflex is stimulated by a reduction of air flow to the baby, caused, for example, by a cloth covering the face or by an accumulation of mucus in the respiratory passages. When confronted with a reduction of air flow, the baby's first reaction is to pull her head back. If this does not remove the eliciting stimulus, the baby will move her hands in a face-wiping motion. If this also fails to remove the eliciting stimulus, then the baby will begin to cry. Crying involves vigorous expulsion of air, which is often sufficient to remove whatever was obstructing the air passages. The respiratory occlusion reflex is obviously essential for survival. If the baby does not get enough air, she may suffocate. A problem arises when the respiratory occlusion reflex is triggered during nursing. While nursing, the baby can get air only through the nose. If the mother presses the baby too close to the breast during feeding so that the baby's nostrils are covered by the breast, the respiratory occlusion reflex will be stimulated. The baby will attempt to pull her head back from the nipple, may paw at her face to get released from the nipple, and may begin to cry. Successful nursing requires a bit of experience. The mother and child have to adjust their positions so that nursing can progress without stimulation of the respiratory occlusion reflex (Gunther, 1961). (See Figure 2.3.)

The Modal Action Pattern

Simple reflex responses, such as pupillary constriction to a bright light and startle reactions to a brief loud noise, are evident in many species of animals. By contrast, other forms of elicited behavior are evident in just one species or in a small group of related species. For example, sucking in response to objects placed in the mouth is a characteristic of mammalian infants. Herring-gull chicks are just as dependent on parental feeding as are human infants. However, the elicited behaviors involved in their infant feeding behavior are very different from those of humans. When a parent returns to the nest from a foraging trip, the baby chicks peck at the tip of the parent's bill (see Figure 2.4). This causes the parent to regurgitate. As the chicks continue to peck, they manage to get some of the parent's regurgitated food, and this provides their nourishment.

Response sequences, such as those involved in infant feeding, that are typical of one species or a small set of species, are referred to as **modal action patterns** or **MAPs.** Such species-characteristic response patterns have been identified in many aspects of animal behavior, including sexual behavior, territorial defense, aggression, and prey capture. Ring doves, for example, begin their sexual behavior with a courtship interaction that culminates in the selection of a nest site and the construction of the nest by both the male and female birds. By contrast, in the three-spined stickleback, a species of small fish, the male first establishes a territory and constructs a nest. Females that enter the territory after the nest has been constructed are courted and induced to lay their eggs in the nest. Once a female has deposited her eggs, she is chased away, leaving the male to care for and defend the eggs until the offspring hatch.

An important feature of modal action patterns is that the threshold for eliciting such activities varies a great deal as a function of circumstances (Camhi, 1984; Baerends, 1988). The same stimulus can have widely different effects depending on the physiological state of the animal and its recent actions. A male stickleback, for example, will not court a female ready to lay eggs until he has completed building his nest. And after the female has deposited her eggs, the male will chase her away rather than court her as he did earlier. In many species, including the stickleback, stimuli that elicit male territorial and sexual behavior do so only during the breeding season.

Modal action patterns were initially identified by *ethologists,* scientists interested in the study of the evolution of behavior. Early ethologists, such as Lorenz and Tinbergen, referred to species-specific action patterns as "fixed action patterns" to emphasize that the activities involved occurred pretty much the same way in all members of a species. However, not all members of a species perform a given activity, such as nest building, in exactly the same fashion. Therefore, the term *modal action pattern* is preferred now (Baerends, 1988).

The modal action pattern has proven to be invaluable in the study of the evolution of behavior. In fact, it has served as the basic unit of behavior in ethological investigations.

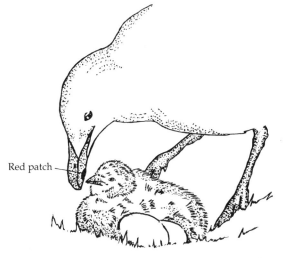

Red patch

Figure 2.4 Feeding of herring-gull chicks. The chicks peck a red patch near the tip of the parent's bill, causing the parent to regurgitate food for the chicks.

Because modal action patterns occur in a similar fashion among members of a given species, they include activities that are informally characterized as instinctive. "Instinctive" behavior is often considered primarily to reflect an individual's genetic history, leading to the impression that modal action patterns are not the product of learning and experience. However, the fact that all members of a species exhibit similar forms of responding does not necessarily mean that the behavior was not learned through experience. As Tinbergen (1951) recognized many years ago, similar behavior on the part of all members of a species may reflect similar learning experiences. In a more recent expression of this sentiment, Baerends (1988) wrote that "learning processes in many variations are tools, so to speak, that can be used in the building of some segments in the species-specific behavior organization" (p. 801). Thus, learning may be involved in what we commonly refer to as "instinctive" behavior (Hailman, 1967).

The Nature of Response-Eliciting Stimuli

The eliciting stimulus is fairly easy to identify in examples of simple reflexes, such as the startle response to a brief loud noise. The stimuli responsible for modal action patterns are often more difficult to identify, especially if the action patterns occur in the course of social interactions among several animals. Let us consider again, for example, the feeding of herring-gull chicks. To get fed, the chicks have to peck the parent's beak to stimulate the parent to regurgitate. Something about the parent elicits pecking on the part of the chicks. However, from a casual observation of the situation, one cannot identify the critical eliciting stimuli. Herring gulls have a long, yellow bill with a striking red patch near the tip. Pecking in the chicks may be elicited by movements of the parent; the color, shape, or length of its bill; the noises the parent makes; or some other stimulus. To isolate which of these features are important for the pecking response,

Tinbergen and Perdeck (1950) tested herring-gull chicks with various artificial models instead of live adult gulls. From this research they concluded that a model had to have several characteristics to strongly elicit pecking. It had to be a long, thin, moving object that was pointed downward and that had a contrasting red patch near the tip. These experiments suggest that the yellow color of the adult's bill, the shape and coloration of its head, and the noises it makes are all unimportant for eliciting pecking in the gull chicks. The specific features that were found to be required to elicit the pecking behavior are called, collectively, the **sign stimulus** or **releasing stimulus** for this behavior.

A sign or releasing stimulus is sufficient for eliciting a modal action pattern. However, a given action pattern may be controlled by several stimulus features in an additive fashion. In addition, the most effective stimulus for eliciting a modal action pattern may not be one that is likely to occur under natural conditions. These principles are nicely illustrated by a study of the egg-retrieval behavior of herring gulls (Baerends & Drent, 1982). Brooding herring gulls will retrieve into their nest eggs placed on the rim of the nest. To determine which features of eggs best stimulates this egg-retrieval behavior, Baerends and Drent tested gulls with wooden eggs of various sizes, colors, and speckling.

Results of this study indicated that the gulls preferred to retrieve green speckled eggs more than yellow ones, yellow eggs more than brown, and brown eggs more than blue. The preference for green and yellow eggs over brown eggs was remarkable because the brown wooden eggs were most similar to a real gull egg. Increases in the number of speckles and their contrast with the background also increased egg-retrieval behavior, as did increases in the size of the wooden eggs.

Color, speckling, and size appeared to control the egg-retrieval behavior in an additive fashion. Thus, the attractiveness of an egg could be increased by making it more green, more speckled, or larger. Optimizing all three of these stimulus dimensions resulted in a green, highly speckled, and abnormally large egg. Interestingly, such an egg was more effective in stimulating egg-retrieval behavior than was a real gull egg. It was shown, then, that once the stimuli controlling a modal action pattern had been identified, they could be combined to form a stimulus that was more effective than a naturally occurring object in eliciting the action pattern. Such an unusually effective stimulus is called a **supernormal stimulus.**

The Role of Feedback in Elicited Behavior

Responses usually produce specific stimulus consequences. This is true for all behavior, including responses elicited by environmental events. When your pupils constrict in bright light, for example, less light reaches the retina as a result. The salivation elicited by food in the mouth makes the food softer and less concentrated. Coughing and sneezing in re-

sponse to irritation of the respiratory passages produce loud noises and rapid expulsion of air and usually remove the irritant. A specific stimulus that results from a particular response is called a **feedback stimulus** for that response. A consideration of the role of feedback stimuli provides important insights into behavior.

Feedback stimuli may arise from sources internal or external to the organism. Internal feedback cues are provided by sensory neurons that allow the animal to feel the muscle and joint movements involved in making the response. If someone tapped your knee in the appropriate place and elicited the knee-jerk reflex, you would feel your leg kick. You would know when you made the response even if you closed your eyes because of sensations provided by sensory neurons in the leg muscles and knee joint. Such internal feedback cues are called **proprioceptive stimuli.** The movement of most skeletal muscles provides proprioceptive sensations. However, not all reflex responses are accompanied by

---

BOX **2.1**

Eliciting Aggression in Sticklebacks

A frequently cited example of a sign stimulus comes from the studies of ter Pelkwijk and Tinbergen (1937), designed to identify the sign stimulus involved in eliciting aggressive behavior in male stickleback fish. During the breeding season, the underside of reproductively active male sticklebacks becomes red. Using models and dead fish as stimuli, ter Pelkwijk and Tinbergen found that the attack behavior of males increased significantly if the underside of the target was painted red. Detailed resemblance to a stickleback was not as important as the red ventral surface. Based on these observations, ter Pelkwijk and Tinbergen concluded that a red ventral surface was a sign stimulus for releasing aggression in male sticklebacks.

More recent research has yielded inconsistent results, with some sticklebacks showing more aggression to models with a red ventral surface and others attacking a plain silver dummy more frequently (Collias, 1990; Rowland, 1982; Rowland & Sevenster, 1985). In trying to interpret these inconsistencies, authors have speculated about the possible role of prior experience and learning in determining the response of male sticklebacks to a red ventral surface (Baerends, 1985; Rowland, 1982; Rowland & Sevenster, 1985). Experiential factors in determining response to sign stimuli have been explicitly investigated in a recent study of the copulatory behavior of male Japanese quail (Domjan, Greene, & North, 1989). Sign stimuli were more effective in eliciting copulatory behavior in a test arena subjects associated with sexual activity than in a test arena subjects had encountered previously in the absence of sexual reinforcement.

proprioceptive cues. For example, constriction of the pupils creates few internal sensations. Rather, the feedback that results from pupillary constriction occurs because less light reaches the retina. This feedback changes the external stimuli to which the organism is exposed. We will discuss only the role of such external feedback cues in elicited behavior. Some response patterns are largely independent of external feedback cues. In other cases, the behavior is almost exclusively controlled by feedback.

Elicited behavior independent of feedback stimuli. Once they are initiated, some responses go to completion largely independent of the consequences of the behavior. Many modal action patterns run to completion regardless of stimulus consequences once the activities have been initiated. Some familiar examples can be observed in common pets. Cats, for example, when they are eating, shake their heads slightly after taking a bite and then proceed to chew and swallow. The shaking response is very useful when the cat is about to eat a live mouse because it helps to kill the mouse. This part of the modal action pattern continues to occur even when the food does not have to be killed. Another common modal action pattern in domestic cats is seen when they use the litter box. Elimination in cats ends with their scratching the litter to cover up their waste. However, this scratching response is independent of its stimulus consequences. Cats scratch for awhile after eliminating whether or not the litter they scratch covers up their waste. In fact, sometimes they scratch on the side of the litter box without moving any litter at all.

Another dramatic example of a modal action pattern is the cocoon-spinning behavior of the spider *Ciprennium salei* (see Eibl-Eibesfeldt, 1970). The spider begins by spinning the bottom of the cocoon; then it spins the sides. It lays its eggs inside the cocoon and then spins the top of the cocoon, thereby closing it. This response sequence is remark-able because it occurs in the specified order even if the usual outcome of the response is altered by an experimenter. For example, the spider will continue to spin the sides of the cocoon and lay the eggs even if the bottom of the cocoon is destroyed and the eggs fall through the cocoon. If the spider is placed on a partly completed cocoon, it will nevertheless begin the spinning response sequence as if it had to start an entirely new cocoon. Another remarkable aspect is that the spinning responses occur in much the same way even if the spider is unable to produce the material with which to construct the cocoon. Thus, although the spider appears to go through the spinning movements in order to have a place to lay its eggs, the consequences of the behavior do not control its occurrence.

Presence or absence of the eliciting stimulus as feedback. Modal action patterns such as those we have just described are generally elicited by discrete sign stimuli. In other situations, responses are elicited by events that may be present for a long time. In some of these cases, the elicited response may either maintain the animal in contact with the eliciting stimulus or remove the animal from the stimulus. Which of these feedback events takes place strongly determines the future occurrence of the response. If the response maintains the animal in contact with the eliciting stimulus, the response will persist. By contrast, if the behavior removes the animal from the eliciting stimulus, the response will cease.

We have already encountered response systems in which the response feedback is provided by the presence or absence of the eliciting stimulus. Consider, for example, the sucking response of newborn babies. When presented with a nipple, the baby begins to suck. This response serves to maintain contact between the baby and the nipple. The continued contact, in turn, elicits further sucking behavior. In other cases, the outcome of the response removes the eliciting stimulus. Reflexive sneezing and coughing, for example, usually result in removal of the irritation in the respiratory passages that originally elicited the behavior. When the irritation is removed, the sneezing and coughing cease.

Feedback involving the presence or absence of the eliciting stimulus is very important in controlling reflexive locomotor movement in many animals. In one type of reflexive locomotion, the eliciting stimulus produces a change in the speed of movement (or the speed of turning), irrespective of direction. Such movement is called a **kinesis.** The behavior of woodlice provides a good example. The woodlouse *(Porcellio scaber)* is a small isopod usually found in damp areas, such as under rocks, boards, and leaves. From a casual observation of the places in which woodlice are found, one might be tempted to conclude that they move toward damp places because they prefer such areas. However, their tendency to congregate in damp places is a result of a kinesis. Low levels of humidity elicit locomotor movement in the lice. As long as the air is dry, the lice continue to move. When they reach more humid places, a higher proportion of them are found to be inactive. Thus, they tend to congregate in areas of high humidity not because they prefer such areas and "voluntarily" seek them out, but because in damp places the stimulus for movement is absent (Fraenkel & Gunn, 1961).

Kinesis determines the resting location of other types of animals as well. In contrast to the woodlice, both adult and larval grasshoppers are more active in moist areas and quiescent in dry places (Riegert, 1959). This response increases the likelihood that they will remain in dry areas. In flatworms kinesis is controlled by illumination rather than humidity. Several types of flatworms are more likely to stop in dark than in well-lit places (Walter, 1907; Welsh, 1933). Another interesting kinesis controlled by light is found in the larvae of the brook lamprey *(Lampetra planeri).* When exposed to light, they wriggle around with the head pointed downward. The greater the illumination, the greater the activity. On a muddy substrate, the wriggling movement results in the animal's burrowing into the ground. The burrowing persists until the light receptors at the tip of the tail become covered up with mud (Jones, 1955).

Kinesis produces movements toward (or away from) particular stimuli as an indirect result of changes in the rate of movement triggered by the stimuli. In another type of reflexive locomotion process, the stimulus directly creates movements toward or away from it. This type of mechanism is called a **taxis** (plural, *taxes*). A taxis is identified by the nature of the eliciting stimulus and whether the movement is toward or away from the stimulus. Earthworms tend to turn away from bright light (Adams, 1903). This is an example of a *negative phototaxis.* The South American bloodsucker orients and goes toward warm bodies (Wigglesworth & Gillett, 1934). In the laboratory, for example, the bloodsucker will go toward a test tube of warm water. This is an example of a *positive thermotaxis.* The tree snail exhibits a *negative geotaxis* (Crozier & Navez, 1930). Pulling of the shell in one direction causes the snail to move in the opposite direction. In nature the result is that the snail climbs trees because gravity pulls its shell toward the ground. The direction of flight in many insects is controlled by taxes. Locusts, for example, have small tufts of hair on the front of the head. The animals always orient their flight so that the hairs are bent straight back (Weiss-Fogh, 1949). Changes in flight orientation produce feedback in the form of changes in the hair tufts, and this feedback stimulates further changes in orientation that make the locust fly directly into the wind.

Taxes and kineses are remarkable because they illustrate how responses that appear to be goal-directed and volitional can be produced by relatively simple and mechanistic reflex processes. To explain the behavior of woodlice, for example, it is not necessary to postulate that they enjoy and seek out damp places. Similarly, it is not necessary to postulate that locusts seek to fly into the wind or enjoy doing so. Rather, these apparently goal-directed movements can be explained in terms of reflex responses controlled by feedback cues involving the presence or absence of the eliciting stimulus. The locomotor/orientation movement will persist as long as the response feedback involves continued contact with the eliciting stimulus; it will cease when other types of feedback cues occur.

Responses elicited and guided by different stimuli. So far, we have discussed elicited behavior that is largely independent of the feedback cues and elicited behavior that is controlled by feedback involving the presence or absence of the eliciting stimulus. There are also responses that are elicited by one stimulus and guided by feedback involving a second stimulus. A good example is provided by the mouthbreeding cichlid *(Tilapia mossambica)*, a basslike fish that incubates its eggs in its mouth. After hatching, the young remain close to the mother for a number of days. The approach of a large object or turbulence in the water causes the young to swim toward the mother. More specifically, they approach her lower parts and dark areas. When they reach the mother, they push on the surface and penetrate into holes, and hence many of them end up in the mother's mouth. If the mother is replaced by a model, the young also approach its lower parts and dark patches and push against these areas (Baerends, 1957). The stimulus that elicits the entire response sequence is the approach of a large object or water turbulence. However, the behavior is guided by other cues—the lower side of the mother (or model) and dark patches.

Certain aspects of the egg-retrieval response of the greylag goose also illustrate how one stimulus may be responsible for eliciting a behavior and another involved in guiding it (Lorenz & Tinbergen, 1939). Whenever an egg rolls out of the nest, the goose reaches out and pulls the egg back with side-to-side movements of its beak. This behavior has two components. One involves extending the body to reach the wayward egg and then moving the beak back toward the nest. The other component is the side-to-side adjustments of the beak involved in rolling the egg. The first component is a pure modal action pattern. Once elicited, it goes to completion regardless of the response feedback that occurs. After the goose has extended its body to reach the egg, it pulls its beak all the way back to the nest even if the egg rolls out from under the beak somewhere along the way. By contrast, the side-to-side movements of the beak occur only if the goose is pulling back a rounded, egg-shaped object. If a straight pipe that does not wobble is substituted, the side-to-side movements do not occur. These movements are closely governed by response feedback. If the egg wobbles in one direction, the goose will move its beak more to that side to support it. This movement may cause the egg to wobble in the other direction, producing another side-to-side adjustment. The sequence of responses guided by feedback continues until the goose has pulled its beak all the way back.

Effects of Repeated Stimulation: Two Examples

Because elicited behavior involves a close relationship between an environmental event and a resulting response, elicited behavior is often considered invariant. We tend to assume that an elicited response—particularly, a simple reflex response—will occur the same way automatically every time the eliciting stimulus is presented. We assume, for example, that a baby will suck with invariant vigor every time a nipple is presented. If elicited behavior did occur the same way every time the stimulus was presented, however, it would be of limited interest, particularly for investigators of learning. Learning is identified by changes in behavior that result from experience. If elicited behavior were invariant, it would not be of much relevance to the study of learning.

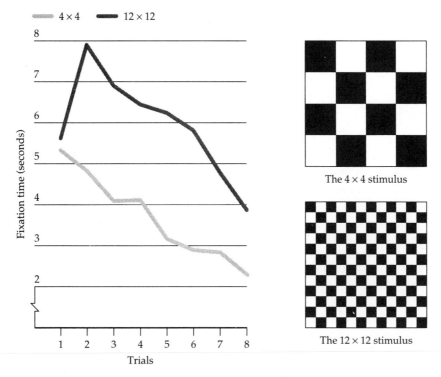

Figure 2.5 Time infants spent looking at a visual stimulus during successive trials. For one group, the stimulus consisted of a 4 × 4 checkerboard pattern. For a second group, the stimulus consisted of a 12 × 12 checkerboard pattern. The stimuli are illustrated to the right of the results. *(From "Determinants of Infant Visual Attention: Evidence For a Two-Process Theory," by Bashinski, Werner and Rudy, 1985,* Journal of Experimental Child Psychology, 39, *pp. 580–598. Copyright © 1985 by Academic Press. Reprinted by permission.)*

Contrary to common assumptions about reflexive and elicited behavior, such behavior is not invariant. One of the most impressive facts about behavior is its plasticity. Even simple elicited responses do not occur the same way each time the eliciting stimulus is presented. Our discussion of the role of feedback cues in elicited behavior indicated that in some cases the nature of the behavior is altered by the feedback cues that result from responding. Alterations in the nature of elicited behavior often also occur simply as a result of repeated presentations of the eliciting stimulus. The following examples illustrate several ways in which elicited behavior can change as a result of repeated stimulation.

Visual Attention in Human Infants

Human infants have a lot to learn about the world. One way they obtain information is by looking at things in their environment. Visual cues elicit a looking response, which can be measured in terms of how long the infant gazes at a stimulus before shifting his eyes elsewhere.

In one study of visual attention (Bashinski, Werner, & Rudy, 1985; see also Kaplan, Werner, & Rudy, 1990), 4-month-old infants were tested with one of two types of visual stimuli that differed in complexity. The stimuli are shown in the right panel of Figure 2.5. Each one was a checkerboard pattern, but one had 4 squares on each side (the 4 × 4 stimulus), and the other had 12 squares on each side (the

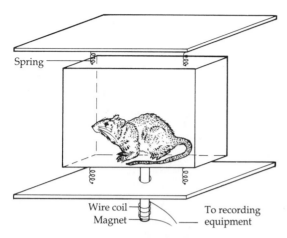

Spring

Wire coil
Magnet

To recording
equipment

Figure 2.6 Stabilimeter apparatus to measure the startle response of rats. A small chamber is balanced on springs between two stationary platforms. A magnet, surrounded by a wire coil, is fixed to the bottom of the chamber. Sudden movements of the rat result in movements of the chamber that produce an electrical current in the wire coil. *(Adapted from Hoffman and Fleshler, 1964.)*

12 × 12 stimulus). Each stimulus lasted for 10 seconds and was presented eight times at 10-second intervals. One group of infants always received the 4 × 4 stimulus, and another group always received the 12 × 12 stimulus.

Both stimuli elicited visual attention initially, with the babies spending an average of about 5.5 seconds looking at the stimuli. With repeated presentations of the 4 × 4 stimulus, visual attention progressively decreased. By contrast, the babies increased the duration of their gaze at the 12 × 12 stimulus during the second trial. After that, visual attention to the 12 × 12 stimulus also decreased.

These results illustrate that visual attention elicited by a novel stimulus changed as the babies gained experience with the stimulus. Furthermore, the nature of the change was determined by the nature of the stimulus. With a relatively simple stimulus, visual attention progressively declined. With a more complex stimulus, attention initially increased and then declined. Thus, far from being invariant, the elicited behavior of looking at

checkerboard patterns changed in different ways as a result of experience with the stimuli.

Startle Response in Rats

Variations in elicited behavior of the type that occur when a stimulus is repeatedly presented to elicit visual attention also occur in many other response systems. One system that has been extensively investigated involves the startle response. The startle response is evident in many species. If someone unexpectedly blows a clown's horn behind your back, you are likely to become startled. The startle response consists of a sudden jump and tensing of the muscles of the upper part of the body, usually involving raising of the shoulders. In rats, the reaction can be measured by placing the animal in a stabilimeter chamber (see Figure 2.6). A stabilimeter is a small enclosure held in place by several springs. When startled, the animal jumps, producing a bouncing movement of the chamber. Sudden movements can be precisely measured to indicate the vigor of the startle reaction.

The startle reaction can be elicited in rats by all sorts of stimuli, including brief tones and lights. In one experiment, Davis (1974) investigated the startle reaction of rats to presentations of a brief (90-millisecond) loud tone (110 decibels [dB], 4,000 cycles per second [cps]). Two groups of rats were tested. Each group received 100 successive tone trials separated by 30 seconds. In addition, a noise generator provided background noise that sounded something like water running from a faucet. For one group, the background noise was relatively quiet (60 dB); for the other, the background noise was rather loud (80 dB), but of lower intensity than the brief tones.

The results of the experiment are shown in Figure 2.7. As was true of the visual-attention response, repeated presentations of the eliciting stimulus (the 4,000-cps tone) did not always produce the same startle response. For subjects tested in the presence of the soft background noise (60 dB), repetitions of the

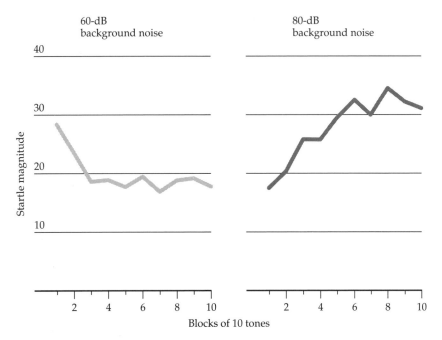

Figure 2.7 Magnitude of the startle response of rats to successive presentations of a tone with background noise of 60 and 80 dB. *(From "Sensitization of the Rat Startle Response by Noise" by M. Davis, 1974,* Journal of Comparative and Physiological Psychology, 87, pp. 571–581. Copyright © 1974 by the American Psychological Association. Reprinted by permission.)*

tone resulted in weaker and weaker startle reactions. This outcome is similar to what was observed when the 4 × 4 stimulus was repeatedly presented to elicit visual attention in babies. By contrast, when the background noise was loud (80 dB), repetitions of the tone elicited more vigorous startle reactions. This outcome is comparable to what was observed at first with the 12 × 12 stimulus. Thus, as with visual attention, repeated elicitations of the startle reflex produced a decrease in the magnitude of the startle reaction in some circumstances and an increase in others.

The Concepts of Habituation and Sensitization

The two studies described in the previous section show that both decreases and increases in responding can occur with repeated presentation of an eliciting stimulus. These changes involve the behavior or performance of human and nonhuman animals. Decreases in responsiveness produced by repeated stimulation are examples of **habituation effects.** Increases in responsiveness are examples of **sensitization effects.** Habituation and sensitization effects represent fundamental forms of behavior change that result from prior experience. They are such fundamental features of how organisms adjust to the environment that they occur in nearly all species and response systems (for example, Peeke & Petrinovich, 1984).

Adaptiveness and Pervasiveness of Habituation and Sensitization

Organisms are constantly being bombarded by a host of stimuli. Imagine yourself sitting at your desk, for example. Even such a simple situation involves a myriad of sensations. You experience the color, texture, and brightness of the paint on the walls; the sounds of the air-conditioning system; noises from other rooms; odors in the air; the color and texture of the desk; the tactile sensations of the chair against your legs, seat, and back; and so on. If you were to respond to all of the stimuli in the situation, your behavior would be disorganized and chaotic. Habituation and sensitization effects reflect how you end up sorting out what to ignore and what to respond to. Habituation and sensitization effects are the end products of processes that help you organize and focus your behavior in the sea of ongoing stimulation.

There are numerous instances of habituation and sensitization in common human experience. Consider the grandfather clock, for example. Most people who own such a clock do not notice each time it chimes. They have completely habituated to the clock's sounds. In fact, they are more likely to notice when the clock misses a scheduled chime. In a sense, this is unfortunate, because they may have purchased the grandfather clock specifically for the beauty of its chime. Similarly, people who live on busy streets, near railroad tracks, or close to an airport may become entirely habituated to the noises that frequently intrude into their homes. On the other hand, visitors would be much more likely to respond to, and be bothered by, such sounds.

Driving a car involves exposure to a large array of complex visual and auditory stimuli. In becoming an experienced driver, a person habituates to the numerous stimuli that are irrelevant to driving, such as details of the color and texture of the road, the kind of telephone poles that line the sides of the street, tactile sensations of the steering wheel, and sounds from the engine. Habituation to irrelevant cues is particularly prominent during long driving trips. If you are driving continuously for several hours, you are likely to become oblivious to all kinds of stimuli that

are irrelevant to keeping the car on the road. If you then come across an accident or arrive in a new town, you are likely to "wake up" and again pay attention to various things that you had been ignoring. Passing a bad accident or coming to a new town is an arousing stimulus that changes your state and sensitizes various orientation responses that were previously habituated.

If you ever had a cat or dog that you brought home when it was young, chances are the animal was extremely agitated and cried a great deal during the first few days. This occurred because most of the stimuli in the animal's new environment were effective in eliciting responses. As the cat or dog got used to its new home — that is, as it became habituated to many of the stimuli in the situation — it stopped being agitated and became generally less active. Humans experience similar effects. If you visit a new place or encounter people you have never dealt with before, you are likely to pay attention to all sorts of stimuli that you ordinarily ignore. In a strange home, you are likely to take notice of the quality of the furniture, the drapes, and some of the knickknacks on the shelves. You are likely to ignore such details in familiar places — so much so that you may not be able to describe the color of the walls in a hallway you pass through every day or to recall the type of knob attached to a door you use regularly.

Distinctions Between Habituation, Sensory Adaptation, and Response Fatigue

As previously noted, in many situations the response that is initially elicited by a stimulus ceases to occur when the stimulus is frequently repeated. This decline in responding is a key characteristic of habituation effects. However, not all instances in which repetitions of a stimulus result in a decline in responding represent habituation. To understand alternative sources of response decrement, we need to return to the concept of a reflex. A reflex consists of three components (see Figure 2.1). First, a stimulus activates one of the sense organs of the body, such as the eyes or ears. This process generates sensory neural impulses that are relayed to the central nervous system (spinal cord and brain). The second component involves relay of the sensory messages to motor nerves. The neural impulses in motor nerves in turn activate the muscles that create the observed response, in the third and last component of the reflex.

Given the three components of a reflex, there are several reasons why an elicited response may decline with repeated stimulation. The elicited response will not be observed if for some reason the sense organs become temporarily insensitive to stimulation. A person may be temporarily blinded by a bright light, for example, or suffer a temporary hearing loss because of repeated exposures to a loud noise. Such decreases in sensitivity are called **sensory adaptation.** The reflex response will also fail to occur if the muscles involved become incapacitated by **fatigue.** Sensory adaptation and response fatigue are impediments to the elicited response that are produced outside the nervous system, in sense organs and muscles.

The likelihood of a response will also be changed if the neural processes involved in the elicited behavior are altered. Various types of changes in the nervous system can hinder or facilitate transmission of neural impulses from sensory to motor neurons. Habituation and sensitization are assumed to involve such neurophysiological changes. Thus, habituation is different from sensory adaptation and response fatigue. In habituation, the subject ceases to respond to a stimulus even though it remains fully capable of sensing the stimulus and of making the muscle movements required for the response. The response fails to occur because, for some reason, the sensory neural impulses are not relayed to the motor neurons.

In studies of habituation, sensory adaptation is ruled out by evidence that habituation is response-specific. An organism may reduce

its responding to a stimulus in one aspect of its behavior while continuing to respond to the stimulus in other ways. When a teacher makes an announcement while you are concentrating on taking a test, you may look up from your test at first, but only briefly. However, you will continue to listen to the announcement until it is over. Thus, your orienting response habituates quickly, but other attentional responses to the stimulus will persist.

Response fatigue as a cause of a response decrement can be ruled out by evidence that the response will quickly recover when a new stimulus is introduced. After your orienting response to the teacher's announcement has habituated, if someone whispers your name you are likely to look in the direction of the whisper. Thus, a new stimulus will elicit the habituated response, indicating that failure of the response was not due to fatigue.

A Dual-Process Theory of Habituation and Sensitization

Now that we have talked about changes in behavior or performance—a habituation effect being a decreased level of responding and a sensitization effect being an increased level of responding—how can we determine the factors responsible for such changes? To answer this question we have to shift our level of analysis from behavior to presumed underlying process. The dual-process theory of habituation and sensitization assumes that different types of underlying neural processes are responsible for increases and decreases in responsiveness to stimulation. One category of changes in the nervous system produces decreases in responsiveness. This category of changes is called a **habituation process.** Another category of changes in the nervous system produces increases in responsiveness. Such changes constitute the **sensitization process.** These two types of processes may occur simultaneously in a given situation. The results observed will depend on which process is stronger. The left-hand graph in

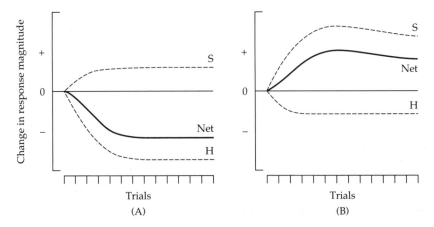

Figure 2.8 Hypothetical data illustrating the dual-process theory of habituation and sensitization. The dashed lines indicate the strength of the habituation (H) and sensitization (S) processes across trials. The solid line indicates the net effects of these two processes. In panel A (left), the habituation process becomes stronger than the sensitization process across trials, which leads to a progressive decrement in responding. In panel B (right), the sensitization process becomes stronger than the habituation process across trials, which leads to a progressive increase in responding.

Figure 2.8 illustrates a hypothetical situation in which repetitions of a stimulus strengthen the habituation process more than the sensitization process. The net effect of these changes is a decline in the elicited response across trials (a habituation effect). The right-hand graph illustrates the opposite outcome. Here, repetitions of a stimulus strengthen the sensitization process more than the habituation process, the result being an increase in the magnitude of the elicited response across trials (a sensitization effect). Thus, the changes in the elicited behavior that actually occur in a particular situation represent the net effect of habituation and sensitization processes.

In a sense it is unfortunate that the underlying *processes* that produce habituation and sensitization *effects* are also called habituation and sensitization. One may be led to think that a habituation effect is produced by a habituation process, and that a sensitization effect is produced by a sensitization process. In fact, as is illustrated in Figure 2.8, a habituation effect is the sum or net result of both habituation and sensitization processes. A sensitization effect is

also the net result of both habituation and sensitization processes. As previously stated, whether the net result is an increase or a decrease in behavior depends on which underlying process is stronger in the given situation. The distinction between *effects* and *processes* in considerations of habituation and sensitization is analogous to the distinction between *performance* and *learning* as discussed in Chapter 1. Recall that performance refers to observable behavior and learning to the presumed underlying mechanism.

On the basis of neurophysiological research, Groves and Thompson (1970) suggested that habituation and sensitization processes occur in different parts of the nervous system (see also Thompson et al., 1973). Habituation processes are assumed to occur in what is called the **S–R system.** This system consists of the shortest neural path that connects the sense organs stimulated by the eliciting stimulus and the muscles involved in making the elicited response. (The S–R system may be viewed as the reflex arc.) By contrast, sensitization processes are assumed to occur in what is called the **state system.** This consists of other parts of the nervous system that determine the organism's general level of responsiveness or readiness to respond. The state system is relatively quiescent during sleep, for example. Drugs such as stimulants or depressants may alter the functioning of the state system and thereby change responsiveness. The state system is also altered by emotional experiences. The jumpiness that accompanies fear is caused by activation of the state system. The state system thus determines the animal's readiness to respond, whereas the S–R system enables the animal to make the specific responses elicited by the stimuli in the situation. The observed behavioral changes reflect the combined actions of these two systems.

The examples of habituation and sensitization illustrated in Figures 2.5 and 2.7 can be easily interpreted in terms of the dual-process theory. Repeated exposure to the 4 × 4 checkerboard pattern produced a decrement in responding. This may be interpreted by assuming that the 4 × 4 stimulus activated primarily the S–R system, and hence activated primarily habituation processes. The more complex 12 × 12 checkerboard pattern presumably activated not only the S–R system but also the state system. The activation of the state system resulted in the increment in visual attention that occurred after the first presentation of the 12 × 12 pattern. However, sensitization processes were not sufficiently activated to entirely counteract the effects of habituation, with the result that after a couple of trials visual attention also declined in response to the 12 × 12 stimulus.

The dual-process theory is also consistent with the habituation and sensitization effects we noted in the startle reaction of rats (Figure 2.7). When subjects were tested with a relatively quiet background noise (60 dB), there was little in the situation to arouse them. Therefore, we can assume that the experimental procedures did not produce changes in the state system. Repeated presentations of the startle-eliciting tone merely activated the S–R system, which resulted in habituation of the startle response. However, the opposite outcome occurred when the animals were tested in the presence of a loud background noise (80 dB). In this case, stronger startle reactions occurred to successive presentations of the tone. Because the identical tone was used to elicit the startle response for both groups, differences in the results cannot be attributed to the tone. Rather, one must assume that the loud background noise increased arousal or readiness to respond. This sensitization of the state system was presumably responsible for the increase in the magnitude of the startle reaction.

The preceding interpretations of changes in visual attention and startle responding illustrate several important features of the dual-process theory. As we have seen, the state and S–R systems are activated differently by repeated presentations of a stimulus. The S–R system is activated every time a stimulus elicits a response because it is the neural circuit that conducts impulses from sensory input to response output. By contrast, the state system becomes involved only in special circumstances. First, some extraneous event (such as an intense background noise) may increase the subject's alertness and sensitize the state system. Second, the state system may be sensitized by the repeated stimulus presentations if the stimulus is sufficiently intense or excitatory (a 12 × 12 checkerboard pattern, as compared with a 4 × 4 pattern). If the complex stimulus is repeated soon enough so that the second presentation occurs while the subject remains sensitized from the preceding trial, an increase in responding will be observed.

The dual-process theory of habituation and sensitization has been very influential in the study of the plasticity of elicited behavior, although it has not been successful in explaining all habituation and sensitization effects. One of the important contributions of the theory has been the assumption that elicited behavior can be strongly influenced by neurophysiological events that take place outside the reflex arc directly involved in a particular elicited response. In dual-process theory, the state system is assumed to modulate the activity of reflex arcs. The basic idea that certain parts of the nervous system serve to modulate S–R systems that are more directly involved in elicited behavior has been also developed in other more recent studies of habituation and sensitization (for example, Borszcz, Cranney, & Leaton, 1989; Davis & File, 1984; Davis, Hitchcock, & Rosen, 1987). (For a detailed discussion of other theories of habituation, see Stephenson & Siddle, 1983.)

Characteristics of Habituation and Sensitization

Much research has been performed to determine how various factors influence habituation and sensitization processes. Although the characteristics of habituation and sensitization are not perfectly uniform across all species and response systems, there are many commonalities. We will describe some of the most important.

Time Course of Habituation and Sensitization

Most of the forms of behavior change we will describe in later chapters are retained for long periods (one or more years). In fact, this is one of the defining characteristics of learning phenomena (see Chapter 1). Instances of habituation and sensitization do not always have this characteristic, and therefore not all instances of habituation and sensitization are properly considered examples of learning.

Time course of sensitization. Sensitization processes generally have temporary effects. Although in some instances sensitization persists for more than a week (for example,

Heiligenberg, 1974), in most situations the increased responsiveness is short-lived. Different sensitization effects may persist for different amounts of time. Davis (1974), for example, investigated the sensitizing effect of a 25-minute exposure to a loud noise (80 dB) in rats. As expected, the loud noise sensitized the startle response to a tone. However, this increased reactivity persisted for only 10–15 minutes after the loud noise was turned off. In other response systems, sensitization dissipates much more rapidly. For example, sensitization of the spinal hindlimb-flexion reflex in cats persists for only about 3 seconds (Groves & Thompson, 1970). However, in all response systems the duration of sensitization effects is determined by the intensity of the sensitizing stimulus. More intense stimuli produce greater increases in responsiveness, and the sensitization effects persist longer.

Time course of habituation. Habituation also persists for varying amounts of time. With sensitization, differences in the time course of the effect usually reflect only quantitative differences in the same underlying mechanism. By contrast, there appear to be two *qualitatively* different types of habituation effects. One type of habituation is similar to most cases of sensitization in that it dissipates relatively quickly—within seconds or minutes. The other type is much longer lasting and may persist for many days. These two types of habituation were nicely illustrated in an experiment on the startle response of rats (Leaton, 1976). The test stimulus was a high-pitched, loud tone presented for 2 seconds. The animals were first allowed to get used to the experimental chamber without any tone presentations. Each rat then received a single test trial with the tone stimulus once a day for 11 days. Because of the long (24-hour) interval between stimulus presentations, any decrements in responding produced by the stimulus presentations were assumed to exemplify the long-lasting habituation process. The transient (short-lasting) habituation process was

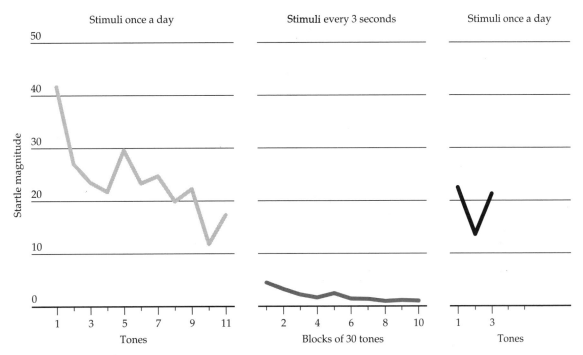

Figure 2.9 Startle response of rats to a tone presented once a day in phase 1, every 3 seconds in phase 2, and once a day in phase 3. *(From "Long-Term Retention of the Habituation of Lick Suppression and Startle Response Produced by a Single Auditory Stimulus" by R.N. Leaton, 1976,* Journal of Experimental Psychology: Animal Behavior Processes, *2, pp. 248–259. Copyright © 1976 by the American Psychological Association. Reprinted by permission.)*

activated in the next phase of the experiment by giving the subjects 300 closely spaced tone presentations (every 3 seconds). Finally, the animals were given a single tone presentation 1, 2, and 3 days later to measure recovery from the short-term habituation.

Figure 2.9 shows the results. The most intense startle reaction was observed the first time the tone was presented. Progressively less intense reactions occurred during the next 10 days. Because the animals were tested only once every 24 hours in this phase, the progressive decrements in responding indicate that the habituating effects of the stimulus presentations persisted throughout the 11-day period. This long-lasting habituation process did not result in complete loss of the startle reflex. Even on the 11th day, the animals still reacted a little. By contrast, startle reactions quickly ceased when the tone pre-

sentations occurred every 3 seconds in the next phase of the experiment. However, this loss of responsiveness was only temporary. When the animals were tested with the tone 1, 2, and 3 days later, the startle response recovered to the level of the 11th day of the experiment. This recovery, known as **spontaneous recovery,** occurred simply because the tone had not been presented for a long time (24 hours). Spontaneous recovery is the identifying characteristic of the short-term, or temporary, habituation effect.

Repeated presentations of a stimulus do not always result in both long-lasting and short-term habituation effects. With the spinal leg-flexion reflex in cats, for example, only the short-term habituation effect is observed (Thompson & Spencer, 1966). In such cases, spontaneous recovery completely restores the animal's reaction to the eliciting stimulus if a long enough period of rest is permitted after habituation. By contrast, spontaneous recovery is never complete in situations that also involve long-term habituation effects, as in Leaton's experiment. As Figure 2.9 indicates, the startle response was restored to some extent in the last phase of the experiment. However, even here the animals did not react as vigorously to the tone as they had the first time it was presented.

Few theories can explain the qualitative differences between the short- and long-term habituation effects. The dual-process theory described earlier was formulated primarily to account for only the temporary aspects of habituation and sensitization. Differences in

the mechanisms of the short- and long-term habituation effects are detailed in a behavioral theory of information processing (for example, Whitlow & Wagner, 1984).

Stimulus Specificity of Habituation and Sensitization

Habituation processes are assumed to be highly specific to the repeated stimulus. A response that has been habituated to one stimulus can be evoked in full strength by a new eliciting stimulus. After you have become completely habituated to the chimes of your grandfather clock, for example, if the clock malfunctions and makes new sounds, your

---

BOX **2.2**

Recovery from Habituation as a Test of Infant Perception

What does the world look like to infants? If we want to know what adults see in a picture or diagram, we can simply ask them. Obviously, such a direct approach will not work with infants because their ability to use language is not sufficiently developed. Cohen and Younger (1984) conducted a study of the habituation of visual attention to solve this problem. The stimuli they used are shown in Figure 2.10. One group of infants received the stimuli in the top row; another group received the stimuli in the bottom row. In each case, the stimuli consisted of two lines that met to form an angle. The experimental question was, Do the infants see the stimuli as two separate lines, or do they integrate the lines and see them as forming an angle? The perception of an angle requires more sophistication because an angle is not a property of either line; rather, it represents the relationship between the two lines.

Each infant was first habituated to viewing one of the stimuli presented on the left side of Figure 2.10. After visual attention had declined significantly to the habituation stimulus, the infants were tested with each of the stimuli shown on the right side of Figure 2.10. Notice that the first of the test stimuli was identical to the training stimulus, and hence no recovery from habituation was expected when this stimulus was presented. The second stimulus involved the same angle as the habituation stimulus, but the lines forming the angle were presented in a novel orientation. The third stimulus employed the same lines as the habituation stimulus, but the lines were now joined to form a new angle. Finally, the fourth test stimulus involved lines in a novel orientation and a new angle.

Three-month-old infants showed no recovery from habituation when the second test stimulus was presented, but they viewed test stimuli #3 and #4 for significantly longer periods. This pattern of results indicates that the 3-month-old infants were responding on the basis of the angle formed by the two lines. When lines in novel orientations formed the familiar angle (stimulus #2), the infants treated the stimulus as familiar, whereas when lines in a familiar orientation formed a new angle (stimulus #3), they responded to the lines as being novel.

Contrasting results were obtained with younger, 6-week-old infants. These younger infants viewed the stimuli as consisting of separate lines and ignored the angle relation between the lines. Thus, they showed no recovery in responding when the lines were left in the original orientation but were put together to form

attention to the clock is likely to become entirely restored. After complete habituation of the orienting response to one stimulus, the response is likely to occur in its normal strength if a sufficiently novel stimulus is presented. Stimulus specificity characterizes all examples of habituation and therefore has been considered one of the defining characteristics of habituation (Thompson & Spencer, 1966).

Although habituation effects are always stimulus-specific, some generalization of the effects may occur. If you have habituated to a particular clock chime, you may also not respond to another clock chime that is only slightly different from the old one. This phenomenon is called **stimulus generalization** of habituation. As the new stimulus is made increasingly different from the habituated stimulus, the subject's reaction will increasingly resemble the response in the absence of habituation.

In contrast with habituation processes, sensitization is less stimulus-specific. If an animal becomes aroused or sensitized for some reason, its reactivity will increase to a range of cues. Pain induced by footshock, for example, increases the reactivity of laboratory rats to both auditory and visual cues. However, the range of stimuli to which an animal may become sensitized by footshock is not unlimited. Shock sensitization does not increase the

a new angle (stimulus #3). However, they increased their attention when lines in novel orientations were used to form the original angle (stimulus #2).

This study demonstrates that 6-week-old infants view the world differently from 3-month-old infants. Rather than seeing relationships between the stimuli they encountered, the younger infants treated the stimuli as consisting of separate and independent line elements. Perceptual integration ability to respond to a relationship between the lines appears to develop later in life. This study illustrates the usefulness of habituation techniques in the pursuit of sophisticated questions about infant perception and categorization (see also Cohen, 1988).

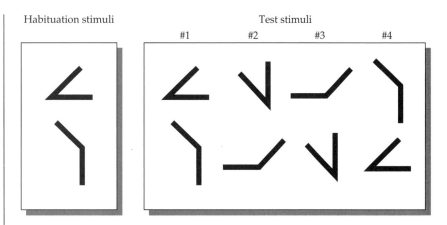

Figure 2.10 Stimuli used in the experiment by Cohen and Younger (1984). One group of infants received the stimuli in the top row. A second group received the stimuli in the bottom row. *(Adapted from Cohen and Younger, 1984.)*

reactivity of rats to novel taste stimuli. Reactivity to novel tastes is sensitized by internal malaise as opposed to cutaneous pain (Miller & Domjan, 1981). Separate sensitization systems appear to exist for exteroceptive and interoceptive stimulation.

Effects of Strong Extraneous Stimuli

As we have noted, changing the nature of the eliciting stimulus can produce recovery of a habituated response. However, this is not the only way to quickly restore responding after habituation. The habituated response can also be restored by sensitizing the subject with exposure to an extraneous stimulus. This phenomenon is called **dishabituation**. Figure 2.11 illustrates the results of a study involving dis-

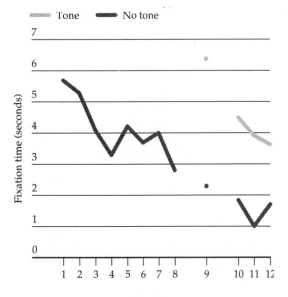

Figure 2.11 Fixation time is plotted as a function of trials for a 4 × 4 checkboard pattern. On the ninth trial, some of the subjects were exposed to a 10-5, 1000-Hz , 75dB tone. This caused an increase in responding to the checkerboard pattern. (*From "Habituation, Sensitization, and Infant Visual Attention" by Kaplan, Werner, and Rudy, 1990,* Advances in Infancy Research, Vol. 6 by C. Rovee-Collier and L.P. Lipsitt (Eds.). Copyright © 1990 by Ablex Publishing Company. Reprinted by permission.)

habituation of the visual-attention response of human infants (Kaplan, Werner, & Rudy, 1990). The infants were shown a 4 × 4 checkerboard pattern during each of the first eight trials of the experiment and displayed a familiar habituation effect. During trial 9, a 75-dB, 1,000-cps tone was sounded along with the visual stimulus for one group of infants, while the other group continued to receive the visual stimulus without the tone as before. The presence of the tone greatly elevated responding. Furthermore, responding continued to be elevated in trials 10, 11, and 12, during which the tone was again omitted and only the 4 × 4 visual stimulus was available.

It is important to keep in mind that *dishabituation* refers to recovery in the response to the previously habituated stimulus—the 4 × 4 pattern in our example. Responding directly to the sensitizing or dishabituating tone is not of interest. In fact, the increased visual fixation that was observed when the tone was presented on trial 9 could not be explained as a response to the tone because the tone was presented through a speaker located above and behind the infant. Thus, if the infant had oriented toward the source of the tone, he or she would have ended up looking away from the visual stimulus.

Effects of Stimulus Intensity and Frequency

Habituation and sensitization effects are closely related to the intensity and frequency of the eliciting stimulus. The intensity of a stimulus is important because more intense stimuli are more likely to activate sensitization processes. The frequency of a stimulus is the number of presentations in a unit of time, such as number per minute. The frequency of a stimulus is important because it determines how much time elapses between successive presentations or trials. With a high stimulus frequency, little time elapses between successive trials. With a low stimulus frequency, trials are more spread out in time.

Each activation of the sensitization process and each activation of the short-term habituation process is assumed to decay with time. The frequency of stimulus presentations determines whether the next trial occurs before the effects of the previous trial have had a chance to dissipate. Rapid repetitions of a stimulus are likely to result in the accumulation or summation of habituation and sensitization effects across trials, whereas slow repetitions of the stimulus will reduce the chances of such cumulative effects. Stimulus intensity and frequency manipulations can produce a variety of outcomes depending on the processes predominantly activated by the stimulus (habituation or sensitization) and the rates of decay of these processes.

Generally, an increase in responding (sensitization) is more likely if the repeatedly presented stimulus is very intense. Furthermore, with intense stimuli, more sensitization occurs as the frequency of the stimulus is increased (for example, Groves, Lee, & Thompson, 1969). By contrast, habituation effects predominate if the repeated stimulus is relatively weak. Furthermore, the rate of habituation increases as the frequency of the weak stimulus is increased because more frequent presentations of the weak stimulus permit summation of the short-term habituation process (see Figure 2.9). Long-term habituation processes are not facilitated by increasing the frequency of stimulus presentations. In fact, there is some evidence that less long-term habituation occurs with more frequent stimulations (for example, Davis, 1970). Because repeated presentations of a stimulus can activate sensitization as well as short-term and long-term habituation processes, the effects of stimulus intensity and frequency in any given situation will depend on the combined effects of these various processes.

Changes in Complex Emotional Responses

To this point, our discussion of changes produced by repetitions of an eliciting stimulus has been limited to relatively simple response systems. However, many stimuli produce much more complex responses than startling or orienting. A stimulus may evoke love, fear, euphoria, terror, satisfaction, uneasiness, or a combination of these emotions. In this section we will describe the standard pattern of emotions evoked by complex emotion-arousing stimuli and how this pattern of emotional responses is altered by repetitions of the stimulus. These issues have been most systematically addressed by the **opponent-process** theory of motivation proposed by Solomon and his collaborators (Hoffman & Solomon, 1974; Solomon, 1977; Solomon & Corbit, 1973, 1974). The theory describes a mechanism for the habituation of primary emotional responses. As we will see in Chapter 4, opponent-process concepts also have been prominently employed in analyses of classical conditioning.

The Opponent-Process Theory of Motivation

What happens when an emotion-arousing stimulus is presented and then removed? Consider the reactions of a 16-year-old who is given a car to drive for the first time. Initially, the teenager will be extremely excited and happy. This excitement will subside a bit as time passes. Nevertheless, the car will continue to give pleasure. If after a day or two the car becomes no longer available, the teenager's emotions will not simply return to neutrality. Rather, for awhile after surrendering the car, a longing for it will persist. This longing will then gradually dissipate.

Obviously, different emotion-arousing stimuli elicit different types of emotional responses. However, the patterns of the emotional changes appear to have certain common characteristics. Solomon and his associates have called these characteristics the **standard pattern of affective dynamics** (Solomon & Corbit, 1974). The key elements of the pattern are shown in Figure 2.12. The onset of the emotion-arousing stimulus, such as receipt of a car, elicits a strong emotional response (happiness) that quickly reaches a *peak*. This

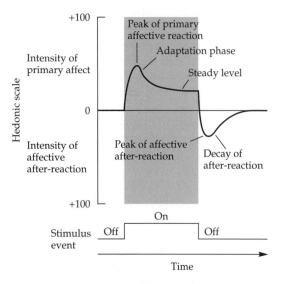

Figure 2.12 Standard pattern of affective dynamics. *(From "An Opponent-Process Theory of Motivation: I. The Temporal Dynamics of Affect" by R.L. Solomon and J.D. Corbit, 1974, Psychological Review, 81, pp. 119–145. Copyright © 1974 by the American Psychological Association. Reprinted by permission.)*

peak reaction is followed by an *adaptation phase* during which the emotional response subsides a bit until it reaches a *steady state*. The stimulus (the car) continues to elicit the emotion (happiness) during the steady state. When the stimulus ceases (the teenager has to surrender the car), the emotional state quickly changes to feelings opposite to those that occurred in the presence of the stimulus. (Now the teenager feels unhappy and has a longing for the car.) This reversal of the emotional state, called the **affective after-reaction,** gradually decays as the subject returns to the normal state.

How will a teenager react to getting a car once such an experience has become routine? If a person has had access to a car many times before, receipt of the car will not elicit the same intense happiness that was experienced the first time. Getting the car is likely to produce only a mild reaction. However, this time, if the car becomes unavailable, the unhappiness and longing for it that result will

be much more intense than the first time. Once a person has become accustomed to having a car, losing access to it creates intense unhappiness. Thus, the pattern of emotional changes to a habituated emotion-arousing stimulus is different from the standard pattern of affective dynamics. This habituated pattern is shown in Figure 2.13. The stimulus elicits only a slight emotional response. However, the affective after-reaction is much stronger than in the standard pattern.

Mechanisms of the Opponent-Process Theory

What underlying mechanisms produce the standard pattern of affective dynamics and modifications of this pattern with habituation to the emotion-arousing stimulus? The opponent-process theory of motivation assumes that neurophysiological mechanisms involved in emotional behavior act to maintain emotional stability. Thus, the opponent-process theory is a *homeostatic* theory. It assumes that an important function of mechanisms that control emotional behavior is to minimize deviations from emotional neutrality or stability. (The concept of homeostasis has been very important in the analysis of behavior. We will discuss other types of homeostatic theories in later chapters.)

How might neurophysiological mechanisms maintain emotional stability or neutrality? Maintaining any system in a neutral or stable state requires that a disturbance that forces the system away from neutrality be met by an opposing force that counteracts the disturbance. Consider, for example, trying to keep a seesaw level. If something pushes one end of the seesaw down, the other end will go up. To keep the seesaw level, a force pushing one end down has to be met by an opposing force on the other side.

The concept of opponent forces or processes serving to maintain a stable state is central to the opponent-process theory of motivation. The theory assumes that an emotion-arousing stimulus pushes a person's emotional state away from neutrality. This shift away from emotional neutrality is assumed to trigger an opponent process that counteracts the shift. The patterns of emotional behavior observed initially and after extensive experience with a stimulus are attributed to various features of the opponent process and when it occurs in relation to when the primary emotional disturbance occurs. Basically, the opponent process is assumed to be a bit inefficient. It lags behind the primary emotional disturbance and becomes effective in substantially counteracting the primary disturbance only after repeated practice.

The opponent-process theory assumes that the presentation of an emotion-arousing stimulus initially elicits what is called the **primary process,** or *a* **process,** which is responsible for the quality of the emotional state (happiness, for example) that occurs in the presence of the stimulus. The primary, or *a*, process is assumed to elicit, in turn, an **opponent process,** or *b* **process,** that generates the opposite emotional reaction (unhappiness, for example). The emotional changes observed when a stimulus is presented and then removed are assumed to reflect the net result of the primary and opponent processes. The strength of the opponent process subtracts from the strength of the primary process to provide the emotions that actually occur.

Figure 2.14 shows how the primary and opponent processes determine the standard pattern of affective dynamics. When the stimulus is first presented, the *a* process occurs unopposed by the *b* process. The primary emotional reaction can therefore reach its peak quickly. The *b* process then becomes activated and begins to oppose the *a* process. The *b* process reduces the strength of the primary emotional response and is therefore responsible for the adaptation phase of the standard pattern. The primary emotional response reaches a steady state when the *a* and *b* processes have each reached their maximum strength during the stimulus presentation. When the stimulus is withdrawn, the *a* process

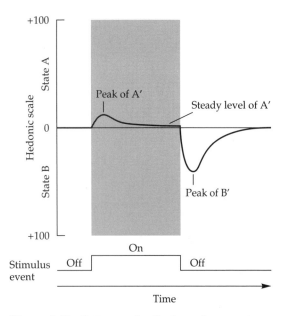

Figure 2.13 Pattern of affective changes to a habituated stimulus. *(From "An Opponent-Process Theory of Motivation: I. The Temporal Dynamics of Affect" by R.L. Solomon and J.D. Corbit, 1974,* Psychological Review, 81, *pp. 119–145. Copyright © 1974 by the American Psychological Association. Reprinted by permission.)*

is quickly terminated, but the *b* process lingers for awhile. Thus, with the *b* process now having nothing to oppose, the emotional responses characteristic of the opponent process become evident for the first time. These emotions are typically opposite to those observed during the presence of the stimulus.

The summation of primary and opponent processes provides a good explanation for the standard pattern of affective dynamics. But how do these underlying processes change during the course of habituation to an emotion-arousing stimulus? As we saw in Figure 2.13, after extensive exposure to the emotion-arousing stimulus, the stimulus ceases to elicit strong emotional reactions and the affective after-reaction becomes much stronger when the stimulus is terminated. The opponent-process theory explains this outcome by assuming simply that the *b* process becomes strengthened by repeated exposures

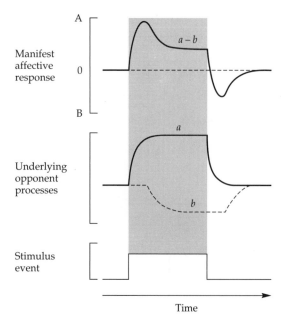

Figure 2.14 Opponent-process mechanism that produces the standard pattern of affective dynamics. *(From "An Opponent-Process Theory of Motivation: I. The Temporal Dynamics of Affect" by R.L. Solomon and J.D. Corbit, 1974, Psychological Review, 81, pp. 119–145. Copyright © 1974 by the American Psychological Association. Reprinted by permission.)*

to the stimulus. The strengthening of the *b* process is reflected in several of its characteristics. The *b* process becomes activated sooner after the onset of the stimulus, its maximum intensity becomes greater, and it becomes slower to decay when the stimulus ceases. On the other hand, the *a* process is assumed to remain unchanged. Thus, after habituation, the primary emotional responses are more strongly opposed by the opponent process. This effect of habituation reduces the intensity of the observed primary emotional responses during presentation of the emotion-arousing stimulus. It also leads to the excessive affective after-reaction when the stimulus is withdrawn (see Figure 2.15).

Examples of Opponent Processes

Love and attachment. The reactions of a teenager to getting a car for a few days, described

earlier, provide just one example of opponent-process mechanisms. Marriage partners may experience corresponding changes. Newlyweds are usually very excited about each other and are very affectionate whenever they are together. This primary emotional reaction habituates as years go by. Gradually, the couple settles into a comfortable mode of interaction that lacks the excitement of the honeymoon. However, this habituation of the primary emotional reaction is accompanied by a strengthening of the affective after-reaction. The more time a couple spends together, the more unhappy the partners become when separated for some reason, and this unhappiness lasts longer. ("Absence makes the heart grow fonder.") After the partners have been together for several decades, the death of one is likely to cause a very extensive grief reaction in the survivor. The intense grief may last a year or two. This strong affective after-reaction is remarkable, considering that by this stage in their relationship the couple may have entirely ceased to show any overt signs of affection.

The predictions of the opponent-process theory for human love and attachment have not been tested experimentally. However, animal research provides strong support for the theory in the area of attachment and separation (see Hoffman & Solomon, 1974; Mineka, Suomi, & DeLizio, 1981; Starr, 1978; Suomi, Mineka, & Harlow, 1983).

Drug addiction. Many drugs are taken mainly for their emotional effects. The emotional changes that result from initial and later drug administrations are accurately described by the opponent-process theory of motivation in many cases (Solomon, 1977). The opponent-process theory predicts that psychoactive drugs will produce a biphasic emotional effect the first few times they are taken. One set of emotional responses is experienced when the drug is active (the primary affective response), and the opposite emotions occur when the drug has worn off (the affective after-reaction). Such biphasic changes are evident with a variety of psychoactive drugs, including alcohol, opiates (such as heroin), amphetamine, and nicotine. The sequence of effects of alcohol is very familiar. Shortly after taking the drug, the person becomes mellow and relaxed because the drug is basically a sedative. The opponent after-reaction is evident in headaches, nausea, and other symptoms of a hangover. With amphetamine, the presence of the drug creates feelings of euphoria, a sense of wellbeing, self-confidence, wakefulness, and a sense of control. After the drug has worn off, the person is likely to be fatigued, depressed, and drowsy.

The opponent-process theory predicts that with repeated frequent uses of a drug, the primary emotional response will weaken and the opponent after-reaction will strengthen. Habituation of the primary drug reactions is an example of **drug tolerance,** in which the effect of a drug declines with repeated doses. Habitual users of alcohol, nicotine, heroin, caffeine, and other drugs are not as greatly affected by the presence of the drug as naive drugtakers. An amount of alcohol that would make a casual drinker a bit tipsy is not likely to have any effect on a frequent drinker. Frequent drinkers have to consume much more alcohol to have the same reactions.

Because of this tolerance, habitual drug users sometimes do not enjoy taking the drug as much as naive users. People who smoke many cigarettes, for example, rarely derive much enjoyment from doing so. Accompanying this decline in the primary drug reaction is a growth in the opponent after-reaction. Accordingly, habitual drug users experience much more severe "hangovers" on termination of the drug than naive users. Someone who stops smoking cigarettes, for example, will experience headaches, irritability, anxiety, tension, and general dissatisfaction. When a heavy drinker stops taking alcohol, he or she is likely to experience hallucinations, memory loss, psychomotor agitation, delirium tremens, and other physiological disturbances. For a habitual user of amphetamine, the fatigue and

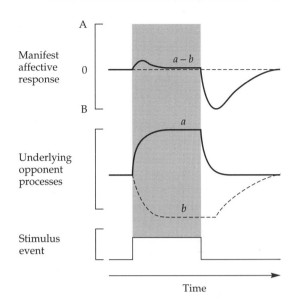

Figure 2.15 Opponent-process mechanism that produces the affective changes to a habituated stimulus. *(From "An Opponent-Process Theory of Motivation: I. The Temporal Dynamics of Affect" by R.L. Solomon and J.D. Corbit, 1974,* Psychological Review, *81, pp. 119–145. Copyright © 1974 by the American Psychological Association. Reprinted by permission.)*

depression that follow the primary effects of the drug may be so severe as to cause suicide.

If the primary pleasurable effects of a psychoactive drug are gone for habitual users, why do they continue to take the drug? Why are they addicted? The opponent-process theory suggests that drug addiction is mainly an attempt to reduce the aversiveness of the affective after-reaction to the drugs—the bad hangovers, the amphetamine "crashes," the irritability that comes from not having the usual cigarette. There are two ways to reduce the aversive opponent after-reactions of drugs. One is to simply wait long enough for them to dissipate. This is what is known as "cold turkey." For heavy drug users, cold turkey may take a long time and may be very painful. The opponent after-reaction can be much more quickly eliminated by taking the drug again. This will reactivate the primary process and stave off the agonies of withdrawal. According to the theory, addicts are not "trapped" by the pleasure they derive from the drug directly. Rather, they take the drug to reduce withdrawal pains.

Concluding Comments

Our complex physical and social environment largely determines all aspects of our functioning. The quality of life and survival itself depend on an intricate coordination of behavior with the complexities of the environment. Elicited behavior represents one of the fundamental ways in which the behavior of all animals—from single-celled organisms to complex human beings—is adjusted to environmental events.

As we have seen, elicited behavior takes many forms, ranging from simple reflexes mediated by just three neurons to complex emotional reactions. Although elicited behavior occurs as a reaction to a stimulus, it is not rigid and invariant. In fact, one of the remarkable features of elicited behavior is that its form is often altered depending on the situation. Some instances of elicited behavior are guided by response-feedback cues. If an eliciting stimulus does not arouse the organism, repeated presentations of the stimulus will evoke progressively weaker responses. This pattern represents the phenomenon of habituation. If the eliciting stimulus is particularly intense or of significance to the subject, repeated presentations will arouse the organism and lead to progressively stronger reactions. This pattern represents the phenomenon of sensitization.

Any environmental event will activate habituation and sensitization processes to varying degrees. The strength of the responses that are observed reflects the net effect of habituation and sensitization. Therefore, if one does not know the past experiences of the organism, it is impossible to predict how strong a reaction will be elicited by a particular stimulus presentation.

Repeated presentations of an eliciting stimulus produce changes in simple responses as well as in more complex emotional reactions. Organisms tend to minimize changes in emotional state caused by external stimuli. According to the opponent-process theory of motivation, emotional responses stimulated by an outside event are counteracted by an opposing process in the organism. This compensatory, or opponent, process is assumed to become stronger each time it is elicited, leading to a reduction of the primary emotional responses if the stimulus is frequently repeated. The strengthened opponent emotional state is evident when the stimulus is removed.

Habituation, sensitization, and changes in the strength of opponent processes are the simplest mechanisms whereby organisms adjust their reactions to environmental events on the basis of past experience.

3 | *Classical Conditioning: Foundations*

Chapter 3 provides an introduction to the fundamental concepts involved in another basic form of learning—classical conditioning. Investigations of classical conditioning began with the work of Pavlov. Since then, the research has been extended to a variety of organisms and response systems. Some of the classical conditioning procedures we will describe establish an excitatory association between two stimuli. Others serve to inhibit the operation of excitatory associations. Following a discussion of how learning can be extinguished, we will conclude the chapter by considering various examples and applications of classical conditioning.

We began our discussion of the principles of behavior in the preceding chapter by describing elicited behavior and the modification of elicited behavior through sensitization and habituation. These relatively simple processes permit organisms to adjust their behavior to a range of environmental challenges. However, if animals had only the behavioral mechanisms described in Chapter 2, they would remain rather limited in the kinds of things they could do. Habituation, for example, involves learning about a single stimulus only. However, events in the world do not take place in isolation or at random with respect to other events. Rather, they occur in a predictable or consistent manner. Habituation processes are not sufficient to allow you to take advantage of predictable relationships between different stimuli in the environment and adjust your behavior accordingly. If you can predict what is going to happen next, you can get ready and deal with the event more effectively than if you are caught off guard.

Cause and effect relationships in the environment ensure that certain events reliably precede others. Your car's engine does not run unless the ignition has been turned on; you cannot walk through a doorway until you have opened the door; it does not rain unless there are clouds in the sky. Social institutions and customs also ensure that events occur in a predictable order. Classes are scheduled at predictable times; you can count on being allowed to pick out what you want to buy in a store before having to pay for it; you can predict whether someone will engage you in conversation by the way the person greets you. Learning to predict events in the environment and learning to respond on the basis of such predictions constitute a very important aspect of behavioral adjustment to the environment. Imagine how much trouble you would have if you could never predict how long something would take to cook, when stores would be open, or whether your car would start in the morning.

The simplest mechanism whereby organisms learn about relations between stimuli and learn to alter their behavior accordingly is **classical conditioning.** Classical conditioning enables animals to take advantage of the orderly sequence of events in the environment and learn which stimuli tend to go with which other events. On the basis of this learning, animals come to make new responses to stimuli. For example, classical conditioning is the process whereby animals learn to approach signals for food and to salivate when they are about to be fed. It is also integrally involved in the learning of such emotional reactions as fear and pleasure to stimuli, which initially do not elicit these emotions. Before further discussing the role of classical conditioning in animals and human behavior generally, we will describe some of the kinds of detailed experimental investigations that have provided us with what we know about classical conditioning.

Pavlov and the Early Years of Classical Conditioning

Systematic studies of classical conditioning began with the work of the great Russian physiologist Ivan P. Pavlov (see Box 3.1, p. 56). The phenomenon of classical conditioning was also independently discovered by Edwin B. Twitmyer in a Ph.D. dissertation submitted to the University of Pennsylvania in 1902 (see Twitmyer, 1974). Twitmyer repeatedly tested the knee-jerk reflex of college students by sounding a bell .5 seconds before hitting the patellar tendon. After awhile, the bell was sufficient to elicit the reflex in some of the students. However, Twitmyer did not develop the implications of his discoveries, and his findings were ignored for many years.

As we noted in Chapter 1, Pavlov's studies of classical conditioning were an extension of his research on the processes of digestion. Pavlov served as a professor in a medical school where students were required to complete a research project before graduating. He

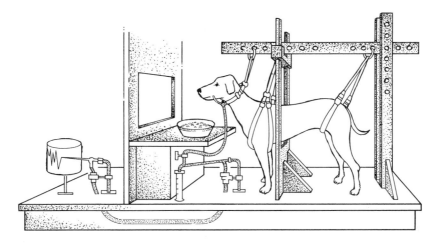

Figure 3.1 Diagram of the Pavlovian salivary conditioning preparation. A cannula attached to the animal's salivary duct conducts drops of saliva to a data-recording device. *(From "The Method of Pavlov in Animal Psychology" by R.M. Yerkes and S. Morgulis, 1909,* Psychological Bulletin, 6, pp. 257–273.)

had many ideas for research, and therefore students were eager to work in his laboratory. Pavlov made major advances in the study of digestion by developing surgical techniques that enabled dogs to survive for many years with artificial tubes or fistulae that permitted the collection of various digestive juices. With the use of a stomach fistula, for example, Pavlov was able to collect stomach secretions in dogs that otherwise lived normally. Technicians in the laboratory soon discovered that the dogs would secrete stomach juices in response to the sight of food, or even just upon seeing the person who usually fed them. The laboratory produced considerable quantities of stomach juice in this manner and sold the excess to the general public. The popularity of this juice as a remedy for various stomach ailments supplemented the income of the laboratory for several years.

Assistants in the laboratory referred to stomach secretions in response to food-related stimuli as "psychic secretions" because they seemed to be a response to the expectation of food. However, for many years the phenomenon of psychic secretions generated little scientific interest.

The first systematic studies of classical conditioning were performed by Stefan Wolfsohn and Anton Snarsky in Pavlov's laboratory (Boakes, 1984). Both of these students focused on the actions of the salivary glands, which are the first digestive glands involved in the breakdown of food. Some of the salivary glands are rather large and have large and accessible ducts that can be easily externalized with a fistula (see Figure 3.1). Wolfsohn studied salivary responses to various substances placed in the mouth: dry food, wet food, sour water, and sand, for example. After the dogs had experienced these substances placed in the mouth, the mere sight of the substances was enough to make them salivate.

Whereas Wolfsohn used naturally occurring substances in his studies, Snarsky's contribution was to extend these observations to artificial substances. In one study, for example, Snarsky first presented sour water (such as strong lemon juice) to the dogs that was artificially colored black. After eliciting salivation with black sour water, Snarsky found that the dogs would also salivate to plain black water or to the sight of any bottle containing a black liquid.

The substances tested by Wolfsohn and Snarsky had both visual and orosensory stimulus features. When sand was initially placed in the mouth, its orosensory features (what the sand felt like in the mouth) elicited salivation. When the dog was subsequently just shown the sand, the visual features of the sand elicited salivation. Presumably the dogs learned to associate the visual features of the sand with its orosensory features. Such learning is referred to as **object learning** because it involves associating different features of the same object.

To study the mechanisms of associative learning, the stimuli to be associated have to be manipulated independently of one another. This is inconvenient to do in an object-learning paradigm where the two stimuli of

---

I. P. Pavlov: Biographical Sketch

BOX **3.1**

Born in 1849 into the family of a priest in Russia, Pavlov dedicated his life to scholarship and discovery. He received his early education in a local theological seminary and planned a career of religious service. However, his interests soon changed, and at 21 he entered the university in St. Petersburg, where his studies focused on chemistry and animal physiology. After obtaining the equivalent of a bachelor's degree, he entered the Imperial Medico-Surgical Academy in 1875 to further his education in physiology. Eight years later, he received his doctoral degree for his research on the efferent nerves of the heart and then began investigating various aspects of digestive physiology. In 1888 he discovered the nerves that stimulate the digestive secretions of the pancreas—a finding that initiated a series of experiments for which Pavlov was awarded the Nobel Prize in Physiology in 1904.

Pavlov did a great deal of original research while a graduate student as well as after obtaining his doctoral degree. However, he did not have a faculty position or his own laboratory until 1890, when he was appointed professor of pharmacology at the St. Petersburg Military Medical Academy. In 1895 he became professor of physiology at the same institution. Pavlov remained very active in the laboratory until close to his death in 1936. In fact, much of the research for which he is famous today was performed after he received the Nobel Prize.

I.P. Pavlov (1849–1936) *(Bettman Archive.)*

interest are properties of the same object. Therefore, in subsequent studies of classical conditioning, Pavlov focused on procedures in which the events or stimuli to be associated came from different sources.

The Classical Conditioning Paradigm

Most people are familiar with the type of procedure Pavlov eventually used to study anticipatory salivation. The procedure typically involved two stimuli of importance. One of these was a noise or a light. On its first presentation, this stimulus might have elicited an orienting response, but it did not elicit salivation. The other stimulus in the situation was food or the taste of a sour solution placed in the mouth. In contrast to the first stimulus, this second one elicited not only orientation movements but also vigorous salivation, even the first time it was presented. Pavlov referred to the tone or light as the **conditional stimulus** because the ability of this stimulus to elicit salivation depended on (was conditional on) pairing it with food presentation several times. By contrast, the food or sour-taste stimulus was called the **unconditional stimulus** because its ability to elicit salivation was not dependent on any prior training of the subjects. The salivation that eventually came to be elicited by the tone or light was called the **conditional response,** and the salivation that was always elicited by the food or sour taste was called the **unconditional response.** Thus, stimuli and responses whose properties and occurrence did not depend on prior training were called "unconditional," and stimuli and responses whose properties and occurrence depended on special training were called "conditional."

In the first English translation of Pavlov's writings, the term *unconditional* was erroneously translated as *unconditioned,* and the term *conditional* was translated as *conditioned.* The -*ed* suffix was used exclusively in English writings for many years. However, the term

conditioned does not capture Pavlov's original meaning of "dependent on" as well as the term *conditional* (Gantt, 1966). The words *conditional* and *unconditional* are more common in modern writings on classical conditioning and are now used interchangeably with *conditioned* and *unconditioned.* Because the terms *conditioned (unconditioned) stimulus* and *conditioned (unconditioned) response* are common in discussions of classical conditioning, they are often abbreviated. *Conditioned stimulus* and *conditioned response* are abbreviated **CS** and **CR**, respectively. *Unconditioned stimulus* and *unconditioned response* are abbreviated **US** and **UR**, respectively.

Experimental Situations

Classical conditioning has been investigated in a wide variety of situations involving many different species. Pavlov did most of his experiments with dogs using the salivary-fistula technique. However, this kind of research is rather costly. Therefore, most contemporary experiments on Pavlovian conditioning are carried out with domesticated rats, rabbits, and pigeons. We will now describe some of the more popular techniques.

Sign Tracking

Pavlov's research concentrated on salivation and other such response systems that may be characterized as highly reflexive. In these systems, a distinctive unconditioned response occurs invariably following presentations of the unconditioned stimulus and comes to be elicited also by the conditioned stimulus as the CS and US are repeatedly paired. Because of Pavlov's work, for quite some time it was believed that classical conditioning procedures could produce learning only in highly reflexive systems. In recent years, however, such a restrictive view of Pavlovian conditioning has been abandoned (for example, Rescorla, 1988b) with growing recognition of the

numerous ways in which associations between conditioned and unconditioned stimuli
can be reflected in changes in behavior. One
experimental paradigm that has contributed
to this broader perspective is called **sign
tracking** or **autoshaping** (Hearst, 1975; Hearst
& Jenkins, 1974; Locurto, Terrace, & Gibbon,
1981).

Animals tend to approach and contact
stimuli that signal the availability of food. In
the natural environment, the availability of
food is usually indicated by some aspect of the
food itself. By approaching and contacting the
food signals, animals in effect come in contact
with the food. For a predator, for example, the
sight, movements, odor, and perhaps noises of
the prey are cue⌄ indicating the possibility of
a meal. By tracking these stimuli, the predator
is likely to catch its prey.

Sign tracking can be investigated in the
laboratory by presenting a discrete, localized
stimulus just before each delivery of a small
amount of food. The first experiment of this
sort was performed by Brown and Jenkins
(1968) with pigeons. The animals were placed
in an experimental chamber that had a small
circular key that could be illuminated and
that the pigeons could peck (see Figure 1.4).
Periodically, the animals were given a small
amount of food. The key light was illuminated for 8 seconds immediately before each
food delivery. The pigeons did not have to
do anything for the food to be presented. The
food was automatically delivered after each
illumination of the response key no matter
what the animals did. Since the animals were
hungry, one might predict that when they
saw the key illuminated, they would go to
the food dish and wait for the forthcoming
food presentation. Interestingly, however,
that is not what happened. Instead of using
the key light to find out when to go to the
food dish, the pigeons started pecking the
key itself. This behavior was remarkable because they were not required to peck the

response key to get food at that point in the
experiment.

Since its discovery, many experiments have
been done on the sign-tracking phenomenon
using a variety of species, including chicks,
quail, goldfish, lizards, rats, rhesus monkeys,
squirrel monkeys, and human adults and
children. (For a recent review, see Tomie,
Brooks, & Zito, 1989.) These experiments
have shown that sign tracking is a very
useful technique for the investigation of how
associations between one stimulus and another are learned. In pigeon sign-tracking
experiments, the conditioned stimulus is illumination of the response key and the
unconditioned stimulus is presentation of
food. As in other conditioning procedures,
learning proceeds most rapidly when the CS
is presented just before the US; learning does
not occur if the CS and US are presented at
random times in relation to each other
(Gamzu & Williams, 1971, 1973).

The tracking of signals for food is dramatically illustrated by instances in which the
signal is located far away from the food-
delivery site. In one such experiment (see
Hearst & Jenkins, 1974), pigeons were placed
in a 6-ft (182-cm) alley that had a food dish
in the middle (see Figure 3.2). Each end of
the alley had a circular disk that could be
illuminated. Presentation of food was always
preceded by illumination of the disk at one
end of the alley. The visual stimulus at the
opposite end was uncorrelated with food.
One other aspect of the experiment is important to point out. The food was available
for only 4 seconds each time it was presented. Therefore, if the animal did not walk
to the food cup within 4 seconds, it did not
get any food on that trial.

After illuminations of the light at one end
of the alley had been paired with delivery
of food a number of times, the pigeons
started doing a most remarkable thing. As
soon as the light came on, they would run

Food dish

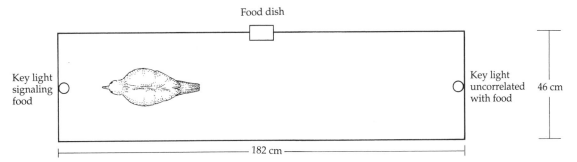

Key light
signaling
food

Key light
uncorrelated
with food

46 cm

182 cm

Figure 3.2 Top view of "long box" used in sign-tracking experiment with pigeons. The conditioned stimulus is illumination of the key light at one end of the experimental chamber. Food is delivered in the middle of the chamber. *(Based on Jenkins, personal communication, 1980.)*

to that end of the alley, peck the illuminated disk, and then run to the center of the alley to get the food. Because the alley was very long, the pigeons did not always get back to the food dish in the middle before the food was removed. This sign-tracking behavior was amazing because it was entirely unnecessary. The animals did not have to peck the lighted disk to get the food reward. They could have just sat in the middle of the alley and waited for the food on each trial. The fact that they did not is evidence of the compelling attraction of classically conditioned signals for food reward. By contrast, the subjects did not consistently approach the light at the other end of the box, which was uncorrelated with food presentations (see also Boakes, 1979).

Sign tracking is possible only in situations where the conditioned stimulus is localized and therefore can be approached and "tracked." In one study, more diffuse spatial and contextual cues of the chamber in which pigeons were given food periodically served as the conditioned stimulus. This time the learning of an association was evident in an increase in activity, rather than in a specific approach response (Rescorla, Durlach, & Grau, 1985). In another experiment (with rats as subjects), a localized light and a sound

were compared as conditioned stimuli for food (Cleland & Davey, 1983). Only the light resulted in conditioned approach or sign-tracking behavior. In response to the sound as a signal for food, the rats were more likely to approach the food cup. These experiments illustrate that for sign tracking to occur the conditioned stimulus has to be of the proper modality and configuration.

Fear Conditioning

Classical conditioning is also involved in the learning of emotional responses. One area of special interest is the acquisition of fear. Laboratory studies of fear conditioning typically are conducted with rats. In most experiments, the aversive unconditioned stimulus is a brief electrical current delivered to the feet through a metal grid floor. We suspect that a large measure of the unpleasantness of the brief shock is that it is startling—unlike anything the animal is likely to have encountered elsewhere. The conditioned stimulus in studies of fear conditioning may be a tone or a light, and conditioned fear is measured indirectly by measuring how the conditioned fear stimulus alters the animal's ongoing activity.

One technique for indirect measurement of conditioned fear is called the **conditioned**

emotional response (or **conditioned suppression**) procedure, abbreviated **CER**. This procedure, devised by Estes and Skinner (1941), has since been used extensively in the study of Pavlovian conditioning (Kamin, 1965). Rats are first trained to press a response lever for food reward in a small experimental chamber (see Figure 3.3A). After sufficient lever-press training, they come to press the lever at a steady rate, earning a food reward every 2–3 minutes. The classical conditioning phase of the experiment is instituted once the lever-press responding has been well established. The duration of the CS is usually 1–2 minutes. The typical conditioning procedure involves presentation of the shock US at the end of the conditioned stimulus. The intertrial interval is usually 15–30 minutes.

The progress of fear conditioning is evident from the disruption of the food-rewarded lever pressing by the conditioned stimulus. If subjects have never encountered the conditioned stimulus before, a slight disruption of lever pressing may occur the first time it is presented. If the CS is not paired with shock, this initial slight response suppression habituates. Within 3–4 trials the CS has no effect whatever on the rats' behavior. However, if the CS reliably signals the footshock, then after several such pairings the animals begin to show evidence that the CS is becoming conditioned, and they suppress their lever-press response when the CS is presented. Within 3–5 conditioning trials, the conditioned suppression of lever pressing can become complete (Kamin & Brimer, 1963). The animals may not press the lever at all when the CS is presented. The response suppression, however, is specific to the CS. Soon after the CS is turned off, the animals resume the food-rewarded behavior.

Becoming motionless, or freezing, is one of the innate reactions of rats to fearful and aversive stimuli (Bolles, 1970). The CER procedure is designed to provide a sensitive measure of the response suppression induced by fear (Bouton & Bolles, 1980; Mast, Blan-

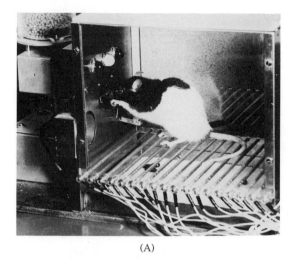

(A)

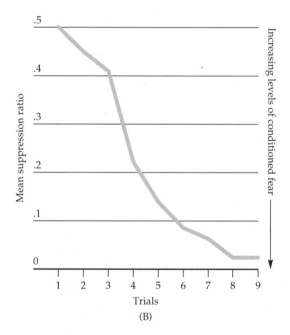

(B)

Figure 3.3   (A) A rat pressing a response lever for food reward in a conditioned suppression experiment. (B) Sample results of a conditioned suppression experiment with rats (from Domjan, unpublished). Three conditioning trials were conducted on each of 3 days of training. The CS was an audiovisual stimulus and the US was a brief shock through the grid floor. A suppression ratio of .5 indicates that subjects did not suppress their lever pressing during the CS. A suppression ratio of 0 indicates total suppression of responding during the CS.

chard, & Blanchard, 1982). Because the animals are first trained to press a response lever at a steady rate for a food reward, deviations from this baseline of responding can be easily measured. A quantitative measure of the degree of response suppression produced by the conditioned stimulus is obtained by dividing the number of lever-press responses the subject makes during the CS by the sum of the number of responses it makes during the CS and during an equally long period preceding presentation of the CS. Thus, the formula for calculating the *suppression ratio* is:

$$\frac{\text{CS response}}{\text{CS response} + \text{pre-CS response}}$$

This index has a value of zero if the subject suppresses lever pressing completely during the CS because the numerator of the ratio is zero. At the other extreme, if the rat does not alter its rate of lever pressing at all when the CS is presented, the index takes on the value of .5.

For example, let us assume that the CS is presented for 3 minutes and that in a typical 3-minute period the rat makes 45 responses. If the CS does not disrupt lever pressing, the animal will make 45 responses during the CS, so that the numerator of the ratio will be 45. The denominator will be 45 (CS responses) + 45 (pre-CS responses), or 90. Therefore, the ratio will be .5. Values of the ratio between 0 and .5 indicate various degrees of response suppression, or conditioned fear.

Figure 3.3B shows sample results of a conditioned suppression experiment with rats. Three conditioning trials were conducted on each of 3 days of training. Very little response suppression occurred the first time the CS was presented, and not much acquisition of suppression was evident during the first day of training. However, a substantial increase in suppression occurred from the last trial on day 1 (trial 3) to the first trial on day 2 (trial 4). With continued training, responding gradually became more and more suppressed,

until the animals hardly ever pressed the response lever when the CS was presented.

Interpreting conditioned suppression data can be confusing because learning is evident in decreasing values of the suppression ratio. The thing to keep in mind is that decreasing values of the suppression ratio indicate increasing levels of fear. The smaller the suppression ratio, the more motionless the subject is, presumably because the CS elicits more conditioned fear.

Eyeblink Conditioning of Rabbits

The eyeblink reflex is a discrete reflex, much like the patellar knee-jerk response. It is easy to demonstrate in a variety of species. To get someone to blink, all you have to do is clap your hands near their eyes or blow a puff of air through a straw directed toward their eyes. If the puff of air is preceded by a brief tone, the person is likely to learn to blink when the tone comes on, in anticipation of the air puff.

Eyeblink conditioning has been the subject of extensive investigation in human subjects. For a study of eyeblink conditioning in human infants, for example, see Little, Lipsitt, and Rovee-Collier (1984). However, in contemporary research, eyeblink conditioning is more frequently conducted with albino laboratory rabbits that provide a convenient preparation for the study of the neurophysiology of learning.

The rabbit eyeblink preparation was developed by I. Gormezano (see Gormezano, 1966; Gormezano, Kehoe, & Marshall, 1983). Large albino rabbits are typically used. Gormezano chose to investigate the eyeblink response because in the absence of special training rabbits rarely blink their eyes. Therefore, if the animal is observed to blink after the presentation of a stimulus, one can be quite certain that the response occurred because of the stimulus and would not have occurred otherwise.

Laboratory rabbits are very sedentary and tend to sit in one place even if they are not restrained. In eyeblink conditioning experiments, the rabbit is placed in a small enclosure and attached to equipment that permits the measurement of the blink response. The unconditioned stimulus to elicit the eyeblink response is provided by a small puff of air or mild irritation of the skin below the eye with a brief (.1-second) electrical current. Various stimuli have been used as conditioned stimuli, including lights, tones, and mild vibration of the animal's abdomen.

In the typical conditioning experiment, the conditioned stimulus is presented for 500 milliseconds (ms) and ends in the delivery of the unconditioned stimulus. The unconditioned stimulus elicits a rapid and vigorous eyelid closure. As the CS is repeatedly paired with the US, the eyeblink response also comes to be made to the CS. Investigators record whether an eyeblink occurs during the CS, before the US is presented, on each trial. The data are presented in terms of the percentage of trials on which a CR is observed in blocks of trials.

Eyeblink conditioning is often a relatively slow process, and even with extensive training subjects do not make a conditioned response on every trial. Figure 3.4 shows a typical learning curve for eyeblink conditioning for a group of 12 rabbits. The animals received 82 conditioning trials each day. By the eighth day of training (656 trials), conditioned responses occurred on about 70% of the trials. Control groups in such experiments, which do not receive the CS paired with the US, typically blink on fewer than 5% of trials.

Taste-Aversion Learning

Another popular procedure for investigating classical conditioning involves taste-aversion learning. Although this learning phenomenon has been known for more than 40 years (see Richter, 1953; Rzoska, 1953), it did not become a popular technique for the study of classical conditioning until the 1970s as the work of John Garcia, James Smith, Paul Rozin, Sam Revusky, and others became well known (see

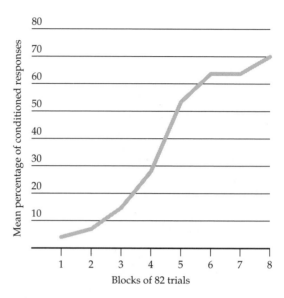

Figure 3.4 A typical learning curve for eyeblink conditioning. *(From "Acquisition and Extinction of the Classically Conditioned Eyelid Response in the Albino Rabbit" by N. Schneiderman, I. Fuentes, and I. Gormezano, 1962,* Science, 136, *pp. 650–652. Copyright © 1962 by the American Association for the Advancement of Science. Reprinted by permission.)*

Barker, Best, & Domjan, 1977; Braveman & Bronstein, 1985).

The taste-aversion conditioning technique takes advantage of an important form of learning that is involved in how animals (and people) select things to eat. Most things in the environment are inedible. Eating such things will make an animal sick, if it doesn't kill it. One of the ways in which animals manage to select safe foods is to learn to avoid poisonous ones. Given the importance of poison-avoidance learning for survival, it is not surprising that such learning can occur in a single trial.

In learning to avoid a poisonous food, the animal must learn to associate its smell or taste with its ill effects. Then it can avoid the food just by smelling or tasting it. Thus, poison-avoidance learning is an instance of "object learning" in that the source of the conditioned and unconditioned stimuli is the same object. We previously discussed object learning in connection with Wolfsohn's pioneering study of conditioned salivation to the sight of sand in dogs. For increased analytical power, studies in Pavlov's laboratory subsequent to Wolfsohn's experiment employed conditioned and unconditioned stimuli that originated in different objects. For the same reason, investigators of poison-avoidance learning have developed procedures that permit presenting taste or odor stimuli independent of the source of the illness that serves as the unconditioned stimulus.

In the taste-aversion conditioning technique, animals are given a flavored solution to drink and are then made to feel sick by injection of a drug or exposure to aversive radiation. As a result of the experience of ill effects after the taste exposure, the animals acquire an aversion for the taste. Their preference for and voluntary ingestion of the taste solution are suppressed by the conditioning treatment.

Taste-aversion learning is a result of the pairing of the CS (in this case a taste) and the US (drug injection or radiation exposure) in much the same manner as in other examples of classical conditioning. When taste-aversion learning was not yet well understood, it was believed that this type of conditioning was governed by some unique laws of learning that did not apply to conditioning situations such as eyeblink and salivary conditioning (see Rozin & Kalat, 1971, for example). Many of the reasons for maintaining this belief are not compelling in light of more recent research (see Domjan, 1980, 1983). However, taste-aversion learning differs from other conditioning situations in some important respects. First, strong taste aversions can be learned in one pairing of the flavor and illness. Although one-trial learning is also observed in fear conditioning, one-trial learning is rarely, if ever, observed in eyeblink conditioning, salivary conditioning, or sign tracking. The second unique feature of taste-aversion learning is that learning is evident even if the animals do not get sick until several hours after exposure to the novel taste. The interval between the CS and the US in eyeblink

conditioning, for example, is usually less than 1 second; very little, if any, conditioning occurs when longer delays separate the two events. In contrast to the short CS–US intervals that are necessary in salivary, fear, and sign-tracking conditioning situations, animals will learn an aversion to a flavored solution even if the unconditioned stimulus is not presented for several hours (Garcia, Ervin, & Koelling, 1966; Revusky & Garcia, 1970).

A dramatic example of long-delay taste-aversion learning in rats is provided by an experiment by Smith and Roll (1967). The animals were first adapted to a water-deprivation schedule so that they would readily drink when a water bottle was placed on their cage. One day when they were thirsty, the rats were allowed to drink a novel .1% saccharin solution for 20 minutes. At various times after the saccharin presentation ranging from 0 to 24 hours, different groups of animals were exposed to radiation from an X-ray machine. Subjects serving as controls were also taken to the X-ray machine but were not irradiated. They were called the sham-irradiated rats. Starting a day after the radiation or sham treatment, each rat was given a choice of saccharin solution or plain water to drink for 2 days.

The preference of each group of animals for the saccharin solution is shown in Figure 3.5. Animals exposed to radiation within 6 hours after tasting the saccharin solution showed a profound aversion to the saccharin flavor in the postconditioning test. They drank less than 20% of their total fluid intake from the saccharin drinking tube. Much less of an aversion was evident in animals irradiated 12 hours after the saccharin exposure, and hardly any aversion was observed in rats irradiated 24 hours after the taste exposure. In contrast to this gradient of saccharin avoidance observed in the irradiated rats, all the sham-irradiated groups strongly preferred the saccharin solution. They drank more than 70% of their total fluid intake from the saccharin drinking tube.

Taste-aversion learning attracted a great deal of attention when it was first discovered

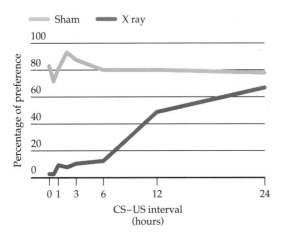

Figure 3.5 Mean percent preference for the CS flavor during a test session conducted after the CS flavor was paired with X irradiation. Different groups of rats were conditioned at each CS–US interval. Percent preference is the percentage of a subject's total fluid intake (saccharin solution plus water) that consisted of the saccharin solution. *(From "Trace Conditioning With X-rays as an Aversive Stimulus" by J.C. Smith and D.L. Roll, 1965,* Psychonomic Science, 9, *pp. 11–12. Copyright © 1965 by Psychonomic Society. Reprinted by permission.)*

that the learning could occur in one trial with very long delays between CS and US. On further reflection, however, it would be more surprising if taste-aversion learning did not have these characteristics. Toxic materials in food often do not have their bad effects until the food is digested, absorbed in the blood, and distributed to various body tissues. This process takes time. Therefore, if animals were not able to associate the taste of bad foods with delayed ill effects, they would not be able to learn to avoid eating toxic materials. Poison-avoidance learning is especially important for such animals as the rat. Rats eat a wide variety of foods and are therefore highly likely to encounter toxic materials.

Excitatory Pavlovian Conditioning

During excitatory conditioning, subjects learn an association between the conditioned and unconditioned stimuli. As a result of this

association, presentation of the conditioned stimulus activates processes related to the unconditioned stimulus—in the absence of the actual presentation of the US. These US-related processes are then responsible for conditioned responses to the CS. Thus, dogs come to salivate in response to the sight of sand or black water, pigeons learn to approach and peck a key light that was followed by food, rats learn to freeze to a sound that preceded footshock, rabbits learn to blink in response to a tone that preceded a puff of air, and rats learn to avoid drinking saccharin that was followed by illness. In all these cases, the conditioned stimulus came to activate behavior that was related to the respective unconditioned stimuli as a result of the pairings of the CS with the US.

Excitatory Conditioning Procedures

One of the most important factors that determines the course of classical conditioning in each of the situations we have described is the relative timing of the conditioned stimulus and the unconditioned stimulus. Seemingly small and trivial variations in how a CS is paired with a US can have profound effects on the rate and extent of classical conditioning. Five classical conditioning procedures that have been frequently investigated are diagramed in Figure 3.6. The horizontal distance in each diagram represents the passage of time; vertical displacements represent the onset and termination of a stimulus. Each configuration of CS and US represents a single presentation of each stimulus—that is, one **conditioning trial.** In the typical classical conditioning experiment, numerous conditioning trials may be presented in one or more training sessions. The interval between conditioning trials is called the **intertrial interval.** By contrast, the interval between the start of the CS and the start of the US within a conditioning trial is called the **interstimulus interval** or **CS–US interval.** The interstimulus interval is always much shorter than the intertrial interval. In many experiments the interstimulus

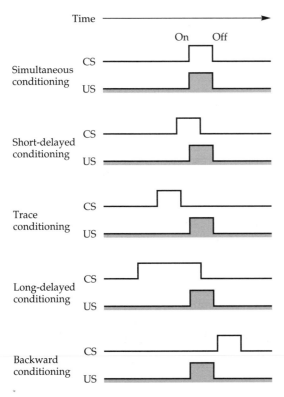

Figure 3.6 Five frequently investigated classical conditioning procedures.

interval is less than 1 minute, whereas the intertrial interval may be 5 minutes or more.

1. *Simultaneous conditioning.* Perhaps the most obvious way to expose subjects to the CS paired with the US is to present the two stimuli at the same time. This procedure, called **simultaneous conditioning,** is the first procedure depicted in Figure 3.6. The critical feature of this procedure is that the conditioned and unconditioned stimuli are presented concurrently.

2. *Short-delayed conditioning.* The CS can be presented slightly before the US. This procedure, called **short-delayed conditioning,** is the most frequently used technique. The critical feature of this procedure is that the onset of the CS precedes the onset of the US by a short period (less than 1 minute) and the US is presented either during the CS or immediately afterward.

3. *Trace conditioning.* The **trace conditioning** procedure is similar to the short-delayed procedure except that in trace conditioning the US is not presented until after the CS has ended. The interval between the end of the CS and the beginning of the US is called the **trace interval.**

4. *Long-delayed conditioning.* This procedure is also similar to the short-delayed conditioning procedure in that the CS precedes the US. However, in **long-delayed conditioning** the CS remains present much longer (5–10 minutes) before the US is delivered.

5. *Backward conditioning.* The last procedure depicted in Figure 3.6 differs from the other procedures in that the CS is presented shortly *after*, rather than before, the US. This technique is called **backward conditioning.**

Measurement of the Conditioned Response

Pavlov and others after him have conducted systematic investigations of procedures of the type depicted in Figure 3.6 to find out how the conditioning of the CS depends on the temporal relation between the CS and US presentations. To make comparisons of how learning proceeds with various procedures, one has to devise some method of measuring conditioning to the CS. Furthermore, this method should be equally applicable to all the procedures. One technique involves measuring how soon the conditioned response occurs after presentation of the conditioned stimulus. This measure of the strength of the response is called the **latency** of the conditioned response. Latency is the amount of time that elapses between presentation of the conditioned stimulus and occurrence of the conditioned response.

Measurement of response latency can tell us about the course of conditioning only if the conditioned response occurs before the US in a particular conditioning procedure. This can be the case in the short-delayed, long-delayed, and trace conditioning procedures because in all these cases the conditioned response can begin before the unconditioned stimulus is presented. However, the latency of the response in the simultaneous and backward conditioning procedures cannot be used as an index of conditioning. In these cases, the behavior observed during the CS is not clearly due to the presence of just the CS. This is particularly true for simultaneous conditioning. Any behavior observed during the CS in that procedure could have been elicited by the US rather than the CS because the US is present at the same time. In backward conditioning, behavior observed during the CS may have been elicited by the US, which occurred before the CS. Measures of the latency of the response in the short-delayed, long-delayed, and trace conditioning procedures similarly may not indicate what learning has taken place if the conditioned response happens to be delayed until after the unconditioned stimulus is presented.

One way to avoid the preceding problems is to test for conditioning by presenting the CS by itself (without the US) periodically during training. Responses elicited by the CS can then be observed without contamination from responses elicited by the US. Such CS-alone trials introduced periodically to measure the extent of learning are called **test trials.**

Test trials permit measurement not only of latency but also of other aspects of the conditioned response. When studying salivation, for example, Pavlov often measured how many drops of saliva were elicited. Such measures of response strength are said to reflect the **magnitude** of the response. One may also calculate the percentage of CS-alone test trials on which a conditioned response is observed. This provides an index of the **probability** of the conditioned response.

Control Procedures in Classical Conditioning

Devising an effective test trial is not enough to obtain conclusive evidence of classical conditioning. As we noted in Chapter 1, learning is an inference about the causes of behavior based on a comparison of at least two condi-

tions. To be certain that a conditioning procedure is responsible for the observed changes in behavior, those changes must be compared to the effects of a control procedure. What should the control procedure be? In studies of habituation and sensitization, we were interested only in the effects of prior exposure to a stimulus. Therefore, the comparison or control procedure was rather simple: it consisted of no prior stimulus exposure. In studies of classical conditioning, our interest is in how conditioned and unconditioned stimuli become associated. This is a more complicated issue than mere exposure to a stimulus. Hence, more complicated control procedures are required.

An association between a CS and a US implies that the two events have become connected somehow. After an association has been established, the CS is able to activate processes related to the US, something it could not do before. An association between the CS and US presumably depends on the two events having been experienced in connection with each other. Therefore, to conclude that an association has been established, we have to make sure that the effect observed could not have been produced by prior experience with the CS or US in isolation.

As we saw in our discussions of sensitization in Chapter 2, presentations of an arousing stimulus, such as food to a hungry animal, can increase the behavior elicited by a more innocuous stimulus, such as a tone, without an association having been established between the two stimuli. (Recall, for example, the phenomenon of dishabituation, discussed under "Characteristics of Habituation and Sensitization" in Chapter 2.) Therefore, increases in responding observed with repeated CS–US pairings can sometimes result from exposure just to the US. Instances in which exposure to the US itself produces responses to the CS that mimic the CR are called **pseudoconditioning.** Control procedures have to be evaluated to ensure that responses that develop to the CS during classical conditioning do indeed represent an association between the CS and US rather than sensitization effects of exposure to the conditioned and unconditioned stimuli.

Investigators have debated at great length about the proper control procedures for classical conditioning. Ideally, a control procedure for the learning of an association would involve the same number and distribution of CS and US presentations as the experimental procedure, but with the CSs and USs arranged so that they could not become associated. One control procedure that has been prominent in recent history involves presenting the conditioned and the unconditioned stimuli in a random order with respect to each other (Rescorla, 1967b). Unfortunately, evidence from a variety of sources indicates that associative learning can result from such a **random control procedure.** (For a detailed discussion, see Papini & Bitterman, 1990.)

Other control procedures that more successfully achieve the goal of exposing subjects to both the CS and the US in a manner that precludes the learning of an association involve presenting the two types of stimuli separately. The CSs and USs should be presented with a time delay of sufficient duration to prevent the learning of an association. Such a procedure is called an **explicitly unpaired control.** Of course, how much time between CSs and USs is sufficient to prevent their becoming associated will depend on the response system. In taste-aversion learning, much longer intervals have to be used than in other forms of conditioning. In one variation of the explicitly unpaired control procedure, only CSs are presented during one session and only USs are presented during a second session. (For a further discussion of control methodology, see Gormezano et al., 1983.)

Effectiveness of Excitatory Conditioning Procedures

Using test trials and measures of response latency, magnitude, or probability, the effectiveness of the various procedures depicted in

Figure 3.6 can be compared. Rarely have all five procedures been compared in the same experiment. Furthermore, the results of the comparisons that have been performed sometimes differ depending on the type of response that is conditioned. However, some generalizations can be made on the basis of the available evidence.

Simultaneous conditioning. Presenting the CS at the same time as the US usually does not result in an observable conditioned response. Some investigators have reported successful conditioning of fear after small numbers of simultaneous conditioning trials (for example, Burkhardt & Ayres, 1978; Mahoney & Ayres, 1976). A more common observation is that simultaneous conditioning is not as effective as short-delayed conditioning (Heth & Rescorla, 1973), and many have observed no conditioned responding as a result of simultaneous conditioning (for example, Bitterman, 1964; Smith, Coleman, & Gormezano, 1969). However, more recent evidence suggests that simultaneous conditioning can produce significant changes in behavior provided that the proper test procedures are used (Matzel, Held, & Miller, 1988; Rescorla, 1980b). Thus, previous failures to observe conditioned responding following simultaneous conditioning may have reflected failures of performance rather than failures of learning.

Short-delayed conditioning. In many situations, the short-delayed conditioning procedure is most effective in producing excitatory conditioning. As we noted earlier, the interval between the start of the CS and the start of the US is called the interstimulus or CS–US interval. The CS–US interval is 0 second in simultaneous conditioning. Generally, as the CS–US interval is increased, conditioning improves up to a point and then declines (for example, Ost & Lauer, 1965; Schneiderman & Gormezano, 1964).

Trace conditioning.   In each trial of the short-delayed procedure, the CS is presented just before the US and persists until the US occurs. The trace conditioning procedure is similar in that here the CS is also presented shortly before the US (see Figure 3.6). However, in the trace procedure the CS is terminated for a short time before the US occurs. Whether there is a trace interval between the CS and the US has a significant effect on learning. The trace procedure is often less effective than the delayed procedure in producing excitatory conditioning (for example, Ellison, 1964; Kamin, 1965), and under certain circumstances the trace procedure results in inhibition rather than excitation of the conditioned response (Hinson & Siegel, 1980; Kaplan, 1984). Because the CS ends before the start of the US in a trace conditioning procedure, the best predictor of the US is the gap between the CS and the US, when the subjects experience just the background contextual cues of the experimental chamber. Perhaps not surprisingly, subjects come to associate those background cues with the US (Marlin, 1981). Interestingly, trace conditioning of the CS is facilitated when the background cues are altered by filling the gap between the CS and US with another stimulus—a gap-filler (Kaplan & Hearst, 1982; Rescorla, 1982a; Thomas, Robertson, & Lieberman, 1990). However, it is not entirely clear how such a gap-filler promotes conditioning.

Long-delayed conditioning.   With the short-delayed and trace conditioning procedures, as training progresses, the magnitude of the conditioned response increases and its latency decreases. Interestingly, with the exception of taste-aversion learning, this does not happen if a longer CS–US interval is used. As the animal begins to learn the conditioned response with a long CS–US interval, the latency of the conditioned response becomes shorter only up to a point. After extensive experience with the procedure, the animal appears to learn that the US is not presented for some time after the beginning of the CS, and it starts

to delay its conditioned response until the presentation of the US. Pavlov referred to this withholding of the conditioned response at the start of the CS in long-delayed conditioning as *inhibition of delay.* Inhibition of delay has been observed in several response systems, including salivary and fear conditioning (for example, Pavlov, 1927; Rescorla, 1967a; Williams, 1965). However, it has not been investigated in some of the more recently developed classical conditioning preparations, such as sign tracking.

Backward conditioning.   Results of studies using the backward conditioning procedure have been mixed. Some investigators have reported that excitatory conditioning occurs with backward pairings of the CS and US (for example, Ayres, Haddad, & Albert, 1987; Hearst, 1989; Shurtleff & Ayres, 1981; Spetch, Wilkie, & Pinel, 1981). Other investigators have reported primarily inhibitory conditioning after backward pairings of the CS and US (for example, Maier, Rapaport, & Wheatley, 1976; Siegel & Domjan, 1971). To make matters even more confusing, in a rather remarkable experiment, Tait and Saladin (1986) reported both excitatory and inhibitory conditioning effects resulting from the same backward conditioning procedure.

The factors that determine the outcome of backward conditioning remain poorly understood. The results appear to be influenced by the number of conditioning trials that are conducted (Heth, 1976); the nature of the presentations of the unconditioned stimulus—signaled or unsignaled (Dolan, Shishimi, & Wagner, 1985; Williams & Overmier, 1988a); the interval between trials (Williams & Overmier, 1988); and the assessment procedure used to evaluate learning (Tait & Saladin, 1986). These various outcomes illustrate the complexities of conditioning processes and may be best understood by assuming that unconditioned stimuli have multiple effects. Different aspects of the US may be captured by different conditioning parameters and test procedures. We will have more to say about this idea in Chapter 4 under the heading "SOP and AESOP."

Contiguity and Signal Relations Between Conditioned and Unconditioned Stimuli

What determines the effectiveness of various procedures in conditioning a new response to the CS? Why are some procedures much more successful than others in producing excitatory classical conditioning? These questions are fundamental to the analysis of classical conditioning and have preoccupied investigators for decades. The simplest answer is that excitatory classical conditioning is produced by experience of the CS and the US at the same time. This is the principle of **stimulus contiguity.** Two events are said to be contiguous if they occur at the same time. The assumption that contiguity is critical for the learning of an association between two stimuli (the CS and US, for example) is one of the earliest and most frequently recurring ideas in the analysis of classical conditioning (see Gormezano & Kehoe, 1981). However, review of the excitatory conditioning procedures we described earlier shows that a simple notion of stimulus contiguity does not provide an adequate account of classical conditioning. Presentation of the CS and US at the same time, as in the simultaneous conditioning procedure, rarely results in an observable conditioned response. Rather, the most successful procedure for excitatory classical conditioning is the short-delayed conditioning procedure, in which the CS is initiated slightly before presentation of the US. This is just one of many findings that are inconsistent with a simple stimulus-contiguity principle of association learning. Because of such findings, the principle of contiguity has undergone various reformulations and refinements to better explain results of classical conditioning experi-

ments. We will discuss some of these theoretical developments in Chapter 4.

Problems with a simple contiguity principle have also encouraged the development of alternative ideas about the mechanisms of classical conditioning. One of the most prominent of these is based on the notion that classical conditioning involves the learning of a signal relation between the conditioned and unconditioned stimuli. According to this idea, organisms are most likely to learn to make the conditioned response to a CS if occurrences of the CS can be used as a signal of the forthcoming presentation of the US. Procedures in which the CS cannot be used as a basis for predicting the US often do not promote rapid acquisition of the conditioned response.

Examples of Signal Relations

The usefulness of the conditioned stimulus in predicting the unconditioned stimulus can be easily assessed by contemplating real-world situations in which signals are used. There are many such situations. One involves sirens that ordinarily signal the approach of an emergency vehicle, such as an ambulance or fire truck. The purpose of the siren is to get people to make way for the emergency vehicle. The siren is analogous to the conditioned stimulus and the arrival of the emergency vehicle is analogous to the unconditioned stimulus. If you always heard the siren just before the ambulance arrived, you would quickly learn to get out of the way. In this case, the siren would be a good predictor, or signal, for the coming ambulance. Such a procedure is analogous to the short-delayed conditioning procedure, in which the CS is a good predictor of the US. By contrast, if you never heard the siren until the ambulance was on the scene, you would have no reason to react to the siren. The siren would not provide useful information about the coming of the ambulance. You could simply get out of the way when the ambulance arrived. This case is analogous to the simultaneous conditioning procedure, in which the signal relation between the CS and the US is not very good. You would have even less reason to get out of the way when the siren sounded if you always heard the siren only after the ambulance had already left. This case is comparable to the backward conditioning procedure. If you learned anything under these circumstances, it would be that the siren indicated the departure of the ambulance.

The analysis is a bit more complicated if the relation between the sounding of the siren and the presence of the ambulance is comparable to the trace conditioning procedure. In this case, the siren would stop before the ambulance arrived. Therefore, the presence of the siren would indicate that the ambulance was not to arrive right away. The coming of the ambulance would be best indicated by the termination of the siren. Thus, with a trace procedure, you would be most likely to make way for the ambulance when the siren ended.

If you experienced something comparable to the long-delayed conditioning procedure, you would always hear the siren for a long time before the arrival of the ambulance. In this case, you would learn to ignore the siren when you first heard it, and you would worry about getting out of the way only after the siren had been on for a while. Most people's experience with sirens and emergency vehicles is closest to the long-delayed conditioning procedure. Perhaps this is why people rarely respond immediately when they hear a siren while driving.

The idea that classical conditioning reflects the signal relation between the CS and the US stimulated much research during the 1970s. However, it has proven to be inadequate to the task of explaining many of the finer details of classical conditioning phenomena. For example, it is difficult to explain instances of excitatory simultaneous conditioning or excitatory backward conditioning in terms of the signal relation between the CS and the US. The idea of signal relations also cannot explain why filling the gap between the CS and the US

in a trace conditioning procedure facilitates conditioning of the CS, or why, in some cases, the same procedure results in conditioned excitation in one test situation and conditioned inhibition in a different type of test (Tait & Saladin, 1986).

Inhibitory Pavlovian Conditioning

When people mention Pavlovian conditioning, they are usually thinking about excitatory conditioning. However, an equally important aspect of Pavlovian conditioning is **inhibitory conditioning.** Much of learning may be viewed as involving regulatory processes—processes that regulate or control how an organism interacts with its environment (for example, Hollis, 1982). As we saw in Chapter 2, regulatory processes require two opposing mechanisms. We will encounter numerous examples of opposing mechanisms during the course of our study. In Chapter 2, we discussed habituation and sensitization, and opponent processes related to the regulation of emotional reactions. In Pavlovian conditioning, two opposing mechanisms are conditioned excitation and conditioned inhibition.

Opposing mechanisms are not necessarily symmetrical opposites of one another. Sensitization is not the symmetrical opposite of habituation. The two are activated by different types of stimuli and involve different neural processes. Even so, the sensitization process can counteract the effects of the habituation process. Analogously, the b process in the opponent-process theory of motivation is not the symmetrical opposite of the a process. The a and b processes differ in their time courses, for example. Nevertheless, the b process can counteract the a process. In a similar fashion, Pavlovian conditioned inhibition does not appear to be the symmetrical opposite of conditioned excitation. But it serves to counteract conditioned excitation. Thus, whereas an excitatory conditioned stimulus comes to *activate* processes related to the US, an inhibitory conditioned stimulus comes to *suppress* processes related to the US. This suppression is evident in decreased levels of excitatory conditioned responding.

Although Pavlov discovered inhibitory conditioning along with excitatory conditioning, inhibitory conditioning did not command the serious attention of psychologists in North America until the mid-1960s (Boakes & Halliday, 1972; Rescorla, 1969b). This relatively long neglect of inhibitory conditioning is puzzling because inhibition of conditioned responding is as important in the organization of behavior as excitatory conditioning. We will now describe some important procedures for producing conditioned inhibition and special test procedures that are used to assess conditioned inhibition. (For a more extensive review of conditioned inhibition, see Fowler, Lysle, & DeVito, 1991; Miller & Spear, 1985.)

Procedures for Inhibitory Conditioning

Prominent inhibitory conditioning procedures involve a negative signal relationship between the CS and the US. The inhibitory CS signals the absence of the US. An important prerequisite for conditioning a stimulus to signal the absence of some US is that the US periodically be presented in that situation. There are many signals for the absence of events in our daily lives. Signs such as "Closed," "Out of Order," and "No Entry" are all of this type. However, these signs provide meaningful information and influence what we do only if they indicate the absence of something we otherwise expect to see. For example, if we encounter the sign "Out of Gas" at a gas station, we may become frustrated and disappointed and will not enter the station. The sign "Out of Gas" provides important information here because we ordinarily expect service stations to have gas. However, the same sign does not tell us anything of interest if it is put up in front of a jewelry store, and it is not likely to discourage

us from going into the store to look at jewelry. This example illustrates the general rule that inhibitory conditioning and inhibitory control of behavior occur only if there is an excitatory context for the unconditioned stimulus in question (for example, Baker & Baker, 1985; Fowler, Kleiman, & Lysle, 1985; LoLordo & Fairless, 1985). This principle makes inhibitory conditioning very different from excitatory conditioning, the latter being not as dependent on a special context in the same way.

Standard procedure for conditioned inhibition.

Pavlov recognized the importance of an excitatory context for the conditioning of inhibitory response tendencies and was careful to provide such a context in his standard procedure for conditioning inhibition (Pavlov, 1927). The technique, diagramed in Figure 3.7, involves two conditioned stimuli and two kinds of conditioning trials repeated in random order. The unconditioned stimulus is presented on some of the trials (trial type A in Figure 3.7). Whenever the US occurs, it is announced by one of the conditioned stimuli, the CS+ (a tone, for example). On the other type of trial (trial type B in Figure 3.7), the CS+ is presented together with the second conditioned stimulus, the CS− (a light, for example). The US does not occur on these trials. As the animal receives repeated trials of CS+ followed by the US and CS+/CS− followed by no US, the CS− gradually acquires inhibitory properties (Marchant, Mis, & Moore, 1972). The trials in which the CS+ and CS− are presented without the US are the inhibitory conditioning trials. The excitatory context for this conditioning is provided by the presence of the CS+ on the inhibitory conditioning trials.

The standard conditioned inhibition procedure is analogous to situations in which something is introduced that prevents an outcome that is otherwise highly likely. A red traffic light at a busy intersection is a signal (CS+) of potential danger (the US). However, if a police officer indicates that you should

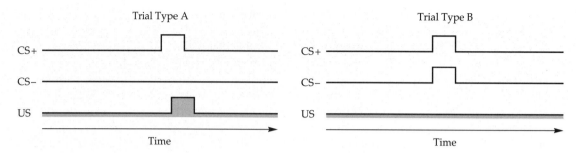

Figure 3.7   Standard procedure for conditioned inhibition. On some trials (type A), the CS+ is paired with the US. On other trials (type B), the CS+ is paired with the CS− and the US is not presented. The procedure is effective in conditioning inhibitory properties to the CS−.

cross the intersection despite the red light (perhaps because the traffic lights are malfunctioning), you will probably not have an accident. The red light (CS+) together with the gestures of the officer (CS−) are not likely to be followed by danger. The gestures act like a CS− to inhibit, or block, your hesitation to cross the intersection because of the red light.

Differential inhibition.   Another frequently used procedure for conditioning inhibition is called **differential inhibition.** This procedure is very similar to the standard procedure just described. As in the standard procedure, the US is presented on some trials and its occurrence is always announced by the presentation of the CS+. On other trials, the US does not occur and animals experience only the CS−. Thus, the differential inhibition procedure involves two types of trials: CS+ followed by the US and CS− followed by no US (see Figure 3.8). As in the standard procedure, the CS− becomes a conditioned inhibitory stimulus (for example, Rescorla & LoLordo, 1965).

The differential inhibition procedure is analogous to having two traffic lights at an intersection, one red and one green. The red light (CS+) signals danger (US) when crossing the intersection, whereas the green light (CS−) signals the absence of danger (no US). If you cross the intersection during the green light (CS−), you can be reasonably confident

that you will not be involved in an accident.

It is not as obvious what provides the excitatory context for the conditioning of inhibition in the differential conditioning procedure as in the standard procedure. In contrast to the standard procedure for conditioned inhibition, the CS+ is not present on the inhibitory conditioning trials of the differential conditioning procedure. In fact, this is the only important difference between the two procedures. However, there is another factor that may produce an excitatory context during the inhibitory conditioning trials (CS−, no US) in the differential conditioning procedure. Because the US is periodically presented, the stimuli of the experimental situation may become conditioned by the US so that the animal has some expectation of the US whenever it is in this situation. Thus, the contextual cues of the experimental situation may provide the excitatory context for the learning of inhibition in the differential inhibition procedure. However, this does not always happen, and therefore the differential inhibition procedure is not always as effective in producing conditioned inhibition as the standard procedure. (See LoLordo & Fairless, 1985, for an extensive discussion of this issue.)

Negative CS–US contingency.   Conditioned inhibition can also result from procedures in which there is only one explicit conditioned stimulus, provided that this CS is presented in

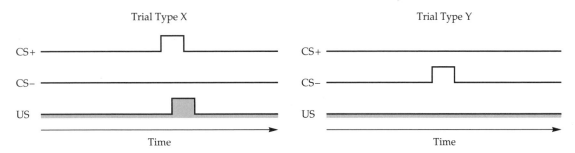

Figure 3.8 Procedure for differential inhibition. On some trials (x), the CS+ is paired with the US. On other trials (y), the CS− is presented alone. The procedure is effective in conditioning inhibitory properties to the CS−.

a negative signal relation to the US. That is, the probability that the US will occur has to be greater in the absence of the CS than in the presence of the CS or immediately after the CS occurs. A sample arrangement that meets this requirement is diagramed in Figure 3.9. The US is periodically presented by itself. However, each occurrence of the CS is followed by a predictable absence of the US.

Conditioned inhibition is reliably observed in procedures in which the only explicit conditioned stimulus is in a negative contingent relation to the US (Rescorla, 1969a). What provides the excitatory context for this inhibition? Since there is no explicit CS+ that predicts occurrences of the US in this procedure, the US is presented in the experimental situation without being signaled. The environmental cues of the experimental chamber therefore become conditioned to predict occurrences of the US. Thus, as in differential inhibition, the excitatory context for the inhibitory conditioning is provided by the contextual cues of the experimental situation (Dweck & Wagner, 1970).

Measuring Conditioned Inhibition

How are conditioned inhibitory processes manifest in behavior? For conditioned excitation, the answer to the corresponding question is straightforward. Stimuli that have become conditioned to activate processes re-

lated to the US usually come to elicit responses related to the US that were not evident in the presence of these stimuli before conditioning. Thus, conditioned excitatory stimuli come to elicit new responses such as salivation, approach, or eye blinking, depending on what the unconditioned stimulus is. One might expect that conditioned inhibitory stimuli would elicit the opposites of these reactions — namely, suppression of salivation, approach, or eye blinking. How are we to measure these response opposites?

Bidirectional response systems. Identification of opposing response tendencies is easy with response systems that can change in opposite directions from baseline (normal) performance. This is characteristic of many physiological responses. Heart rate, respiration, and temperature, for example, can either increase or decrease from normal. Certain behavioral responses are also bidirectional. For example, animals can either approach or withdraw from a stimulus, and their rate of lever pressing for a food reward can either increase or decrease. In these cases, conditioned excitation results in a change in behavior in one direction, and conditioned inhibition results in a change in behavior in the opposite direction. The sign-tracking procedure has been most often used to provide evidence of inhibitory conditioning through bidirectional responses. As noted earlier, pigeons approach

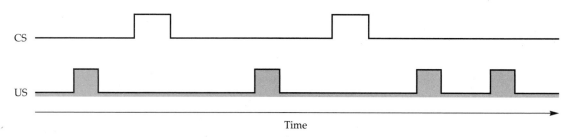

Figure 3.9 Negative CS–US contingency procedure for conditioning inhibitory properties to the CS.

visual stimuli associated with the forthcoming presentation of food. If an inhibitory conditioning procedure is used instead, the pigeons withdraw from the CS (Hearst & Franklin, 1977; Wasserman, Franklin, & Hearst, 1974). Evidence of inhibitory conditioning through bidirectional responses has also been obtained with the conditioned suppression technique with rats. As we saw, stimuli that have been associated with forthcoming shock suppress the rate of food-rewarded lever pressing in rats. By contrast, stimuli that have become associated with the absence of shock increase the rate of food-rewarded lever pressing (Hammond, 1966; see also Wesierska & Zielinski, 1980). Another good example of bidirectionality involves taste preference. We noted that animals reduce their preference for a taste that has been paired with sickness. However, animals increase their preference for tastes that have been associated with the absence of illness (for example, Best, Dunn, Batson, Meachum, & Nash, 1985).

It is important to note that the simple observation of a response opposite to the reaction to a conditioned excitatory stimulus is sometimes not sufficient to conclude that inhibitory conditioning is involved. One must make certain that the topography, or form, of the opposing response was due to the inhibitory conditioning procedure. Mere exposure to the CS sometimes results in a reaction to the CS that is opposite to what is typically observed with conditioned excitatory stimuli. This is true, for example, for taste preferences. Mere exposure to a flavor often increases

preference for it (Domjan, 1976). Inhibitory conditioning with poisoning also increases taste preference (Best et al., 1985). Therefore, inhibitory conditioning has to produce higher taste preferences than are observed with mere taste exposure if one is to be sure that conditioned inhibition is responsible for the outcome.

The compound-stimulus, or summation, test. Inhibitory conditioning can be investigated directly in bidirectional response systems. However, many responses cannot change in both directions. Eye blinking in rabbits is a good example. In the absence of an eliciting stimulus, rabbits rarely blink. If a stimulus had been conditioned to inhibit the eyeblink response, we would not observe eyeblinks when this stimulus was presented. But, then again, the animal also would not blink when the stimulus was absent. Therefore, we could not be sure whether the lack of responding reflected an active suppression of blinking or merely the low baseline level of this behavior in the absence of any stimulation. Thus, before concluding that a stimulus actively inhibits blinking, more sophisticated techniques must be used. The most versatile procedure for assessing inhibition is the **compound-stimulus test,** or **summation test.** This procedure was particularly popular with Pavlov (for example, Pavlov, 1927) and is becoming regarded as the most acceptable procedure for the measurement of conditioned inhibition in contemporary research (see Miller & Spear, 1985).

Difficulties created by low baseline levels of

responding are overcome in the compound-stimulus test by presenting an excitatory conditioned stimulus that elicits the conditioned response. Conditioned inhibition is then measured in terms of the reduction or inhibition of this conditioned responding. Thus, the test involves observing the effects of an inhibitory CS − *in compound with* an excitatory CS +. We may also conceptualize the procedure as one that involves observing the *summation* of the effects of an inhibitory stimulus (CS −) and an excitatory stimulus (CS +).

An experiment by Reberg and Black (1969) illustrates the use of the compound-stimulus test to evaluate inhibition in a conditioned suppression experiment. Subjects in the conditioned inhibition group received differential conditioning in which a CS + was periodically presented ending in a brief shock and a CS − was periodically presented in the absence of shock. (Visual and auditory stimuli were used as CS + and CS −.) The comparison group received only the CS + paired with shock during this part of the experiment, so that for them the CS − did not become associated with the absence of shock. Then, both groups received two types of test trials. During one test trial, only the CS + was presented so as to determine the degree of response suppression the animals learned to this stimulus. During the other test trial, the CS + was presented simultaneously with the CS −. The results are summarized in Figure 3.10. For the conditioned inhibition group, less response suppression occurred when the CS − was presented simultaneously with the CS + than when the CS + was presented alone.

Thus, the CS − inhibited the response suppression produced by the CS +. Such an inhibition effect did not occur in the comparison group. For these subjects, the CS − had not been conditioned to signal the absence of shock. In fact, the CS − was presented for the first time during the test trials. The presence of the CS − did not inhibit the response suppression produced by the CS + in the comparison group.

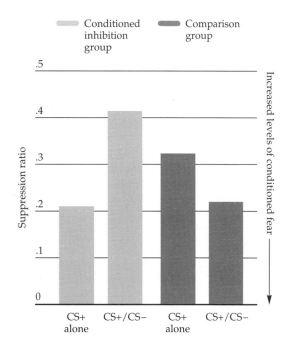

Figure 3.10 Compound-stimulus test of inhibition in a conditioned suppression experiment. For the conditioned inhibition group, the CS − was a predictor of the absence of shock. For the comparison group, the CS − was a novel stimulus. The CS − reduced the degree of response suppression produced by a shock-conditioned CS + in the conditioned inhibition group, but not in the comparison group. *(Adapted from Reberg and Black, 1969.)*

The retardation-of-acquisition test. Another frequently used indirect test of conditioned inhibition is the **retardation-of-acquisition test** (for example, Hammond, 1968; Rescorla, 1969a). The rationale for this test is also rather straightforward. If a stimulus actively inhibits a particular response, then it should be unusually difficult to condition that stimulus to elicit the behavior. In other words, the rate of acquisition of a particular conditioned response should be retarded if the stimulus initially elicits an inhibition of the response.

Although the retardation-of-acquisition test has been frequently employed in research on conditioned inhibition, it may not be as useful for the assessment of conditioned inhibition as the compound-stimulus test. One serious difficulty is that many factors can slow down the course of excitatory classical conditioning. We will discuss some of these factors in Chapter 4. The existence of numerous sources of retardation of acquisition makes it difficult to identify a particular instance of retarded acquisition as a consequence of conditioned inhibition (see, for example, Baker & Baker, 1985). Another difficulty is that the retardation-of-acquisition test fails to detect certain forms of conditioned inhibition (for example, Holland, 1985).

Extinction

So far, our discussion of classical conditioning has centered on various aspects of the acquisition of new associations between conditioned and unconditioned stimuli and the resultant new responses or behavioral tendencies that the conditioned stimuli come to elicit. The question arises, Are the results of such conditioning permanent, or are there ways to reverse the effects of excitatory conditioning? Many investigators, including Pavlov, have puzzled over this question.

One highly effective procedure for reducing conditioned responses that result from excitatory conditioning procedures is **extinction.** In an extinction procedure, the conditioned stimulus is repeatedly presented by itself, without the unconditioned stimulus, and in the absence of any kind of signal relation with the US. If the subject had been conditioned to approach a CS for food, for example, repeated presentations of the CS without food would result in loss of the conditioned approach response.

The loss of the conditioned response that occurs as a result of extinction is not the same as the loss of behavior that may occur because of **forgetting.** In extinction, the repeated presentations of the CS by itself are responsible for the gradual decline of the conditioned response. Forgetting, by contrast, is a decline in the strength of the conditioned response

that may occur simply because of the passage of time. Extinction involves a particular experience with the conditioned stimulus. Forgetting occurs with prolonged absence of exposure to the conditioned stimulus.

Extinction and Habituation

The procedure for extinction of conditioned stimuli is very similar to the procedures we discussed in Chapter 2 for producing habituation. Both extinction and habituation involve repeated presentation of a stimulus. The critical difference between them is that in extinction the stimulus involved had been previously conditioned. An earlier phase of conditioning is not required for habituation. Because of the similarity in the procedures for extinction and habituation, we might expect that there would also be similarities in the results observed. Such similarities are indeed being uncovered. For example, it has been shown that the effects of the interval between successive presentations of a stimulus are similar in habituation and extinction paradigms (Westbrook, Smith, & Charnock, 1985).

Another important characteristic of habituation is that the habituated stimulus recovers its ability to evoke the response with the passage of time. As noted in Chapter 2, this phenomenon is called the "spontaneous recovery" of habituation. A similar effect is observed with extinguished stimuli or responses. If, after a series of extinction trials, the animal is given a period of rest away from the experimental environment, *spontaneous recovery* of the extinguished response may occur (Pavlov, 1927; Robbins, 1990). Less spontaneous recovery would be expected after successive series of extinction trials, as was true of habituation. Eventually, there would be no recovery after the rest period.

Habituation and extinction are also similar in the effects of novel stimuli on the loss of responsiveness. In Chapter 2 we described how presentation of a novel stimulus often results in recovery of the response elicited by the habituated stimulus (dishabituation). A comparable effect occurs in extinction. If, after a series of extinction trials, a novel stimulus is presented, recovery may occur in the response to the extinguished CS (Pavlov, 1927). This recovery in the conditioned response produced by novelty is called **disinhibition.** It is important to differentiate disinhibition from spontaneous recovery. Even though both processes are forms of recovery of the conditioned response, in spontaneous recovery the recovery occurs simply because of the passage of time. In disinhibition it occurs because of the presentation of a novel stimulus.

The Learning Involved in Extinction

The phenomenon of extinction fits our definition of learning in that it involves a change in behavior (loss of responsiveness to a stimulus) as a result of experience (repeated presentations of the CS). However, one may wonder what is actually learned. One possible answer is that extinction does not involve the learning of something new but, rather, the unlearning of the previously conditioned response tendency. According to this view, the gradual decline in the conditioned response in extinction simply reflects the loss of whatever was learned earlier. Rather than adopt this view of extinction, Pavlov (1927) suggested that during extinction animals somehow learn to inhibit making the conditioned response to the CS. According to this view, extinction does not involve the loss or unlearning of the original CS–US association, but rather the acquisition of a new inhibitory process that prevents the appearance of the conditioned response.

The primary evidence for Pavlov's inhibition interpretation of extinction was provided by the phenomenon of disinhibition. Pavlov reasoned that if extinction involved inhibition of the conditioned response, then the response should recover if this inhibition was disrupted somehow. Presentation of a novel stimulus presumably disrupts the inhibition, and thereby produces recovery of the conditioned response in the disinhibition phenomenon.

Despite the phenomenon of disinhibition, extinction does not appear to involve the same type of active inhibition that occurs when a CS becomes associated with the absence of a US (Rescorla, 1969b). An extinguished CS does not have any of the three identifying properties of a conditioned inhibitory stimulus that we discussed earlier (see "Measuring Conditioned Inhibition").

Extinguished conditioned stimuli have not been observed to elicit responses opposite to those elicited by excitatory conditioned stimuli in bidirectional response systems. In fact, after extinction the CS is not likely to elicit any change in behavior from the baseline conditions. An extinguished conditioned stimulus is also no more difficult to condition than a novel stimulus. Indeed, the opposite result is usually observed; that is, conditioning proceeds more rapidly with previously extinguished conditioned stimuli than with novel stimuli (Konorski & Szwejkowska, 1950, 1952). Finally, an extinguished stimulus does not inhibit the conditioned responses elicited by an effective conditioned stimulus in a compound test. Rather, it is not unusual to observe some facilitation of responding when the extinguished CS is presented together with an effective CS (Reberg, 1972).

The preceding evidence indicates that extinction does not produce the same kind of inhibition of behavior that is learned in conditioned inhibition procedures. Evidently, extinction procedures produce suppression of behavior through some other type of response-inhibiting mechanism. Although the precise nature of that process is not well understood, investigators are becoming increasingly convinced that Pavlov was correct in suggesting that extinction involves *new learning* rather than the *unlearning* of a CS–US association. This conclusion is supported by growing evidence that extinction does not eliminate previously conditioned associations and responses. Evidence that the original association is not lost during the course of extinction is provided by the phenomena of dishabituation and spontaneous recovery. Recent evidence indicates that responding to an extinguished stimulus also can be recovered by reinstituting contextual and other stimuli that were present during original acquisition (Bouton, 1991).

Applications of Classical Conditioning

Classical conditioning is typically investigated in laboratory situations. However, we do not have to know much about classical conditioning to realize that it often occurs outside the laboratory and is applicable to a wide range of situations. Classical conditioning is most likely to develop when one event reliably precedes another in a short-delayed CS–US pairing. This occurs in many aspects of life. As we mentioned at the beginning of the chapter, stimuli in the environment occur in an orderly temporal sequence. One reason is the physical constraints of causation. Some events simply cannot happen before other events have taken place. Social institutions and customs are also usually arranged to make things happen in a predictable order. Because of these factors, in many situations certain stimuli reliably precede others, and whenever that is the case, classical conditioning may take place (Turkkan, 1989).

We will describe a variety of examples and applications of classical conditioning in concluding the present chapter. Paying tribute to Pavlov's background as a physiologist, we will begin with several illustrations of the role of classical conditioning in the control of physiological processes. We will then describe some interesting examples of classical conditioning in human behavior.

Digestion

One clear example of a temporal sequence of events necessitated by the physical arrange-ment of causes and effects is the digestive system. Food does not enter the mouth until the subject has seen it, approached it, smelled it, and put it in the mouth. Food is not swallowed until it is chewed, and it does not appear in the stomach until it has been swallowed. Similarly, it does not enter the small intestine until it has been in the stomach, and it does not enter the large intestine until it has been in the small intestine. This sequence of events makes the digestive system a prime candidate for the involvement of classical conditioning (Woods, 1991).

Although not all the conditioning processes involved in digestion have been experimentally verified, it is not difficult to speculate about the role of classical conditioning in digestion. We know that different types of food require secretion of different combinations of digestive juices into the alimentary canal. It takes certain combinations and amounts of stomach and intestinal secretions to digest a large, tasty steak, and it takes other combinations and amounts to digest scrambled eggs. Because food always passes through the alimentary canal in the same sequence (mouth to stomach to small intestine to large intestine), one may speculate that the stimuli involved in one stage of the process become signals for where the food will be and what will happen in the next stage. In this way, the relevant digestive juices can be secreted in each part of the alimentary tract in anticipation of the arrival of food there. Thus, the stomach can begin to secrete the relevant digestive materials when the food is in the mouth or when the subject first smells the food. Similarly, the small intestine can become prepared for the arrival of food on the basis of the stimuli provided by food in the mouth and stomach. Such anticipatory secretions could substantially speed up the digestive process.

One example of a digestive conditioned response that has been investigated is the release of insulin in response to sweet tastes. Insulin is involved in the digestion of sugars. It is released by the pancreas as an uncondi-tioned response to the presence of sugar in the digestive tract. The presence of sugar in the stomach and small intestine is always preceded by the taste of sugar in the mouth. Therefore, the taste of sugar can become conditioned to stimulate the release of insulin as an anticipatory conditioned response. After such conditioning, insulin may also be released as an anticipatory response when subjects taste artificial sweeteners, such as saccharin. If a real sugar is ingested (sucrose or glucose, for example), the released insulin is used up in the digestion of the sugar. However, if the subject ingests only saccharin, the released insulin is not used up because there is no sugar to digest. Therefore, ingestion of saccharin results in excessive amounts of circulating insulin. This causes a drop in blood sugar level and is responsible for the "heady" feeling people sometimes get after having a diet drink on an empty stomach. Interestingly, the drop in blood sugar level elicited as a conditioned response by the taste of sweets can become extinguished if the subject receives extensive exposure to an artificial sweetener (Deutsch, 1974). Because insulin is not required for the digestion of saccharin, the release of insulin following ingestion of saccharin becomes extinguished with extensive exposure to saccharin.

Control of Pain Sensitivity

A second physiological system that can be influenced by classical conditioning is the neural mechanisms involved in pain perception. In Chapter 4 we will describe results of classical conditioning experiments in which painkilling drugs such as morphine are used as unconditioned stimuli. Pain sensitivity can also be reduced by exposure to stressful or painful events. The brain contains its own painkiller substances, called *endorphins,* which are released by exposure to stress (for example, Willer, Dehen, & Cambier, 1981). Interestingly, the release of these endogenous, or internal, painkillers can be classically conditioned to stimuli that signal presentation of an aversive stimulus. Fanselow and Baackes (1982), for ex-

ample, administered shock to rats in a distinctive chamber and then measured conditioned fear (as indexed by the rats' becoming motionless) and pain sensitivity when the rats were exposed to this environment again. Exposure to the shock-conditioned stimuli elicited both fear and reduced pain sensitivity. Such results were not obtained when the rats were exposed to stimuli that had not been conditioned with shock. Subsequent research indicated that the reduction of pain sensitivity stimulated by exposure to a fear-conditioned stimulus was probably caused by the same neurophysiological processes that are activated by an injection of morphine (see also Chance, 1980; MacLennan, Jackson, & Maier, 1980; Oliverio & Castellano, 1982).

Conditioned reductions in pain sensitivity (hypoalgesia) serve to regulate the course of aversive classical conditioning. As the CS comes to elicit the hypoalgesic conditioned response, the painfulness of the unconditioned stimulus is reduced, and the unconditioned stimulus becomes less effective in producing further learning. Hypoalgesic conditioned responses also help to prevent pain-related responses from getting in the way of defensive behaviors (fleeing an anticipated predator, for example) that may be necessary to cope with the upcoming aversive event. (For a recent review of research on conditioned hypoalgesia, see Fanselow, 1991.)

Control of Disease Resistance

The immune system is involved in mobilizing physiological defenses against germs and other foreign substances that sometimes enter the body so that these substances do not cause disease. Traditionally, the immune system has been regarded as independent of the nervous system. That is, the production and release of antibodies were assumed to be the result of chemical and hormonal reactions—not neural activity. This view of the immune system as autonomous of the nervous system is being challenged by research indicating that the presentation of a conditioned stimulus can influence immune function. Since conditioned stimuli act through the nervous system, these results suggest that the immune system is subject to neural control.

Research on conditioned modifications of the immune system developed from work on taste-aversion conditioning. As we noted earlier, taste aversions are conditioned by exposing animals to a novel taste, followed by an aversive experience. Injection of a wide variety of drugs can provide the aversive experience (Gamzu, Vincent & Boff, 1985). One drug that is particularly effective in producing conditioned taste aversions in rats is cyclophosphamide. An important physiological effect of cyclophosphamide is that it suppresses the immune system, making subjects more prone to disease by interfering with the production of antibodies. In an elegant series of experiments, Robert Ader and his associates have shown that this suppression of the immune system can also be elicited as a conditioned response to a taste stimulus previously conditioned with cyclophosphamide. (See Ader, 1985, for a review.) In one experiment (Ader, Cohen, & Bovbjerg, 1982), for example, rats were first permitted to drink a novel saccharin solution and were then injected with cyclophosphamide. Several days later, the animals were injected with a foreign tissue (blood cells from sheep), and the production of antibodies was measured in response to the introduction of these "germs." If the rats were reexposed to the saccharin conditioned stimulus, their immune response to the foreign tissue was suppressed. The conditioned stimulus suppressed the production of antibodies to combat the foreign blood cells. Other research demonstrated that such conditioned immunosuppression effects could be extinguished using the usual Pavlovian extinction procedure of repeatedly presenting the flavor CS by itself without the drug US (Bovbjerg, Ader, & Cohen, 1984; see also Ader & Cohen, 1982; Klosterhalfen & Klosterhalfen, 1990).

More recent research with cyclophosphamide as the unconditioned stimulus has indicated that the responses conditioned by this drug serve to protect subjects from the immunosuppressive effects of cyclophosphamide. The conditioned stimulus increases immunological function (Krank & MacQueen, 1988; MacQueen & Siegel, 1989; MacQueen, Siegel, & Landry, 1990). We do not know yet why some investigators have observed a suppression of immune function as a result of conditioning with cyclophosphamide whereas others have observed enhancement of immune function. Regardless of the form of the conditioned physiological changes, these studies clearly show that the immune system can be altered by classical conditioning processes. Such findings indicate that some immune system functions are mediated by the nervous system. The findings also indicate that classical conditioning can control resistance to disease.

Acquired Food Preferences and Aversions in People

The normal course of eating provides numerous opportunities for the learning of associations. Rozin and Zellner (1985) concluded a review of the role of Pavlovian conditioning in the food likes and dislikes of people with the note that "Pavlovian conditioning is alive and well, in the flavor–flavor associations of the billions of meals eaten each day, . . . in the associations of foods and offensive objects, and in the associations of foods with some of their consequences" (p. 199).

Taste-aversion and taste-preference learning as examples of Pavlovian conditioning have been extensively investigated in various animal species (see Riley & Tuck, 1985). A growing body of evidence indicates that many human taste aversions are also the result of Pavlovian conditioning. Much of the evidence of human taste-aversion learning has been provided by the results of questionnaire surveys (Garb & Stunkard, 1974; Logue, Ophir, & Strauss, 1981; Logue, 1985, 1988a). Many people report having acquired at least one food aversion during their lives. Interestingly, the reported circumstances of food-aversion learning in people are often comparable to circumstances that have been shown to facilitate aversion learning in animals. For example, the aversions are more likely to have resulted from a forward pairing of the food with subsequent illness than from simultaneous or backward pairings. As in the animal experiments, the aversions are often learned in one trial, and learning can occur even if illness is delayed several hours after ingestion of the food. Another interesting aspect of the results is that in a sizable proportion of instances (21%) the subjects were certain that their illness was not caused by the food they ate. Nevertheless, they learned an aversion to the food. This finding indicates that food-aversion learning in people can be independent of rational thought processes and can go against a person's conclusions about the causes of their illness. Experimental demonstrations of taste-aversion learning in human subjects are also available (for example, Cannon, Best, Batson, & Feldman, 1983).

The fact that food aversions can be acquired to novel foods eaten prior to illness even if the illness is not caused by the food can create serious problems. One common form of treatment of cancer is chemotherapy, which involves taking strong doses of debilitating drugs. Chemotherapy procedures often cause nausea as a side effect. This raises the possibility that chemotherapy procedures might condition aversions to food ingested before a therapy session even though the patients realize that their illness is not caused by the food. Recent research indicates that this indeed happens. Both child and adult cancer patients have been shown to acquire aversions to foods eaten before a chemotherapy session (Bernstein, 1978; Bernstein & Webster, 1980; Carrell, Cannon, Best, & Stone, 1986). These results suggest an explanation for the lack of appetite commonly found among chemotherapy patients. The lack of appetite, or anorexia, may reflect aversions learned to foods eaten before therapy sessions. This Pavlovian conditioning analysis suggests that some of the anorexia may be prevented by changing the schedule of meals relative to therapy sessions,

by varying the diet so that the subject has access to foods that were not associated with chemotherapy, and by providing highly familiar and bland foods that are not as likely to become conditioned.

Conditioned food aversions also may contribute to the suppression of food intake or anorexia observed in situations other than cancer chemotherapy. (See Bernstein & Borson, 1986, for a review.) The anorexia that accompanies some tumors may result from food-aversion learning. Animal research indicates that the growth of tumors can result in the conditioning of aversions to food ingested during the disease. Food-aversion learning may also contribute to anorexia nervosa, a disorder characterized by severe and chronic weight loss. Suggestive evidence indicates that people suffering from anorexia nervosa experience digestive disorders that may increase their likelihood of learning food aversions. Increased susceptibility to food-aversion learning may also contribute to loss of appetite evident in people suffering from severe depression. Finally, animal research suggests that food-aversion learning may be involved in the suppression of food intake that results from two surgical procedures—intestinal bypass surgery and vagotomy—sometimes used to treat human cases of morbid obesity.

Alcohol-Aversion Therapy

As research on taste-aversion learning indicates, people can acquire strong aversions to the flavor of a particular food if that flavor is paired with subsequent illness. Such aversion learning can be problematic, as in chemotherapy. Aversion conditioning can also be beneficial. One important therapeutic application of aversion conditioning is alcohol-aversion therapy (Boland, Mellor, & Revusky, 1978; Cannon & Baker, 1981; Cannon, Baker, Gino, & Nathan, 1986; Elkins, 1975).

Conditioned aversion treatment of alcoholism became available in 1935 at Shadel Hospital in Seattle, Washington (Lemere & Voegtlin, 1950). The basic procedure involves pairing the taste and smell of alcohol with nausea. The nausea is caused by an injection of a drug (usually emetine). Just before the onset of nausea, the patient is asked to smell and taste various alcoholic beverages. In a typical procedure, five conditioning trials are conducted, with one day of rest separating successive treatments. The client is asked to return for a booster conditioning trial 2–3 weeks after the initial trials. Further trials are periodically conducted during the next year as required by the client's progress.

Aversion conditioning has been remarkably successful in the treatment of excessive alcohol ingestion, but it does not work for everyone seeking help. Lemere and Voegtlin (1950) reported that 60.5% of patients remained abstinent for 1 year and 38.5% remained abstinent for 5 years or more. In a more recent evaluation (Wiens & Menustik, 1983), 63% were found to remain abstinent for a year and about a third for 3 years. Males and females respond equally well to treatment, and success does not depend on educational level, employment status, type of employment, or prior history of treatment for alcoholism. However, older male patients are more likely to show improvement than younger male patients, and married males respond to treatment better than single males.

Infant and Maternal Responses Involved in Nursing

Nursing can start within an hour of an infant's birth and is an important aspect of how infants and mothers interact with each other. During the course of nursing, the infant provides stimuli that control responses on the part of the mother, and the mother provides stimuli that control responses on the part of the infant. Placement of a nipple in the baby's mouth, for example, stimulates the baby to suck. The sucking responses of the infant in turn stimulate the milk let-down reflex. Both of these reflexes can come to be conditioned to

additional stimuli the infant and mother provide each other, and such conditioning facilitates the nursing interaction.

Nursing requires holding the infant in a particular position, which provides special tactile stimuli for the infant. Such tactile stimuli may become conditioned to elicit orientation, and pucker-suck responses on the part of the infant. In a study of human infants 2–48 hours old, Blass, Ganchrow, and Steiner (1984) employed a small squirt of sucrose solution to the lips as an unconditioned stimulus. This stimulus elicited orientation and sucking as unconditioned responses. A tactile conditioned stimulus was used, consisting of stroking the forehead at a rate of about once per second for 10 seconds. For babies in the experimental group, the US was delivered at the end of the 10-second CS. For babies in the control group, the US was presented unpaired with the CS. After just 18 trials of conditioning, infants in the experimental but not the control group showed strong conditioned orientation and pucker-suck responses to the tactile CS.

Tactile stimuli provided by the baby to the mother may also become conditioned, in this case to elicit the milk let-down response in anticipation of having the infant nurse. Mothers who nurse their babies frequently may experience the milk let-down reflex when the baby cries or after the usual period between feedings has elapsed. All these stimuli (special tactile cues, the baby's crying, and the time of normal feedings) reliably precede sucking by the infant. Therefore, they may become conditioned by the sucking stimulation and come to elicit milk secretion as a conditioned response.

Conditioning of Sexual Behavior

Pavlovian conditioning is also important in learning about sexual situations. Although clinical observations indicate that human sexual behavior is shaped by learning experiences, the best experimental evidence of sexual conditioning has been obtained with animal subjects. In these studies, males typically serve as subjects, and the unconditioned stimulus is provided either by the sight of a sexually receptive female or by physical access to a female.

Sexual Pavlovian conditioning has been investigated using a variation of the sign-tracking procedure in which a localized stimulus, such as a light, is used as a signal for visual or physical access to a female. As we noted earlier, subjects come to approach a localized conditioned stimulus that has become associated with the presentation of food. Similar results are obtained when a localized visual stimulus becomes associated with access to a potential sexual partner. In one study (Domjan, Lyons, North, & Bruell, 1986), a red light was presented briefly to male Japanese quail immediately before access to a female quail. Within a few trials, the male birds came to approach and remain near the light conditioned stimulus. Similar conditioned approach behavior has been observed in studies of sexual conditioning with the blue gourami, a fish species (Hollis, Cadieux, & Colbert, 1989).

In addition to eliciting conditioned approach behavior, the presentation of sexually conditioned stimuli also has been observed to facilitate copulation between males and females in bird, fish, and rodent species (Domjan et al., 1986; Hollis et al., 1989; Zamble, Hadad, Mitchell, & Cutmore, 1985). The facilitation of copulatory behavior was evident in that the male subjects were quicker to perform copulatory responses and were more likely to engage in courtship and appeasement behaviors. Some of these results of conditioning may have been mediated by sexually conditioned hormonal changes. Sexually conditioned stimuli have been observed to stimulate the release of testosterone and leuteinizing hormone in male rats (Graham & Desjardins, 1980).

The preceding studies illustrate how "arbitrary" conditioned stimuli can become associated with sexual reinforcement. Such conditioning may be involved in the acquisition of sexual fetishes in people. For some people, seemingly nonsexual stimuli (lace and rubber boots, for example) are sexually arousing. Such sexual fetishes may develop through the association of the nonsexual stimuli with sexual reinforcement. (For a relevant animal experiment, see Domjan, O'Vary, & Greene, 1988.)

Animal research also suggests that conditioning may be involved in making certain natural features of females sexually attractive to males. During a sexual encounter, the male experiences olfactory and visual cues provided by the female. These stimuli are then followed by sexual reinforcement. This sequence of events permits the association of natural female olfactory and visual stimuli with sexual reinforcement. Thus, sexual encounters allow for the occurrence of *object learning*.

We previously encountered the concept of object learning in connection with the pioneering studies of Wolfsohn and Snarsky in Pavlov's laboratory. As you may recall, object learning involves associating one aspect of an object with other features of the same object (visual cues of sand with sand in the mouth in Wolfsohn's studies, for example). Sexual situations provide ample opportunities for object learning.

Consistent with the object-learning hypothesis, studies have shown that, as a result of sexual experience with females, male rats, mice, and dogs come to prefer the odor of sexually receptive females over the odor of nonreceptive females (Carr, Loeb, & Dissinger, 1965; Doty & Dunbar, 1974; Hayashi & Kimura, 1974). In quail, sexual experience increases the response of males to the visual cues provided by the female's plumage, and these effects of sexual experience have been shown to be the result of associative learning (Domjan, 1992).

Concluding Comments

As we have seen, classical conditioning processes are involved in a wide variety of important aspects of behavior. Depending on the procedure used, the learning may occur quickly or slowly. With some procedures, excitatory response tendencies are learned, whereas with other procedures subjects learn to inhibit a particular response in the presence of the conditioned stimulus. In both cases, subjects learn a relation between the conditioned and unconditioned stimuli. Organisms can learn to associate a CS with the impending presentation of the US or with the absence of the US for awhile. Finally, if the CS is repeatedly presented without the US after conditioning, it will become extinguished and lose most of its response-evoking properties.

4

Classical Conditioning: Mechanisms

Chapter 4 is devoted to further detailing the mechanisms and outcomes of classical conditioning. The discussion is organized in three parts. First, we will describe the kinds of events that can become associated with one another. Then we will discuss the determining factors for the types of responses that come to be made to conditioned stimuli. In the third and final section of the chapter, we will focus on the mechanisms involved in the formation of associations between conditioned and unconditioned stimuli.

What Makes Effective Conditioned and Unconditioned Stimuli?

The question of what makes some stimuli effective as conditioned stimuli and what makes others effective as unconditioned stimuli is perhaps the most basic question about classical conditioning. Traditionally, Western investigators have been concerned mainly with how classical conditioning is influenced by various temporal arrangements and signal relations between conditioned and unconditioned stimuli. The issue of what makes stimuli effective as CSs and USs was originally addressed by Pavlov and is also increasingly attracting the attention of contemporary researchers.

Initial Response to the Stimuli

Pavlov addressed the question of effectiveness criteria for conditioned and unconditioned stimuli in his definitions of the terms *conditioned* and *unconditioned*. According to these definitions, the conditioned stimulus is one that does not elicit the conditioned response initially, but comes to do so as a result of association with the unconditioned stimulus. By contrast, the unconditioned stimulus is one that is effective in eliciting that response without any special training experiences. It is important to note that these definitions are stated in terms of the elicitation of a particular response—the one to be conditioned. The conditioned stimulus is usually not entirely behaviorally silent before conditioning. It elicits orientation and perhaps other responses. At first, however, the conditioned stimulus does not elicit the response to be conditioned.

Because Pavlov defined conditioned and unconditioned stimuli in terms of the elicitation of a particular response, identifying potential CSs and USs involves comparing the responses elicited by each before conditioning. Such a comparison makes the identification of CSs and USs a relative matter. A particular stimulus may serve as a CS relative to some stimuli and as a US relative to other stimuli. Consider, for example, a palatable saccharin solution for thirsty rats. This stimulus may serve as a *conditioned* stimulus in a taste-aversion experiment with illness serving as the US. In this case, conditioning trials would consist of exposure to the saccharin flavor followed by injection of a drug that induces malaise, and animals would learn to stop drinking the saccharin solution. A palatable saccharin solution may also serve as an *unconditioned* stimulus—in a sign-tracking experiment, for example. The conditioning trials in this case might involve the illumination of a light just before each presentation of a small amount of saccharin. After a number of trials of this sort, the animals would begin to approach the light CS. Thus, whether the saccharin solution is considered a US or a CS depends on its relation to other stimuli in the situation. In the sign-tracking experiment, the saccharin solution serves as the US because it elicits the response in question (approach) without conditioning. In the taste-aversion experiment, the saccharin solution serves as the CS because it elicits the conditioned response (withdrawal or aversion) only after pairings with sickness.

The Novelty of Conditioned and Unconditioned Stimuli

If a conditioned stimulus were to elicit the response of interest at the start of conditioning, new learning would be difficult to detect. Therefore, consideration of the initial response to a stimulus is important for the measurement of learning. However, the absence of the target response at first is not enough for a stimulus to be an effective conditioned stimulus. As we saw in studies of habituation, the behavioral impact of a stimulus is very much dependent on its novelty. Highly familiar stimuli often do not elicit as vigorous reactions as novel stimuli do. Novelty is also very important in classical conditioning. If either the conditioned or the unconditioned stimulus is highly familiar, Pavlovian conditioning proceeds much more slowly than if the CS and US are novel.

Investigations of the role of novelty in classical conditioning are usually conducted in two phases. In experiments that address the issue of CS novelty, for example, animals are first given repeated exposure to the stimulus that is later to be used as the CS. During this initial phase of the experiment, the CS-to-be is always presented by itself. After this stimulus familiarization, the CS is paired with an unconditioned stimulus using conventional classical conditioning procedures. Animals that have received preconditioning exposures to the CS are usually slower to learn the conditioned response than animals for which the CS is novel. This phenomenon is called the **CS-preexposure** or **latent-inhibition effect** (Albert & Ayres, 1989; Lubow, 1989).

Experiments that address the issue of US novelty are conducted in a manner similar to the CS-preexposure experiments. In the first phase of the study, animals are given repeated exposures to the unconditioned stimulus presented alone. The US is then paired with a conditioned stimulus, and the progress of learning is monitored. Animals familiarized with an unconditioned stimulus are slower to associate the US with a conditioned stimulus than animals for which the US is novel during classical conditioning. This result is called the **US-preexposure effect** (Randich, 1981; Randich & LoLordo, 1979; Saladin, ten Have, Saper, Labinsky, & Tait, 1989).

The mechanisms of CS- and US-preexposure effects have been the subject of extensive research and debate. Although several mechanisms have been proposed, two are especially prominent. One focuses on the fact that during preexposure subjects are repeatedly exposed to the CS or the US in the presence of particular background cues (cues of the experimental chamber, for example). The hypothesis assumes that presentations of the CS or US in a particular situation result in the learning of an association between the CS or US and the background cues of that situation. This association is then assumed to interfere with the subsequent learning of an association between the CS and the US (for example, Wagner, 1976). Thus, this first mechanism attributes the CS- and US-preexposure effects to the learning of interfering associations during preexposure. The second mechanism focuses on the fact that preexposure to the CS or US involves repeatedly presenting this stimulus by itself. Because the preexposed stimulus is presented by itself, subjects are assumed to learn that the CS or US is not related to anything of significance. This learning of irrelevance is then assumed to disrupt subsequent learning that the CS signals the US (for example, Baker & Mackintosh, 1977).

Much evidence in support of the associative-interference account of the US-preexposure effect has been obtained (for example, Domjan & Best, 1980; Hinson, 1982; Randich & Ross, 1984, 1985; Saladin & Tait, 1986). Evidence in support of the learned-irrelevance interpretation is also available (for example, Baker & Mercier, 1982; Baker, Singh, & Bindra, 1985; Channell & Hall, 1983), suggesting that both associative interference and learned irrelevance can degrade the effectiveness of potential conditioned and unconditioned stimuli. An especially strong learned-irrelevance interference effect occurs if subjects are exposed to both the CS and the US randomly with respect to each other before an attempt at excitatory conditioning (Dess & Overmier, 1989; Matzel, Schachtman, & Miller, 1988).

CS and US Intensity

Another important stimulus variable for classical conditioning is the intensity of the conditioned and unconditioned stimuli. Most biological and physiological effects of stimulation are related to the intensity of the stimulus input. This is also true for conditioning. The association of a CS with a US occurs more rapidly, and the final amount of conditioning achieved is greater, when more intense stimuli are used (for example, Kamin & Brimer, 1963; Kamin & Schaub, 1963; Scavio & Gormezano, 1974). This relation is observed over a broad range of stimulus intensities. However, if the CS or US intensity is too high, conditioning may be disrupted, probably because very intense stimuli elicit strong unconditioned reactions that may make it difficult for the animal to engage in the conditioned response. Experiments on classical conditioning rarely involve such extreme CS and US intensities.

The fact that conditioning is facilitated by increasing the intensity of the CS and US may be related to the novelty of the conditioned and unconditioned stimuli. Animals and people rarely encounter stimuli that are very intense. Therefore, high-intensity conditioned and unconditioned stimuli may be more novel than lower intensity stimulation. Novelty may be at least partly responsible for the stimulus-intensity effects in classical conditioning (see Kalat, 1974).

CS–US Relevance, or Belongingness

We noted earlier that whether a stimulus can serve as a CS is often relative to what stimulus serves as the US and vice versa. The relation we discussed earlier involved initial responses to the CS and US. Another variable that governs the rate of classical conditioning is the degree of relevance, or belongingness, in the CS–US relationship. Certain conditioned stimuli are more easily associated with certain types of unconditioned stimuli, whereas other types of CSs are more easily associated with other USs. Apparently, some CSs are more relevant to, or belong better with, certain USs.

Stimulus relevance in aversion conditioning. The phenomenon of CS–US relevance was first clearly demonstrated by Garcia and Koelling (1966) in one of the classic experiments in conditioning. They used two types of CSs (tastes and audiovisual cues) and two types of

USs (shock and sickness). The experiment, diagrammed in Figure 4.1, involved having rats drink from a drinking tube before administration of one of the unconditioned stimuli. The drinking tube was filled with flavored water, either salty or sweet. In addition, each lick on the tube activated a brief audiovisual stimulus (the click of a relay and a flash of light). Thus, the conditioned stimulus was complex, involving both taste and audiovisual components. After exposure to this complex CS, the animals either received shock through the grid floor or were made sick with radiation exposure or drug injections.

Because all the unconditioned stimuli used were aversive, it was expected that the animals would learn some kind of aversion. The experimenters measured the response of the animals to the taste and audiovisual stimuli separately after conditioning. During tests of response to the taste CS, the water was flavored as before, but now licks did not activate the audiovisual stimulus. During tests of response to the audiovisual CS, the water was unflavored, and the audiovisual stimulus was briefly turned on whenever the animal drank. The degree of conditioned aversion to the taste or audiovisual CS was inferred from the amount of suppression of drinking.

The results of the experiment are summarized in Figure 4.2. Before this experiment was performed, there was no reason to expect that one of the unconditioned stimuli would be more effective than the other in conditioning an aversion to one aspect of the conditioned-stimulus complex. However, that is precisely what happened. Animals conditioned with shock subsequently suppressed their drinking much more when tested with the audiovisual stimulus than when tested with the taste CS. The opposite result occurred when animals were conditioned with sickness. These rats suppressed their drinking much more when the taste CS was present than when drinking produced the audiovisual stimulus. Thus, stronger aversions were conditioned to audio-

Conditioning   Test

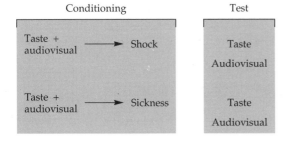

Figure 4.1 Diagram of Garcia and Koelling's (1966) experiment. A compound taste–audiovisual stimulus was first paired with either shock or sickness. The subjects were then tested with the taste and audiovisual stimuli separately.

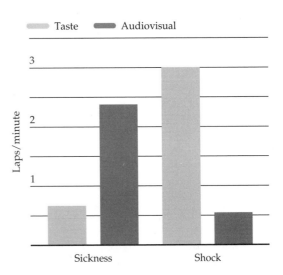

Figure 4.2 Results of Garcia and Koelling's (1966) experiment. Rats conditioned with sickness learned a stronger aversion to taste than to audiovisual cues. By contrast, rats conditioned with shock learned a stronger aversion to audiovisual than to taste cues. (*Adapted from Garcia and Koelling, 1966.*)

visual cues than to taste cues when the US was shock, and stronger aversions were conditioned to tastes than to audiovisual cues when the US was internal malaise.

Garcia and Koelling's experiment demonstrates the principle of CS–US relevance, or belongingness. Conditioning in this experiment was governed by the *combination* of the CS and US involved in the association. The audiovisual CS, for example, was not generally more effective than the taste CS. Rather, the audiovisual CS was more effective only when shock served as the US. Correspondingly, the shock US was not generally more effective than the sickness US. Rather, shock conditioned stronger aversions than sickness only when the audiovisual cue served as the CS. The only way to explain the results Garcia and Koelling observed is to acknowledge that certain combinations of conditioned and unconditioned stimuli (tastes with illness, audiovisual cues with shock) are more easily associated than other combinations (tastes with shock, audiovisual cues with illness).

The effect of CS–US relevance demonstrated by Garcia and Koelling has since been observed in numerous experiments. (For a review, see Domjan, 1983.) Some have suggested that the effect occurs only when subjects receive exposure to the taste and the audiovisual stimuli simultaneously before the US

during conditioning trials. However, the phenomenon is apparent even if the animals are exposed to only one or the other CS, not both, during conditioning (for example, Domjan & Wilson, 1972). The phenomenon also occurs in rats 1 day after birth (Gemberling & Domjan, 1982). This last finding indicates that extensive experience with tastes, sickness, audiovisual cues, and peripheral pain is not necessary for the stimulus-relevance effect. Rather, the phenomenon appears to reflect a genetic predisposition for the selective association of certain combinations of CSs and USs.

The stimulus-relevance relation observed by Garcia and Koelling is also evident in human behavior. Surveys of the conditions under which people learn food aversions indicate that they usually learn such aversions as a result of gastrointestinal illness, not as a result of hives or accidents such as breaking an arm or scraping a knee. Furthermore, illness is much more likely to condition aversions to foods than to nonfood stimuli such as the location where the food was eaten (Garb & Stunkard, 1974; Logue et al., 1981; Pelchat & Rozin, 1982).

It is important to note that the principle of CS–US relevance identified by Garcia and Koelling does not mean that associations between CSs and USs that are not relevant to each other are impossible. The Garcia–Koelling experiment and similar studies do not purport to show that rats cannot learn aversions to tastes paired with shock or to exteroceptive cues paired with sickness. In fact, both these types of associations have been demonstrated (for example, Best, Best, & Henggeler, 1977; Krane & Wagner, 1975; but see Hankins, Rusiniak, & Garcia, 1976). Rather, stimulus relevance rests on the demonstration that associations are learned *more easily* between the CSs and USs that are relevant to each other than between other combinations of CSs and USs. In addition, aversions conditioned with shock and sickness appear to be qualitatively different (Delamater & Treit,

1988; Pelchat, Grill, Rozin, & Jacobs, 1983). Taste aversions conditioned with sickness appear to make the taste unpalatable to subjects, whereas aversions conditioned with shock make the CS a signal of danger without changing its palatability.

Stimulus-relevance generality. For several years, the stimulus-relevance effect just described was the only known instance of CS–US relevance in classical conditioning. Consequently, some theorists suggested that the relevance of tastes to toxicosis and of audiovisual cues to footshock in rats is an adaptive specialization of learning (for example, Rozin & Kalat, 1971). However, research has uncovered other stimulus-relevance relations. For example, LoLordo and his associates found that pigeons associate visual cues with food much more easily than they associate auditory cues with food. By contrast, if the conditioning situation involves shock, auditory cues are more effective as the CS than

---

BOX **4.1**

Behavior Approaches to the Control of Smoking

A variety of aversion conditioning procedures have been developed to discourage cigarette smoking (Hall, Hall, & Ginsberg, 1990). Early efforts involved aversion therapy in which smoking was associated with pain induced by electric shock. More recently, techniques have been developed based on findings indicating that the aversion conditioning is more effective if the aversive stimulus is "relevant" to the situation. In these procedures, cigarette smoking itself is used to provide the aversive stimulus. A frequently employed procedure is called "rapid smoking." This procedure requires the subject to inhale every 6 seconds for either a fixed period or until nausea or dizziness develops. Such rapid smoking is aversive and serves to condition an aversion to smoking.

Aversion conditioning procedures are most effective in discouraging smoking when they are combined with other behavior modification techniques. Rapid smoking, for example, may be effectively combined with training in self-monitoring and self-management procedures. Subjects are first required to maintain accurate records of the number of cigarettes smoked and the time, place, and circumstances of smoking. Once information has been obtained on the frequency and circumstances of a subject's usual smoking behavior, goals can be introduced with the intent of gradually reducing smoking behavior. Two types of goals are adopted. One goal is to reduce the total number of cigarettes smoked each day. The other goal is to reduce the number of situations in which the person is allowed to smoke. These goals act in concert to restrict smoking behavior. Compliance with the goals can be encouraged by setting up a contract system. For example, the subject may deposit a sizable sum of money at the start of treatment and receive portions of this deposit back each time a specified goal is met.

visual cues. Thus, visual cues are relevant to food and auditory cues are relevant to shock for pigeons (see LoLordo, Jacobs, & Foree, 1982; Kelley, 1986; Shapiro, Jacobs, & LoLordo, 1980; Shapiro & LoLordo, 1982). To what extent such findings are specific to pigeons remains to be determined.

The importance of CS–US similarity. Although there is no doubt that CS–US relevance is a major factor in classical conditioning, at present it is not known what makes a CS relevant to a US. One promising answer is that similarity in the time course of conditioned and unconditioned stimuli is important (Testa, 1974). This idea explains the results of the Garcia–Koelling experiment by assuming that tastes and illness have similar time courses, as do audiovisual cues and shock. Tastes are generally considered long-duration stimuli because even if presented briefly, they often leave a slow-fading aftertaste or trace. This is particularly true of certain tastes, such as garlic and onion. Malaise induced by radiation or drug treatment is also lengthy. The similarity in the length of taste and sickness experiences may be critical to their rapid association. The relevance between audiovisual cues and shock may be explained in comparable terms. Audiovisual cues are typically short-lasting and do not have long traces. The footshock used in these experiments was also brief, and that is perhaps why audiovisual cues became rapidly associated with shock.

The CS–US similarity hypothesis has been difficult to test in aversion conditioning experiments because of difficulties in specifying and experimentally manipulating the time course of taste and illness stimuli. Although we are probably correct in assuming that tastes and sickness are both long-lasting, we do not know exactly how long-lasting they are in particular cases. Good evidence for the CS–US similarity hypothesis has been obtained in other conditioning situations (for example, Rescorla & Cunningham, 1979; Rescorla & Furrow, 1977; Rescorla & Gillan, 1980). However, the applicability of these results to stimulus relevance in aversion learning remains a subject for speculation.

The Concept of Biological Strength

In all the examples of classical conditioning discussed so far, the CS did not elicit as strong responses as the US prior to conditioning. The familiar example of salivary conditioning is a good case in point. In this situation, the conditioned stimulus (a tone) initially elicits only orientation movements. By contrast, the US (food) elicits vigorous approach, ingestion, salivation, chewing, swallowing, and so on. Pavlov was aware of this large difference in the "biological strength" of conditioned and unconditioned stimuli before the start of training and considered the difference necessary for the selection of conditioned and unconditioned stimuli (Pavlov, 1927). Pavlov suggested that for a stimulus to become conditioned, it had to be a weaker biological stimulus than the unconditioned stimulus with which it was to be paired. By "weaker biological stimulus" he meant one that initially elicited fewer and weaker responses.

Higher order conditioning. One implication of Pavlov's criteria for conditioned and unconditioned stimuli is that a stimulus may serve in the role of an unconditioned stimulus after it has become conditioned. Consider, for example, a tone that is repeatedly paired with food. After a sufficient number of trials, the tone will come to elicit salivation. Because of its association with food, the tone will also result in stronger biological reactions than novel tones or lights. It will elicit orientation movements and approach responses, and the animal will become generally aroused when the tone is presented. According to the concept of biological strength, the tone should be effective in conditioning salivation to other stimuli that do not initially elicit salivation.

Pairings of the previously conditioned tone with a novel light, for example, should gradually result in the conditioning of salivation to the light. Indeed, this effect is often observed and is called **higher order conditioning**. Figure 4.3 diagrams the sequence of events that brings about higher order conditioning.

As the term implies, higher order conditioning may be considered to operate at different levels. In the preceding example, conditioning of the tone with food is considered first-order conditioning. Conditioning of the light with the previously conditioned tone is considered second-order conditioning. If the conditioned light were then used to condition yet another stimulus—say, an odor—that would be third-order conditioning. Although there is no doubt that second-order conditioning is a robust phenomenon (for example, Rescorla, 1980a), little research has been done to evaluate the mechanisms of third and higher orders of conditioning. However, even the existence of second-order conditioning is of considerable significance because it greatly increases the range of situations in which classical conditioning can take place. With higher order conditioning, classical conditioning can occur without a primary unconditioned stimulus. The only requirement is that a previously conditioned stimulus be available.

Counterconditioning. Many instances of association learning, including higher order conditioning, satisfy the criterion of differential biological strength. However, this criterion is not met in all situations that permit the learning of associations between stimuli. Two stimuli can become associated with each other even though both elicit strong responses initially, or both are of considerable biological strength. This occurs in **counterconditioning**. In counterconditioning the response an animal makes to a stimulus is reversed, or "countered," by associating this stimulus with a US that promotes the opposite type of reaction.

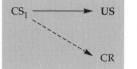 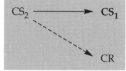

Figure 4.3 Procedure for higher order conditioning. CS_1 is first paired with the US and comes to elicit the conditioned response. A new stimulus (CS_2) is then paired with CS_1 and also comes to elicit the conditioned response.

In one study of counterconditioning (Pearce & Dickinson, 1975), the aversive properties of brief shock were reduced or reversed by associating the shock with food. In the first phase of the experiment, rats in the counterconditioned group received shock periodically, but each shock delivery ended in a food pellet. Subjects in control groups received the shocks and food pellets either unpaired, or they received only one or the other of the USs. How these treatments changed the aversiveness of shock was then measured by using the shock in a conditioned-suppression procedure. As expected, subjects that previously had shock paired with food showed less development of conditioned suppression than the control groups. This result indicates that the counterconditioning procedure had reduced the aversive properties of the shock.

In the preceding counterconditioning experiment, an association was established between two unconditioned stimuli, shock and food. (For other examples of counterconditioning, see Dickinson & Dearing, 1979.) Both of these stimuli have considerable "biological strength." One cannot argue that one of the stimuli is biologically weaker than the other. Therefore, the concept of relative biological strength is not useful in considering counterconditioning procedures.

Sensory preconditioning. Counterconditioning involves the learning of an association between two stimuli, each of which elicits a vigorous response before conditioning. Associations can also be learned between two stimuli, each of which elicits only a mild orienting response before conditioning. One situation in which this type of learning is often investigated is called **sensory preconditioning,** the procedure for which is shown in Figure 4.4. Animals first receive repeated exposures of two biologically weak stimuli presented together. The stimuli may be two visual cues—a triangle presented close to a square, for example. No response conditioning is evident in this phase of training. Neither the triangle nor the square comes to elicit new responses. Response conditioning takes place in the second phase of the experiment, in which a triangle is now paired with an unconditioned stimulus, such as food. An approach response becomes conditioned to the triangle as a result of this conditioning with food. The significant finding is that once the triangle elicits sign tracking, the square also elicits this response because of its prior association with the triangle. Thus, the association of the two innocuous visual cues with each other becomes evident when one of the stimuli is conditioned to elicit a vigorous response. (For additional examples, see Berridge & Schulkin, 1989; Lavin, 1976; Rescorla & Durlach, 1981.)

Differential biological strength as an aid to measuring learning rather than producing it. The example of sensory preconditioning suggests that differential biological strength may

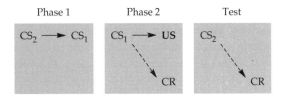

Figure 4.4 Procedure for sensory preconditioning. First CS$_2$ is paired with CS$_1$ without an unconditioned stimulus in the situation. Then CS$_1$ is paired with a US and comes to elicit a conditioned response. In a later test session, CS$_2$ is also found to elicit the conditioned response, even though CS$_2$ was never paired with the US.

be important in instances of association learning because it permits observing the effects of learning more easily—not because it actually facilitates the learning process. The phenomenon of sensory preconditioning indicates that organisms are fully capable of learning to associate two innocuous stimuli, CS$_1$ and CS$_2$, with each other. However, this learning is not directly evident. The association is behaviorally silent until one of the stimuli (CS$_1$) is made to elicit a strong response—until one of the stimuli is made biologically strong, in Pavlov's terminology. The association can then be seen by a corresponding response being elicited by the second stimulus (CS$_2$).

The somewhat roundabout method used to give behavioral expression to a learned association in the sensory-preconditioning procedure is not necessary in other procedures we

---

<table>
<tr><td rowspan="2">BOX **4.2**</td><td>*Higher Order Conditioning of Fear*</td></tr>
<tr><td>Irrational fears sometimes develop through higher order conditioning. For example, Wolpe (1990) describes the case of a woman who initially developed a fear of crowds. How this fear was originally conditioned is unknown, but</td></tr>
</table>

somehow crowds became conditioned fear-eliciting stimuli. To avoid arousing her fear, the subject would go to the movies only in the daytime when few people were present. On one such visit, the theater suddenly filled with students. The subject became extremely upset by this, and came to associate moviehouses with crowds. Thus, one fear-conditioned stimulus (crowds) had conditioned fear to other stimuli (moviehouses) that previously were innocuous, as in higher order conditioning. After her frightening experience in the moviehouse, the subject avoided going to the movies even when she was unlikely to encounter many other people there. Furthermore, her newly acquired fear of moviehouses generalized to other public places, such as restaurants, churches, and public buildings. She also avoided these, even if they were empty.

have considered because in these other procedures cues are associated with stimuli that already elicit strong responses. In standard first-order conditioning (salivary conditioning, for example), an innocuous stimulus (CS) is associated with a biologically strong event (US); by virtue of this association, the CS comes to elicit a response corresponding to US. Higher order conditioning is similar in that an initially "neutral" stimulus becomes associated with one that already elicits stronger responses. In counterconditioning, the associated stimulus is likewise biologically strong, so that associations with it result in an observable change in elicited behavior.

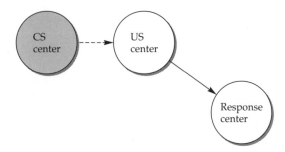

Figure 4.5 Diagram of Pavlov's stimulus-substitution model. The solid arrow indicates an innate neural connection. The dashed arrow indicates a learned neural connection. The CS comes to elicit a response by activating the US center, which innately elicits the response.

What Determines the Nature of the Conditioned Response?

In the present and preceding chapters, we have described numerous examples of classical conditioning. In all of our discussion, conditioning was identified by the development of new responses to conditioned stimuli. We have described a large variety of responses that can become conditioned, including salivation, eye blinking, fear, locomotor approach and withdrawal, and aversion responses, as well as physiological processes involved in digestion, pain sensitivity, and immunological defense. However, we have not yet considered explicitly why one set of responses becomes conditioned in one situation and other responses become conditioned in other circumstances. What factors determine what responses are acquired during the course of classical conditioning? Several answers to this question have been suggested. We will now describe some of the important models and discuss the evidence that supports or contradicts each.

The Stimulus-Substitution Model

The oldest idea about what animals learn in classical conditioning is based on a model of

conditioning proposed by Pavlov. As we noted earlier, Pavlov was primarily a physiologist. Not unexpectedly, therefore, his model of conditioning has a decidedly physiological orientation. For purposes of theorizing, Pavlov viewed the brain as consisting of discrete neural centers, as illustrated in Figure 4.5. He suggested that one brain center was primarily responsible for processing the unconditioned stimulus and that a different center was primarily responsible for processing the conditioned stimulus. A third brain center was assumed to be responsible for generating the unconditioned response. Because the unconditioned response occurred whenever the unconditioned stimulus was presented, Pavlov assumed there was a neural connection between the neural center for the US and the neural center for the UR. Furthermore, because the reaction to the US did not have to be learned, the functional pathway between the US and UR centers was assumed to be innate (see Figure 4.5).

According to Pavlov's model, the learning of conditioned responses takes place through the establishment of new functional neural pathways. During the course of repeated pairings of the conditioned and unconditioned stimuli, a connection develops between the brain center for the CS and the brain center for the US. Presentation of the conditioned stimulus then results in excitation of the US neural center by way of this new neural pathway. Excitation of the US center in turn generates the unconditioned response because of the preexisting connection between the US and UR centers. Therefore, conditioning enables the conditioned stimulus to elicit the unconditioned response. The response to the conditioned stimulus may not always be identical to the response to the unconditioned stimulus. Differences between the two may occur if, for example, the conditioned stimulus is not as intense as the unconditioned stimulus and therefore produces less excitation of the UR center. However, the Pavlovian model predicts that the general nature and form of the conditioned response will be similar to those of the unconditioned response. Because of the new functional pathway established between the CS center and the US center, the conditioned stimulus comes to have effects on the nervous system similar to those of the unconditioned stimulus. In a sense, the CS becomes a surrogate US—a substitute for the US. That is why the model is called **stimulus substitution.**

The US as a determining factor for the CR. According to the stimulus-substitution model, each unconditioned stimulus is assumed to have its own unique brain center, which is connected to a unique unconditioned response center. If conditioning turns a CS into a surrogate US, the model predicts that CSs conditioned with different USs will come to elicit different types of conditioned responses. This is obviously true. Animals learn to salivate when conditioned with food and to blink when conditioned with a puff of air to the eye. Salivation is not conditioned in eyeblink conditioning experiments, and eyeblink responses are not conditioned in salivary conditioning experiments.

The unconditioned stimuli involved in salivary and eyeblink conditioning differ in numerous respects. For example, food is a desirable or appetitive stimulus, whereas a

puff of air to the eyes is a mildly aversive stimulus. What would happen if the two unconditioned stimuli were more similar? For example, would two different appetitive unconditioned stimuli also support different conditioned responses? The available evidence indicates that the answer is yes. However, some of the changes in behavior produced by conditioning will be common to the two USs.

Consider, for example, food and water as USs. Food and water are both desirable, appetitive stimuli. However, they elicit different unconditioned responses. A pigeon eating grain makes rapid, hard pecking movements directed at the grain with its beak slightly open at the moment of contact. By contrast, it drinks by lowering its beak into the water, sucking up some water, and then raising its head gradually to allow the water to flow down its throat. Thus, the unconditioned responses of eating and drinking differ in both speed and form.

Jenkins and Moore (1973) compared sign tracking in pigeons with food and with water as the unconditioned stimulus. In both experimental situations, the conditioned stimulus was illumination of a small disk or response key for 8 seconds before delivery of the unconditioned stimulus. With repeated pairings of the key light with presentation of grain, the pigeons gradually became conditioned to peck the illuminated key. Pecking also developed with repeated pairings of the key light with presentation of water. However, the form of the conditioned response was very different in the two situations. In the food experiment, the pigeons pecked the response key as if eating: the pecks were rapid with the beak slightly open at the moment of contact. In the water experiment, the pecking movement was slower, made with the beak closed, and was often accompanied by swallowing. Thus, the form of the conditioned response was determined by and resembled the form of the unconditioned response. Eatinglike pecks occurred in conditioning with food, and drinkinglike pecks occurred in conditioning with water (see also Spetch, Wilkie, & Skelton, 1981).

Similar findings have been obtained with food pellets and milk as unconditioned stimuli with rat subjects. In one study, the insertion of a response lever into the experimental chamber 10 seconds before the delivery of a food pellet or milk served as the conditioned stimulus. With both USs, the rats learned to approach and touch the response lever. However, they were much more likely to lick the lever when it was associated with milk as opposed to food pellets (Davey & Cleland, 1982; Davey, Phillips, & Cleland, 1981). (For additional examples of conditioned responses determined by the nature of the US, see Meachum & Bernstein, 1990; Parker, 1988; Pelchat et al., 1983; Peterson, Ackil, Frommer, & Hearst, 1972; Zalaquett & Parker, 1989.)

Difficulties with the stimulus-substitution model. Doubts arose about the stimulus-substitution model very early in North American investigations of classical conditioning. The problem was that in many situations the forms of the conditioned and unconditioned responses are significantly different. Hilgard reviewed several examples many years ago (Hilgard, 1936). He noted, for example, that whereas the unconditioned response to shock is an increase in respiration rate, the conditioned response to a CS paired with shock is a decrease in respiration. Detailed study of the form of conditioned eyeblink responses also showed that humans blink differently in response to conditioned and unconditioned stimuli. In other research of this type, Zener (1937) carefully observed both salivation and motor responses to a bell that had been paired with food in dogs. The unconditioned response to food always involved lowering the head to the food tray and chewing one or more pieces of food. After conditioning, the bell rarely elicited chewing movements; and if chewing occurred, it was not sustained. The

conditioned response to the bell only sometimes included orientation to the food tray. On some trials the dog looked toward the bell instead. On other trials the dog's orientation vacillated between the food tray and the bell, and on still other occasions the dog held its head between the food tray and the bell when the bell sounded. Thus, the conditioned responses elicited by the bell were often different from the unconditioned responses elicited by the food.

Modern approaches to stimulus substitution. Because the form of the conditioned response is not invariably similar to the form of the unconditioned response, some researchers have become skeptical about the stimulus-substitution model. In addition, modern theorists believe that neural mechanisms of learning are much more complex than the stimulus-substitution model implies. Nevertheless, the unconditioned stimulus remains one of the factors that determines the nature of conditioned responding. Some modern theorists have therefore proposed a variant of the stimulus-substitution model. This model retains the idea that the conditioned response is elicited by way of a US "center" of some sort. However, in an effort to avoid misleading implications about neural mechanisms, the contemporary view does not make reference to the nervous system. Rather, it is stated in more abstract language. The new model states that animals learn two things from repeated pairings of a CS with a US. First, they learn an association between the CS and the US. Second, they form an image, or representation, of the unconditioned stimulus. According to the model, the conditioned response depends on both these factors. The CS elicits the CR because of its association with the US representation. If either the CS–US association or the US representation is weak, the conditioned response will not occur.

Strong evidence for the importance of the US representation in classical conditioning is

Phase 1 Phase 2 Test

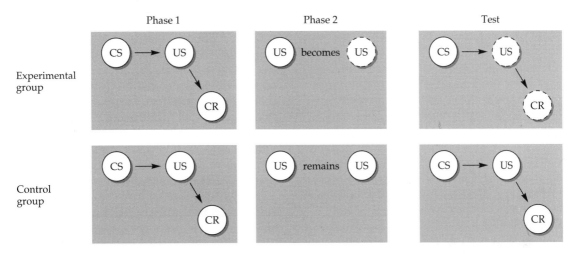

Figure 4.6 Basic strategy and rationale involved in US-devaluation experiments. In phase 1 the experimental and control groups receive conventional conditioning to establish an association between the CS and the US and to lead subjects to form a representation of the US. In phase 2 the US representation is devalued for subjects in the experimental group. The US representation remains unchanged for subjects in the control group. If the conditioned response (CR) is elicited by way of the US representation, devaluation of the US representation in the experimental group is expected to reduce responding to the CS.

provided by experiments in which the US representation is manipulated without changing the CS–US association. One set of these studies involved reducing the value of the US representation after conditioning. The basic strategy and rationale involved are illustrated in Figure 4.6. In one experiment, for example, Holland and Rescorla (1975a) first conditioned two groups of mildly food-deprived rats using an appetitive conditioning procedure in which a tone was repeatedly paired with pellets of food. This initial phase of the experiment was assumed to establish an association between the tone CS and the food US as well as to get the subjects to form a representation of the food US. Conditioned responding was evident in increased activity elicited by the tone.

In the next phase of the experiment, the experimental group received a treatment designed to devalue the US representation. The subjects were given sufficient free food to completely satisfy their hunger. Food satiation presumably reduces the value of food and

thus devalues the US representation. The deprivation state of the control group was not changed in phase 2. Thus, the US representation was assumed to remain intact for the control group (see Figure 4.6). Both groups then received a series of test trials with the tone-conditioned stimulus. During these tests, the experimental group showed significantly less conditioned responding than the control group. These results show that devaluation of the US representation reduced the power of the tone CS to elicit the activity-conditioned response. The experiment demonstrates in an ingenious way that the conditioned response is elicited by way of a US representation.

The preceding experiment, together with other research (for example, Bouton, 1984; Cleland & Davey, 1982; Holland & Straub, 1979; Rescorla, 1973, 1974; Rescorla & Cunningham, 1977; Rescorla & Heth, 1975), shows that the status of the US representation can be very important in classical conditioning. Subjects learn an association between the CS and a representation of the US, and the conditioned response is elicited by way of the US representation.

S–S versus S–R learning. In the example we have presented, whether or not the conditioned stimulus elicited a CR critically depended on the status of the US representation. Classical conditioning did not result in the formation of a new reflex connection between the CS and CR such that the CR was elicited whenever the CS was presented. Rather, conditioning resulted in an association between the CS and a representation of the US. Presentation of the CS elicited the US representation and the CR was simply a reflection of this US representation. This type of outcome is called stimulus–stimulus learning, or **S–S learning.** In S–S learning subjects learn an association between two stimuli (the CS and the US, for example). The conditioned response is only an indirect reflection of this association. Whether the conditioned response occurs depends on the behavioral impact of the associated stimulus (the US) at the time. If the associated stimulus is reduced in behavioral impact (by food satiation, for example), the elicited conditioned response will also be reduced.

Studies involving US devaluation provide one type of evidence for S–S learning. We previously encountered evidence of S–S learning in a different type of conditioning situation—sensory preconditioning (see Figure 4.4). In sensory preconditioning, subjects first learn an association between two innocuous stimuli, CS_2 and CS_1. Whether CS_2 elicits an observable conditioned response as a result of this association depends on the behavioral impact of the associated stimulus, CS_1. If the behavioral impact of the associated stimulus is increased (by pairing CS_1 with a biologically strong US), a conditioned response to CS_2 appears. In sensory preconditioning experiments, the behavioral impact of the associated stimulus is increased. In US-devaluation experiments, the behavioral impact of the associated stimulus is decreased. Both types of

experiments illustrate S–S learning because in both cases the conditioned response is elicited by way of the behavioral impact of the associated stimulus.

Although evidence of S–S learning is available from a variety of classical conditioning situations, not all instances of classical conditioning involve S–S learning. In some cases, subjects appear to learn a direct association between a CS and a CR. This type of learning is called stimulus–response learning, or **S–R learning.** Some evidence for S–R learning is available from studies of second-order conditioning.

S–S versus S–R learning in second-order conditioning. How might we test whether second-order conditioning involves the learning of S–S or of S–R associations? Recall that, in second-order conditioning, learning occurs because of the pairings of a novel second-order stimulus, CS_2, with a previously conditioned stimulus, CS_1 (see Figure 4.3). The relation of CS_2 and CS_1 in second-order conditioning is procedurally comparable to the relation of CS_1 to the US in first-order conditioning. If second-order conditioning involved S–S learning, CS_2 would evoke a conditioned response by way of the representation of CS_1. This possibility is illustrated to the left in Figure 4.7. If CS_2 evoked a conditioned response by way of the associated representation of CS_1, then changing the behavioral impact of CS_1 should also change the response evoked by CS_2. The behavioral impact of CS_1 can be altered simply by extinguishing CS_1. According to the S–S learning interpretation, extinguishing CS_1 after second-order conditioning should also weaken the subjects' response to CS_2.

If second-order conditioning involved S–R learning, CS_2 would elicit the conditioned response directly. This possibility is illustrated to the right in Figure 4.7. If CS_2 came to elicit the conditioned response directly through an S–R association, then once this association had been established, changes in the behavioral

S–S learning   S–R learning

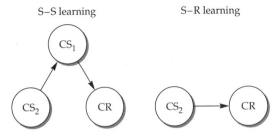

Figure 4.7 Two possible mechanisms of second-order conditioning. In S–S learning, the conditioned response is elicited by way of the representation of CS_1. In S–R learning, the conditioned response is elicited directly by CS_2.

impact of CS_1 should have no effect on the response to CS_2. Thus, according to the S–R learning interpretation, extinguishing CS_1 after second-order conditioning should not weaken the subjects' response to CS_2.

Studies of the effects of extinguishing CS_1 following second-order conditioning have provided a diversity of outcomes. In some situations, second-order conditioning has been shown to involve S–R learning (Archer & Sjoden, 1982; Holland & Rescorla, 1975a, 1975b; Rizley & Rescorla, 1972). In other cases, evidence indicates that second-order conditioning involves S–S learning (Hittesdorf & Richards, 1982; Leyland, 1977; Rashotte, Griffin, & Sisk, 1977; Rescorla, 1979). It appears that S–S learning is more likely in second-order conditioning if CS_2 and CS_1 are presented simultaneously rather than successively during training, and if the two CSs are both visual cues, rather than one being a visual cue and the other an auditory stimulus (Nairne & Rescorla, 1981; Rescorla, 1982b).

The Compensatory-Response Model

Pavlov's idea that conditioning involves stimulus substitution has not remained useful in light of modern research. The CS does not become a substitute for the US in that it always elicits a response similar to the unconditioned response. The closest that modern conceptions of classical conditioning come to

the idea of stimulus substitution is that the CS activates a representation of the US, and the conditioned response is an indirect reflection of this US representation. However, the US-representation view does not specify the form that the conditioned response will take. Several other ideas have been proposed to explain the nature of conditioned responses. One prominent proposal, the **conditioned-compensatory-response** model, was stimulated by research on conditioning involving drugs as unconditioned stimuli.

The conditioned-compensatory-response model is a radical proposal because it assumes, contrary to the stimulus-substitution model, that conditioned responses are opposite in form to the responses elicited by the unconditioned stimulus. We previously encountered the idea of compensatory or opposing responses in connection with the opponent-process theory of motivation, in Chapter 2. The opponent-process theory of motivation provides a mechanism for minimizing the disruptive effects of an emotion-arousing stimulus. According to the theory, an emotion-arousing stimulus produces a primary reaction, which is soon counteracted by an opponent process that activates responses opposite those initially elicited by the stimulus (see Figures 2.13 and 2.14).

The conditioned-compensatory-response model takes advantage of some of the same ideas as the opponent-process theory of motivation. Like the opponent-process theory, it is a homeostatic model in that it provides a mechanism for minimizing disruptive effects of stimuli. In this case, the disruptions are produced by drug stimuli. Also like the opponent-process theory, the basic mechanism for reducing the disruptive effects of stimuli involves elicitation of a compensatory or opponent response. The primary difference between the two models concerns the source of the opponent response. In the opponent-process theory of motivation, the opponent response is an aftereffect of the unconditioned stimulus. Thus, in a sense it is a delayed unconditioned response. By contrast, in the compensatory-response model, the opponent response is a reaction to a conditioned stimulus that has become associated with the US. Thus, the opponent response is a drug-anticipatory conditioned response.

The compensatory-response model was stimulated in response to the fact that in many classical conditioning situations involving drugs as unconditioned stimuli, the form of the conditioned response is opposite in form to the unconditioned response. For example, epinephrine causes a decrease in gastric secretion as an unconditioned response. By contrast, the response to a CS for epinephrine is increased gastric secretion (Guha, Dutta, & Pradhan, 1974). Dinitrophenol causes increased oxygen consumption and increased temperature. The response to a CS for dinitrophenol involves decreased oxygen consumption and decreased temperature (Obál, 1966). Compensatory conditioned responses also have been observed as a result of conditioning with morphine, lithium, ethanol, chlorpromazine, and amphetamine, among other drugs. (For reviews, see Siegel, 1977, 1989.)

The compensatory-response model has attracted attention because it has been used as the basis for an innovative explanation of the development of drug tolerance. Tolerance to a drug is said to develop when repeated administrations of the drug have progressively less effect. Development of drug tolerance is often a serious problem in the use of drugs because progressively higher doses are required to produce a given effect. Traditionally, drug tolerance has been considered to result from pharmacological processes. In contrast to this traditional approach, Shepard Siegel has proposed a model of drug tolerance based on classical conditioning (see Siegel, 1983, 1989). The model assumes that each time a drug is administered constitutes a classical conditioning trial in which the stimuli that accompany the drug administration become associated with the effects of the drug. These conditioned stimuli might be the time of day, the sensations involved in preparing a syringe, or the distinctiveness of the place where the drug is usually taken. As a result of association with the drug effects, the drug-administration cues are assumed to elicit conditioned responses that are opposite to the unconditioned reactions to the drug. Because the conditioned responses compensate for the effects of the drug itself, those responses reduce the reaction otherwise elicited by the drug. Therefore, the response to the drug is attenuated when the drug is taken in the presence of these conditioned stimuli (see Figure 4.8).

The conditioning model of drug tolerance attributes tolerance to compensatory responses conditioned to environmental stimuli paired with drug administration. If the model is valid, then manipulations of the external environment should influence the effectiveness of drugs. Various aspects of this prediction have been confirmed by Siegel and his colleagues as well as by numerous other investigative teams in studies with opiates (morphine and heroin), alcohol, scopolamine, benzodiazepines, and amphetamine. (See reviews by Siegel, 1989; Stewart & Eikelboom, 1987.)

Conditioning with morphine has been studied most extensively. Morphine has a long history of medical use as a painkiller. However, patients quickly develop tolerance to the drug, so that a given dosage becomes progressively less effective in reducing pain. The compensatory-response model suggests that environmental variables that influence the acquisition and extinction of conditioned responses will have corresponding effects on the expression of drug tolerance. Many predictions of the conditioning theory have been confirmed. Thus, the effectiveness of morphine in reducing pain may be restored if the usual drug-administration cues are removed, as by administering the drug with a novel procedure or in a new room. Drug tolerance is also less likely if subjects are made highly familiar with the drug-administration stimuli before being treated with the drug because

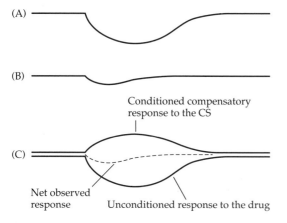

Figure 4.8 Diagram of the Pavlovian-conditioning model of drug tolerance. The strength of the drug reaction is represented by deviations from the horizontal line. (A) Reaction to the CS plus the drug before conditioning, illustrating the unconditioned response to the drug. (B) Attenuated reaction to the CS plus the drug after extensive experience with the drug, illustrating drug tolerance. (C) Components of the reaction after conditioning, showing that the net attenuated drug response is due to a compensatory conditioned response to the CS that counteracts the unconditioned response to the drug.

such CS familiarity interferes with conditioning. Once drug tolerance has developed, it can be reversed by extinguishing the drug-administration cues by repeatedly presenting them without the drug. Other learning effects that are evident in drug conditioning include conditioned inhibition, blocking, and sensory preconditioning. (For recent research on the conditioning model of drug tolerance, see, for example, Dafters, Hetherington, & McCartney, 1983; Hinson & Siegel, 1986; King, Bouton, & Musty, 1987; MacRae & Siegel, 1987; Rochford & Stewart, 1987; Schnur & Martinez, 1989; Shapiro & Nathan, 1986; Tiffany & Maude-Griffin, 1988.)

Numerous studies of the conditioned-compensatory-response model of drug tolerance have confirmed that variables that influence other forms of classical conditioning also influence the effectiveness of many psychoactive drugs. A truly remarkable body

of evidence has been developed in this area. However, several aspects of drug conditioning studies have been problematic for the compensatory-response model. One recurrent problem is that contrary to the model, not all learned modifications of drug effects are accompanied by the predicted conditioned drug-compensatory responses (for example, Falls & Kelsey, 1989; MacRae & Siegel, 1987; Paletta & Wagner, 1986; Tiffany, Petrie, Baker, & Dahl, 1983). Such findings have led some to advocate application of a behavioral model of habituation to the phenomena of conditioned drug tolerance that makes no commitment about the form of conditioned responses (Baker & Tiffany, 1985). However, this approach is limited in its ability to explain evidence of conditioned drug-withdrawal effects (for example, Falls & Kelsey, 1989). Another approach is to assume that drug-compensatory responses exist but may be difficult to observe (Siegel, 1989). Such responses may involve physiological changes that are not expressed in behavior (King et al., 1987), or they may require special test procedures for their expression (Hinson, Poulos, & Cappell, 1982; Krank, 1987).

Another potential problem for the conditioned-compensatory-response model is that drug tolerance is not always eliminated by administering the drug in the absence of the usual drug-conditioned environmental stimuli. For example, if morphine is always administered while a rat is in its customary wire-mesh home cage, some tolerance to morphine also may be observed if the subject is moved to a distinctively different room and placed in a smooth plastic cage. A change in the circumstances of drug administration usually produces some but not total recovery of the drug response. If drug tolerance is produced by compensatory responses elicited by drug-conditioned cues, what accounts for tolerance observed in the absence of the conditioned stimuli?

One possibility is that some of the drug tolerance is not mediated by conditioning processes. A more interesting possibility is that environmental cues associated with drug administration are not the only stimuli that become conditioned by drug experiences. Internal sensations related to the onset of a drug experience (starting to feel drowsy, for example) may constitute an important component of the stimulus complex that becomes conditioned to elicit the conditioned compensatory response (Greeley, Lé, Poulos, & Cappell, 1984). When this occurs, tolerance will transfer to new situations as long as the drug-onset sensations are the same.

As the preceding considerations illustrate, the conditioned-compensatory-response model can be extended to make it consistent with some types of evidence that at first glance appear to be inconsistent with the model.

However, the model is not likely to provide a comprehensive explanation for all classically conditioned drug responses. The problem is that not all drug-conditioned responses are opposite to the apparent effects of the unconditioned stimulus. For example, amphetamine causes increased activity as an unconditioned response—behavior that can be conditioned to stimuli that reliably precede the presence of amphetamine (Pickens & Dougherty, 1971). Insulin causes decreased activity, convulsions, and unresponsiveness to applied stimulation; this pattern of behavior also occurs in response to a CS for insulin (Siegel, 1975). In yet other cases, measurement of several response systems indicates that some conditioned responses are similar to the unconditioned response and others are opposite to it. For exam-

---

Heroin Overdose from the Absence of Drug-Conditioned Stimuli

BOX **4.3**

Heroin overdose is a leading cause of death among heroin users. It is also one of the most perplexing causes of death. Victims rarely take more heroin before they die than they usually use. On occasion, death occurs while the syringe is still in the victim's arm—before he or she has finished injecting the intended amount. Therefore, heroin-related deaths are rarely caused by excessive amounts of the drug. Why do the addicts die, then? One answer is suggested by the conditioning model of drug tolerance. Long-term users of heroin have a set ritual they go through when taking the drug. They may use the drug only at certain times, only in the company of certain people, or only in special locations. These drug-related stimuli are expected to become conditioned by the heroin use. The conditioning model predicts that heroin-compensatory physiological reactions will come to be elicited by the usual drug-administration ritual. If experienced users take heroin at an unusual time, with a new group of people, or in a new place, the conditioned compensatory responses will not occur. Hence, the usual amount of heroin will have a much greater physiological effect than it would have ordinarily. This unexpectedly large drug effect may be sufficient to cause physical complications and death.

Not all people who experience heroin overdose die. Prompt medical attention can be a lifesaver. Interviews with survivors of heroin overdose indicate that the adverse reaction to the drug often occurs when the heroin is taken in unusual circumstances (Siegel, 1984). Animal research also indicates that the absence of drug-conditioned stimuli places subjects at increased risk of heroin-induced death (Siegel, Hinson, Krank, & McCully, 1982). Rats in this research first received several heroin injections in connection with a distinctive set of environmental stimuli. The animals were then given a higher test dose of the drug. For some subjects the test dose was administered in the presence of the usual drug-administration stimuli. For another group, the drug was given in an environment where the subjects had never received heroin before. The test dose of heroin resulted in a greater proportion of deaths among animals that received the drug in the absence of the drug-conditioned environmental cues. These findings support an explanation of the heroin-overdose phenomenon in terms of the conditioning model of drug tolerance. (For additional applications of conditioning theory to problems of drug addiction and treatment, see Poulos, Hinson, & Siegel, 1981; Siegel, 1989; Stewart & Eikelboom, 1987.)

ple, after conditioning with anticholinergic drugs, the conditioned stimulus elicits pupillary dilation and increased salivation (Korol, Sletten, & Brown, 1966; Lang, Brown, Gershon, & Korol, 1966). The pupillary dilation CR is similar to the unconditioned response to the drugs, whereas the increased salivation is opposite to the direct effects of the anticholinergic agents. These diverse findings make the compensatory-response model inadequate as a general account of the form of classically conditioned responses.

Various efforts have been made to provide a more comprehensive account of the form of conditioned responses (see Eikelboom & Stewart, 1982; Stewart & Eikelboom, 1987). One promising direction of inquiry involves combining concepts of the opponent-process theory of motivation, which emphasizes opponent *unconditioned* responses, and concepts of the compensatory-response model, which emphasizes opponent *conditioned* responses (Schull, 1979; Wagner, 1981). Following this approach, the responses conditioned to a stimulus are expected to mimic the behavioral aftereffects of the US with which the CS has become associated. If the US produces an opponent aftereffect, that opponent response will appear as a compensatory conditioned response to the CS. By contrast, if the US does not produce an opponent aftereffect, the conditioned response is not expected to be compensatory. Evidence consistent with this idea is available (see Paletta & Wagner, 1986). However, it remains to be seen whether all of the diverse drug-conditioned responses can be explained in terms of this formulation. We will have more to say about this kind of theorizing later in this chapter (see "SOP and AESOP" and Figure 4.14).

The CS as a Determinant of the Form of the CR

According to the models of conditioning we have considered so far, the form of the conditioned response is determined by the unconditioned stimulus or its representation. The compensatory-response model assumes that the CR will "compensate" for the effects of the US. The US-representation model is not as specific about the form of the CR, but it also assumes that the nature of the conditioned response will depend on the US and its representation. Although these models have identified important influences on the nature of the conditioned response, they are incomplete because recent research indicates that the form of the CR also depends on the nature of the conditioned stimulus.

Earlier in this chapter we discussed how the speed of learning of the conditioned response is influenced by various aspects of the conditioned stimulus. The *rate* of learning depends on the intensity and novelty of the CS and the relevance of the CS to the US. Aspects of the conditioned stimulus also influence the *form* of the conditioned response. In an unusual experiment, for example, Timberlake and Grant (1975) investigated classical conditioning in rats with food as the unconditioned stimulus. One side of the experimental chamber was equipped with a sliding platform that could be moved in and out of the chamber through a flap door (see Figure 4.9). Instead of using a conventional light or tone as the conditioned stimulus, the experimenters restrained a live rat on the stimulus platform. Ten seconds before each delivery of food, the platform was moved into the experimental chamber, thereby transporting the stimulus rat through the flap door. The stimulus rat was withdrawn from the chamber at the end of the trial. Thus, presentation of the stimulus rat served as the conditioned stimulus for food.

The stimulus-substitution model predicts that the experimental subjects will come to respond to the CS for food as they respond to food. Therefore, they are expected to gnaw or bite the stimulus rat that serves as the CS. It is unclear what the compensatory-response model predicts in this situation. In fact, as the CS rat was repeatedly paired with food, the CS came to elicit orientation, approach, and sniff-

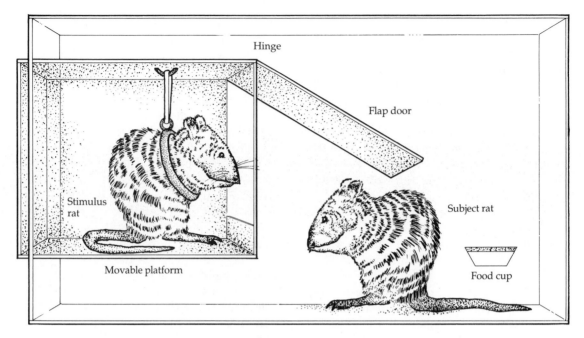

Figure 4.9   Diagram of the experiment by Timberlake and Grant (1975). The conditioned stimulus for food is presentation of a stimulus rat on a movable platform through a flap door on one side of the experimental chamber.

ing movements, as well as social contacts. Such responses did not develop if the CS rat was not paired with food or was presented at random times with respect to food. This outcome does not support any model that explains the form of the conditioned response solely in terms of the unconditioned stimulus used. The pattern of conditioned responses, particularly the social behavior elicited by the CS rat, was no doubt determined by the unusual conditioned stimulus used in this experiment (see also Timberlake, 1983a). Other kinds of food-conditioned CSs elicit different conditioned responses. For example, Peterson et al. (1972) inserted an illuminated response lever into the experimental chamber immediately before presenting food to rats. As reported in this study, with the protruding metal lever as a conditioned stimulus, the conditioned responses were "almost exclusively oral and consisted mainly of licking . . . and gnawing" (p. 1010).

One of the most careful and systematic investigations of the role of the conditioned stimulus in determining the nature of the conditioned response was performed by Holland (1977). He compared visual and auditory stimuli in experiments involving a food US in rats. Conditioned auditory cues of various types invariably resulted in head-jerk and startle movements and standing by the food dish. The conditioned head-jerk and startle reactions were not evident with conditioned visual stimuli. When diffuse light was paired with food, the predominant conditioned response was standing by the food dish. When a conditioned visual stimulus was localized at the top of the experimental chamber, conditioned rearing on the hind legs was also often observed (see also Holland, 1980, 1984; Sigmundi & Bolles, 1983).

The Behavior Systems Approach

The approaches to the form of the conditioned response we have been discussing have their intellectual roots in Pavlov's physiological model systems approach to the study of learning. As we noted in Chapter 1, in this approach, a small range of the animal's activities are isolated for investigation. The focus of the investigation is not on the animal's activities, but rather on how changes in an isolated response can be used to gain information about underlying learning mechanisms. This approach is continuing to provide rich dividends in new knowledge about learning mechanisms. However, it is becoming evident that answers to questions about the nature of conditioned behavior and performance will require considering the animal's behavior from a broader perspective. Holland (1984), for example, has commented that a comprehensive account of the form of conditioned responses will require "knowledge of the normal functions of behavior systems engaged by the various CSs, the natural, unlearned organization within those systems, and the ontogeny of those systems" (p. 164).

It is convenient to conceptualize the full range of things animals do as being organized in different behavior systems. There are behavior systems for procuring and eating food, for territorial defense, for sexual behavior, for maintaining warmth (thermoregulation), and so on. Each behavior system consists of a series of response modules, each with its own controlling stimuli and responses, arranged spatially and/or temporally. For example, in territorial defense, the distant approach of an intruder initially provides only weak stimuli that elicit corresponding mild responses of vigilance and orientation. As the intruder moves closer, the stimuli it provides become more intense and distinctive, and the elicited responses also change, perhaps to vigorous patrolling. Finally, as the intruder enters the defended territory, the elicited responses change again, to threat gestures and aggression.

The behavior systems approach recognizes that the unconditioned responses elicited by

common unconditioned stimuli are part of a spatially and temporally organized behavior system. Food unconditioned stimuli activate the behavior system involved in foraging and feeding. By contrast, aversive unconditioned stimuli activate the predatory-defensive behavior system. Classical conditioning procedures involve superimposing a CS–US relationship on the preexisting behavioral system activated by the US.

The conditioned stimuli we use in laboratory studies of classical conditioning do not activate particular responses in a behavior system before conditioning. However, as a CS becomes associated with the US, it becomes integrated into the behavioral system activated by the US and comes to elicit component responses of that system. Thus, food-conditioned stimuli come to elicit component responses of the feeding system, and shock-conditioned stimuli come to elicit component responses of the defense system. The CS may become incorporated into the behavioral system at various points in the spatial–temporal organization of the US-activated system. The particular conditioned responses that are learned depend on the point of integration. If the CS becomes integrated into early components of the territorial defensive system, for example, it will only elicit vigilance and orientation conditioned responses. By contrast, if the CS becomes integrated into later components, it may elicit threat gestures and aggressive responses. According to this view, then, the CS does not come to either substitute for or compensate for the US. Rather, it comes to substitute for a stimulus at some point in the behavior system activated by the US.

An experiment on the conditioning of baby chicks with heat as the unconditioned stimulus nicely illustrates some of the concepts of the behavior systems approach. To predict what might happen in such a situation, we first have to consider the thermoregulatory behavior system of chicks. When baby chicks are cold and seek warmth in their natural environment, they approach the mother hen, peck at the feathers on the underpart of her body, and snuggle up to her (rub and push their heads up into her feathers). Once they have nestled in under the mother hen's feathers, the chicks stop moving, twitter, and close their eyes. Thus, the behavior system involves first approach-and-pecking responses, then snuggling responses, and finally quiescence and closing of the eyes upon attainment of warmth.

Wasserman (1973) used a small lighted disk as the conditioned stimulus and paired this with brief exposure to heat in young chicks. As the light became conditioned, the chicks started to approach and peck it. Later the pecking responses became less forceful as the chicks pushed the lighted disk and shook their heads in a snuggling type of movement. These conditioned responses were very different from the reactions to the heat unconditioned stimulus itself, which included napping. However, the conditioned responses resembled what chicks do when they seek warmth from a mother hen in the barnyard. Thus, the conditioned stimulus became integrated into early portions of the thermoregulatory behavior system of the chicks (see also Hogan, 1974; Jenkins, Barrera, Ireland, & Woodside, 1978; Wasserman, 1974, 1981).

The behavior systems approach has been most extensively developed by Timberlake (see Timberlake, 1983a, 1983b; Timberlake & Lucas, 1989) and is consistent with much of what we know about the nature of classically conditioned behavioral responses. (The theory has not been extended to conditioned physiological responses.) The view is clearly consistent with numerous findings indicating that the form of conditioned responses is determined by the nature of the unconditioned stimulus. Since different unconditioned stimuli activate different behavior systems, CSs integrated into these systems will also elicit different conditioned responses. However, the behavior systems view does not require that the form of the conditioned

response be the same as the form of the unconditioned response.

The behavior systems view is also consistent with the fact that the form of conditioned responses is determined by the nature of the conditioned stimulus. Certain types of stimuli may be more effective in eliciting particular component responses of a behavior system than other types of stimuli. Therefore, the nature of the CS may determine the component of the behavior system that comes to be elicited as a conditioned response.

Finally, the behavior systems view is consistent with the finding that the form of the conditioned response is determined by the CS–US interval that is used in classical conditioning (Holland, 1980). With a long CS–US interval, the CS may become incorporated into early components of the behavior system. With a short CS–US interval, later response components may become conditioned (Timberlake & Lucas, 1989).

A Functional/Adaptive Approach to the CR

The models of the conditioned response we have considered so far have provided suggestions about the mechanisms of conditioned behavior and have identified individual factors that determine the form of the conditioned response. However, they have not addressed explicitly the issue of why these mechanisms exist—why these mechanisms shape the form of conditioned behavior rather than some others. This issue is the focal point of a functional/adaptive approach to the conditioned response (see Hollis, 1982, 1984b; Shettleworth, 1983a).

Casual reflection reveals that classically conditioned responses are often of benefit to the subject. Anticipatory salivation speeds up digestion, aversion learning to poisonous food reduces subsequent intake of the harmful food, conditioned analgesia reduces the discomfort from a painful stimulus, and conditioned compensatory drug responses reduce the physiological disturbance caused by the administration of a drug. The beneficial effects of conditioned responses have been evident for a long time. As Culler (1938) explained:

> [Without a signal] the animal would still be forced to wait in every case for the [shock] stimulus to arrive before beginning to meet it. The veil of the future would hang just before his eyes. Nature began long ago to push back the veil. Foresight proved to possess high survival-value, and conditioning is the means by which foresight is achieved. Indeed, this provision gave the distance-receptors most of their value. Neither sight nor sound of an approaching enemy is intrinsically hurtful; without conditioning, these exteroceptors would have lost their phylogenetic significance. (p. 136)

According to this interpretation, animals have evolved to make conditioned responses because these responses allow them to make the necessary adjustments in preparation for an unconditioned stimulus.

Why should animals prepare themselves for oncoming stimuli? As the preceding quotation implies, the biological "benefits" of conditioned responses are measured by their contribution to fitness and reproductive success. By responding in a particular way to the impending delivery of an unconditioned stimulus, subjects increase the likelihood that they will survive to reproduce and pass their genes on to future generations. Thus, the form of the conditioned response is assumed to be adaptive and to contribute to the biological fitness of the organism.

It is important to note that the functional/adaptive approach is not an alternative to determinants of the conditioned response we discussed previously. The claim that conditioned responses are adaptive does not specify how the form of the conditioned response is determined by various antecedent factors such as the nature of conditioned and unconditioned stimuli. In a sense, the functional/adaptive approach specifies the biological uses that conditioned responses can serve (fit-

ness)—not the mechanisms that create conditioned responses. An analogy to an automobile may clarify this distinction. The function of an automobile is to transport people and goods. However, specifying this function does not tell us about the mechanisms of the automobile—whether it has a diesel or a gasoline engine, for example.

Because the functional/adaptive view focuses on the functions of conditioned responses rather than on the mechanisms that produce CRs, it addresses the issue of conditioned behavior from a different perspective than that of other models we have considered. This new perspective can lead to innovative investigations of conditioning. Shettleworth (1983a) has suggested that a consideration of the functions of learning may provide suggestions about possible mechanisms involved in its production (see Chapter 1, p. 10). Consideration of the functions of conditioned responses has also stimulated studies of interesting new forms of conditioning. Hollis (1984a), for example, has found that territorial male fish (gouramis) are more successful in defending their territory if an intruder is signaled by a CS than if the intruder appears without warning. Courtship behavior in males of this species is also more likely if presentation of a female is signaled by a CS than if the female is unexpected (Hollis et al., 1989). Sexual behavior also has been found to be enhanced by sexually conditioned stimuli in laboratory rats and Japanese quail (see Domjan, 1992).

How Do Conditioned and Unconditioned Stimuli Become Associated?

We have described numerous situations in which classical conditioning occurs, including discussion of various factors that determine what responses result from this learning.

However, we have yet to address in detail the critical issue of how conditioned and unconditioned stimuli become associated. What are the mechanisms of association learning—the underlying processes that are strongly activated by conditioning procedures that produce rapid learning and weakly activated by procedures that are less effective in producing learning? This question has been the subject of intense scholarly work over the past 25 years. From this effort have emerged many new ideas that have radically altered our conceptions of classical conditioning. The evolution of theories of classical conditioning continues today as investigators strive to formulate comprehensive accounts of the mechanisms of association learning that can embrace all the diverse research results.

The Blocking Effect

The modern era in theories of classical conditioning got under way about 25 years ago with the discovery of several provocative phenomena that stimulated the application of information processing ideas to the analysis of classical conditioning (for example, Rescorla, 1967b, 1968b; Wagner, Logan, Haberlandt, & Price, 1968). One of the most prominent of these phenomena was the **blocking effect.**

To get an intuitive sense of the blocking effect, consider the following scenario. Each Sunday afternoon your parents take you to visit your grandmother, who always serves a rice pudding that slightly disagrees with you. Not wanting to upset her, you politely eat the pudding during each visit, and consequently acquire an aversion to rice pudding. One of the visits falls on a holiday, and to make the occasion a bit more festive, your grandmother serves tea cookies with the rice pudding this time. As usual, you eat some of everything that is offered, and as usual you get a bit sick to your stomach. Will you now learn an aversion to the tea cookies? Probably not. Knowing that rice pudding disagrees with you, you probably will attribute your illness to the proven culprit and not acquire an aversion to the tea cookies.

The blocking effect involves a similar sequence of events. First, subjects are conditioned to associate one stimulus (CSA) with a US. Once that association has become well established, a second stimulus (CSB) is added to CSA during the conditioning trials. The basic finding is that prior conditioning of stimulus A interferes with or blocks the conditioning of the added stimulus B.

The blocking effect was initially investigated using the conditioned suppression technique with rats (Kamin, 1968, 1969). The basic procedure involved three phases (see Figure 4.10). Two conditioned stimuli were employed, a tone and a light. In phase 1, the experimental group received repeated pairings of one of the CSs (stimulus A) with the unconditioned stimulus. This phase of training was continued until stimulus A was completely conditioned, and the animals totally suppressed their lever-press responses whenever stimulus A occurred. In the next phase of the experiment, stimulus B was presented together with stimulus A and paired with the US. After several such conditioning trials, stimulus B was presented alone in a test trial to see if it had become conditioned to elicit fear. Interestingly, very little suppression to stimulus B was observed on this test trial.

The control group in the blocking design received the same kind of conditioning trials with stimulus B as the experimental group, as indicated in phase 2 of Figure 4.10. That is, for the control group, stimulus B was also presented simultaneously with stimulus A during its conditioning trials. However, for the control group, stimulus A was not conditioned to elicit fear prior to these compound-stimulus conditioning trials. In many replications of the experiment, stimulus B invariably produced less conditioned suppression in the experimental group than in the control group.

Since the time of Aristotle, temporal contiguity has been considered the primary means

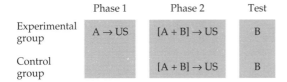

	Phase 1	Phase 2	Test
Experimental group	A → US	[A + B] → US	B
Control group		[A + B] → US	B

Figure 4.10 Diagram of the blocking procedure. During phase 1, stimulus A is conditioned with the US in the experimental group, while the control group does not receive conditioning trials. During phase 2, both the experimental and control groups receive conditioning trials in which stimulus A is presented simultaneously with stimulus B and paired with the US. A later test of response to stimulus B alone shows that less conditioning occurs to stimulus B in the experimental than in the control group.

by which stimuli become associated. The blocking effect has become a landmark phenomenon in classical conditioning because it put to rest the idea that temporal contiguity is sufficient for conditioning. The blocking effect clearly indicates that classical conditioning does not occur merely because of the presentation of a CS together with a US. During phase 2 of the blocking experiment, stimulus B is paired with the US in an identical fashion for the experimental and the control groups. If pairing of CS and US were sufficient for conditioning, stimulus B should become conditioned equally in both groups. The fact that stimulus B becomes conditioned only in the control group is strong evidence that pairing of a CS with a US is not enough to produce learning.

In addition to demonstrating the blocking effect, Kamin (1968, 1969) performed many experiments to find out what aspects of this procedure were responsible for interference with the conditioning of stimulus B in the experimental group. These and other experiments have shown that the conditioning of stimulus B will be blocked if stimulus B is redundant—that is, if B adds no new information about the US. Two aspects of the blocking procedure are critical in meeting this requirement. First, stimulus A must be present together with stimulus B. Second, stimulus A

has to be an adequate predictor of the US during the conditioning trials for stimulus B. These features ensure that stimulus A alone is sufficient to signal the US and that B is redundant (unnecessary).

If the conditions that make stimulus B redundant are not met, blocking will not occur. For example, stimulus A does not block the conditioning of stimulus B if stimulus A is not present during phase 2. Blocking also does not occur if stimulus A is not conditioned with the US during phase 1, or if the conditioned properties of stimulus A are extinguished between phases 1 and 2. In both these cases, the result is that stimulus A does not signal occurrences of the US during phase 2, and therefore stimulus B is not redundant.

Why is it that a redundant stimulus does not become conditioned by the US? The presence of stimulus A during the conditioning trials for stimulus B in phase 2 of the blocking procedure makes the US entirely expected. Thus, the US is not surprising in phase 2. These considerations suggested to Kamin that the unconditioned stimulus has to be *surprising* to produce conditioning. Kamin reasoned that if the unconditioned stimulus is not surprising, it will not startle the animal and stimulate the "mental effort" needed for the formation of an association. Unexpected events are events to which the organism has not yet adjusted. Therefore, unexpected events are much more likely to create new learning.

The Rescorla–Wagner Model

The idea that the surprisingness of an unconditioned stimulus determines its effectiveness in producing new learning was developed into a formal mathematical model of conditioning by Robert Rescorla and Allan Wagner (Rescorla & Wagner, 1972; Wagner & Rescorla, 1972). With the use of this model, the implications of the concept of US surprisingness were extended to a wide variety of conditioning phenomena. Consequently, the Rescorla–

Wagner model dominated research on classical conditioning for about 10 years after its formulation.

We will not describe details of the mathematical treatment Rescorla and Wagner provided; rather, we will describe the conceptual basis and implications of the theory.

How might we measure the surprisingness of an unconditioned stimulus? What does it mean to say that something is surprising? By definition, an event is surprising if it is different from what we expected. A big difference between what you expect and what actually occurs makes the outcome very surprising. If you expect a small gift for your birthday, and you receive a car, you will be very surprised. By contrast, if the difference between what is expected and what actually occurs is small, the outcome is not very surprising. If you expect to receive a small gift and that is what you get, you will not be greatly surprised. Rescorla and Wagner formalized these notions in the assumption that the surprisingness and hence the effectiveness

of a US depend on how different the US is from what the subject expects. Furthermore, they assumed that expectation of the US is related to the conditioned or associative properties of the stimuli that precede the US. If the conditioned stimuli present on a trial do not permit accurate prediction of the US that occurs, the US will be surprising. If those CSs permit accurate prediction of the US, the US will not be surprising.

The Rescorla–Wagner model views learning as the adjustment of expectations to what actually happens. If current expectations do not accurately predict the US that is presented, the expectations will be readjusted. This readjustment of expectations will continue until the expectations perfectly match the outcome of conditioning trials. Learning ceases when discrepancies between expectations and outcomes no longer exist.

The basic ideas of the Rescorla–Wagner model clearly predict the blocking effect. In applying the model, it is important to keep in mind that expectations of the US are based on

---

The Picture–Word Problem in Teaching Reading: A Form of Blocking

BOX **4.4**

Early instruction in teaching reading often involves showing children a written word, along with a picture of what that word represents. Thus, two stimuli are presented (picture and word). The children have already learned what the picture is called (a "horse," for example). Therefore, the two stimuli in the picture–word compound include one that is already known (the picture) and one that is not (the word). This makes the picture–word compound much like the compound stimulus in a blocking experiment: a previously conditioned stimulus is presented along with a new stimulus, not yet conditioned. Animal research on the blocking effect indicates that the presence of a previously conditioned stimulus disrupts conditioning of the added stimulus. Singh and Solman (1990) recently tested whether a similar effect occurs with picture–word compounds in teaching reading to mentally retarded students. The children were taught to read words such as knife, lemon, radio, stamp, and chalk. Some of the words were taught using a variation of the blocking design in which the picture of the object was presented first and the subject was asked to name it. The picture was then presented, together with its written word, and the subject was asked, "What is that word?" In other conditions, the words were presented without their corresponding pictures. All 8 students in the experiment showed the slowest learning of the words that were taught in the blocking procedure. By contrast, 6 of the 8 students showed the fastest learning of the words that were taught without their corresponding pictures. (The remaining 2 students learned most rapidly with a modified procedure.) These results suggest that processes akin to blocking may occur in learning to read. The results also suggest that pictorial prompts should be used with caution in reading instruction because they may disrupt rather than facilitate learning.

all of the cues available to the subject during the conditioning trial.

As we saw in Figure 4.10, the experimental group in the blocking design first receives extensive conditioning of stimulus A so that it acquires a perfect expectation that the US will occur whenever it encounters stimulus A. In phase 2, stimulus B is presented together with stimulus A, and the two CSs are followed by the US. According to the Rescorla–Wagner model, no conditioning of stimulus B occurs in phase 2 because the US is fully expected in phase 2 on the basis of the presence of stimulus A. Subjects in the control group receive the identical training in phase 2, but the presence of stimulus A does not lead to an expectation of the US for them. Therefore, the US is surprising for the control group and produces new learning.

Loss of associative strength despite continued presentation of the US.

Although the Rescorla–Wagner model is consistent with fundamental facts of classical conditioning such as acquisition and the blocking effect, much of the importance of the model has come from its unusual predictions about learning. It predicts, for example, that under certain circumstances conditioned stimuli will lose associative strength despite continued pairings with the US. How might this happen? Recall that the model views learning as the adjustment of expectancies to outcomes. At the start of conditioning, for example, the CS fails to predict the US that occurs. Thus, the subject receives *more* of a US than what is expected, and the resulting adjustment is an *increase* in expectation of the US. The opposite result occurs if the subject receives *less* of a US than what is expected. In this case, the resulting adjustment is a *decrease* in US expectation or associative strength. This can occur even if the US continues to be presented, as in the experiment outlined in Figure 4.11.

Figure 4.11 outlines a 2-phase experiment. In phase 1 subjects receive conditioning trials in which stimulus A is paired with the US and

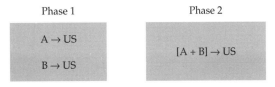

Figure 4.11 Loss of associative strength despite continued presentations of the US. Stimuli A and B are conditioned separately to asymptote in phase 1 so that each CS perfectly predicts the US. In phase 2, stimuli A and B are presented simultaneously and paired with the same US that was used in phase 1. This produces an overexpectation of the US. Because the US is surprisingly small at the start of phase 2, the associative strengths of stimuli A and B decrease until the simultaneous presentation of the two CSs no longer produces an overexpectation.

trials in which stimulus B is paired with the same US (one pellet of food, for example). The conditioning of stimuli A and B on separate trials continues in phase 1 until both stimuli have been conditioned completely—until both stimuli predict perfectly the one-food-pellet US. Phase 2 is then initiated. In phase 2 stimuli A and B are presented simultaneously, followed by the same US—one food pellet. The question is what happens to the individual associative strengths of stimuli A and B as a result of the phase 2 training. Note that the same US that was used in phase 1 continues to be presented in phase 2. Given that there is no change in the US, informal reflection suggests that the associative strengths of stimuli A and B should also remain unchanged during phase 2. In contrast to this common-sense prediction, the Rescorla–Wagner model predicts that the associative strengths of the individual stimuli A and B will decrease in phase 2.

As a result of training in phase 1, stimuli A and B both come to predict the one-food-pellet US. When stimuli A and B are presented simultaneously for the first time, in phase 2, the expectations based on each are assumed to add together, with the result that subjects expect a two-food-pellet US. This is an overexpectation because the US remains only one food pellet. Thus, there is a discrepancy between what is expected and what occurs. At the start of phase 2, subjects find the US surprisingly small. To bring their expectations of the US in line with what actually occurs in phase 2, subjects have to decrease their expectancy of the US based on stimuli A and B. Thus, stimuli A and B are predicted to lose associative strength despite continued presentations of the same US. The loss in associative strength is predicted to continue until A and B presented together predict only one food pellet. The predicted loss of conditioned response to the individual stimuli A and B in this type of procedure is highly counterintuitive but has been verified experimentally (see Kremer, 1978).

Conditioned inhibition. How does the Rescorla–Wagner model explain the development of conditioned inhibition? Consider, for example, the standard inhibitory conditioning procedure (see Figure 3.7). This procedure involves two kinds of trials—those on which the US is presented (reinforced trials) and those on which the US is omitted (nonreinforced trials). On reinforced trials, a conditioned excitatory stimulus (CS+) is presented. On nonreinforced trials, the CS+ is presented together with the conditioned inhibitory stimulus, CS−.

Application of the Rescorla–Wagner model to such a procedure requires considering reinforced and nonreinforced trials separately. To accurately anticipate the US on reinforced trials, the CS+ has to gain excitatory properties. The development of such conditioned excitation is illustrated in the left-hand panel of Figure 4.12. Excitatory conditioning involves the acquisition of positive associative value and ceases once the subject predicts the US perfectly on each reinforced trial.

What happens on nonreinforced trials? On nonreinforced trials, both the CS+ and CS−

occur. Once the CS+ has acquired some degree of conditioned excitation (because of its presentation on reinforced trials), the subject will expect that the US will occur on a nonreinforced trial. However, the US does not happen on these trials. Therefore, this is a case of overexpectation, similar to the example illustrated in Figure 4.11. To accurately predict the absence of the US on nonreinforced trials, the associative value of the CS+ and the CS− has to sum to zero. How can this be achieved? Given the positive associative value of the CS+, the only way to achieve a net zero expectation of the US on nonreinforced trials is to make the associative value of the CS− negative. Hence, the Rescorla–Wagner model explains conditioned inhibition by assuming that the CS− acquires negative associative value (see the left-hand panel of Figure 4.12).

Extinction of conditioned excitation and conditioned inhibition. Predictions of the Rescorla–Wagner model for extinction are illustrated in the right-hand panel of Figure 4.12. The standard procedure for extinction involves omitting the unconditioned stimulus on each trial. If a CS has acquired excitatory properties (see CS+ in Figure 4.12) at the start of extinction, it will lead to an overexpectation of the US. The expectation elicited by the CS gradually will be brought in line with the absence of the US during extinction by reduction of the associative value of the CS+ to zero.

The Rescorla–Wagner model posits an analogous scenario for extinction of conditioned inhibition. At the start of extinction, the CS− has negative associative value. This may be thought of as creating an underprediction of the US; the subject predicts less than the zero US that occurs on extinction trials. To bring expectations in line with the absence of the US, the negative associative value of the CS− is gradually lost and the CS− ends up with zero associative strength.

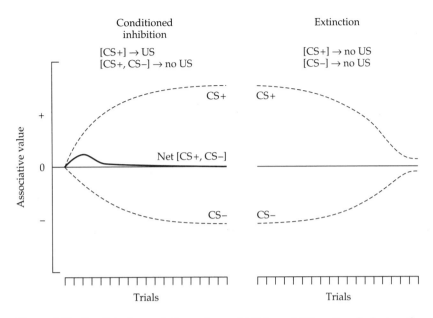

Figure 4.12 Predicted associative values of CS + and CS − stimuli during the course of conditioned inhibition training (left) and extinction (right). During conditioned inhibition training, when the CS + is presented alone, it is followed by the US; by contrast, when the CS + is presented with the CS −, the US is omitted. The net associative value of CS + and CS − is the sum of the associative values of the individual stimuli. During extinction, the conditioned stimuli are presented alone and the US never occurs.

Major features of the Rescorla–Wagner model.
The preceding illustrations of the operations of the Rescorla–Wagner model included a number of major features. The following is a list of these features:

1. Conditioned excitation and conditioned inhibition are assumed to represent different points on a continuum of associative value that ranges from positive to negative. The associative value of a particular conditioned stimulus is assumed to be a point somewhere on this continuum. Therefore, according to the theory, a conditioned stimulus cannot have both excitatory and inhibitory value at the same time. This is called the *single-associative-value assumption.*

2. On a conditioning trial involving just one CS, what a subject learns about the stimulus is assumed to depend on the differ-

ence between expectation aroused by that CS (its associative value) and the outcome of the trial. How the expectation (or associative value) was acquired is assumed to be irrelevant. Another way to express this idea is that the path used to reach a particular associative value is assumed to be insignificant. Hence, this is called the *path-independence assumption.*

3. In a situation involving multiple conditioned stimuli, each of those conditioned stimuli is assumed to contribute independently to the US expectation that is aroused. The effectiveness of one stimulus in arousing expectation of the US serves to block conditioning of the other cues. In this manner, conditioned stimuli compete for association with the US. Hence, this is called the *stimulus-competition assumption.*

4. The model analyzes learning in situations with more than one conditioned stimu-

lus in terms of the association of each CS with the US. This is called the *exclusive-US-learning assumption.*

5. As we saw in Figure 4.12, an extinction procedure involving the absence of the US is assumed to result in a loss of both positive and negative associative value. The same extinction procedure is assumed to be effective in eliminating conditioned excitation and conditioned inhibition. This is called the *universal-extinction assumption.*

6. Finally, as was also illustrated in Figure 4.12, the Rescorla–Wagner model assumes that extinction is the opposite of acquisition. Whereas in acquisition, associative values diverge from zero, in extinction associative values return to zero. This is called the *extinction-as-unlearning assumption.*

Difficulties with the Rescorla–Wagner model. The Rescorla–Wagner model stimulated a great deal of research and led to the discovery of many new and important phenomena of classical conditioning. However, the model is not without its shortcomings. In fact, evidence is now available that contradicts each of the six assumptions we have listed. It is instructive to discuss these violations of the model because the exceptions serve to further illustrate the richness and complexity of classical conditioning phenomena.

Contrary to the single-associative-value assumption, several studies have yielded evidence indicating that under certain conditions, a particular conditioned stimulus may have both excitatory and inhibitory properties (Matzel, Gladstein, & Miller, 1988; Robbins, 1990; Tait & Saladin, 1986). Other research has revealed violations of the path-independence assumption (Brown-Su, Matzel, Gordon, & Miller, 1986).

The stimulus-competition assumption is consistent with most research findings. However, in ingestional aversion learning the presence of a well-conditioned or easily conditioned stimulus has been found to *facilitate,* rather than interfere with, the conditioning of

another CS. This phenomenon is known as **potentiation.** In general, the presence of an easily conditioned taste stimulus will facilitate or potentiate the learning of an ingestional aversion to a less salient, nongustatory conditioned stimulus. Numerous investigators have reported that taste cues potentiate the conditioning of odor stimuli with poisoning in rodents (for example, Bouton, Jones, McPhillips, & Swartzentruber, 1986; Rusiniak, Palmerino, & Garcia, 1982; Rusiniak, Palmerino, Rice, Forthman, & Garcia, 1982). Taste cues also have been found to potentiate conditioning of visual cues, environmental stimuli, and other taste stimuli in rats. (For potentiation of visual aversion learning, see Galef & Osborne, 1978; for potentiation of environmental conditioning, see Best, Brown, & Sowell, 1984; Best, Batson, Meachum, Brown, & Ringer, 1985; Westbrook, Harvey, & Swinbourne, 1988; and for potentiation of aversion learning to other tastes, see Bouton, Dunlap, & Swartzentruber, 1987; Davis, Best, & Grover, 1988.) Finally, taste cues also have been found to potentiate ingestional aversion learning to visual cues in bird species (Jackson & Fritsche, 1989; Lett, 1980).

In its approach to the learning that takes place in situations involving more than one conditioned stimulus (blocking, conditioned inhibition, and potentiation), the Rescorla–Wagner model directs attention only to how each CS becomes associated with the US. This *exclusive-US-learning assumption* also has turned out to be an oversimplification. More recent evidence suggests that in compound-CS situations subjects also may learn associations between the individual conditioned stimuli. In addition to learning CS–US associations, subjects may learn CS–CS associations. For example, some instances of potentiation appear to be the result of such CS–CS associations (Best et al., 1985; Davis et al., 1988; Durlach & Rescorla, 1980; Miller, McCoy, Kelly, & Bardo, 1986; but see Lett, 1982). The potentiated odor or other cue may become associated with the taste CS during compound conditioning. This odor–taste CS–CS association enhances the ingestional aversion to the odor because the odor activates the memory of the associated taste, which is aversive because of its own association with the toxicosis US. Moreover, within-compound associations have been discovered to develop in several other paradigms, including blocking, conditioned inhibition, and overshadowing procedures (Cunningham, 1981; Matzel, Shuster, & Miller, 1987; Rescorla, 1981, 1982b, 1983; Speers, Gillan, & Rescorla, 1980; Williams & Overmier, 1988b; Williams, Travis, & Overmier, 1986). (For a discussion of overshadowing, see Chapter 8, "Effects of Relative Ease of Conditioning Various Stimuli.")

The universal-extinction assumption of the Rescorla–Wagner model also has been called into question in light of more recent research findings. As we noted in Chapter 3, repeated nonreinforcement of a conditioned excitatory stimulus produces a decline in excitatory conditioned responding. By contrast, contrary to the Rescorla–Wagner model, in most studies of the extinction of a conditioned inhibitory (CS−) stimulus, repeated nonreinforced presentations of the CS− have not been found to reduce its conditioned inhibitory properties (for example, Zimmer-Hart & Rescorla, 1974). In fact, some investigators have found that repeated nonreinforcement of a CS− can enhance its conditioned inhibitory properties (for example, DeVito & Fowler, 1987). Curiously, an effective procedure for reducing conditioned inhibitory properties of a CS− does not involve presenting the CS− at all. Rather, it involves extinguishing the excitatory properties of the CS+ with which the CS− was presented during inhibitory conditioning trials (Best et al., 1985; Lysle & Fowler, 1985). (For a more complete discussion of procedures for extinguishing conditioned inhibition, see Fowler et al., 1991.)

Finally, as noted in Chapter 3, a growing body of evidence indicates that extinction should not be viewed as simply the reverse of acquisition. Extinction appears to produce the learning of a new relationship between the CS and the US (that the US no longer follows the CS) rather than the unlearning of a previously acquired relationship (see Bouton, 1991).

Additional challenges for a comprehensive theory of classical conditioning. In addition to dealing with the findings we have mentioned that are problematic for the Rescorla–Wagner model, a comprehensive theory of classical conditioning must also explain various other features of classical conditioning that the Rescorla–Wagner model fails to address. For example, the theory should incorporate time as a variable so that it may explain why simultaneous, delayed, trace, and backward conditioning procedures produce different results. It should allow for sensory preconditioning and higher order conditioning and explain the effects of changing the value of the US. A comprehensive theory also must address issues of performance and provide an explanation for differences in the form of the conditioned response as a function of the CS, the US, and other conditioning parameters. Finally, as we will see in later chapters, a comprehensive theory also must incorporate memory and reminder effects.

Other Models of Classical Conditioning

The formulation of a comprehensive theory of classical conditioning is a formidable challenge. Given the nearly 100 years of research on classical conditioning, a comprehensive theory must account for many diverse findings. No theory available today has been entirely successful in accomplishing that goal. Nevertheless, interesting new ideas about classical conditioning have been proposed. Some of these new models serve to complement the Rescorla–Wagner model; others are alternative formulations.

CS-modification models. In the Rescorla–Wagner model, differences in how much is learned from a conditioning trial are explained in terms of differences in the effectiveness of the unconditioned stimulus. If the US is surprising, much more conditioning occurs than if the US is expected. The outcome of various procedures is explained by how those procedures alter the surprisingness of the outcome or unconditioned stimulus on a trial. Therefore, the Rescorla–Wagner model is a **US-modification model** of classical conditioning. North American psychologists have favored US-reduction models. By contrast, British psychologists have approached phenomena such as the blocking effect by assuming that the effectiveness or ability of the CS to enter into an association is altered under various circumstances (Mackintosh, 1975; Pearce & Hall, 1980). Thus, they have attempted to explain differences in learning in terms of changes in the effectiveness of the conditioned stimulus. Such models are called **CS-modification models.**

CS-modification models emphasize that for conditioning to take place, the conditioned stimulus has to be noticeable, or salient; it has to attract the subject's attention. The salience of a CS on a conditioning trial is assumed to determine how much conditioning takes place on that trial. If a stimulus has lost its salience and is no longer noticeable, subjects will not learn much that is new about it.

CS-modification models differ in their assumptions about what determines the salience, or noticeability, of the CS on a given trial. Pearce and Hall (1980), for example, assume that how well subjects pay attention to the CS on a given trial is determined by how surprising the US was on the preceding trial (see also Hall, Kaye, & Pearce, 1985). Subjects have a lot to learn in situations where the US is surprising. Therefore, if a CS is followed by a surprising US, the subjects will pay closer attention to that CS on the next trial. A surprising US is assumed to increase the salience of the CS. In contrast, if a CS is followed by an expected US, the subjects will pay less attention to that CS on the next trial.

An expected US is assumed to decrease the salience of the CS.

The Pearce and Hall model is consistent with many common findings in classical conditioning. For example, it explains the typical course of acquisition of a conditioned response by assuming that the surprisingness of the US at the start of conditioning makes subjects pay close attention to the CS, and this results in large increments in conditioning. As learning proceeds, the US becomes less surprising. This reduces the amount of attention subjects pay to the CS, with the result that less learning takes place. The asymptote, or limit, of conditioning is reached when the US is perfectly predicted because perfect predictability completely reduces the salience of the CS.

CS-modification models of conditioning differ from US-reduction models in other ways as well. Not only do CS-modification models emphasize changes in the salience of the CS, they also assume that the surprisingness of the US on a given trial affects only what happens on the next trial. If trial 10, for example, ends in a surprising US, that outcome increases the salience of the CS on the next trial, trial 11. The surprisingness of the US on trial 10 is not assumed to determine what is learned on trial 10. How much attention the CS attracts on trial 10 is assumed to have been determined by events prior to trial 10. Thus, US surprisingness is assumed to have only a prospective influence on conditioning. This is an important contrast to US-reduction models, in which the surprisingness of the US determines what is learned on the same trial the US is presented. The assumption that the US on a given trial influences only what is learned on the next trial has permitted CS-reduction models to explain certain findings (for example, Mackintosh, Bygrave, & Picton, 1977). However, that assumption has made it difficult for the models to explain other results. In particular, the models cannot explain blocking that occurs in one trial (for example, Azorlosa & Cicala, 1986; Balaz, Kasprow, & Miller, 1982; Dickinson, Nicholas, & Mackintosh, 1983; Gillan & Domjan, 1977). According to CS-reduction models, blocking occurs because the lack of surprisingness of the US on compound-CS trials reduces the salience of the blocked CS. However, that reduction in salience occurs only after the first compound-CS trial. Therefore, CS-reduction models cannot explain blocking that occurs on the first compound-CS trial.

The relative-waiting-time hypothesis. Neither the Rescorla–Wagner model nor CS-modification models were designed to explain temporal factors in conditioning. By contrast, temporal factors are the focus of the **relative-waiting-time hypothesis** (Gibbon & Balsam, 1981; Jenkins, Barnes, & Barrera, 1981). This hypothesis, also referred to as the *scalar expectancy hypothesis,* was developed to explain the results of studies of sign tracking in which the duration of the conditioned stimulus and the interval between trials or successive food presentations were systematically varied. The findings from these studies were consistent with the generalization that the strength of conditioned responding to a stimulus is determined by a comparison of two factors: how long the subject has to wait for food in the presence of the CS *(CS waiting time),* and how long the subject has to wait for food in an experimental situation irrespective of the conditioned stimulus *(context waiting time).* A conditioned stimulus is informative about the presentation of the US only if the US occurs sooner during the CS than in the experimental situation irrespective of the CS. The relative-waiting-time hypothesis predicts that if the CS waiting time is much less than the waiting time for food in the situation in general, then the subject will show a high level of conditioned responding to the CS. By contrast, if the CS waiting time is similar to the context waiting time, conditioned responding will not be observed.

The relative-waiting-time hypothesis has been tested in studies of the effects of introducing extra unconditioned stimuli between trials involving the pairing of the CS and US. These extra USs during the intertrial interval should decrease the context waiting time and thereby reduce the ratio between the context and CS waiting times. A smaller ratio of context-to-CS waiting times should result in less conditioned responding to the CS. This prediction of the relative-waiting-time hypothesis has been confirmed. Extra intertrial USs invariably result in less responding to the CS. However, an important corollary of the hypothesis has yielded more controversial results. The corollary is that context waiting time is to be measured independent of any signals that might permit prediction of the extra intertrial USs. Some studies have reported that extra intertrial USs disrupt conditioned responding whether or not these USs are signaled (for example, Jenkins et al., 1981), whereas others have observed that signaling the extra USs makes them less effective in disrupting conditioned responding (for example, Durlach, 1983; see also Balsam & Gibbon, 1988; Cooper, Aronson, Balsam, & Gibbon, 1990; Durlach, 1989; Goddard & Jenkins, 1987).

The comparator hypothesis. The relative-waiting-time hypothesis was developed to explain certain temporal features of excitatory conditioning and manipulations of CS–US contingency. One of its important contributions was to emphasize that accurate prediction of conditioning effects may require a comparison of what happens during the CS to what happens in the experimental situation in general. The idea that such comparisons are critical to the understanding of many learning phenomena has been developed in greater detail by R. Miller and his collaborators in the **comparator hypothesis** (Miller & Matzel, 1988, 1989). As does the relative-waiting-time hypothesis, the comparator hypothesis assumes that conditioned responding depends not only on associations between a target CS and the US but also on possible associations the subject may learn between other cues and the US. The associative strength of other cues present during training with the target CS is especially important.

As Figure 4.13 illustrates, a comparison is made between the associative strength of the CS and the associative strength of the other cues present during the training of the CS. If the associative strength of the CS exceeds the associative strength of the other cues, the balance of the comparison is tipped in favor of excitatory responding to the target CS. As the associative strength of the other cues becomes stronger, the balance of the comparison becomes less favorable for excitatory responding and may tip in favor of inhibitory responding to the CS if the relative associative strength of the other cues becomes sufficiently strong.

Unlike the relative-waiting-time hypothesis, the comparator hypothesis emphasizes associations rather than time. It assumes that subjects learn three associations during the course of conditioning: an association between the target CS and the US, an association between other contextual stimuli and the US, and an association between the target CS and those other contextual cues. When the target CS is presented, all three of these associations are activated, permitting the subject to compare the CS–US association to the context–US association. That comparison determines conditioned responding. It is important to note that the hypothesis makes no commitment about how associations become established. Rather, it describes how CS–US and context–US associations determine responding to the target CS. Thus, unlike US-modification and CS-modification models, the comparator hypothesis is a theory of performance, not a theory of learning.

An important corollary to the comparator hypothesis is that the comparison of CS–US and context–US associations is made at the time of testing for conditioned responding.

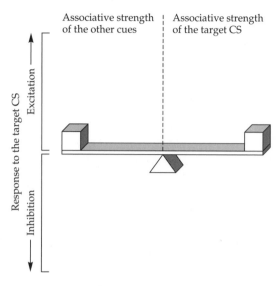

Figure 4.13 Illustration of the comparator hypothesis. Responding to the target CS is represented by the height of the left side of the seesaw. If the associative strength of the CS exceeds the associative strength of the other cues present during training of the CS, the comparison tips in favor of excitatory responding to the CS. As the associative strength of the other cues increases, the comparison becomes less favorable for excitatory responding and may tip in favor of inhibitory responding.

Because of this assumption, the comparator hypothesis is able to predict that extinction of context–US associations following conditioning of a target CS will enhance responding to that target CS (for example, Hallam, Matzel, Sloat, & Miller, 1990; Matzel, Brown, & Miller, 1987).

The comparator hypothesis has been most extensively tested in studies of conditioned inhibition (see Kasprow, Schachtman, & Miller, 1987; Schachtman, Brown, Gordon, Catterson, & Miller, 1987). The hypothesis attributes inhibitory responding to situations in which the association of the target CS with the US is weaker than the association of contextual cues with the US. The contextual cues in this case are the stimuli that provide the excitatory context for inhibitory conditioning. Interestingly, the hypothesis predicts that extinction of these conditioned excitatory stimuli following inhibitory conditioning will eliminate evidence of conditioned inhibition. Thus, the comparator hypothesis is unique in predicting that extinction of conditioned inhibition is best accomplished not by presenting the CS− alone but by extinguishing the CS+ cues that provided the excitatory context for inhibitory conditioning. As we noted earlier, this unusual prediction has been confirmed (Best et al., 1985; Lysle & Fowler, 1985).

SOP and AESOP.   Each of the new models we have described emphasizes a different aspect of classical conditioning and the production of conditioned responding. The relative-waiting-time hypothesis addresses a fairly small range of phenomena. The comparator hypothesis is more ambitious, but it is not a theory of learning and therefore it does not provide an explanation of how associations are acquired. CS-modification models attempt to address the same wide range of phenomena as does the Rescorla–Wagner model, but they have some of the same difficulties as the Rescorla–Wagner model. All of these models have been important in directing our attention to previously ignored aspects of classical conditioning. However, none of them has come to dominate the study of classical conditioning as the Rescorla–Wagner model did in the 1970s.

The last two models we will consider, **SOP** and **AESOP,** are the most ambitious in attempting to provide a new, comprehensive approach to classical conditioning (Wagner, 1981; Wagner & Brandon, 1989; Wagner & Larew, 1985). These models provide not only an account of the acquisition of conditioned excitation and inhibition, but also an explanation of the form of conditioned responses (Paletta & Wagner, 1986). Thus, unlike the other models that characterize only learning or performance, these models provide an account of both aspects of classical conditioning. Furthermore, SOP and AESOP are "real time" models, and hence can explain conditioning effects that depend on the precise timing of conditioned and unconditioned stimuli.

SOP.   SOP is an acronym for "standard operating procedures" of memory and "sometimes opponent process." The SOP model provides a general characterization of how stimuli are processed by the nervous system. Its starting assumptions bear striking resemblance to opponent-process ideas that we have already encountered in discussions of the opponent-process theory of motivation in Chapter 2 and compensatory conditioned responses earlier in this chapter. As illustrated in Figure 4.14, each stimulus is presumed to have a primary (A1) and a secondary (A2) effect. The A1 and A2 states are analogous to the primary (*a*) and opponent (*b*) states of the opponent-process theory of motivation. When the stimulus starts, the A1 state predominates; the A2 state then gradually takes over, followed by its own decay.

An excitatory association between a CS and a US is presumed to develop if the A1 state of the CS overlaps with the A1 state of the US, as is the case for the CS and US diagramed in Figure 4.14. Once a CS–US association has been learned the CS continues to elicit its own A1 and A2 states, as shown in the upper right-hand graph of Figure 4.14. Moreover, the CS comes to activate neural processes related to the US as well. After excitatory conditioning, however, the CS does not come to act as a substitute for the US. Rather, it activates only the A2 state of the US.

Because excitatory conditioning is presumed to occur only if the A1 states of the CS and the US overlap, the model predicts systematic changes in the degree of excitatory conditioning as a function of variations in the CS–US interval. None of the other models we have considered explain such effects.

The SOP model also explains why backward conditioning results in excitatory conditioning under certain conditions and inhibitory conditioning under other circumstances. As we discussed in Chapter 3, in backward

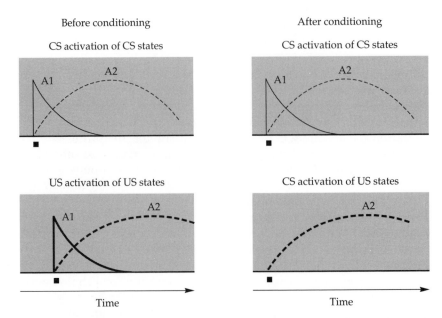

Figure 4.14 Mechanisms of the SOP model. Before the CS has been conditioned (left), the CS and the US elicit their own respective A1 and A2 states. After the CS has been conditioned (right), the CS continues to elicit its own A1 and A2 states. In addition, the CS elicits the A2 state of the US.

conditioning the CS is presented after the US. Excitatory backward conditioning is predicted to occur if the CS is presented soon enough after the US so that the A1 state of the US has not yet decayed when the A1 state of the CS occurs. Inhibitory conditioning of the CS is presumed to occur if the A1 state of the CS overlaps with the A2 state of the US. This circumstance can be arranged by delaying the presentation of the CS until most of the A1 state of the US has decayed and only the A2 state of the US remains (Wagner & Larew, 1985).

SOP also provides rules for predicting the form of the conditioned response. Before conditioning, the CS is not a biologically significant stimulus. Hence, the A1 and A2 states of the CS are not manifest in strong behavioral reactions. By contrast, the A1 and A2 states of the US create easily observed behavior. The initial reaction to an injection of morphine, for example, is a decrease in activity, which is followed by hyperactivity as a

delayed or secondary response. Because an excitatory conditioned stimulus is presumed to elicit the A2 state of the US, the conditioned response to morphine is expected to be the hyperactivity response. Thus, in cases where the secondary effects of the US are opposite the initial reactions to the US, the conditioned response is expected to be similar to this opposing response.

As we have seen, however, not all unconditioned stimuli produce biphasic unconditioned responses. For example, an aversive stimulus elicits a reduction in pain sensitivity, which is not followed by enhanced pain sensitivity. Therefore, in such a case the conditioned response, which mimics the delayed effects of the US, will not be opposite in form to the initial effects of the US. SOP predicts that the form of the conditioned response will be opposite the form of the unconditioned response only with USs that have biphasic behavioral effects. Hence, SOP is a "sometimes-opponent-process" theory that predicts when the conditioned response will be similar to or opposite the initial responses to the unconditioned stimulus. These predictions have been confirmed in studies of conditioned morphine effects and conditioned hypoalgesia. (For a review of these studies, see Wagner & Brandon, 1989.) However, the generality of these ideas remains to be tested.

AESOP. Recently SOP has been extended in recognition of the fact that unconditioned stimuli are complex events that have multiple aspects of potential significance for learning. In particular, unconditioned stimuli may be viewed as having motivational–emotional aspects as well as simple sensory features. AESOP is an extension of SOP designed specifically to incorporate the motivational–emotional aspects of unconditioned stimuli. Thus, AESOP is an "*affective extension*" of SOP. The basic assumption of AESOP is that unconditioned stimuli activate two sets of A1 and A2 processes—one set related to sensory features of the US and the other set related to the emotional features of the US. Emotional reactivity is generally slower than the simple sensation of a stimulus. (If someone tells you that your best friend is sick and will not be able to visit you, your disappointment may not be immediate and will last longer than your awareness of the spoken message.) Therefore, the A1 and A2 processes related to emotional effects of a US are also presumed to be longer lasting.

The added assumption that unconditioned stimuli have multiple features with different time courses enables AESOP to explain a greater range of findings concerning the nature of conditioned responses (see Wagner & Brandon, 1989). In addition, it provides an account for the puzzling finding that a given conditioned stimulus can have both conditioned excitatory and conditioned inhibitory properties (for example, Tait & Saladin, 1986). The CS can have excitatory associations with one aspect of the US and inhibitory associa-

tions with other US features at the same time.

SOP and AESOP have been remarkably successful in explaining a wide range of phenomena and offer an approach to integrating issues relevant to both learning and performance. However, even these models leave many important phenomena unaccounted for. For example, it is not clear how SOP and AESOP would explain potentiation in excitatory conditioning or comparator effects in inhibitory conditioning. The models also may have difficulty with findings concerning extinction. For example, they assume that extinction of excitation occurs by the same process responsible for conditioned inhibition, even though empirical evidence fails to support a conditioned inhibition view of extinction. The models also cannot explain how the nature of the conditioned stimulus determines the form of the conditioned response or why, in some situations, the conditioned response appears to bear little resemblance to the unconditioned responses. Thus, the task of integrating all of our knowledge about classical conditioning remains a challenge as we approach the second century of research in this area.

Concluding Comments

Traditionally, classical conditioning has been regarded as a relatively simple and primitive type of learning that is involved in the regulation only of glandular and visceral responses, such as salivation. The establishment of CS–US associations was assumed to occur fairly automatically with the pairing of a CS and a US. Given the simple and automatic nature of the conditioning and its limitation to glandular and visceral responses, it was not viewed as important in explaining the complexity and richness of human experience. This view of classical conditioning is no longer tenable.

The research reviewed in Chapters 3 and 4 has shown that classical conditioning is a rather complex process and that it is involved in the conditioning of a wide variety of responses, including emotional behavior and locomotor movements. The learning does not occur automatically with the pairing of a CS with a US. Rather, it depends on the subject's prior experience with each of these stimuli, the presence of other stimuli during the conditioning trial, and the extent to which the CS and US are relevant to each other. Furthermore, the processes of classical conditioning are not limited to CS–US pairings. Learned associations can occur between two biologi-cally weak stimuli (sensory preconditioning), in the absence of an unconditioned stimulus (higher order conditioning), or in the absence of conventional conditioned stimuli (counter-conditioning).

Given these and other complexities of classical conditioning processes, it is a mistake to disregard classical conditioning in attempts to explain complex forms of behavior. The richness of classical conditioning mechanisms makes them potentially quite relevant to the richness and complexity of human experience.

5 | *Instrumental Conditioning: Foundations*

This chapter begins a discussion of instrumental conditioning and goal-directed behavior. In this type of conditioning, presentations of stimuli depend on the prior occurrence of designated responses. We will first consider origins of research on instrumental conditioning and the investigative methods used in contemporary research. This discussion lays the groundwork for the following section on four basic types of instrumental conditioning procedures. We will conclude the chapter with a discussion of three fundamental elements of the instrumental conditioning paradigm: the instrumental response, the goal event, and the relation between the instrumental response and the goal event.

In the preceding chapters we discussed various aspects of how responses are elicited by discrete stimuli. Studies of habituation, sensitization, and classical conditioning are all concerned with analyses of the mechanisms whereby stimuli trigger responses. Because of this emphasis, experiments on habituation, sensitization, and classical conditioning use procedures in which animals have no control over the stimuli to which they are exposed. Certain events, such as CSs and USs, are periodically introduced into the situation according to a schedule determined by the experimenter. The organism's adjustment to these stimulus presentations involves habituation, sensitization, and/or classical conditioning.

The procedures for studying and modifying elicited behavior are not unusual. There are many situations in which an organism has no control over the events or stimuli that it encounters. However, there are also many circumstances in which events are a direct result of the individual's behavior. By studying hard, a student can learn the material in a course and get a good grade; by turning the car key in the ignition, a driver can start the engine; by putting a coin in a vending machine, a child can obtain a piece of candy. In all these instances, some aspect of the subject's behavior is instrumental in producing a consequent stimulus. Furthermore, the behavior occurs because of the consequences it produces. Students would not study if studying did not yield interesting information or result in good grades; drivers would not turn the ignition key if this did not start the engine; and children would not put coins in a candy machine if they did not get something in return. Responses that occur mainly because they are instrumental in producing certain consequences are called **instrumental behavior.**

Because instrumental behavior is governed mainly by the events it produces, such behavior can be characterized as goal-directed. Instrumental responses occur because the goal would not be reached without them. Goal-

directed behavior represents a large proportion of all animal and human behavior. Consider our morning routine. We get out of bed in order to go to the bathroom and get cleaned up. We get cleaned up to be ready to get dressed. We get dressed to keep warm and avoid social embarrassment. The next step may involve making breakfast to reduce hunger. Then we may drive a car to get to work. On the job, we perform various tasks to receive praise and a salary. Our daily life is filled with actions, large and small, that are performed to produce certain consequences.

The fact that the consequences of an action can determine future occurrences of that action is obvious to everyone. If you happen to find a dollar bill when you glance down, you will keep looking at the ground as you walk. How such consequences influence future behavior is not so readily apparent. Much of the remainder of this text is devoted to a discussion of the mechanisms responsible for the control of behavior by its consequences. In the present chapter, we will describe some of the history, basic techniques, procedures, and issues in the experimental analysis of instrumental, or goal-directed, behavior.

How might we investigate instrumental behavior? One way would be to go to the natural environment and look for examples of goal-directed behavior. However, this approach is not likely to lead to definitive results because factors responsible for goal-directed behavior are difficult to isolate without experimental manipulation. Consider, for example, a dog sitting comfortably in its yard at home. When an intruder approaches, the dog starts to bark vigorously, with the result that the intruder goes away. Because the dog's barking has a clear consequence (departure of the intruder), we may conclude that the dog barked in order to produce this consequence — that barking was goal-directed. However, an equally likely possibility is that barking was elicited by the novelty of the intruder and persisted as long as the eliciting stimulus was present. The response consequence — departure of the intruder—may have been incidental to the dog's barking. Deciding between these alternatives is difficult without experimental manipulations of the relation between barking and its consequences.

The type of research we will discuss brings instrumental behavior into the laboratory. The idea, as with elicited behaviors, is to study representative instrumental responses in the hope of discovering general principles. However, it will become apparent that the task is complicated by a number of factors.

Elicited behavior is relatively simple to produce for investigation. One has only to select a stimulus that elicits the response of interest. Getting an instrumental response to occur for investigation can be considerably more difficult because the goal that motivates the behavior occurs *after* the response has been made. Accordingly, the experimenter first has to induce the organism to make the response so that the consequences of the behavior can occur and gain control of its future occurrence. In this sense instrumental behavior is voluntary, or, as Skinner (1953) suggested, it is *emitted* rather than elicited. We can do things to increase or decrease the likelihood that the response will occur. However, the ultimate initiation of the response belongs with the organism. Because instrumental behavior is emitted, to investigate it in the laboratory requires providing a situation in which the behavior will be likely to occur.

Early Investigations of Instrumental Conditioning

Laboratory and theoretical analyses of instrumental conditioning began in earnest with the work of E.L. Thorndike. Thorndike's original intent was to study animal intelligence (Thorndike, 1898, 1911). The publication of Darwin's theory of evolution had led people to speculate about the extent to which human intellectual capacities, such as reasoning, were present in animals.

Thorndike pursued his studies by devising a series of puzzle boxes. He would place a hungry cat (or dog or chicken) in the puzzle box with some food left outside in plain view of the animal. The task for the cat was to learn to escape from the box and obtain the food.

Different puzzle boxes required different responses by the cat to get out. Some were easier than others. In the simplest boxes, the cat's random movements initially led to escape and access to the food. With repeated trials, the cat escaped more and more quickly. In more complicated boxes, such as box "K" shown in Figure 5.1, escape also improved with practice, but more slowly. In "K," the cat had to pull a string, depress a pedal, and open one of two latches to get out. Figure 5.1 shows the median times for escape for 5 cats. None of the cats escaped on the first trial in the 10-minute maximum time that was allowed. The cats' performance improved on later trials; toward the end of the experiment they escaped in 2–3 minutes.

Thorndike interpreted the results of his studies as reflecting the learning of an association. When a cat was initially placed in a box, it displayed a variety of responses typical of a confined animal. Eventually, some of these responses resulted in opening the door. Thorndike believed that such successful escapes led to the learning of an association between the stimuli inside the puzzle box and the escape responses. As the association, or connection, between the box and the successful responses became stronger, the cat came to make those responses whenever it was confined in the puzzle box. The consequence of the successful responses—escaping the box—strengthened the association between the box stimuli and those responses.

On the basis of his research, Thorndike formulated the **law of effect**. The law of effect states that *if a response in the presence of a stimulus is followed by a satisfying event, the association between the stimulus and the response is strengthened. If the response is followed by an annoying event, the association is weakened. It is*

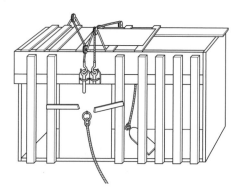
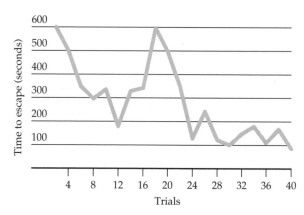

Figure 5.1 Thorndike's puzzle box "K" and the median escape times of 5 cats tested in the box on 40 successive trials. The cats took less and less time to get out of the box with practice. *(Left: From "Animal Intelligence: An Experimental Study of the Association Processes in Animals" by E.L. Thorndike, 1898,* Psychological Review Monograph, 2 *(Whole no. 8). Right: Adapted from "Thorndike's (1898) Puzzle-Box Experiments Revisited" by H. Imada and S. Imada, 1983,* Kwansie Gakuin University Annual Studies, 32, *pp. 167–184.)*

important to stress here that, according to the law of effect, animals learn an association between the response and the stimuli present at the time of the response. The consequence of the response is not involved in the association. The satisfying or annoying consequence simply serves to strengthen or weaken the bond, or association, between the response and the stimulus situation. Thus, Thorndike's law of effect involves S–R learning.

Modern Approaches to the Study of Instrumental Conditioning

Thorndike used 15 different puzzle boxes in his investigations, each box requiring different manipulations for the cat to get out. As more scientists became interested in studying learning with animal subjects, the range of situations investigated became much smaller. Certain experimental situations became "standard" and have been used repeatedly to facilitate comparison of results obtained in different laboratories. Some popular contemporary techniques for studying instrumental behavior are similar to Thorndike's procedures in that they involve **discrete trials**:

subjects are repeatedly placed in an apparatus and can perform the instrumental response only once with each placement. By contrast, other procedures involve the **free-operant** method, in which the response of interest can occur repeatedly (freely) once the subject has been placed in the experimental chamber.

Discrete-Trial Methods

Discrete-trial investigations of instrumental behavior are often conducted in some type of maze. The use of mazes in investigations of learning was introduced at the turn of the twentieth century by W.S. Small (1899, 1900), an American psychologist. Small was interested in studying rats and was stimulated to use a maze by an article he had read in *Scientific American* describing the complex system of underground burrows that kangaroo rats typically build in nature. Small reasoned that a maze would take advantage of the rats' "propensity for small winding passages."

Figure 5.2 shows two mazes frequently used in contemporary research. The **runway,** or straight-alley maze, contains a start box at one end and a goal box at the other. The rat is placed in the start box at the beginning of each trial. The movable barrier separating the start box from the main section of the runway is then lifted. The rat is allowed to make its way down the runway until it reaches the goal box, which usually contains a reward, such as food or water.

Improvement in the instrumental behavior is usually evaluated using a measure of re-

---

E.L. Thorndike: Biographical Sketch

BOX 5.1

Edward Lee Thorndike was born in 1874 and died in 1949. As an undergraduate at Wesleyan University, he became interested in the work of William James, then at Harvard. Thorndike himself entered Harvard as a graduate student in 1895. During his stay he began his research on instrumental behavior, at first using chicks as subjects. Since there was no laboratory space at Harvard at that time, he set up his project in William James's cellar. After a short time, he was offered a fellowship at Columbia University. This time his laboratory was located in the attic of psychologist James Cattell. Thorndike received his Ph.D. from Columbia in 1898 for his work entitled "Animal Intelligence: An Experimental Analysis of Associative Processes in Animals." This included the famous puzzle-box experiments. Thorndike stayed on in New York at Columbia University Teachers College, where for many years he served as professor of educational psychology. Among other things, he attempted to apply to children the principles of trial-and-error learning he had uncovered with animals. He also became interested in psychological testing and became a leader in this newly formed field. Several years before his death, Thorndike returned to Harvard as the William James Lecturer—a fitting honor for this great psychologist, considering the origins of his interests in psychology.

E.L. Thorndike (1874–1949) *(UPI/Bettman Archive.)*

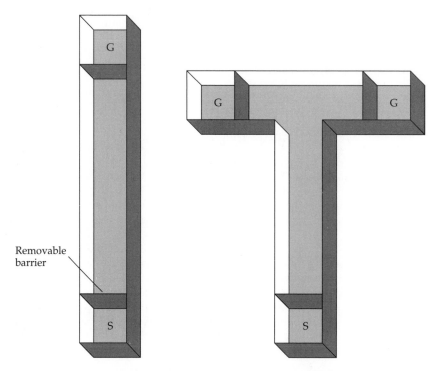

Removable
barrier

Figure 5.2   Top view of a runway and a T maze. S is the start box; G, the goal
box.

sponse vigor. We can measure, for example, how long the animal takes to traverse the alley and reach the goal box. This is called the **running time.** With repeated trials, animals typically require progressively less time to get to the goal box. Some experimenters prefer measuring the **running speed** at which the animals move down the alley. Running time can be easily converted to running speed by dividing the length of the runway by the running-time measure. Another common measure of behavior in runways is **latency.** The latency of the running response is the time it takes the animal to leave the start box and begin moving down the alley. Typically, latencies become shorter as training progresses.

Another frequently used maze is the **T maze,** shown to the right of Figure 5.2. The T maze consists of a start box and alleys arranged in the shape of a T. A goal box is located at the end of each arm of the T. Because it has two goal boxes, the T maze is well suited to studying instrumental *choice* behavior. For example, the experimenter may bait one goal box with plain food and the other goal box with food flavored with NutraSweet®. By repeatedly placing the rat in the T maze and seeing which arm it chooses, the experimenter can measure preference for one food over the other. The latency and speed of running down the stem of the T maze to the choice arms can also provide important information. If neither of the alternatives provided in the goal boxes is palatable, the rat may have a long latency and may run slowly.

Free-Operant Methods

In a runway or a T maze, a subject has limited opportunities to respond. After reaching the goal box, the subject is removed for awhile before being returned to the start box for another trial. By contrast, free-operant methods allow the subject to repeat the instrumental response "freely" over and over again. Free-operant methods were devised by B.F. Skinner (1938) to study behavior in a more continuous manner than is possible with mazes. Skinner (Figure 5.3) was interested in the laboratory analysis of a form of behavior that is representative of all naturally occurring ongoing activity. However, before behavior can be experimentally analyzed, a measurable unit of behavior must be defined. Casual observations of ongoing behavior indicate that behavior is continuous; that is, one activity leads to another. Behavior does not fall neatly into units as do molecules of a chemical solution. Skinner proposed the concept of the *operant* as a way of dividing behavior into meaningful and measurable units.

Figure 5.4 shows a typical **Skinner box** used to study free-operant behavior in rats. (A Skinner box used to study pecking in pigeons is presented in Figure 1.4). The Skinner box is a small experimental chamber that contains something like a lever that the rat can manipulate. The chamber also has a mechanism that can deliver a reward, such as food or water. In the simplest experiment, a hungry rat is placed in the chamber. The lever is electronically connected to the food-delivery system. When the rat depresses the lever, a pellet of food falls into the food cup.

Operant responses, such as the lever press, are defined in terms of the effect that they have on the environment. Activities that have the same effect on the environment are considered to be instances of the same operant. The critical thing is not the muscles involved in the behavior but the way in which the behavior "operates" on the environment. For example, the lever-press operant response in rats is typically defined as a depression of the lever sufficient to cause the closure of a microswitch. The subject may press the lever with its right paw, its left paw, or its tail. All

Figure 5.3 B.F. Skinner (1904–1990) *(Bettman Archive.)*

these different muscle responses constitute the same operant if they all depress the lever the required amount. Various ways of pressing the lever are assumed to be functionally equivalent because they all have the same effect on the environment—namely, closing the microswitch.

Most rats, when placed in a Skinner box, do not press the lever frequently. There are two preliminary steps for establishing the lever-press behavior. First the animals are taught when food is available in the food cup. This is done by repeatedly pairing the sound of the food-delivery device with the delivery of a food pellet into the cup. After enough such pairings, the sound of the delivery of food

Figure 5.4 A Skinner box equipped with a response lever and an automatic food-delivery device. Electrical equipment is used to program procedures and record responses automatically. *(Omikron/Photo Researchers, Inc.)*

comes to serve as a conditioned stimulus for the presence of food in the cup. This preliminary phase of conditioning is called **magazine training.**

Learning new responses. After magazine training, the subject is ready to learn the required instrumental response. If the response is not already in the subject's repertoire, the subject may never "discover" on its own what it has to do to obtain food. To facilitate acquisition of a new operant response, experimenters employ a strategy used by animal trainers for centuries. At first food is given if the subject merely approximates the final desired response. For example, at first a rat may be given a food pellet each time it gets up on its hind legs anywhere in the experimental chamber. Once the rearing response has been established, the food pellet may be given only if the rat rears over the response lever. Rearing in other parts of the chamber would no longer be reinforced. Once rearing over the lever has been established, the food

pellet may be given only after the rat actually depresses the lever. Such a sequence of training steps is called **shaping.** Shaping involves two complementary tactics: *reinforcement of successive approximations to the required response* and *nonreinforcement of earlier response forms.*

As is illustrated in the preceding example, the shaping of a new operant requires training response components or approximations to the final behavior. Once an operant response such as lever pressing has become established, the manner in which the subject accomplishes the required operation on the environment does not matter. Nevertheless, the steps used in shaping the behavior continue to influence how the subject performs the operant. For example, if rearing was one of the reinforced approximations during shaping, the subject is likely to continue to rear as it presses the lever (Stokes & Balsam, 1991). With extensive training, responding becomes more efficient and comes to involve less energy expenditure (Brener & Mitchell, 1989; Mitchell & Brener, 1991).

Shaping procedures can be used not only to train new operants but also to train new features or parameters of an operant response. For example, after a child has been taught how to hit a baseball with a bat properly, the teacher may want to shape increases in the force of the batting response to enable the child to hit the ball farther. Many aspects of sports involve such training of response parameters: learning to throw or kick a football farther, to jump off a higher diving board, to swim faster, to hold a bow and arrow more steadily, and so forth.

In a laboratory study, Deich, Allan, and Zeigler (1988) shaped the gape response of pigeons pecking for food reinforcement. Pigeons peck for food with their beaks opened a bit. Deich and his associates used a special transducer to measure how far pigeons kept their beaks open as they pecked a response key. In a baseline phase, the pigeons were reinforced for pecking irrespective of their gape. In another phase of the experiment, food was provided only if their beaks were opened wider than a criterial value. The criterion was chosen based on the previous day's performance so that at least 20% of the birds' pecks would be reinforced. As the birds met each new criterion, the criterion was

made more stringent, thereby shaping the birds to peck with increasingly wider gapes. In a comparable manner, decreases in the gape response were shaped in another phase of the experiment.

Figure 5.5 indicates the results of the gape-response study for one pigeon in terms of the percentage of pecks that occurred with various gape sizes. During the baseline phase, when reinforcement was independent of how wide the beaks were opened, subjects showed intermediate gape responses. After the shaping procedure in which the criterion for reinforcement required progressively wider gapes, the pigeons learned to peck with more open beaks. By contrast, after shaping in which the criterion for reinforcement involved progressively smaller gapes, the pigeons learned to peck with their beaks more tightly closed. These changes occurred fairly rapidly. The data in the middle panel of Figure 5.5 were obtained during the fifth training session, and the data in the bottom panel came from the seventh session of that condition. (Each session had 32 trials.)

The results presented in Figure 5.5 illustrate several important aspects of the process of shaping. Most responses are like the gape response in that they occur with some vari-

---

Defining Responses in Behavior Therapy

BOX **5.2**

The concept of the operant is useful in defining behaviors in the clinic as well as in the laboratory. A mother brings her son to the clinic complaining that the child is hyperactive or undisciplined. She describes her child with comments like "He wreaks havoc whenever he enters the room" or "He drives me crazy" or "He is completely uncontrollable." Similarly, a distraught husband and wife may seek help because they feel the love has disappeared from their marriage. Both the mother and the married couple describe their problem in general terms, although the difficulty comes from a series of specific responses. Treatment in many cases must start with a more precise definition of the activities that are problematic. What does the child actually do when he enters a room? What specific behaviors lead the husband and wife to conclude that love is lost? Sometimes defining the specific problem responses is enough to alleviate the difficulty. At other times the clinician has to help the clients find out what kinds of events or situations promote the problem responses. It may then be possible to change the environment in a way that encourages more desirable responses to replace the problematic activities.

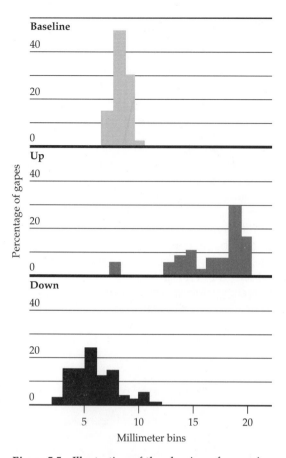

Figure 5.5 Illustration of the shaping of gape size in pigeons. Each panel shows the relative frequency of gapes of various sizes observed in the pecking behavior of a pigeon. During the baseline phase (top panel), pecking was reinforced with food irrespective of the size of the gape. In the other phases, pecking was reinforced only if it occurred with gapes that either exceeded a progressively increasing criterion (middle panel) or were less than a progressively decreasing criterion (bottom panel). *(From "Conjunctive Differentiation of Gape During Food-Reinforced Keypecking in the Pigeon" by J.D. Deich, R.W. Allan, and H.P. Zeigler, 1988,* Animal Learning & Behavior, 16, *pp. 268–276. Copyright © 1988 by the Psychonomic Society. Reprinted by permission.)*

ability. The gape response was most uniform during the baseline phase. However, even then, the pigeons pecked with a range of gapes—their beaks during different pecks

were 7–10 mm apart. This variability in responding helps to ensure that at least a few responses occur that are in the direction you may want to shape. Thus, shaping takes advantage of the inherent variability of behavior. Without such variability, shaping procedures could not succeed.

When a gape-size criterion was introduced, the distribution of gape sizes changed in the direction of the reinforcement criterion. Presenting food only if the gape exceeded a certain size, for example, served to shift the distribution of gape sizes to higher values. However, it was important to set each criterion so that at least some of the subject's existing responses could be reinforced. For example, the first shaping criterion could not have been set at 15 mm because during the baseline phase the pigeon had never made a peck with its beak more than 10 mm apart.

With the proper choice of response criteria during shaping, the distribution of the subject's responses was shifted to values the bird had never displayed prior to training. For example, after the pigeon was trained to peck with progressively larger gapes, it pecked with its beak opened 20 mm some of the time. By contrast, during the baseline phase, gapes had never exceeded 10 mm. In an analogous fashion, shaping of small gape sizes produced pecks with gapes as small as 4 mm, which never had been observed during the baseline phase. These aspects of the results illustrate that shaping can produce new response forms never before performed by the organism. (For additional discussions of shaping, see Galbicka, 1988; Midgley, Lea, & Kirby, 1989; Pear & Legris, 1987; Platt, 1973.)

Response rate as a measure of operant behavior. The major advantage of free-operant methods over discrete-trial techniques for studying instrumental behavior is that free-operant methods permit continuous observation of behavior over long periods. With continuous opportunity to respond, the subject rather than the experimenter determines the fre-

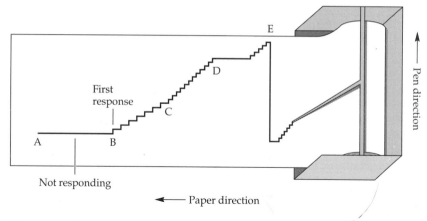

Figure 5.6 Cumulative recorder used for the continuous recording of behavior. The paper moves out of the machine toward the left at a fixed rate. Each response causes the pen to move up the paper one step. No responses occurred between points A and B. A moderate rate of responding occurred between points B and C and a rapid rate occurred between points C and D. At point E, the pen reset to the bottom of the page.

quency of occurrence of the instrumental response. Hence, free-operant techniques provide a special opportunity to observe changes in the likelihood of behavior over time. How should we take advantage of this and measure the probability of an operant response? Measures of response latency and speed that are commonly used in discrete-trial procedures provide detailed information about individual responses but do not characterize the likelihood of repetitions of a response. Skinner proposed that the rate of occurrence of operant behavior (frequency of the response in a particular interval) be used as a measure of response probability. If the rate of responding is high, probability of the response is said to be high. If the rate of responding is low, probability of the response is said to be low.

The cumulative recorder. Free-operant investigations are typically concerned with measuring the rate of behavior over time. Skinner devised a data-recording instrument—the **cumulative recorder**—that is ideally suited to recording and displaying such information. As shown in Figure 5.6, the cumulative recorder consists of a rotating drum that pulls paper out of the recorder at a constant speed. A pen rests on the surface of the paper. If no responses occur, the pen remains stationary and makes a horizontal line as the paper comes out of the machine. If the animal performs a lever-press response, the pen moves one step vertically on the paper. Since each lever-press response causes the pen to move one step up the paper, the total vertical distance traveled by the pen represents the cumulative (total) number of responses the subject has made. Because the paper comes out of the recorder at a constant speed, the horizontal distance on the cumulative record is a measure of how much time has elapsed in the session. The slope of the line made by the cumulative recorder represents the rate of responding.

The **cumulative record** provides a complete visual representation of when and how frequently the animal responds during a session. In the record of Figure 5.6, for example, the animal did not perform the response between points A and B and a slow rate of responding occurred between points B and C. Responses occurred more frequently between points C and D, but the subject paused at D. After responding resumed, the pen reached the top of the page (at point E) and reset to the bottom for additional responses.

The behavioral-baseline technique. When first put in a Skinner box, a subject engages in a wide variety of activities. Each activity has a particular rate of occurrence before conditioning. A naive rat, for example, exhibits a high rate of sniffing and a low rate of lever pressing. This initial rate of responding before the introduction of experimental manipulations is called the **free-operant baseline**, or the **operant level.** The free-operant baseline can be used to assess the change in behavior that occurs when a conditioning procedure is introduced. Reinforcement of lever pressing, for example, will increase the rate of this response from its low operant level to a much higher rate.

The free-operant baseline, or operant level, is useful in revealing the effects of procedures that *increase* the rate of responding, such as reinforcement. However, if the operant level of a response is low to begin with, it cannot be used to detect the effects of experimental manipulations that might further *decrease* the rate of the behavior. In such cases, it is desirable to regularly reinforce the operant response so that it will occur at a stable rate higher than the operant level. This level of responding maintained by reinforcement is also called a baseline. The baseline rate of a reinforced operant response can be used to evaluate the effects of procedures, stimuli, or other manipulations that may either increase or decrease the rate of operant behavior. The effects of the experimental manipulations are revealed by changes in the baseline rate of the operant response.

In Chapter 3 we described the use of a **behavioral baseline** to evaluate the effects of aversive classical conditioning procedures. The technique, known as conditioned suppression or the conditioned emotional response procedure, first involves getting rats to lever-press for food reinforcement at a steady rate. A light or tone CS is then paired with shock. The effects of this classical conditioning are then evaluated by presenting the conditioned stimulus while the subject is pressing the response lever. The common outcome is that the animal stops lever pressing during the shock-conditioned stimulus. Thus, fear conditioning is evident in suppression of baseline food-reinforced lever pressing.

The behavioral-baseline technique has been used extensively to study learning and behavior. It is also a powerful method for studying the effects of physiological manipulations and drug effects on behavior. Egli and Thompson (1989), for example, used the technique to investigate the behavioral effects of methadone, a synthetic opioid used in the detoxification and treatment of heroin addicts. Pigeons were first trained to peck a response key for intermittent food reinforcement. After the key-pecking behavior had stabilized, the birds were given test sessions with and without various doses of methadone.

Figure 5.7 indicates the results of the drug-effect study for one bird. The cumulative record of key pecking during a test session without methadone is shown on the left; the results with 3.0 mg/kg of methadone are shown on the right. Each session lasted 45 minutes. In the absence of the drug, the bird pecked at a high and steady rate. Each time it completed 400 pecks, the pen reset to the bottom of the page. Resets occurred 9 times during the no-drug session, indicating that the pigeon pecked more than 3,600 times. By contrast, far fewer pecks occurred during the methadone session. This time the pen reset 3 times and the pigeon pecked only a little more than 1,200 times.

The cumulative records also show how the methadone disrupted behavior. In the absence of the drug (left), the pigeon's high rate of pecking was fairly steady throughout the

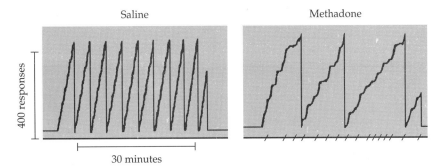

Figure 5.7 Cumulative record of key pecking in a pigeon during a no-drug session (left) and during a test with 3.0 mg/kg methadone (right). Notice that methadone results in less responding overall because of the intrusion of periods of no responding and periods of low rates of responding. *(From "Effects of Methadone on Alternative Fixed-Ratio Fixed-Interval Performance: Latent Influences on Schedule-Controlled Responding" by M. Egli and T. Thompson, 1989,* Journal of the Experimental Analysis of Behavior, 52, *pp. 141–153. Copyright © 1989 by Journal of the Experimental Analysis of Behavior. Reprinted by permission.)*

session. Ignoring the vertical reset lines, the cumulative record for the no-drug session consists of a series of nearly straight lines, each with a similar steep slope. By contrast, the cumulative record for the methadone session (right) is rather irregular. There are short horizontal line segments (indicating no responses) scattered among short line segments with steep slopes (indicating high response rates) and segments with more shallow slopes (indicating lower response rates). These differences in slope indicate that the subjects were not responding steadily throughout the methadone session. Rather, they displayed more of a run–stop pattern in which high (and moderate) response rates were separated by the total absence of pecking. Thus, the overall suppression of pecking during methadone was achieved by breaking up the high steady rate evident in the no-drug session with pauses and lower rates of responding.

The behavioral-baseline technique popularized by Skinner and his students provides a novel method for the analysis of behavior because it permits evaluation of the effects of an experimental manipulation on the behavior of individual subjects (see Sidman, 1960).

Until the behavioral-baseline technique was developed, studies of learning typically involved investigating groups of subjects exposed to each experimental condition. The effects of these conditions were then evaluated by comparing statistical summaries of the performance of each group. For example, the results might be expressed in terms of the average performance of the various groups.

Skinner objected to this group-statistical approach and advocated exposing individual subjects to the same reinforcement procedure until the behavior was stable and predictable. He then observed how a manipulation influenced this stable baseline. As long as the baseline was indeed stable, the results of the experimental manipulations could be easily detected. Given that the effects of manipulations can be observed in individual subjects with the behavioral-baseline technique, Skinner argued that the science of behavior should be based on the analysis of individual subjects rather than on statistical averages of the behavior of groups of individuals. It is now recognized that both the group-statistical and individual-subject approaches have their place in the experimental analysis of behavior.

Some questions are more easily answered using a single-subject baseline technique. For other types of questions, groups of subjects are needed. Throughout the remainder of the text we will discuss both types of research.

Instrumental Conditioning Procedures

In all instrumental conditioning situations, the subjects' behavior results in some type of environmental consequence. Instrumental conditioning procedures can be categorized according to the nature of the environmental event controlled by the behavior. The event may be pleasant or unpleasant. A pleasant event is technically called an **appetitive stimulus.** An unpleasant event is technically called an **aversive stimulus.** Another important factor in the classification of instrumental conditioning procedures is the relationship, or contingency, between the response and the environmental event that it controls. The instrumental response may produce the event (in which case a *positive contingency* is said to be in effect) or eliminate it (in which case a *negative contingency* is said to be in effect). Table 5.1 describes four common instrumental conditioning procedures. The procedures differ in what type of stimulus (appetitive or aversive reinforcer) is controlled by the instrumental response and whether the response produces or eliminates the stimulus.

Positive Reinforcement

The term **positive reinforcement** refers to a class of situations in which there is a positive contingency between the instrumental response and an appetitive reinforcing stimulus. In other words, if the subject performs the instrumental response, it receives the reinforcing stimulus; if the subject does not perform the response, the reinforcing stimulus is not presented. Giving a hungry rat a food pellet whenever it presses a response lever but not when it does not press the lever is a laboratory

TABLE 5.1 *Types of instrumental conditioning procedures*

Name of Procedure	Effect of the Instrumental Response
Positive reinforcement	Response produces an appetitive stimulus that is not as likely to occur otherwise.
Punishment	Response produces an aversive stimulus that is not as likely to occur otherwise.
Negative reinforcement (escape or avoidance)	Response eliminates or prevents the occurrence of an aversive stimulus that is more likely otherwise.
Omission training	Response eliminates or prevents the occurrence of an appetitive stimulus that is more likely otherwise.

example of positive reinforcement. There are many examples of positive reinforcement outside the laboratory. A father may give his daughter a cookie only when she puts away her toys; a teacher may praise a student only when the student hands in a good report; or an employee may receive a bonus check only when he performs well on the job. The intention of the father, the teacher, and the employer is to make sure that the instrumental response continues to occur and to encourage increases in responding.

Sometimes continuous rewarding events are used in positive reinforcement procedures. In these cases, the rewarding event continues (or may even increase) as long as the instrumental response is being performed. If the instrumental response stops, the rewarding stimulus also stops or is decreased. In an interesting application of this type of positive reinforcement, infants were conditioned to kick in order to operate a mobile suspended over the crib (Rovee & Rovee, 1969). The harder they kicked, the more movement they could produce in the mobile. The infants showed a rapid and sustained increase in kicking under these circumstances.

Laboratory procedures in which a continuous reinforcing stimulus is used resemble situations outside the laboratory in which there is a direct mechanical connection between behavior and the environment. For example, as long as you pedal a bicycle, it continues to move; as long as you stoke a fire on a cold winter day, it continues to provide enjoyable warmth; as long as a child pumps her feet on a swing, she continues to enjoy the back-and-forth motion of the swing. Although these examples involve continuous reinforcers, they nevertheless represent positive reinforcement because there is a positive contingency in each case between the instrumental response and the reinforcer. When the instrumental responses are terminated, the reinforcing stimuli are also terminated.

Punishment

The term **punishment** refers to a class of situations in which there is a positive contingency between the instrumental response and an unpleasant, or aversive, stimulus. If the subject performs the instrumental response, it receives the aversive stimulus; if it does not perform the instrumental response, the aversive stimulus is not presented. A mother may reprimand her child for running into the street but not for playing quietly in the yard; your boss may criticize you for being late to a meeting; your teacher may give you a failing grade for answering too many test questions incorrectly. Such procedures decrease the future likelihood of the instrumental response.

Laboratory experiments on punishment usually also involve some type of positive reinforcement to get the instrumental behavior to occur occasionally. The subject may be initially trained to make some response for positive reinforcement, such as pressing a lever or running down a runway for food. Once the lever response has been established,

an aversive stimulus, such as shock, may be presented after each lever press. In the runway, the subject may receive a brief shock in the goal box. The result is a decrease in lever pressing or running.

Negative Reinforcement

The first two situations we described involved a positive contingency between the instrumental response and the reinforcer. If the response occurred, the reinforcer was delivered; if the response did not occur, the reinforcer was not delivered. In positive reinforcement, the reinforcer was a rewarding, or pleasant, stimulus; in punishment, the reinforcer was an unpleasant, or aversive, stimulus. We now turn to procedures that involve a negative contingency between the instrumental response and reinforcer. In a negative contingency the response turns off or prevents the presentation of the reinforcer. If the response occurs, the reinforcer is withheld; if the response does not occur, the reinforcer is delivered. Such a procedure increases the likelihood of behavior if the reinforcer is an aversive stimulus. Situations in which the occurrence of an instrumental response terminates or prevents the delivery of an aversive stimulus involve **negative reinforcement.**

There are two types of negative reinforcement procedures. In one case the aversive stimulus is continuously present but can be terminated by the instrumental response. This type of procedure is called **escape.** Prisoners may escape the unpleasantness of a jail by breaking out. You may escape the unpleasant static of a radio by turning it off. People may leave a movie theater to escape the experience of a bad movie. In the laboratory, a rat may be exposed to a continuous loud noise at the beginning of a trial. By jumping over a barrier or pressing a lever, the rat can escape the noise. In all these cases, the presence of the aversive stimulus sets the occasion for the instrumental response. The instrumental response is reinforced by termination of the aversive stimulus only if the response occurs during the aversive stimulus. If the rat presses the lever when the noise is off, the lever press cannot be reinforced by termination of the noise.

The second type of negative reinforcement procedure involves an aversive stimulus that is scheduled to be presented sometime in the future. In this case the instrumental response prevents delivery of the aversive stimulus. This type of procedure is called **avoidance.** There are many things we do to prevent the occurrence of something bad. Students often study before an examination to avoid receiving a bad grade; responding to a fire alarm may permit a person to avoid injury; people get their cars tuned up regularly to avoid unexpected breakdowns. In the laboratory, a rat may be scheduled to receive shock at the end of a warning stimulus. However, if it makes the instrumental response during the warning stimulus, the shock will not be delivered. We will have much more to say about avoidance behavior in Chapter 9.

Omission Training

Another type of situation that involves a negative contingency between the instrumental response and the reinforcer is called **omission training.** In this case, the instrumental response prevents the delivery of a pleasant event, or appetitive reinforcer. If the subject makes the instrumental response, the appetitive reinforcer is not delivered; if the subject does not respond, the appetitive reinforcer is presented. Thus, the reinforcer is delivered only if the subject withholds the instrumental response. As you might suspect, this type of procedure leads to a decrease in the likelihood of the instrumental behavior.

Omission training is often a preferred method of discouraging human behavior because it does not involve delivering an aversive stimulus (as punishment does). Omission training is being used when a child is told to go to his room after doing something bad. The

parents are not introducing an aversive stimulus when they tell the child to go to his room. There is nothing aversive about the child's room. Rather, by sending the child to the room, the parents are withdrawing sources of appetitive reinforcement, such as playing with friends or watching television. Suspending someone's driver's license for drunken driving also constitutes omission training (withdrawal of the reinforcement or privilege of driving).

Omission-training procedures are also sometimes called **differential reinforcement of other behavior,** or **DRO.** This term highlights the fact that in omission training the subject periodically receives the reinforcer provided it is engaged in behavior *other* than the response specified by the procedure. Making the target response results in omission of the reward that would have been delivered had the subject performed some "other" behavior. Thus, omission training involves the reinforcement of "other" behavior.

A Final Note on Terminology

The terms used to describe instrumental conditioning procedures may result in considerable confusion. Several comments may help clarify matters. First, in the terms *positive* and *negative reinforcement, positive* and *negative* do not refer to pleasant and unpleasant outcomes. Rather, they refer to positive and negative contingencies between the instrumental response and its environmental consequence. Positive reinforcement involves a positive contingency between behavior and an environmental event (*presentation* of a rewarding stimulus); negative reinforcement involves a negative contingency between behavior and an environmental event (*removal* of an aversive stimulus). The term *reinforcement* is used in both cases because both positive and negative reinforcement produce increases in the rate of the instrumental response.

There also may be confusion regarding negative reinforcement and punishment. An aversive stimulus is used in both procedures. However, the relation of the instrumental response to the aversive stimulus is drastically different in the two cases. In what is commonly called punishment, there is a positive contingency between the instrumental response and the aversive stimulus. (The response results in delivery of the aversive stimulus.) By contrast, in negative reinforcement, there is a negative response–reinforcer contingency. (The response either terminates or prevents the delivery of the aversive stimulus.) This difference in the contingencies produces very different outcomes. The instrumental response is decreased by the punishment procedure and increased by negative reinforcement.

Fundamental Elements of Instrumental Conditioning

As we will see in the coming chapters, analysis of instrumental conditioning involves

numerous factors and variables. However, the essence of instrumental behavior is that it is controlled by its consequences. Thus, instrumental conditioning fundamentally involves three elements: a response, an outcome (the reinforcer), and a relation, or contingency, between the response and the reinforcer. In the remainder of this chapter, we will discuss the effects of each of these fundamental elements on instrumental conditioning.

The Instrumental Response

The outcome of instrumental conditioning procedures depends in part on the nature of the response being conditioned. Some responses are more easily modified by certain instrumental conditioning procedures than other responses are. In Chapter 9 we will describe how the nature of the response influences the outcome of negative reinforcement (avoidance) and punishment procedures. In the present section we will describe how the nature of the response determines

---

BOX **5.3**

Omission Training as a Therapeutic Procedure

Omission-training procedures involve the delivery of reinforcement when the subject fails to perform a target response. Therefore, such procedures can be used to encourage subjects to withhold undesired responses. In one study (Barton, Brulle, & Repp, 1986), omission-training procedures were tested with mentally retarded students of elementary school age. The reinforcer selected for each student was based on recommendations from teachers, aides, and parents or caretakers; reinforcers included apples, raisins, grapes, and juice. One student engaged in recurrent handflapping (moving the hand up and down or back and forth). The rate of this behavior was first observed under baseline conditions (in the absence of special intervention) for 12 days. Then, an omission-training procedure was introduced for the next 29 days. Omission training consisted of providing a reinforcer whenever a 1-minute period elapsed without any handflapping. The omission-training phase was then followed by return to the baseline condition, followed by reintroduction of omission training.

The results of the study are summarized in Figure 5.8. During the first baseline phase, the student engaged in handflapping about once a minute. This rate of responding declined to near zero during the first omission-training phase. Return to the baseline condition resulted in recovery of the handflapping response. Reintroduction of omission training at the end of the study produced another decline in responding. Interestingly, responding dropped to close to zero faster the second time the omission contingency was introduced. These results indicate that omission training is an effective procedure for suppressing responding and illustrate that the suppression of responding is easily reversed by removing the omission procedure.

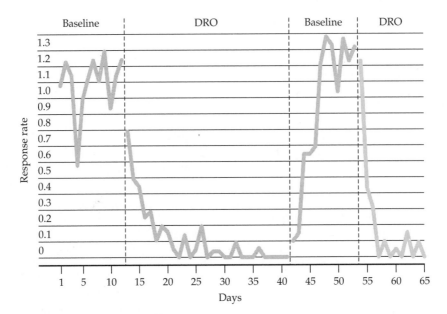

Figure 5.8 Rate of handflapping (responses per minute) by a mentally retarded student during baseline conditions, when reinforcement is not provided, and during omission-training phases, when reinforcement is provided for 1-minute periods without handflapping. *(From "Maintenance of Therapeutic Change By Momentary DRO" by L.E. Barton, A.R. Brulle, and A.C. Repp, 1986,* Journal of Applied Behavior Analysis, 19, *pp. 277–282. Copyright © 1986 by the Journal of Applied Behavior Analysis. Reprinted by permission.)*

the results of positive reinforcement procedures.

We have already described two contemporary techniques for the study of instrumental conditioning that involve different types of responses. In discrete-trial runway studies, subjects have to go from the start to the goal box in a runway to obtain the reinforcer. Subjects in these experiments do not have to learn the response involved in the task—locomotion. The animals used in these experiments are typically old enough that they are already able to walk and run. Runway studies involve teaching the animal where to run and what to run for.

In contrast to the runway situation, free-operant lever-press training does not involve a response already in the subjects' repertoire. Most of the rats that serve in lever-press experiments have never had the opportunity to press a lever before. Therefore, as we noted

earlier, under "Free-Operant Methods," the lever-press behavior has to be shaped by the reinforcement of successive approximations. Exactly how is this shaping done and what does it accomplish? Although rats may come into a lever-press experiment never having pressed a lever before, they are not entirely inexperienced in the various behavioral components of pressing a lever. Lever pressing requires that the rat get up on its hind legs, that it reach out a paw, and that it press down. All these responses are likely to be in the rat's repertoire already. What, then, does a rat learn that is new? It learns to make various components of the lever-press behavior in a coordinated fashion so that the lever gets depressed and it earns the reward. Unless rearing, reaching out a paw, and pressing down occur in the correct sequence and in the correct place in the experimental chamber, these actions do not constitute pressing the lever.

Thus, instrumental conditioning of lever pressing involves the rearrangement of components of the rat's behavior. Reinforcement can lead to the *creation of a new response unit made up of the set and sequence of response components that result in reinforcement* (for example, Schwartz, 1981, 1982, 1986; Midgley et al., 1989).

The response components that become incorporated into a new behavioral unit—a new operant—are usually observable actions, such as the leg, body, and hand movements involved in bowling. Interestingly, however, operant behavioral units also can become organized in terms of more abstract dimensions. For example, subjects can learn to obtain reinforcement in a situation where they are required to do something new for each reinforcer. Thus, response variability can serve as an operant.

In one study of variability as an operant (Page & Neuringer, 1985), pigeons had to peck two response keys eight times to obtain food reinforcement. The eight pecks could be distributed between the two keys in any manner. All the pecks could be on the left or the right key, or the pigeons could alternate between the keys in various ways (two pecks on the left, followed by one on the right, one on the left, three on the right, and one on the left, for example). However, to obtain food reinforcement on a given trial, the sequence of left-right pecks had to be different from the pattern of left-right pecks the bird made on the preceding 50 trials. Thus, to obtain reinforcement, the pigeons had to generate novel patterns of left-right pecks and not repeat any pattern for 50 trials. In a control condition, food reinforcement was provided at the same frequency for eight pecks distributed between the two keys, but now the sequence of right and left pecks did not matter. The pigeons did not have to generate novel response sequences in the control condition.

Sample results of the experiment are presented in Figure 5.9 in terms of the percentage of response sequences performed during each

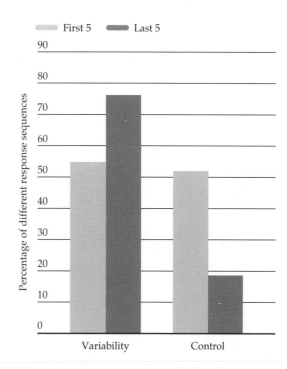

Figure 5.9 Percentage of novel left-right response sequences pigeons performed when variability in response sequences was required for food reinforcement (left) and when food reinforcement was provided regardless of response sequence (right). Data are presented separately for the first five and last five sessions of each procedure. *(From "Variability Is An Operant" by S. Page and A. Neuringer, 1985,* Journal of Experimental Psychology: Animal Behavior Process, 11, *pp. 429–452. Copyright © 1985 by the American Psychological Association. Reprinted by permission.)*

session that were different from each other. Results for the first and last 5 days on each procedure are presented separately. About 50% of the response sequences performed were different from each other during the first five sessions of each procedure. When the instrumental conditioning procedure required response variability, variability in responding increased to about 75%. By contrast, when subjects were reinforced regardless of the sequence of left-right pecks they made, variability in performed sequences dropped to less than 20%.

This study illustrates two interesting facts about instrumental conditioning. First, it shows that variability in responding can be maintained and increased by reinforcement. Thus, response variability can be established as an operant (see also Machado, 1989; Morgan & Neuringer, 1990; Morris, 1987; Neuringer, 1991). The results also show that in the absence of explicit reinforcement of response variability, responding becomes more stereotyped with continued instrumental conditioning. Subjects in the control condition decreased the range of different response sequences they performed as training progressed. Thus, the typical consequence of instrumental reinforcement is a decrease in response variability. (For other studies of the development of response stereotypy in instrumental conditioning, see Pisacreta, 1982; Schwartz, 1980, 1985, 1988.)

Response constraints on instrumental conditioning. As we saw in the preceding discussion, instrumental conditioning can act on already existing behavioral units (as in running down a runway). It can also result in the creation of new response units. How far do these processes extend? Can instrumental conditioning come to control the frequency of all already existing behaviors? Are there any limits on the types of new behavioral units that can be created with instrumental conditioning? A growing body of evidence indicates that there are important limitations or constraints both on the instrumental conditioning of existing behavioral units and on the creation of new behavioral units.

In Chapter 4 we saw that classical conditioning occurs at different rates depending on the combination of CS and US that is used. Rats readily learn to associate tastes with sickness, for example, whereas associations between tastes and shock are not so easily learned. Such examples suggest that a CS has to "belong" with a US, or be "relevant" to the US, for conditioning to occur rapidly. Analogous belongingness, or relevance, relations occur in instrumental conditioning.

Thorndike was the first to observe differences in the conditionability of various responses with reinforcement. In many of the puzzle-box experiments, the cat had to manipulate a latch or string to escape from the box. However, Thorndike also tried to condition such responses as yawning and scratching. The cats could learn to make these responses; however, interestingly, the form of the responses changed as training proceeded. At first, the cat would scratch itself vigorously to be let out of the box. On later trials, it would only make "aborted" scratching movements. It might put its leg to its body but would not make a true scratch response. Similar results were obtained in attempts to condition yawning. As training progressed, the animal might open its mouth to be let out of the box, but it would not give a bona fide yawn.

Thorndike proposed the concept of **belongingness** to explain the failures to train such responses as scratching and yawning. According to this concept, certain responses naturally belong with certain reinforcers because of the subject's evolutionary history. Operating a latch and pulling a string are manipulatory responses that naturally belong with release from confinement. By contrast, scratching and yawning characteristically do not help animals escape from confinement and therefore do not belong with release from the puzzle box. Presumably this is why scratching and yawning do not persist as vigorous bona fide responses when reinforced by release from the box.

The concept of belongingness in instrumental conditioning is nicely illustrated by the results of a study involving the three-spined stickleback fish (*Gasterosteus aculeatus*). During the mating season each spring, male sticklebacks establish territories from which they chase away and fight other males and court females. Sevenster (1973) used the presentation of another male or a female as a reinforcer in instrumental conditioning of a male stickleback. One group of subjects was required to bite a rod to obtain access to the reinforcer.

Biting is a component of the aggressive behavior that occurs when a resident male encounters an intruder male. When the reinforcer was another male, biting behavior increased; access to another male was an effective reinforcer for the biting response. By contrast, biting did not increase when it was reinforced with courtship opportunity. However, courtship opportunity was an effective reinforcer for other responses, such as swimming through a ring. Evidently, a belongingness relation exists between biting and the consequent presentation of another male. By contrast, biting does not "belong with" presentation of a female, which typically elicits courtship rather than aggression.

Various limitations on instrumental conditioning were also observed by Breland and Breland (1961) in attempts to condition instrumental responses with food reinforcement in several species. Their goal was to train animals to perform amusing response chains for displays to be used in amusement parks and zoos. During the course of this work, they observed dramatic behavior changes that were not consistent with the reinforcement procedures they were using. For example, they describe a raccoon that was reinforced for picking up a coin and depositing it in a coin bank.

> We started out by reinforcing him for picking up a single coin. Then the metal container was introduced, with the requirement that he drop the coin into the container. Here we ran into the first bit of difficulty: he seemed to have a great deal of trouble letting go of the coin. He would rub it up against the inside of the container, pull it back out, and clutch it firmly for several seconds. However, he would finally turn it loose and receive his food reinforcement. Then the final contingency: we [required] that he pick up [two] coins and put them in the container.
>
> Now the raccoon really had problems (and so did we). Not only could he not let go of the coins, but he spent seconds, even minutes, rubbing them together (in a most miserly fashion), and dipping them into the container. He carried on this behavior to such an extent that the practical application we had in mind—a display featuring a raccoon putting money in a piggy bank—simply was not feasible. The rubbing behavior became worse and worse as time went on, in spite of nonreinforcement. (p. 682)*

The Brelands had similar difficulties with other species. Pigs, for example, also could not learn to put coins in a piggy bank. After initial training, they began rooting the coins along the ground. The Brelands called the development of such responses as rooting in the pigs and rubbing coins together in the raccoons **instinctive drift.** As the term implies, the extra responses that developed in these food-reinforcement situations were activities the animals instinctively perform when obtaining food. Pigs root along the ground in connection with feeding, and raccoons rub and dunk food-related objects. These innate food-related responses are apparently very strong and can take over to the extent that they compete with the responses required by the experimenter. The Brelands emphasized that such instinctive response tendencies have to be taken into account in the analysis of behavior.

The behavior systems approach to constraints on instrumental conditioning. The concepts of "belongingness" and "instinctive drift" suggest that different reinforcers belong to different behavior systems, each with its own response organization. If the instrumental response selected by the experimenter does not "belong" in the behavior system of the reinforcer, it will be difficult to increase that target response with instrumental conditioning. Moreover, in such cases other responses that are already a part of the behavior system will emerge, producing "instinctive drift." Thus, Thorndike and the Brelands recognized that instrumental conditioning procedures are superimposed on a preexisting behavioral organization. The outcome of the conditioning procedures depends on how well these

* From "The Misbehavior of Organisms," by K. Breland and M. Breland, 1961. In *American Psychologist, 16,* 682.

procedures fit with existing behavioral structures.

The relevance of behavior systems for the analysis of learning has been developed in greater detail by Timberlake (1983a; see also Timberlake & Lucas, 1989). We previously encountered the behavior systems approach in analyses of the form of classically conditioned responses (see Chapter 4). The approach also provides important insights into response limitations on instrumental conditioning.

Common reinforcers, such as food and water, are assumed to be part of behavior systems involved in feeding and drinking. These behavior systems become organized during the course of evolution and development and consist of a series of modules or components, each with its own controlling stimuli and responses. When an animal is food-deprived and is in a situation where it might encounter food, its feeding system becomes activated, and it begins to engage in foraging and other food-related responses. An instrumental conditioning procedure is superimposed on this behavior system. The effectiveness of the procedure in increasing the target response will depend on the compatibility of the target response with the preexisting organization of the feeding system. Furthermore, the nature of other responses that emerge during the course of training will depend on the behavioral components of the feeding system that become activated by the instrumental conditioning procedure.

According to the behavior systems approach, we should be able to predict which responses will increase with food reinforcement and which responses will not increase by studying what animals do when their feeding system is activated in the absence of instrumental conditioning. In a study of hamsters, Shettleworth (1975) found that food deprivation decreases the probability of self-care responses, such as face washing and scratching, but increases the probability of environment-directed activities, such as digging, scratching at a wall (scrabbling), and rearing on the hind legs. These results suggest that self-care responses (face washing and scratching) are not part of the feeding system activated by hunger, whereas environment-directed activities (digging, scrabbling, and rearing) do belong to the feeding system. Based on this analysis, we should find that face washing and scratching are not increased by instrumental food reinforcement. However, food reinforcement should result in increases in digging, scrabbling, and rearing. This pattern of results is precisely what has been observed in studies of instrumental conditioning (Shettleworth, 1975). Thus, the susceptibility of various responses to food reinforcement can be predicted from how those responses are altered by food deprivation, which presumably reflects their compatibility with the feeding system.

As we saw in Chapter 4, another way to diagnose whether a response is a part of a behavior system is to perform a classical conditioning experiment. Through classical conditioning, a CS comes to elicit component responses of the behavior system activated by the US. If "instinctive drift" reflects responses of the behavior system, responses akin to instinctive drift should be evident in a classical conditioning experiment. Timberlake and his associates (see Timberlake, 1983b; Timberlake, Wahl, & King, 1982) tested this prediction with rats in a modification of the coin-handling studies conducted by Breland and Breland. Instead of a coin, the apparatus delivered a ball bearing into the experimental chamber at the start of each trial. The floor of the chamber was angled so that the ball bearing rolled from one end to the other and into a hole if the rat did not get in its way. In one condition, the rats were required to make contact with the ball bearing to obtain food reinforcement. Other conditions employed a classical conditioning procedure: food was provided after the ball bearing rolled across the chamber whether or not the rat touched the ball bearing. Consistent with the behavior systems view, rats in both types of conditioning procedures came to touch and extensively handle the ball bearings instead of letting them roll into the hole. (Some animals picked up the bearing, put it in their mouth, carried it to the other end of the chamber, and sat and chewed it.) Such "instinctive drift" developed with both instrumental and classical conditioning procedures. These results indicate that touching and handling the ball bearing are manifestations of the feeding behavior system in rats. Thus, instinctive drift represents the intrusion of responses appropriate to the behavior system activated during the course of instrumental conditioning.

According to the behavior systems approach, differences in the preexisting responses of the behavior system activated by a conditioning procedure will lead to differences in the type of responses that are easily conditioned by that procedure. The preexisting responses of a behavior system may vary across species and reinforcers. The behavior systems approach predicts that such differences should lead to corresponding differences in the ease of conditioning certain responses. This prediction has been confirmed in comparisons of the conditioning of carnivorous versus herbivorous species of rodents and in a comparison of conditioning with food versus water in rats (Timberlake, 1983b; Timberlake & Washburne, 1989).

The Instrumental Reinforcer

The second fundamental element of instrumental conditioning we will consider is the reinforcer. Several aspects of a reinforcer determine its effects on the learning and performance of instrumental behavior. We will first consider the direct effects of the quantity and quality of a reinforcer on instrumental behavior. We will then discuss how response to a particular reward amount and type depends on the subject's past experience with other reinforcers.

Quantity and quality of the reinforcer. Many studies have evaluated the influence of the quantity and quality of the reinforcer in both reinforcement and punishment situations. In punishment situations, the effects are as might be expected; that is, longer and more intense aversive stimuli are more effective in suppressing behavior. Positively reinforced runway behavior is also directly related to the magnitude of the reinforcer. Rats, for example, run faster for larger rewards. In free-operant situations, however, the effects of reinforcer magnitude are more complex and depend on the schedule of reinforcement in effect (for example, Reed, 1991; Reed & Wright, 1989). (We will consider schedules of reinforcement in Chapter 6.)

Although the quantity and quality of the reinforcer are logically different characteristics, it is often difficult to separate them experimentally. A change in the quantity of the reinforcer may also make the reinforcer qualitatively different. An increase in shock intensity, for example, may result in a qualitatively different type of discomfort. In an interesting experiment involving positive reinforcement, Hutt (1954) tried to isolate the effects of quantity and quality on instrumental behavior. Nine groups of rats were trained to press a bar for a liquid reinforcer. The reinforcer was varied in both quantity and quality for the various groups. Three of the groups received a small amount of fluid, three a medium amount, and three a large amount. The fluid was a mixture of water, milk, and flour. One of the three groups given a particular amount of fluid received this basic mixture. For another group, the quality of the mixture was improved by adding saccharin. For the third group, the quality of the fluid was reduced by adding a small amount of citric acid. Figure 5.10 shows the average rate of bar pressing for each group. Increases in either the quality or the quantity of the reinforcer produced higher rates of responding.

Shifts in the quality or quantity of the reinforcer. In the study by Hutt (1954), a given subject received only one particular quantity and quality of food throughout the experiment. What would happen if subjects were

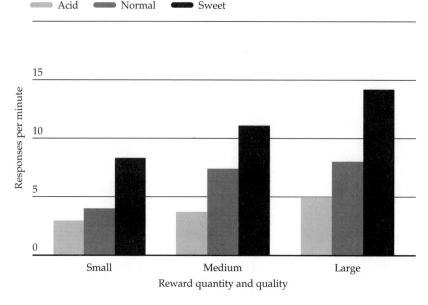

Figure 5.10 Average rates of responding in groups of subjects for which responding was reinforced with reinforcers varying in quantity and quality. *(From "Rate of Bar Pressing as a Function of Quality and Quantity of Food Reward" by P.J. Hutt, 1954,* Journal of Comparative and Physiological Psychology, 47, *pp. 235–239.)*

shifted from one type of reward to another? This is a particularly interesting question because it raises the possibility that the effectiveness of a particular reinforcer depends not only on its physical properties but also on how the reward compares with others the subject has had. We saw in Chapter 4 that the effectiveness of an unconditioned stimulus in classical conditioning depends on how the US compares with the subject's expectations based on prior experience. If the US is larger (or more intense) than expected, it will support excitatory conditioning. By contrast, if it is smaller (or weaker) than expected, the US will support inhibitory conditioning. Are there analogous effects of reward quantity and quality in instrumental conditioning? Evidently, yes. Numerous studies have shown that the effects of a particular amount and type of reward on instrumental behavior depend on the quantity and quality of the reinforcer the subject had experienced previ-

ously. (For reviews, see Flaherty, 1982, 1991.) Speaking loosely, the research has shown that a good reward is treated as especially good after reinforcement with a poor reward, and a poor reward is treated as especially poor after reinforcement with a good reward.

Effects of a shift in the quantity of reward were first described by Crespi (1942). The basic results are also nicely illustrated by a more recent study by Mellgren (1972). Four groups of rats served in a runway experiment. During phase 1, two of the groups received a small reward (2 food pellets) each time they reached the end of the runway. The other two groups received a large reward (22 pellets) for each trip down the runway. (Delivery of the reward was always delayed for 20 seconds after the subjects had reached the end of the runway so that they would not run at their maximum speed.) After 11 trials of training in phase 1, one group of rats receiving each reward quantity was shifted to the alternate quantity. Thus, some rats were shifted from small to large reward (S-L), and others were shifted from large to small reward (L-S). The remaining two groups continued to receive the same amount of reward in phase 2 as they had received in phase 1. (These groups were designated as L-L and S-S.)

Figure 5.11 summarizes the results of the experiment. At the end of phase 1, subjects receiving the large reward ran slightly, but not significantly, faster than subjects receiving the small reward. For groups that continued to receive the same amount of reward in phase 2 as in phase 1 (groups L-L and S-S), instrumental performance did not change much when phase 2 was introduced. By contrast, significant deviations from these baselines of running were observed in groups of subjects that received shifts in reward magnitude with the start of phase 2. Subjects shifted from large to small reward (group L-S) rapidly decreased their running speeds and subjects shifted from small to large reward (group S-L) soon increased their running speeds. The most significant finding was that, following a shift in reward magnitude, the subjects' behavior was not solely a function of the new reward magnitude. Rather, response to the new reward was enhanced by the subjects' previous history with a contrasting reward magnitude. Subjects shifted from a small to a large reward (group S-L) ran faster for the large reward than subjects that had always received the large reward (group L-L). Correspondingly, subjects shifted from a large to a small reward (group L-S) ran more slowly for the small reward than subjects that had always received the small reward (group S-S).

The results Mellgren obtained illustrate the phenomena of successive positive and negative behavioral contrast. **Positive behavioral contrast** refers to an outcome in which subjects respond more for a favorable reward if they previously received a less favorable reward than if they did not have this prior experience. More informally, the favorable reward looks especially good to the subjects in

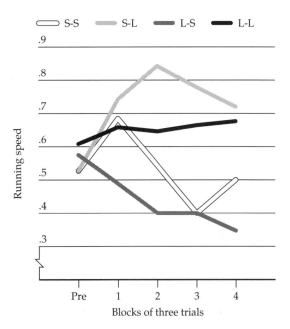

Figure 5.11   Running speeds of four groups of rats in blocks of three trials. Block "Pre" represents running speeds at the end of phase 1. Blocks 1–4 represent running speeds in phase 2. At the start of phase 2, groups S-L and L-S experienced a shift in amount of reward from small to large and large to small, respectively. Groups S-S and L-L received small and large rewards, respectively, throughout the experiment. *(From "Positive and Negative Contrast Effects Using Delayed Reinforcement" by R.L. Mellgren, 1972,* Learning and Motivation, *3, pp. 185–193. Copyright © 1972 by Academic Press. Reprinted by permission.)*

contrast to the worse reward they previously experienced. **Negative behavioral contrast** refers to an outcome in which subjects respond less for an unfavorable reward if they previously received a better reward than if they did not have this prior experience. In this case, the unfavorable reward looks especially bad to the subjects in contrast to the better reward they previously experienced.

Mellgren's results illustrate *successive behavioral contrast* effects because the two reward conditions were presented in different phases of the experiment, and only one shift in reward magnitude occurred for shifted groups. Positive and negative behavioral contrast are also obtained if reward conditions are shifted frequently, with a different cue signaling each reward condition. (For a review, see Williams, 1983.) Such contrast effects are called *simultaneous behavioral contrast* because of the frequent reward shifts. The procedures used to produce simultaneous contrast are also called *multiple schedules of reinforcement.* We will consider multiple schedules further in Chapter 8.

Crespi (1942) suggested that positive and negative successive behavioral contrast phenomena reflect emotional reactions to the shift in reward conditions. A shift from small to large reward may create "joy," which facilitates instrumental responding. Correspondingly, a shift from large to small reward may create "anger" or frustration, which disrupts responding. Although different types of contrast effects appear to be the result of different processes (for example, Flaherty & Rowan, 1986), explanations that emphasize emotional reactions are still attractive. Such explanations have been most extensively developed for negative contrast effects. For example, consistent with such accounts, tranquilizers have been found to reduce the magnitude of successive negative contrast. (For a review, see Flaherty, 1991.)

The emotional processes involved in negative behavioral contrast may be conceptualized in terms of frustration theory (Amsel, 1958, 1962, 1967). Among other things, frustration theory provides a technical definition of frustration. The essence of the definition is that frustration occurs when subjects experience less reward than they expect. Frustration produced by the encounter of less than an expected quantity or quality of reward is called **primary frustration.** Primary frustration is considered to be an unconditioned stimulus, much like other unconditioned stimuli we have encountered. Like other unconditioned stimuli, primary frustration elicits innate responses, which in this case consist in avoiding the goal area where the disappointing reward was encountered. How do these ideas help

explain negative behavioral contrast? Negative behavioral contrast occurs when subjects are shifted from a large to a small reward (L-S). While they are reinforced with the large reward, subjects presumably learn to expect that particular type of reward. When they are then shifted to a small reward, the reward they encounter is smaller than what they expect, and therefore primary frustration is elicited. Primary frustration leads to avoidance of the goal box and hence slower running speeds. Such slow running speeds are not observed with subjects that are always given the small reward (S-S). These subjects never receive a large reward in the situation and therefore do not learn to expect one. Consequently, the small reward for them never constitutes less of a reward than what they expect, and hence they never experience frustration.

The Response–Reinforcer Relation

As we have said, instrumental behavior produces and is controlled by its consequences. Animals and people perform all kinds of responses that have various consequences. In some cases, a direct relation exists between what a person does and the consequence that follows. If you put 50¢ into a coffee machine, you get a cup of coffee. As long as the machine is working, you will get a cup of coffee every time you put in the required 50¢. In other cases, no relation may exist between behavior and an outcome. You may wear a red shirt to an examination and receive a good grade. However, the grade would not be related to your having worn the red shirt. In yet other situations, the relation between behavior and its consequences may be imperfect. An animal may search for food often, but be successful only some of the time.

From the organism's point of view, figuring out the relation between its behavior and the consequences of its behavior is an epistemological problem. Animals and people perform a continual stream of responses and experience all kinds of environmental events. You are continually doing something, even if it is just sitting still, and things are continually happening in your environment. For any organism, a critical problem is to figure out how its behavior is related to the environmental events it experiences. An organism must organize its behavior to meet various challenges, and it must do so in a way that makes the best use of its time and energy. To be efficient, an animal has to know the ways in which it can and cannot control its environment. There is no point in working hard to make the sun rise each morning, because that will happen anyway. It makes more sense to devote energy to building a shelter or hunting for food — things that do not become available without effort. You have to know what events are under your control to be able to distribute your efforts efficiently.

The relation between behavior and its consequences is one of the most important factors in the control of instrumental behavior. When we study the acquisition of instrumental behavior in the laboratory, we typically arrange for the instrumental response to produce the reinforcer without delay. If a pigeon pecks a key in the required fashion, it immediately receives grain; if a rat makes the correct turn in a T maze, it finds food right away. We casually think of such instrumental conditioning situations as involving cause and effect. Pecks cause delivery of grain, and correct turns cause access to food. In fact, however, two relations are involved in such situations. The first of these is a temporal relation between the instrumental response and the reinforcer. If the reinforcer is presented immediately after the response, we call this relation **temporal contiguity.** The second relation involves the extent to which the instrumental response is necessary and sufficient for the occurrence of the reinforcer. This is called the **response–reinforcer contingency.** Put another way, the response–reinforcer contingency is the extent to which delivery of the reinforcer is dependent on the prior occurrence of the response.

Investigators have been very interested in analyzing the importance of both temporal contiguity and response–reinforcer contingency in instrumental conditioning.

Effects of temporal contiguity. The importance of temporal contiguity in instrumental conditioning has been investigated by systematically varying the delay between occurrence of the instrumental response and subsequent delivery of the reinforcer. Early investigations of the effects of delay of reinforcement on instrumental conditioning were conducted with the use of the T maze, in which the instrumental response was making a right or left turn. Groups of rats were used, each receiving a different delay of reinforcement. Reinforcement was delayed by confining the rat to a compartment after it made its choice but before it was allowed to enter the goal box and gain access to the reinforcer. Figure 5.12 summarizes results from two such studies. In both experiments, learning was best with no delay of reinforcement and declined thereafter with longer delays. The data from Wolfe (1934) show a much flatter gradient than the data from Grice (1948). Delays of reinforcement did not disrupt learning nearly as much in Wolfe's study as they did in Grice's. What accounts for this difference in results?

Unlike Wolfe's experiment, Grice's was specifically designed to eliminate cues other than the food reinforcer that might signal to the rat that it had made the correct response. Stimuli that signal the forthcoming presentation of food are called **secondary** or **conditioned reinforcers.** A variety of cues can become conditioned as reinforcers. If the food reward is always given in the left arm of the T maze, for example, the left arm can become a conditioned reinforcer. Subjects that enter this arm will be exposed to the conditioned reinforcer immediately; therefore, they will not experience a delay of reward even if presentation of the food is delayed. Thus, conditioned reinforcers can enable subjects to "bridge" a delay between the instrumental

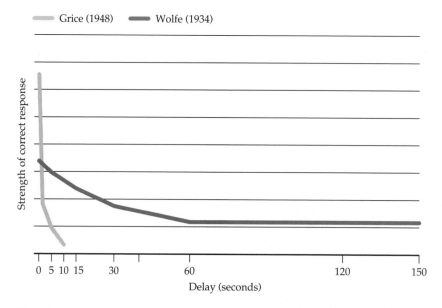

Figure 5.12 Strength of the correct response as a function of delay of reinforcement in two experiments. *(From "The Effect of Delayed Reward Upon Learning in the White Rat" by J.B. Wolfe, 1934,* Journal of Comparative and Physiological Psychology, *17, pp. 1-21; also from "The Relation of Secondary Reinforcement to Delayed Reward in Visual Discrimination Learning" by G.R. Grice, 1948,* Journal of Experimental Psychology, *38, pp. 1–16.)*

response and delivery of the primary reinforcer (see Cronin, 1980; Winter & Perkins, 1982).

In Grice's experiment, the reinforced response was choosing the white arm of a T maze. However, the white arm was sometimes on the right and sometimes on the left. Therefore, secondary cues from turning right or left were not predictive of the food reward and did not become conditioned as reinforcers. The procedure ensured that groups of rats for which delivery of food was delayed after the choice response would not receive immediate feedback from conditioned reinforcers. Procedures like Grice's that minimize the possibility of immediate conditioned reinforcement typically result in a very steep delay-of-reinforcement gradient (but see Lattal & Gleeson, 1990).

Grice showed that instrumental conditioning can be disrupted by delays of reinforcement as short as .5 second. Why is instrumen-

tal conditioning so sensitive to a delay of reinforcement? A potential answer to this question is provided by realizing that behavior consists of an ongoing, continual stream of activities. When reinforcement is delayed after performance of a specified response R_A, the subject does not stop responding. After performing R_A, the subject performs other activities—R_B, R_C, R_D, and so on. A delayed reward may be delivered immediately after response R_M. The problem for the subject then is to distinguish R_A, the target instrumental response, from other responses it performed during the delay interval. If the subject has no way of distinguishing R_A from its other actions, one of these other actions (probably the one closest to reward delivery) will become associated with the reinforcer.

The preceding considerations suggest that if the instrumental response were marked in some way to make it distinguishable from the ongoing stream of other actions of the subject, delay of reinforcement would not have such deleterious effects on instrumental conditioning. Lieberman, McIntosh, and Thomas (1979) tested this prediction in a study with rats, using the maze shown at the top in Figure 5.13. After release from the start box, the rats had a choice between entering a white or a black side arm. Entering the white side arm was designated as the correct instrumental response and was reinforced with access to

Conditioned Reinforcement and Human Behavior: Bridging a Delay of Reinforcement and Conditioning Industriousness

BOX **5.4**

Conditioned reinforcers are common in human instrumental conditioning situations. Verbal praise ("You did a good job"), grades, and money are all familiar powerful conditioned reinforcers. In applied situations, conditioned reinforcers are often used to provide immediate reinforcement when practical considerations require delaying delivery of the primary reinforcer. An elementary school teacher, for example, may set up a point system for reinforcing children in a classroom. The system may involve giving children points for doing a good job on assigned classroom tasks as soon as they turn in their work. These points can then be exchanged for candy, small toys or stickers, extra recess time, a class party, or other primary reinforcers, at a later time.

Conditioned reinforcement can also be used to promote certain styles of behavior. Eisenberger (1991) recently proposed that "industriousness," or the willingness to work hard, can result from having the sensations of effortful responding become conditioned as reinforcers. The effortfulness of a response can depend on the physical force involved in making the response (pressing a heavy response lever as compared to a light one). Effortfulness can also be related to cognitive difficulty (a difficult as compared to an easy crossword puzzle, for example). Learned-industriousness theory assumes that the sensations of response effort can be easily turned into conditioned reinforcers. Subjects who are required to perform effortful behavior to obtain reinforcement presumably learn to associate effortfulness with the primary reinforcer. Thus, reinforcement for performing a difficult task makes the sensations of working hard reinforcing. Once effortfulness has become a conditioned reinforcer, subjects will be more likely to work hard in other situations. In a sense, working hard becomes its own source of reward.

Building on a large body of evidence consistent with the idea that the sensations of effort acquire conditioned reinforcing properties when subjects are reinforced for performing a difficult task, the theory of learned industriousness has been extended in a variety of interesting ways (see Eisenberger, 1991). One unusual prediction is that people reinforced for effortful behavior will be less likely to cheat than people reinforced for performing an easy task. Cheating typically involves trying to obtain a difficult goal without doing the necessary work; for example, trying to get a good grade on a hard test without spending the time needed to learn the material. If working hard becomes its own reward (becomes a conditioned reinforcer), then people who have been reinforced for working hard should persist in a difficult task, and therefore should be less likely to cheat. This prediction has been confirmed by Eisenberger and his colleagues (Eisenberger & Masterson, 1983; Eisenberger & Shank, 1985).

College students were first given either easy or difficult cognitive tasks to work on. The problems involved mentally adding 2-digit or 7-digit numbers and identifying one or five differences between very similar cartoon drawings. Each correct response was acknowledged by the experimenter. If the student got an item wrong, he or she was permitted to try again. After this preliminary training, the students were given a series of difficult anagram problems to solve (scrambled letters that had to be rearranged to form a word). The task was made nearly impossible by allowing only 5 seconds for each anagram. At the end of each trial, the experimenter provided the correct answer, and the student had to indicate whether the answer he or she was thinking of matched the one provided by the experimenter. Cheating was easily achieved by claiming to have thought of the correct answer. Consistent with the theory of learned industriousness, students who had worked on the high-effort math and perceptual identification tasks were less likely to cheat on the anagram task than students who had worked on the low-effort tasks.

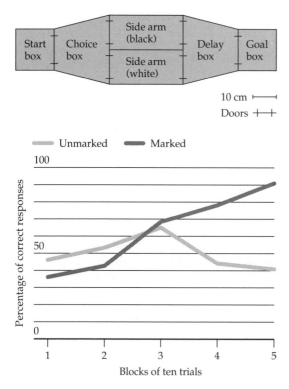

Figure 5.13 Top view of apparatus and results of an experiment to test the effects of marking an instrumental response on instrumental conditioning with reinforcement delayed 60 seconds. Choosing the white side arm was designated as the correct instrumental response. Subjects spent the delay interval in the delay box. "Marked" subjects were placed in the delay box after each choice response. "Unmarked" subjects were allowed to walk into the delay box undisturbed. *(From "Learning When Reward Is Delayed: A Marking Hypothesis" by D.A. Lieberman, D.C. McIntosh, and G.V. Thomas, 1979,* Journal of Experimental Psychology: Animal Behavior Processes, 5, *pp. 224–242. Copyright © 1979 by the American Psychological Association. Reprinted by permission.)*

food in the goal box after a delay of 60 seconds. The two groups were differentiated by what happened to them immediately after making the correct choice. Subjects in the "marked" group were picked up by the experimenter and placed in the delay box. By contrast, subjects in the "unmarked" group were undisturbed. After they made the correct re-

sponse, the door at the end of the choice alley was opened for them, and they were allowed to walk into the delay box. Thus, for them the correct choice response was not distinguished in a special way in their stream of other activities. Sixty seconds after the instrumental response, subjects in both groups were picked up and placed in the goal box to obtain the reinforcer. The same sequence of events occurred when the subjects made an incorrect response except that in these cases they were not reinforced at the end of the delay interval.

Results of the experiment are shown in the graph in Figure 5.13. Subjects in the marked group learned the instrumental response with the 60-second delay of reinforcement much better than subjects in the unmarked group. At the end of 50 training trials, marked subjects were making the correct choice 90% of the time. By contrast, unmarked subjects were making the correct choice about 50% of the time, which is chance performance. In another experiment, Lieberman and his colleagues demonstrated successful learning with delayed reinforcement when the instrumental response was marked by a brief, intense light or noise (Lieberman et al., 1979). These effects of marking cannot be explained in terms of secondary or conditioned reinforcement, because the marking stimulus was presented after both correct and incorrect choice responses. Thus, the marking stimulus itself did not provide information that the subject had made a correct response (see also Lieberman, Davidson, & Thomas, 1985; Lieberman & Thomas, 1986; Thomas & Lieberman, 1990; Urcuioli & Kasprow, 1988).

The response–reinforcer contingency. As we noted earlier, the response–reinforcer contingency refers to the extent to which the delivery of the reinforcer is dependent on the prior occurrence of the response. The contingency is defined in terms of two probabilities: the probability that the reinforcer (S^{R+}) will occur given that the instrumental response (R) has been performed [$p(S^{R+}/R)$] and the probability that the reinforcer will occur given that the instrumental response has not been performed [$p(S^{R+}/noR)$]. A perfect positive contingency exists if the reinforcer is delivered after each occurrence of the instrumental response [$p(S^{R+}/R) = 1.0$] but is never delivered in the absence of the response [$p(S^{R+}/noR) = 0$]. A negative contingency exists if the reinforcer is more likely to occur when the instrumental response is not performed than when the response is performed [$p(S^{R+}/noR) > p(S^{R+}/R)$]. Finally, a zero contingency exists if the reinforcer is equally likely whether or not the instrumental response has been performed [$p(S^{R+}/R) = p(S^{R+}/noR)$].

The studies of delay of reinforcement we have reviewed all involved a perfect positive contingency between response and reinforcement. Although reinforcement was delayed for some groups, the probability of reinforcement was always 1.0 given that the instrumental response occurred, and reinforcement was never provided if the instrumental response did not occur. Delaying the presentation of the reinforcer following the response did not change the fact that reinforcement was always entirely dependent on prior performance of the instrumental response. Studies of delay of reinforcement show that such a perfect contingency between response and reinforcer is not sufficient to produce instrumental conditioning. Even with total dependence of reinforcement on prior responding, conditioning typically does not occur if reinforcement is delayed too long. Does this mean that the contingency between response and reinforcer is unimportant in instrumental conditioning?

Skinner's superstition experiment. Skinner (1948) was the first to investigate whether instrumental conditioning is possible in the absence of a positive response–reinforcer contingency. He placed several pigeons in separate experimental chambers and set the equipment to deliver a bit of grain every 15 seconds irrespective of what the pigeons were doing. The birds were not required to peck a key or perform any other response to get the food. After some time, Skinner returned to see what the pigeons were doing. He described some of what he saw as follows:

> In six out of eight cases the resulting responses were so clearly defined that two observers could agree perfectly in counting instances. One bird was conditioned to turn counterclockwise about the cage, making two or three turns between reinforcements. Another repeatedly thrust its head into one of the upper corners of the cage. A third developed a "tossing" response, as if placing its head beneath an invisible bar and lifting it repeatedly. (p. 168)

The pigeons appeared to Skinner to be responding as if their behavior controlled delivery of the reinforcer when, in fact, the rewards were delivered independently of behavior. Accordingly, Skinner called this **superstitious behavior.**

Skinner's explanation of superstitious behavior rests on the idea of **accidental,** or **adventitious, reinforcement.** Animals are always doing something even if no particular responses are required to obtain reinforcers. Skinner suggested that whatever response a pigeon happens to make just before a reinforcer is delivered becomes strengthened and subsequently increases in frequency because of the reward. Hence, the term *adventitious reinforcement* in reference to the accidental pairing of a response with delivery of the reinforcer. One accidental pairing with a reinforcer increases the chance that the same response will occur just before the next delivery of reward. A second fortuitous response–reinforcer contiguity further strengthens the probability of the response. In this way, each accidental pairing helps to "stamp in" a particular response. After awhile, the response will occur frequently enough to be identified as superstitious behavior.

Skinner's interpretation of his experiment was appealing and consistent with views of reinforcement that were widely held at the time. Impressed by studies of delay of reinforcement, theoreticians thought that temporal contiguity was the main factor responsible for learning. Skinner's experiment appeared to support this view and suggested that a positive response–reinforcer contingency is not necessary for instrumental conditioning.

Reinterpretation of the superstition experiment. Skinner's bold claim that response–reinforcer contiguity rather than contingency is most important for instrumental conditioning has been challenged by subsequent empirical evidence. In a landmark study, Staddon and Simmelhag (1971) reported their attempt to replicate Skinner's experiment with pigeons. Staddon and Simmelhag's observations were much more extensive and systematic, however. They defin_d and measured the occurrence of many responses, such as orienting to the food hopper, pecking the response key, wing flapping, turning in quarter circles, and preening. They recorded the frequency of each response according to when it occurred during the interval between successive deliveries of the reinforcer.

Figure 5.14 shows the data obtained by Staddon and Simmelhag for several responses for one pigeon. We see that some of the responses occurred predominantly toward the end of the interval between successive reinforcers. For example, R₁ and R₇ (orienting to the food magazine and pecking at something on the magazine wall) were much more likely to occur at the end of the interreinforcement interval than at other times. Staddon and Simmelhag called these **terminal responses.** Other activities increased in frequency after the delivery of a reward and then decreased as the time for the next reward drew closer. The pigeons were most likely to engage in R₈ and R₄ (moving along the magazine wall and making a quarter turn) somewhere near the middle of the interreinforcement interval. These activities were called **interim responses.** Which actions were terminal responses and which were interim responses did not vary much from one pigeon to another. Furthermore, Staddon and Simmelhag failed to find evidence of acciden-

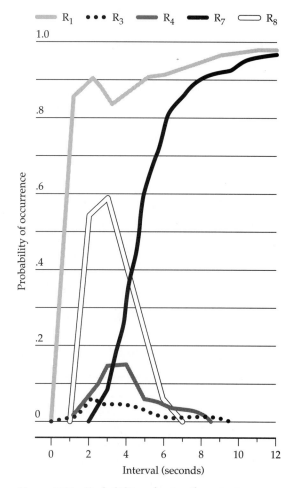

Figure 5.14 Probability of several responses as a function of time between successive deliveries of a food reinforcer. R_1 (orienting toward the food magazine wall) and R_7 (pecking at something on the magazine wall) are terminal responses, having their highest probabilities at the end of the interreinforcement interval. R_3 (pecking at something on the floor), R_4 (a quarter turn), and R_8 (moving along the magazine wall) are interim responses, having their highest probabilities somewhere near the middle of the interreinforcement interval. *(From "The 'Superstition' Experiment: A Reexamination of Its Implications for the Principles of Adaptive Behavior" by J.E.R. Staddon and V.L. Simmelhag, 1971,* Psychological Review, *78, pp. 3–43. Copyright © 1971 by the American Psychological Association. Reprinted by permission.)*

tal reinforcement effects. Responses did not always increase in frequency merely because they occurred coincidentally with food delivery. Food delivery appeared to influence only the strength of terminal responses, even in the initial phases of training.

Subsequent research has provided much additional evidence that periodic presentations of a reinforcer produce behavioral regularities, with certain responses predominating late in the interval between successive food presentations and other responses predominating earlier in the interfood interval (Anderson & Shettleworth, 1977; Innis, Simmelhag-Grant, & Staddon, 1983). It is not clear why Skinner failed to observe such regularities in his pigeons. One possibility is that he focused on different aspects of the behavior of different birds in an effort to document that each bird responded idiosyncratically. For example, he may have focused on the terminal response of one bird and different interim responses in other birds. Subsequent investigators have also noted some variations in behavior across subjects but have emphasized what are even more striking similarities among animals given food periodically, independent of their behavior.

What is responsible for the development of similar terminal and interim responses in subjects exposed to the same schedule of response-independent food presentations? Staddon and Simmelhag (1971) suggested that terminal responses represent species-typical responses that reflect the anticipation of food as time draws nearer to the next food presentation. By contrast, they viewed interim responses as reflecting other sources of motivation that come to the fore during portions of the interfood interval when food presentation is unlikely. More recent investigators have favored approaches in which terminal and interim responses are considered to be different manifestations of the same motivational state (for example, Innis, Reberg, Mann, Jacobson, & Turton, 1983; Matthews, Bordi, & Depollo, 1990). The best developed of these alternative formulations is the behavior systems approach (Lucas, Timberlake, & Gawley, 1988; Timberlake & Lucas, 1985).

According to the behavior systems approach, the foraging–feeding system is activated in food-deprived subjects given periodic small portions of food. The animals' behavior under these circumstances is assumed to be a reflection of their preorganized foraging and feeding behavior. Just before the delivery of food, behavior is expected to be directed toward the place where food is about to appear. Notice that in Figure 5.14 the terminal responses, R_1 and R_7, involved orienting and pecking something on the feeder wall. By contrast, just after food delivery (R_4 in Figure 5.14), turning and moving away from the feeder area were likely to occur (see also Timberlake & Lucas, 1985; Matthews et al., 1990). These turning-away responses reflect earlier components of foraging behavior — responses pigeons make when food has become depleted in one place and the subject has to move on to look for food elsewhere.

Consistent with the behavior systems approach, the distribution of activities that develops with periodic deliveries of a reinforcer depend on the nature of that reinforcer. For example, different patterns of behavior develop with food versus water presentations (Innis et al., 1983; Reberg, Innis, Mann, & Eizenga, 1978), presumably because food and water activate different behavior systems.

Direct detection of a response-outcome contingency. Skinner's analysis of superstitious behavior also has been called into question by evidence that animals are able to detect whether or not their behavior causes an environmental outcome. Killeen (1981) devised an ingenious procedure for getting pigeons to tell him whether an outcome was caused by their behavior (see also Killeen & Smith, 1984). The pigeons were placed in an experimental chamber with three pecking keys arranged in a row along one wall. Pecking the center key caused its light to go off 5% of the time. Occasionally, however, the center key light was also turned off by signals from a computer independently of the pigeons' behavior. Each time the center key

TABLE 5.2 *The triadic design used in studies of the learned-helplessness effect*

Group	Exposure Phase	Conditioning Phase
Group E	Escapable shock	Escape–Avoidance
Group Y	Yoked inescapable shock	Escape–Avoidance
Group R	Restricted to apparatus	Escape–Avoidance

darkened, the pigeons were "asked" to report whether they or the computer had caused the light to go off. When the center key darkened, the two side keys were illuminated. If the pigeons had caused the light to go off, pecks at the left key were reinforced with food; if the computer had caused the center key light to go off, pecks at the right key were reinforced with food. Thus, by pecking on the left or right (the "I did it" or the "computer did it" side key), the pigeons could signify whether their behavior was responsible for the darkening of the center key.

The pigeons were remarkably accurate in their assessment of causality. They reported correctly 80–90% of the time. How they accomplished this was evident in some aspects of their behavior. For example, one bird pecked the center key in short quick bursts. If the light went off while it was pecking, it would choose the "I did it" side key. Between bursts of pecking on the center key, the pigeon stood in front of the "computer did it" side key. If the center light went off while the pigeon stood in front of the "computer did it" side key, it would peck that side key.

Effects of the controllability of reinforcers. A strong contingency between an instrumental response and a reinforcer essentially means that the response controls the reinforcer. With a strong contingency, whether the reinforcer occurs depends on whether the instrumental response has occurred. Studies of the effects of control over reinforcers have provided the most extensive body of evidence on the sensitivity of behavior to response–reinforcer contingencies. Although some of these studies

have involved positive reinforcement (for example, Caspy & Lubow, 1981; Job, 1987, 1989), most of the research has focused on the effects of control over aversive stimulation (see Maier & Jackson, 1979; Maier & Seligman, 1976; Minor, Dess, & Overmier, 1991; Seligman & Weiss, 1980).

Contemporary research on the effects of the controllability of aversive stimulation on learning originated with the pioneering studies of Seligman, Overmier, and Maier (for example, Overmier & Seligman, 1967; Seligman & Maier, 1967), who investigated the effects of exposure to uncontrollable shock on subsequent escape–avoidance learning. The typical finding was that exposure to uncontrollable shock disrupts subsequent learning. This phenomenon has come to be called the **learned-helplessness effect.**

Learned-helplessness experiments are usually conducted using the triadic design presented in Table 5.2. The experiment involves two phases, an exposure phase and a conditioning phase. During the exposure phase, one group of subjects (E) is exposed to periodic shocks that can be terminated by performing an escape response (rotating a small wheel or tumbler, for example). Each subject in the second group (Y) is yoked to a subject in group E and receives the same shocks as its group E partner. However, subjects in group Y cannot do anything to turn off the shocks. The third group (R) receives no shocks during the exposure phase but is restricted to the apparatus for as long as the other groups. During the conditioning phase, all subjects receive escape–avoidance training. This is usually conducted in a shuttle apparatus that has two adjacent compartments (see Figure 9.4, p. 265). The animals have to go back and forth between the two compartments to avoid shock (or escape any shocks that they did not avoid).

The remarkable finding in experiments on the learned-helplessness effect is that the effects of aversive stimulation during the exposure phase depend on whether or not shock is escapable. Exposure to uncontrollable shock in group Y during the exposure phase produces a severe disruption in subsequent escape–avoidance learning. By contrast, often little or no deleterious effects of exposure to escapable shock occur. In the conditioning phase of the experiment, group Y typically shows much less escape–avoidance learning than groups E and R. Similar detrimental effects of exposure to yoked inescapable shock have been reported on subsequent responding for food reinforcement (for example, De-Cola & Rosellini, 1990; Rosellini & DeCola, 1981; Rosellini, DeCola, & Shapiro, 1982).

The fact that group Y shows a deficit in subsequent learning in comparison to group E indicates that the subjects are sensitive to the procedural differences between escapable and yoked inescapable shock. The primary procedural difference between group E and Y is the presence of a response–reinforcer contingency in group E but not in group Y. Therefore, one may conclude that the subjects are sensitive to this contingency. The first major explanation of studies employing the triadic design — the **learned-helplessness hypothesis** — was based on this conclusion (Maier & Seligman, 1976; Maier, Seligman, & Solomon, 1969). The learned-helplessness hypothesis assumes that during exposure to uncontrollable shocks, animals learn that the shocks are independent of their behavior — that there is nothing they can do to control the shocks. Furthermore, they come to expect that the contingency between their behavior and future reinforcers will also be zero. This expectation of lack of control undermines their subsequent learning in two ways. First,

it makes it more difficult for them to learn a positive response–reinforcer contingency. Second, it reduces their motivation to respond and try to control future reinforcers.

It is important to distinguish the learned-helplessness *hypothesis* from the learned-helplessness *effect*. The learned-helplessness effect is the pattern of results obtained with the use of the triadic design (poorer learning in group Y than in groups E and R). The learned-helplessness effect has been replicated in numerous studies and is a well-accepted finding in conditioning and learning. By contrast, the learned-helplessness hypothesis, which explains the learning deficit in group Y as a consequence of the learning of a zero response–reinforcer contingency, has been a provocative but controversial explanation of the learned-helplessness effect since its introduction (see Black, 1977; Levis, 1976).

Early in the history of research on the learned-helplessness effect, investigators became concerned that the learning deficit observed in group Y was a result of these subjects learning to be inactive in response to shock during the exposure phase. Consistent with this hypothesis, in some situations, inescapable shock produces a decrease in motor movement, or response perseveration, and this is responsible for subsequent performance deficits (Anderson, Crowell, Cunningham, & Lupo, 1979; Anisman, de Catanzaro, & Remington, 1978; Anisman, Hamilton, & Zacharko, 1984; Irwin, Suissa, & Anisman, 1980). However, there are also situations in which effects on learning are not likely to be due to the suppression of movement caused by inescapable shock (for example, Jackson, Alexander, & Maier, 1980; Rosellini, DeCola, Plonsky, Warren, & Stilman, 1984). Therefore, a learned-inactivity hypothesis cannot explain all instances of learned-helplessness effects (Maier & Jackson, 1979).

Another difficulty with the learned-helplessness hypothesis is that it takes a restricted view of what might be responsible for the outcome of experiments based on the triadic design. In its explanation of the learning deficit observed in group Y, the learned-helplessness hypothesis focuses only on the zero response–reinforcer contingency that group Y receives during the exposure phase. However, there are many other possible factors that might impede subsequent escape–avoidance learning. One interesting possibility, for example, is that inescapable shock causes subjects to pay less attention to their actions. If a subject fails to pay attention to its behavior, it will have difficulty associating its actions with reinforcers in escape-avoidance or other forms of instrumental conditioning.

In a fascinating experiment, Maier, Jackson, and Tomie (1987) tested this attention-deficit hypothesis with rats. They reasoned that an animal that fails to pay attention to its behavior because of exposure to inescapable shock is faced with the same problem as an animal that receives delayed reinforcement. In both cases, the animals have difficulty figuring out which of their actions causes the delivery of the reinforcer. This analogy suggested to Maier and his colleagues that manipulations that facilitate learning with delayed reinforcement might also help subjects exposed to inescapable shock. As we saw earlier in this chapter, the problem of identifying which response is responsible for delayed reinforcement can be solved by marking the target response with an immediate external feedback stimulus of some sort. Maier and his colleagues reasoned that reduced attention to instrumental behavior also may be alleviated by introducing an external response feedback cue. Thus, their prediction was that subjects given inescapable shock will not be disrupted in their subsequent escape learning if each instrumental response was marked by an external stimulus.

Human Applications of the Concept of Helplessness

BOX **5.5**

The fact that a history of lack of control over reinforcers can severely disrupt subsequent instrumental performance has important implications for human behavior. The concept of helplessness has been extended and elaborated to a variety of areas of human concern, including intellectual achievement, susceptibility to heart attacks, aging and death, and victimization and bereavement (see Garber & Seligman, 1980). Perhaps the most prominent area to which the concept of helplessness has been applied is depression (Seligman, 1975). Recent formulations view depression as a consequence of a special form of helplessness, called *hopelessness* (Abramson, Metalsky, & Alloy, 1989).

Although the ideas that gave rise to theories of human helplessness originated in animal research, the human applications of the concept were developed and extended without further reference to animal research on the effects of uncontrollable aversive stimulation. An interesting aspect of these formulations is that, with people, the uncontrollability of aversive events is considered to be just a contributing factor—not a sufficient cause—for the development of helplessness (see Abramson et al., 1989; Peterson & Seligman, 1984). The way in which someone's mood and behavior changes as a result of an uncontrollable aversive event is assumed to depend primarily on the person's interpretation of the causes of the bad event, the importance attached to the bad event, and the extent to which the bad event is viewed as reflecting poorly on the individual's personality (his or her worth, desirability, and abilities).

Consider, for example, receiving a low grade on a test. The extent to which this experience will make you lethargic and depressed is assumed to depend on how you interpret this experience. You may become depressed if you consider the test to be very important (if you think your grade determines whether you will be able to continue working toward your chosen career) and if you consider a low grade as reflecting poorly on your intelligence and your general worth as a person. By contrast, if you think you got a poor grade because you were given the wrong test form or that the test was unfair, or if you consider the test to be just one of many you have to take as a part of your education, the low grade will be less likely to make you depressed.

The relevant results of their experiment are presented in Figure 5.15. The figure shows the latency of escape responses performed by various groups during the second phase—the conditioning phase—of the experiment. Higher values indicate slower escape responses, and hence poorer escape learning. Groups E, Y, and R were the standard groups of the triadic design and yielded the usual learned-helplessness effect. Group E, which received escapable shocks during the exposure phase, performed with as short latencies as group R, which was not given shock during phase 1. By contrast, group Y, which received inescapable shocks in phase 1, had significantly longer escape latencies.

The fourth group of subjects, group Y-M (yoked-marker) received the same type of shocks as group Y during the exposure phase. During the conditioning phase, group Y-M received a marking stimulus after each escape response. The marker consisted of turning off the house lights for .75 second and having the floor tilt slightly as the rat crossed from one side of the shuttle box to the other. The presence of this marker completely eliminated the deficit in learning that was otherwise produced by prior exposure to inescapable shock. Group Y-M performed much better than group Y and as well as groups R and E. (Other aspects of the experiment ruled out nonspecific effects of the marking stimulus.) Thus, as predicted, marking the instrumental response overcame the learned-helplessness deficit. This outcome suggests that one of the sources of the learning deficit is a reduction in attention to the responses subjects perform (see also Lee & Maier, 1988).

Another contemporary approach to the learned-helplessness effect takes an even broader and more radical approach to analyzing the outcome of the triadic design than the attentional approach. The focus of interest in the triadic design has been on the difference between groups E and Y, since these groups receive the same exposure to aversive stimulation in phase 1. The learned-helplessness

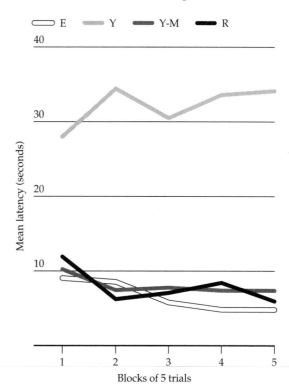

Figure 5.15 Mean escape latency during the conditioning phase for four groups of rats in a learned-helplessness experiment. During the exposure phase, group E received escapable shocks, groups Y and Y-M received yoked inescapable shocks, and group R received no shock. During the conditioning phase, a brief marking stimulus was presented after each escape response for subjects in group Y-M. *(From "Potentiation, Overshadowing, and Prior Exposure to Inescapable Shock" by S.F. Maier, R.L. Jackson, and A. Tomie, 1987,* Journal of Experimental Psychology: Animal Behavior Processes, 13, *pp. 260–270. Copyright © 1987 by the American Psychological Association. Reprinted by permission.)*

hypothesis has encouraged us to think about the difference between groups E and Y in terms of group Y showing a deficit in learning compared with group E. However, the same results can be looked at in terms of group E showing facilitated learning in comparison to group Y. In a chapter called "Inverting the Traditional View of Learned Helplessness," Minor et al. (1991) recently suggested that instead of focusing on what goes wrong with

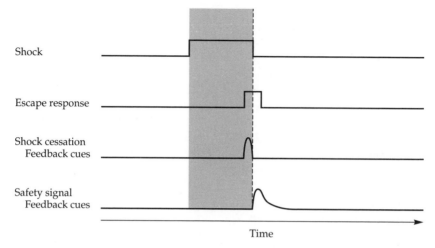

Figure 5.16 Stimulus relations in an escape conditioning trial. Shock-cessation feedback cues are experienced at the start of the escape response, just before the termination of shock. Safety-signal feedback cues are experienced just after the termination of shock, at the start of the intertrial interval.

group Y, we should focus on what goes right with group E—what allows subjects given initial escape training to cope better with shock during the subsequent conditioning phase. In a sense, Minor and his colleagues suggested that we consider the triadic design as an experiment on learned mastery or coping rather than as an experiment on learned helplessness.

This "inversion" of the traditional view of learned helplessness has stimulated a closer look at what happens when subjects are permitted to escape shock in the exposure phase of the triadic design. It is apparent that escape training is far more complex than it appears to be at first glance.

We are accustomed to thinking about escape conditioning as involving a response that results in the termination of an aversive stimulus. However, there are also special stimulus relations in an escape procedure that are potentially very important. These are illustrated in Figure 5.16. Making the escape response results in internal response feedback cues. Some of these response-produced stimuli are experienced at the start of the escape response, just before the shock is turned off,

and are called *shock-cessation feedback cues.* Other response-produced stimuli are experienced as the subject completes the response, just after the shock has been turned off at the start of the intertrial interval. These are called *safety-signal feedback cues.*

Analyses of stimulus factors in subjects given escapable shock first centered on the possible significance of safety-signal feedback cues. Safety-signal feedback cues are reliably followed by the intertrial interval, and hence by the absence of shock. Therefore, such feedback cues can become conditioned inhibitors of fear and limit or inhibit fear elicited by contextual cues of the experimental chamber. No such safety signals exist for subjects given yoked inescapable shock because, for them, shocks and shock-free periods are not predictable. Therefore, contextual cues of the chamber in which shocks are delivered are more likely to become conditioned to elicit fear in inescapably shocked subjects. These considerations have encouraged analyzing the triadic design in terms of group differences in signals for safety rather than in terms of differences in response–reinforcer contingencies.

This approach has yielded some startling results. Jackson and Minor (1988), for example, introduced a brief signal after each inescapable shock given to yoked subjects. Because this stimulus reliably signaled the shock-free periods between trials, it was expected to become conditioned as a safety signal. Providing this cue to yoked subjects served to completely eliminate the learning deficit that was otherwise produced by the inescapable shocks. Thus, the safety signal produced the same results as an escape response. However, such findings have not been always observed (DeCola, Rosellini, & Warren, 1988; Maier & Warren, 1988; Rosellini, Warren, & DeCola, 1987), and the learned-helplessness effect is not necessarily correlated with fear conditioning of contextual cues (Maier, 1990). These considerations have encouraged focusing on other aspects of escape responding that may be responsible for facilitated performance (see Minor et al., 1991). Recent evidence suggests, for example, that the critical aspect of an escape response may not be that it signals a safe period but that it indicates that the shock is being terminated. Thus, cessation signals may model critical features of an escape response more effectively than safety signals (Minor, Trauner, Lee, & Dess, 1990).

Focusing on signal relations in the triadic design rather than on response–reinforcer contingencies has not yet yielded a comprehensive account of all of the results. However, the available evidence indicates that significant differences in how subjects cope with aversive stimulation can result from differences in signal relations. The more restricted focus of the learned-helplessness hypothesis cannot explain such findings. On balance, the triadic design has been invaluable in focusing attention on the possible importance of response–reinforcer contingencies. However, research has uncovered many factors other than the response–reinforcer contingency that also determine the effects of exposure to aversive stimulation.

Concluding Comments

As we have seen, organisms are sensitive to the contiguity as well as the contingency between an instrumental response and a reinforcer. Typically, these two aspects of the relation between response and reinforcer act jointly to produce learning (Davis & Platt, 1983). Both factors serve to focus the effects of reinforcement on the instrumental response. The dependency, or contingency, relation ensures that the reinforcer is delivered only after occurrence of the specified instrumental response. The immediacy relation ensures that other activities do not intrude between the specified response and the reinforcer to disrupt conditioning of the target response.

6 | Schedules of Reinforcement and Choice Behavior

In Chapter 6 we will continue our discussion of the importance of the response–reinforcer relation in instrumental behavior by describing the effects of various schedules of reinforcement. Schedules of reinforcement are programs, or rules, that determine how instrumental behavior is related to reinforcement. To begin, we will consider simple fixed and variable ratio and interval schedules of reinforcement and the ways in which these schedules determine patterns of instrumental responding. We will also describe how the schedule of reinforcement in effect during the conditioning and maintenance of a response determines the persistence of the response during extinction, when reinforcement is no longer provided. In conclusion, we will describe how concurrent and concurrent-chain schedules of reinforcement are used in the empirical and theoretical analyses of choice.

We ended Chapter 5 with a discussion of the importance of the response–reinforcer relation in instrumental conditioning. The present chapter is devoted to a further discussion of this fundamental aspect of instrumental conditioning. In describing various instrumental conditioning procedures in Chapter 5, we may have given the impression that every occurrence of the instrumental response results in delivery of the reinforcer in these procedures. Casual reflection suggests that such a perfect contingency between response and reinforcement is rare outside the laboratory. You do not get a high grade on a test every time you spend many hours studying. You cannot get on a bus every time you go to the bus stop. Inviting someone over for dinner does not always result in a pleasant evening. In fact, in most cases the relation between instrumental responses and consequent reinforcement is rather complex. Attempts to study how these complex relations control the occurrence of instrumental responses have led to laboratory investigations of schedules of reinforcement.

A **schedule of reinforcement** is a program, or rule, that determines how and when the occurrence of a response will be followed by a reinforcer. There are an infinite number of ways that such a program could be set up. The delivery of a reinforcer may depend on the occurrence of a certain number of responses, the passage of time, the presence of certain stimuli, the occurrence of other responses of the animal, or any number of other things. One might expect that cataloging the behavioral effects produced by the various possible schedules of reinforcement would be a very difficult task. However, research so far has shown that the job is quite manageable. Reinforcement schedules that involve similar relations among stimuli, responses, and reinforcers usually produce similar patterns of behavior. The exact rate of responding may differ from one situation to another. However, the *pattern* of response rates is usually amazingly predictable. This regularity has made the study of the effects of reinforcement schedules both interesting and fruitful.

Schedules of reinforcement influence both how an instrumental response is learned and how it is then maintained by reinforcement. Traditionally, however, investigators of schedule effects have been concerned primarily with the maintenance of behavior. Reinforcement schedules are typically investigated in Skinner boxes that permit continuous observation of behavior so that fluctuations in the rate of responding can be readily observed and analyzed (for example, Ferster & Skinner, 1957). The manner in which the operant response is initially shaped and conditioned is rarely of interest. Often a given schedule of reinforcement will produce its characteristic pattern of instrumental behavior irrespective of how the operant response was originally learned. Thus, investigations of reinforcement schedules have provided a great deal of information about the factors that control the maintenance and performance, rather than the learning, of instrumental behavior.

Investigation of the mechanisms of reinforcement that maintain instrumental responding is just as important for the understanding of behavior as investigation of the mechanisms that promote the learning of new responses. More of an animal's behavior is devoted to repeating responses that were previously learned than to acquiring new responses. Humans also spend much of their day doing highly familiar things. Conditions of reinforcement that maintain behavior are of great concern to managers, who have to make sure their employees continue to perform the jobs they learned earlier. Even teachers are more often concerned with encouraging the occurrence of already learned responses than with teaching new responses. Many students who do poorly in school know how to do their homework and how to study, but simply choose not to. Teachers can use information about the effects of reinforcement schedules to motivate more frequent studying.

Simple Schedules of Intermittent Reinforcement

Schedules of reinforcement are important in the analysis of instrumental behavior because they are largely responsible for variations in the frequency and pattern of instrumental responding. Processes that organize and direct instrumental performance are activated in different ways by different schedules of reinforcement. The simplest schedule is a **continuous reinforcement schedule,** in which every occurrence of the instrumental response results in delivery of the reinforcer. Continuous reinforcement rarely occurs outside the laboratory because the world is not perfect. Pushing an elevator button usually brings the elevator. But all elevators occasionally malfunction, so that nothing may happen when you push the button. Instrumental behavior often results in reinforcement only some of the time. Situations in which responding is reinforced only some of the time are said to involve a **partial** or **intermittent reinforcement schedule.** There are many ways to arrange for responding to be reinforced intermittently. We begin with a discussion of "simple" schedules of reinforcement. In simple schedules, a single factor determines which response is reinforced.

Ratio Schedules

The defining characteristic of **ratio schedules** is that reinforcement depends only on the number of responses made by the subject. The program relating responses to reinforcement requires merely counting the responses and delivering the reinforcer each time the required number is reached. One might, for example, deliver the reinforcer after every tenth lever-press response in rats. In such a schedule, there would be a fixed ratio between the number of responses the subject made and the number of reinforcers it got. (There would always be ten responses per reinforcer.) This makes such a procedure a **fixed-ratio sched-**ule. More specifically, the procedure would be called a fixed-ratio 10 schedule (abbreviated FR 10). Fixed-ratio schedules are found in daily life wherever a fixed number of responses are always required for reinforcement. The delivery person who always has to visit the same number of houses to complete his route is working on a fixed-ratio schedule. Piecework in factories is usually set up on a fixed-ratio schedule: workers get paid for every so many "widgets" they put together. Flights of stairs provide another example. In a given staircase, you always have to go up the same number of steps to reach the next landing.

Strictly speaking, a continuous reinforcement schedule is also a fixed-ratio schedule. Reinforcement depends only on the number of responses the subject makes. Furthermore, there is a fixed ratio of responses to reinforcements: one response per reinforcer. Therefore, continuous reinforcement is a fixed ratio of 1.

On a continuous reinforcement schedule, subjects typically respond at a steady and moderate rate. Only brief and unpredictable pauses occur. A pigeon, for example, will peck a key for food steadily at first and slow down as it becomes satiated. A very different pattern of responding occurs when an intermittent fixed-ratio schedule of reinforcement is in effect. Figure 6.1 shows the cumulative record of a pigeon that had learned to respond on a fixed-ratio 120 schedule. To obtain food reinforcement, 120 pecks were required. Each food delivery is indicated by the small downward deflections of the recorder pen. As you can see, the bird stopped responding after each food delivery. However, when it resumed pecking, it responded at a high and very steady rate. Responding on a fixed-ratio schedule has two characteristics. The zero rate of responding that occurs just after reinforcement is called the **postreinforcement pause.** The high and steady rate of responding that completes each ratio requirement is called the **ratio run.** If the ratio requirement is increased a little (from FR 120 to 150, for example), the

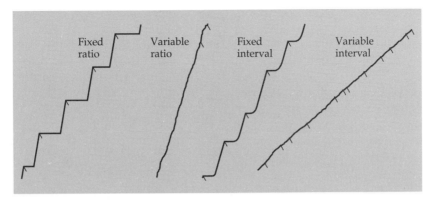

Figure 6.1 Sample cumulative records of different pigeons pecking a response key on four simple schedules of food reinforcement: fixed-ratio 120, variable-ratio 360, fixed-interval 4 minute, and variable-interval 2 minute. *(From Schedules of Reinforcement by C.B. Ferster and B.F. Skinner, 1957, Appleton-Century-Crofts.)*

rate of responding during the ratio run may remain the same. However, with higher ratio requirements, the postreinforcement pause becomes longer (for example, Felton & Lyon, 1966). If the ratio requirement is suddenly increased a great deal (from FR 120 to FR 500, for example), the animal is likely to pause periodically before the completion of the ratio requirement. This effect is called **ratio strain.** In extreme cases, ratio strain may be so great that the animal stops responding altogether. When training an organism, one must be careful not to raise the ratio requirement (or, more generally, the difficulty of a task) too quickly, or ratio strain may occur and the organism may give up altogether.

The postreinforcement pause in fixed-ratio schedules is a result of the predictably large number of responses required for the next delivery of the reinforcer. Given enough experience with a fixed-ratio procedure, the subject learns that after reinforcement it always has to make a certain number of responses to receive the next reinforcer (Griffiths & Thompson, 1973). This predictability can be disrupted by varying the number of responses required for reinforcement from one occasion to the next. Such a procedure is still a ratio schedule because reinforcement

still depends on how many responses the subject makes. However, a different number of responses is counted for the delivery of each reward. Such a procedure is called a **variable-ratio schedule.** We may, for example, require the subject to make 10 responses to earn the first reward, 13 to earn the second reward, 7 for the next one, and so on. The numerical value of a variable-ratio schedule indicates the average number of responses required per reinforcement. Thus, our procedure would be a variable-ratio 10 schedule (abbreviated VR 10). Because the number of responses required for reinforcement is no longer predictable, there are no predictable pauses in the rate of responding on a variable-ratio schedule. Rather, the subject responds at a fairly steady rate. Figure 6.1 shows a cumulative record for a pigeon whose pecking behavior was maintained on a VR 360 schedule of reinforcement. Notice that even though on average the VR 360 schedule required many more pecks for each reinforcer than the FR 120 schedule shown in Figure 6.1, the VR 360 schedule maintained a much more steady pattern of responding.

Although postreinforcement pauses can occur on variable-ratio schedules (see Blakely & Schlinger, 1988; Schlinger, Blakely, & Kaczor, 1990), such pauses are longer and more prominent with fixed-ratio schedules. The overall response rate on fixed- and variable-ratio schedules is similar provided that, on average, similar numbers of responses are required. However, the overall response rate tends to be distributed in a pause–run pattern with fixed-ratio schedules, whereas a more steady pattern of responding develops with variable-ratio schedules (for example, Crossman, Bonem, & Phelps, 1987).

Variable-ratio schedules are found in daily life whenever an unpredictable amount of effort is required to obtain a reinforcer. Each time a custodian goes into a room on his rounds, he knows that some amount of cleaning will be necessary, but he does not know exactly how dirty the room will be. Gamblers playing a slot machine are also responding on a variable-ratio schedule. They have to play the machine to win. However, they never know how many plays will produce the winning combination. Variable-ratio schedules are also common in sports. A certain number of strokes are always required to finish a hole in golf, for example. However, players can never be sure how many strokes they will need to use when they start.

Interval Schedules

Reinforcement does not always depend solely on the amount of effort or the number of responses the subject makes. Sometimes responses are reinforced only if they occur at certain times. **Interval schedules** illustrate this type of situation. In a simple interval schedule, a response is reinforced only if it occurs more than a set amount of time after the last reinforcer delivery. In a **fixed-interval schedule,** the set time is constant from one occasion to the next. Consider, for example, a fixed-interval 4-minute schedule (FI 4 min) for pecking in pigeons. A bird on this schedule would get reinforced for the first peck it made after 4 minutes had passed after the last food delivery. Because pecks made shortly after a

reinforcer never result in food, animals on a fixed-interval schedule learn to wait to respond until the end of the FI 4-min interval (see Figure 6.1). Very few responses occur at the beginning of the interval after a reward. As the time for the availability of the next reinforcer draws closer, the response rate increases. The animal responds at a high rate at the end of the 4-minute interval and therefore usually receives the reinforcer as soon as the 4 minutes are up. There is a curve in the cumulative record as the animal speeds up responding toward the end of the interval. The pattern of response that develops with fixed-interval reinforcement schedules is accordingly called the **fixed-interval scallop.**

It is important to realize that a fixed-interval schedule of reinforcement does not ensure that the animal will be reinforced at fixed intervals of time. Thus, pigeons on an FI 4-min schedule do not automatically receive the reinforcer every 4 minutes. Instrumental responses are required for the reinforcer in interval schedules, just as in ratio schedules. The interval determines only when the reinforcer becomes available. In order to receive the reinforcer when it becomes available, the subject still has to make the instrumental response.

Fixed-interval schedules are found in situations in which a fixed amount of time is required to prepare or set up the reinforcer. Consider, for example, washing clothes in an automatic washer. A certain amount of time is required to complete the wash cycle. No matter how many times you open the washing machine before the required amount of time has passed, you will not be reinforced with clean clothes. Once the cycle is finished, the reinforcer becomes available, and you can pick up your clean clothes any time after that. Making Jell-O provides another example. After the gelatin is mixed in hot water, it has to chill for a certain amount of time to gel. To be able to eat the Jell-O, you have to wait until it is ready. No matter how many times you check the refrigerator before the required amount of time has elapsed, the Jell-O will not have the proper consistency. If you are particularly eager to eat the Jell-O, the rate of your opening the refrigerator door will be similar to an FI scallop.

Like ratio schedules, interval schedules can be unpredictable. In a **variable-interval schedule,** the reinforcer is provided for the first response that occurs after a variable amount of time has elapsed since the previous reward. We may set up a schedule, for example, in which one reward is delivered when the animal makes a response after 1 minute following the last reward, the next reinforcer is given for the first response that occurs after 3 minutes following that reward, and the next one is given for the first response that occurs at least 2 minutes later. In this procedure, the average interval that has to pass before successive rewards become available is 2 minutes. Therefore, the procedure is a variable-interval 2-minute schedule, abbreviated VI 2 min. Like variable-ratio schedules, variable-interval schedules maintain steady and stable rates of responding without pauses (see Figure 6.1).

Variable-interval schedules are found in situations in which an unpredictable amount of time is required to prepare or set up the reinforcer. A mechanic who cannot tell you when your car will be ready has imposed a variable-interval schedule on you. You have to wait a certain amount of time before attempts to get your car will be reinforced. However, the amount of time involved is unpredictable. A taxi dispatcher is also controlled by variable-interval schedules. After a cab has completed a trip, it is available for another assignment, and the dispatcher will be reinforced for sending the cab on another errand. However, once an assignment is made, the cab is unavailable for an unpredictable period, during which time the dispatcher cannot use the same cab for other trips.

In simple interval schedules, once the reward becomes available, the subject can receive the reward any time thereafter, provided it makes the required response. On a fixed-interval 2-minute schedule, for example, reward becomes available 2 minutes after the previous reinforcement. If the animal responds at exactly this time, it will be reinforced. If it waits to respond for 90 minutes after the previous reinforcement, it will still get the reward. Outside the laboratory, it is more common for reinforcers to become available for only limited periods in interval schedules. Consider, for example, a dormitory cafeteria. Meals are served only at certain times. Therefore, going to the cafeteria is reinforced only if you wait long enough after the last meal. However, once the next meal becomes available, you have a limited amount of time in which to get it. This kind of restriction on how long reward remains available is called a **limited hold.** Limited-hold restrictions can be added to both fixed-interval and variable-interval schedules.

Comparison of Ratio and Interval Schedules

There are striking similarities between the patterns of responding maintained by simple ratio and interval schedules. As we have seen, both fixed-ratio and fixed-interval schedules produce a predictable pause in responding after each reinforcement. By contrast, variable-ratio and variable-interval schedules both maintain steady rates of responding, without predictable pauses. Despite these similarities, there is a very important difference between ratio and interval schedules. This involves the feedback loop between the rate of responding and the frequency of reinforcement. The relation between the rate of responding and the frequency of reinforcement is technically called the **feedback function.** Each schedule of reinforcement has its own feedback function. In ratio schedules, the feedback loop between responses and reinforcers is very strong. Because the only thing that determines whether the subject will be reinforced is the number of responses it makes, the rate of responding totally determines the frequency of reinforcement. By responding at a higher rate, the subject can always earn reinforcers at a higher rate.

In interval schedules, the rate of response does not determine the frequency of reinforcement in the same manner as in ratio schedules. Consider, for example, an FI 2-min schedule. Each reward becomes available 2 minutes after the last reward. If the subject responds right away when the reward is set up, the reward is delivered and the next cycle begins. However, no matter how frequently the subject responds, it will never be reinforced any more often than once every 2 minutes. Therefore, the interval schedule sets a maximum limit on the frequency of reinforcers the subject can earn. In the FI 2-min example, the limit is 30 reinforcers per hour. If the subject does not respond as soon as each reward becomes available, it will not earn reinforcers as often as possible. Therefore, the rate of responding determines the frequency of reinforcement to some extent. However, the de-

The Postreinforcement Pause, Procrastination, and Cramming for Exams

BOX **6.1**

The postreinforcement pause that occurs in fixed-ratio and fixed-interval schedules is a very common human experience. In fixed-ratio schedules, the pause occurs because a predictably large number of responses are always required to produce the next reward. In a sense, the animal is "procrastinating" before embarking on the large effort necessary for reinforcement. Similar procrastination is legendary in human behavior. Consider, for example, a term in which you have several papers to write. You are likely to work on one term paper at a time. However, when you have completed one paper, you probably will not start working on the next one right away. Rather, there will be a postreinforcement pause. After completing a large project, people tend to take some time off before starting the next task. In fact, procrastination between tasks or before the start of a new job is the rule rather than the exception. Laboratory results provide a suggestion for overcoming such procrastination. Fixed-ratio-schedule performance in the laboratory indicates that once animals begin to respond on a ratio run, they respond at a high and steady rate until they complete the ratio requirement. This suggests that if somehow you got yourself to start on a job, chances are you would not find it difficult to keep working to finish it. Only the beginning is hard. One technique that works pretty well in getting started is to tell yourself that you will begin with only a small part of the new job. If you are trying to write a paper, tell yourself that you will write only one paragraph to start with. You may very well find that once you have completed the first paragraph, it will be easier to write the second one, then the one after that, and so on. If you are procrastinating about spring cleaning, instead of thinking about doing the entire job, start with a small part of it, such as washing the kitchen floor. The rest will then come more easily.

On a fixed-interval schedule, postreinforcement pauses may occur because once a reward has been delivered, there is no chance that another will be available for some time. Scheduling of tests in college courses has important similarities to the basic fixed-interval schedule. In many courses there are few tests, and the tests are evenly distributed during the term. There may be a midterm and a final exam. The pattern of studying that such a schedule maintains is very similar to what is observed in the laboratory. There is no studying at all at the beginning of the semester or just after the midterm exam. Many students begin to study only a week or so before each test, and the rate of studying rapidly increases as the day of the test approaches. Studying at the beginning of the term or after the midterm exam is not reinforced by the receipt of good grades on tests at that time. Therefore, students do not study at these points in the term. More frequent studying can be motivated by giving more frequent tests. The highest rate of responding would occur if unannounced tests were given at unpredictable times, in a manner analogous to a variable-interval schedule. This is the "pop quiz" technique.

livery of reward depends more on exactly *when* the subject responds than on how often it responds.

Because the rate of responding does not entirely determine the frequency of reinforcement in interval schedules, such schedules typically do not motivate as high response rates as ratio schedules, even if subjects receive the same number of reinforcements in the two types of schedules. In an important experiment on this topic, Reynolds (1975) compared the rate of key pecking in pigeons reinforced on variable-ratio and variable-interval schedules. Two pigeons were trained to peck the response key for food reinforcement. One of the birds was reinforced on a variable-ratio schedule. Therefore, for this bird the frequency of reinforcement was entirely determined by its rate of response. The other bird was reinforced on a variable-interval schedule. In this case, however, the availability of the reinforcer was controlled by the behavior of the other pigeon. Each time the variable-ratio pigeon was just one response short of the required number, the experimenter reinforced the next response that each subject made. Thus, the variable-ratio bird controlled the variable-interval schedule for its partner. This yoking procedure ensured that the frequency of reinforcement was virtually identical for the two subjects.

Figure 6.2 shows the pattern of responding exhibited by each subject. Even though the two subjects received the same frequency of reinforcers, they behaved very differently. The pigeon reinforced on the variable-ratio schedule responded at a much higher rate than the pigeon reinforced on the variable-interval schedule. The variable-ratio schedule motivated much more vigorous instrumental behavior (see also Peele, Casey, & Silberberg, 1984).

Ratio schedules motivate higher rates of responding than interval schedules outside the laboratory as well. Doctors, for example, usually work on a schedule that has very strong ratio characteristics. The more patients they see, the more money they make. Every patient whom they refuse to see represents the loss of a certain amount of income. This direct relation between rate of response and rate of reinforcement may contribute to their diligence. Because ratio characteristics in a schedule of reinforcement provide a strong impetus for responding, such schedules are usually strongly resisted by employees. In a labor–management negotiation, management is likely to want to build ratio characteristics into the contract, whereas representatives of labor will insist that interval-schedule characteristics be instituted.

Theoretical analyses of why variable-ratio schedules produce higher response rates than variable-interval schedules initially focused on the relative benefits of waiting between responses on the two schedules (see, for example, Peele, Casey, & Silberberg, 1984). How long a subject waits between successive responses is technically referred to as the **interresponse time**, abbreviated **IRT**. On variable-interval schedules there is a benefit to waiting a long time between responses because the longer the animal waits, the more likely it is that the reinforcer will be ready when it responds again. Therefore, variable-interval schedules involve differential reinforcement of longer interresponse times, which results in low rates of responding. The converse of this argument has been made to explain the results of variable-ratio schedules. The argument has been that VR schedules differentially reinforce short interresponse times, and that results in the high rates of responding. However, recent analyses have indicated that the differences between VR and VI schedules cannot be explained solely in terms of the reinforcement of different types of interresponse times (Dawson & Dickinson, 1990; Wearden & Clark, 1988). Other factors also have to be considered, such as the feedback loop between response rate and reinforcement rate (McDowell & Wixted,

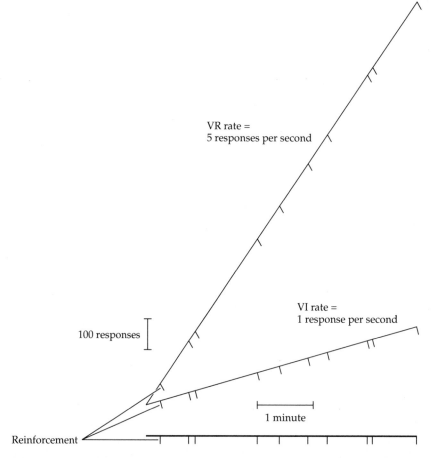

Figure 6.2 Cumulative records for two pigeons, one reinforced on a variable-ratio (VR) schedule and the other yoked to it on a variable-interval (VI) schedule. Although subjects received the same reinforcements at about the same time, the VR bird responded five times as fast as the VI bird. *(From* A Primer of Operant Conditioning 2nd ed. *by G.S. Reynolds, Scott, Foresman, 1975. Reprinted by permission of the author.)*

1988). As we noted earlier, this feedback function is much stronger on VR than on VI schedules.

Response-Rate Schedules of Reinforcement

Although ratio schedules produce higher rates of responding than comparable interval schedules, neither type of schedule requires that subjects perform at a specific rate in order to get reinforced. Therefore, differences in the rate of responding are indirect effects of the schedules. By contrast, other types of procedures specifically require that subjects respond at a particular rate to get reinforced. Such procedures are called **response-rate schedules.**

In response-rate schedules, whether a response is reinforced depends on how soon it occurs after the preceding response. A reinforcement schedule could be set up, for example, in which a response is reinforced only if it occurs within 5 seconds following the preceding response. If the subject makes a response every 5 seconds, its rate of response will be 12 per minute. Thus, the schedule provides reinforcement if the rate of response is 12 per minute or greater. The subject will not be reinforced if its rate of response is less than 12 per minute. As you might suspect, this procedure encourages responding at high rates. Therefore, it is called **differential reinforcement of high rates,** or **DRH.**

In DRH schedules, a response is reinforced only if it occurs *before* a certain amount of time

has elapsed following the preceding response. The opposite result is achieved if a response is reinforced only if it occurs *after* a certain amount of time has elapsed following the previous response. This type of procedure is called **differential reinforcement of low rates,** abbreviated **DRL.** As you might suspect, DRL schedules encourage subjects to respond slowly.

Response-rate schedules are found outside the laboratory in situations that require particular rates of responding. DRH schedules are in effect in sports where speed is of the essence. For example, running from home plate to first base in a baseball game is

---

Wage Scales and Schedules of Reinforcement

BOX **6.2**

The basis for determining the wages paid for work performed in a company constitutes a schedule of reinforcement. Laboratory research indicates that different schedules of reinforcement maintain different patterns and rates of responding. To the extent that these effects occur outside the laboratory, we may expect different wage systems to produce different rates of responding in work situations as well. A recent study of productivity among waitpersons at three family restaurants illustrates such effects (George & Hopkins, 1989).

As is customary, the waitpersons were paid an hourly wage. Most earned the federal minimum wage for servers, $1.90 plus tips, and a few earned more based on seniority. The employees complained that they were underpaid. The owners decided that they could not increase wages without an increase in productivity because the restaurants were already losing money. However, the servers claimed that they had no incentive to increase productivity because of their low wages. Thus, the two sides found themselves stuck in a common labor–management dispute. Following the advice of behavioral consultants, the owners adopted a performance-contingent pay scale. Such a system is a variant of a fixed-ratio schedule in which rate of reinforcement is directly related to rate of responding. In a performance-contingent pay scale, each server is paid a fixed proportion of his or her gross sales. The proportion was set at 7%. Servers could easily make at least $1.90 per hour at 7% of gross sales, and 7% seemed to be the break-even point for profitability of the restaurant.

Introduction of the performance-contingent pay scale increased the hourly earning of the servers 24–30% in the three restaurants. The new schedule of reinforcement also increased productivity. Gross sales per labor hour increased 18–36%. This increase occurred primarily because of increases of 18–26% in the number of customers served per labor hour, rather than because of how much was purchased by each customer.

A common criticism of efforts to increase productivity by changing the schedule of reinforcement is that increased productivity is used to boost profits at the expense of the workers. How the benefits of increased productivity are distributed is an important and complex issue. In the present study, the benefits accrued primarily to the servers. Wage rates increased. However, labor costs as a proportion of gross sales did not change after the performance-contingent pay system had been introduced. Thus, the increased productivity of the servers did not contribute to higher profits. However, the owners may have benefited from the new pay scale in other ways, such as from having servers who were more satisfied and more likely to remain on the job. Measuring such secondary benefits would have provided interesting additional data.

reinforced only if it occurs faster than the time it takes to throw the ball to first base. In other circumstances, responding is reinforced only if it occurs at a specified rate. This is typically the case in dancing and music. Another obvious example is an assembly line, where the speed of movement of the line dictates the rate of response for the workers. If an employee responds more slowly than the specified rate, he or she will not be reinforced and may, in fact, get fired. However, workers have to be careful not to work too rapidly, because of social pressure imposed by fellow workers. Those who respond at very high rates are likely to earn the enmity of their peers. Social pressure in some work situations differentially reinforces low rates of responding.

Extinction

So far we have discussed how organisms behave when their responses are reinforced according to various schedules of reinforcement. A related and very important issue concerns what responses occur when reinforcement is no longer available. Not many reinforcement schedules in nature remain in effect throughout the organism's lifetime. Responses that are successful in producing reinforcement at one time may cease to be effective as circumstances change. Children, for example, are praised for drawing crude representations of people and objects, but the same type of drawing is not considered good if made later in life. Dating someone may be extremely pleasant and rewarding until the person finds another special friend and no longer encourages your approaches. The nonreinforcement of a response that was previously rewarded is called **extinction.** We encountered extinction in Chapter 3 in connection with classical conditioning. There, *extinction* referred to the reduction in a response when the conditioned stimulus was no longer followed by the unconditioned stimu-

lus. In instrumental conditioning, extinction is the reduction in an instrumental response when it is no longer followed by the reinforcer.

Effects of Extinction Procedures

Instrumental extinction procedures — withdrawal of reinforcement — have two important types of effects on the organism. First, of course, the procedure results in a gradual decrease in the rate of the instrumental response. During the first extinction session, the subject may respond rapidly at first and then gradually slow down until it stops making the instrumental response. If the subject is placed back in the experimental situation the next day, there may be a slight and temporary recovery in rate of responding. This is called **spontaneous recovery.** However, the amount of spontaneous recovery decreases with repeated extinction sessions, until the subject ceases to make the instrumental response altogether. Extinction and spontaneous recovery are illustrated in Figure 6.3.

In addition to the expected decline in the instrumental response, extinction procedures also produce strong emotional effects and behavioral arousal. If the subject has become accustomed to receiving reinforcement for a particular response, it may become extremely upset and aggressive when rewards are no longer delivered. This emotional reaction induced by withdrawal of rewards is called **frustration.** Frustrative aggression induced by extinction procedures is dramatically demonstrated by experiments in which two animals (pigeons, for example) are placed in the same Skinner box (Azrin, Hutchinson, & Hake, 1966). One of them is initially rewarded for pecking a response key, while the other animal is restrained in a corner of the experimental chamber. The key-pecking bird largely ignores the other one as long as reinforcement is provided. However, when

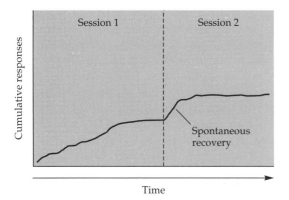

Figure 6.3 Cumulative record of responding during the first and second sessions of extinction. The burst of responding at the beginning of the second session is spontaneous recovery. (Hypothetical data.)

reinforcement ceases, the previously rewarded animal is likely to attack its innocent partner. Similar aggression occurs if a stuffed model instead of a real animal is placed in the Skinner box. (See Nation and Cooney, 1982, for an experimental study of extinction-induced aggression in human subjects.)

Frustrative reactions to withdrawal of rewards are also common outside the laboratory. When a vending machine breaks down and no longer delivers a soft drink or candy for the coins that are put into it, people often become abusive and pound and kick the machine. Vending machines have to be built very sturdily to withstand this frustrative aggression. Frustration is also common in interpersonal interactions when extinction is introduced by one of the parties. If a secretary has a cup of coffee ready for the boss every morning, the first time the secretary fails to prepare the cup of coffee, the boss is likely to become angry. If a child is accustomed to being driven to school every day by her parents, she is likely to become upset if one day she has to walk or take the bus. If you and your special friend usually go on a date every Saturday evening, you will surely be very

disturbed if unexpectedly your friend calls off the date.

Determinants of Extinction Effects

The most important variable that determines the magnitude of both the behavioral and emotional effects of an extinction procedure is the schedule of reinforcement in effect for the instrumental response before the extinction procedure is introduced. Various subtle features of reinforcement schedules can influence the subsequent extinction of instrumental responses. However, the dominant schedule characteristic that determines extinction effects is whether the instrumental response was reinforced every time it occurred (continuous reinforcement) or only some of the times it occurred (intermittent, or partial, reinforcement). Most of the schedules of reinforcement described earlier in the chapter involved partial reinforcement. We discussed these schedules in great detail because the pattern of responding that occurs when reinforcement is available closely depends on the special features of each schedule. However, the difference between continuous and partial reinforcement is much more important in the study of extinction effects than differences between the various possible partial reinforcement schedules. The general finding is that extinction is much slower and involves fewer frustration reactions if the subjects previously experienced partial reinforcement than if they previously experienced continuous reinforcement (see Figure 6.4). This phenomenon is called the **partial-reinforcement extinction effect,** or **PREE.**

The persistence in responding that is created by intermittent reinforcement can be remarkable. Aspiring actors and actresses study hard and persist in their eagerness to pursue an acting career even though they may get very few important roles. Habitual gamblers are similarly at the mercy of intermittent reinforcement. The few times they win big

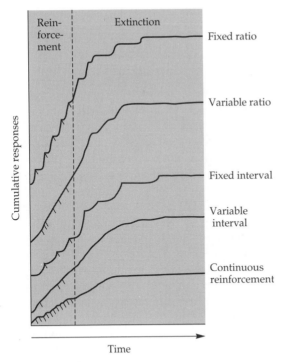

Figure 6.4 Cumulative records of extinction of instrumental behavior following various simple schedules of reinforcement. (Hypothetical data.)

strongly encourage them to continue gambling during long strings of losses. Partial reinforcement also occurs often in interpersonal situations. If you are not really interested in dating someone who finds you extremely attractive, you may accept only a small proportion of his or her invitations. By doing this, you are reinforcing the person intermittently, which may make the person much more persistent in trying to win your favor. Intermittent reinforcement can also have undesirable consequences if parents give in to various demands from a child only after the child has made the request repeatedly. Consider, for example, a child riding in a grocery cart while the parent is shopping. The child asks the parent to buy a piece of candy. The parent says no. The child asks again and again and then begins to throw a temper tantrum because the parent continues to say

no. At this point, the parent is likely to give in to avoid public embarrassment. By buying the candy, the parent will have reinforced the temper tantrum and also provided intermittent reinforcement for the repeated demands for candy. The schedule of reinforcement the parent used will make the child very persistent in making requests in the future, and will also encourage tantrums.

Mechanisms of the Partial-Reinforcement Extinction Effect

Perhaps the most obvious explanation of the PREE is that more responses occur when reward is withdrawn after intermittent reinforcement than after continuous reinforcement because the withdrawal of reward is more difficult to detect in the former case. If the subject does not receive reward after each response during training, it may not immediately notice when reward ceases. The change in reinforcement conditions is presumably much more dramatic if reward ceases after continuous reinforcement. This explanation of the partial-reinforcement extinction effect is called the **discrimination hypothesis.**

Although the discrimination hypothesis provides an intuitively satisfactory explanation of the PREE, the phenomenon is not so straightforward. In an ingenious test of the discrimination hypothesis, Jenkins (1962) and Theios (1962) first trained one group of animals with partial reinforcement and another group with continuous reinforcement. Both groups then received a period of continuous reinforcement before reinforcement for each group was withdrawn. Because the extinction procedure was introduced immediately after continuous reinforcement training for both groups, it was presumably equally noticeable or discriminable. Nevertheless, the subjects that initially received partial reinforcement training responded more during the extinction period. This study indicates that the advantage of partial reinforcement does not come from greater difficulty in detecting the start of the extinction procedure. Rather, it seems that subjects learn something important during partial reinforcement training that is not lost if they also receive continuous reinforcement before the extinction procedure.

What do organisms learn during partial reinforcement training that makes them respond more often when rewards are no longer available? Numerous complicated experiments have been performed in attempts to answer this question. These studies indicate that partial reinforcement training promotes persistence during extinction in two ways. One of the mechanisms of the partial-reinforcement extinction effect was proposed by Amsel (for example, 1958, 1962, 1967, 1986) and has come to be known as **frustration theory.** Frustration theory assumes that animals reinforced on an intermittent schedule go through several stages in their training. During the course of partial reinforcement, subjects receive some rewarded and some nonrewarded trials. Consequently, they develop conflicting expectations. Rewarded trials lead them to expect reinforcement and nonrewarded trials lead them to expect nonreinforcement. Initially, the anticipation of reward encourages the subjects to go ahead and make the instrumental response, whereas the anticipation of nonreinforcement discourages them from making the instrumental response. Thus, early in training the subjects are in a conflict about what to do. However, on some occasions when the subjects expect nonreward, performance of the instrumental response may in fact be followed by the reinforcer. Because of such experiences, performance of the instrumental response becomes conditioned to the expectation of nonreward. According to frustration theory, this is the key to persistent responding in extinction. Because animals learn to make the instrumental response in expectation of nonreward, subjects trained with intermittent reinforcement continue to make the response when extinction procedures are introduced. By contrast, there is nothing about the ex-

perience of continuous reinforcement that teaches animals to respond when they expect not getting rewarded. Therefore, these subjects stop responding much sooner in extinction.

The second prominent mechanism that explains responding in extinction after intermittent reinforcement was proposed by Capaldi (for example, 1967, 1971) and is known as **sequential theory.** Sequential theory relies heavily on memory mechanisms. It assumes that animals can remember very well whether or not they were reinforced for performing the instrumental response in the recent past. The theory further assumes that animals on a partial reinforcement schedule learn to make the instrumental response when they remember not having been rewarded on the preceding trials. Thus, the memory of nonreward becomes a cue for performing the instrumental response. Precisely how this happens depends a great deal on the sequence of rewarded (R) and nonrewarded (N) trials that are administered in the intermittent reinforcement schedule.

Consider the following sequence of trials: RNNRRNR. In this sequence the subject is rewarded the first time it makes the instrumental response, not rewarded on the next two occasions, then rewarded twice, then not rewarded, and then rewarded again. The fourth and last trials are critical in this schedule. The subject is reinforced for responding on the fourth trial. It is assumed that on this trial the subject remembers not having been rewarded on the preceding two trials. Because of the reinforcement on the fourth trial, it is assumed the subject learns that it will be reinforced for responding when it remembers not having been reinforced on the preceding two trials. A similar mechanism is activated by the reinforcer on the last trial of the preceding sequence. Here, the subject is rewarded for responding when it remembers that it was not reinforced on the single trial immediately preceding. With enough experiences of this type, subjects learn to respond whenever they remember not having been reinforced on the preceding trials. This learning, in turn, creates persistent responding in extinction after intermittent reinforcement. A continuous reinforcement schedule does not permit animals to learn such persistence. On a continuous reinforcement schedule, subjects are rewarded for every occurrence of the instrumental response. Therefore, they cannot learn that they will be rewarded for responding on occasions when they remember not having been reinforced on preceding trials. Nonreinforced trials during extinction therefore do not motivate them to continue responding.

Some have regarded frustration theory and sequential theory as competing explanations of the partial-reinforcement extinction effect. However, since the two mechanisms were originally proposed, a very large and impressive body of evidence has been obtained in support of each theory. Therefore, we cannot regard one of the theories as correct and the other as incorrect. Rather, the two theories point out two different ways in which partial reinforcement can promote responding during extinction. In some situations one or the other mechanism may be operative; in other cases, both processes could be contributing to persistent responding in extinction.

Concurrent Schedules: The Study of Choice

The reinforcement schedules we have discussed thus far have involved an analysis of the relation between occurrences of a particular response and reinforcement of that response. However, the study of situations in which only one response is being measured is not likely to provide us with a complete understanding of behavior. Animal and human behavior involves a great deal more than just the repetition of individual responses. Even in a simple situation such as a Skinner box, organisms engage in a variety of activities and are continually choosing between the various responses they are able to perform. Furthermore, the occurrence of a particular response depends to a great extent on the availability of other response alternatives. A teenager may trim the neighbor's grass for $25 if the sky is overcast and his friends are out of town. However, if the weather is good and his friends are home, he is more likely to spend the afternoon at the beach with them. We are constantly having to make choices about what to do. Should we go to the movies or stay at home and study? Should we go shopping tonight or watch television tonight and go shopping tomorrow? Understanding the mechanisms of response choice is fundamental to the understanding of behavior because the choices organisms make determine the occurrence of individual responses.

The choice situations available to animals and people can be very complex. For example, a person may have a choice of 12 different responses (reading the newspaper, watching television, going for a walk, playing with the dog, and the like), each of which produces a different type of reinforcer according to a different reinforcement schedule. Analyzing all the factors that control the individual's behavior in such a situation would be formidable, if not impossible. Therefore, psychologists have begun experimental investigations of the mechanisms of choice by studying simpler situations. The simplest choice situation is one in which the subject has two response alternatives and each response is followed by a reinforcer according to some schedule of reinforcement.

Historically, much of the research on choice behavior has been conducted using mazes, particularly the T maze. Choice can be measured by the frequency with which the subjects turn to the left or right. In a classic paper entitled "The Determiners of Behavior at a Choice Point," Tolman (1938) advanced the argument that all behavior is essentially choice behavior. The choice may be one response or another or, more simply, responding or not responding. (For a good review of the choice experiments using T mazes, see Woodworth & Schlosberg, 1954.)

More recent approaches to the study of choice use Skinner boxes equipped with two manipulanda, such as two response levers. In the typical experiment, responding on each manipulandum is reinforced on some schedule of reinforcement. The two schedules are in effect at the same time and the subject is free to switch from one manipulandum to the other. This type of procedure is called a **concurrent schedule.** Concurrent schedules of reinforcement allow for continuous measures of choice because the subject is free to change back and forth between the response alternatives. Preference (choice) is measured by the rates of response on each manipulandum or the time spent responding on each.

Figure 6.5 shows an example of a concurrent schedule for pigeons. The experimental chamber has two response keys. If the pigeon pecks the key on the left, it receives food reinforcers according to a variable-interval 60-second schedule. Pecks on the right key produce food reinforcers according to a fixed-ratio 10 schedule. The animal is free to peck either response key at any time. The point of the experiment is to see how the animal distributes its pecks on the two keys and how the schedule of reinforcement on each key influences its choices.

On some concurrent schedules, particularly those involving interval-schedule components, the pigeon may be reinforced for the very first peck it makes after switching from one key to the other. This "accidental" reinforcement may encourage the subject to change frequently from one key to the other regardless of its preference for the reinforcement schedules on the two keys. Since the object is to measure preference, switching merely for the sake of switching has to be discouraged. This is accomplished by adding a **change-over delay** (abbreviated **COD**) to the choice procedure. A change-over delay specifies a certain amount of time after a switch

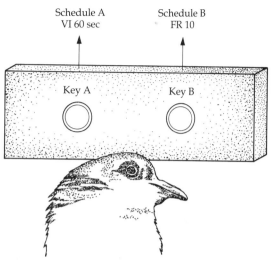

Figure 6.5 Diagram of a concurrent schedule. Pecks on key A are reinforced according to a VI 60-sec schedule of reinforcement. Pecks on key B are reinforced according to an FR 10 schedule of reinforcement.

from one response key to the other during which pecks are not reinforced. For example, a 5-second COD may be imposed, which ensures that responses occurring during the first 5 seconds after a switch are not reinforced. Such a contingency is usually sufficient to avoid the direct reinforcement of switching behavior.

Measures of Choice Behavior

The animal's choice in a concurrent schedule is reflected in the distribution of its behavior between two response alternatives. This can be measured in several ways. One common technique is to calculate the **relative rate of responding** on each alternative. The relative rate of responding on key A, for example, is calculated by dividing the response rate on key A by the total rate of responding (rate on key A plus rate on key B): $R_A/(R_A + R_B)$, where R_A is the rate of responding on key A and R_B is the rate on key B. If the subject pecks equally often on the two response keys, this ratio will be .5. If the rate of responding on key A is greater than the rate of responding on key B, the ratio will be greater than .5. If the rate of responding on key A is less than the rate of responding on key B, the ratio will be less than .5. The relative rate of responding on key B can be calculated in a comparable manner.

The Matching Law

As you might suspect, the distribution of the subject's behavior between the two response alternatives is greatly influenced by the reinforcement schedule for each alternative. For example, if the same variable-interval reinforcement schedule is available for each response alternative, as in a concurrent VI 60-sec VI 60-sec procedure, the pigeon will peck the two keys equally often. The relative rate of responding for pecks on each side will be .5. This result is intuitively reasonable. If the pigeon spent all its time pecking on one side, it would receive only the reinforcers programmed for that side. The subject can get more reinforcers by pecking on both sides. Since the VI reinforcement schedule available on each side is the same, there is no advantage in spending more time on one side than on the other.

By responding equally often on each side of a concurrent VI 60-sec VI 60-sec schedule, the subject will also earn reinforcers equally often on each side. The **relative rate of reinforcement** earned for each response alternative can be calculated in a manner comparable to the relative rate of response. For example, the relative rate of reinforcement for alternative A is the rate of reinforcement of response A divided by the total rate of reinforcement (the sum of the rate of reward earned on side A plus the rate of reward earned on side B). This is expressed in the formula $r_A/(r_A + r_B)$, where r_A and r_B represent the rates of reinforcement earned on each response alternative. On a concurrent VI 60-sec VI 60-sec schedule, the relative rate of reinforcement for each response alternative will be .5 because the subject earns rewards equally often on each side.

Effects of variations in the concurrent schedule. As we have seen, in the concurrent VI 60-sec VI 60-sec schedule, both the relative rate of responding and the relative rate of reinforcement for each response alternative are .5. Thus, the relative rate of responding is equal to the relative rate of reinforcement. Will this equality also occur if the two response alternatives are not reinforced according to the same schedule in the concurrent procedure? This important question was asked by Herrnstein (1961). Herrnstein studied the distribution of responses on various concurrent VI VI schedules in which the maximum total rate of reinforcement the subject could earn was 40 per hour. However, depending on the exact value of each VI schedule, different proportions of the total 40 rewards per hour could be obtained by each response alternative. For example, with a concurrent VI 6-min VI 2-min schedule, a VI 6-min schedule is in effect on the right key and a VI 2-min schedule on the left key. A maximum of 10 reinforcers per hour could be obtained by responding on the right, and a maximum of 30 reinforcers per hour could be obtained by responding on the left.

Herrnstein studied the effects of a wide variety of concurrent VI VI schedules. There was no constraint on which side the pigeons could peck. They could respond exclusively on one side if they chose, or they could distribute their pecks between the two sides in any proportion they chose. In fact, however, the pigeons distributed their responding in a uniform and predictable fashion. The results, summarized in Figure 6.6, indicate that the relative rate of responding on a given alternative was always very nearly equal to the relative rate of reinforcement earned on that alternative. If the pigeons earned a greater proportion of their reinforcers on alternative A, they made a greater proportion of their responses on alternative A. Thus, *the relative rate of responding on an alternative matched the relative rate of reinforcement on that alternative.* Similar findings have been obtained in a variety of situations, which encouraged Herrnstein to state the relation as a law of behavior.

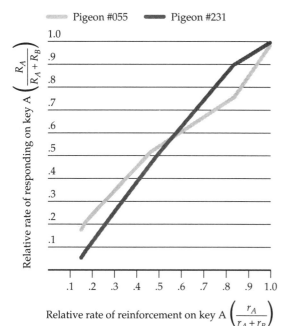

Relative rate of responding on key A $\left(\dfrac{R_A}{R_A + R_B}\right)$

Relative rate of reinforcement on key A $\left(\dfrac{r_A}{r_A + r_B}\right)$

Figure 6.6 Various combinations of VI schedules were tested whose combined reinforcement rate was 40 reinforcements per hour. Note that throughout the range of schedules, the relative rate of responding nearly equals (matches) the relative rate of reinforcement. *(From "Relative and Absolute Strength of Response as a Function of Frequency of Reinforcement" by R.J. Herrnstein, 1961,* Journal of the Experimental Analysis of Behavior, 4, *pp. 267–272. Copyright © 1961 by the Society for the Experimental Analysis of Behavior, Inc. Reprinted by permission.)*

It is called the **matching law** and is expressed as follows:

$$\frac{R_A}{R_A + R_B} = \frac{r_A}{r_A + r_B} \tag{6.1}$$

where R_A and R_B are the rates of responding on side A and side B, and r_A and r_B are the rates of reinforcement earned on each side.

Undermatching, overmatching, and response bias.   The matching law clearly indicates that choices are not made capriciously; they are, rather, an orderly function of rates of reinforcement. However, the precise characterization of the function is the subject of continuing research. (See reviews by Baum, 1979; Davison

& McCarthy, 1988; Wearden & Burgess, 1982; Williams, 1988.) Although the matching law has enjoyed considerable success and has guided much research over the past 20 years, relative rates of responding do not always match relative rates of reinforcement perfectly.

Deviations from matching can be measured quantitatively with the use of an alternate expression of the matching law. Equation (6.1) is algebraically equivalent to the equation

$$\frac{R_A}{R_B} = \frac{r_A}{r_B} \tag{6.2}$$

In this expression of the matching law, the relative rate of responding is represented simply as a ratio of the individual response rates (R_A/R_B); the relative rate of reinforcement is represented by a corresponding ratio (r_A/r_B). The idea that relative rates of responding match relative rates of reinforcement is stated simply as an equivalence between these two ratios.

Most instances in which choice behavior does not correspond perfectly to the matching relation can be accommodated by eq. (6.2) with the introduction of two parameters, *a* and *b*. This generalized form of the matching law (Baum, 1974) is as follows:

$$\frac{R_A}{R_B} = b \left(\frac{r_A}{r_B}\right)^a \tag{6.3}$$

The parameter *a* represents sensitivity of the choice behavior to the relative rates of reinforcement for the response alternatives. Perfect matching occurs if *a* is equal to 1.0. In that case, relative response rates are a direct function of relative rates of reinforcement. One type of deviation from perfect matching involves reduced sensitivity of the choice behavior to the relative rate of reinforcement. Such results are referred to as **undermatching** and can be accommodated by eq. (6.3) by making the exponent *a* less than 1.0. (Notice that if the exponent *a* is less than 1.0, the value of the term representing relative reinforcer rates, $(r_A/r_B)^a$, becomes smaller, indicating the reduced sensitivity to the relative rate of reinforcement.) In other instances, the relative rate of responding is more sensitive to the relative rate of reinforcement than what is predicted by perfect matching. Such outcomes are called **overmatching** and can be accommodated by eq. (6.3) by making the exponent *a* greater than 1.0. (In this case, the value of the term representing the relative rate of reinforcement, $(r_A/r_B)^a$, is increased, indicating the increased sensitivity to this factor.)

Choices are more likely to exhibit some lack of sensitivity to relative reinforcement rates than they are to exhibit enhanced sensitivity to reinforcement rates. Therefore, undermatching is found more often than overmatching. A common cause of undermatching is the use of an inadequate change-over delay (see Williams, 1988). As we noted earlier, without an adequate change-over delay, switching behavior may become directly reinforced. This reduces the independence of the two response alternatives and thereby reduces the subject's sensitivity to the relative rate of reinforcement. Making it more difficult for the subject to switch from one alternative to another helps to increase the independence of the two response alternatives. If switching from one schedule to the other is made sufficiently difficult, subjects tend to overmatch — they exhibit an exaggerated bias for the alternative with the higher rate of reinforcement (see, for example, Davison, 1991a).

In Herrnstein's original experiment (and in most others that have followed), the two alternative responses involved in the choice were similar activities (both involved pecking a response key). The reinforcer provided for each alternative was also the same (a short period of access to food). The parameter *b* in the generalized matching law becomes important when the response alternatives are different (one may be pecking a key and the other stepping on a treadle). Parameter *b* is also important when the reinforcer provided for the two responses is different. In the case of pigeons, one reinforcer may be buckwheat and the other hemp (seed). A preference (or

bias) for one response or one reinforcer over the other is represented as a change in the value of *b* (see Hanson & Green, 1986; Miller, 1976). In the absence of bias, *b* is equal to 1.0. Depending on the nature of the bias or preference, *b* will be greater or less than 1.0.

Extension of the matching law to other aspects of reinforcers. The matching relation has been extended to aspects of reinforcers other than their rate of presentation. For example, relative rate of responding has been found to be related to the relative amounts of each reinforcer (Catania, 1963). Under certain circumstances, matching also has been found with delays of reinforcement. Shorter relative delays of reinforcement have been associated with higher relative response rates (Chung & Herrnstein, 1967). Features of a reinforcer such as amount and delay can be considered to be aspects of the quality or value of the reinforcer. Larger and more immediate reinforcers presumably are of greater value. Such considerations have encouraged the suggestion that relative rates of responding reflect the relative value of reinforcers. However, more recent research has indicated that relative rates of responding depend not only on the relative rate, amount, and delay of reinforcement but also on absolute values of these various reinforcer features (Davison, 1988; Logue & Chavarro, 1987). For example, relative responding for the more immediate reinforcer has been shown to decrease as the absolute values of the alternative delays of reinforcement were decreased. These findings suggest that a complete characterization of reinforcer value will have to take into consideration not only relative features of reinforcers but also absolute features.

Extension of the matching law to simple reinforcement schedules. If the matching law represents a fundamental fact about behavior, then it should also characterize responding on simple schedules of reinforcement. In a simple reinforcement schedule, only one response manipulandum is provided (such as a lever or a key) and the subject is reinforced for responses on this manipulandum according to some program. The matching law describes the distribution of responses among several alternatives. How can it be applied to single-response situations? As Herrnstein (1970) pointed out, even single-response situations can be considered to involve a choice. The choice is between making the specified response (bar pressing or pecking a key, for example) and engaging in other possible activities (grooming, walking around, pecking the floor, sniffing holes in the experimental chamber). Subjects receive explicit reinforcers programmed for occurrences of the specific operant response. In addition, they no doubt receive intrinsic rewards for the other activities in which they engage. Hence, the total reinforcement in the situation has to be considered to include the programmed rewards and the intrinsic rewards. This type of analysis permits application of the matching law to single-response reinforcement schedules. Consider R_A to represent the rate of the specified operant response in the schedule, R_O the rate of the animal's other activities, r_A the rate of the explicit programmed reinforcement, and r_O the rate of the intrinsic reinforcement for the other activities. The matching law for single-response situations can be stated as follows:

$$\frac{R_A}{R_O} = \frac{r_A}{r_O} \qquad (6.4)$$

Extensions of the matching law to single-response situations have enjoyed some success (for example, Heyman & Monaghan, 1987). However, the results do not always fit the matching equation as well as one would like (Dougan & McSweeney, 1985; Warren-Boulton, Silberberg, Gray, & Ollom, 1985).

Mechanisms of the Matching Law

The matching law describes how subjects distribute their responses in a choice situation but does not explain what mechanisms are responsible for this response distribution. Relative rates of responding on two alternatives and relative rates of reward earned on those two response alternatives are both measures of the subject's behavior. What independent variable, or outside factor, is responsible for the choices described by the matching law? This question has stimulated extensive experimentation and theoretical debate (see Commons, Herrnstein, & Rachlin, 1982; Davison & McCarthy, 1988; Williams, 1988).

Matching and maximizing rates of reinforcement.   The most extensively investigated explanations of choice behavior are based on the intuitively reasonable idea that animals distribute their actions among response alternatives so as to receive the maximum amount of reinforcement possible in the situation. According to this idea of **maximizing**, subjects switch back and forth between response alternatives so as to receive as many reinforcers as they possibly can. The idea that subjects maximize reinforcement has been used to explain choice behavior at two levels of analysis. *Molecular theories* use the idea of maximizing to explain behavior at the level of individual choice responses; *molar theories* use it to explain overall levels of responding rather than individual choice responses.

Molecular theories.   According to molecular theories of maximizing, animals always choose whichever response alternative is most likely to be reinforced at the time. Shimp (1966, 1969) proposed an early version of molecular matching: that, in a concurrent schedule of reinforcement with two schedule alternatives, the subject switches from one schedule to the other as the probability of reinforcement for the other schedule increases. Consider, for example, a pigeon working on a concurrent VI VI schedule. As the pigeon pecks key A, the timer controlling reinforcement for key B is still operating. The longer the pigeon stays on key A, the greater the probability that the requisite interval for key B will elapse and reinforcement will become available for pecking key B. By switching, the pigeon can pick up the reinforcer on key B. Now, the longer it continues to peck key B, the more likely key A will become set for reinforcement. Shimp proposed that the matching relation is a by-product of prudent switching when the probability of reinforcement on the alternative response key becomes greater than the probability of reinforcement on the current response key.

Detailed studies of the patterns of switching from one to another response alternative have not always supported the molecular maximizing theory proposed by Shimp. Some of these studies have also shown that matching is possible in the absence of momentary maximizing (for example, Nevin, 1969, 1979). Other experiments have provided strong ev-

idence that momentary maximizing can occur in concurrent schedules (Hinson & Staddon, 1983a, 1983b). However, as Williams (1988) has pointed out, these experiments were conducted under circumstances that did not produce the matching relation. Therefore, the role of molecular maximizing in explaining the matching relation remains unresolved.

Molar theories.   Molar theories of maximizing assume that animals and people distribute their responses among various alternatives so as to maximize the amount of reinforcement they earn over the long run (for example, Rachlin, Battalio, Kagel, & Green, 1981; Rachlin, Green, Kagel, & Battalio, 1976). How long the "long run" is assumed to be is not clearly specified. However, in contrast to molecular

---

The Matching Law, Human Behavior, and Behavior Therapy

BOX **6.3**

The matching law and its implications have been found to apply to a wide range of human behavior situations, including pressing a button for monetary rewards, detecting signals on a screen in a vigilance task, conducting conversation with several persons in a group situation, engaging in self-injurious behavior maintained by social reinforcement, and working on assigned classroom tasks (see, for example, Baum, 1975; Conger & Killeen, 1974; Martens, Lochner, & Kelly, 1992; McDowell, 1982). In addition, the matching law has important conceptual and technological implications for applications of reinforcement principles (McDowell, 1982). According to the matching law, the tendency to make a particular response depends not only on the rate of reinforcement for that response but also on the rates of reinforcement available for alternative activities. This implies that analysis of a problematic behavior (truancy from school, for example) has to include not only consideration of the rewards available for that particular behavior but also rewards the subject can obtain in other ways. Thus, the matching law suggests that accurate assessment of a behavior problem requires consideration of the subject's full range of activities and sources of reinforcement. The matching law also suggests novel techniques for decreasing the frequency of a particular undesired behavior and increasing the frequency of a desired response. According to the matching law, the rate of an undesired response can be decreased by increasing the rate of reinforcement for other activities or by simply increasing the rate of "free" reinforcements available to the subject. Conversely, the matching law implies that the rate of a desired response can be increased by decreasing the rate of reinforcement available otherwise.

Implications of the matching law for behavior therapy are illustrated by the treatment of a mildly retarded 22-year-old man to decrease his oppositional behavior (McDowell, 1981). The person periodically became very uncooperative, and his oppositional behavior sometimes escalated to the point of assault. Given the potential for aggression in the situation, punishment was judged to be an unsuitable technique for decreasing the oppositional behavior. The undesired behavior was successfully treated by introducing a system that permitted the subject to earn positive reinforcement by engaging in a variety of other activities. He could earn points for performing various personal hygiene, job, and educational tasks and then exchange the points for money. Increasing the rate of reinforcement for other activities significantly decreased the rate of oppositional behavior.

theories, molar theories focus on aggregates of behavior over some period of time rather than on individual choice responses. Molar-maximizing theory was originally formulated to explain choice behavior in concurrent schedules involving ratio components. In concurrent ratio schedules, subjects rarely switch back and forth between response alternatives. Rather, they choose the ratio component that requires the fewest responses for reinforcement and respond only on this alternative. On a concurrent FR 20 FR 10 schedule, for example, the subject is likely to respond only on the FR 10 alternative. In this way it maximizes the rate of reinforcement it receives. Why should anyone work on the leaner FR 20 schedule if the same reinforcer can be earned with the same type of response on an FR 10 schedule?

Molar maximizing predicts that subjects will work to obtain the maximum possible amount of reinforcement in a situation. To determine whether they have achieved this requires determining what actually constitutes optimal performance. However, optimal performance is often difficult to determine. What constitutes optimal performance depends on how deliveries of the reinforcer are related to behavior, or, more generally, on the relation between behavior and the feedback consequences provided by the environment. As we noted earlier, this relation is the *feedback function*. The feedback function is easy to specify in the case of ratio schedules. Consider, for example, a fixed-ratio 10 schedule of reinforcement. The subject receives the reinforcer for every tenth response. Therefore, the rate of reinforcement (environmental feedback) will be directly related to the rate of responding. More specifically, the rate of reinforcement will be equal to one-tenth the rate of responding. This equation describes perfectly the feedback function, the relation between behavior and the consequences provided by the environment. With feedback functions for various ratio schedules determined in a comparable manner, figuring out

which response strategy provides the maximum amount of reinforcement is relatively easy for concurrent ratio schedules.

Whether subjects are obtaining the maximum possible reinforcement in the long run is much more difficult to determine in situations that involve complex relations between behavior and environmental feedback consequences. Consider, for example, fishing from a small pond—a fishing hole. What is the optimal rate of fishing? How frequently should you take fish out to obtain the maximum number of fish in the long run? To answer this question, we have to know the feedback function relating how many fish you can get to how rapidly you remove them. The feedback function is rather complicated and difficult to determine. If you remove fish at a high rate, you may soon deplete the pond, leaving no fish behind to breed and create the next generation. Therefore, a very high rate of fishing would provide a limited rate of return in the long run. If you fish very slowly, while you will not run into the problem of depletion, you may have a lower rate of return than what is optimally possible. An intermediate rate of fishing would produce the best outcome. The feedback function has to be known precisely to determine exactly which intermediate rate of responding will provide the maximum rate of return.

Evaluations of molar maximizing have been complicated by the difficulty of specifying feedback functions for various schedules of reinforcement. On a variable-interval schedule, for example, reinforcement depends not only on the occurrence of a response but on *when* that response is made. If the subject makes a lot of responses just after each reward, it will receive few rewards for a high response rate. By contrast, if it waits after each reward and then spaces out its responding more evenly, it will earn many more rewards for the same overall response rate. Therefore, the temporal distribution of behavior is important in specifying the feedback function for interval schedules. The relation between responding and reinforcement is even more complicated in concurrent schedules. Here we have to consider the distribution of responses between the two alternatives in addition to their individual characteristics.

In many situations, molar maximizing and matching formulations predict the same type of choice behavior. However, certain aspects of choice behavior present difficulties for maximizing theories. One difficulty arises from results of concurrent VI VI schedules of reinforcement. On a concurrent VI VI schedule, subjects can earn close to all of the available rewards on both schedules, provided they occasionally sample each alternative. Therefore, the total amount of reinforcement obtained on a concurrent VI VI schedule can be close to the same despite wide variations in how subjects distribute their behavior between the two alternatives. The matching relation is only one of many different possibilities that yield close to maximal rates of reinforcement. Because other response distributions can yield similar amounts of total reward, molar maximizing cannot explain why choice behavior is distributed so close to the matching relation on concurrent VI VI schedules and not in other equally effective ways (Heyman, 1983).

Another challenge for molar matching is provided by results of studies of concurrent variable-ratio and variable-interval schedules. On a variable-ratio schedule, the rate of reinforcement is directly related to the rate of responding. By contrast, on a variable-interval schedule, the subject has only to sample the schedule occasionally to obtain close to the maximum number of rewards. Given these differences in feedback relations for the two schedules, for maximum return on a concurrent VR VI schedule, subjects should concentrate their responses on the variable-ratio alternative and respond only occasionally on the variable-interval component. Evidence shows that animals do favor the VR component but not as strongly as molar maximizing

predicts (Baum, 1981; DeCarlo, 1985; Herrnstein & Heyman, 1979; Heyman & Herrnstein, 1986). (For other findings inconsistent with molar maximizing, see Davison & Kerr, 1989; Ettinger, Reid, & Staddon, 1987; Mazur & Vaughan, 1987; Zeiler, 1987.)

Possible interpretations of violations of molar maximizing. The available evidence clearly indicates that animals do not always respond in ways that maximize the benefits they reap from their efforts. Nevertheless, the hypothesis that choice is governed by molar maximizing has been too attractive for some investigators to abandon. Animals that respond so as to maximize reinforcers are presumably more successful in life than animals that do not respond optimally. Therefore, evolution should lead to the selection of behavioral processes that facilitate maximizing reinforcers. Based on such reasoning, one may accept the idea of molar maximizing as axiomatic. That is, regardless of the evidence, one may assume that animals respond so as to maximize reinforcers.

Given this assumption, how should we interpret evidence contrary to molar maximizing? If we assume that animals maximize reinforcers, then evidence to the contrary simply indicates that we have not calculated the benefits the animal derives from its choices correctly. One source of error may be the existence of previously unsuspected sources of reinforcement. Rachlin et al. (1981), for example, suggested that in addition to working for food reinforcement, the choices animals make are also governed by their interest in leisure. That is, nonresponding can have its own source of reinforcement (leisure), which is lost when the subject makes an instrumental response. In calculating optimal behavior, one has to consider not only food reinforcers earned but also how much leisure is thereby lost and the value of leisure time. However, if violations of molar maximizing are always attributed to incorrect analyses of what is optimal from the subject's perspective, the hypothesis of molar maximizing becomes impossible to disprove.

Another approach is to use molar maximizing as a guide to the study of the functions or benefits of behavior rather than treat it as a hypothesis, subject to verification or disproof (Rachlin, Green, & Tormey, 1988). This approach recognizes that not all aspects of a subject's behavior can occur in a way that will optimize all aspects of the environment. Instead of trying to prove whether maximizing is or is not a universal rule, maximizing is used as a tool with which to investigate the functions or benefits of behavior—to determine the circumstances under which subjects manage to optimize reinforcers and when they do not. With this approach, maximizing is not treated as a mechanism or process determining choice but as an analytical technique for the study of behavioral function. (We will return to this approach to maximizing in discussions of optimal foraging theory in Chapter 7.)

Melioration. Another mechanism used to explain choice behavior, **melioration,** was proposed in 1980 by Herrnstein and Vaughan (see also Vaughan, 1981, 1985). Melioration refers to bettering a situation. Herrnstein and Vaughan suggested that animals change from one response alternative to another to improve on the local rate of reinforcement they are receiving. Adjustments in the distribution of behavior between alternatives are assumed to continue until the subject is obtaining the same local rate of reward on all alternatives. It can be shown mathematically that when subjects distribute their responses so as to obtain the same local rate of reinforcement on each alternative, they are behaving in accordance with the matching law. Therefore, the mechanism of melioration results in matching.

To see how melioration works, consider a VI 1-min VI 3-min concurrent schedule. During the first hour of exposure to this schedule,

the subject will switch back and forth between the two alternatives and may end up spending a total of 30 minutes responding on each component, earning all of the available rewards. On a VI 1-min schedule, 60 rewards are available in one hour. If the subject manages to get all of these during the course of spending a total of 30 minutes on the VI 1-min schedule, the local rate of reinforcement on the VI 1-min schedule will be 60 rewards for 30 minutes of responding, or 120 per hour. On a VI 3-min schedule, 20 rewards are available in one hour. If the subject gets all of these during the course of spending a total of 30 minutes on the VI 3-min schedule, its local rate of reinforcement on the VI 3-min component will be 20 rewards in 30 minutes, or 40 per hour. Since the local rate of reinforcement on the VI 1-min schedule (120/hr) is much higher than on the VI 3-min schedule (40/hr), the subject will shift its behavior in favor of the VI 1-min alternative. However, if it shifts too far and spends too much time on the VI 1-min schedule and samples the VI 3-min schedule only rarely, it may be rewarded every time it pecks the VI 3-min key. This would make the local rate of reward on the VI 3-min key higher than the local rate of reward on the VI 1-min alternative, with a resulting shift in favor of the VI 3-min schedule. Such shifts back and forth will continue until the local rates of reinforcement earned on the two alternatives are equal.

The melioration mechanism is related to previously proposed mechanisms of the matching law in that it involves shifts in behavior to more favorable rates of return. It provides an analysis of choice behavior at a level somewhere between molecular and molar theories of maximizing. Molecular theories emphasize control by the probability of reinforcement at a given moment. If the momentary probability of reinforcement is higher on another alternative, the subject is assumed to switch to that alternative at that moment. Melioration is stated in terms of the *local rate of reinforcement* rather than in terms of momentary probability of reinforcement. Thus, it considers outcomes over a longer term than molecular maximizing theories. But it is not concerned with overall rates of reinforcement, as molar theories of maximizing are.

Although tests of the melioration hypothesis have yielded confirmatory evidence (for example, McSweeney, Melville, Buck, & Whipple, 1983), the hypothesis has also encountered some major difficulties (see Williams, 1988). Therefore, investigators are continuing their exploration of alternative approaches to explaining how organisms choose between different sources of reinforcement (for example, McDowell & Wood, 1985; Myerson & Hale, 1988; Staddon, 1988).

Concurrent-Chain Schedules: The Study of Complex Choice

In the choice situations described in the previous section, animals had two response alternatives and could switch from one to the other at any time. Many choice situations outside the laboratory are of this type. If you are eating a dinner of roast beef, vegetables, and mashed potatoes with gravy, you can switch from one food to another at any time during the meal. You can similarly switch back and forth between radio stations you listen to or parts of the newspaper you read. However, other situations involve much more complex choices. Choosing one alternative may make other alternatives unavailable, and the choice may involve assessing complex, long-range goals. Should you go to college and get a degree in engineering or start in a full-time job without a college degree? One cannot switch back and forth between these two alternatives frequently. Furthermore, to make the decision, you need to consider more than merely whether you enjoy taking engineering courses more or less than you enjoy holding a job. This choice also involves long-range goals. A degree in engineering may enable you to get

a higher paying job eventually, but it may require significant economic sacrifices initially. Getting a job would enable you to make money sooner, but in the long run you might not be able to earn as much money.

Obviously, we cannot conduct experiments that directly involve such complex choices as choosing between college and employment. However, simplified analogous questions may be posed to laboratory animals. For example, does a pigeon prefer to work on an FR 10 schedule of reinforcement for 15 minutes, or does it prefer to work on a VI 60-sec schedule for the same amount of time? Answers to such questions can be obtained with the use of **concurrent-chain schedules.** A concurrent-chain schedule of reinforcement involves at least two components (see Figure 6.7). In the first component, the subject is allowed to choose between two alternatives by making one of two responses. In the example diagramed in Figure 6.7, the pigeon makes its choice by pecking either response key A or response key B. Pecking key A produces alternative A, the opportunity to peck key A for 15 minutes on an FR 10 schedule of reinforcement. If the pigeon pecks key B at the beginning of the cycle, it thereby produces alternative B, which is the opportunity to peck key B for 15 minutes on a VI 60-sec schedule. Responding on either key A or key B during the initial component of the schedule does not produce reinforcement. The opportunity for reinforcement occurs only after the initial choice has been made and the pigeon has produced one or the other terminal component. Another important feature of the concurrent-chain schedule is that once the subject has made a choice between A and B, it is stuck with that choice until the end of the terminal link of the schedule (in our hypothetical example, for 15 minutes). Thus, concurrent-chain schedules involve *choice with commitment.*

The pattern of responding that occurs in the terminal component of a concurrent-chain schedule is characteristic of whatever sched-

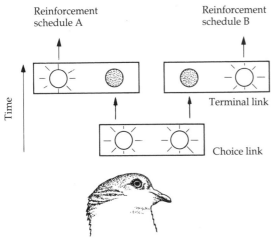

Figure 6.7 Diagram of a concurrent-chain schedule. Pecking key A in the choice link puts into effect reinforcement schedule A in the terminal link. Pecking key B in the choice link puts into effect reinforcement schedule B in the terminal link.

ule of reinforcement is in effect during that component. In our example, if the pigeon has produced alternative A, its pattern of pecking during the terminal component will be similar to the usual response pattern in FR 10 schedules. If the pigeon has produced alternative B, its pattern of pecking during the terminal component will be characteristic of a VI 60-sec schedule.

The animal's choice between the schedules of reinforcement in effect in the terminal components of a concurrent-chain schedule is measured by the proportions in which it chooses key A and key B during the initial choice component. Studies of concurrent-chain schedules focus on how choice in the initial component of the chain is determined by the schedules of reinforcement in effect in the terminal components. In this manner, concurrent-chain schedules can help answer many interesting questions about how various aspects of reinforcement combine to influence choice. For example, the early work of Autor (1969) has led to the extensive use of the concurrent-chain methodology to study conditioned reinforcement (see recent studies by

Dunn & Spetch, 1990; Fantino, Freed, Preston, & Williams, 1991; Preston & Fantino, 1991; Williams & Dunn, 1991). In studies of conditioned reinforcement, each terminal link is associated with a different exteroceptive stimulus (different colored lights, for example). These exteroceptive stimuli can serve as conditioned reinforcers for responding during the choice component of the schedule. Choice in the initial link is determined not only by primary reinforcement (food, for example) provided in the terminal link but also by conditioned reinforcement provided by the exteroceptive stimuli associated with each terminal link.

Concurrent-chain schedules also can be used to determine the relative value of schedules of reinforcement. We noted earlier, in discussing extensions of the matching law to other aspects of reinforcers, that simple concurrent schedules have been used to assess the relative value of reinforcers. For example, the relative value of a large as opposed to a small amount of food may be measured in terms of the relative rate of responding that occurs when the large and small rewards are each available at the same time (concurrently) on a VI 30-sec schedule. In an analogous fashion, relative rates of responding on key A versus key B in the choice link of a concurrent-chain schedule can be used to measure the relative value of the reinforcement schedules that are in effect on key A versus key B in the terminal link of the concurrent chain. A preference for responding on key A as opposed to key B during the choice link may be taken as evidence that the terminal schedule on key A is of greater value to the subject than the terminal schedule on key B.

One particularly interesting question concerning the relative value of reinforcement schedules is whether subjects prefer a predictable source of reinforcement over one that is unpredictable. Do animals play it safe and put greater value on predictable schedules, or do they prefer unpredictable or risky schedule alternatives? Furthermore, under what circumstances are animals *risk averse,* selecting the safe and predictable alternative, and when are they *risk prone,* preferring the unpredictable alternative? Many life decisions involve a choice between predictable and unpredictable situations. Concurrent-chain schedules are ideal for investigating the processes responsible for choices in such situations.

In one experiment (Hamm & Shettleworth, 1987, Experiment 2), pigeons were always reinforced with 8 food pellets for responding on one terminal-link schedule. Responding on the other terminal link schedule resulted in either 16 pellets or zero pellets. These two possible outcomes occurred equally often on the second terminal link. Thus, across trials, the average amount of food reinforcement was identical on the two schedules, but one schedule was predictable whereas the other one was not. The pigeons were sensitive to this aspect of the schedules and consistently preferred the more reliable source of reinforcement. They were risk averse, which is the typical outcome obtained in such experiments.

Can animals be made risk prone by making the unreliable reinforcer more attractive even though it occurs less often? Will animals prefer a large unpredictable source of reinforcement over a smaller but predictable reinforcer? Evidently the answer is yes. In one study (Hastjarjo, Silberberg, & Hursh, 1990b), rats faced a choice between two response levers. If they selected the "risky" lever, they received 15 food pellets one-third of the time and no pellets the rest of the time; if they selected the "safe" lever, they got 3 pellets every time. Faced with such choices, the rats usually selected the risky lever (see also Mazur, 1988).

Another interesting application of concurrent-chain schedules is the experimental investigation of self-control. As every dieter knows, self-control is often a matter of choosing the greater delayed reward (being thin) over the immediate smaller reward (eating the piece of cake). When the piece of cake is in plain view, it is very difficult to choose the delayed reward. Rachlin and Green (1972) set up a laboratory analog of self-control with pigeons. When given a direct choice between an immediate small reward or a delayed large reward, pigeons often chose the small immediate reward. However, under certain circumstances they could be trained to exhibit self-control. The basic concurrent-chain schedule used in this research is shown in Figure 6.8. In the terminal components of the schedule, responding was rewarded by either immediate access to a small amount of grain (alternative A) or access to a large amount of grain that was delayed by 4 seconds (alternative B). The pigeons could choose between these two alternatives by pecking either key A or key B during the initial component of the schedule.

Under what circumstances did the pigeons show self-control? Everyone who diets knows that it is easier to refuse a piece of cake that is to be eaten at tomorrow's luncheon than to refuse one that is to be eaten in the next few minutes. A similar effect occurred in the pigeons. The subjects were more likely to choose the delayed large reward over the immediate small reward if the terminal components of the concurrent-chain schedule were delayed after the pigeons made their initial choice. This was accomplished by requiring the subjects to respond 10 times on the choice keys instead of only once during the initial component of the schedule.

The phenomenon of self-control as illustrated by the Rachlin and Green experiment has stimulated much research and theorizing. Numerous investigators have found, in agreement with Rachlin and Green, that preferences shift in favor of the more remote large reward as subjects are made to wait longer to receive either reward after making their choice. If rewards are delivered shortly after a choice response, subjects generally favor a more immediate small reward over a more remote large reward. However, if a constant delay is added to the delivery of both rewards, subjects are more likely to show self-control and favor the more remote large reward. This

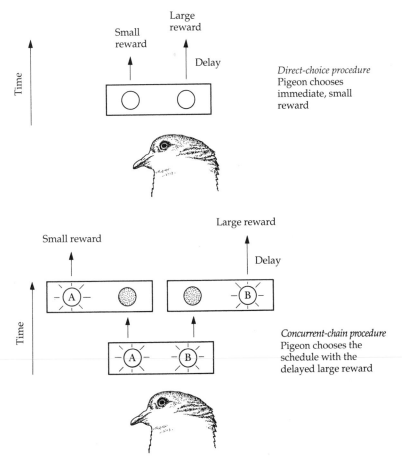

Figure 6.8 Diagram of the experiment by Rachlin and Green (1972) on self-control. The direct-choice procedure is shown at the top; the concurrent-chain procedure, at the bottom.

crossover in preference has been obtained in experiments with both people and nonhuman subjects and thus represents a general property of choice behavior. (For a review, see Logue, 1988b.)

Theoretical efforts to explain choice behavior in self-control paradigms have been based on the principles of matching and maximizing. As we noted earlier, the matching approach assumes that the value of a reinforcer is directly related to its size or amount and inversely related to how long the subject has to wait to obtain the reinforcer. The longer the subject has to wait for the reinforcer, the more

its value is discounted. These relationships are illustrated in Figure 6.9 for a small and a large reward. The size of the reinforcer is represented by the height of the vertical bars. Time is represented by distance along the horizontal axis. Decay of reinforcer value as a function of time is illustrated by the curves that decrease toward the left from each reinforcer. Notice that the figure is set up so that the large reinforcer is given later than the small one.

Figure 6.9 also identifies two points in time, T_1 and T_2, before delivery of the small and large rewards. The waiting time to reward delivery is much less for T_1 than for T_2. The reward-value curves shown in Figure 6.9 predict the choice behavior that is typically observed in self-control experiments. When the waiting time for reward delivery is short (T_1), the value of the small reward is greater than the value of the large reward. Hence, subjects will choose the small reward. By contrast, when waiting time is long (T_2), the value of the large reward is greater than the value of the small reward, and the subject will choose the large reward. Thus, the model depicted in Figure 6.9 predicts the crossover from preference for the small reward to preference for the more remote large reward

Can Self-Control Be Trained?

BOX **6.4**

A person who cannot tolerate the delay involved in obtaining certain large rewards has to forgo obtaining those reinforcers. Self-control, or the selection of a larger delayed reward, is often a sensible strategy. In fact, some have suggested that self-control is a critical component of socialization and emotional adjustment. This raises an interesting question: Can self-control be trained? The answer seems to be yes.

Training people with delayed reward appears to have generalized effects in increasing their tolerance for delayed reward. In one study (Eisenberger & Ardonetto, 1986), second- and third-grade students in a public elementary school were first tested for self-control by being asked whether they wanted to get 2¢ immediately or 3¢ at the end of the day. Children who elected the immediate reward were given 2¢. If the delayed reward was elected, 3¢ was placed in a cup to be given to the child later. The procedure was repeated eight times to complete the pretest. The students then received three sessions of training with either immediate or delayed reward. During each session, various problems were presented: one involved counting objects on a card, another was a picture-memory task, and the third was a shape-matching task. For half the students, correct responding was reinforced immediately with 2¢. For the remaining students, correct responses resulted in 3¢ being placed in a cup that was given to the child at the end of the day. After the third training session, preference for small immediate versus larger delayed reward was measured as in the pretest. Provided that the training tasks involved low effort, the children who had been trained with delayed reward were more likely to select the larger delayed reward during the posttest than were the children who had been trained with small immediate reinforcement. Thus, the experiment provided evidence of generalized self-control resulting from training with delayed reinforcement.

Other studies have demonstrated that gradually changing the delay of reinforcement can promote self-control choice responding. In one study (Logue, Rodriguez, Peña-Correal, & Mauro, 1984), pigeons were first trained using a procedure in which both large and small reward (6-second and 2-second access to food, respectively) were delayed 6 seconds after the choice response. Under these conditions, the subjects selected the large reward nearly exclusively. The delay to the smaller reward then was gradually reduced, with the hope that the birds would continue to select the larger reward (which was now delayed more). The procedure was effective in promoting selection of the delayed large reinforcer over the smaller more immediate reinforcer (see also Mazur & Logue, 1978). However, even with this special training, the birds ended up selecting the smaller reward on a majority of the trials when the smaller reward was delivered immediately.

More impressive learning of self-control was obtained in a study of impulsive or hyperactive preschool children (Schweitzer & Sulzer-Azaroff, 1988). Instead of starting with both small and large rewards delivered after a long delay, the children were first trained with small and large rewards presented immediately after the choice response. Under these conditions, the children quickly learned to choose the large reward nearly exclusively. A delay was then introduced in the delivery of the large reward. Each time a child adjusted to the delay and continued to select the large reward, the delay was increased. The small reward continued to be delivered immediately. The training procedure was effective in increasing the self-control behavior of 4 of the 5 children in the study. By gradually introducing increasing delays in the delivery of the large reward, the children's choice of the large reward was maintained. This resulted in increased choice of the large delayed reward over the small immediate reinforcer in 4 of the 5 children.

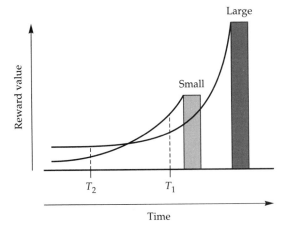

Figure 6.9 Hypothetical relations between reward value and waiting time to reward delivery for a small reward and a large reward presented some time later.

as the waiting time for both rewards is increased.

The approach based on the matching law illustrated in Figure 6.9 accurately characterizes the results of many animal experiments (see Logue, 1988b). Various outcomes can be accommodated by changing the rates of decay of the reinforcer-value functions. For example, in some situations animals seem to be more sensitive to reinforcer amounts than to reinforcer delays, and this increases the likelihood of their choosing the large delayed reward (see Box 6.4). Such cases can be accommodated by assuming that the decay functions for reinforcer value do not drop off as rapidly as the functions shown in Figure 6.9.

In contrast to the animal studies, which are well characterized by the generalized matching law, experiments conducted with normal adult humans typically have yielded results that are better explained in terms of maximizing (for example, King & Logue, 1987; Logue, King, Chavarro, & Volpe, 1990; Logue, Peña-Correal, Rodriguez, & Kabela, 1986). The reinforcer in these studies was the accumulation of points on a counter, which were exchanged for money at the end of the experimental session. The adult humans were

much more likely than pigeons to select the large delayed reward. The results observed across a variety of experimental manipulations could be explained more parsimoniously by assuming that choice of the large delayed reward was motivated by an effort to maximize obtained reinforcers rather than an effort to match choices to relative reinforcer value (see also Sonuga-Barke, Lea, & Webley, 1989a).

Interestingly, preference for the large delayed reward in humans emerges with age. Four-year-old children are more likely to respond like pigeons, selecting the small immediate reward, than are 6- or 9-year-old children, who exclusively select the large delayed reward (Sonuga-Barke, Lea, & Webley, 1989b). The bases of these species and developmental differences remain to be determined.

Concluding Comments

The basic principle of instrumental conditioning is very simple: reinforcement increases (and punishment decreases) the future probability of an instrumental response. However, as we have seen, the experimental analysis of instrumental behavior can be rather intricate. Many important aspects of instrumental behavior are determined by the schedule of reinforcement. There are numerous schedules by which responses can be reinforced. Reinforcement can depend on how many responses have occurred, the passage of time, or the rate of responding. Furthermore, more than one reinforcement schedule may be available to the subject at the same time. The pattern of instrumental behavior, as well as choices between various response alternatives, is strongly determined by the schedule of reinforcement that is in effect. Reinforcement schedules also determine the extent to which subjects persist in responding when rewards become unavailable. These various findings have told us a great deal about how reinforcement controls behavior in a variety of circumstances.

7 Reinforcement: Theories and Experimental Analysis

Chapter 7 is devoted to a detailed discussion of the mechanisms whereby reinforcement increases the future probability of certain responses. Following a discussion of some fundamental issues in reinforcement theory, we will consider two approaches to a theory of reinforcement. The first approach considers reinforcement to be the presentation of a special kind of stimulus and attempts to identify the special properties of reinforcing stimuli. The second approach views reinforcement as behavioral regulation and is concerned with how instrumental contingencies produce a redistribution in the actions of the organism.

Chapters 5 and 6 described how instrumental behavior is influenced by various kinds of experimental manipulations. This research has provided much information about the characteristics of instrumental behavior in a variety of circumstances. The present chapter will analyze the mechanisms of reinforcement in greater detail. We will consider why certain events are effective reinforcers and what kind of learning takes place during the course of instrumental conditioning. The answers to these questions involve some of the most exciting and important aspects of behavior theory today.

We are witnessing a major reorientation in how theoreticians conceptualize the mechanisms of reinforcement. Early investigators followed Thorndike in assuming that reinforcement involved the strengthening of a particular response by the presentation of a special kind of stimulus (a reinforcer) after occurrences of the response. Thus, the emphasis was on changes in a single response brought about by delivery of a particular type of stimulus. More recent conceptualizations of the reinforcement process take a broader view of the animal's behavior. They recognize that reinforcement involves much more than the presentation of a stimulus. Reinforcing events usually also involve an activity of some sort, such as eating a food pellet. In addition, modern views are concerned not only with changes in the reinforced response that results from instrumental conditioning but also with changes in the activities related to the reinforcer. Thus, instrumental conditioning is viewed as creating a new distribution or balance of activities, not just as strengthening a particular response. This shift in perspective has involved a change from thinking about reinforcement as a form of physiological regulation to thinking about reinforcement as a form of behavioral regulation.

Fundamental Issues in Reinforcement Theory

If we were to name all the stimuli that have been used as reinforcers, our list would be very long. Included would be familiar reinforcers, such as food, water, and access to a social partner. The list would also include oxygen and a comfortable temperature, as well as less obvious things such as diet drinks, watching a moving electric train, playing pinball, running, and even exposure to electrical shock. We might also include reinforcers that are difficult to define, such as the approval of others, self-satisfaction, and the like. What do all these things have in common that makes them effective reinforcers? We might presume that where there is reinforcement, there is pleasure. Thorndike used a slightly different wording. In the law of effect, he described what we now call reinforcing stimuli as events that produce "satisfying states of affairs" (see p. 125). What, though, is a satisfying state of affairs? Or, what is pleasurable? It is tempting to define *pleasure* or *satisfying state of affairs* as any event or stimulus that the subject will work for—in other words, whatever will reinforce behavior. However, this makes the definition of a reinforcer circular. We cannot define a reinforcer as something that provides pleasure if we define something that provides pleasure as a reinforcer. What is needed is a definition of *pleasure* or *satisfying state of affairs* that is not stated in terms of a reinforcement effect.

One way out of the circularity in the answer to What makes reinforcers reinforce? is to restrict the scope of the question. Instead of trying to answer the question for all circumstances, we can try to provide an answer for only a particular reinforcing stimulus that is used to strengthen a particular response in a unique situation. For example, what makes food an effective reinforcer for lever pressing in rats placed in a Skinner box? A circular answer to this question would be that food reinforces lever pressing because it is a reinforcer in that situation. Obviously, this is not an informative statement. Meehl (1950) suggested that the **principle of transsituationality** can be of help in cases like this. The principle of transsituationality assumes that reinforcers are effective in strengthening behavior in a variety of situations. Food, for example, is expected to reinforce not only lever pressing in a Skinner box but also running in a runway and swimming in a tank of water. Given such transsituationality, one can use the outcome of the effects of reinforcement in one situation to explain the effects in another. Thus, we can say that food strengthens behavior in a lever-press experiment because food has been identified as a reinforcer in a runway experiment. This explanation is not circular. The reinforcing properties of food are identified in a situation (the runway experiment) that is different from the situation in which we are trying to explain the reinforcement effect (the lever-press experiment).

Although the principle of transsituationality helps to avoid circularity, it is not entirely satisfactory. Assume that we use the fact that food is an effective reinforcer in a runway experiment to explain why food strengthens behavior in a lever-press experiment. Such an explanation would not provide much insight into behavior. The fundamental question of why reinforcers work would remain unanswered until we knew why food is an effective reinforcer in a runway experiment. Another weakness of this approach is that reinforcers are not always effective across a broad range of situations. As we discussed in Chapter 5, there are serious constraints on operant conditioning. A reinforcer that is effective in strengthening one response may not be useful in reinforcing other types of behavior.

The theories of reinforcement that we will examine in the coming pages represent a more analytical approach to the question of what

makes a reinforcer work. Basically, there are two central problems. One problem is to determine the essential characteristics of reinforcers. If these were known, one could identify reinforcers readily by the presence or absence of the critical characteristics. The second problem is describing the mechanism involved. That is, what does the reinforcer do, and how does it do it?

The theories of reinforcement we will discuss analyze the characteristics of reinforcers and the mechanisms of reinforcement in different ways. We will begin by discussing traditional and rather familiar ideas that conceptualize reinforcement as the presentation of special types of stimuli. Some theories of this type also view reinforcement as satisfying particular physiological needs. We will then discuss reinforcement conceptualized as behavioral regulation, contributing to the satisfaction of behavioral "goals" or "needs."

Reinforcement as Stimulus Presentation

Traditionally, reinforcement has been viewed as the presentation of particular types of stimuli contingent on performance of a particular instrumental response. Various suggestions have been made about the special characteristics a stimulus must have for it to serve as a reinforcer. However, all theories of reinforcement that consider the reinforcer as a stimulus share the view that reinforcement "strengthens" the instrumental response. The various conceptions differ on how this is accomplished. Thorndike, for example, proposed that "strengthening" of the instrumental response is a secondary result of the formation of an association between the instrumental response and the stimulus context in which the response is performed. By contrast, Skinner placed much greater emphasis on the relationship between the instrumental response and the reinforcer. He suggested that reinforcement strengthens whatever behavior happens to occur just before delivery of the reinforcer. We will discuss these issues in greater detail in Chapter 10.

Physiological Homeostasis and Drive Reduction

In much of the research on instrumental learning, biologically important stimuli such as food and water are used as reinforcers. Subjects are first deprived of a substance such as food; the return of this substance then serves as the reinforcer. Because these stimuli are necessary to the animal's survival, many theories of reinforcement have emphasized physiological factors in reinforcement.

Some reinforcement theorists have described the procedures of deprivation and reinforcement as two opposing processes that alter the organism's physiological state. The concept of **physiological homeostasis** is useful here to describe the results of these two processes. By *physiological homeostasis* we mean that state of the organism in which all physiological systems are in proper balance. Deprivation procedures upset this balance. By contrast, reinforcement returns the organism to homeostasis — the balanced state. The motivation to perform the instrumental response arises from the shift away from homeostasis that is caused by deprivation. According to this view, reinforcement works because organisms always seek to return to homeostasis.

One of the first theorists to make extensive use of a physiological homeostatic mechanism was Clark Hull. (For a contemporary review of Hullian theory, see Amsel & Rashotte, 1984.) Hull believed that the deprivation procedures used in experiments that employ food and water as reinforcers create a biological drive state. Reinforcers were assumed to have the common characteristic of reducing this drive state. Since the mechanism of reinforcement involved reducing a drive state, the view was called **drive-reduction theory.** According to drive-reduction theory, each time the subject obtains the reinforcer, it moves a step closer to

homeostasis. The inborn tendency of the organism to return to homeostasis is the motivation for the response. Therefore, according to Hull, the degree of drive determines (in part) the degree of responding.

Physiological needs or drives are assumed to be related to elements of the environment that are necessary for survival of the individual. Therefore, need or drive states presumably can be identified with physiology experiments. Consistent with this view, food, water, and return to a more comfortable temperature have all been used successfully as instrumental reinforcers.

Primary Motivation and Incentive Motivation

Drive-reduction theory exemplifies the fact that the analysis of reinforcement is often cast as part of the broader field of motivation. Reinforcement is one way of forcing behavior to change. Where, though, does the force originate? Sometimes the force seems to lie within the organism as a drive state. Motivation induced by a drive state is called **primary motivation.** Motivation for behavior may also come from the reinforcer itself. Sometimes just the presence of food, water, or a sexual partner can trigger behavior. Such motivation created by the reinforcer itself is called **incentive motivation.**

For example, in a recent T-maze experiment conducted with laboratory rats, 300 mg of food was found to be a more effective reinforcer if it was given as four 75-mg pellets than if it was given as one 300-mg pellet to equally food-deprived subjects (Capaldi, Miller, & Alptekin, 1989). Given the equivalent levels of food deprivation, such results cannot be explained in terms of differences in drive level and illustrate the importance of incentive motivation. Evidently, four food pellets are more attractive to hungry rats than a single large pellet that contains the same amount of food.

We thus have two possible sources of motivation: (1) the drive state and (2) the incentive properties of the reinforcer. The role of each of these sources has been discussed at length in the psychology literature (see Bolles, 1975). At present it appears that reinforcement is neither solely drive reduction nor solely incentive motivation. Both aspects play a role. Miller and Kessen (1952), for example, compared the reinforcement effects of food delivered directly into the stomach through a fistula and food consumed in the normal fashion. They found that fistula feeding could serve effectively as a reinforcer. Drive reduction from fistula feeding appears to be sufficient. However, the effect was not as powerful as that produced by normal eating. Normal eating may have been more effective in increasing the instrumental response because it provided both drive-reduction reinforcement and incentive motivation.

Sensory Reinforcement

The distinction between primary and incentive motivation illustrates that drive-reduction mechanisms are not sufficient to explain all reinforcement effects. External stimuli also have an important role in the motivation of instrumental behavior. Other lines of evidence suggest that drive reduction may not even be necessary for reinforcement. Sheffield, Wulff, and Backer (1951), for example, demonstrated that a male rat will run down a runway in order to gain access to a female even though it is not allowed to ejaculate with the female. In this case, the instrumental behavior was performed to obtain a stimulus without drive reduction. In fact, the drive level or excitement of the male was probably increased by encounter with the female without copulation. Thus, a reinforcement effect was obtained in the face of an increase rather than a decrease in drive.

The lack of importance of drive reduction in reinforcement is also illustrated by numerous examples of the reinforcing effects of stimuli that are not biologically or physiologically significant in any obvious sense. One

prominent reinforcement theorist has commented that "virtually anything can act as a reward in suitable circumstances" (Berlyne, 1969, p. 182). Activities such as watching a moving electric train can be used to reinforce the behavior of monkeys. Turning on a light, opportunity for exploration, and drinking a saccharin solution, which has no nutritive value and therefore does not reduce a physiological need, can also be effective rewards. Motivation of behavior by the sensory properties of stimuli is a common human experience. Fine works of art and music, for example, provide primarily sensory reinforcement.

To explain the effectiveness of sensory reinforcers, one might hypothesize the existence of corresponding drive states. For example, one might hypothesize the existence of a curiosity drive to explain the reinforcing effect of watching a moving electric train. However, this approach is not very productive. The only evidence for the existence of a curiosity drive is that moving trains and the like are effective reinforcers. This reintroduces the same type of circularity problem we discussed earlier. We would be saying that a moving train reinforces behavior because it reduces the curiosity drive and that we know that there is a curiosity drive because the sight of a moving train reinforces behavior. Drive-reduction theory compels us to add an item to our list of drives each time we find a reinforcer that does not satisfy a biological drive that has been identified by other means. However, if we do this, we will not have a way to identify reinforcers independent of the outcome of instrumental conditioning. Therefore, the drive-reduction hypothesis has not been entirely successful in specifying a common feature of all reinforcers independent of their reinforcement effects.

Brain-Stimulation Reinforcement and Motivation

Two physiological psychologists, James Olds and Peter Milner, implanted electrodes in the septal area of the brain of rats. The rats were then observed in a large compartment where they were given brief, mild electrical pulses to the brain through the electrodes. The rats tended to move toward the area of the chamber where they had last received the brain stimulation. Olds and Milner then connected a response lever to the electrical stimulator and discovered that the rats would press the lever at extremely high rates for many hours to receive the brain stimulation. The phenomenon was called **intracranial self-stimulation** (Olds & Milner, 1954). Olds and Milner's study sparked a great deal of interest and raised the hope that a mechanism common to all reinforcers could be analyzed on a physiological level.

Many experiments have been performed to map out the various areas of the brain that, when stimulated, yield a reinforcement effect. In addition, studies have documented the neurochemical pathways that are involved. (For a review, see Vaccarino, Schiff, & Glickman, 1989.) Another set of experiments has explored the similarity of self-stimulation to other types of reinforcers. One outstanding feature of self-stimulation is that it is persistent, with high response rates relative to other types of instrumental responding. In other respects, self-stimulation appears to be similar to the traditional reinforcers when the two are compared under carefully controlled situations. (For a review, see Mogenson & Cioe, 1977.) Thus, explanations for the effects of self-stimulation have followed the explanations for traditional reinforcers. In general, it is assumed that one physiologically based explanation can serve for both.

One early explanation of brain-stimulation reinforcement involved drive reduction. It was hypothesized that brain stimulation activated the neural circuits that are involved when drives are reduced by consummatory behavior. However, this explanation turned out to be simplistic. It was discovered that the same electrical stimulation of the brain that reinforces lever pressing can also elicit responses such as eating, drinking, and

sexual behavior when the appropriate stimulus (food, water, or a sexual partner) is available (for example, Caggiula & Hoebel, 1966; Herberg, 1963; Hoebel & Teitelbaum, 1962; Margules & Olds, 1962; Mogenson & Stevenson, 1966). Thus, brain stimulation appears in part to *induce* rather than *reduce* drives. Based on such evidence, Glickman and Schiff (1967) suggested that brain-stimulation reward is dependent on the activation of neural circuits involved in the elicitation of species-typical behavior (see also Vaccarino et al., 1989).

As with traditional reinforcers, research on brain stimulation supports the idea that reinforcement is the result of both drive state and incentive motivation. Evidence for this point of view arises from the fact that the rate of self-stimulation can be enhanced or reduced by altering either the drive state or incentive stimuli. For example, a rat will self-stimulate faster if it is also food-deprived (Olds, 1958). If the site of stimulation also induces drinking, self-stimulation is enhanced if water is available (Mendelson, 1967; Mogenson & Kaplinsky, 1970; Mogenson & Morgan, 1967). If the water is made tastier by adding saccharin, the response rate is enhanced even more (Phillips & Mogenson, 1968). Results such as these have led theorists to conclude that reinforcement occurs when an external stimulus (such as water) is present in conjunction with an overall drive state (such as thirst). This is, of course, what happens in the typical instrumental situation. Both elements also appear to be involved with brain stimulation (Mogenson & Huang, 1973).

Reinforcement as Behavioral Regulation

The stimulus theories of reinforcement we considered in the preceding section either were directly concerned with physiological mechanisms of reinforcement or were formulated in response to theories that viewed reinforcement as a mechanism for the regulation of internal physiological systems. The theories share the assumption that reinforced behavior is trained, or stamped into the organism's behavioral repertoire. The underlying assumption of the next set of theories we will consider is much different. These theories are not concerned with the physiological substrates of reinforcement. Rather, reinforcement is described in terms of how the organism must adjust its behavior to meet the demands of a particular situation. The effects of reinforcement are not viewed as the stamping in of a particular response but as the reorganization of behavior. The various theories describe different ways in which this reorganization may take place.

Homeostasis, as we have said, is a balanced physiological state of the organism. Homeostasis becomes relevant to reinforcement when deviations from the stable state occur and the organism attempts to rectify the situation. The behavioral regulation theories we will consider in this section assume that a similar homeostatic mechanism exists with respect to behavior. That is, we may consider the behaving organism as having a particular balance of responses to maintain. The organism has particular things to do: it must eat, breathe, drink, keep warm, exercise, entertain itself, and so on. All these activities have to occur in particular proportions. If the normal or optimal balance of activities is upset, behavior is assumed to change so as to correct the deviation from behavioral homeostasis. The actual behavioral balance may, in fact, serve to maintain physiological homeostasis. Eating, drinking, and exercise are all part of maintaining physiological homeostasis. However, behavior regulation theories of reinforcement are stated in terms of behavioral rather than physiological processes. Another major innovation of behavioral regulation theories is that they view reinforcement as involving changes in the opportunity to engage in particular responses. Rather than focusing on the "stamping in" of a particular response, the emphasis

here is on relations between the instrumental response and responses made possible by presentation of the "reinforcer."

The Precursors of Behavioral Regulation Theories

Behavioral regulation theories evolved from ideas about reinforcement formulated by David Premack in the mid-1960s. Premack developed the idea that opportunities to engage in particular types of responses can serve as reinforcers. The possibility that certain responses may serve as reinforcers was first recognized by Sheffield and his co-workers, who formulated the **consummatory-response theory.** The consummatory-response theory was proposed in an effort to explain why particular incentive stimuli, such as food, are effective reinforcers. Many reinforcers, like food and water, elicit species-typical unconditioned responses, such as chewing, licking, and swallowing. The consummatory-response theory attributes reinforcement to these species-typical behaviors. It asserts that species-typical consummatory responses—eating, drinking, and the like—are themselves the critical feature of reinforcers. Drive reduction might follow a consummatory response, but it was assumed to be unimportant in strengthening the instrumental response. Research on the consummatory-response theory focused on demonstrations that consummatory responses could reinforce instrumental behavior in the absence of drive reduction. Famous experiments were performed showing that saccharin is an effective reinforcer for rats (for example, Sheffield, Roby, & Campbell, 1954). A mild solution of saccharin has a pleasant taste and stimulates consummatory behavior but is not nutritive and therefore presumably does not reduce a drive state.

Premack's Theory of Reinforcement

The consummatory-response theory represents a step away from stimulus theories of reinforcement in that it considers reinforcement as the opportunity to engage in a particular type of response. However, the consummatory-response and stimulus theories of reinforcement all share the assumption that the responses that accompany reinforcing stimuli are fundamentally different in some way from responses that can serve as instrumental behavior. Consummatory responses (chewing and swallowing, for example) are assumed to be fundamentally different from various potential instrumental responses, such as running, jumping, or manipulating something. Premack took issue with this distinction and suggested that instrumental responses and responses accompanying reinforcing stimuli differ only in their likelihood of occurrence. He pointed out that responses involved with commonly used reinforcers are activities that the subject is highly likely to pursue. For example, animals in a food-reinforcement experiment are highly likely to engage in eating behavior. Deprivation procedures serve to ensure that eating will be the most likely behavior in the situation. By contrast, instrumental responses are typically low-probability activities. An experimentally naive rat, for example, is quite unlikely to press a response lever. Premack (1965) proposed that this difference in response probabilities is critical for reinforcement. Formally, his reinforcement principle can be stated as follows: *Given two responses, the opportunity to perform the higher probability response after the lower probability response will result in reinforcement of the lower probability response. However, the opportunity to perform the lower probability response after the higher probability response will not result in reinforcement of the higher probability response.* This is known as the **differential probability principle.**

Eating will reinforce bar pressing because eating is typically more probable than bar pressing. Under ordinary circumstances, bar pressing cannot reinforce eating. However, Premack's theory suggests that if for some reason bar pressing became more probable

than eating, it would reinforce eating. Thus, Premack's theory denies that there is a fundamental distinction between reinforcers and instrumental responses. The particular characteristic that makes a reinforcer act as such is not something intrinsic to the reinforcing response. Rather, the reinforcing response is simply a response that is more likely to occur than the instrumental response. Consequently, it is possible to use a wide variety of responses as reinforcers.

Experimental evidence. Premack and his colleagues conducted many experiments to test his theory (see Premack, 1965, 1971a). One of the early studies was conducted with young children. Premack first gave the children two response alternatives (eating candy and playing a pinball machine) and measured which response was more probable for each child. Some of the children preferred eating candy over playing pinball; others preferred the pinball. In a second phase of the experiment (see Figure 7.1), the children were tested with one of two procedures. In one procedure, eating was specified as the reinforcing response and playing pinball was the instrumental response. That is, the children had to play the pinball machine in order to gain the opportunity to eat the candy. The question was whether all the children would increase their pinball playing. Consistent with Premack's theory, only those children who preferred eating to playing pinball showed a reinforcement effect under these circumstances. In the second procedure, the roles of the two responses were reversed. Eating was the instrumental response, and playing pinball was the reinforcing response. The children had to eat candy to gain the opportunity to play pinball. In this situation, only those children who preferred playing pinball to eating showed a reinforcement effect.

In another experiment, Premack (1962) altered the probabilities of the responses by changing deprivation conditions. Rats were tested using the responses of drinking and

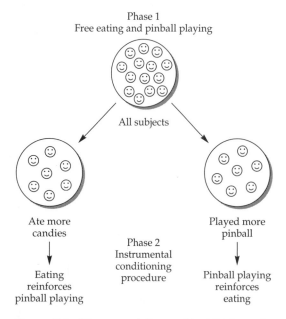

Phase 1
Free eating and pinball playing

All subjects

Ate more
candies

Eating
reinforces
pinball playing

Phase 2
Instrumental
conditioning
procedure

Played more
pinball

Pinball playing
reinforces
eating

Figure 7.1 Diagram of Premack's (1965) study. [See the accompanying discussion for details.]

running in a rotating wheel. The experiment is illustrated in Figure 7.2. In one study the rats were water-deprived but not deprived of the opportunity to run in the wheel. Under these circumstances drinking was more probable than running, and the opportunity to drink could be effectively used to reinforce running. In the second study, the rats were not deprived of water. Under these circumstances, they were more likely to run in the wheel than to drink. Now the opportunity to run in the wheel could be effectively used to reinforce drinking. However, drinking could no longer be used to reinforce running. Thus, running and drinking could be interchangeably used as instrumental and reinforcing responses, depending on the animal's state of water deprivation.

Measuring response probability.   Both of the preceding experiments had two parts. In the first part, behavior was measured in a situation in which the subject had unlimited opportunity to engage in either of the responses to be used later as the instrumental and the

reinforcing responses. This situation is assumed to reveal the behavioral homeostatic balance of the organism in the absence of any constraints on responding. We call this the *baseline phase*. In the second part of the experiments, the *instrumental conditioning phase,* the opportunity to engage in the high-probability reinforcer response was provided only when the subject made the lower probability instrumental response. As we saw, what happened in the second phase depended on the relative probabilities of the two responses during the baseline phase. Therefore, before we can make precise predictions about how one response will (or will not) reinforce another, we must have some way to measure and compare the baseline probabilities of the two responses.

One possible measure of response probability is the frequency with which each response occurs in a set amount of time. This measure serves well as long as we are comparing responses that require similar amounts of time, such as pressing two alternative but otherwise identical response levers. What would we do, however, if we wanted to compare the probability of two very different responses, such as doing a crossword puzzle and eating? Comparing frequencies of response here would be very cumbersome and difficult. One would have to specify what constituted an instance, or unit, of puzzle-solving behavior and an instance, or unit, of eating. Would completing one word in a crossword puzzle constitute a unit of puzzle-solving behavior, or would completing all the items in a certain direction (horizontal or vertical) constitute one unit of this behavior? Would a unit of eating mean taking one bite, completing one course, or eating an entire meal?

As suggested by the preceding discussion, it is difficult to formulate comparable units of behavior for diverse activities. However, a common dimension to all responses is *time*. Premack suggested that response probability may be measured in terms of the amount of time the subject spends engaged in the response during a specified period. We can express this idea in the following equation:

EXPERIMENT 1

1. Rat is water deprived

2. Rat drinks more than it runs

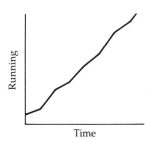

3. Drinking reinforces running

EXPERIMENT 2

1. Rat is not water deprived

2. Rat runs more than it drinks

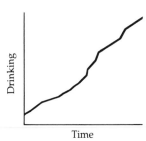

3. Running reinforces drinking

Figure 7.2 When a rat is water deprived (Experiment 1), it drinks more than it runs. Therefore, drinking reinforces running. When a rat is not water deprived (Experiment 2), it runs more than it drinks. This time, running reinforces drinking.

$$\text{Probability of response} = \frac{\text{time spent on response}}{\text{total time}}$$

By this definition, responses taking up a greater proportion of the available time are considered more probable than responses on which the subject spends less time. If in an hour you spend 45 minutes eating and 15 minutes working on a puzzle, we would say that eating was more probable than working on the puzzle during this hour. Therefore, eating should reinforce working on the puzzle.

Although time as a measure of response probability provides a common dimension for measuring the likelihood of diverse activities, it has its own difficulties. The first problem is empirical. Several studies have shown that the duration of an activity is not as basic to behavior, or as important to the subject, as

other dimensions of behavior such as response frequency (for example, Allison, Moore, Gawley, Mondloch, & Mondloch, 1986; Davison, 1991b). Other difficulties with time as a measure of response probability are conceptual. With certain activities, it is difficult to decide how to identify the duration of the behavior. For example, rats drink in a series of momentary licks. We may agree that the first lick is the start of a bout of drinking, but the end of the bout is more difficult to identify. How long does the rat have to pause between licks for us to decide that the bout is finished? There is no easy answer to this question.

Another decision to be made concerns the observation period during which the duration of an activity is measured. A long observation period can yield results very different from a short observation period. Consider, for example, a comparison between sexual behavior and studying. A student may spend a good deal more time reading than engaging in sexual behavior. Nevertheless, most students would find sexual behavior more pleasant and reinforcing. This paradox may be resolved if we take into account the duration of the baseline observations. Given an unlimited choice between sex and reading in a 2-hour period, sex will most likely predominate. However, over a 2-year period, reading may be the more probable response. The baseline observation period is also critical for assessing the proba-

bility of responses that occur only periodically. For example, although you spend a good deal of time eating during a 24-hour period, eating is not uniformly distributed over the course of a day. Rather, it is highly likely only at certain times. In addition, the more time you devote to an activity such as eating, the less likely the response becomes for awhile. After an hour has been spent in gastronomic pursuits, eating can become very *un*likely.

Because response probabilities vary with time itself, Premack went on to suggest that momentary probability is the best measure for

Applications of the Premack Principle

BOX **7.1**

Efforts to use reinforcement procedures to encourage appropriate behavior in normal school children or mentally retarded or autistic students require identifying an effective reinforcer. Food is often used as the reinforcer with considerable success in research with mildly food-deprived animal subjects. However, practical and ethical considerations have encouraged investigators to identify other forms of reinforcement for human subjects. The Premack principle has been a great help in this regard because it suggests that any activity that is more likely than the response to be reinforced can serve as an effective reinforcer. Therefore, effective reinforcers may be identified by determining which are high-probability responses.

Individuals differ in their preferred activities. Some may prefer playing ball after school; others may prefer talking to friends on the phone. By measuring the relative probability of different activities for each individual, reinforcement procedures can be personalized to take advantage of each person's own unique response preferences. This may result in some rather unusual responses serving as reinforcers.

Children with autism often engage in repetitive aberrant behaviors. One form of these, called **stereotypy,** involves repeated responses such as hand waving, making noises, rubbing objects, tapping objects, or snapping fingers. Another form of aberrant behavior, called **delayed echolalia,** involves verbal repetitions. For example, one autistic child was heard to say over and over again, "Ding! ding! ding! You win again," and "Match Game 83." A third form of aberrant behavior, **perseverative behavior,** involves persistent manipulation of an object. For example, the child may repeatedly manipulate only certain plastic toys. The high probability of stereotypy, echolalia, and perseverative behavior in children with autism suggests that these responses may be effectively used as reinforcers in treatment procedures. This possibility has been explored by several investigators. In a recent study by Charlop, Kurtz, and Casey (1990), the effectiveness of different forms of reinforcement was compared in training various academic-related skills in autistic children. The tasks included identifying which of several objects was the same or different from the one held up by the teacher, adding up coins, and correctly responding to sentences designed to teach receptive pronouns or prepositions. In one experimental condition, a preferred food (such as a small piece of chocolate, cereal, or a cookie) served as the reinforcer, in the absence of programmed food deprivation. In another condition, the opportunity to perform an aberrant response for 3 to 5 seconds served as the reinforcer.

Some of the results of the study are illustrated in Figure 7.3. Each panel represents the data for a different student. Notice that in each case, the opportunity to engage in some form of aberrant behavior resulted in making predictions about reinforcement. Opportunity to perform response A will serve to reinforce another response B only if at that moment the probability of A is higher than the probability of B.

The Response-Deprivation Hypothesis

In most instrumental conditioning procedures, the momentary probability of the reinforcer response is kept at a high level by restricting access to the reinforcing response. A rat lever-pressing for food, for example, typically comes into the experimental situation not having eaten much and does not receive a whole meal for each lever-press response. These limitations on the reinforcing response are very important. If we were to give the rat a full meal for making one lever press, chances are we would not increase its rate of pressing very much. Restrictions on the opportunity to engage in the reinforcing response serve to increase its effectiveness as a reinforcer.

Premack (1965) recognized the importance of restricting access to the reinforcer response for instrumental conditioning. He regarded response deprivation as a necessary condition

better performance on the training tasks than food reinforcement. Stereotypy, delayed echolalia, and perseverative behavior all served to increase task performance above what was observed with food reinforcement. These results indicate that high-probability responses can serve to reinforce lower probability responses, even if those high-probability responses are not characteristic of normal behavior.

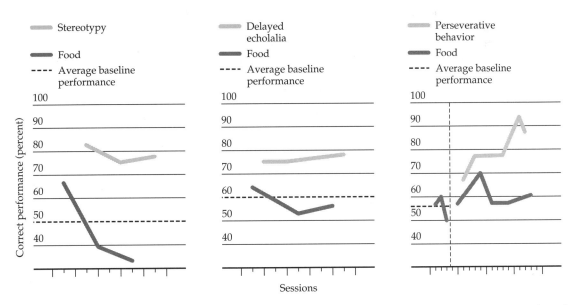

Figure 7.3 Task performance data for three children with autism. One student's behavior was reinforced with food or the opportunity to engage in stereotyped behavior. The second child's behavior was reinforced with food or the opportunity to engage in delayed echolalia. The third student's behavior was reinforced with food or the opportunity to engage in perseverative responding. (Responding during baseline periods was also reinforced with food.) *(From "Using Aberrant Behaviors as Reinforcers for Autistic Children" by M.H. Charlop, P.F. Kurtz, and F.G. Casey, 1990,* Journal of Applied Behavior Analysis, *23, pp. 163–181. Copyright © 1990 by Journal of Applied Behavior Analysis. Reprinted by permission.)*

for reinforcement. However, he regarded it as an adjunct to the differential probability principle. In his view, the reinforcer response still had to be a more likely behavior than the instrumental response. By contrast, Timberlake and Allison (1974) abandoned the differential probability principle altogether. They argued that restriction of the reinforcer response was sufficient for instrumental reinforcement—an idea known as the **response-deprivation hypothesis.**

In several studies, investigators found that depriving subjects of a low-probability response can make access to that response an effective reinforcer, even if the initial probability of the instrumental response is higher (Allison & Timberlake, 1974; Eisenberger, Karpman, & Trattner, 1967). Such evidence indicates that with response deprivation, a low-probability response can be used to reinforce a higher probability response. Thus, response deprivation can lead to reinforcement effects even if Premack's differential probability principle is violated. This shows that response deprivation is more basic to reinforcement than the differential probability principle.

Depriving the subject of access to the reinforcer response disrupts the natural flow of behavior. The subject can no longer allocate time to its various activities in the way it would have otherwise. This disruption of the natural flow of behavior appears to be critical for obtaining reinforcement effects.

Behavioral Bliss Points and Behavioral Regulation

The idea that instrumental conditioning involves restricting the free flow of behavior has been developed further in behavioral regulation theories of reinforcement (see Allison, 1983, 1989; Hanson & Timberlake, 1983; Timberlake, 1980, 1984). Behavioral regulation theories do not focus on the relative probabilities of the instrumental and reinforcing responses but on the extent to which an instrumental

response–reinforcer contingency disrupts behavioral stability and forces the subject away from its behavioral "bliss point."

Every situation provides various response opportunities. In an experimental situation, for example, an animal can run in a wheel, drink, eat, scratch itself, sniff holes, or manipulate a response lever. Behavioral regulation theory assumes that if animals are free to distribute their responses among the available alternatives, they will do so in a way that is most comfortable or in some sense "optimal" for them. This response distribution can be considered to define a behavioral "bliss point." The particular distribution of activities that constitutes the bliss point will vary from one situation to another. For example, if the running wheel is made very difficult to turn or the subject is severely deprived of water, the relative likelihood of running and drinking will change. However, for a given circumstance, the behavioral bliss point, as revealed in unconstrained choices among response alternatives, is assumed to be fixed. Behavioral regulation theory assumes further that the behavioral bliss point will be defended against disruptions caused by limitations on the opportunity to engage in particular responses. Such limitations often result from instrumental conditioning procedures because instrumental procedures do not permit subjects access to the reinforcer response unless the subjects have previously performed the instrumental response in the required fashion.

Behavioral regulation theory is analogous in some respects to homeostatic physiological regulation. Consider, for example, homeostatic mechanisms for maintenance of body temperature. In humans, normal core body temperature is 98.6° F. This optimal temperature is defended against disruption by various homeostatic mechanisms. If you enter a walk-in freezer, your body temperature is defended by constriction of surface blood vessels, shivering, and the like. If you go into a sauna, your body temperature is defended by vasodilation and sweating. Usually, the homeostatic mechanisms defending body temperature are so successful that core body temperature does not change despite large variations in environmental temperature. A behavioral bliss point is analogous to optimal body temperature. It is defended against disruptions in the opportunity to engage in various responses. As we will see, however, unlike physiological homeostatic mechanisms that can successfully maintain a fixed optimal point, behavioral regulation cannot always get the animal back to its free-baseline behavioral bliss point in the face of disruptions caused by instrumental response–reinforcer contingencies.

The behavioral bliss point can be defined in terms of the relative frequency of occurrence of all the responses of an organism in an unconstrained situation. To simplify analysis, let us just focus on two responses, running and drinking, as in Premack's experiments illustrated in Figure 7.2. If no restrictions are placed on running and drinking, these activities may occur in any relation to each other. The animal may run a lot and drink a lot, run a lot and drink little, run little and drink a lot, or run little and drink little. Figure 7.4 represents amount of running on the horizontal axis and amount of drinking on the vertical axis. Without constraints, a subject's running and drinking could fall at any point on this set of axes. Let us assume that the subject's behavior in a free-baseline situation is represented by the open circle. The subject drinks for 15 seconds and runs for 15 seconds in our observation period. This defines the subject's behavioral bliss point in this situation. How would the introduction of an instrumental contingency between running and drinking disrupt the behavioral bliss? That depends on the nature of the contingency.

Figure 7.4 shows three possible contingent relations between running and drinking. These are represented by the solid lines emanating from the origin in the figure. These lines specify how much the animal has to run to obtain a particular amount of drinking time.

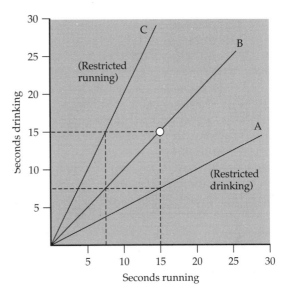

Figure 7.4 Allocation of behavior between running and drinking. The open circle shows the optimal allocation, or behavioral bliss point, obtained in a free-baseline session. Lines A, B, and C represent different contingent relations imposed between running and drinking. The contingency represented by line A restricts drinking by requiring twice as much running to maintain the optimal amount of drinking. The contingency represented by line C restricts running by requiring twice as much drinking to maintain the optimal amount of running. Line B, which passes through the bliss point, requires only that the organism do what it most prefers; therefore, it exerts no restriction.

Thus, these lines are feedback functions (see Chapter 5). Line B represents a contingency in which one second of running is required for each second of drinking opportunity. Line B passes through the bliss point of running and drinking obtained in the free-baseline condition. This makes the contingency represented by line B rather special because it permits subjects to reach the behavioral bliss point and satisfy the response–reinforcer contingency at the same time. The contingencies represented by lines A and C do not allow that.

Line A specifies a contingency in which the subject has to run twice as much as it drinks. For 7.5 seconds of drinking, it has to run for 15 seconds. Because the behavioral bliss point is

15 seconds of drinking for 15 seconds of running, the contingency specified by line A involves a restriction of drinking. Line C represents a different kind of restriction. Here the subject has to drink twice as much as it runs. Thus, for 7.5 seconds of running, it has to drink for 15 seconds. In this case, the response–reinforcer contingency involves a restriction of running relative to the behavioral bliss point. Lines A and C represent instrumental conditioning procedures that challenge maintenance of the behavioral bliss point.

Behavioral regulation theory states that subjects will defend against challenges to the behavioral bliss point, just as physiological regulation involves defense against challenges to a physiological set point. However, the interesting thing is that the free-baseline behavioral bliss point cannot always be reestablished after an instrumental contingency is introduced. In our example, the behavioral bliss point was 15 seconds of drinking and 15 seconds of running in a standard observation period. Consider the possibilities when the schedule of reinforcement represented by line C in Figure 7.4 is imposed on the free-response situation. Now the subject cannot achieve "bliss" with respect to running without strongly deviating from the optimal level for drinking, and vice versa. Since the line C contingency requires twice as much drinking as running, to achieve the optimal level of 15 seconds of running, the subject would have to drink for 30 seconds, twice its optimal level. Or if the subject achieved its optimal 15 seconds of drinking, its running would be at 7.5 seconds, half the optimal level. Line A represents similar problems in returning to the behavioral bliss point. The constraint of the response–reinforcer contingency prevents the subject from achieving "bliss" with respect to one response without strongly deviating from the optimal level for the other behavior.

Schedules of reinforcement such as those represented by lines A and C in Figure 7.4 preclude subjects from returning to their behavioral bliss point. However, this does not mean that return to the behavioral set point is irrelevant in such cases; to the contrary, it is the force that drives motivated behavior. Behavioral regulation theory assumes that returning to the behavioral set point remains a goal of response allocation. When this goal cannot be reached, the redistribution of responses between the instrumental and contingent behaviors becomes a matter of compromise. Although the resulting distribution of behavior cannot be optimal for either response considered separately, it can be the optimal in terms of what is possible for both responses together, given the constraints of the instrumental conditioning procedure. Staddon, for example, has proposed a **minimum-deviation model** of behavioral regulation (Staddon, 1979; see also Staddon, 1983). According to this model, introduction of a response–reinforcer contingency causes subjects to redistribute their behavior between the instrumental and contingent responses in a way that minimizes the total deviation of the two responses from the optimal point. For situations in which the free-baseline behavioral bliss point cannot be achieved, the minimum-deviation model provides one view of how subjects settle for the next best thing.

How are reinforcement effects produced by behavioral regulation? We have discussed behavioral regulation as the defense of a behavioral bliss point in the face of restrictions on response opportunities imposed by a response–reinforcer contingency, noting that often this defense involves settling not for the free-baseline bliss point but for the next best thing possible in the situation. How do these mechanisms lead to increases in instrumental behavior in typical instrumental conditioning procedures? A reinforcement effect is identified by an increase in the occurrence of an instrumental response above levels that would occur in the absence of the response–reinforcer contingency. As Figure 7.4 illustrates, feedback functions that do not go through the behavioral bliss point invariably restrict access to a response below the level specified by the bliss point. In line A of Figure 7.4, for example, the subject's drinking is restricted relative to running. To move as close as possible to the behavioral bliss point, the subject has to increase its running so as to gain more opportunity to drink. This is precisely what occurs in typical instrumental conditioning procedures. Access to the reinforcer is restricted; to gain more opportunity to engage in the reinforcer response, the subject has to increase performance of the instrumental response. Increase in performance of the instrumental response (a reinforcement effect) results from behavioral regulatory mechanisms that function to minimize deviations from the behavioral bliss point.

Problems with the bliss-point approach. The bliss-point approach has done much to change the way we think about reinforcement and about instrumental conditioning procedures. However, recent experimental evidence suggests that the approach has two major shortcomings, which we will now describe.

1. As we have seen, at the start of behavioral regulation experiments, the behavioral bliss point is determined by giving subjects access to two response alternatives without restriction. The bliss point is based on a measure of each response totaled over the entire free-baseline session. Thus, the behavioral bliss point is a *molar* feature of behavior. A given molar bliss point could be achieved in a variety of ways. In the hypothetical example given in Figure 7.4, subjects were allowed to choose between drinking from a water spout and running in a wheel and ended up spending 15 seconds on each activity during the free-baseline session. This could have been achieved by the subject doing all of its drinking before it did any of its running. Another possibility is that the subject could have frequently switched back and forth between the two activities in the process of accumulating 15 seconds on each response. According to

the behavioral-bliss-point approach, such differences should not matter.

One way to test this assumption is to introduce contingencies between running and drinking that allow the subject to reach its molar bliss point but require different patterns of switching between the two responses. Such schedules are called **nondepriving**, or **equilibrium**, **schedules** because they do not require the subject to perform more or less of either response overall than is specified by the molar bliss point. Contrary to predictions of behavioral regulation theories, subjects do not respond so as to maintain their molar bliss point on all nondepriving schedules (for example, Gawley, Timberlake, & Lucas, 1987; Tierney, Smith, & Gannon, 1987). The evidence indicates that the outcome of instrumental contingencies depends on constraints on the subject's preferred pattern of switching back and forth between response alternatives. Thus, an adequate characterization of "behavioral bliss" requires information about molecular response patterns.

2. Another, and perhaps more serious, difficulty for the behavioral-bliss-point approach is that responses that occur in an unconstrained situation do not appear to have the same "value" as responses that occur as a part of an instrumental contingency. In behavioral regulation theory, the outcome of instrumental contingencies is predicted from the free-baseline distribution of responses. For such predictions to work, one has to assume that responses performed in the absence of contingency constraints are basically the same as the responses that occur when an instrumental contingency is imposed. For example, running in a wheel in the absence of response constraints (free running) has to be considered to be the same as running in order to gain access to a water spout (contingent running). This assumption has been found to be incorrect in several experiments (Allison, Buxton, & Moore, 1987; Gawley et al., 1987; Tierney et al., 1987).

Doing something when there are no requirements (jogging for your own pleasure, for example) appears to be different from doing the same thing when it is required by an instrumental contingency (jogging in a physical education class, for example). In a 1987 experiment by Gawley and his associates, rats were required to run in a wheel to obtain water ("contingent running") but also were permitted to engage in "free running" that was unnecessary for water reinforcement. Under these conditions, the rats ran more than they did during the free-baseline condition. The contingent running did not appear to count toward their behavioral bliss point. If contingent responses do not count toward the

bliss point, it is difficult to see how one can predict the outcome of instrumental contingencies based on the bliss point.

The conceptual legacy of behavioral regulation theory. Although the bliss-point approach has encountered some serious difficulties, behavioral regulation theory has contributed significantly to how we think about instrumental reinforcement. Therefore, it is instructive to review some of its conceptual contributions. First, behavioral regulation theory has moved us away from thinking about reinforcers as special kinds of stimuli or as special kind of responses. Rather, we are more

---

Behavioral Regulation and Human Behavior

BOX 7.2

Although most of the research on behavioral regulation theories of reinforcement has been performed with animal subjects, the principles also apply to human behavior (Timberlake & Farmer-Dougan, 1991). In a given situation, people also have a favorite way of distributing their activities among the available alternatives. For each person, there is an optimal way. If a response–reinforcer contingency is introduced, people readjust their behavior to find the most comfortable new distribution of activities given the restrictions imposed by the instrumental procedure.

Bernstein and Ebbesen (1978) investigated response reallocation in three adults who were paid to live individually in a laboratory room 24 hours a day for several weeks. One subject was a 19-year-old female undergraduate, another was a 39-year-old female homemaker, and the third was a 26-year-old unemployed male construction worker. The laboratory provided all the amenities of a comfortable small apartment—tables, chairs, sofa, bed, refrigerator, bathroom with shower, cooking utensils, and so on. Subjects were observed from an adjacent room through a one-way-vision window. After observing the free-baseline distribution of behavior in the situation, the experimenters imposed a response–reinforcer contingency. Figure 7.5 shows the results of one such experiment involving sewing or knitting and studying Russian. The open circle represents the free-baseline levels of these activities. The subject spent much more time sewing and knitting than studying. An instrumental contingency was then imposed requiring the subject to spend a certain amount of time studying before gaining the opportunity to sew or knit. The solid line in Figure 7.5 illustrates the contingency. The contingency placed a restriction on sewing and knitting. If the subject studied only as much as during the free-baseline condition, she could sew and knit far less than during baseline. The filled circle in Figure 7.5 illustrates the reallocation of behavior that resulted from the contingency. The subject increased her studying but not quite enough to be able to spend as much time sewing and knitting as during the baseline phase. Thus, the instrumental contingency produced a shift in both responses: the low-probability behavior (studying) increased and the high-probability behavior (sewing and knitting) decreased.

Another fascinating observation in this series of experiments was that subjects redistributed their behavior in accordance with an instrumental contingency even though they resented the contingency and sometimes tried to resist complying with it. One subject attempted to resist the schedule of reinforcement by not using

likely to look for the causes of reinforcement in how instrumental contingencies constrain the organism's free flow of behavior. Reinforcement effects are seen as related to the animal's ongoing activities and therefore are assumed to be a function of those activities. This is in sharp contrast to drive-reduction theory, in which reinforcers were regarded as absolutes and as transsituational.

A second major contribution of behavioral regulation theory is that instrumental conditioning procedures are not considered to "stamp in" (to use Thorndike's term) or to "strengthen" instrumental behavior. Rather, instrumental conditioning is seen as creating a new distribution, or allocation, of responses. Typically, the reallocation of behavior involves an increase in the instrumental response and a decrease in the reinforcer response. These two changes are viewed as equally important features of the redistribution of behavior. Furthermore, behavioral regulation theory makes no fundamental distinctions between instrumental and reinforcer responses. Reinforcer responses are not assumed to be more likely than instrumental responses. They are not assumed to provide any special physiological benefits or to have any inherent characteristics that make them different from instrumental responses. Rather,

up the opportunity that she had earned to sew. After not sewing for 11 hours, she finally gave in and did some sewing, whereupon she quickly returned to the instrumental response. Apparently, the prospect of life without sewing was worse than giving in to the response limitations imposed by the schedule of reinforcement.

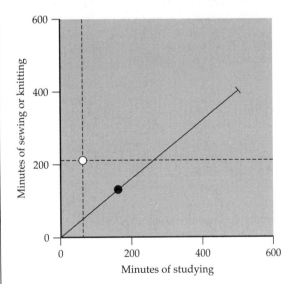

Figure 7.5 Allocation of behavior between studying Russian and sewing or knitting in the free-baseline condition and under the instrumental contingency imposed by the experimenters (solid line). The open circle represents the free-baseline levels observed; the filled circle represents the levels observed after the contingency was imposed. *(From J. Allison,* Behavioral Economics *[Praeger Publishers, New York, an imprint of Greenwood Publishing Group, Inc., 1983], p. 45. Reprinted with permission; all rights reserved.)*

instrumental and reinforcer responses are distinguished only by the roles assigned to them by an instrumental contingency.

The behavioral regulation approach also embraces the major idea that organisms respond so as to maximize their benefits or behavioral "bliss." The idea of optimization is not original with behavioral regulation theory. We have encountered it already in discussions of concurrent schedules and choice, and it will come up again in the following sections. In drive-reduction theories of reinforcement, optimization referred to a return to physiological homeostasis and a drive-free state. The behavioral regulation approach suggests a much broader view of optimization in theories of reinforcement. The "optimal" distribution of activities is assumed to be determined not only by physiological needs but also by the subject's ecological niche and natural or phylogenetically determined response tendencies. These additional aspects of optimization are developed further in optimal foraging theory, to be discussed shortly.

Finally, behavioral regulation theory views reinforcement effects as just one manifestation of the ways in which animals strive to distribute their responses among alternatives so as to make the best of their opportunities and circumstances. Thus, behavioral regulation is a part of an organism's overall adaptation to its environment. (See Staddon, 1983, for a comprehensive treatment of instrumental behavior as adaptation.)

Economic Concepts and Response Allocation

As we have seen, the outcome of instrumental conditioning procedures depends on an interplay between the subject's preexisting behavioral repertoire and restrictions imposed by the instrumental response–reinforcer contingency. Psychologists have been interested in discovering principles that describe how behavior changes as a result of schedule constraints. Students who have studied economics may recognize a similarity here to problems of labor supply and consumer demand in microeconomics. Economists, like psychologists, strive to understand changes in behavior in terms of preexisting preferences and restrictions on fulfilling those preferences. Some psychologists have become interested in this commonality of concerns. It is appealing to "borrow" economic ideas in the analysis of behavior because economics provides highly developed theories and mathematical models. We will now consider how economic ideas have influenced reinforcement theories, specifically behavioral regulation. For the sake of simplicity, we will concentrate on the basic ideas that have had the most impact on understanding reinforcement. (For further details, see Allison, 1983; Hursh, 1980, 1984; Lea, 1978; Rachlin et al., 1976; Staddon, 1980.)

Labor supply. In 1953 Skinner suggested that schedules of reinforcement could be compared to human labor for wages. For example, we can think of a rat's bar-press response as a way to earn food, just as piecework in a factory is a way to earn money. The number of bar presses required per food pellet is then analogous to the rate of pay, or wage rate. Economists have studied how various wage rates influence the amount a person will work (the labor supply). The relationship between how much work is performed at various wage rates and the total amount earned at those wage rates is called a **labor supply curve.** Figure 7.6 shows a theoretical labor supply curve. Each of the lines radiating from the origin represents a different wage rate. Line 1 (L_1), for example, represents a high wage rate because here earnings increase quickly with only small increases in labor. Line 5 (L_5), by contrast, represents very poor wages. Here very little additional money is earned for even large increases in work. The points on each line represent the total amount earned at each wage rate. These points connected together constitute a labor supply curve.

Let us consider what happens according to a theoretical labor supply curve as we move from high to low wages (as we go from L_1 to

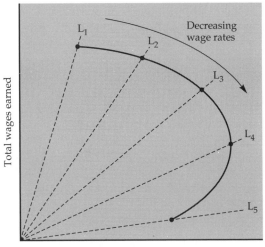

Figure 7.6 An idealized standard labor supply curve showing total work that someone would be willing to perform and total wages earned as a function of different wage rates (represented by the straight lines radiating from the origin). Line L_1 represents the highest wage rate; line L_5, the lowest.

L_5 in Figure 7.6). Going from a high wage rate (L_1) to a slightly lower rate (L_2), we see that people presumably try to maintain their total earnings by working more (increasing total work performed). As wage rates continue to fall (L_2 to L_4), people continue to increase their work output to offset the lower rates of pay. However, the increased effort is not sufficient to maintain total earnings at the original level. When wage rates are made very low (line 5 in Figure 7.6), total work performed no longer increases to compensate for the low wages. In fact, just the opposite happens. Total work performed decreases for the first time. Thus, decreases in wage rates are assumed to result in increases in total work performed up to a point (L_1 to L_4), after which total work performed decreases (L_5). Because of this reversal, the labor supply curve is characterized as "backward-bending."

What determines the shape of the labor supply curve? Analyses of the labor supply curve are based on the idea of optimization — the assumption that individuals distribute their efforts so as to get the most out of a situation. However, in calculating what is optimal, one has to consider not only wages earned but also the value of leisure. When the wage rate decreases, in order to maintain the same level of earnings a person must spend more time working and sacrifice leisure time. Whether that person is willing to forgo leisure in favor of working depends on the relative value of the two activities. At high wage rates, the benefits of working are much greater than the benefits of leisure. Therefore, a person is willing to give up leisure in favor of working, and decreases in the wage rate are compensated by increased responding. This is the case for wage rates L_1 through L_4 in Figure 7.6. However, it is interesting to note that even with very high wage rates (L_1 and L_2), individuals do not compensate perfectly for a decrease in the wage rate. They do not give up all of the leisure time that would be necessary to maintain their original level of earnings.

When the wage rate becomes very low, the benefits of working become much less relative to the benefits of leisure. Under such circumstances, it is no longer so advantageous to give up leisure time in favor of working. At the extreme, the marginal benefit of increased work may be less than the marginal benefit of increased leisure. At that point, work output actually decreases as the individual seeks more leisure time; hence, the labor supply curve bends backward.

Backward-bending labor supply curves, such as the one in Figure 7.6, are predicted by microeconomic theory. Such curves have also been obtained in instrumental conditioning research with animal subjects. Kelsey and Allison (1976), for example, performed an experiment with rats pressing a bar for sucrose reward. "Wage rate" was varied by changing the number of lever presses that were required to obtain ten licks of sucrose. As the lever-press requirement was increased, the total number of lever presses (total work performed) increased at first but then declined, as in backward-bending labor-supply curves.

Borrowing from economic analyses, results of instrumental conditioning procedures may be interpreted in terms of the relative values of work and leisure. In the study by Kelsey and Allison (1976), for example, rats allocated their time between leisure and lever pressing for sucrose. Leisure activities in a Skinner box include sniffing, exploring, grooming, and the like. When the number of lever presses required to obtain sucrose became too high, leisure activities predominated and the rats decreased their bar pressing (see also Green, Kagel, & Battalio, 1987).

Consistent with other rules for response reallocation, labor supply theory assumes that how an organism responds to schedule constraints will depend on its preexisting preferences. However, this approach differs in a fundamental way from the bliss-point approach. The bliss-point approach considers only the instrumental and the reinforcer responses involved in an instrumental conditioning procedure. Labor supply theory introduces a third type of behavior—leisure activity.

Consumer demand.   In the previous section we made use of economic theory in an analogy between instrumental behavior and labor. Another analogy may be made between instrumental behavior and the consumption of goods. The theory of consumer demand describes factors that influence how much money a person will spend on various commodities. In borrowing from consumer demand theory, psychologists have equated time spent responding (or number of responses performed) with money. In this analogy, total time available to respond or the total number of responses the subject can make is analogous to income—the total amount of money someone has available to spend. The "price" of a reinforcer is the time or number of responses required to obtain it as specified by the instrumental conditioning procedure. The goal is to determine how instrumental behavior ("spending") is controlled by instrumental contingencies ("prices").

The relation between how much of some commodity is purchased and its price is expressed as a **demand curve.** Sometimes the consumption of a commodity is very easily influenced by its price. If the price of "penny candy" increases, you may buy less of it. Other commodities are less responsive to price changes. The degree to which price influences consumption is called **elasticity of demand.** Demand for penny candy is elastic. The more penny candy costs, the less candy you will buy. Demand for water, however, is much less elastic. People continue to purchase water even if the price increases a great deal.

We can think of demand for reinforcers in an instrumental conditioning procedure as being elastic or inelastic in an analogous fashion. Here, price is determined by the effort required to obtain a given amount of the reinforcer. In a recent study of cigarette smokers, for example, the instrumental response was pushing a plunger, and the reinforcer was the opportunity to take puffs on a cigarette (Bickel, DeGrandpre, Hughes, & Higgins, 1991). Price was increased by requiring more responses for each reinforcer (using fixed-ratio schedules) or by decreasing the number of puffs the subjects could take with each access to the reinforcer. Increases in the price of smoking decreased the amount subjects smoked, regardless of how the price was determined. Thus, cigarette smoking was highly sensitive to price in the laboratory situation. It showed high elasticity.

Would working for food be similarly sensitive to the price of food? This question was addressed in an experiment with laboratory rats by Hursh, Raslear, Shurtleff, Bauman, & Simmons (1988). The price of food was varied by increasing the number of lever presses required for each food pellet, by increasing the force required to make each lever-press response, or by decreasing the amount of food that was provided each time the ratio requirement was met. Different ways of changing the "price" of food had similar effects on how much food rats worked to obtain. As the price of food increased, the rats at first increased their instrumental responding to obtain the same amount of food. Thus, over a range of low prices, the demand for food was inelastic. However, responding failed to keep up with further increases in price, and food consumption declined. This outcome is remarkable because it shows that over a high range of prices, even the demand curve for food shows some elasticity.

Food is such a basic commodity that it may seem surprising that food intake would be influenced by price. Animals cannot do without food. However, food intake is just one factor determining the organism's energy balance. Energy balance depends on the relationship between energy intake and energy expenditure. An organism can compensate for decreased food intake by reducing energy expenditure. Just such an outcome was recently discovered by Rashotte and Henderson (1988). In a study with pigeons, they found, as usual, that a large increase in the price of food (as determined by a fixed-ratio schedule of reinforcement) resulted in a decrease in food intake. However, the effect of the decrease in food intake on energy balance was "corrected" to some extent by a decrease in the nighttime body temperature of the birds. Thus, energy balance was defended by decreased energy utilization when the price of food was very high.

Elasticity of demand is a measure of the impact of price on behavior, and price is determined by response–reinforcer contingencies. Therefore, the effects of response–reinforcer contingencies may be investigated by studying the factors that determine the elasticity of demand. This has made elasticity of demand a critical issue in behavioral economics.

Economists have identified three important factors that determine the elasticity of demand. One is the level of income. If you are very wealthy, you may continue to purchase balloons even if the price skyrockets. (For recent demonstrations of income effects in animal research, see Hastjarjo et al., 1990a;

Silberberg, Warren-Boulton, & Asano, 1987). A second factor is the price itself. Demand for so-called penny candies may be inelastic at prices under 25¢ but elastic at higher prices. We saw such a relationship in the effects of price on food intake. Food intake was insensitive to variations in price only as long as prices remained fairly low. When the response costs of obtaining food became excessive, food intake declined. The third important factor determining elasticity of demand is the availability of substitutes.

Substitutability. In general, if the price of something goes up, purchases or consumption will decrease if people can obtain an acceptable substitute for it at a lower cost. Many people find tea a good substitute for coffee. Therefore, when the price of coffee increases, they will switch to tea. However, if you happen to dislike tea, you may continue to buy coffee at the higher prices because, for you, tea is not an acceptable substitute. Thus, the elasticity of the demand for coffee is influenced by the availability of tea as a substitute for coffee. In an analogous fashion, the elasticity of demand for food in an instrumental conditioning situation will depend on the availability of acceptable lower cost substitutes. If an acceptable alternative food source is available on an easier schedule of reinforcement, the demand for food pellets will show much more elasticity or sensitivity to schedule requirements (Lea & Roper, 1977).

Two experiments performed in 1975 by Kagel and his associates nicely illustrate the effects of substitutability (see also Rachlin et al., 1976). Rat subjects lived in Skinner boxes with two levers. Each rat was allowed a fixed number of lever presses it could perform, or "spend," each day (daily income). In the first experiment, pressing one lever produced dry food pellets, whereas pressing the other lever produced water. In the second study, lever presses could be "spent" on two sweet drinks. Food pellets and water are poor substitutes for each other. In fact, these commodities are *complementary.* The more dry food pellets one eats, the more one needs to drink. By contrast, the two sweet drinks used in the second study were presumed to be good substitutes.

In each experiment, the "price" of one of the reinforcers was increased by increasing the schedule requirement. In the first experiment, changes in "price" were not accompanied by changes in food consumption. The rats did not substitute the "cheaper" water for the more "expensive" food. Demand for food was inelastic. By contrast, substitution occurred in the second experiment. As the price of one sweet drink increased, the rats spent more of their responses obtaining the other drink. Demand for the sweet drinks was elastic. (For further studies of substitutability in rats, see Allison & Moore, 1985; Green & Rachlin, 1991. For a study of substitutability in instrumental conditioning with children, see Burkhard et al., 1978.)

Behavioral economists have focused on the substitutability of alternative reinforcers in considering the effects of response cost in analyses of the elasticity of demand. However, the availability of alternative response or physiological strategies may also influence elasticity of demand. As we noted earlier in Rashotte and Henderson's (1988) study, when the cost of obtaining food became too high for pigeons, the birds conserved energy by decreasing their nighttime body temperature. Lowering nocturnal body temperature is a physiological strategy for maintaining energy balance that can serve as a substitute for responding to obtain additional food when the energetic costs of responding for food are very high.

The importance of economic models for behavioral regulation.
As we have seen, economic theory has provided psychologists with new ways of analyzing behavioral regulation. Like other approaches to behavioral regulation, economic models assume that behavior changes so that something is maximized.

What that "something" is depends on what we are looking at. In the labor supply analogy, the distribution of earnings and leisure is maximized. In the consumer demand analogy, the value of total behavioral output is maximized. Economic theory has provided new and precise ways of describing constraints that various instrumental conditioning procedures impose on the organism's repertoire of behavior. More important, it suggests that instrumental behavior cannot be described in a vacuum. Rather, the entire repertoire of the organism at a given time must be considered as a system (Rachlin, 1978; Rachlin & Burkhard, 1978). Changes in one part of the system influence changes in other parts. Constraints imposed by instrumental procedures are more or less effective depending on the characteristics of the nonconstrained behavior. Psychologists are just beginning to document substitutability effects and other interactions in behavioral systems.

Optimal Foraging Theory and Behavioral Regulation

One area in which a system of behaviors has been extensively studied is foraging. **Foraging** refers to behaviors involved in the search for and procurement of food. Foraging is a rather complex system of behaviors that may involve specialized perceptual mechanisms for recognizing foodstuffs, motor responses for getting to the food and handling it, memory mechanisms for remembering which food sources have already been depleted or locations where food might have been stored, and social behavior such as avoidance of competitors and predators or defense of a feeding area (see Commons, Kacelnik, & Shettleworth, 1987; Kamil, Krebs, & Pulliam, 1987; Kamil & Sargent, 1981). In Chapter 11 we will discuss some special memory mechanisms involved in the foraging behavior of food-hoarding birds. The aspect of foraging that is relevant to analyses of instrumental behavior is the relation between effort expended and food obtained (Shettleworth, 1988).

Research on foraging behavior has been dominated by theories of optimal foraging (see Krebs & McCleery, 1984; Stephens & Krebs, 1986). The basic assumption of optimal foraging theories is that animals search and obtain food in a manner that maximizes their energy intake *(E)* per unit time *(T)* spent foraging. Thus, animals are assumed to maximize E/T.

Comparisons with other optimality approaches. Optimal foraging theories are similar in some ways to other optimality theories that we have already discussed, such as molar maximizing models of choice (see Chapter 6), behavioral-bliss-point models, and behavioral economics. However, unlike the behavioral-bliss-point and behavioral economics approaches, which are applicable to a variety of responses and reinforcers, optimal foraging theories are restricted to analyses of activities involved in procuring and consuming nutrients. Another important difference is that optimal foraging theories were introduced by zoologists and field biologists interested in understanding foraging behavior in the wild. For this reason, a recurrent issue in studies of optimal foraging is ecological validity. Investigators are concerned with the extent to which experimental studies of optimal foraging accurately represent the behavior of animals in their natural environment (Mellgren, 1982; Shettleworth, 1989).

The roots of research on optimal foraging in zoology and field biology have also stimulated a more comparative approach to the study of response allocation than has occurred in the other areas we previously discussed. Foraging behavior occurs in diverse forms in the animal kingdom. Some species of animals feed only in certain seasons. Deer and moose, for example, eat a lot in the spring and summer to build up fat and mineral reserves for the winter. Animals that eat only plants (herbivores) have to eat a great deal to obtain enough nutrition from their relatively poor-quality food. The response cost of procuring plants to eat is usually low, but herbivores have to eat frequent meals. By contrast, animals that hunt and eat mostly meat (carnivores) can get by with far less food because the nutritional quality of their food is so much better. However, their procurement costs (effort required to capture a prey) are much greater. Foraging theory, with its biological perspective, highlights that a complete theory of response allocation must address such species differences.

Key elements of the foraging problem. For most animals, food is distributed in patches. For example, a hummingbird forages among patches of flowers for nectar, and a squirrel forages among tree branches for nuts. Foraging involves two essential decisions: first, whether to enter a patch in search of food — to visit a clump of flowers or a tree branch — and then whether to continue looking for food in that location or to go elsewhere in the hope of finding a richer source of food. Both of these aspects of foraging have been investigated in great detail.

Other things being equal, animals will, of course, elect to enter a rich patch over one that has little food. However, animals rarely have the luxury of choosing between two simultaneously available food sources in their environment. Rather, patches of food are encountered in succession, one after another, and there may be a long waiting period between encounters or a long distance between the patches. This makes foraging choices more difficult. Upon encountering a lean patch, should the animal continue on its way in the hope of finding a richer source of food in the near future, or should it stop and harvest the food from the lean patch that it found? Optimal foraging theory predicts that choice of the leaner patch will depend on the likelihood of encountering a richer patch. If you are likely to find a better source of food soon, there is no need to accept the poorer alternative.

Ito and Fantino (1986) tested this prediction by simulating the foraging situation with a complex schedule of reinforcement in experiments with pigeons. Going from one patch to the next ("searching") was simulated by a variable-interval schedule. Completion of the VI schedule represented arrival at a food patch. The patch was either rich or lean, as signaled by distinct colors on a pecking key. One color represented a rich food patch (6-second access to grain); the other color represented a leaner patch (3-second access to grain). When one of the colors came on, the pigeon could either accept that patch of food or return to the search state and go for the next patch. (If the pigeon accepted a patch, it had to peck on a VI 20-sec schedule to actually obtain the programmed reinforcer.)

As a simulation of the probability of encountering the next patch of food, the VI schedule in effect during the search state of the procedure was changed across different parts of the experiment. In one part of the experiment, each search state was relatively short (VI 5 sec). In other parts of the experiment, the search states were longer (VI 15 and VI 30 sec). The longer the VI schedule in the search state, the less likely the subject was to encounter the next patch of food. The prediction was that as the probability of encountering a patch of food decreased, the likelihood that the pigeons would accept the lean patch would increase. The results, summarized in Figure 7.7, confirmed the prediction. The percentage of short-duration patches accepted by the pigeons increased as the duration of the VI schedule in the search state became longer (see also Fantino & Preston, 1988). This study illustrates some of the complexities involved in making an optimal decision about entering a food patch.

As we have noted, the second major decision involved in foraging is whether or not to remain in the selected patch or go to another

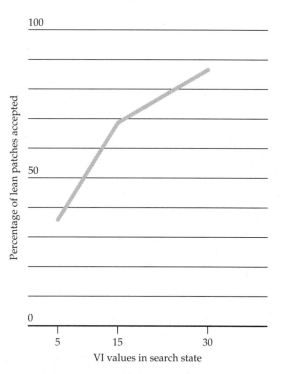

Figure 7.7 Mean percentage of lean patches of food accepted as a function of the probability of encountering the next food patch, as determined by the VI schedule in the search state. *(From "Choice, Foraging, and Reinforcer Duration" by M. Ito and E. Fantino, 1986, Journal of the Experimental Analysis of Behavior, 46, pp. 93–103. Copyright © 1986 by Journal of the Experimental Analysis of Behavior. Reprinted by permission.)*

one. Interestingly, the considerations involved in this decision are similar in some respects to those involved in entering a patch. In the natural environment, patches of food have a fixed amount of food in them, so that the longer an animal harvests food from a chosen patch, the less food remains there. As the patch becomes depleted, the animal has to decide whether to remain there or try to find a richer source of food. The decision is a difficult one. Optimality requires leaving at just the right time. If the animal leaves too early, it will give up food that is readily at hand. By contrast, if it stays too long, it will be wasting its time on a depleting patch when it could be harvesting a richer one. As in the decision to enter a patch, optimality in leaving a patch requires comparing the current situation to possible future gains.

Various laboratory procedures have been devised to investigate the foraging problem posed by a depleting patch (see Shettleworth, 1988). In one approach, animals are given a choice between two patches of food. One patch always provides food at a moderate rate and is therefore a nondepleting patch. The second patch starts out much richer in food but becomes depleted (see for example, Bhatt & Wasserman, 1987; Redhead & Tyler, 1988; Wanchisen, Tatham, & Hineline, 1988). Optimal choice in this situation requires selecting the depleting patch at first (since it is richer in food initially). However, as food becomes harder to get in the depleting patch, the animal should switch to the nondepleting patch.

Kamil, Yoerg, and Clements (1988) tested this prediction in a study of the foraging behavior of blue jays using a variation on a concurrent-chain schedule (see also Kamil & Clements, 1990). Blue jays eat insects, including moths. In this experiment encounter with an insect was simulated by presenting a picture of a moth. The birds faced a wall with two small rectangular panels on which pictures could be projected from the back (see Figure 7.8). The pictures either showed a conspicuous black and white moth on a pink background or just showed the background. If a picture of a moth appeared, the birds got a bit of food. The right panel represented a nondepleting patch and the left panel represented a depleting patch. Both patches were available throughout the experiment.

The birds selected the depleting or the nondepleting patch by pecking a small circular pecking key below the rectangular picture panels. If they selected the nondepleting patch, a picture of a moth appeared 25% of the time, each appearance followed by access to food reinforcement. Thus, selection of the nondepleting patch was reinforced intermit-

tently. No matter how often the birds encountered a moth on the nondepleting side, the probability of finding another one in that patch (and hence the probability of reinforcement) remained 25%.

If the birds selected the depleting patch, finding a prey item was more likely at first. The birds encountered a picture of a moth (and food reinforcement) 50% of the time. However, the depleting side had a limited number of moths available during each session. After the birds had obtained the available number, no more moths were to be had there for the remainder of the session. In different parts of the experiment, each session started with 9, 6, or 3 moths in the depleting patch. Thus, initially the probability of reinforcement on the depleting side was greater than on the nondepleting side (50% as compared to 25%). However, as the session progressed and all the moths on the depleting side were found, the relative probabilities reversed, with the depleting side now having a lower probability of reinforcement (0%) than the nondepleting side (25%).

As expected, the choice behavior of the blue jays tracked the probabilities of reinforcement in the two patches. At the start of a session, the blue jays were more likely to select the depleting patch. However, as each session progressed, they switched to the nondepleting patch. The birds learned to respond quite efficiently, obtaining more than 90% of all possible moths in each session.

Optimality: Description rather than mechanism. Deciding when to enter a patch and when to depart from it in a way that optimizes the rate of obtaining food involves complex judgments. The food density of the current and possible future patches has to be accurately assessed, impending changes in the current patch (depletion) have to be correctly judged, the likelihood of encountering another patch soon has to be determined, and the effort and risk involved in traveling to the next patch have to be considered in compar-

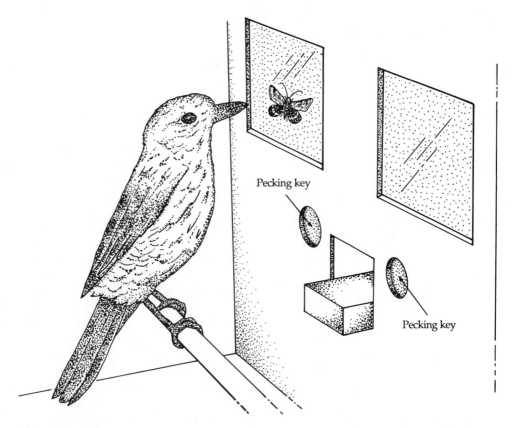

Figure 7.8   A blue jay in an experiment on the effects of patch depletion on foraging behavior. Patches were represented by slides projected from the rear on the rectangular displays on either side of the food dish above the pecking keys. The slides sometimes showed a black and white *Cotocala relicta* moth. *(Drawing based on a photograph provided by A. Kamil.)*

ison to the likely benefits. Optimal foraging theories say nothing about the mechanisms animals use to accomplish all of this successfully. Rather, optimal foraging theories describe what constitutes optimal performance.

To assume that optimality is a mechanism of foraging, one would have to assume that animals have fabulous abilities to calculate probabilities and weigh costs and benefits over a large span of time. However, optimality calculations often require complex mathematics, something animals are not likely to do. If animals do not make complex optimality calculations, how do they manage to approximate optimal choice performance? Answers

to this question are beginning to emerge from the interactive efforts of biologists and psychologists. Psychologists are beginning to explore the behavioral processes that might be involved in foraging situations and the ways in which those behavioral processes may contribute to near-optimal performance (for example, Fantino & Abarca, 1985; Gibbon, Church, Fairhust, & Kacelnik, 1988; Timberlake, Gawley, & Lucas, 1987, 1988).

One interesting conclusion that has emerged from considerations of the mechanisms animals use in foraging is that animals do not have to make complicated optimality calculations in order to perform near optimally. Following some simple *rules of thumb* often can lead to nearly the same outcome as more complicated optimality calculations. Consider, for example, the study of foraging in blue jays we used as an example of choice behavior. Recall that in this experiment the animals had to decide when to switch from a depleting to a nondepleting patch. Kamil and his associates (1988) discovered that the probability of leaving the depleting patch was determined by two factors. One of these was the number of times in a row the birds failed to find a moth in the depleting patch. This factor is called the *run of bad luck.* According to the rule of thumb, the longer the run of bad luck in the depleting patch, the more likely the birds were to switch to the nondepleting patch. The other rule of thumb was related to the number of moths the birds had already found in the depleting patch. The depleting patch had a limited number of moths at the start of each session. When all of those had been found, there were no more for the rest of the session. The blue jays evidently detected this aspect of the situation and were more likely to switch to the nondepleting patch once they had obtained close to the total number of moths available on the depleting patch that day. The two rules of thumb (run of bad luck and number of prey already found) were used in combination. The birds were more likely to switch in response to a particular run of bad luck if they had already obtained most of the available prey.

Studies of foraging behavior have enriched our knowledge of the mechanisms of response allocation in the same manner as behavioral economics; that is, such studies have focused attention on some previously ignored factors that are important determinants of choice. Studies of foraging behavior have also expanded the conceptual framework for the investigation of instrumental conditioning by emphasizing the ecological validity of laboratory studies and by raising questions about species differences in response allocation.

Concluding Comments

The research and theories about reinforcement discussed in this chapter represent several points of view. No one approach is comprehensive. Each approach starts from a particular set of ideas about what a reinforcer is. The choice of whether to regard a reinforcer as a stimulus or as a response leads, as we have seen, in different directions. In fact, a reinforcer in most cases involves both stimuli and responses. Determining a common feature for all reinforcers is therefore an extremely complex task.

Explaining the mechanism of reinforcement likewise rests on a set of starting assumptions about instrumental behavior. The instrumental response was originally viewed as a single behavior that increases in frequency with reinforcement. Drive-reduction theorists suggested a physiologically based mechanism to account for this "stamping in" effect. However, with more research it became clear that the motivating circumstances are not so simple. As we have seen, more comprehensive approaches to the problem of reinforcement take a broader view of the organism's behavior. An instrumental conditioning procedure is considered to be a constraint on the organism's free-flow of behavior, and increases in the instrumental response are regarded as by-products of a comprehensive response reorganization or reallocation. The nature of the response reallocation depends on the availability of substitutes and the costs and benefits of alternative strategies. So far, the most productive working assumption has been that the response reallocation results in optimality in some sense. However, what is being optimized and how the optimization is achieved remain subjects of investigation and theoretical controversy.

The story of the development of theories of reinforcement is an exciting illustration of the course of scientific inquiry. It spans intellectual developments from simple stimulus–response drive-reduction formulations to comprehensive considerations of how the organism's repertoire is constrained by instrumental contingencies and how organisms solve complex ecological problems. In this aspect of the study of conditioning and learning, perhaps more so than in any other, investigators have moved boldly to explore radically new conceptions when older ideas did not meet the challenges posed by new empirical findings.

8

Stimulus Control of Behavior

Chapter 8 is organized around the principles of stimulus control. Although most of the chapter deals with the ways in which instrumental behavior comes under the control of particular stimuli that are present when the response is reinforced, the concepts we will discuss are equally applicable to classical conditioning. We will begin with the definition of stimulus control and the basic concepts of stimulus discrimination and generalization and go on to discuss factors that determine the extent to which behavior comes to be restricted to particular stimulus values. Along the way, we will describe special forms of stimulus control (intradimensional discrimination) and control by special categories of stimuli (compound stimuli and contextual cues). We will conclude this chapter with a discussion of the learning of conditional and hierarchical relations in both instrumental and classical conditioning.

In our discussion of instrumental behavior so far, we have emphasized the relation between the instrumental response and the reinforcer. As we have seen in Chapters 5–7, the response–reinforcer relation is a very important aspect of instrumental conditioning. However, it is not the only factor that determines the occurrence of instrumental behavior. Responses and reinforcers do not occur in a vacuum; rather, they occur in the presence of particular stimuli. Such stimuli can come to determine whether or not the subject performs the instrumental response. Responding may come under the control of the stimuli that are present when the response is reinforced. In this section we will describe the stimulus control of instrumental behavior and some of the processes that are responsible for it.

Stimulus control of instrumental behavior is evident in many spheres of life outside the laboratory. For most students, for example, studying is under the strong control of school-related stimuli. College students who have fallen behind in their work often make determined resolutions to do a lot of studying when they return home during Thanksgiving, Christmas, or spring vacation. However, despite their good intentions, it is not likely that much work gets accomplished during these holidays. The stimulus context of the holidays is usually very different from the stimulus context when classes are in session. Therefore, the holiday stimuli do not evoke effective studying behavior. Traveling businesspeople often have a similar problem. They may find it difficult to get much work done on airplanes because the stimulus context of an airplane is too different from the stimuli of their offices.

Stimulus control of behavior is an important aspect of behavioral adjustments to the environment. The survival of animals in the wild frequently depends on their ability to perform responses that are appropriate to the stimulus circumstances. With seasonal changes in their food supply, for example, animals may have to change their foraging responses to obtain food. Within the same season, one type of behavior is required in the presence of predators or intruders and other types of responses are reinforced in the absence of nearby danger. In cold weather, animals may seek comfort by going to areas warmed by the sun; on rainy days, they may seek comfort by going to sheltered areas. To be effective in obtaining comfort and avoiding pain, animals always have to behave in ways that are appropriate to their changing circumstances.

Performance of instrumental responses appropriate to the stimulus situation is so important that failure to do this is often considered abnormal. Many instrumental acts that are evident in psychologically disturbed persons are pathological only in that they occur in situations where they should not. Getting undressed, for example, is acceptable instrumental behavior in the privacy of your bedroom. The same behavior on a public street is considered highly abnormal. Staring at a television set is considered appropriate if the set is turned on. Staring at a blank television screen may be a symptom of behavior pathology. If you respond in a loving way in the presence of your spouse or other family members, your behavior generally has positive consequences. The same behavior directed toward strangers on the street can have quite different effects. Yelling and screaming are reinforced by social approval at football games. The same responses are frowned on if they occur in a church, a classroom, or a supermarket.

As we have noted, reinforcement of an instrumental response typically occurs in the presence of particular stimuli, and these stimuli may come to control the performance of the instrumental behavior. How can we tell that instrumental behavior has come under the control of such stimuli? How do stimuli gain control over instrumental behavior? In what sense do these stimuli control behavior, and what do subjects learn about the stimuli? Questions such as these have been extensively discussed and investigated. Some of the highlights of this research will be reviewed in the present chapter. (For a more detailed discussion of the stimulus control of behavior, see Balsam, 1988.)

Differential Responding and Stimulus Discrimination

The first problem that has to be solved in an investigation of stimulus control is how to identify and measure instances of this effect. How can we tell that an instrumental response has come under the control of certain cues? Consider, for example, a pigeon pecking for food on a variable-interval reinforcement schedule in a Skinner box. While in the Skinner box, the pigeon is exposed to a wide variety of stimuli, including the color and texture of the walls of the chamber, the sight of the nuts and bolts holding the chamber together, the odor of the chamber, and the noises of the ventilating fan. In addition, let us assume that the circular response key in the box is illuminated by a pattern consisting of a white triangle on a red background. The pigeon in this situation is probably also stimulated by internal sensations relating to its degree of food deprivation and its general physical well-being. How can we determine whether these external and internal stimuli control the pigeon's key-pecking behavior?

Reynolds (1961) conducted an experiment using stimuli similar to those we have just described. Two pigeons were reinforced on a variable-interval schedule for pecking a circular response key. Reinforcement for pecking was available whenever the response key was illuminated by a visual pattern consisting of a white triangle on a red background (see Figure 8.1). The stimulus on the key thus had two components—the white triangle and the red color of the background. Reynolds was interested in finding out which of these stimulus components gained control over the pecking behavior. Therefore, after the pigeons learned to peck steadily at the triangle on the red background, Reynolds measured the amount of pecking that occurred when only one of the component stimuli was presented. On some of the test trials, the white triangle was projected on the response key without the red color. On other test trials, the red background color was projected on the response key without the white triangle.

The results are summarized in Figure 8.1. One of the pigeons pecked a great deal more when the response key was illuminated with the red light than when it was illuminated with the white triangle. This outcome shows that its pecking behavior was much more strongly controlled by the red color than by the white triangle. By contrast, the other pigeon pecked a great deal more when the white triangle was projected on the response key than when the key was illuminated by the red light. Thus, for this subject, the pecking behavior was more strongly controlled by the triangle than by the color stimulus.

Reynolds' experiment illustrates several important ideas. First, it shows how we can experimentally determine whether instrumental behavior has come under the control of a particular stimulus. *Stimulus control of instrumental behavior is demonstrated by differential responding in the presence of different stimuli.* If a subject responds in one way in the presence of one stimulus and in a different way in the presence of another stimulus, we can conclude that its behavior has come under the control of the stimuli involved. Such differential responding was evident in the behavior of both pigeons Reynolds tested. Both animals responded more frequently in the presence of one of the stimuli (red color or triangle) than in the presence of the other.

Differential responding to two or more stimuli also indicates that the subjects are discriminating among the stimuli—that they are treating each stimulus as different from the other cues. Such stimulus discrimination does not always occur. If the pigeons had ignored the visual cues projected on the response key or had been blind, they would have responded the same way to the white triangle and the red background. The fact that they responded differently to the two stimuli

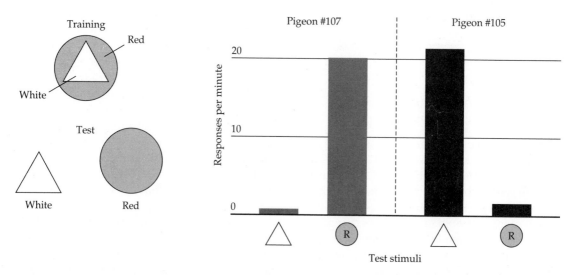

Figure 8.1 Summary of procedure and results of experiment by Reynolds (1961). Two pigeons were first reinforced for pecking whenever a compound stimulus consisting of a white triangle on a red background was projected on the response key. The rate of pecking was then observed in each subject when the white triangle and the red background stimuli were presented separately.

shows that they discriminated between the two cues. Thus, *stimulus discrimination exists whenever subjects respond differently to different stimuli*. Stimulus discrimination and stimulus control are two ways of considering the same phenomenon. One cannot have one without the other. If a subject does not discriminate between two stimuli, its behavior is not under the control of those cues.

Another interesting aspect of the results of Reynolds' experiment was that the pecking behavior of each animal came under the control of a different stimulus component. The behavior of one bird came under the control of the red color and the behavior of the other bird came under the control of the triangle. The procedures used in the experiment did not direct the animals to attend especially to either the red light or the triangle. Therefore, it is not surprising that different stimuli came to control pecking behavior in the two subjects. The experiment was comparable to showing a group of children a picture of a cowboy grooming a horse. Some of the children may focus on the cowboy, whereas others may find the horse more interesting. In

the absence of special procedures of the sort we will discuss shortly, one cannot always predict which of the various stimuli an organism experiences will gain control over its instrumental behavior.

Although only one of the stimulus components evoked much pecking in each of the pigeons, we cannot conclude from this information that the other stimulus had no effect whatever. Measures of some other response to the stimuli or other tests of key pecking may provide evidence of control by both stimulus components (Wilkie & Masson, 1976). As the experiment was conducted, it yielded information only about the stimulus control of key pecking in an extinction test. The conclusions that can be reached from the study are also limited to the stimulus features that were varied in the tests. The fact that one pigeon responded more frequently to the white triangle than the red background allows us to conclude only that some property or properties of the triangle were important. It does not tell us that the shape of the triangle was the critical feature of the stimulus. The pecking behavior may have been controlled instead by the color or brightness of the triangle. Further tests are required to identify exactly which of these stimulus characteristics controlled the pecking behavior. These considerations indicate that the conclusions that can be reached about stimulus control are limited to the particular responses, stimuli, and test procedures that are used.

Stimulus Generalization

In our discussion so far, we have treated stimuli as if they were clearly identifiable and distinguishable entities in the world. However, identifying and differentiating various stimuli is not a simple matter. Stimuli may be defined in all kinds of ways. Sometimes widely different objects or events are considered instances of the same stimulus because they all share the same function. A wheel, for example, may be small or large; may be spoked or not spoked; may be made of wood, rubber, or metal; and may or may not have a tire on it. By contrast, in other cases stimuli are identified and distinguished in terms of precise physical features, such as the frequency of sound waves or the wavelength of light. The color red, for example, refers to a small range of wavelengths of light. Light that fails to fall within this restricted range (reddish orange, for example) is not considered red even if it misses the criterion range only slightly.

Psychologists and physiologists have long been concerned with how organisms identify and distinguish different stimuli. In fact, some have suggested that this is the single most important question in psychology (Stevens, 1951). The problem is central to the analysis of stimulus control. As we will see, numerous factors are involved in the identification and differentiation of stimuli. Experimental analyses of the problem have depended mainly on the phenomenon of **stimulus generalization.** In a sense, stimulus generalization is the opposite of differential responding, or stimulus discrimination. Stimulus generalization is said to exist *whenever the subject fails to respond*

differently to various stimuli — whenever the same level of behavior is observed in the presence of different stimuli.

The phenomenon of stimulus generalization was first observed by Pavlov. He found that after a particular stimulus was conditioned, subjects would also make the conditioned response to other, similar stimuli. That is, they failed to respond differentially to stimuli that were similar to the original conditioned stimulus. Stimulus generalization has also been investigated in instrumental conditioning. In a landmark experiment, Guttman and Kalish (1956) first reinforced pigeons on a variable-interval schedule for pecking a response key illuminated by a yellowish-orange light with a wavelength of 580 nanometers (nm). After training, the animals were tested with a variety of other colors presented in a random order without reinforcement, and the rate of responding in the presence of each color was recorded. The results of the experiment are summarized in Figure 8.2. The highest rate of pecking occurred in response to the original 580-nm light. The subjects also made substantial numbers of pecks when lights of 570- and 590-nm wavelength were tested: the responding generalized to the 570-nm and 590-nm stimuli. However, as the color of the test stimuli became increasingly different from the color of the original training stimulus, progressively fewer responses occurred. The results show a gradient of responding as a function of how similar each test stimulus was to the original training stimulus. This type of outcome is called a **stimulus generalization gradient.**

Stimulus Generalization Gradients as a Measure of Stimulus Control

Stimulus generalization gradients are often used to evaluate stimulus control because they provide information about how sensitive the subject's behavior is to variations in a particular aspect of the environment (see Honig & Urcuioli, 1981). With the use of stimulus

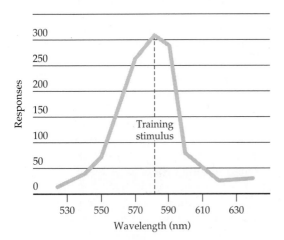

Figure 8.2 Stimulus generalization gradient for pigeons that were trained to peck in the presence of a colored light of 580-nm wavelength and then tested in the presence of other colors. *(From "Discriminability and Stimulus Generalization" by N. Guttman and H.I. Kalish, 1956,* Journal of Experimental Psychology, 51, *pp. 79–88.)*

generalization gradients, we can determine exactly how much the environment has to be changed to produce a change in behavior. Consider, for example, the gradient in Figure 8.2. Subjects responded much more when the original 580-nm training stimulus was presented than when the response key was illuminated by lights whose wavelengths were 520, 540, 620, and 640 nm. Thus, differences in color controlled different levels of responding. However, this control was not very precise. Responding to the 580-nm color generalized to the 570- and 590-nm stimuli. The wavelength of the 580-nm training stimulus had to be changed by more than 10 nm before a decrement in performance was observed. This aspect of the stimulus generalization gradient provides precise information about how much the wavelength of the light had to be changed for the pigeons to treat the colors as different from the training stimulus.

The fact that substantial rates of responding occurred in the presence of stimuli between 570 and 590 nm indicates that the color of the response key did not have to have a wavelength of exactly 580 nm to evoke the pecking

response. How do you suppose pigeons would have responded in this experiment if they had been color-blind? If the subjects had been color-blind, they could not have distinguished lights of different wavelengths. Therefore, they would have responded in much the same way regardless of what color was projected on the response key. Figure 8.3 presents hypothetical results of an experiment of this sort. If the pigeons did not respond on the basis of the color of the key light, similar high rates of responding would have occurred as different colors were projected on the key. Thus, the stimulus generalization gradient would have been flat.

A comparison of the results obtained by Guttman and Kalish and our hypothetical experiment with color-blind pigeons indicates that *the steepness of a stimulus generalization gradient can be used as a measure of the extent to which the stimulus feature being varied controls the behavior of the subjects.* A flat generalization gradient (Figure 8.3) is obtained if subjects respond in the same way to a variety of stimuli. This lack of differential responding shows that the stimulus feature that is varied in the generalization test does not control the

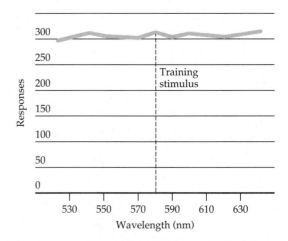

Figure 8.3 Hypothetical stimulus generalization gradient for color-blind pigeons trained to peck in the presence of a colored light of 580-nm wavelength and then tested in the presence of other colors.

instrumental behavior. By contrast, a steep generalization gradient (Figure 8.2) is obtained if subjects respond more to some of the test stimuli than to others. This differential responding is evidence that the instrumental behavior is under the control of the stimulus feature that is varied among the test stimuli. We may think of generalization and differential responding as opposites. If a great deal of generalization occurs, there is little differential responding. If responding is highly differential to stimuli, little generalization is obtained.

Effects of Sensory Capacity and Orientation on Stimulus Control

As we shall see, numerous factors determine whether, and to what extent, a particular stimulus will come to control responding. Consideration of these factors has to begin with the organism's sensory capacity and orientation. The range of stimuli that potentially can come to influence behavior is determined by the organism's sensory world — the world of sensations a particular subject experiences. Sensory capacity and orientation determine which stimuli are included in an organism's sensory world. Presentation of an environment with certain features of interest to us does not guarantee that the subject will respond to these same features. One must always consider the subject's own (and possibly unique) point of view or sensory world in analyzing stimulus control.

One of the most obvious determinants of how the subject perceives its environment is the organism's sensory capacities. A subject's behavior can come under the control of a particular stimulus only if the organism is sensitive to that stimulus. Events outside the range of what the subject can detect with its sense organs simply do not exist for that individual unless the stimuli are amplified or transduced into something the organism can detect. People, for example, cannot detect sounds whose pitch is above about 20,000 cycles per second. Such stimuli are called "ultrasounds" because they are outside the

Figure 8.4 An infant looking up at a mobile.

range of human hearing. Because ultrasounds are inaudible to people, such sounds cannot come to control human behavior. Other species, however, are able to hear ultrasounds. Dogs, for example, can hear whistles outside the range of human hearing and therefore can be trained to respond to such sounds.

Limitations on the stimuli that can come to control behavior are also set by whether the subject comes in contact with the stimulus. Consider, for example, a child's crib. Parents often place mobiles and other decorations on and around the crib to provide interesting stimuli for the child to look at. The crib shown in Figure 8.4 is decorated with such a mobile. The mobile consists of several thin needlework animal figures mounted on cardboard (including a giraffe, a seal, and a lion). Which aspects of this stimulus complex can potentially control the child's behavior? To answer this question, one first has to consider what the child sees about the mobile rather than what the mobile looks like to adults. From the child's vantage point under the mobile, only the bottom edges of the animal figures are visible. The shapes of the animals and surface decorations cannot be seen very well from below. Therefore, these other features are not likely to gain control of the child's looking behavior. These considerations illustrate that the subject's orientation with respect to the various features of its environment greatly influences which stimuli can gain control over its behavior. (For research findings illustrating the importance of orientation for the acquisition of stimulus control, see,

---

BOX **8.1**

Generalization of Treatment Outcomes

Behavioral treatment procedures, as other forms of treatment or therapy, are typically conducted under specific circumstances (with special stimuli, on a particular training ward, or with a particular therapist). For the resultant modifications of behavior to be maximally useful, what is learned during treatment has to generalize outside the training situation. An autistic student, for example, who is taught certain communicative responses in interactions with a particular therapist should also exhibit those responses in interactions with caretakers and others. In promoting generalization of treatment outcomes, the following approaches may be used (for example, Schreibman, Koegel, Charlop, & Egel, 1990; Stokes & Baer, 1977):

1. One approach is to try to *make the treatment situation as similar as possible to the natural environment.* Thus, if the natural environment provides reinforcement only intermittently, a good idea is to reduce the frequency of reinforcement during treatment sessions as well. Another way to increase the similarity of the treatment procedure to the natural environment is to use the same reinforcers as those the subject is likely to encounter in the natural environment.

2. Generalization also may be increased by *conducting the treatment procedure in new settings.* This strategy is called *sequential modification.* After a behavior has been conditioned in one situation (a classroom), training is conducted in a new situation (the playground). If that does not result in sufficient generalization, training can be extended to a third environment (the school cafeteria).

3. Another effective procedure is to *use sufficient numbers of exemplars during training.* In trying to extinguish or countercondition fear of elevators, for example, training should be conducted with a sufficient number of different types of elevators. In training retarded students how to use a spoon properly, training with different types of spoons and with different types of foods (applesauce, ice cream, and soup) will encourage generalization.

4. Generalization may be also encouraged by *conditioning the new responses to stimuli that are common to various situations.* Language provides effective mediating stimuli. Responses conditioned to verbal or instructional cues are likely to generalize to new situations in which those instructional stimuli are encountered.

5. Another approach is to *make the training procedure indiscriminable or incidental to other activities.* In one study (McGee, Krantz, & McClannahan, 1986), for example, the investigators took advantage of the interest that autistic children showed in specific toys during a play session to teach the children how to read the names of the toys.

6. Finally, generalization outside a training situation is achieved if the training helps to *bring the subject in contact with contingencies of reinforcement available in the natural environment* (Baer & Wolf, 1970). Once a response is acquired through special training, the behavior often can be maintained by naturally available reinforcement. Once a child learns to swim or ride a bicycle with the help of special instruction, these behaviors are maintained by pleasures provided by the activities. Similarly, teaching children rudimentary social skills involved in cooperative play may enable them to derive enjoyment from playing with other children outside the training situation. To take advantage of naturally occurring reinforcement in maintaining newly acquired behavior, the naturally available contingencies of reinforcement must be identified and treatment procedures must focus on teaching the skills necessary to procure those reinforcers.

for example, Gillette, Martin, & Bellingham, 1980.)

Effects of Experience on Stimulus Control

One of the most important determinants of stimulus control is the subject's past experience. The suggestion that experience with stimuli may determine the extent to which those stimuli will come to control behavior originated in an early theoretical dispute about the mechanisms of stimulus generalization. The first model of stimulus generalization was offered by Pavlov. Pavlov observed stimulus generalization effects in his classical conditioning experiments. He noted, for example, that if a tactile stimulus applied to one part of the skin was conditioned with a US, tactile stimuli applied to nearby areas of the skin would also elicit the conditioned response. However, the strength of the conditioned response was less as the test stimuli were applied to areas farther and farther from the location of the original CS. From such observations, Pavlov formulated a model of stimulus generalization based on the **irradiation of excitation.**

Pavlov assumed that every stimulus produces excitation in a particular area of the cortex and that similar stimuli activate physically adjacent areas. He proposed that when a CS is presented and paired with reinforcement, excitation occurs in the brain locus corresponding to the CS, and this excitation irradiates to adjacent brain locations, much as circular waves irradiate from the point of contact when a pebble is tossed into a calm lake. The irradiation of excitation was assumed to grow progressively weaker with increasing distance from the center of excitation. You may recall from Chapter 4 that simultaneous excitation of the CS and US centers was assumed to result in an association between the two stimuli. Because of the irradiation of excitation, whenever the CS was presented, nearby areas also became activated, and Pavlov assumed that these nearby areas of the brain also became associated with the US center. Thus, during the course of conditioning, the US was assumed to become associated not only with the CS but also with stimuli that were similar to the CS.

The neural mechanism Pavlov proposed to explain stimulus generalization was greeted with skepticism, but the basic idea that effects of training spread to stimuli similar in some way to the training cues was adopted by such major behavior theorists as Hull and Spence. However, some psychologists argued that even this formulation was unacceptable. Consider, for example, our hypothetical experiment on stimulus generalization in color-blind pigeons. We suggested that such animals would respond equally to stimuli of various colors. They would show perfect stimulus generalization. Such a result could not be explained in terms of the spread of effect of excitation because, in color-blind animals, the presentation of a particular color during training presumably does not produce excitation of a brain area corresponding to that color. A much more reasonable explanation of the results with color-blind subjects is that they respond similarly to all the colors because they cannot distinguish differences between them. This type of alternative account of stimulus generalization was proposed by Lashley and Wade (1946) in a spirited attack on the irradiation-of-excitation hypothesis. Lashley and Wade suggested that the generalization of a conditioned response from one stimulus to another reflects a failure of subjects to discriminate differences between the stimuli. They suggested that animals have to learn to treat stimuli as similar to or different from one another. Thus, in contrast to Pavlov, they considered the shape of a stimulus generalization gradient to be determined entirely by the subject's previous sensory experiences rather than by the physical properties of the stimuli tested.

Encouraged in part by Lashley and Wade's proposals, investigators have shown considerable interest in the effects of experience on stimulus control. Lashley and Wade assumed that animals learn to distinguish similarities and differences between stimuli by experiencing natural variations of the stimuli. Exposure to various colors during one's normal course of activities, for example, was assumed to produce color discrimination. If this is true, then animals raised in a colorless environment should show less differential responding based on color than animals previously exposed to color stimuli. This prediction has been confirmed (see, for example, Rudolph, Honig, & Gerry, 1969). However, limiting the exposure of animals to color stimuli does not block the development of stimulus control entirely.

Stimulus discrimination training. A possible reason that animals raised in a colorless environment do not show strong stimulus control is that they have not had different types of experiences with color stimuli. For example, color cues have not distinguished various objects in the environment for them. This possibility can be tested by means of **stimulus discrimination procedures.** In a stimulus discrimination procedure, the subject is exposed to at least two different stimuli—let us say a red and a green light. However, reinforcement for performing the instrumental response is available only in the presence of one of the colors. For example, the subject could be reinforced for responding on trials when the red light is on but not when the green light is on. In this procedure, diagramed in Figure 8.5, the red light signals the availability of reinforcement for responding. The green light signals that responding will not be reinforced. The stimulus that signals the availability of reinforcement is often called the **S+** or **S^D** (pronounced "ess dee"). By contrast, the stimulus that signals the lack of reinforcement is often called the **S−** or **S$^\Delta$** (pronounced "ess delta").

With sufficient exposure to a discrimination procedure, subjects will come to respond whenever the S+ is presented and withhold responding whenever the S− is presented.

The acquisition of this pattern of responding is illustrated in the graph of Figure 8.5. Initially, subjects respond similarly in the presence of the S+ and the S−. However, as training progresses, responding in the presence of the S+ persists and responding in the presence of the S− declines. The fact that the subjects respond much more to the S+ than to the S− indicates differential responding to the S+ and S− stimuli. Thus, stimulus discrimination procedures establish control by the stimuli that signal when reinforcement is and is not available. Once S+ and S− have gained control over the subject's behavior, they are called **discriminative stimuli.** S+ is a discriminative stimulus for performing the instrumental response, and S− is a discriminative stimulus for not performing the response.

The procedure diagramed in Figure 8.5 is the standard procedure for stimulus discrimination training in instrumental conditioning. Stimulus discriminations can be also established with the use of classical conditioning procedures. In this case one CS (the CS+) is paired with the unconditioned stimulus and another CS (the CS−) is presented in the absence of the US. With repeated pairings of the CS+ with the US and presentations of the CS− by itself, subjects will gradually learn to make the conditioned response to the CS+ and inhibit the conditioned response when the CS− is presented. (We discussed this procedure in Chapter 3; see Figure 3.8.) Instrumental stimulus discrimination procedures are different from classical conditioning procedures only in that the subject has to perform the instrumental response in the presence of the S+ in order to receive reinforcement. Thus, the S+ does not signal that reinforcement will be automatically provided. Rather, the S+ indicates that performance of the instrumental response will be reinforced.

Multiple schedules of reinforcement. The stimulus discrimination procedure shown in Figure 8.5 is just one way in which differential responding can be established. Differential

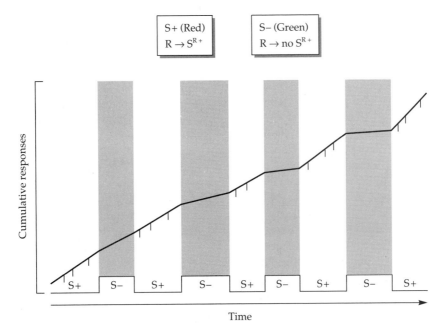

Figure 8.5 Procedure and hypothetical results (presented as a cumulative record) of stimulus discrimination training. Responding is reinforced on a variable-interval schedule in the presence of the S+ (a red light) and is not reinforced in the presence of the S− (a green light). Differential responding gradually develops to the two stimuli. (Hatch marks on the cumulative record indicate reinforcements.)

responding to two (or more) stimuli can develop whenever each stimulus signals a different schedule of reinforcement for the instrumental response. For example, we could reinforce responding in the presence of a red light on a variable-ratio 5 schedule of reinforcement (VR 5) and reinforce responding in the presence of a green light on a fixed-interval 1-minute schedule (FI 1 min). Such a procedure is diagramed in Figure 8.6. You may recall from Chapter 6 that a variable-ratio schedule maintains a stable rate of responding. By contrast, on a fixed-interval schedule subjects pause just after each reinforcement and gradually increase their rate of responding after that until the next reinforcement (producing a scalloped pattern). In a multiple schedule, subjects will gradually come to perform the appropriate pattern of instrumental behavior in the presence of each stimulus.

Whenever the red light is on, a steady rate of responding will occur, corresponding to the variable-ratio schedule; whenever the green light is on, a scalloped pattern will be evident, corresponding to the fixed-interval schedule. This outcome is illustrated in Figure 8.6. The different patterns of responding that occur in the presence of the red and green lights indicate that these stimuli control differential responding. To conclude that there is differential responding to stimuli, one does not necessarily have to see responding to one stimulus and no responding to a different stimulus.

A procedure of the sort shown in Figure 8.6 is called a **multiple schedule of reinforcement.** In a multiple schedule, different schedules of reinforcement are in effect consecutively in the presence of different stimuli. Stimulus discrimination procedures are a special type of multiple schedule in which the reinforcement schedule provided in the presence of one of the stimuli is extinction. The general result with multiple schedules is that the pattern of responding that occurs in the presence of a particular stimulus corresponds to whatever reinforcement schedule is in effect with that stimulus. Multiple schedules illustrate that the patterns of responding produced by various schedules of reinforcement can come under the control of stimuli present when each schedule is in effect.

Stimulus discrimination and multiple schedules outside the laboratory. Nearly all reinforcement schedules that exist outside the laboratory are in effect only in the presence of

particular stimuli. Playing a game yields reinforcement only in the presence of enjoyable or challenging partners. Hurrying is reinforced in the presence of stimuli that indicate that you will be late and is not reinforced in the presence of stimuli that indicate that you will not be late. Driving rapidly is reinforced when you are on the highway but not when you are on a city street. Loud and boisterous discussions with your friends are reinforced at a party Saturday night. The same type of behavior is not reinforced during a sermon in church. Eating with your fingers is reinforced when you are on a picnic but not when you are in a fine restaurant. Getting dressed in your best clothes is reinforced when you are going to the senior prom but not when you are

---

Stimulus Control of Sleeping in Children

BOX **8.2**

Getting young children to go to sleep in the evening and remain asleep during the night is often a challenge for parents. Night wakings by young children can be stressful for parents and have been linked to increased maternal malaise, marital discord, and child abuse. Behavioral approaches to the treatment of night waking have stressed the concepts of stimulus control and extinction.

In the absence of special intervention, the child typically wakes up at night and cries or calls a parent. The parent visits with the child and tries to put him or her back to sleep either in the child's own bed or in the parent's bed, where the child eventually falls asleep. This scenario may serve to maintain the sleep disturbance in two ways. First, parental attention upon waking may serve to reinforce the child for waking up. Second, special efforts the parent makes to encourage the child to go back to sleep (taking the child into the parent's bed, for example) may introduce special discriminative stimuli for getting back to sleep. In the absence of those cues, getting back to sleep may be especially difficult.

In a 1990 study of behavioral treatment of night waking in infants from 8 to 20 months old, France and Hudson gave parents the following instructions:

At bedtime, carry out the usual bed-time routine (story, song, etc.). Then place *(child's name)* in bed. Bid him or her "Good night" and immediately leave the room. Do not return unless absolutely necessary. If absolutely necessary, check your child (when illness or danger is suspected), but do so in silence and with a minimum of light. (p. 93)

This procedure was intended to minimize reinforcement of the child for waking up. The procedure was also intended to make the child's own bed in the absence of parental interaction a discriminative stimulus for getting back to sleep should the child wake up at night. With the introduction of these procedures, all 7 infants in the study were reported to decrease the number of times they woke up and cried or called for their parents during the night. Prior to introduction of the procedure, the mean number of nightly awakenings was 3.3. After the treatment procedure, this declined to .8. A similar decrease was observed in the total duration of nightly awakenings. These gains were maintained during follow-up tests conducted 3 months and 2 years later.

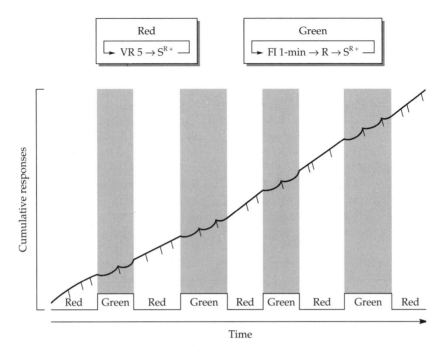

Figure 8.6 Procedure and hypothetical results (presented as a cumulative record) of a multiple schedule of reinforcement. Responding is reinforced on a variable-ratio 5 schedule in the presence of a red light and is reinforced on a fixed-interval 1-minute schedule in the presence of a green light. A steady rate of responding characteristic of a VR 5 schedule occurs during the red light and a scalloped pattern of responding characteristic of an FI 1-min schedule occurs during the green light. (Hatch marks on the cumulative record indicate reinforcements.)

preparing to paint the garage. Your daily activities typically consist of going from one situation to another (to the kitchen to get breakfast, to the bus stop, to your office, to someone else's office, to the grocery store, and so on), and in each situation reinforcement is provided on different schedules.

Effects of discrimination training on stimulus control. We have noted that discrimination training brings the instrumental response under the control of the stimuli used. We reached this conclusion because discrimination training produces differential responding to the S+ and S− stimuli. How precise is the control that S+ acquires over the instrumental behavior, and what factors determine the precision of the stimulus control that is

achieved? To answer such questions, it is not enough to note differential responding to S+ versus S−. One must also find out how steep the generalization gradient is when subjects are tested with stimuli that systematically vary from the S+ along some stimulus dimension. Furthermore, one must find out which aspect of the discrimination training procedure is responsible for the type of stimulus generalization gradient obtained. These issues were first addressed in classic experiments by Jenkins and Harrison (1960, 1962).

Jenkins and Harrison investigated how auditory stimuli of different frequencies (pitches) come to control the pecking behavior of pigeons reinforced with food. They measured how pigeons responded to tones of various frequencies after three types of training procedures. One group of subjects was reinforced during training for pecking in the presence of a 1,000-cycle-per-second tone and received no reinforcement when the tone was off. Therefore, for these subjects the 1,000-cps tone served as the S+ and the absence of tones served as the S−. A second group of pigeons also received discrimination training. The 1,000-cps tone again served as the S+. However, for the second group the S− was a 950-cps tone. Thus, these pigeons were reinforced for pecking whenever the 1,000-cps tone was presented and were not reinforced whenever the 950-cps tone was presented. The third group of pigeons served as a control group and did not receive discrimination training. The 1,000-cps tone was continuously turned on for these animals, and they could always receive reinforcement for pecking in the experimental chamber.

Upon completion of the preceding training procedures, each pigeon was tested for pecking in the presence of tones of various frequencies to see how precisely pecking was controlled by the pitch of the tones in each group. Figure 8.7 shows the generalization gradients obtained in the experiment. The control group, which had not received discrimination training, responded nearly equally in the presence of all the test stimuli: the pitch of the tones did not control behavior. Each of the other two training procedures produced control over the pecking behavior by the frequency of the tones. The strongest stimulus control (steepest generalization gradient) was observed in animals that had been reinforced for responding in the presence of the 1,000-cps tone (S+) and not for responding to the 950-cps tone (S−). Subjects that had received discrimination training between the 1,000-cps tone (S+) and the absence of tones (S−) showed an intermediate degree of stimulus control by tonal frequency.

Jenkins and Harrison's experiment shows that *discrimination training increases the stimulus control of instrumental behavior.* Furthermore, a particular stimulus dimension, such as tonal frequency, is most likely to gain control over responding if the S+ and S− stimuli used in the discrimination procedure differ along that stimulus dimension. The most precise control by tonal frequency was observed in subjects that had received discrimination training in which the S+ was a tone of one frequency (1,000 cps) and the S− was a tone of another frequency (950 cps). Discrimination training did not produce as strong control by pitch if the S+ was a 1,000-cps tone and the S− was the absence of tones. In this case, subjects learned a discrimination between the presence and absence of the 1,000-cps tone and could have been responding in part on the basis of the loudness or timbre of the tone in addition to its frequency.

Some investigators have used results of the sort obtained by Jenkins and Harrison to argue that stimuli come to control instrumental behavior only if subjects experience differential reinforcement in connection with the stimuli (for example, Terrace, 1966). According to this suggestion, if subjects are not exposed to different reinforcement schedules in the presence of different stimuli, these stimuli will not gain control over their behavior.

In analyzing why a particular type of stimulus has gained control over instrumental behavior, it is important to consider not only the differential reinforcement that is provided during an experiment but also the differential reinforcement that may occur outside the experimental context. Thomas, Mariner, and Sherry (1969), for example, replicated the control group tested by Jenkins and Harrison and confirmed that the generalization gradient for tonal frequencies is flat when subjects do not receive discrimination training. They also tested a second group of pigeons that had received experience with a 1,000-cps tone in the home cage. For these subjects the 1,000-cps tone was sounded every time food was delivered in the home cage. Key-peck training in the experimental chamber was conducted in the same way for these animals as for the

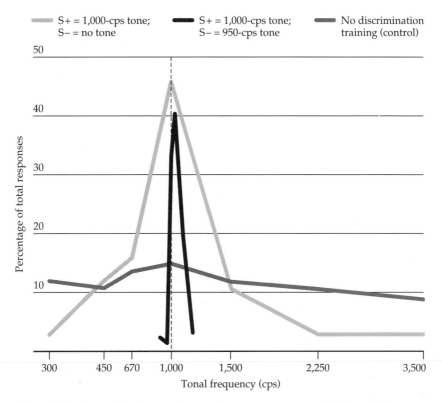

Figure 8.7 Generalization gradients of response to tones of different frequencies after various types of training. One group received discrimination training in which a 1,000-cps tone served as the S+ and the absence of tones served as the S−. Another group received training in which a 1,000-cps tone served as the S+ and a 950-cps tone served as the S−. The control group did not receive discrimination training before the generalization test. *(From "Effects of Discrimination Training on Auditory Generalization" by H.M. Jenkins and R.H. Harrison, 1960.* Journal of Experimental Psychology, 59, *pp. 246–253; Also from "Generalization Gradients of Inhibition Following Auditory Discrimination Learning" by H.M. Jenkins and R.H. Harrison, 1962.* Journal of the Experimental Analysis of Behavior, 5, *pp. 435–441.)*

control group. Tests of stimulus generalization using tones of various frequencies resulted in a steep generalization gradient for the group that had experienced the tone paired with food delivery. Thus, the effects of differential training conducted in the home cage with the 1,000-cps tone transferred to the experimental chamber and resulted in greater stimulus control of pecking by the frequency of the tones.

The idea that differential reinforcement is necessary for the development of stimulus

control is intuitively attractive. However, the hypothesis is also nearly impossible to refute with experimentation. Any time we find a case in which stimulus control occurs in the absence of explicit differential training, one can always postulate a possible source of inadvertent differential training that might have occurred outside the experimental situation. The mere fact, for example, that different responses are required to obtain food in a Skinner box than in the home cage may be sufficient to produce control by the stimuli in the Skinner box. (For a further discussion of this issue, see Balsam, 1988.)

Range of possible discriminative stimuli.   Discrimination procedures can be used to bring a subject's instrumental behavior under the control of a wide variety of stimuli. For example, Eslinger and Ludvigson (1980) used the odors left by rewarded versus nonrewarded rats as discriminative stimuli for other rats (see also Batsell, Ludvigson, & Kunko, 1990). Spetch and Wilkie (1981) used 10-second versus 5-second presentations of food as discriminative stimuli for pigeons. Capaldi, Nawrocki, and Verry (1984) showed that internal cues of recently having been rewarded or not rewarded can serve as discriminative stimuli for future instrumental responses. D'Amato and Salmon (1982) used two different tunes as discriminative stimuli for rats and monkeys, and Porter and Neuringer (1984) showed that pigeons are able to discriminate the music of Bach from that of Stravinsky and generalize this discrimination to music of other composers from the same periods in musical history. Others have trained pigeons to discriminate the sound of different spoken words (Pisacreta, Gough, Redwood, & Goodfellow, 1986) and uniform from mixed arrays of dots (Honig, 1991).

The fact that stimulus discrimination procedures can be used to bring behavior under the control of a wide variety of stimuli makes these procedures powerful tools for the investigation of how animals process information. We will see some impressive fruits of this research in our discussions of animal cognition in Chapters 11 and 12. Studies of discrimination learning have also yielded some unexpected information about animal social behavior.

In several bird and mammalian species, sexually inexperienced males fail to discriminate males and females of their own species. Male ruffed grouse, for example, have been observed to respond similarly to male and female grouse (Allen, 1934), and young male red-winged blackbirds have been observed to copulate with taxidermic models of various bird species, seemingly unaware of the sex of the models (Noble & Vogt, 1935). In more recent research, male Japanese quail have been observed to copulate with both male and female quail, also apparently unaware of the sex of the other birds (for example, Wilson & Bermant, 1972). However, they can learn which quail is a male and which is a female if they are exposed to a discrimination training procedure in which exposure to females is paired with sexual reinforcement (in the form of copulatory opportunity) and exposure to males is provided without reinforcement (Domjan & Ravert, 1991; Nash, Domjan, & Askins, 1989). Thus, if female quail serve as an S+ and male quail serve as an S− for sexual reinforcement, subjects learn to discriminate females from males and come to prefer remaining near females. Interestingly, in many respects learning to discriminate the sex of other quail occurs in much the same way as other more conventional forms of discrimination learning. The critical factor is differential reinforcement of the female and male cues (see also Nash & Domjan, 1991).

What Is Learned in Discrimination Training?

As we have seen, if an instrumental response is reinforced in the presence of one stimulus (S+) and not reinforced in the presence of another stimulus (S−), these stimuli will come to control occurrences of the instrumental behavior. Because of the profound effect that discrimination training has on stimulus control, investigators have been interested in what subjects learn during discrimination training. Consider the following relatively simple situation: Responses are reinforced whenever a red light is turned on (S+) and not reinforced whenever a loud tone is presented (S−). What strategies could the subject use to make sure that most of its responses were reinforced in this situation? One possibility is that the subject will learn simply to respond whenever the S+ is present and will not learn anything about the S−. If it adopted the strategy "Respond only when S+ is present," the subject would end up responding much more to S+ than to S− and would obtain the available reinforcers. Another possibility is that the subject will learn to not respond during S− but will not learn anything about S+. This would constitute following the rule "Suppress responding only when S− is present." If the subject took this approach, it would also end up responding much more to S+ than to S−. A third possibility is that the subject will learn both to respond to S+ and to not respond to S−. Thus, it may learn something about the significance of both the stimuli in the discrimination procedure.

Spence's Theory of Discrimination Learning

One of the first and most influential theories of discrimination learning was proposed by Kenneth Spence in 1936. Spence advocated the last of the possibilities we have just described. According to his theory, reinforcement of a response in the presence of the S+ conditions excitatory properties to the S+ that come to evoke the instrumental behavior on future presentations of this stimulus. By contrast, nonreinforcement of responding during presentations of S− is assumed to condition inhibitory properties to S− that serve to inhibit the instrumental behavior on future presentations of S−. Differential responding to S+ and S− is assumed to reflect the excitation and inhibition that become conditioned to S+ and S−, respectively.

How can we experimentally evaluate the excitation–inhibition theory of discrimination learning? As we have noted, mere observation that subjects respond more to S+ than to S− is not sufficient to argue that they have learned something about both of these stimuli.

More sophisticated experimental tests are required. One possibility is to use stimulus generalization gradients. If an excitatory tendency has become conditioned to S+, then stimuli that increasingly differ from S+ should be progressively less effective in evoking the instrumental response. In other words, we should observe a steep generalization gradient, with the greatest amount of responding occurring to S+. Such an outcome is called an **excitatory stimulus generalization gradient.** If an inhibitory tendency has become conditioned to S−, then stimuli that increasingly differ from S− should be progressively less effective in inhibiting the instrumental response. Such an outcome is called an **inhibitory stimulus generalization gradient.**

Behavioral techniques were not sufficiently sophisticated when Spence proposed his theory to allow direct observation of the kind of excitatory and inhibitory stimulus generalization gradients his theory assumed. However, experimental tests conducted decades later proved that his ideas were substantially correct. In one important experiment, two groups of pigeons received discrimination training with visual stimuli before tests of stimulus generalization (Honig, Boneau, Burstein, & Pennypacker, 1963). One group of subjects was reinforced for pecking when the response key was illuminated by a white light that had a black vertical bar superimposed on it (S+) and was not reinforced when the white light was presented without the vertical bar (S−). The second group of animals received the same type of discrimination training; however, for them the S+ and S− stimuli were reversed. The black vertical bar served as the S− and white key without the bar served as the S+. After both groups had learned to respond much more to S+ than to S−, Honig and his colleagues conducted tests of stimulus generalization to see how much control the vertical bar had gained over the instrumental behavior in the two groups. The test stimuli consisted of the black bar on a white back-

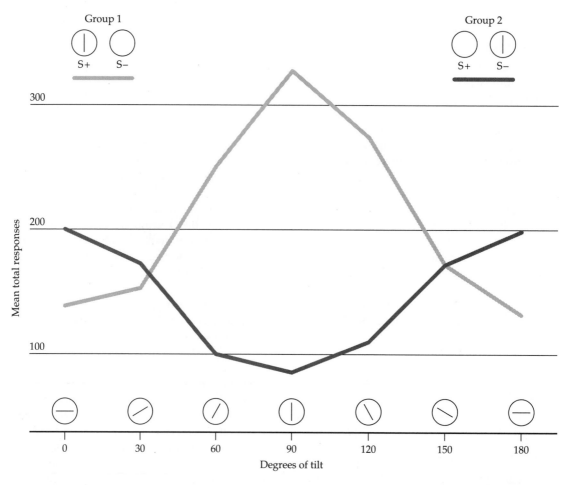

Figure 8.8 Stimulus generalization gradients for line-tilt stimuli in two groups of subjects after discrimination training. For group 1 a vertical black bar on a white background served as the S+ and the white light without the bar served as the S−. For group 2 the functions of the stimuli were reversed. *(From "Positive and Negative Generalization Gradients Obtained Under Equivalent Training Conditions" by W.K. Honig, C.A. Boneau, K.R. Burstein, and H.S. Pennypacker, 1963,* Journal of Comparative and Physiological Psychology, 56, *pp. 111–116.)*

ground, with the bar tilted at various angles away from the vertical position.

The results of the experiment are summarized in Figure 8.8. Let us first consider the outcome for group 1. Recall that for this group the vertical bar had served as the S+ during discrimination training. Therefore, these subjects came to respond in the presence of the vertical bar. During the generalization test, the highest rate of responding occurred when the bar was presented in the original vertical position, and progressively less responding was observed when the bar was tilted farther and farther away from the vertical. These results indicate that the position of the vertical bar had gained control over the pecking behavior when the stimulus served as S+. Let us consider next the results for group 2. For these subjects the vertical bar had served as the S− during discrimination training. At the end of discrimination training, these subjects did not peck when the vertical bar was projected on the response key. Results of the generalization test indicated that this failure to respond to the vertical bar was due to active inhibition of the pecking behavior in response to the position of the vertical bar. As the bar was tilted farther and farther away from the original vertical position, progressively more pecking occurred. Stimuli that were increasingly different from the original S− produced progressively less inhibition of the pecking behavior.

This experiment shows that discrimination training can produce both excitatory conditioning to S+ and inhibitory conditioning to S−. An excitatory stimulus generalization gradient around the vertical bar was obtained when the bar served as the S+, and an inhibitory gradient of generalization around the vertical bar was obtained when the bar served as the S−. The excitatory gradient had an inverted-U shape, with greatest responding occurring to the original S+. The inhibitory gradient had the opposite shape, with the least responding occurring to the original S−. The fact that gradients of excitation and inhibition can occur around S+ and S− provides strong support for Spence's theory of discrimination learning.

The choice of the stimuli that served as S+ and S− in this experiment was very important for the conclusions that were reached. Consider, for example, group 2, which received the vertical bar on a white background as the S− and the white background without a bar as the S+. Responding in the inhibitory generalization gradient increased as the bar was tilted away from vertical. This outcome could not be explained by claiming that tilting the black bar made the test stimuli more similar to the S+. Changing the orientation of the black bar does not make a bar stimulus more or less similar to the white background

alone (the S+). The bar stimuli are qualitatively different from the background alone. As we will discuss later in this chapter, different results occur if the S+ and S− stimuli differ quantitatively rather than qualitatively (see "Effects of Intradimensional Discrimination Training").

Errorless Discrimination Training

The results of the experiment we have just described show that discrimination training can result in excitatory tendencies conditioned to the S+ and inhibitory tendencies conditioned to the S−. However, this experiment does not tell us whether all discrimination training procedures produce both kinds of learning. In fact, subsequent research has shown that discrimination training does not always result in inhibitory tendencies conditioned to the S−. In the typical discrimination procedure, the S+ and S− stimuli remain unchanged during the course of training. Initially, subjects respond both during presentations of the S+ and presentations of the S− (see Figure 8.5). However, because reinforcement is not available during S−, responding during S− gradually becomes extinguished. In a series of important experiments, Terrace (1964, 1966) investigated whether subjects can learn a discrimination without ever making a response to S− and experiencing the fact that responses are not reinforced during S−.

Terrace developed a novel discrimination procedure in which subjects make very few if any responses during S− ("errors"). The technique involves gradually fading in the S− stimulus. Let us assume that we wish to train pigeons to peck when the response key is illuminated by a red light and to not peck when the key is illuminated by a green light. If we used a standard discrimination procedure, we would present the red and green stimuli on alternate trials and reinforce the pecking response only during the red light. The intensity and duration of the S+ and S−

stimuli would remain the same during the course of training. In Terrace's errorless discrimination procedure the S+ is presented at the same intensity and duration on every S+ trial throughout training (for example, Terrace, 1972). However, this is not true for the S−; the S− is gradually faded in. During the initial trials of the discrimination procedure, the S− is presented so briefly and at such a low intensity that the subject does not respond to it. The duration and intensity of the S− are gradually increased in small steps on successive S− trials as discrimination training progresses. If these fading steps are small enough, subjects may never respond to the S−. Thus, the fading procedure enables the discrimination to be learned without errors.

Early results suggested that errorless discrimination training leads to fundamentally different types of reactions to S− than more standard discrimination techniques. As we have seen, during the course of conventional discrimination training, the S− comes to actively inhibit the instrumental response (see Figure 8.8). The S− also becomes aversive to the subject and may elicit aggressive responses and attempts to escape and avoid the S−. Another possible result of conventional discrimination training is the peak-shift effect, to be described in the next section. Terrace found that, after errorless discrimination training, the S− does not come to actively inhibit responding or to produce aggression or escape and avoidance attempts; moreover, the peak-shift effect does not occur. He therefore proposed that the performance of nonreinforced responses to S− ("errors") during the course of discrimination training is necessary for the S− to actively inhibit responding and produce the various other side effects of conventional discrimination training (for example, Terrace, 1972). However, subsequent research has shown that the absence of errors is probably not the critical factor. Rather, the fading technique used to introduce the S− in the errorless procedure may be what prevents the S− from becoming conditioned to actively

inhibit responding and produce the emotional effects of more conventionally trained S− stimuli (Rilling, 1977).

Effects of Intradimensional Discrimination Training

So far we have discussed general characteristics of stimulus discrimination training that can be found with any combination of stimuli serving as the S+ and the S− in a discrimination procedure. In addition to the effects already described, certain special problems and phenomena arise if the S+ and S− in a discrimination procedure differ from each other in only one stimulus characteristic, such as color, brightness, or pitch. Training procedures in which the S+ and S− are identical except in one stimulus characteristic involve **intradimensional discrimination.** Consider, for example, discrimination training in which the S+ and S− are identical in every respect except color. What effect will the similarity in the colors of S+ and S− have on the control of S+ over the instrumental behavior? Will the rate of response to S+ be determined mainly by the availability of reinforcement in the presence of S+, or will the rate of response to S+ also be influenced by how similar the color of S+ is to the color of S−?

The peak-shift phenomenon. In an important experiment, Hanson (1959) investigated the effects of intradimensional discrimination training on the extent to which various colors controlled the pecking behavior of pigeons. All the subjects in the experiment were reinforced for pecking in the presence of a light whose wavelength was 550 nanometers. Thus, the S+ was the same for all animals. The groups differed in how similar the S− was to the S+. One group, for example, received discrimination training in which the S− was a color of 590-nm wavelength. For another group the S− was much more similar to the S+; the wavelength of the S− was 555 nm, only 5 nm away from the S+. The performance of these subjects was compared with the behavior of a control group that did not receive discrimination training but was also reinforced for pecking in the presence of the 550-nm S+ stimulus. After these different types of training, all subjects were tested for their rate of pecking in the presence of stimuli of various wavelengths.

The results are shown in Figure 8.9. Let us consider first the performance of the control group. These animals showed the highest rates of response to the S+ stimulus, and progressively lower rates of responding occurred as the subjects were tested with stimuli increasingly different from the S+. Thus, the control group showed the usual excitatory stimulus generalization gradient around the S+. Animals that had received discrimination training with the 590-nm color as S− yielded slightly different results. They also responded at high rates to the 550-nm color that had served as the S+. However, these subjects showed much more generalization of the pecking response to the 540-nm color. In fact, their rate of response was slightly higher to the 540-nm color than to the original 550-nm S+. This shift of the peak responding away from the original S+ was even more dramatic in subjects that had received discrimination training with the 555-nm color as S−. These subjects showed much lower rates of responding to the original S+ (550 nm) than either of the other two groups. Furthermore, their highest response rates occurred to colors of 540- and 530-nm wavelength. This shift of the peak of the generalization gradient away from the original S+ is remarkable because in the earlier phase of discrimination training, responding was never reinforced in the presence of the 540-nm or 530-nm stimuli. The highest rates of pecking occurred to stimuli that had never even been presented during the original training.

The shift of the peak of the generalization gradient away from the original S+ is called the **peak-shift phenomenon**. The results of Hanson's experiment indicate that the peak-

shift effect occurs following intradimensional discrimination training. A shift in the peak of the generalization gradient did not occur in the control group, which had not received discrimination training. The peak of the generalization gradient is shifted away from S+ in a direction opposite the stimulus that was used as the S− in the discrimination procedure. In addition, the peak-shift effect was a function of the similarity of the S− to the S+ used in discrimination training. The greatest shift in peak responding occurred in subjects for which the S− had been very similar to the S+ (555 nm and 550 nm, respectively). The peak-shift effect was much less for subjects that had received discrimination training with more widely different colors (590 nm compared with 550 nm). A small peak-shift effect is also evident in Figure 8.7 for subjects that received intradimensional discrimination training (bold lines). (For other, more recent examples of the peak-shift effect, see Moye & Thomas, 1982; Weiss & Schindler, 1981.)

The Spence model of intradimensional discrimination learning. The peak-shift effect is remarkable because it shows that the only stimulus in whose presence responding is reinforced (the S+) is not necessarily the stimulus that evokes the highest rate of responding. How can this be? We previously described the 1963 findings of Honig and his colleagues, which showed that reinforcing responding in the presence of an S+ results in an excitatory stimulus generalization gradient centered around the S+ (see Figure 8.8). That seems inconsistent with the peak-shift phenomenon. How can peak shift be explained in terms of the excitatory and inhibitory gradients that we have assumed develop as a result of discrimination training? In an ingenious analysis, Spence (1937) suggested that excitatory and inhibitory gradients may in fact produce the peak-shift phenomenon. His analysis is particularly remarkable because it was proposed more than 20 years before the peak-shift effect was experimentally demonstrated.

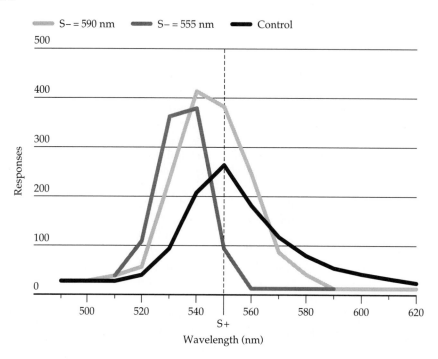

Figure 8.9 Effects of intradimensional discrimination training on stimulus control. All three groups of pigeons were reinforced for pecking in the presence of a 550-nm light (S+). One group received discrimination training in which the S− was a 590-nm light. Another group received discrimination training in which the S− was a 555-nm light. The third group served as a control and did not receive discrimination training before the test for stimulus generalization. *(From "Effects of Discrimination Training on Stimulus Generalization" by H.M. Hanson, 1959,* Journal of Experimental Psychology, 58, *pp. 321–333.)*

Spence's explanation is based on two assumptions. First, Spence assumed that intradimensional discrimination training produces excitatory and inhibitory stimulus generalization gradients centered at S+ and S−, respectively, in much the same way as other types of discrimination training. Second, he assumed that the tendency to respond to a particular stimulus is determined by the generalized excitation to that stimulus *minus* the generalized inhibition to that stimulus. By subtracting the assumed gradient of inhibition centered at S− from the assumed gradient of excitation centered at S+, Spence was able to predict the phenomenon of peak shift under certain circumstances.

Consider for example, Hanson's peak-shift experiment in which two similar colors served

as S+ and S− (see Figure 8.9). What is learned about the S+ and S− stimuli will presumably generalize along the color dimension (wavelength of light). Figure 8.10 shows the excitatory and inhibitory generalization gradients that will presumably develop around the S+ and S− stimuli. Notice that because S+ and S− are close together on the stimulus dimension, the excitatory and inhibitory gradients overlap a great deal. To predict the level of response that will occur to various wavelengths of light, one simply has to subtract the level of inhibition that is assumed to be generalized to a particular stimulus from the level of excitation generalized to that stimulus. The inhibitory gradient in Figure 8.10 does not extend to stimuli S_3 and S_4. Therefore, no generalized inhibition is subtracted from the gener-

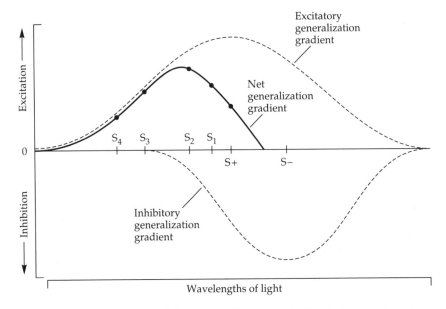

Figure 8.10 Spence's model of intradimensional discrimination learning. Excitatory and inhibitory stimulus generalization gradients (dashed curves) are assumed to become established around S+ and S−, respectively. The subject's behavior is assumed to reflect the net generalization gradient. The net gradient is calculated by subtracting the level of inhibition that is assumed to be generalized to a particular stimulus from the level of excitation that is assumed to be generalized to that stimulus. (See the accompanying text for further explanation.)

alized excitation for these test stimuli. The greatest amount of inhibition is subtracted from the generalized excitatory strength of stimulus S−, with lesser amounts subtracted from the S+ and test stimuli S_1 and S_2. The dots connected with a solid line in Figure 8.10 represent the net excitatory strength of S−, S+, and test stimuli S_1 through S_4.

The net excitatory gradient in Figure 8.10 is a prediction of the subject's behavior. This prediction is consistent with the peak-shift effect. Note that the peak of the net generalization gradient in Figure 8.10 is not at the S+ but is displaced away from S+ in a direction opposite S−. This is precisely what is observed in peak-shift experiments (see Figure 8.9).

Predictions from Spence's model depend on the exact shape of the excitatory and inhibitory gradients that are assumed to exist around S+ and S−, respectively. The shift in the peak of the net excitatory gradient away from S+ depends on the inhibitory generalization gradient extending to S+. If the S+ and S− stimuli are too far apart for this to happen (or the inhibitory gradient is not broad enough to extend to S+), the excitatory potential of S+ will not be reduced by generalized inhibition, and the peak-shift effect will not be observed. As mentioned previously, experimental techniques were unavailable to obtain direct evidence of excitatory and inhibitory gradients and their net effects at the time Spence proposed his model. However, more recent research conducted with modern operant conditioning techniques has provided impressive evidence for the types of generalization gradients Spence assumed served as the basis for peak shift (see Hearst, 1968, 1969; Klein & Rilling, 1974; Marsh, 1972).

A relational adaptation-level explanation of peak shift. As we noted earlier, studies of stimulus control can tell us a great deal about how animals (and people) view the world. An important question that has been a source of debate for decades is whether we view stimuli in terms of their individual and absolute properties or in terms of their relation to other stimuli that we experience (for example, Köhler, 1939). Evidence consistent with each of these approaches to the analysis of stimulus control is available, suggesting that both types of mechanisms are involved in how we respond.

Spence's model of discrimination learning is an absolute stimulus learning model. It predicts behavior based on the net excitatory properties of individual stimuli. Evidence of relational processes in stimulus control is illustrated by a recent experiment conducted with college students (Thomas, Mood, Morrison, & Wiertelak, 1991, Experiment 2). The experiment was relatively simple, consisting of discrimination training followed by a test of stimulus generalization. The factor manipulated in the experiment was the range of stimuli to which the subjects were exposed during the generalization test. One group of subjects received a wider range of test stimuli than another group. This manipulation should not change the results if behavior is governed by the absolute feature of each stimulus. However, if a given stimulus is viewed in relation to others that are experienced, the range of the test stimuli should influence the degree of stimulus control.

The training and test stimuli consisted of a black line in a circular field. The line was tilted to a different degree in each of 11 line tilts (numbered 1 through 11). Stimulus 1 was the steepest line (70° counterclockwise from the horizontal) and stimulus 11 was the flattest (only 20° from the horizontal). For all subjects, stimulus 1 was the S− and stimulus 4 (55° from horizontal) was the S+.

Training consisted of presenting the S+ and S− stimuli briefly, one at a time. At the start of the experiment, the subject was shown the S+ and told to press a button whenever that stimulus appeared again. During training the experimenter said "correct" each time a correct response was made. After the discrimination had been well learned, the subjects were given a generalization test with a variety of line-tilt stimuli. No feedback for responding was provided during the generalization test. For group 1, stimuli 1–7 (70°–40°) were presented during generalization testing. For group 2, stimuli 1–11 (70°–20°) were presented. Thus, the range of stimuli did not differ by much, but the second group was exposed to a wider range of test stimuli than the first.

The results of the experiment are presented in Figure 8.11. For the narrow-range group, the peak of the generalization gradient was at the S+, stimulus 4, and subjects favored higher numbered stimuli only slightly. Group 2 favored higher numbered stimuli much more than group 1 did. In fact, it favored responding to higher numbered stimuli so much that the peak of the generalization gradient was shifted away from the S+ and was at stimulus 6 instead of 4. These results are difficult to explain in terms of the generalization of conditioned excitation and inhibition because the two groups received the identical discrimination training procedures. Only the range of stimuli presented during the generalization test differed between them, and no response feedback or reinforcement was provided during generalization testing.

The peak shift illustrated in Figure 8.11 is consistent with a relational adaptation-level explanation (see Thomas et al., 1991). According to this explanation, stimuli are judged not in response to their absolute properties but in relation to all the other stimuli experienced in that situation. The range of stimuli experienced determines the *adaptation level* of the subject, and individual stimuli are judged in relation to this adaptation level. The adaptation level is a kind of average of the stimuli encountered. Exposure to higher numbered

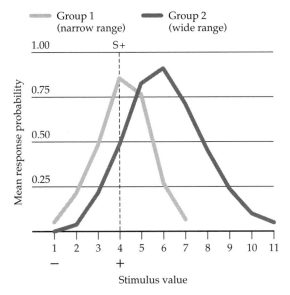

Figure 8.11 Mean line-angle generalization gradients obtained from college students. The S− was stimulus 1 and the S+ was stimulus 4 for all subjects. Group 1 was tested with stimuli 1–7, whereas group 2 was tested with stimuli 1–11. *(From "Peak Shift Revisited: A Test of Alternative Interpretations" D.R. Thomas, K. Mood, S. Morrison, and E. Wiertelak, 1991,* Journal of Experimental Psychology: Animal Behavior Processes, *17, pp. 130–140. Copyright © 1991 by the American Psychological Association. Reprinted by permission.)*

stimuli shifts the adaptation level to those stimuli.

During discrimination training, only the S+ and the S− were presented (stimuli 1 and 4). Thus, the adaptation level was presumably a value somewhere between stimuli 1 and 4. Because responding to stimulus 4 was reinforced, the subjects presumably learned to respond to a stimulus that exceeded their adaptation level by a certain amount. When the range of test stimuli was extended from stimulus 7 to stimulus 11, the adaptation level presumably also shifted to higher stimulus values. Because subjects learned to respond to a stimulus based on the stimulus exceeding the adaptation level, when the adaptation level shifted to higher stimulus values, responding also shifted to higher stimulus val-

ues and a peak-shift effect was observed. (For related evidence of stimulus-range effects in animal discrimination learning, see Hinson & Lockhead, 1986.)

Control of Behavior by Compound Stimuli

So far in our discussion of stimulus control, we have addressed how organisms respond to individual stimuli—a red or a green light, for example, or a vertical or horizontal line. However, stimuli never occur individually. Even such a simple stimulus as a circular pecking key illuminated with a red light is more appropriately considered a compound stimulus with various stimulus elements. These elements include, for example, the wavelength of the red light, its brightness, the shape of the response key, and the location of the key. Situations outside the laboratory are usually even more complex. During a football game, for example, cheering is reinforced by social approval if the people near you are all rooting for the same team as you are. The discriminative stimulus for cheering consists of a rich array of visual stimuli indicating that your team has scored, the sound of the announcer stating the score, and the complex visual and auditory cues provided by others around you cheering. As another example, consider the discriminative stimulus that tells you that pushing your grocery cart up to the checkout counter is appropriate. The customer before you has to have finished checking out, the checkout counter area has to be free of other carts, the checkout person is likely to glance in your direction, and if you hesitate, the people behind you in line are likely to have something to say.

What determines which and how many of the elements of a compound stimulus gain control over the instrumental behavior? Although all perceptible stimuli present at the time the response is made may gain some control over the behavior, certainly not all stimulus elements gain *equal* control over the instrumental response. Some elements come to exert much stronger influence on the instrumental behavior than others. In the present section we will consider some of the factors that determine which elements of a compound stimulus come to predominate in determining the occurrence of the instrumental behavior.

Compound stimuli as complex as those found at a football game or a checkout counter are difficult to analyze experimentally. Laboratory studies of how elements of a compound stimulus come to control instrumental behavior have been most often conducted with compounds that consist of only two simple elements, such as a light and a tone. Research has shown that which of the elements of a compound gains predominant control over the instrumental behavior depends on their relative effectiveness as signals for reinforcement, the type of reinforcement used, the responses subjects are required to perform for reinforcement, and the relative ease of conditioning of the stimulus elements.

Relative Effectiveness of Stimulus Elements as Signals for Reinforcement

We noted in the study of classical conditioning that the signal value of the CS is an important factor for conditioning. Simply pairing the CS with the US does not necessarily result in conditioning. If the US occurs both in the presence and in the absence of the CS, the CS may not become conditioned, even though it is periodically paired with the US. Similar findings have been observed with discriminative stimuli. The procedures used in one such investigation (Wagner et al., 1968) are summarized in Figure 8.12. Two groups of rats were conditioned with a discrete-trial procedure in which the subjects were reinforced on 50% of the trials for pressing a lever in the presence of a compound stimulus consisting of a light and one of two tones. For both groups, one of the

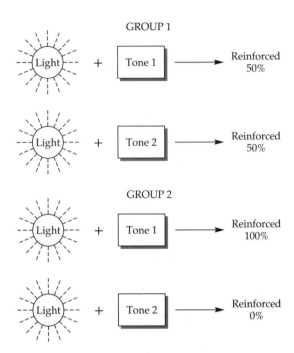

Figure 8.12 Diagram of experiment by Wagner, Logan, Haberlandt, and Price (1968). Relative to the two tones, the light was a better predictor of reinforcement for group 1 than for group 2. Consequently, subjects responded to the light more in group 1 than in group 2.

tones (tone 1) was presented simultaneously with the light on half of the trials, and the other (tone 2) was presented simultaneously with the light on the remaining trials. For group 1, responding was reinforced on 50% of the trials on which the light/tone-1 compound stimulus was presented and on 50% of the trials on which the light/tone-2 compound stimulus was presented.

Before describing the procedure for group 2, let us consider the relative predictive value of the two tones and the light stimulus in the procedure for group 1. Note that the subjects received reinforcement for responding 50% of the time when tone 1 was presented. The procedure also provided reinforcement 50% of the time when tone 2 was presented. Finally, the subjects were also reinforced 50% of the time when the light appeared, even though the light was presented on a greater total number of trials than the tones. Because reinforcement was delivered on 50% of the trials on which tone 1, tone 2, and the light were each presented, the three stimuli were equally good predictors of reinforcement in the situation.

The procedure for group 2 was similar to that for group 1 in many respects. Again tone 1 was presented with the light on half the trials and tone 2 was presented with the light on the remaining trials. However, this time reinforcement was always available on trials with the light/tone-1 compound stimulus. By contrast, responses were never reinforced on trials with the light/tone-2 stimulus. This procedure ensured that, as in group 1, reinforcement was available 50% of the time when the light stimulus was presented. However, this time the light stimulus was not as good a predictor of the availability of reinforcement as tone 1. Of the three stimuli, tone 1 was the best predictor of reinforcement because subjects could obtain reinforcement on 100% of the trials on which tone 1 was presented. Tone 2 was the least valid predictor of reinforcement because subjects were never reinforced on tone-2 trials. The value of the light as a signal for reinforcement was intermediate between the two tones.

Relative to the tones in the experiment, the light stimulus was a better predictor of the availability of reinforcement for group 1 than for group 2. Therefore, if the relative predictive value of the cues is important in determining stimulus control, we would expect the light to have greater control over the behavior of the animals in group 1 than in group 2. This is precisely what Wagner and his associates observed. In tests with the light stimulus presented alone at the end of the experiment, subjects in group 1 responded much more than subjects in group 2. It is important to realize that this outcome cannot be explained in terms of the percentage of time that reinforcement was available when the light stimulus was presented. In both groups 1 and

2, subjects could obtain reinforcement on 50% of the trials on which the light was presented. The critical difference between groups 1 and 2 was that, relative to the other stimuli in the situation (tones 1 and 2), the light was a better predictor of reinforcement for group 1 than for group 2.

Results of the sort obtained in the experiment just described clearly indicate that discriminative stimuli have a powerful effect on behavior not only because they are paired with the reinforcement but also because they signal how or when a reinforcer is to be obtained. Other things being equal, if a stimulus is a better predictor of the availability of reinforcement than another cue, it is more likely to gain control of instrumental behavior.

Effects of Type of Reinforcement on Stimulus Control

Stimulus control depends not only on the relative effectiveness of a stimulus as a signal for reinforcement but also on the nature of the reinforcer. Certain types of stimuli are more likely to gain predominant control over the instrumental response with positive than with negative reinforcement. This relation has been most clearly demonstrated in experiments with pigeons (see LoLordo, 1979).

In one study in this area (Foree & LoLordo, 1973), two groups of pigeons were given discrimination training to press a foot treadle in the presence of a compound stimulus consisting of a red light and a 440-cps tone. Responses in the absence of the light/tone compound were not reinforced. For one group of animals, reinforcement for treadle pressing in the presence of the light/tone S+ stimulus consisted of food. For the other group, treadle pressing was reinforced by the avoidance of shock. If these subjects pressed the treadle in the presence of the S+, no shock was delivered on that trial; if they failed to respond during the S+, a brief shock was periodically applied until a response occurred. Both groups of pigeons learned the discrimi-

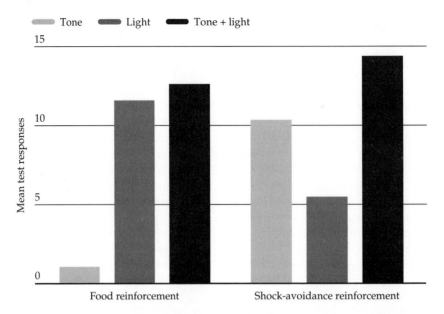

Figure 8.13 Effects of type of reinforcement on stimulus control. A treadle-press response in pigeons was reinforced in the presence of a compound stimulus consisting of a tone and a red light. With food reinforcement, the light gained much more control over the behavior than the tone. With shock-avoidance reinforcement, the tone gained more control over behavior than the light. *(Adapted from Foree, D.D., & LoLordo, V.M., 1973.)*

nation. The animals pressed the treadle much more frequently in the presence of the light/tone stimulus than in its absence. Once this occurred, Foree and LoLordo sought to determine which of the two components of the complex S+, the light or the tone, was primarily responsible for the response during the S+. Subjects received test trials in which the light or the tone stimulus was presented alone. Responding during these tests with the stimulus elements was then compared with the subjects' behavior when the light and the tone were presented simultaneously, as during the initial discrimination training.

The results are summarized in Figure 8.13. Pigeons that had received discrimination training with food reinforcement responded much more when tested with the light stimulus alone than when tested with the tone alone. In fact, their rate of treadle pressing in response to the isolated presentation of the

red light was nearly as high as when the light was presented simultaneously with the tone. We can conclude that the behavior of these subjects was nearly exclusively controlled by the red-light stimulus. A very different pattern of results occurred with the animals that had received discrimination training with shock-avoidance reinforcement. These animals responded much more when tested with the tone alone than when tested with the light alone. Thus, with shock-avoidance reinforcement the tone acquired more control over the treadle response than the red light.

Similar results have been obtained in a variety of experiments (for example, Kelley, 1986; Kraemer & Roberts, 1985; Schindler & Weiss, 1982; Shapiro et al., 1980; Shapiro & LoLordo, 1982). These findings indicate that stimulus control of instrumental behavior is determined in part by the type of reinforcement used. Visual stimuli appear to be more

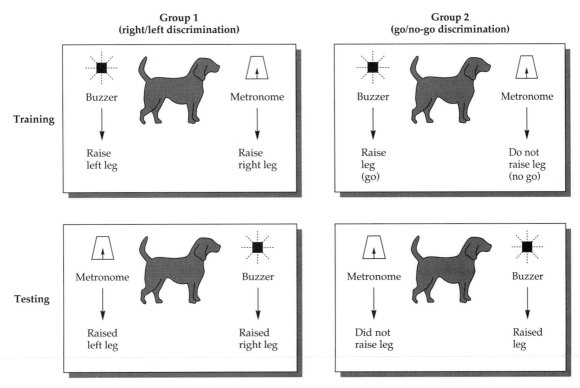

Figure 8.14 Diagram of experiment by Dobrzecka, Szwejkowska, and Konorski (1966). Dogs were conditioned in a left/right or go/no-go discrimination (groups 1 and 2, respectively) with auditory stimuli that differed both in location (in front or in back of the subjects) and in quality (the sound of a buzzer or a metronome). During testing, the location of the two sounds was reversed. The results showed that the left/right differential response was controlled mainly by the location of the sounds, whereas the go/no-go differential response was controlled mainly by the quality of the sounds.

likely to gain control over positively reinforced behavior than auditory cues, and auditory cues are more likely to gain control of negatively reinforced behavior than visual cues. This dependence of stimulus control on type of reinforcement is probably the result of the evolutionary history of pigeons. Responding to visual cues may be particularly useful for pigeons in seeking food, whereas responding to auditory cues may be particularly adaptive in avoiding danger. Unfortunately, we do not know enough about the evolutionary history of pigeons to be able to identify the evolutionary advantages of different types of stimulus control in different situations. We also do not know much about how stimulus control varies as a function of type of reinforcement in other species. This question is a fertile area for future research.

Effects of Type of Instrumental Response on Stimulus Control

Another factor that can determine which of several components of a discriminative stimulus gains control over behavior is the nature of the response required for reinforcement. The importance of the instrumental response for stimulus control is illustrated by an experiment by Dobrzecka, Szwejkowska, and Konorski (1966). These investigators studied discrimination learning in dogs with auditory stimuli. The dogs were gently restrained in a harness, with a metronome placed in front of them and a buzzer placed behind them. The metronome and buzzer provided qualitatively different types of sounds: the metronome produced a periodic beat and the buzzer produced a continuous rattle. The two stimulus sources also differed in location, one in front of the animal and the other behind it. Dobrzecka and his colleagues were interested in which of these two stimulus characteristics (quality of the sound or its location) would come to control behavior.

Two groups of dogs served in the experiment (see Figure 8.14). The two groups differed in what responses were required for reinforcement in the presence of the buzzer and the metronome stimuli. Group 1 received training on what can be called a right/left discrimination. When the metronome was sounded, subjects in this group were reinforced for raising the right leg; when the buzzer was sounded, they were reinforced for raising the left leg. Thus, the location of the response (right/left) was important for reinforcement in this group. Group 2 received training on what may be called a go/no-go discrimination. In this case the subjects learned to raise the right leg to the buzzer $(S+)$ but to leave it down when the metronome $(S-)$ was on. Thus, the quality of the response (go/no-go) was important for reinforcement for this group rather than its location.

What aspect of the sounds of the metronome and buzzer—quality or location—gained control over the instrumental behavior in the two groups of subjects? To answer this question, the animals were tested with the positions of the metronome and buzzer reversed. During these tests, the buzzer was placed in front of the animals and the metronome behind them (see Figure 8.14). This manipulation produced very different results in the two groups. Subjects trained on the right/left discrimination (in which the location of the response was critical for reinforcement)

had learned to respond mainly on the basis of the location of the auditory cues rather than their quality. Subjects in group 1 raised their right leg in response to sound from the front, regardless of whether the sound was made by the metronome or the buzzer. When the sound came from the back, they raised the left leg, again regardless of whether the sound was made by the metronome or the buzzer. Thus, the location of the sounds controlled their behavior much more than sound quality. The opposite outcome was observed in subjects trained on the go/no-go discrimination. These dogs responded mainly on the basis of the quality of the sound rather than its location. They raised a leg in response to the buzzer regardless of whether the sound came from the front or the back, and they did not raise a leg when the metronome was sounded, again irrespective of the location of the metronome.

These results indicate that responses that are differentiated by location (right/left) are more likely to come under the control of the location of discriminative stimuli. By contrast, responses that are differentiated by quality (go/no-go) are more likely to come under the control of the quality of discriminative stimuli (see also Bowe, Miller, & Green, 1987; Williams, Butler, & Overmier, 1990). Although some suggestions have been made for why such relations exist (see Neill & Harrison, 1987), a definitive explanation has yet to be found. However, the research to date clearly indicates that the activities required for reinforcement can determine which aspects of discriminative stimuli come to control the instrumental behavior.

Effects of Relative Ease of Conditioning Various Stimuli

Research on the effects of the type of reinforcement and the type of instrumental response on stimulus control has not been very extensive. Therefore, the range of discrimination situations in which these variables are important is not yet known. Another determinant of stimulus control, the relative ease of conditioning the various stimuli in the situation, has been known for a long time and is likely to be important in most instances of stimulus discrimination learning. As we noted in Chapter 4, Pavlov (1927) observed that if two stimuli are presented simultaneously, the presence of the stimulus that is easier to condition may hinder the conditioning of the other stimulus. This phenomenon is called **overshadowing.** The presence of the stimulus that becomes conditioned rapidly overshadows the conditioning of the other stimulus. In many of Pavlov's experiments, the two stimuli were of the same modality (two tones, for example) but differed in intensity. Generally, more intense stimuli become conditioned more rapidly. Pavlov found that a low-intensity stimulus could become conditioned (somewhat slowly) if it was presented by itself and repeatedly paired with the US. However, much less conditioning occurred if the weak stimulus was presented simultaneously with a more intense stimulus. Later research has shown that overshadowing can occur between stimuli of different modalities as well, provided that one stimulus is more easily conditioned than the other (for example, Kamin, 1969).

Although the phenomenon of overshadowing was first discovered in classical conditioning, it also occurs in instrumental discrimination procedures. (For a review, see Sutherland & Mackintosh, 1971.) If a stimulus is composed of two components, acquisition of control by the weaker component may be disrupted by the presence of the more effective component. From the research of LoLordo and his associates, for example, we would expect that in food-reinforcement situations the acquisition of control by an auditory stimulus would be overshadowed by the presence of a visual stimulus. We previously discussed studies of auditory-stimulus control of food-reinforced pecking in pigeons by Jenkins and Harrison (1960,

1962). The response key in these experiments was always illuminated with a white light, and unless one of the auditory cues was used as a discriminative stimulus, the pecking behavior did not come to be controlled by the auditory cues. This result was interpreted as showing that a stimulus must be an S+ in order to acquire control over behavior. However, a later experiment by Rudolph and Van Houten (1977) challenges this conclusion. They found steep auditory generalization gradients, indicating strong control by the auditory cues, provided that the pigeons pecked a dark key. This finding suggests that Jenkins and Harrison may not have found stimulus control of pecking by auditory cues in the absence of discrimination training (see Figure 8.7) because the response key they used was illuminated with a light. Perhaps the light overshadowed the auditory stimulus during training.

Theoretical Approaches to the Control of Behavior by Compound Stimuli

Having described some important empirical phenomena involving the control of behavior by compound stimuli, let us now turn to theoretical issues. How should we analyze the behavioral processes that are responsible for compound-stimulus effects? Historically, two different approaches have been taken in solving this problem. The first, and perhaps most familiar, strategy is to assume that organisms respond to a compound stimulus in terms of the elements that make up the compound. This is called the **stimulus-element** approach. It is exemplified by models that assume that elements of a compound stimulus compete with one another for association with the reinforcer or for the attention of the subject. We described this type of model in Chapter 4. Success in the competition may be considered to be a function of the various factors we noted as being relevant to the control of behavior by elements of a compound stimulus—relative effectiveness in predicting reinforcement, the nature of the reinforcer, the nature of the required response, and the relative ease of conditioning the stimulus elements.

An important alternative conceptual strategy assumes that subjects treat a compound stimulus as an integral whole that is not divided into parts or elements. This is called the **configural-cue** approach. According to the configural-cue approach, subjects respond to a compound stimulus in terms of the unique configuration of its elements. It is assumed that the elements are not treated as separate entities. In fact, they may not even be identified. Rather, stimulus elements are important only in terms of how they contribute to the entire configuration of stimulation provided by the compound.

The concept of a configural cue may be illustrated by considering the sound made by a symphony orchestra. The orchestral sound originates from the sounds of the individual instruments. However, the sound of the entire orchestra is very different from the sound of any of the individual instruments, many of which are difficult to identify when the entire orchestra is playing. We primarily hear the configuration of the sounds made by the individual instruments.

The configural-cue approach to the analysis of control by compound stimuli has enjoyed considerable success (Pearce, 1987). Under certain conditions, animals clearly seem to respond to compound stimuli in terms of the configuration of the elements that make up the compound. (For some recent examples, see Kehoe, 1986; Kehoe & Graham, 1988; Pearce & Wilson, 1990a, 1990b; Rescorla, Grau, & Durlach, 1985.) Consider, for example, a *positive patterning* procedure. In such a procedure, reinforcement is available whenever two stimuli are presented together (AB+) but is never presented when each of the stimulus elements appears by itself (A−, B−). Thus, the pattern or configuration of the elements A and B is the signal for reinforcement. Successful

responding under these circumstances requires treating the compound AB differently from its elements A and B.

The configural-cue approach is also consistent with some results obtained when reinforcement does not require responding to the configuration created by a stimulus compound. Consider, for example, an overshadowing experiment involving two stimulus elements, one weak (a) and the other intense (A). The two stimuli are presented together (aA) as cues for reinforcement during conditioning, but nothing in the contingencies of reinforcement requires attending to the configuration of the two stimulus elements. Following conditioning with the compound, tests are conducted with each of the elements presented alone, and the more intense or salient of the elements (A) is found to control more behavior.

According to the configural-cue approach, this outcome should be viewed as reflecting different degrees of stimulus generalization (Pearce, 1987) because the stimulus elements presented by themselves (a or A) are different from the two elements presented as a compound (aA) during conditioning. The more intense stimulus element (A) is presumably more similar to the compound (aA) present during training than the weaker stimulus element (a). Therefore, more of the behavior conditioned to the compound generalizes to the intense stimulus (A) than to the weak stimulus (a), producing the overshadowing effect.

Despite its considerable successes, the configural-cue approach cannot explain all of the results of compound-stimulus experiments. For example, the configural-cue approach is basically incompatible with findings indicating that stimulus control is a function of the type of reinforcer used or the response required. The most prudent conclusion at this point is that organisms respond to stimulus compounds both in terms of the stimulus elements that make up the compound and in terms of unique stimulus configurations created by the stimulus elements.

Control of Instrumental Behavior by Contextual Cues

So far we have been discussing the control of behavior by discrete stimuli, such as a tone, light, or buzzer, presented individually or compounded with each other. A stimulus is said to be discrete if it is presented for a brief period and has a clear beginning and end. The use of discrete stimuli in studies of stimulus control has its roots in reflexology. In the study of a reflex, a discrete stimulus (a puff of air) is employed to elicit a specific response (an eyeblink). As we have seen, instrumental behavior can also come under the control of discrete stimuli, especially when a discrimination training procedure is employed. For example, if a pigeon is reinforced for pecking a key when a vertical line is presented and not reinforced when a horizontal line appears, the pecking behavior will come to be controlled by the line-angle stimuli. Presentation of the S+ will stimulate pecking, in a manner analogous (but not identical) to the elicitation of an eyeblink response by a puff of air.

Although studies with discrete stimuli have provided much information about the stimulus control of instrumental behavior, such studies do not tell the whole story. A more comprehensive analysis of the stimuli organisms experience during the course of instrumental conditioning indicates that discrete discriminative stimuli occur in the presence of background contextual cues. The contextual cues may be provided by visual, auditory, or olfactory cues of the room or place where the discrete discriminative stimuli are presented. Recent research indicates that contextual cues can provide an important additional source of control of learned behavior.

Several of the examples of stimulus control we described at the beginning of this chapter involve the control of behavior by contextual cues. It is easier to concentrate on your studies when you are in the school library rather than at home during holidays because of contextual control of studying behavior. Yelling and screaming at a football game but not during a church sermon also illustrates the power of contextual cues.

Contextual cues can come to control behavior in a variety of ways. (For reviews, see Balsam, 1985; Balsam & Tomie, 1985.) For example, contextual cues can be used in place of discrete discriminative stimuli in a discrimination procedure and thereby come to function in much the same manner as discrete stimuli. Consider a procedure in which a pigeon is placed alternately in a noisy and a silent experimental chamber and is reinforced for pecking a key in one chamber (the S+ context) but not in the other (the S− context). With such a procedure, the pigeon will learn to make the pecking response only in the S+ context. The S+ and S− contexts will come to function in much the same way as if a discrete red light had served as the S+ and a green light had served as the S−. This example of contextual control of behavior is perhaps not surprising because here the contextual cues served as signals for the availability of reinforcement.

Do contextual cues come to control behavior when they do not serve as a signal for the availability of reinforcement — when they are "background" stimuli that the subject is not specifically required to pay attention to? This is one of the major questions in the stimulus control of instrumental behavior. Much work has been devoted to it, and the answer appears to be yes.

In one experiment, for example, Thomas, McKelvie, and Mah (1985) first trained pigeons on a line-orientation discrimination in which a vertical line (90°) served as the S+ and a horizontal line (0°) served as the S−. The pigeons were reinforced with food for pecking on a VI 30-sec schedule on S+ trials and were not reinforced on S− trials. The training took place in a standard Skinner box (context 1), but the availability of reinforcement was signaled by the S+ and S− line-orientation stimuli rather than by the contextual cues.

After the discrimination had been well learned, the contextual cues of the experimental chamber were changed by altering both the lighting and the type of noise in the chamber. In the presence of these new contextual cues (context 2), the discrimination training contingencies were reversed. Now, the horizontal line (0°) served as the S+ and the vertical line (90°) served as the S−. Notice that the subjects were not specifically required to pay attention to the contextual cues. They were simply required to learn a new discrimination problem in which the original S+ and S− stimuli were reversed. (They could have learned this new problem just as well had the contextual cues not been changed.)

The subjects then received generalization tests in which lines of various orientations between 0 and 90° were presented. One such generalization test was conducted in context 1, and another was conducted in context 2. The results of these tests are presented in Figure 8.15. Remarkably, the shape of the generalization gradient in each context was appropriate to the discrimination problem that was experienced in that context. Thus, in context 1, subjects responded most to the 90° stimulus, which had served as the S+ in that context, and least to the 0° stimulus, which had served as the S−. The opposite pattern of results occurred in context 2. Here, the pigeons responded most to the 0° stimulus and least to the 90° stimulus, appropriate to the reverse discrimination contingencies that had been in effect in context 2.

These results clearly illustrate that contextual cues can come to control instrumental behavior. The results also illustrate that contextual stimulus control can occur without one context being more strongly associated with reinforcement than another. In both context 1 and context 2, subjects received discrimination

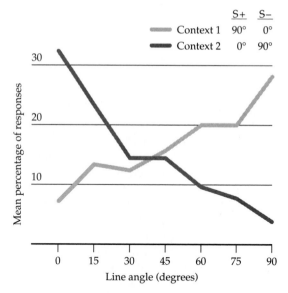

Figure 8.15 Generalization obtained with various line-angle stimuli following training in context 1 and context 2. In context 1, the 90° stimulus served as the S+ and the 0° stimulus served as the S−. In context 2, these functions were reversed, with the 0° stimulus serving as the S+ and the 90° stimulus serving as the S−. *(From "Context as a Conditional Cue in Operant Discrimination Reversal Learning" by D.R. Thomas, A.R. McKelvie, and W.L. Mah, 1985, Journal of Experimental Psychology: Animal Behavior Processes, 11, pp. 317–330. Copyright © 1985 by the American Psychological Association. Reprinted by permission.)*

training involving reinforced (S+) and non-reinforced (S−) trials. Therefore, one context was not a better signal for the availability of reinforcement than the other context. (For other studies of contextual stimulus control in the absence of differential reinforcement of the contextual cues, see Hall & Honey, 1989; Honey, Willis, & Hall, 1990.)

Control of Behavior by Conditional, or Hierarchical, Relations

Another interesting aspect of the results presented in Figure 8.15 is that they suggest that the subjects learned a **conditional,** or hierarchical, relation between the contextual and discriminative stimuli. In a conditional, or hierarchical, relation the significance of one type of stimulus or event depends on the status of another type of stimulus. In the experiment illustrated in Figure 8.15, the significance of a particular line-orientation stimulus (0 or 90°) depended on the context in which that line orientation was presented. In one context, a given line orientation was a signal for reinforcement; in the alternate context, the same line orientation was a signal for nonreinforcement. The availability of reinforcement could not be predicted from the line stimulus by itself. Similarly, the availability of reinforcement could not be predicted from the contextual cues alone. Rather, the contextual cues determined the significance of the line-orientation stimuli. Thus, the availability of reinforcement was signaled by a hierarchical relation between contextual and line-orientation stimuli.

Although the results summarized in Figure 8.15 illustrate the learning of a hierarchical relation, it is worth reemphasizing that the procedures employed did not require subjects to learn such a relation. While in context 1, subjects were not required to attend to the background cues of that context to predict reinforcement. They could have learned the original discrimination just as well without learning anything about the contextual cues. Once subjects entered context 2, there was no requirement that they remember what they had learned in context 1. The reversal problem in context 2 also did not require learning anything about the contextual cues present during the reversal training. The results illustrate that contextual control can develop even if such control is not necessary for subjects to optimize reinforcement in a particular experiment.

Control of behavior by hierarchical relations is typically observed in situations that require responding to the conditional relations between events. We have already encountered one such situation, instrumental discrimination training. In an instrumental discrimination procedure, subjects are reinforced for responding in the presence of S+ but are not reinforced in the presence of the S−. Thus, an instrumental discrimination procedure consists of three basic components: a cue (S+ or S−), a response, and a reinforcer. These three components are arranged in a special way so that the first component (the S+ or S−) signals the relation between the second and third events (the response and the reinforcer). Another way to think about this procedure is that the relation that exists between the response and the reinforcer is dependent, or conditional, on the presence of the S+ and S−. One response–reinforcer relation exists when the S+ is present (positive reinforcement), and a different relation exists when the S− is present (extinction). Thus, instrumental discrimination procedures in fact involve conditional control of the relation between the response and the reinforcer (Davidson, Aparicio, & Rescorla, 1988; Goodall & Mackintosh, 1987; Holman & Mackintosh, 1981; Jenkins, 1977; Skinner, 1938).

The mechanisms involved in the control of behavior by conditional or hierarchical relations have been investigated in greatest detail in classical conditioning. The fundamental concept of conditional control is that one event signals the relation between two other events. Classical conditioning is typically conceived as involving a relation between a conditioned and an unconditioned stimulus. The CS may be brief illumination of a localized response key with an orange light, and the US may be food. A strong relation exists between the CS and US if the food is presented immediately after each occurrence of the CS but not at other times. How could we establish conditional control over such a CS–US relation?

By analogy with instrumental discrimination procedures, we should have a third event indicate whether presentation of the key light will end in food. For example, we could use a noise stimulus, in the presence of which the key light would be followed by food. In the absence of the noise stimulus, the key light would not end with the food US. This procedure is diagramed in Figure 8.16. As in instrumental discrimination procedures, subjects receive both reinforced and nonreinforced trials. During reinforced trials, the noise stimulus is turned on for 15 seconds. Ten seconds after onset of the noise, the orange key-light CS is turned on for 5 seconds and is immediately followed by the food US. During nonreinforced trials, the noise stimulus is not presented. The key-light CS is simply turned on alone for 5 seconds without the food US.

The procedure just described is similar to one that was tested in a sign-tracking (autoshaping) experiment with pigeons by Rescorla, Durlach, and Grau (1985). In this experiment, the noise stimulus was used as the conditional cue on reinforced trials for half the pigeons. For the other half, a diffuse flashing light was used in place of the noise. The conditioned response that was measured was pecking the response key when it was illuminated with the orange key-light CS. Since pecking is not elicited by diffuse auditory or visual cues, the key-peck behavior could be interpreted as a response only to the orange key-light CS.

The results of the experiment are illustrated in Figure 8.17. Subjects pecked the orange key much more when it was presented in compound with a conditional cue than when it was presented as an isolated element. Thus, the presence of the conditional cue facilitated responding to the key-light CS. It is important to keep in mind that the conditional cues themselves did not elicit pecking because pigeons do not peck in response to diffuse auditory and visual stimuli. Rather, the conditional cues increased the ability of the orange key-light CS to elicit pecking. The diffuse conditional cues had gained conditional control over the ability of the key-light CS to elicit the conditioned response. Just as a discriminative stimulus facilitates instrumental behavior, the diffuse conditional cues

Reinforced trials	Nonreinforced trials
Noise	No noise
Key light → food	Key light → no food

Figure 8.16 Procedure for establishing conditional stimulus control in classical conditioning. On reinforced trials, a noise stimulus is presented and a key-light CS is paired with food. On nonreinforced trials, the noise stimulus is absent and the key-light CS is presented without food.

facilitated CS-elicited responding in the present study.

In instrumental discrimination procedures, the conditional cues (S+ and S−) are called "discriminative stimuli." In Pavlovian conditioning, some investigators have called conditional control of responding **facilitation** because the conditional cue facilitates elicitation of the CR by the CS (Rescorla, 1985; Rescorla et al., 1985). In this terminology, the conditional cue is called a *facilitator*. Others have preferred to call conditional control in classical conditioning **occasion setting** because the conditional cue sets the occasion for pairing of the CS with the US (Holland, 1985; Ross, 1983; Ross & Holland, 1981). In this terminology, the conditional cue is called an *occasion-setter*.

The procedure outlined in Figure 8.16 establishes the noise stimulus as a positive occasion-setter, or a stimulus that signals that the key light will result in presentation of the food US. It is interesting to note that this procedure is the converse of the standard procedure for inhibitory conditioning (see Figure 3.7). To turn the procedure outlined in Figure 8.16 into one that will result in the conditioning of inhibitory properties to the noise, all one has to do is to reverse the type of trial on which the noise is presented. Instead of the noise stimulus being presented on reinforced trials, it would be presented on nonreinforced trials. As we noted in Chapter 3, conditioned inhibition develops if a stimulus signals the absence of the US that is otherwise expected to occur. Presenting the noise stimulus on nonreinforced trials would

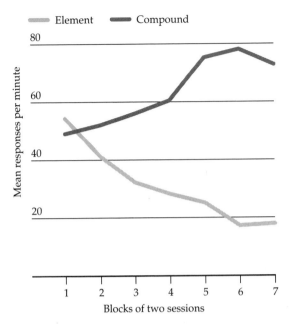

Element — Compound

Figure 8.17 Acquisition of pecking to an orange key light in a study of conditional stimulus control of classically conditioned key pecking in pigeons. The orange key-light CS was paired with food in the presence of a diffuse auditory or visual stimulus (compound trials) and was presented without food in the absence of the diffuse auditory or visual stimulus (element trials). *(From "Contextual Learning in Pavlovian Conditioning" by R.A. Rescorla, P.J. Durlach, and J.W. Grau, in P. Balsam & A. Tomie (eds.), 1985,* Context and Learning. *Copyright © 1985 Erlbaum.)*

make the noise a signal for nonreinforcement of the key light, and would make the noise a conditioned inhibitor. This illustrates that the procedure for inhibitory Pavlovian conditioning involves conditional relations, just as positive occasion-setting and facilitation procedures do. This argument also suggests that conditioned inhibition may be the conceptual opposite of facilitation rather than the opposite of conditioned excitation. In certain circumstances, this indeed appears to be the case (Rescorla, 1987, 1988a).

Facilitation, or occasion setting, is an important aspect of classical conditioning not only because it illustrates that classical condi-

tioning is subject to conditional control, but also because it appears to involve different mechanisms of learning from those we have considered so far. As discussed in Chapter 4, during pairings of a CS with a US, subjects learn an association between the two events such that presentation of the CS comes to activate a representation of the US. We have referred to this kind of learning as the conditioning of excitation to the CS. A facilitator, by contrast, has properties that are different from conditioned excitation. A facilitator does not appear to function by activating a representation of the US. Rather, it has higher order properties that appear to involve activating representations of CS–US relations.

Several lines of evidence support the conclusion that facilitators have unique properties that involve hierarchical relations rather than simple conditioned excitatory properties. In several studies, attempts to obtain evidence of conditioned excitatory properties of facilitators failed to reveal such evidence (for example, Bouton & Swartzentruber, 1986; Puente, Cannon, Best, & Carrell, 1988). These experiments indicate that a stimulus can set the occasion for conditioned responding elicited by another cue without itself eliciting visible conditioned responding. Other studies have shown that conditioning simple excitatory properties to a stimulus does not make that stimulus a facilitator (see Holland, 1985; Rescorla, 1985).

Another line of evidence indicating that facilitation does not involve simple conditioned excitation is based on the effects of an extinction procedure. As we noted in Chapter 3, a conditioned excitatory stimulus that is repeatedly presented by itself gradually loses the capacity to elicit the conditioned response; it undergoes extinction. The same procedure applied to a facilitator has no effect. Once a stimulus has become established as a conditional cue signaling a CS–US relation, repeated presentations of the stimulus by itself do not reduce its ability to facilitate conditioned responding to the CS (for example, Holland, 1989a; Rescorla, 1985; Ross, 1983).

The difference in the effects of extinction on conditioned excitatory stimuli and facilitators may be related to what is signaled. A conditioned excitatory stimulus signals the forthcoming presentation of the US. The absence of the US following presentation of the CS during extinction is a violation of the expectancy conditioned to the CS. Hence, the signal value of the CS has to be readjusted in extinction to bring it in line with the new reality. Such a readjustment is not required by an extinction procedure for a facilitator stimulus. A facilitator signals a relation between two other events (a CS and a US). The absence of those events when the facilitator is presented in extinction does not mean that the relation between them has changed. The information signaled by a facilitator is not proved incorrect by presenting the facilitator by itself during extinction. Therefore, the ability of the facilitator to promote responding elicited by another CS remains intact during extinction. However, a facilitator's effectiveness is reduced if the CS–US relation signaled by the facilitator is altered (Rescorla, 1986).

The last type of evidence that we will consider that supports the conclusion that facilitation and occasion-setting procedures involve special forms of learning rather than simple conditioned excitation has been obtained from transfer tests. These tests were conducted to determine whether a stimulus that has been conditioned to set the occasion for responding to a particular target CS will also increase responding to other CSs. Evidence of successful transfer of the effects of an occasion-setter to new target CSs has been obtained. Of particular interest is the type of properties transfer targets must have in order to be subject to the influence of an occasion-setter. In several studies, transfer effects were obtained only if the new targets had previously served as targets in other occasion-setting procedures (Holland, 1986, 1989a, 1989c; Lamarre & Holland, 1987; Wilson &

Pearce, 1990). No transfer was obtained if the new target previously had served as a conditioned excitatory stimulus, or if it had a history of reinforcement and nonreinforcement but was not a part of a conditional hierarchical relation. These results suggest that stimuli involved in hierarchical relations acquire unique properties different from the properties they have in simple conditioned excitation. These unique properties facilitate transfer of occasion-setting effects.

Finally, it should be pointed out that not all conditional discrimination procedures of the type illustrated in Figure 8.16 result in the learning of a hierarchical relation between the stimuli involved. On reinforced trials in this procedure, a compound stimulus consisting of the noise and the key light was presented. As we noted earlier, subjects can respond to a compound stimulus either in terms of the elements that make up the compound, or in terms of the unique stimulus configuration produced by the elements. For subjects to respond to a conditional discrimination in terms of the hierarchical relation that exists between the stimuli, the stimuli must be treated as independent elements. Thus, occasion-setting and facilitation processes require responding to stimulus compounds as consisting of independent stimulus elements.

To encourage subjects to treat stimulus compounds as consisting of independent elements, investigators have presented the elements one after the other, rather than simultaneously, in what is called a **serial compound.** On reinforced trials, the occasion-setter is usually presented first, followed by the target CS and reinforcement. In many of his experiments on occasion setting, Holland has even inserted a 5-second gap between the occasion-setter and the target CS. Such procedures discourage the perception of a stimulus configuration based on the occasion-setter and the target CS. In numerous studies, Holland and his associates have found that subjects respond to conditional discriminations involving serial compounds in terms of hierarchical relations. By contrast, the use of simultaneous compounds in conditional discriminations often does not result in occasion-setting effects (for example, Holland, 1986, 1989a, 1989c; Ross & Holland, 1981; see also Holland, 1989b; Thomas, Cook, & Terrones, 1990; Thomas, Curran, & Russell, 1988).

Concluding Comments

Stimulus control refers to how precisely tuned an organism's behavior is to specific features of the environment. Therefore, issues concerning the stimulus control of behavior are critical for understanding how an organism interacts with its environment. Stimulus control is measured in terms of the steepness of generalization gradients. A high degree of stimulus control is evidenced by a steep generalization gradient, which indicates that small variations in a stimulus produce large differences in responding. Weaker stimulus control is evidenced by flatter generalization gradients. The degree of stimulus control is determined by numerous factors, including the sensory capacity and sensory orientation of the organism. Stimulus control is also a function of past experience.

Discrimination training increases the stimulus control of behavior whether that training involves stimuli that differ in several respects or stimuli that differ in only one respect. However, intradimensional discrimination training produces more precise stimulus control and may lead to the counterintuitive outcome that the peak level of responding is shifted away from the reinforced stimulus. Stimulus control is also determined by the relative validity of stimuli as signals for reinforcement, the type of instrumental response that is employed, and the relative ease of conditioning individual stimuli. Not only discrete stimuli, but also background contextual cues, can come to control behavior. Furthermore, stimulus control by contextual cues can develop even if attention to contextual cues is not required to optimize reinforcement. Finally, behavior can come to be influenced by conditional or hierarchical relations among stimuli.

9

Aversive Control: Avoidance and Punishment

In Chapter 9 we will discuss how behavior can be controlled by aversive stimulation. Our presentation will focus on two types of instrumental aversive control—avoidance and punishment. Avoidance conditioning increases the performance of a target behavior, and punishment decreases the target behavior. However, in both cases subjects learn to minimize their exposure to aversive stimulation. Because of this similarity, theoretical analyses of avoidance and punishment share some of the same concepts. Nevertheless, for the most part, experimental analyses of the two types of conditioning have proceeded independently of each other. We will describe the major theoretical puzzles and empirical findings in both areas of research.

Aversive stimulation is a fact of life and influences much of what we do. It is natural, then, that we should be interested in how behavior is controlled by aversive stimulation. Two procedures have been extensively investigated in studies of aversive control—avoidance and punishment. In an avoidance procedure, the subject has to make a specific response to prevent an aversive stimulus from occurring; for example, grabbing a handrail to avoid slipping. Thus, an avoidance procedure involves a negative contingency between a particular response and the aversive stimulus. If the response occurs, the aversive stimulus is not presented. By contrast, a punishment procedure involves a positive contingency between the response and the aversive stimulus. Here, if the subject performs the response, the aversive stimulus occurs; for example, someone frowns at you for talking during a sermon in church. Avoidance procedures increase the occurrence of instrumental behavior, whereas punishment procedures result in a decrease in the instrumental behavior.

In addition to these differences in contingencies and behavioral outcomes, avoidance and punishment differ in the attitudes and investigative approaches that they have engendered. Avoidance situations are regarded as necessary evils of life—having to take an umbrella to avoid getting rained on, jumping onto the curb to avoid being hit by a fast-approaching car, throwing out spoiling food to avoid having it create a foul odor. It would be difficult to imagine a world in which avoidance responses were not necessary. On the other hand, we rarely regard punishment situations as similarly inevitable. In fact, we are accustomed to believe that we should not have to tolerate punishment. We should not have to tolerate a teacher who slaps children for not doing their homework or a boss who explodes every time we make a small mistake.

Research on avoidance behavior has focused primarily on theoretical issues. What mechanisms are responsible for behavior for which the primary consequence is the absence of aversive stimulation? By contrast, research on punishment has focused on practical considerations. What procedures are effective in suppressing behavior? What factors influence their effectiveness? In applied situations, investigators have focused on the origins of avoidance and aversion responses and on techniques to reduce such responses. By contrast, applied studies of punishment have focused on the effectiveness of punishment procedures and on possible undesirable side effects of punishment. In addition, applied scientists have been greatly concerned with ethical issues involved in the use of punishment in the treatment of behavior problems.

These differences between avoidance and punishment belie an important commonality between them. With both procedures, the behavior that develops serves to minimize contact with an aversive stimulus. The critical difference is that, in avoidance, taking specific action is required to prevent the aversive stimulus whereas, in punishment, refraining from action minimizes contact with the aversive stimulus. Because of this, avoidance behavior is sometimes referred to as **active avoidance** and punishment is sometimes referred to as **passive avoidance.** The terms *active avoidance* and *passive avoidance* emphasize the fact that both avoidance and punishment involve minimizing contact with an aversive stimulus.

Avoidance Behavior

As we have noted, avoidance involves a negative contingency between a response and an aversive stimulus. If you make the appropriate avoidance responses, you will not fall, bump into things, or drive off the road. No particular pleasure is derived from these experiences. You simply don't get hurt.

The absence of an aversive situation is presumably the reason that avoidance responses are made. However, how can the absence of something provide reinforcement for instrumental behavior? This is the fundamental question in the study of avoidance. Mowrer and Lamoreaux (1942) pointed out a half-century ago that "not getting something can hardly, in and of itself, qualify as rewarding" (p. 6). Since then, much intellectual effort has been devoted to figuring out what else is involved in avoidance conditioning procedures that might provide reinforcement for the behavior. In fact, the investigation of avoidance behavior has been dominated by this theoretical problem.

Origins of the Study of Avoidance Behavior

The study of avoidance behavior was initially closely allied to investigations of classical conditioning. The first avoidance conditioning experiments were conducted by the Russian psychologist Vladimir Bechterev (1913) as an extension of Pavlov's research. Unlike Pavlov, however, Bechterev investigated conditioning mechanisms in human subjects. In one situation, participants were asked to place a finger on a metal plate. A warning stimulus (the CS) was periodically presented, followed by a brief shock (the US) through the plate. As you might suspect, the subjects quickly lifted their finger off the plate upon being shocked. With repeated conditioning trials, they also learned to make this response to the warning stimulus. The experiment was viewed as a standard example of classical conditioning. However, in contrast to the standard classical conditioning procedure, in Bechterev's method the subjects determined whether they were exposed to the US. If they lifted their finger off the plate in response to the CS, they did not experience the shock scheduled on that trial. This aspect of the procedure constitutes a significant departure from Pavlov's methods because in standard classical conditioning the delivery of the US does not depend on the subject's behavior.

The fact that Bechterev and others who followed his example did not use a standard classical conditioning procedure went unno-

Figure 9.1 Modern running wheel for rodents.

ticed for many years. Starting in the 1930s, several investigators attempted a direct comparison of the effects of a standard classical conditioning procedure with those of a procedure that had the added instrumental avoidance component (for example, Schlosberg, 1934, 1936). One of the most influential of these comparisons was performed by Brogden, Lipman, and Culler (1938). They tested two groups of guinea pigs in a rotating wheel apparatus (see Figure 9.1). A tone served as the CS, and shock again served as the US. The shock stimulated the guinea pigs to run and thereby rotate the wheel. For one group of subjects, the shock was always presented 2 seconds after the beginning of the tone (classical group). The second group (avoidance group) received the same type of CS–US pairings when they did not make the conditioned response (a small movement of the wheel). However, if these subjects moved the wheel during the tone CS before the shock occurred, the scheduled shock was omitted. Figure 9.2 shows the percentage of trials on which each group made the conditioned response. It is evident from the results that the avoidance group quickly learned to make the conditioned response and was responding on 100% of the trials within eight days of training. The classical group never achieved this high level of performance even though training was continued much longer for them.

These results indicate a big difference between standard classical conditioning and a procedure that includes an instrumental avoidance component. The avoidance procedure produced a much higher level of responding than was observed with mere pairings of the CS with shock. This facilitation of behavior cannot be explained solely by what is known about classical conditioning. In fact, the results obtained by Brogden and his colleagues are paradoxical when viewed just in terms of classical conditioning. For the avoidance group, the CS was often presented without the US because subjects often prevented the occurrence of shock. These CS-alone trials constitute extinction trials; hence, they should have attenuated the development of the conditioned response. By contrast, the classical group never received CS-alone trials because it could never avoid shock. Therefore, if CS–US pairings were the only important factor in this situation, the classical group should have performed better than the avoidance group. The fact that the opposite result occurred indicates that analysis of avoidance behavior requires more than classical conditioning principles.

The Discriminated Avoidance Procedure

Although avoidance behavior is not just another case of classical conditioning, the classical conditioning heritage of the study of avoidance behavior has greatly influenced its experimental and theoretical analysis. Investigators have been greatly concerned with the importance of signals for the aversive event in avoidance conditioning and with the relation of the warning signal to the instrumental response and the aversive US. Experimental issues of this type have been extensively investigated with procedures similar to that used by Brogden and his colleagues. This method is called **discriminated,** or **signaled, avoidance** and its standard features are diagramed in Figure 9.3.

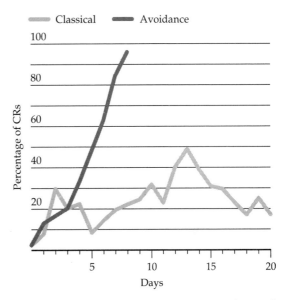

Figure 9.2 Percentage of trials with a conditioned response on successive days of training. The conditioned response prevented shock delivery for the avoidance group but not for the classical group. (*From "The Role of Incentive in Conditioning and Extinction" by W.J. Brogden, E.A. Lipman, and E. Culler, 1938.* American Journal of Psychology, 51, *pp. 109–117.*)

The first thing to note about the signaled avoidance technique is that it involves discrete trials. Each trial is initiated by the CS. The events that occur after that depend on what the subject does. There are two possibilities. If the subject makes the response required for avoidance during the CS but before the shock is scheduled, the CS is turned off and the US is omitted on that trial. This is a successful **avoidance trial.** If the subject fails to make the required response during the CS–US interval, the scheduled shock is presented and remains on until the response occurs, whereupon both the CS and the US are terminated. In this case, the instrumental response results in escape from the shock; hence, this type of trial is called an **escape trial.** During early stages of training, most of the trials are escape trials. Once the avoidance response has been well established, avoidance trials predominate.

Discriminated avoidance procedures can be conducted in a variety of experimental situa-

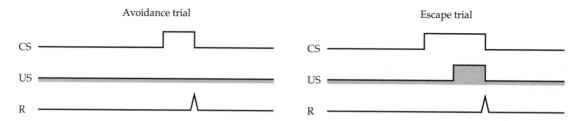

Figure 9.3   Diagram of the discriminated, or signaled, avoidance procedure. *Avoidance trial:* If the subject makes the response required for avoidance during the CS (the signal) but before the US (for example, shock) is scheduled, the CS is turned off, and the US is omitted on that trial. *Escape trial:* If the subject fails to make the required response during the CS–US interval, the scheduled shock is presented and remains on until the response occurs, whereupon both the CS *and* the US are terminated.

tions. One may, for example, use a Skinner box in which a rat has to press a response lever during a tone to avoid shock (Hoffman, 1966). In a more common experimental situation, the shuttle box is employed (see Figure 9.4). The shuttle box consists of two compartments separated by an archway with a small opening. The animal is placed on one side of the apparatus. At the start of a trial, the CS is presented (a light or a tone, for example). If the animal crosses over to the other side before the shock occurs, no shock is delivered and the CS is turned off. At the end of the intertrial interval, the next trial can be administered starting with the animal in the second compartment. With this procedure, the animal shuttles back and forth between the two sides on successive trials. The response is therefore called **shuttle avoidance.**

In the shuttle avoidance procedure, the animal can be shocked on either side of the apparatus. For example, if the subject is on the left side when a trial starts and it fails to make the shuttle response, it will receive shock on the left side. If it is on the right side when a trial begins and it again fails to cross, it will receive shock on the right side. In a variation of the shuttle avoidance procedure, which also has been extensively investigated, the subject is always placed on the same side of the shuttle box at the start of each trial. For example, it may be always placed in the left compartment. In this case, the animal would have to run to the right compartment on each

trial to avoid (or escape) shock. At the end of the trial it would be removed from the right compartment and replaced in the left compartment to start the next trial. Such a procedure is called **one-way avoidance** because the animal always has to cross in the same direction. An important aspect of the one-way procedure is that the animal can be shocked in only one of the two compartments (the one it is placed in at the start of each trial). This part of the apparatus is called the **shock compartment,** whereas the other side is called the **safe compartment.** Because there is a consistently safe compartment in one-way avoidance procedures, one-way avoidance behavior is usually learned more rapidly than shuttle avoidance.

The Two-Process Theory of Avoidance

It is clear from the results of such experiments as that conducted by Brogden and his colleagues in 1938 that avoidance procedures can produce much more responding than procedures in which a warning signal is repeatedly paired with shock but avoidance is not possible. The avoidance contingency provides some kind of instrumental reinforcement for the avoidance response. Exactly what this source of reinforcement is has been the central question in investigations of avoidance learning. The first and most influential answer to the puzzle, proposed by Mowrer (1947) and elaborated by Miller (for example, 1951) and

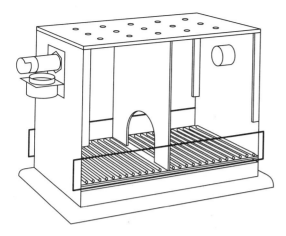

Figure 9.4 A shuttle box. The box has a metal grid floor and is separated into two compartments by an archway with a small opening. The instrumental response consists of crossing back and forth (shuttling) from one side of the box to the other.

others is known as the *two-process theory of avoidance*. In one form or another, this two-process theory has been the dominant theoretical viewpoint on avoidance learning for many years and continues to enjoy success and support (Levis, 1989; McAllister & McAllister, 1991). Because other approaches deal more directly with certain findings, the two-process theory is no longer viewed as a complete explanation of avoidance learning. Nevertheless, the theory remains the standard against which all other explanations of avoidance behavior are always measured.

As its name implies, two-process theory assumes that two mechanisms are involved in avoidance learning. The first is a classical conditioning process activated by pairings of the warning stimulus (CS) with the aversive event (US) on trials when the subject fails to make the avoidance response. Because the US is an aversive stimulus, through classical conditioning the CS also becomes aversive. Being aversive, Mowrer (1947) assumed that it comes to elicit fear. Thus, the first component of two-process theory is the *classical conditioning of fear to the CS*.

Fear is an emotionally arousing state that motivates the organism. It is also unpleasant, so that a reduction in fear can provide negative reinforcement. Since fear is elicited by the CS, termination of the CS presumably results in a reduction in the level of fear. The second process in two-process theory is based on these considerations. Mowrer assumed that learning of the instrumental avoidance response occurred because the response terminated the CS and thereby reduced the conditioned fear elicited by the CS. Thus, the second component is *instrumental reinforcement of the avoidance response through fear reduction*.

There are several noteworthy aspects of two-process theory. First, and perhaps most important, is that the classical and instrumental processes are not assumed to provide independent sources of support for the avoidance behavior. Rather, the two processes are very much interdependent. Instrumental reinforcement through fear reduction is not possible until fear has been conditioned to the CS. Therefore, the classical conditioning process has to occur first. After that, the instrumental conditioning process may create extinction trials for the classical conditioning process. This occurs because each successful avoidance response prevents the occurrence of the US. Thus, two-process theory predicts a constant interplay between classical and instrumental processes. Another important aspect of two-process theory is that it explains avoidance behavior in terms of escape from conditioned fear rather than in terms of the prevention of shock. The fact that the avoidance response prevents shock is seen as a by-product in two-process theory, not as the critical event that motivates avoidance behavior. Escape from conditioned fear provides the critical reinforcement for avoidance behavior. Thus, according to two-process theory, the instrumental response is reinforced by a tangible event (fear reduction) rather than merely the absence of something (aversive stimulation).

Experimental Analysis of Avoidance Behavior

A great deal of research has been conducted concerning avoidance behavior, much of it stimulated in one way or another by two-process theory. We cannot review all the evidence. However, we will consider several important types of results that must be considered in any effort to fully understand the mechanisms of avoidance behavior.

Acquired-drive experiments. In the typical avoidance procedure, classical conditioning of fear and instrumental reinforcement through fear reduction occur intermixed in a series of trials. However, if these two processes make separate contributions to avoidance learning, it should be possible to demonstrate their operation in situations where the two types of conditioning are not intermixed. This is the goal of acquired-drive experiments. The basic strategy is to first condition fear to a CS with a "pure" classical conditioning procedure in which the organism's responses do not influence whether the US is presented. In the next phase of the experiment, the animals are periodically exposed to the fear-eliciting CS and allowed to perform an instrumental response that is effective in terminating the CS (and thereby reducing fear). No shocks are scheduled in this phase. Therefore, the instrumental response is not required to avoid shock presentations. If two-process theory is correct and escape from the fear-eliciting CS can reinforce instrumental behavior, then subjects should be able to learn the instrumental response in the second phase of the experiment. This type of experiment is called an **acquired-drive** study because the drive to perform the instrumental response (fear) is learned through classical conditioning. (It is not an innate drive, such as hunger or thirst.)

One of the first and most famous acquired-drive experiments was performed by Miller (1948). However, because of certain problems with that study, we will describe a follow-up experiment by Brown and Jacobs (1949) in which rats were tested in a shuttle box. During the first phase of the procedure, the door between the two shuttle compartments was closed. The rats were individually placed on one side of the apparatus and a pulsating-light/tone CS was presented, ending in shock through the grid floor. Twenty-two such Pavlovian conditioning trials were conducted, with the rats confined on the right and left sides of the apparatus on alternate trials. The control group received the same training except that no shocks were delivered. During the next phase of the experiment, each subject was placed on one side of the shuttle box and the center barrier was removed. The CS was then presented and remained on until the subject turned it off by crossing to the other side. The animal was then removed from the apparatus until the next trial. No shocks were delivered during the second phase of the experiment, and a one-way procedure was used, with the animals placed on the same side of the apparatus at the start of each trial. The investigators were interested to see whether the rats would learn to cross rapidly from one side to the other when the only reinforcement for crossing was termination of the previously conditioned light/tone CS.

The amount of time each subject took to cross the shuttle box and turn off the CS was measured for each trial. Figure 9.5 summarizes these response latencies for both the shock-conditioned and the control group. The two groups had similar response latencies at the beginning of instrumental training. However, as training progressed, the shock-conditioned animals learned to cross the shuttle box faster (and thus turn off the CS sooner) than the control group. This outcome shows that termination of a fear-conditioned stimulus is sufficient to provide reinforcement for an instrumental response. Such findings have been obtained in a variety of experimental situations (for example, Dinsmoor, 1962; McAllister & McAllister, 1971). In addition, other experiments have shown that delaying the termination of the CS after the instrumen-

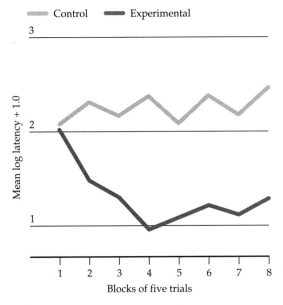

Control ▬▬ Experimental

Figure 9.5 Mean latencies to cross from one side to the other in the shuttle box for control and experimental groups. The shuttle crossing resulted in termination of the CS on that trial. For the experimental group, the CS was previously conditioned with shock. Such conditioning was not conducted with the control group. *(From "The Role of Fear in the Motivation and Acquisition of Responses" by J.S. Brown and A. Jacobs, 1949. Journal of Experimental Psychology, 39, pp. 747–759.)*

tal behavior reduces the reinforcement effect, just as it does with instrumental responses maintained by positive reinforcement (for example, Delprato, 1969; Israel, Devine, O'Dea, & Hamdi, 1974; Katzev, 1967, 1972). These results provide strong support for two-process theory.

Independent measurement of fear during acquisition of avoidance behavior. Another important strategy that has been used in investigations of avoidance behavior involves independent measurement of fear and instrumental avoidance responding. This approach is based on the assumption that if fear motivates and reinforces avoidance responding, then the conditioning of fear and the conditioning of instrumental avoidance behavior

should go hand in hand. Contrary to this prediction, conditioned fear and avoidance responding are not always highly correlated (Mineka, 1979). Fairly early in the investigation of avoidance learning, it was noted that animals become less fearful as they learn the avoidance response (Solomon, Kamin, & Wynne, 1953; Solomon & Wynne, 1953). Since then, more systematic measurements of fear have been used. One popular behavioral technique for measuring fear involves the conditioned suppression procedure described in Chapters 3 and 5. In this technique, animals are first conditioned to make an instrumental response (such as lever pressing) for a food reward. A shock-conditioned CS is then presented while the subjects are responding to obtain food. Generally, the CS produces a suppression in the lever-press behavior, and the extent of this response suppression is assumed to reflect the amount of fear elicited by the CS. If the warning signal in an avoidance procedure comes to elicit fear, then presentation of that warning stimulus in a conditioned suppression experiment should result in suppression of food-reinforced behavior. This possibility was first investigated in a famous experiment by Kamin, Brimer, and Black (1963).

Kamin and his colleagues initially trained their rats to press a response lever for food reinforcement on a variable-interval schedule. The animals were then trained to avoid shock in response to an auditory CS in a shuttle box. Training was continued for independent groups of subjects until they successfully avoided shock on 1, 3, 9, or 27 consecutive trials. The animals were then returned to the lever-press situation. After their rate of responding had stabilized, the auditory CS that had been used in the shuttle box was periodically presented to see how much suppression in responding it would produce. The results are summarized in Figure 9.6. Lower values of the suppression index indicate greater disruptions of the lever-press behavior by the shock-avoidance CS. Increasing degrees of response

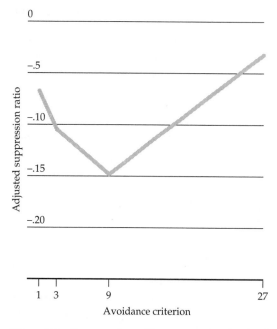

Figure 9.6 Suppression of lever pressing for food during a CS that was previously conditioned in a shock-avoidance procedure. Independent groups received avoidance training until they met a criterion of 1, 3, 9, or 27 consecutive avoidance responses. The suppression scores were adjusted for the degree of suppression produced by the CS before avoidance conditioning. Lower values of the adjusted ratio indicate greater suppression of lever pressing. *(From "Conditioned Suppression as a Monitor of Fear of the CS in the Course of Avoidance Training" by L.J. Kamin, C.J. Brimer, and A.H. Black, 1963,* Journal of Comparative and Physiological Psychology, 56, *pp. 497–501.)*

suppression were observed among groups of subjects that had received avoidance training until they successfully avoided shock on 1 to 9 successive trials. With more extensive avoidance training, however, response suppression declined. Subjects trained until they avoided shock on 27 consecutive trials showed less conditioned suppression to the avoidance CS than subjects trained to a criterion of 9 consecutive avoidances. This outcome indicates that fear as measured by conditioned suppression decreases during extended avoidance training and is at a minimal level after exten-

sive training (see also Cook, Mineka, & Trumble, 1987; Neuenschwander, Fabrigoule, & Mackintosh, 1987; Starr & Mineka, 1977). However, the decrease in fear is not accompanied by a decrease in the strength of the avoidance response (Mineka & Gino, 1980).

The decline in fear to the CS with extended avoidance training presents a puzzle for two-process theory. However, recent evidence and theoretical argument suggest that the scope of two-process theory can accommodate this finding. Although it is well accepted that fear declines as avoidance conditioning proceeds, declining levels of fear do not preclude continued reinforcement of the avoidance response. McAllister and McAllister (1991) pointed out that as long as the CS elicits some degree of fear, CS termination can result in fear reduction and hence reinforcement of the avoidance behavior (see also Levis, 1989). Furthermore, as the avoidance response becomes well learned, a small degree of fear reduction may be sufficient to maintain the response.

Further insights into the paradox of increased avoidance responding in the face of declining levels of fear elicited by the CS are provided by considering the role of fear elicited by the contextual cues of the experimental chamber. To the extent that these contextual cues elicit fear, termination of the CS will not reduce the level of fear to zero, because the contextual cues of the experimental chamber remain after the CS has been turned off. If the level of fear elicited by the experimental context decreases with training, termination of the CS can produce more complete fear reduction. McAllister, McAllister, and Benton (1983) found that as avoidance training progresses, subjects come to discriminate between the CS and the background cues, and fear to the background cues declines more rapidly than the decline in fear to the CS. Under these circumstances, the fear reduction produced by termination of the CS actually increases as training progresses and as fear of the CS declines. Thus, by considering the contribution of contextual cues to the elicitation of fear in an avoidance situation, one can show that the common finding of increased avoidance responding in the face of declining levels of fear to the CS is not necessarily at odds with two-process theory.

Asymptotic avoidance performance. Two-process theory of avoidance not only specifies the mechanisms of the acquisition process for avoidance behavior but also makes predictions about the nature of performance once the response has been well learned. More specifically, it predicts that the strength of the avoidance response will fluctuate in cycles. Whenever a successful avoidance response occurs, the shock is omitted on that trial. This is assumed to be an extinction trial for the conditioned fear response. Repetition of the avoidance response (and thus the CS-alone extinction trials) should lead to extinction of fear. As the CS becomes extinguished, there will be less reinforcement resulting from the reduction of fear, and the avoidance response will also become extinguished. As this happens, the avoidance response will cease to occur in time to prevent the US. However, when shock is not avoided, the CS is paired with the US. This pairing should reinstate fear to the CS and reestablish the potential for reinforcement through fear reduction. Hence, the avoidance response should become reconditioned. Thus, the theory predicts that after initial acquisition, the avoidance response will go through cycles of extinction and reacquisition. Although evidence of this sort has been observed on occasion (for example, Sheffield, 1948), such findings are not always observed. In fact, some have argued that one of the hallmark features of avoidance behavior is its persistence. Avoidance responding may continue for many trials after shocks are discontinued, as long as the response continues to be effective in terminating the CS. In one experiment (Solomon et al., 1953), for example, a dog was reported to have performed the avoidance response on 650 successive trials after only a few shocks. However, such persistence is not a common finding (see Levis, 1989; McAllister & McAllister, 1991).

In terms of two-process theory, there are several approaches to explaining instances in which avoidance behavior persists after the unconditioned aversive stimulus is no longer delivered. One approach is based on the observation that once an avoidance response has been well learned, it occurs with a short latency. Because the animal responds quickly to turn off the CS, later segments of the CS are never experienced and therefore do not have the opportunity to undergo extinction. The short latency of well-learned avoidance responses serves to protect later segments of the CS from becoming extinguished and thereby contributes to the persistence of avoidance behavior. This mechanism, first proposed by Solomon and Wynne (1953), is called **conservation of fear.** (For elaborations on this idea, see Levis, 1981, 1989, 1991.)

Another approach to explaining the persistence of avoidance behavior is based on the role of response feedback stimuli in avoidance conditioning. In all avoidance conditioning procedures, the avoidance response is followed by a period free from shock. There are also always distinctive feedback stimuli that accompany the instrumental response. These may be provided by a change in location, as when a rat moves from one side to the other in a shuttle box; they may be tactile or other external stimuli involved in making the response, such as those provided by touching and manipulating a response lever. The response feedback stimuli may also be proprioceptive (internal) cues provided by the muscle movements involved in making the response. Regardless of what they are, because the instrumental response produces a period free from shock, the stimuli accompanying the response are negatively correlated with shock. As we discussed in Chapter 3, this is one of the circumstances that leads to the development of conditioned inhibition. Therefore, response feedback cues can become conditioned inhibitors of fear (for example, Morris, 1974; Rescorla, 1968b).

The preceding analysis suggests that, after extensive avoidance training, subjects experience two conditioned stimuli in succession on each trial of a discriminated avoidance procedure: the fear-eliciting warning stimulus for shock (CS+), followed by fear-inhibiting feedback cues from the avoidance response (CS−). Therefore, asymptotic avoidance trials should not be viewed as extinction trials in which the CS+ is presented alone, but rather as trials in which the CS+ is followed by fear-inhibitory response feedback cues. Recent evidence indicates that the presentation of fear-inhibiting stimuli following a CS+ can block extinction of the CS+ (Soltysik, Wolfe, Nicholas, Wilson, & Garcia-Sanchez, 1983). This type of blocking can be conceptualized in a manner analogous to the blocking of excitatory conditioning discussed in Chapter 5. Because an inhibitory stimulus is a signal for the absence of shock, occurrence of the CS− makes the absence of shock on avoidance trials fully expected, and this protects the CS+ from any changes in associative strength. Another way to think about this effect is that the absence of shock on avoidance trials is attributed to the CS−. This makes revaluation of the CS+ unnecessary, thus leaving its fear-eliciting properties unchanged. If response feedback cues protect the CS+ from extinction on avoidance trials, the CS+ can continue to elicit fear and motivate the avoidance response. Therefore, this mechanism makes the persistence of avoidance behavior in the face of numerous no-shock trials less puzzling in the context of two-process theory.

Extinction of avoidance behavior through response blocking and CS-alone exposure. As we have noted, if the avoidance response is effective in terminating the CS and no shocks are presented, avoidance responding persists for a long time. Is avoidance behavior always highly resistant to extinction, or are there procedures that result in fairly rapid extinc-

tion? The answer is very important not only for a theoretical analysis of avoidance behavior but also for extinguishing maladaptive or pathological avoidance responses in human patients. An effective and extensively investigated extinction procedure for avoidance behavior is called **flooding,** or **response prevention** (Baum, 1970). It involves presenting the CS in the avoidance situation, but with the apparatus altered in such a way that the subject is prevented from making the avoidance response. Thus, the subject is exposed to the CS without being permitted to terminate it. In a sense, it is "flooded" with the CS.

One of the most important variables determining the effects of a flooding procedure is the duration of the forced exposure to the CS. This is nicely illustrated in an experiment by Schiff, Smith, and Prochaska (1972). Rats were trained to avoid shock in response to an auditory CS warning signal in a one-way avoidance situation. After all the animals had avoided shock on 10 consecutive trials, the safe compartment was blocked off by a barrier and subjects received various amounts of exposure to the CS without shock. Independent groups of subjects received 1, 5, or 12 blocked trials, and on each of these trials the CS was presented for 1, 5, 10, 50, or 120 seconds. The barrier blocking the avoidance response was then removed and all subjects were tested for extinction. At the start of each extinction trial, the subject was placed in the apparatus and the CS was presented until the animal crossed into the safe compartment. Shock never occurred during the extinction trials, and subjects were tested until they took at least 120 seconds to cross into the safe compartment on three consecutive trials. The strength of the avoidance response was measured by the number of trials subjects took to reach this extinction criterion.

As expected, blocked exposure to the CS facilitated extinction of the avoidance response. Furthermore, this effect was determined mainly by the total duration of exposure to the CS. The number of flooding trials

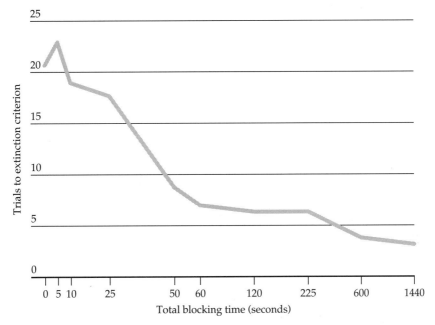

Figure 9.7 Trials to extinction criterion for independent groups of animals that previously received various durations of blocked exposure to the CS. *(From "Extinction of Avoidance in Rats as a Function of Duration and Number" by R. Schiff, N. Smith, and J. Prochaska, 1972,* Journal of Comparative and Physiological Psychology, 81, *pp. 356–359. Copyright © 1972 the American Psychological Association. Reprinted by permission.)*

administered (1, 5, or 12) facilitated extinction only because each trial added to the total amount of time the subjects were exposed to the CS without being allowed to escape from it. The results of the experiment are summarized in Figure 9.7. Increases in the total duration of blocked exposure to the CS resulted in more rapid extinction (see also Baum, 1969; Weinberger, 1965).

Two-process theory predicts that flooding will extinguish avoidance behavior because forced exposure to the CS is expected to produce extinction of fear. The fact that more extensive exposure to the CS results in more rapid extinction (for example, Schiff, Smith, & Prochaska, 1972) is consistent with this view. However, detailed investigations of the role of fear in flooding procedures have also provided evidence contrary to two-process theory. Independent measurements of fear (with

the conditioned suppression technique, for example) have shown that in some situations flooding extinguishes avoidance behavior more rapidly than it extinguishes fear, whereas in other situations the reverse holds (see, for example, Coulter, Riccio, & Page, 1969; Mineka & Gino, 1979; Mineka, Miller, Gino, & Giencke, 1981). These results suggest that extinction of fear is only one factor responsible for the effects of flooding procedures. Other variables may be related to the fact that, during flooding, subjects not only receive forced exposure to the CS but are prevented from making the avoidance response.

Blocking of the avoidance response also can contribute to extinction of the avoidance behavior independent of CS exposure. One demonstration of this fact was performed by Katzev and Berman (1974). After first conditioning rats to avoid shock in a shuttle box, Katzev and Berman conducted 50 extinction trials. Pairs of subjects were set up for this phase of the experiment. For one subject of each pair, the shuttle response was not blocked during the extinction trials so that the rat could turn off the CS by crossing to the other side. The other subject of each pair received the same CS exposures as the first rat, except that the shuttle response was blocked by a barrier. Thus, CS exposure was equal for the two types of subjects, but only one of the subjects in each pair could terminate the CS by making the shuttle response. A third group of rats served as a control group and was not exposed to the CS (or the shuttle box) during this phase. All the subjects were then given a series of standard extinction trials. The barrier was removed altogether and the CS was periodically presented until the subjects crossed to the other side of the apparatus.

The results of this experiment are summarized in Figure 9.8. The control group made the greatest number of shuttle crossings. The fewest responses occurred in subjects that had received blocked exposure to the CS. In fact, these animals were much less likely to respond than animals that had received the identical exposure to the CS but could always terminate the CS presentations by making the shuttle response. These results show that response blocking can facilitate extinction of avoidance behavior independent of variations in CS exposure. Thus, it would appear that the flooding procedure involves more than just Pavlovian extinction of the CS. (For a more detailed discussion, see Baum, 1970; Mineka, 1979.) Response blocking may facilitate extinction by preventing the experience of response feedback cues which, as we noted earlier, can block extinction of fear because of their conditioned inhibitory properties (Soltysik et al., 1983).

Nondiscriminated (free-operant) avoidance. As we have seen, two-process theory places great emphasis on the role of the warning signal, or CS, in avoidance learning. Could

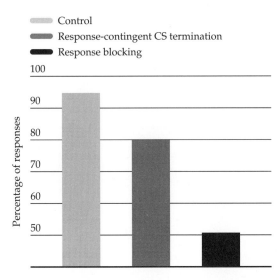

Figure 9.8 Percentage of shuttle responses that occurred during the first 10 test trials conducted at the end of the experiment by Katzev and Berman (1974). All subjects received discriminated avoidance training initially. Then, the control group was not exposed to the CS, the response-contingent CS termination group received CS exposures that it could terminate by a shuttle response, and the response-blocking group received similar CS exposures that it could not control. The figure shows the results of these different extinction treatments. *(Adapted from R.D. Katzev and J.S. Berman, 1974.)*

animals also learn to avoid shock even if there were no external warning stimulus in the situation? Within the context of two-factor theory, this is a heretical question. However, progress in science requires posing bold questions, and Sidman (1953a, 1953b) did just that. He devised a procedure initially called **Sidman avoidance,** which has come to be called **nondiscriminated,** or **free-operant avoidance.** In this procedure, shock is scheduled to occur periodically without warning—let us say every 10 seconds. Some behavior is specified as the avoidance response, and each occurrence of this response prevents the delivery of the scheduled shocks for a fixed period—say, 30 seconds. Animals will learn to avoid shocks under these conditions even though there is no warning stimulus. The procedure is constructed from only two time intervals (see

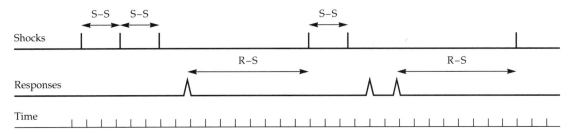

Figure 9.9 Diagram of the nondiscriminated, or free-operant, avoidance procedure. Each occurrence of the response initiates a period without shock, as set by the R–S interval. In the absence of a response, the next shock occurs a fixed period after the last shock, as set by the S–S interval. Shocks are not signaled by an exteroceptive stimulus and are usually brief and inescapable.

Figure 9.9). One of these is the interval between shocks in the absence of a response. This is called the **S–S** (shock–shock) **interval.** The other critical time period is the interval between the response and the next scheduled shock. This is called the **R–S** (response–shock) **interval.** The R–S interval is the period of safety created by the response. In our example, the S–S interval is 10 seconds and the R–S interval is 30 seconds.

In addition to lacking a warning stimulus, the free-operant avoidance procedure differs from discriminated avoidance in allowing for avoidance responses to occur at any time. In discriminated avoidance procedures, the avoidance response is effective in preventing the delivery of shock only if it is made during the CS. Responses in the absence of the CS (the intertrial interval) have no effect. In fact, in some experiments (particularly those involving one-way avoidance), the animals are removed from the apparatus between trials. By contrast, in the free-operant procedure, an avoidance response occurring at any time will reset the R–S interval. If the R–S interval is 30 seconds, shock is scheduled 30 seconds after each response. However, by always responding just before this R–S interval is over, the subject can always reset the R–S interval and thereby prolong its period of safety indefinitely.

There are several striking characteristics of free-operant avoidance experiments. First, these studies generally involve much longer periods of training than discriminated avoid-

ance experiments. It is rare, for example, for a discriminated avoidance procedure in a shuttle box to run long enough for the animals to receive 100 shocks. However, 100 shocks are not excessive in free-operant avoidance studies. Sometimes it takes a lot of experience with shock before subjects learn to make the avoidance response regularly. Extensive training also is often used because the investigators are specifically interested in the steady-state adjustment the animals will make to such schedules of aversive stimulation. Thus, in many cases the initial learning of the avoidance behavior is not the primary focus of the experiment. Another general characteristic of these experiments is that animals often never get good enough to avoid all shocks, even after extensive training. Finally, subjects often differ greatly in how they respond to the identical free-operant avoidance procedure.

Figures 9.10 and 9.11 illustrate the kinds of results that can be obtained with free-operant avoidance training. Each figure shows the cumulative record of lever pressing by a rat in successive 1-hour periods during the rat's first exposure to the avoidance procedure. In the absence of lever presses, the subjects received shock every 5 seconds (the S–S interval). Each lever-press response initiated a 20-second period without shocks (the R–S interval). Shocks are indicated by downward deflections of the cumulative-recorder pen. Rat H-28 (Figure 9.10) received a lot of shocks at first but started to press the lever even during the first hour of training. It responded a great deal

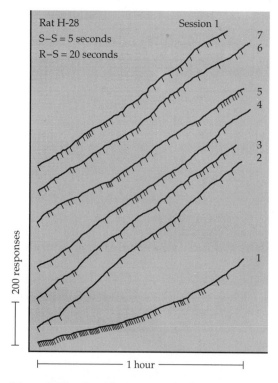

Figure 9.10 Cumulative record of lever pressing for a rat the first time it was exposed to a nondiscriminated avoidance procedure. Numerals at the right label successive hours of exposure to the procedure. Oblique slashes indicate delivery of shock. *(From "Avoidance Behavior" by M. Sidman, in W.K. Honig (Ed.), 1966,* Operant Behavior. *Copyright © 1966 by Prentice-Hall. Reprinted by permission.)*

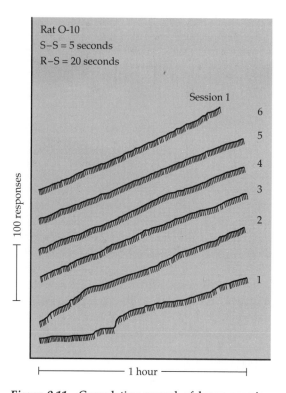

Figure 9.11 Cumulative record of lever pressing for a rat the first time it was exposed to a nondiscriminated avoidance procedure. Numerals at the right label successive hours of exposure to the procedure. Oblique slashes indicate delivery of shock. *(From "Avoidance Behavior" by M. Sidman, in W.K. Honig (Ed.), 1966,* Operant Behavior. *Copyright © 1966 by Prentice-Hall. Reprinted by permission.)*

during the second hour of the session and then settled down to a steady rate of lever pressing for the next 5 hours that the procedure was in effect. This was its stable response pattern under these conditions. Rat H-28 was a particularly fast learner. However, even at the end of the 7 hours of training it received more than 25 shocks per hour.

Rat O-10 (Figure 9.11) did not perform as well as rat H-28. It received a great many more shocks and never achieved a high rate of responding. Its stable pattern of behavior after several hours of training involved responding just after shock delivery and then not responding again until the next shock occurred

at the end of the R–S interval. Therefore, it ended up receiving a shock about every 20 seconds, as set by the R–S interval.

Numerous experiments have been conducted on free-operant avoidance behavior (see Hineline, 1977; Sidman, 1966). The rate of responding is controlled by the values of the S–S and R–S intervals. The more frequently shocks are scheduled in the absence of responding (the S–S interval), the more likely the animal is to learn the avoidance response. Increasing the periods of safety produced by the response (the R–S interval) also promotes the avoidance behavior. In addition, the relative values of the S–S and R–S intervals are important. For example, the animal is not likely to make the instrumental response if the R–S interval is shorter than the S–S interval.

Nondiscriminated avoidance behavior presents a challenge for two-process theory because there is no explicit CS to elicit conditioned fear and it is not clear how the avoidance response reduces fear. However, two-process theory has not been entirely abandoned in attempts to explain free-operant avoidance (see Anger, 1963). The S–S and R–S intervals used in effective procedures are usually rather short (less than 1 minute). Furthermore, they remain fixed during an experiment, so that the intervals are highly predictable. Therefore, it is not unreasonable to suggest that the animals might learn to respond to the passage of time as a signal for shock. This assumption of temporal conditioning permits application of the mechanisms of two-process theory to free-operant avoidance procedures. The basic strategy is to assume that the passage of time after the last shock (in the case of the S–S interval) or after the last response (in the case of the R–S interval) becomes conditioned to elicit fear. Since the timing starts anew with each occurrence of the avoidance response, the response effectively removes the fear-eliciting temporal cues. Termination of these time signals can then reinforce the avoidance response through fear reduction. Thus, the temporal cues involved in nearing the end of the S–S or R–S interval are assumed to have the same role that the explicit CS has in discriminative avoidance procedures.

The preceding analysis of free-operant avoidance in terms of two-process theory predicts that subjects will not distribute their responses randomly in time. Rather, they will be more likely to respond as the end of the R–S interval draws near because it is here that the temporal cues presumably elicit fear. Results consistent with this prediction have been obtained. However, many animals successfully avoid a great many shocks without distributing their responses in the manner

predicted by two-process theory. Furthermore, the predicted distribution of responses often develops only after extensive training — after the subjects are avoiding a great many of the scheduled shocks (see Sidman, 1966). In addition, avoidance behavior has been successfully conditioned with the use of free-operant procedures in which the S–S and R–S intervals are varied throughout the experiment (for example, Herrnstein & Hineline, 1966). When the S–S and R–S intervals are of unpredictable duration, subjects are much less likely to be able to learn to use the passage of time as a signal for shock. It is therefore difficult to adapt two-process theory to explain their avoidance learning. These types of results have discouraged some investigators from accepting two-process theory as an explanation of free-operant avoidance learning. (For further discussion, see Herrnstein, 1969; Hineline, 1977, 1981.)

Alternative Theoretical Accounts of Avoidance Behavior

In the preceding discussion of experimental investigations of avoidance behavior, we used two-process theory to provide the conceptual framework. This was reasonable because many of the research questions were stimulated in one way or another by two-process theory. However, alternative approaches to the analysis of avoidance learning also have been proposed, as investigators have gradually moved away from using traditional discrete-trial discriminated avoidance procedures. We will now discuss some of the more important of these alternative theories.

In two-process theory, reinforcement for the avoidance response is assumed to be provided by the reduction of fear. This is a case of negative reinforcement — reinforcement due to removal of an aversive state. Several recent theoretical treatments have proposed that avoidance procedures also provide for positive reinforcement of the avoidance response, whereas others have suggested that neither negative nor positive reinforcement is important in avoidance learning.

Positive reinforcement through conditioned inhibition of fear.   As we noted earlier, performance of an avoidance response always results in distinctive feedback stimuli, such as spatial cues involved in going from one side to the other in a shuttle box or tactile and other external stimuli involved in pressing a response lever. Because the avoidance response produces a period of safety in all avoidance conditioning procedures, response feedback stimuli may acquire conditioned inhibitory properties and become signals for the absence of aversive stimulation. Since a shock-free period is desirable, a conditioned inhibitory

stimulus for shock may serve as a positive reinforcer. Thus, according to the *safety-signal hypothesis,* the stimuli that accompany avoidance responses may provide positive reinforcement for avoidance behavior.

In most avoidance experiments, no special steps are taken to ensure that the avoidance response is accompanied by vivid feedback stimuli that could become conditioned inhibitors. Spatial, tactile, and proprioceptive stimuli that are not specifically programmed but inevitably accompany the avoidance response serve this function. However, any avoidance procedure can easily be modified to provide a distinctive stimulus, such as a brief light or tone, after each occurrence of the avoidance response. The conditioned inhibition rein-

---

Observational Learning of Fears and Phobias

BOX **9.1**

Excessive fears and phobias can be debilitating and may require therapeutic intervention. Some of the most successful treatment procedures, such as flooding and systematic desensitization, were designed on the basis of conditioning principles. A persistent problem for theoretical analyses of such fears is that people with clinically significant fear and anxiety often have no known history of conditioning with traumatic events. Many people, for example, have an intense fear of snakes even though they have never been bitten by a snake.

If an individual has no known experience with traumatic events, how might that person have acquired a fear or phobia? Recent research with rhesus monkeys *(Macaca mulatta)* suggests that significant fears may be acquired through observational learning. (For a review, see Mineka & Cook, 1988.) Rhesus monkeys reared in the wild have an intense fear of snakes. In response to the sight of a snake, they exhibit a variety of fear responses, including fear grimacing, ear flapping, clutching the cage, averting their eyes, and piloerection (erection of the hair follicles). Fear is also evident in their reluctance to reach over the snake to obtain a food treat. By contrast, monkeys reared in the laboratory do not show these behaviors. Mineka and her colleagues investigated whether laboratory-reared monkeys could acquire a fear of snakes by observing the fear reactions of wild-reared monkeys in response to a snake.

A discriminative observational conditioning procedure was used. During preliminary training, the demonstrator monkeys were taught to reach over a clear plastic container to obtain a food treat. Observer monkeys were then given the opportunity to watch the reactions of the demonstrator monkeys. On some trials, a live or toy snake was placed in the plastic container. During other trials, the plastic container held a neutral object (a block of wood, for example). The demonstrator subjects showed intense fear of the snake stimuli but not of the neutral objects. After as few as two fear-observation trials, most of the observer subjects showed similar fear reactions to the snake stimuli. The level of fear they acquired was closely related to the level of fear shown by the demonstrator monkeys. Furthermore, once the observer monkeys became fearful of the snakes, they could serve effectively as demonstrator subjects in the observational conditioning of other rhesus monkeys. These results indicate that observational learning could be the basis for wide social transmission of fear among members of a monkey troupe or other social group (see also Cook & Mineka, 1990).

forcement model predicts that introducing an explicit feedback stimulus will facilitate the learning of an avoidance response. Numerous experiments have found this to be true (for example, Bolles & Grossen, 1969; D'Amato, Fazzaro, & Etkin, 1968; Keehn & Nakkash, 1959). Other studies have shown that, during the course of avoidance training, a response feedback stimulus becomes a conditioned inhibitor of fear (for example, Morris, 1974; Rescorla, 1968a). Furthermore, there is also direct evidence that a feedback stimulus that has been conditioned to inhibit fear during avoidance training thereby becomes an effective positive reinforcer for new responses (Morris, 1975; Weisman & Litner, 1972; see also Dinsmoor & Sears, 1973). Thus, there is considerable evidence for the conditioned inhibition reinforcement factor in avoidance learning.

There are important similarities and differences between positive reinforcement of avoidance behavior through conditioned inhibition and the negative reinforcement process assumed by two-process theory. Both mechanisms involve a reduction of fear. However, the manner in which this occurs is different in the two cases. Whereas a conditioned inhibitor actively inhibits fear, CS termination is assumed to lead to the passive dissipation of fear. Because both mechanisms involve fear reduction, the operation of both processes depends on the existence of fear. However, the conditioned inhibition reinforcement process is less restrictive about the source of the fear. The fear may be elicited by an explicit warning stimulus or CS. The fear also may be elicited by contextual cues or cues of the environment in which the avoidance procedure is conducted.

The fact that fear elicited by situational cues can provide the basis for conditioned inhibition reinforcement makes the safety-signal hypothesis particularly well suited to explain free-operant avoidance behavior. Subjects often experience numerous shocks during acquisition of free-operant avoidance behavior.

This and the absence of an exteroceptive warning stimulus make it highly likely that the entire experimental situation becomes conditioned to elicit fear. Because shocks never occur for the duration of the R–S interval after a response is made, the proprioceptive and tactile stimuli that accompany the response can become conditioned inhibitors of fear. Thus, the response-associated feedback cues can come to provide positive reinforcement for the free-operant avoidance response (Dinsmoor, 1977; Rescorla, 1968a).

It is important to realize that the conditioned inhibition reinforcement mechanism is not incompatible with or necessarily a substitute for the negative reinforcement process assumed by two-process theory. That is, negative reinforcement through CS termination and positive reinforcement through conditioned inhibitory feedback cues could well be operative simultaneously, both processes contributing to the strength of the avoidance behavior (see Cicala & Owen, 1976; Owen, Cicala, & Herdegen, 1978).

Reinforcement of avoidance through reduction of shock frequency.   As we have seen, the conditioned inhibition reinforcement mechanism does not represent a radical alternative to the two-process theory of avoidance. However, another reinforcement mechanism, **shock-frequency reduction**, has been proposed as an alternative to two-process theory (deVilliers, 1974; Herrnstein, 1969; Herrnstein & Hineline, 1966; Hineline, 1981; Sidman, 1962). By definition, avoidance responses prevent the delivery of shock and thereby reduce the frequency of shocks the subject receives. The theories of avoidance we have discussed so far have viewed the reduction of shocks almost as an incidental by-product of avoidance responses rather than as an immediate primary cause of the behavior. By contrast, the *shock-frequency-reduction hypothesis* views avoidance of shock as critical to the reinforcement of avoidance behavior.

Shock-frequency reduction as the cause of avoidance behavior was first entertained by Sidman (1962) to explain results he obtained in a concurrent free-operant avoidance experiment. Rats were exposed to two free-operant avoidance schedules at the same time. Responses on one response lever prevented shocks on one of the schedules and responses on the other lever prevented shocks on the second schedule. Sidman concluded that the subjects distributed their responses between the two response levers so as to reduce the overall frequency of shocks they received. The idea that shock-frequency reduction can serve to reinforce avoidance behavior was later encouraged by evidence of learning in a free-operant avoidance procedure specifically designed to minimize the role of fear-conditioned temporal cues (Herrnstein & Hineline, 1966). In addition, studies of the relative importance of various components of the discriminated avoidance procedure have also shown that the avoidance component significantly contributes to the learning (for example, Bolles, Stokes, & Younger, 1966; see also Bolles, 1972a; Kamin, 1956).

Although the evidence just cited clearly indicates that avoidance of shock is important, the mechanisms responsible for these results are debatable. Several experiments have shown that animals can learn to make an avoidance response even if the response does not reduce the frequency of shocks delivered (Gardner & Lewis, 1976; Hineline, 1970; see also Hineline, 1981). Responding in these studies delayed the onset of the next scheduled shock but did not prevent its delivery. Thus, overall shock frequency was unchanged by the instrumental response. Such results can be explained in terms of the shock-frequency-reduction hypothesis by assuming that subjects calculate shock frequencies over only a limited period following an avoidance response. However, the hypothesis does not specify the duration of these intervals, leaving them to be determined experimentally (see, for example, Logue, 1982).

In evaluating the shock-frequency-reduction hypothesis, one must also consider the extent to which evidence consistent with the hypothesis can be explained in other ways — specifically, by means of conditioned inhibition reinforcement or by means of punishing effects of shocks in the absence of an avoidance contingency. If a response reduces the frequency of shocks, external and proprioceptive stimuli involved in making the response will come to signal the absence of shock and become a conditioned inhibitor. The conditioned inhibitory properties of these stimuli can then reinforce the behavior. This conditioned inhibition mechanism is a plausible alternative to the shock-frequency interpretation, particularly for free-operant avoidance experiments (for example, Herrnstein & Hineline, 1966). In fact, it is a more broadly applicable explanation. Unlike the shock-frequency hypothesis, the conditioned inhibition account can also explain the results reviewed in the preceding section concerning the properties of response feedback cues in avoidance experiments.

SSDR theory.   In the theories discussed so far, the main emphasis is on how the events that precede and follow the avoidance response control avoidance behavior. The exact nature of the instrumental response required to prevent scheduled shocks is not a primary concern of these theories. In addition, the reinforcement mechanisms assumed by the theories all require some time to develop. Before fear reduction can be an effective reinforcer, fear first must be conditioned to the CS; before feedback cues can come to serve as reinforcers, they must become signals for the absence of shock; and before shock-frequency reduction can work, subjects must experience enough shocks to be able to assess shock frequencies. Therefore, these theories tell us very little about what determines the organism's behavior during the first few trials of avoidance training. The lack of concern with what the subject does during the first few trials is a serious weakness. For an avoidance mechanism to be useful to an animal in its natural habitat, the mechanism has to generate successful avoidance responses very quickly. Avoidance learning that requires numerous training trials is obviously of no use to an animal that fails to avoid being eaten by a predator during its initial encounters.

In contrast to the theories we considered earlier, the account of avoidance behavior we will discuss in the present section focuses on the specific nature of the instrumental response required to prevent shock and addresses the question of what controls the subject's behavior during the early stages of avoidance training. As proposed by Robert Bolles (1970, 1971), the theory first recognizes that aversive stimuli and situations elicit strong unconditioned, or innate, responses in animals. These innate responses are assumed to have evolved because they enable an animal to defend itself successfully against pain and injury. Therefore, Bolles called these **species-specific defense reactions (SSDRs).** In rats, for example, prominent species-specific defense reactions include flight (running); freezing (remaining vigilant but motionless, except for breathing); and defensive fighting. Other reactions to danger include thigmotaxis (approaching walls); defensive burying (covering up the source of aversive stimulation); and increasingly seeking out dark areas.

Originally, Bolles proposed that the configuration of the environment determined the particular SSDR that occurred. For example, flight may predominate when an obvious escape route is available and freezing may predominate if there is no way out of the situation. This must be true to some extent. Defensive fighting, for example, is not possible without an opponent and defensive burying is not possible if something like sand is not available for burying the source of danger. However, other factors, such as the imminence and intensity of the danger, also determine which SSDR occurs (Fanselow, 1989; Fanselow & Lester, 1988).

The SSDR theory of avoidance behavior states that species-specific defense reactions predominate during the initial stages of avoidance training. If the most likely SSDR is successful in preventing shocks, this behavior will persist as long as the avoidance procedure is in effect. If the first SSDR is not effective, it will be followed by shock, which will suppress the behavior through punishment. The animal will then make the next-most-likely SSDR. If shocks persist, this second SSDR will also become suppressed by punishment, and the organism will make the third-most-likely SSDR. The process will end when a response is found that is effective in avoiding shocks, so that the behavior will not be suppressed by punishment. Thus, according to the SSDR account, punishment is responsible for the selection of the instrumental avoidance response from other activities of the organism. Reinforcement, be it positive or negative, is assumed to have a minor role, if any, in avoidance learning. The correct avoidance response is not strengthened by reinforcement. Rather, it occurs because other SSDRs are suppressed by punishment.

One obvious prediction of the SSDR theory is that some types of responses will be more easily learned in avoidance experiments than other types. Consistent with this prediction, Bolles (1969) found that rats can rapidly learn to run in a running wheel to avoid shock. By contrast, their performance of a rearing response (standing on the hind legs) did not improve much during the course of avoidance training. Presumably, running was learned faster because it was closer to the rat's species-specific defense reactions in the running wheel. In another study, Grossen and Kelley (1972) initially documented the subjects' responses to shock before selecting the avoidance response. The rats were placed on a large, flat grid surface. When shocked, the animals were highly likely to freeze near the side walls of the apparatus. A platform was then placed on the grid floor, either in the center or near the side walls, and the animals were required to jump onto the platform to avoid shock. Faster learning occurred when the platform was near the sides of the apparatus than when it was in the center of the grid surface. Thus, the avoidance performance was accurately predicted from the subjects' innate reactions to shock. In an important follow-up experiment, Grossen and Kelley also showed that the position of the platform did not make any difference if the subjects were reinforced with food for making the jump response.

Predatory imminence and the distinction between defensive and recuperative behavior. The SSDR theory has made significant contributions to the understanding of avoidance learning by calling our attention to the importance of species-typical behavior in aversive situations. However, it has not been entirely successful in explaining experimental findings. For example, contrary to the SSDR theory, defensive responses that are ineffective in avoiding aversive stimulation are not necessarily suppressed by punishment. In fact, it has been proposed that punishment may actually promote the occurrence of species-specific defense responses (for example, Bolles & Riley, 1973; Melvin & Ervey, 1973; Walters & Glazer, 1971).

The SSDR theory has also failed to provide a sufficiently detailed account of how animals cope with painful stimuli and the anticipation of danger. More recent formulations recognize that what an animal does in response to danger depends on the imminence of the danger (Fanselow & Lester, 1988; Fanselow, 1989). These formulations also make a distinction between responses to the anticipation of a painful event or injury and responses to the actual occurrence of the damaging event. In the SSDR theory, species-specific defense re-

sponses are considered to be unconditioned responses to aversive stimuli that also could become elicited by conditioned aversive stimuli. In more recent formulations (Bolles & Fanselow, 1980), species-specific defense responses are considered to be responses to fear or to the anticipation of danger, whereas recuperative responses are assumed to be performed after the actual occurrence of a damaging event.

Consider a rat, for example. This small rodent is a potential source of food for cats, coyotes, snakes, and other predators. The rat is presumably safest in its nest in a burrow, but it has to go out periodically to forage for food. When it is out foraging, it is not in much danger as long as no cats or snakes are around. When a snake appears, the rat's level of danger increases, but not by much if the snake is far away. However, as the snake approaches the rat, the level of danger rises. The situation is very dangerous when the snake is about to strike, and maximum danger is encountered when the strike actually occurs. This progression of increasing levels of danger is called **predatory imminence** and is illustrated in Figure 9.12.

An important aspect of the *predatory-imminence hypothesis* is that different species-typical defense responses are assumed to occur as the situation becomes progressively more dangerous. If a rat is forced to forage for food in a location where it periodically encounters snakes, it is likely to go out of its burrow for food less often but to eat larger meals each time (Fanselow, Lester, & Helmstetter, 1988). Thus, the response to a low level of predatory imminence may be an adjustment of meal patterns. When a snake appears but is not yet about to strike, the rat's defensive behavior is likely to change to freezing. Freezing may very well reduce the chances that a predator will see or hear the rat; moreover, many predators will strike only at moving prey. Freezing by the prey also may result in the predator shifting its attention to something else (Suarez & Gallup, 1981).

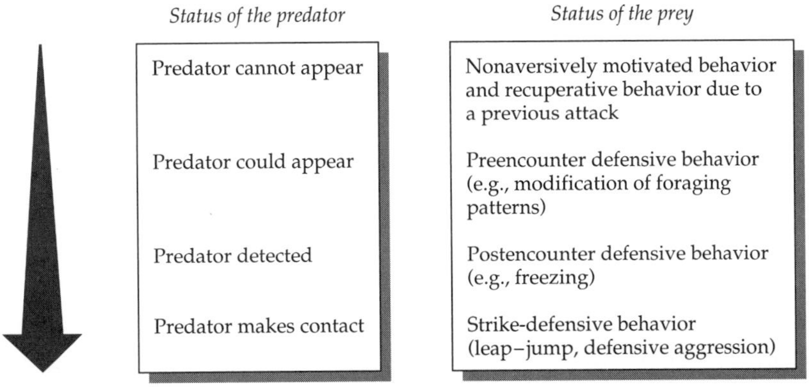

Status of the predator	Status of the prey
Predator cannot appear	Nonaversively motivated behavior and recuperative behavior due to a previous attack
Predator could appear	Preencounter defensive behavior (e.g., modification of foraging patterns)
Predator detected	Postencounter defensive behavior (e.g., freezing)
Predator makes contact	Strike-defensive behavior (leap–jump, defensive aggression)

Figure 9.12 The predatory-imminence continuum. *(From "A Functional Behavioristic Approach to Aversively Motivated Behavior: Predatory Imminence as a Determinant of the Topography of Defensive Behavior" by M.S. Fanselow and L.S. Lester, in R.C. Bolles and M.D. Beecher (Eds.), 1988,* Evolution and Learning, *(pp. 185–212). Copyright © 1988 by Erlbaum. Reprinted by permission.)*

When the snake is about to strike, the rat is likely to leap into the air. It is as if the rat's freezing behavior prepares it to explode into the air when it is then touched. If the rat does not successfully escape the predator at this point, it is likely to engage in defensive aggressive activities. Finally, assuming that the defensive behavior is successful and it manages to get away from the snake, the rat is likely to engage in grooming and other recuperative responses that should promote healing from its injuries.

The predatory-imminence hypothesis differs from the SSDR theory in two important respects. First, as our scenario illustrates, species-specific defense responses such as freezing, fleeing, and aggression are most likely to occur in anticipation of injury rather than in response to the injury itself. The actual injury stimulates recuperative responses. Thus, unlike the SSDR theory, the predatory-imminence hypothesis makes a distinction between defensive and recuperative responses to aversive stimulation. Secondly, in the predatory-imminence hypothesis, the primary determinant of the particular defense response that is observed is assumed to be the level of predatory imminence rather than the

configuration of the environment. Thus, selection among possible SSDRs is not through suppression of ineffective SSDRs by punishment, as the SSDR theory proposes, but by assessment of the level of danger.

Despite these differences, both the SSDR theory and the predatory-imminence hypothesis assume that defensive behavior initially occurs as unconditioned responding. Stimuli that become associated with an aversive event can come to elicit the defense responses as well. The available evidence suggests that in rats the defense response that comes to be elicited by a conditioned stimulus is usually one level lower on the predatory-imminence scale than the response elicited by the unconditioned stimulus (Fanselow, 1989). Thus, if the unconditioned stimulus elicits the leap and jump characteristic of peak predatory imminence, the conditioned stimulus is likely to elicit the freezing behavior of the level just below. Whether this characterization is applicable to other species as well remains to be seen.

Another important similarity between the predatory-imminence hypothesis and the SSDR theory is that neither of them assumes that positive reinforcement is involved in the development of avoidance behavior. In fact, the predatory-imminence hypothesis takes a more radical position than the SSDR theory in rejecting the importance of instrumental conditioning in the response of animals to aversive situations, since it does not even include a punishment mechanism. However, the predatory-imminence hypothesis was developed as an explanation of defensive behavior—not as an explanation of the diverse findings that have been obtained in avoidance learning experiments. Therefore, it was not intended to serve as a complete account of what happens in avoidance conditioning experiments.

The Avoidance Puzzle: Concluding Comments

We have learned a great deal about avoidance behavior in the 50 years since Mowrer and Lamoreaux (1942) puzzled about how "not getting something" can motivate avoidance responses. As we saw, numerous ingenious answers to this puzzle have been provided. Two-process theory, conditioned inhibition reinforcement, and shock-frequency-reduction reinforcement all provide different views of what happens after an avoidance response to reinforce it. By contrast, the SSDR account suggests a punishment alternative to reinforcement theories and the concept of predatory imminence characterizes defensive responses entirely without reference to instrumental contingencies. None of these theories can explain everything that occurs in aversive conditioning situations. However, each provides ideas that are useful for understanding various aspects of avoidance behavior. For example, none of the more recent formulations is as useful in explaining the acquired-drive experiments as two-process theory. The safety-signal theory is particularly useful in explaining free-operant avoidance behavior, the role of response feedback stimuli in avoidance conditioning, and the maintenance of avoidance behavior in the absence of an explicit warning stimulus. Finally, the concept of predatory imminence provides the most useful account of what happens during early stages of avoidance training. Given the complexities of the various avoidance learning paradigms that experimenters have devised, we may have to use several conceptual frameworks to explain all of the available data.

Punishment

Although most of us engage in avoidance behavior of one sort or another every day, there is little public awareness of it. As a society, we are not particularly concerned about what is involved in making avoidance responses. This may be because avoidance conditioning is rarely used to control others' behavior. By contrast, the other aversive conditioning process we will discuss, punishment, has always been of great concern to people. In some situations punishment is used as a form of retribution or as a price for undesirable behavior. The threat of punishment also is frequently used to encourage adherence to religious and civil codes of conduct. Many institutions and rules have evolved to ensure that punishment will be administered in ways that are deemed ethical and acceptable to society. Furthermore, what constitutes justified punishment in the criminal justice system, in childrearing, in schools, and elsewhere is a matter of continual debate.

Despite long-standing societal concerns about punishment, for many years experimental psychologists did not devote much attention to the topic. On the basis of a few experiments, Thorndike (1932) and Skinner (1938, 1953) concluded that punishment was not a very effective method for controlling behavior and that it had only temporary effects at best (see also Estes, 1944). This claim was not seriously challenged until the 1960s, when punishment processes began to be much more extensively investigated (Azrin & Holz, 1966; Campbell & Church, 1969; Church, 1963; Solomon, 1964). We now know that punishment can be an effective technique for modifying behavior. Given the appropriate procedural parameters, responding can be suppressed nearly totally in just one or two trials. With less severe parameters, the suppression of behavior may be incomplete, and responding may recover.

Experimental Analysis of Punishment

The basic punishment procedure involves presenting an aversive stimulus after a specified response. The usual outcome of the procedure is that the specified response becomes suppressed. By not making the punished response, the subject avoids the aversive stimulation. Because punishment involves the suppression of behavior, it can be observed only with responses that are likely to occur in the absence of punishment. To ensure occurrence of the behavior, experimental studies of punishment usually also involve reinforcement of the punished response with something like food or water. Therefore, the subjects frequently face a conflict between responding to obtain positive reinforcement and not responding to avoid punishment. The degree of response suppression that occurs is determined both by variables related to presentation of the aversive stimulus and by variables related to the availability of positive reinforcement.

Characteristics of the aversive stimulus and its method of introduction. A great variety of aversive stimuli have been used in punishment experiments, including electric shock, a blast of air, loud noise, verbal reprimands, a physical slap, a squirt of lemon juice in the mouth, and a cue previously conditioned with shock (Azrin, 1958; Hake & Azrin, 1965; Hall, Axelrod, Foundopoulos, Shellman, Campbell, & Cranston, 1971; Masserman, 1946; Sajwaj, Libet, & Agras, 1974; Skinner, 1938). Other response-suppression procedures have involved the loss of positive reinforcement, time out from positive reinforcement, and overcor-

rection (Foxx & Azrin, 1973; Thomas, 1968; Trenholme & Baron, 1975). **Time out** refers to removal of the opportunity to obtain positive reinforcement. Time out is often used to punish children, as when a child is told "Go to your room" after doing something bad. **Overcorrection** involves requiring a person not only to rectify what was done badly but to overcorrect for the mistake. For example, a child who has placed an object in his mouth may be asked to remove the object and also to wash out his mouth with an antiseptic solution.

The response suppression produced by punishment depends in part on certain features of the aversive stimulus. The effects of various characteristics of the aversive event have been most extensively investigated with shock. The general finding has been that more intense and longer shocks are more effective in suppressing responding. (See reviews by Azrin & Holz, 1966; Church, 1969; Walters & Grusec, 1977.) Low-intensity aversive stimulation produces only moderate suppression of responding, and the disruption of behavior may recover with continued exposure to the punishment procedure (for example, Azrin, 1960). By contrast, if the aversive stimulus is sufficiently intense, responding may be completely suppressed for a long time. In one experiment, for example, high-intensity punishment completely suppressed the instrumental response for 6 days (Azrin, 1960).

Another very important factor in punishment is how the aversive stimulus is introduced. If a high intensity of shock is used when the punishment procedure is first introduced, the instrumental response will be severely suppressed. Much less suppression of behavior will occur if a mild punishment is used initially, with the shock intensity gradually increased during the course of continued punishment training (Azrin, Holz, & Hake, 1963; Miller, 1960; see also Banks, 1976). Thus, subjects can be protected from the effects of intense punishment by first being exposed to lower levels of shock that do not produce much response suppression. It appears that because a low intensity of punishment does not disrupt responding very much, subjects learn to persist in making the instrumental response in the presence of the aversive stimulation. This learning then generalizes to higher intensities of shock, with the result that the instrumental response continues to be made when the more aversive punishment is used.

The preceding findings suggest that subjects adopt a particular mode of responding during their initial exposure to punishment, and this type of behavior generalizes to new punishment situations (Church, 1969). This idea has an interesting implication. Suppose that subjects are first exposed to intense shock that results in a very low level of responding. The mode of behavior adopted during initial exposure to punishment is severe suppression of responding. If the shock intensity is subsequently reduced, the severe suppression of behavior should persist, resulting in less responding than if the mild shock had been used from the beginning. Results such as this have been obtained by Raymond (reported in Church, 1969). Thus, initial exposure to mild aversive stimulation that does not disrupt behavior very much *reduces* the effects of later intense punishment. By contrast, initial exposure to intense aversive stimulation *increases* the suppressive effects of later mild punishment.

Response-contingent versus response-independent aversive stimulation. Another important variable that determines the extent to which aversive stimulation suppresses behavior is whether the aversive stimulus is presented contingent on a specified response or independently of behavior. Response-independent aversive stimulation can result in some suppression of instrumental behavior. However, the general finding is that significantly more suppression of behavior occurs if the aversive stimulus is produced by the instrumental response (for example, Azrin,

1956; Bolles, Holtz, Dunn, & Hill, 1980; Camp, Raymond, & Church, 1967; Frankel, 1975).

In one study demonstrating the importance of the response contingency in punishment, Goodall (1984) compared a CER, or conditioned suppression, procedure (in which footshock during a CS was delivered independent of behavior) and a discriminative punishment procedure (in which shock during the CS was delivered contingent on lever pressing). One group of subjects was trained initially to press a lever for food reinforcement on a VI 60-sec schedule. After responding had stabilized, the treatment procedure of interest was introduced. Two conditioned stimuli were used, a tone and a light. One of the stimuli was designated as the punishment cue (let's say the tone), and the other stimulus was designated as the cue for response-independent aversive stimulation (the light). Two trials with each of the CSs were presented each day in alternation, starting with the punishment cue. During the punishment stimulus, the subjects received a brief shock after every third lever-press response. Thus, punishment was delivered on an FR 3 schedule. Each CER trial was yoked to the preceding punishment trial, so that subjects received the same number and distribution of shocks during the CER cue as they had received during the immediately preceding punishment trial. However, shocks during the CER cue were always delivered independent of the subjects' lever-press behavior.

The results obtained with these procedures are presented in Figure 9.13 in terms of suppression of lever pressing during the CER and punishment cues. Given the brief and mild shocks that were used (.5 mA, .5 sec), not much suppression of behavior was evident during the CER stimulus. By contrast, the same number and distribution of shocks substantially suppressed responding during the punishment stimulus. This difference illustrates that delivering shocks contingent on an instrumental response is more effective in suppressing that response than de-

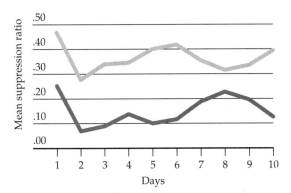

FR 3 CER   FR 3 PUN

Figure 9.13 Suppression of lever pressing during punishment and CER stimuli during 10 successive sessions. During the punishment cue, lever pressing was punished on an FR 3 schedule. During the CER cue, the same number and distribution of shocks was delivered independent of behavior. *(From "Learning Due to the Response-Shock Contingency in Signalled Punishment" by G. Goodall, 1984, The Quarterly Journal of Experimental Psychology, 36B, pp. 259–279. Copyright © 1984 by Erlbaum. Reprinted by permission.)*

livering aversive stimulation independent of behavior.

Effects of delay of punishment. In response-independent procedures, the aversive stimulus may occur immediately after the instrumental response on some occasions and a long time after the response on other occasions. Explicit investigation of the interval between instrumental behavior and aversive stimulation has shown that this variable greatly influences the degree of response suppression. The general finding is that increasing the interval between the instrumental response and delivery of punishment results in less suppression of behavior (for example, Baron, 1965; Camp et al., 1967). This relation is particularly important in attempts to use punishment to modify behavior outside the laboratory. Inadvertent delays may occur if the undesired response is not detected right away, if it takes time to investigate who is actually at fault for an error, or if preparing the aversive stimulus requires time. Such delays can make punishment totally ineffective in modifying the undesired behavior.

Effects of schedules of punishment. Just as positive reinforcement does not have to be provided for each occurrence of the instrumental response, as we saw in the experiment by Goodall, punishment may also be delivered only intermittently. In the Goodall study, punishment was delivered on an FR 3 schedule. More systematic studies have shown that the degree of response suppression produced by punishment depends on the proportion of responses that are punished.

In a study of fixed-ratio punishment by Azrin and his colleagues (1963), pigeons were first reinforced with food on a variable-interval schedule for pecking a response key. When the key-pecking behavior was occurring at a stable and high rate, punishment was introduced. Various fixed-ratio punishment procedures were tested while food reinforcement continued to be provided for the pecking behavior. The results are summarized in Figure 9.14. When every response was shocked (FR 1 punishment), key pecking ceased entirely. With the other punishment schedules, the rate of responding depended on the frequency of punishment. Higher fixed-ratio schedules allowed more responses to go unpunished. Not surprisingly, therefore, higher rates of responding occurred when higher fixed-ratio punishment schedules were used. However, some suppression of behavior was observed even when only every thousandth response was followed by shock. (Because responding was reinforced on a VI 3-min schedule, substantial suppressions of key pecking could occur without loss of food reinforcement.)

Effects of schedules of positive reinforcement. As we noted earlier, in most studies of punishment the instrumental response is simultaneously maintained by a positive reinforce-

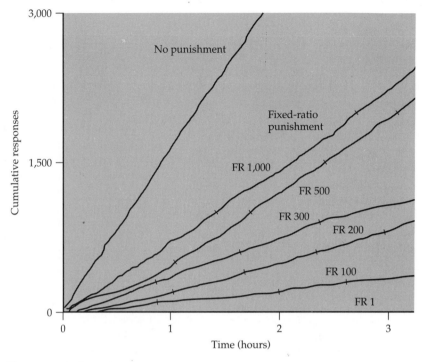

Figure 9.14 Cumulative record of pecking when the response was not punished and when the response was punished according to various fixed-ratio schedules of punishment. The oblique slashes indicate the delivery of punishment. Responding was reinforced on a variable-interval 3-min schedule. *(From "Fixed-Ratio Punishment" by N.H. Azrin, W.C. Holz, and D.R. Hake, 1963,* Journal of the Experimental Analysis of Behavior, 6, *pp. 141–148.)*

ment schedule so that there is some level of responding available to be punished. As it turns out, the effects of a punishment procedure are in part determined by this positive reinforcement. When behavior is maintained by either a fixed- or a variable-interval schedule of positive reinforcement, punishment produces a decrease in the overall rate of responding. However, the temporal distribution of the behavior is not disturbed. That is, during the punishment procedure, variable-interval positive reinforcement produces a suppressed but stable rate of responding (see Figure 9.14), whereas fixed-interval positive reinforcement produces the typical scalloped pattern of responding (for example, Azrin & Holz, 1961). The outcome is considerably different if the behavior is maintained by a

fixed-ratio positive reinforcement schedule. As we noted in Chapter 6, fixed-ratio schedules produce a pause in responding just after reinforcement (the postreinforcement pause), followed by a high and steady rate of responding to complete the number of responses necessary for the next reinforcement (the ratio run). Punishment usually increases the length of the postreinforcement pause but has little effect on the ratio run (Azrin, 1959). The initial responses of a fixed-ratio run are much more susceptible to punishment than later responses. Thus, shock delivered early in a ratio run increases the postreinforcement pause more than shock delivered later in the completion of the ratio (Dardano & Sauerbrunn, 1964; see also Church, 1969). Another important aspect of positive reinforcement schedules is the frequency of reinforcement provided. Generally, punishment has less effect on instrumental responses that produce more frequent positive reinforcement (for example, Church & Raymond, 1967).

Availability of alternative responses for obtaining positive reinforcement. In many experiments, the punished response is also the only response the subject can perform to obtain positive reinforcement, such as food. By decreasing its rate of responding, the subject may decrease the number of food pellets it receives. Therefore, the subject is conflicted as to whether to suppress its behavior to avoid punishment or to respond to obtain positive reinforcement. This predicament does not exist if alternative responses for obtaining positive reinforcement are available. In this case, the subject can entirely cease making the punished response without having to forgo positive reinforcement. As one might expect, the availability of an alternative source of reinforcement greatly increases the suppression of responding produced by punishment. In a study by Herman and Azrin (1964), for example, adult males were seated in front of two response levers. Pressing either response lever was reinforced with a cigarette on a variable-interval schedule. After the behavior was occurring at a stable rate, responses on one of the levers resulted in a brief obnoxious noise. In one experimental condition, only one response lever was available during the punishment phase. In another condition, both response levers were accessible, and responding on one of them was punished with the loud noise. Figure 9.15 shows the results. When the punished response was the only way to obtain cigarettes, punishment produced a moderate suppression of behavior. By contrast, when the alternative response lever was available, responding on the punished lever ceased altogether. Thus, the availability of an alternative response for obtaining positive reinforcement greatly increased the suppressive effects of punishment. Similar results

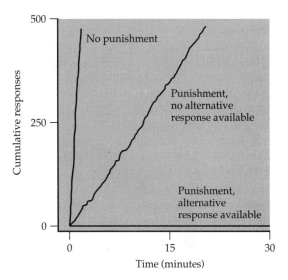

Figure 9.15 Cumulative record of responding when responses are not punished, when responses are punished and there is no alternative source of reinforcement, and when responses are punished but an alternative reinforced response is available. *(From "Punishment" by N.H. Azrin and W.C. Holz, in W.K. Honig (Ed.), 1966,* Operant Behavior. *Copyright © 1966 by Prentice-Hall.)*

have been obtained in other situations. For example, children punished for playing with certain toys are much less likely to play with these if they are allowed to play with other toys instead (Perry & Parke, 1975).

Effects of a discriminative stimulus for punishment. As we saw in Chapter 8, if positive reinforcement is available for responding in the presence of a distinctive stimulus but is not available in its absence, the subject will learn to respond only when the stimulus is present. The suppressive effects of punishment can also be brought under stimulus control. This occurs if responding is punished in the presence of a discriminative stimulus but is not punished when the stimulus is absent. Such a procedure is called **discriminative punishment**. With continued exposure to discriminative punishment, the suppressive effects of punishment will come to be limited to the presence of the discriminative stimulus.

In one of the first experiments of this type, Dinsmoor (1952) reinforced rats with food on a variable-interval 2-min schedule for pressing a response lever. After responding had stabilized, successive 5-minute periods of punishment were alternated with 5-minute periods of no punishment. During the punishment periods, the lights in the experimental chamber were turned off and each lever-press response resulted in a brief shock. During the safe periods, the lights were turned on and no shocks were delivered. (Food reinforcement continued during both the punishment periods and the safe periods.) The rats quickly learned to restrict their lever-press responses to the safe periods. When the lights were turned off, signaling that the punishment procedure was in effect, responding was suppressed. However, responding resumed whenever the lights were turned back on, signaling that responses would not be punished.

The fact that the suppressive effects of punishment can be limited to the presence of discriminative stimuli is often problematic in applications of punishment. In many situations, the person who administers the punishment also serves as a discriminative stimulus for punishment, with the result that the undesired behavior is suppressed only as long as the monitor is present. For example, children learn which teachers are strict about discipline and learn to suppress their rambunctious behavior in those classes more than in other classes. As another example, a highway patrol car is a discriminative stimulus for punishment for speeding. Drivers are more likely to obey speed laws in areas where they see many patrol cars than in unpatrolled stretches of highway.

Punishment as a signal for the availability of positive reinforcement.

Punishment does not always suppress behavior. In fact, in certain situations people seem to seek out punishment. Does this represent a breakdown of the normal mechanisms of behavior, or can such behavior be explained by the principles we have discussed so far? Experimental evidence suggests that conventional behavioral mechanisms may lead to such seemingly abnormal behavior. Punishment seeking can result from a situation in which positive reinforcement is available only when the instrumental response is also punished. In such circumstances, punishment may become a signal, or discriminative stimulus, for the availability of positive reinforcement. If this occurs, punishment will increase rather than suppress responding.

In one demonstration of the discriminative stimulus properties of punishment, pigeons were first trained to peck a response key for food reinforcement on a variable-interval schedule (Holz & Azrin, 1961). Each response was then punished by a mild shock sufficient to reduce the response rate by about 50%. In the next phase of the experiment, periods in which the punishment procedure was in effect were alternated with periods in which punishment was not scheduled. In addition, the pecking response was reinforced with food only during the punishment periods. The punishment and safe periods were not signaled by an exteroceptive stimulus, such as a light or a tone. Therefore, the only way for subjects to tell whether reinforcement was available was to see whether they were punished for pecking. Under these circumstances higher rates of pecking occurred during punishment periods than during safe periods. Punishment became a discriminative stimulus for food reinforcement.

Other instances of self-punitive behavior.

Self-punitive behavior is of considerable interest because it occurs in many forms of human behavior pathology and sometimes is highly ritualized. During the Middle Ages in Europe, for example, flagellants traveled from place to place beating themselves and one another to purge themselves of sin.

Making punishment a discriminative stimulus for positive reinforcement is one way to create self-punitive behavior. Self-punitive behavior can also result from prior escape training. This phenomenon, sometimes called **vicious-circle behavior,** has been extensively investigated in runway situations with rats (see Brown, 1969; Brown & Cunningham, 1981; Melvin, 1971). In a typical experiment, the animals are first given escape training in which the entire runway is electrified and they have to run the length of the alley to escape shock and reach a safe goal box. After the subjects have learned the runway escape response, an extinction procedure is introduced for control subjects; shock is no longer presented in any segment of the runway. For experimental subjects, a portion of the runway (usually the middle third of the alley) remains electrified. Thus, the experimental subjects encounter shock if they run during extinction, whereas the control subjects do not receive punishment. The remarkable finding is that punishment increases the resistance to extinction of the running response in the experimental subjects. Instead of suppressing behavior, punishment of conditioned escape behavior facilitates responding, evidently by maintaining conditioned fear to early alley segments (see Dean & Pittman, 1991).

Response limitations on the effectiveness of punishment. The vicious-circle behavior we have described illustrates the resistance to punishment of a learned defensive response (a conditioned escape response). Other studies have provided evidence that unlearned, or innate, defensive responses are also somewhat resistant to punishment. Shettleworth (1978, 1981), for example, investigated the susceptibility to punishment of various response patterns in hamsters and found that open-rearing (rearing up on the hind legs without touching a wall of the experimental chamber) was significantly less susceptible to punishment than was scrabbling (moving the forepaws rapidly against a side wall of the experimental chamber, as in a digging motion). This difference appeared to be due to

the fact that, unlike scrabbling, open-rearing is an innate defensive behavior in hamsters—it is increased by response-independent shocks. (For additional examples of the resistance of defensive behavior to punishment, see Melvin & Ervey, 1973; Walters & Glazer, 1971.)

Punishment and response reallocation. In Chapter 7 we discussed how reinforcement of a particular response may cause a reorganization, or reallocation, of the organism's entire behavioral repertoire. Reinforcement often increases the future likelihood of the reinforced response and decreases some other activities the subject might perform. Punishment likewise produces a reallocation of the subject's behavior. Suppression of the punished response may be accompanied by increases in some other activities and, possibly, decreases in certain nonpunished responses. In one experiment, for example, thirsty rats were given access to a running wheel and a drinking tube at the same time (Dunham, 1972). The rats were then punished for drinking. As expected, punishment suppressed the drinking response. However, punishment also increased the amount of time the rats spent running in the wheel. Such compensatory increases in nonpunished responses have been observed in a variety of situations. Typically, not all of the animal's nonpunished responses increase when one response is selected out for punishment. Rather, it is often the most likely of the nonpunished responses that shows an increase (Dunham, 1971, 1978). Reorganization of the subject's response profile can also involve decreases in the rate of nonpunished responses. For example, in hamsters, the punishment of certain responses (open-rearing, scrabbling, or face washing) results in an increase in freezing and a walk–sniff behavior, as well as a decrease in unpunished wall rearing and gnawing (Shettleworth, 1978). Research on such reorganizations of behavior illustrates that a comprehensive account of the effects of punishment requires consideration of more than just the response involved in the punishment contingency (Delprato & Rusiniak, 1991).

Theories of Punishment

In contrast to the study of avoidance behavior, investigations of punishment, by and large, have not been motivated by theoretical considerations. Most of the evidence available about the effects of punishment has been the product of empirical curiosity. The investigators were interested in finding out how punishment is influenced by various manipulations rather than in testing certain theoretical formulations. In fact, there are few systematic theories of punishment, and most of these were formulated in some form over 40 years ago. We will now describe three of the most prominent theories.

The conditioned emotional response theory of punishment. One of the first theories of punishment was proposed by Estes (1944) and is based on the observation by Estes and Skinner (1941) that a conditioned stimulus that has been paired with shock will suppress the performance of food-reinforced instrumental behavior. We discussed this conditioned suppression, or conditioned emotional response, procedure earlier in this chapter as well as in Chapters 3 and 5. The standard conditioned suppression experiment involves first conditioning animals to make an instrumental response, such as lever pressing, for food rein-

---

BOX **9.2**

When Punishment Doesn't Work

Sometimes children are brought to a therapist because their behavior is out of control. In a typical example the child is unruly and does not respond to the disciplinary practices of parents or teachers. Even punishment, used as a last resort, does not work. The parents or teachers complain that punishing the child only makes the behavior worse. It is not uncommon for children with a severe problem of this type to be diagnosed as hyperactive or emotionally disturbed. These labels suggest there is something fundamentally wrong with the child. Behavior therapists, however, have found that in some cases the problem may be nothing more than the result of mismanaged discipline. The parents or teachers may have inadvertently established punishment as a discriminative stimulus for positive reinforcement. Instead of decreasing some undesirable behavior, punishment increases it. How can this happen?

Let us take the hypothetical situation of Johnny, who lives in a home with two busy parents. Johnny, like most children, is rather active. If he is quietly playing in his room, the parents are likely to ignore him and engage in activities of their own. By contrast, if Johnny behaves badly or makes demands, the parents are forced to attend to him. The parents may be giving Johnny attention only when he is misbehaving or making demands. Any time he is not being a problem, the parents may be thankfully relieved to have a moment's peace. Thus, rather than reinforcing cooperative or peaceful behavior, the parents can come to ignore Johnny at these times. What we have then is a vicious circle. The more Johnny misbehaves, the less attention he is given for nondisruptive behavior, because the parents increasingly come to cherish quiet moments as a chance to do something on their own. Misbehavior becomes Johnny's main means of obtaining attention. The punishments and reprimands that go with the behavior signal to him that his parents are caring and attending.

In actuality, the therapist does not have the opportunity to observe how behavior problems of this type originate. The "discriminative value of punishment" explanation is supported by the outcome of attempts to change the situation. The hypothesis suggests that if one changes the attention patterns, the behavior problem can be alleviated. Indeed, clinical psychologists often show parents how to attend to appropriate and constructive activities and how to administer punishment with a minimum of attention directed toward the child. In many cases dramatic improvement ensues when parents are able to positively reinforce cooperative behavior with their attentions and ignore disruptive activities as much as possible.

forcement. Classical conditioning is then conducted in which a CS (a tone or light, for example) is paired with a brief shock. The conditioned aversive stimulus is then presented while the animal is allowed to lever-press for the food reinforcement. The usual result is that responding is disrupted during presentations of the CS. This response suppression was originally interpreted as resulting from competing responses elicited by the CS. The basic idea was that the conditioned stimulus came to elicit certain emotional responses (such as freezing) by virtue of being paired with shock. These conditioned emotional responses were presumably incompatible with making the lever-press response (the rat could not freeze and press the lever at the same time). Therefore, the rate of lever pressing was suppressed during presentations of the CS.

Estes (1944) proposed that punishment suppresses behavior through the same mechanism that produces conditioned suppression to a shock-paired CS. In contrast to the conditioned suppression experiment, however, punishment procedures usually do not involve an explicit CS that signals the impending delivery of shock. Estes suggested that the various stimuli the subject experiences just before making the punished response serve this function. For example, just before the rat presses a response lever, it experiences the visual and other spatial cues that exist near the lever, the tactile cues of the lever, and perhaps proprioceptive stimuli that result from its posture just as it is about to make the lever press. When the response is punished, all these stimuli become paired with shock. With repetition of the punishment episode, the various preresponse stimuli become strongly conditioned by the shock. As these cues acquire conditioned aversive properties, they will come to elicit conditioned emotional responses that are incompatible with the punished behavior. Thus, the punished response will become suppressed.

The conditioned emotional response theory can explain a great many facts about punishment. For example, the fact that more intense and longer duration shocks produce more response suppression can be explained by assuming that the stimuli conditioned by these aversive events elicit more vigorous conditioned emotional responses. The theory can also explain why response-contingent aversive stimulation produces more response suppression than response-independent delivery of shock. If shock is produced by the instrumental response, the stimuli that become conditioned by the shock are more likely to be closely related to performance of this behavior. Therefore, the conditioned emotional responses are more likely to interfere with the punished response.

In a reformulation of the conditioned emotional response theory, Estes (1969) proposed an alternative account of the mechanisms of conditioned suppression. The new formulation may be paraphrased in motivational terms. The basic idea is that a shock-conditioned stimulus disrupts food-reinforced responding because it evokes an emotional or motivational state (let us say fear) that is incompatible with the motivation maintaining the food-reinforced behavior. The shock-conditioned stimulus is assumed to inhibit the motivation to respond based on positive reinforcement. This revision is compatible with modern two-process theory, which we will discuss in Chapter 10. As we will see, modern two-process theory also assumes that motivational states elicited by a classically conditioned stimulus can interact with, or influence, the motivational state created by an instrumental conditioning procedure.

The avoidance theory of punishment. Another alternative to the conditioned emotional response theory regards punishment as a form of avoidance behavior. This theory is most closely associated with Dinsmoor (1954, 1977) and follows the tradition of the two-process theory of avoidance. Dinsmoor accepted the notion that the stimuli that set the occasion for the instrumental response become conditioned by the aversive stimulus when the response is punished. Thus, these stimuli were assumed to acquire conditioned aversive properties in much the same manner as stated in the conditioned emotional response theory. However, Dinsmoor added a second process to the mechanism of punishment. He proposed that subjects learn to escape from the conditioned aversive stimuli related to the punished response by engaging in some other behavior that is incompatible with the punished activity. Since this other behavior is incompatible with the punished response, performance of the alternative activity results in suppression of the punished behavior. Thus, the avoidance theory explains punishment in terms of the acquisition of incompatible avoidance responses.

The avoidance theory of punishment is an ingenious proposal. It suggests that all changes produced by aversive instrumental conditioning, be they increases or decreases in the likelihood of a response, can be explained by the same response-strengthening mechanisms. Suppression of behavior is not viewed as reflecting the weakening of the punished response. Rather, it is explained in terms of the strengthening of competing responses that effectively avoid the aversive stimulation. Thus, a single theoretical framework is used to analyze the outcomes of both punishment and avoidance procedures. Such economy is always considered desirable in scientific explanations.

Despite its cleverness and parsimony, the avoidance theory of punishment is not uniformly applauded. First, because it explains punishment in terms of avoidance mechanisms, all the theoretical problems that have been troublesome in the analysis of avoidance behavior become problems that have to be solved in the analysis of punishment as well. Another challenge for the theory is that its critical elements are not stated in a way that makes them easily accessible to experimental verification (Rachlin & Herrnstein, 1969; Schuster & Rachlin, 1968). The stimuli that are assumed to acquire conditioned aversive properties are not under the direct control of the experimenter. Rather, they are events that the subject is assumed to experience when it is about to make the punished response. Similarly, the activities the subject learns to perform to avoid making the punished response are ill specified. The theory does not tell us what these responses will be in a given situation or how one might look for them. The theory also provides a rather cumbersome explanation of the outcome of experiments on concurrent-chain schedules of punishment (for example, Schuster & Rachlin, 1968). However, the theory has remained compatible with most of the facts about punishment, perhaps because it is stated in a way that makes experimental tests of it difficult.

Punishment and the negative law of effect. The third and last concept about punishment that we will consider is also the oldest. Thorndike (1911) originally proposed that positive reinforcement and punishment involve symmetrically opposite processes. Just as positive reinforcement strengthens behavior, so punishment weakens it. In later years Thorndike abandoned the idea that punishment weakens behavior because he failed to find supporting evidence in some of his experiments (Thorndike, 1932). However, the belief that there is a negative law of effect that is comparable but opposite to the familiar positive law of effect has retained favor with some investigators (for example, Azrin & Holz, 1966; Rachlin & Herrnstein, 1969).

One approach to the analysis of the negative law of effect has been initiated by Premack and his colleagues. As we discussed in Chapter 7, Premack proposed that positive reinforcement occurs when the opportunity to engage in a highly valued activity is made dependent on the prior performance of an activity of lower value. The subject allocates time according to this restriction. The instrumental response is increased and the reinforcing behavior is decreased by the contingency.

According to Premack, the punishment contingency reverses this relation. Here, a low-valued activity is made to occur contingent on the performance of a higher valued behavior. Undergoing shock, for example, has a much lower probability than pressing a lever for food. Hence, shock can punish lever pressing.

Premack and his colleagues tested this idea about punishment using a motor-driven running wheel equipped with a drinking tube. In one experiment (Weisman & Premack, 1966), rats were deprived of water, so that drinking was more probable than running. Then a punishment procedure was introduced in which a bout of drinking was followed by a period of forced running. (The motor attached to the running wheel was turned on to force the rats to run.) Under these conditions, drinking was suppressed by running. Thus, a punishment effect was obtained. This and other experiments (see Premack, 1971a) illustrate that the punishing effects of forced running are similar to those of shock. The studies by Premack and his colleagues also illustrate the comparability of reinforcement and punishment. In the Weisman–Premack experiment, the same contingency (running after drinking) produced opposite effects depending on the relative values of running and drinking. When running was made more likely than drinking (by no longer water-depriving the rats), running reinforced drinking. Thus, running after drinking punished or reinforced drinking, depending on whether running was less or more valuable than drinking.

With a reinforcement procedure, the instrumental response is increased and the reinforcing response is decreased relative to a baseline free-responding situation. With a punishment procedure, the instrumental response is decreased and the reinforcing or punishing response is increased relative to a baseline condition. Moreover, in both cases the response that increases is the low-valued behavior and the one that decreases is the higher valued behavior. Viewed in this way, the procedures of reinforcement and punishment

produce the same effects. Operationally, there is only one significant difference. In punishment the subject has to be forced to engage in the lower valued activity. Rats do not ordinarily apply electrical shocks to themselves or run more than they want. In reinforcement the subject is "induced" to engage in the lower valued activity by the contingency itself.

The similarity between punishment and reinforcement we have just described was tested in an interesting experiment involving toy-playing behavior in children (Burkhard et al., 1978). In a baseline phase, children were observed playing with three toys. The toys were ranked high, medium, and low on the basis of how much time the children spent with each one. The children were assigned to reinforcement and punishment groups. For the reinforcement group, 1 minute of playing with the high-ranked toy was allowed after 1 minute of play with the low-ranked toy. For the punishment group, 1 minute of play with the low-ranked toy was required after 1 minute of play with the high-ranked toy. In both cases, the toy ranked as medium provided background activity and could be used freely. If Premack's punishment hypothesis is correct, the reinforcement and punishment procedures should have produced the same new distribution of time among the three toys. This in fact was the result. The reinforcement and punishment groups were indistinguishable in how much time they ended up playing with each toy. Playing with the low-ranked toy increased and playing with the high-ranked toy decreased to comparable levels for the two groups.

Research along the lines Premack has proposed is continuing. As in the case of positive reinforcement, the work suggests that punishment imposes a restriction against which behavior has to be adjusted. The negative law of effect, in light of this approach, is a statement of the way behavior changes under these restrictions: a low-valued activity produces a decrease in a higher valued activity. Economically minded theorists propose, as in the case of positive reinforcement (see Chapter 7), that the subject responds so as to maximize overall value. The maximization process, with both reinforcement and punishment procedures, involves an increase in a low-valued activity balanced against a decrease in a high-valued activity and may include effects on other behaviors as well.

Punishment Outside the Laboratory

As we have seen, punishment can be a highly effective procedure for rapidly suppressing behavior. However, the effectiveness of punishment in laboratory studies is not sufficient to justify the use of punishment outside the laboratory. Punishment procedures are easily misused, and even if the procedures are administered effectively there are serious ethical constraints on their application.

Punishment is typically not employed in an effective manner. Often punishment is first introduced at low intensities (a reprimand for the first offense, for example). The aversive stimulus may not be administered rapidly after the target response but delayed until it is convenient to administer it ("Wait until I tell your parents about this"). Punishment is usually administered on an intermittent schedule, and the chances of getting "caught" may not be high. Appropriate alternative behavior may not be recognized and positively reinforced at the same time that transgressions or errors are punished. Often there are clear discriminative stimuli for punishment. The undesired behavior may be monitored only at particular times or by a particular person, making it likely that the punished response will be suppressed only at those times. Finally, punishment may be the only source of attention for someone, making punishment a discriminative stimulus for positive reinforcement.

The preceding problems with the uses of punishment outside the laboratory can be overcome. However, it is difficult to guard against these pitfalls in common interpersonal interactions. People who punish others often do so because they are frustrated and angry. A frustrative act of punishment is likely to violate many of the guidelines for effective use of punishment. Punishing someone in an act of anger and frustration is a form of abuse — not a form of systematic training.

Abuse is not as likely in the hands of professionals if punishment is used as part of a systematic training or therapeutic program for the treatment of severe behavior problems. In such cases, punishment is usually attempted only after other treatment efforts have failed. In one study, for example, punishment was used to suppress recurrent vomiting by a nine-month-old infant (Linscheid & Cunningham, 1977). The recurrent vomiting had resulted in excessive weight loss and malnutrition. Without treatment, the infant risked potentially fatal medical complications. Brief (.5-second) shocks sufficient to elicit a startle response, but not sufficient to elicit crying, were used as the aversive stimulus. Within three days, vomiting was nearly totally suppressed by the punishment procedure. The suppression of vomiting persisted after discharge from the hospital. The infant started gaining weight again and was soon within normal range.

Cases like the preceding illustrate that punishment can be beneficial. However, even in such instances there are serious ethical dilemmas that have to be resolved. There is an ongoing debate about when, if ever, punishment is justified as a treatment procedure, and therapists are continuing their search for alternative ways to deal with potentially life-threatening behavior problems. (For a recent review, see Repp & Singh, 1990.) Many states have adopted stringent procedures to review and monitor the use of aversive control procedures in therapeutic settings and have banned certain forms of aversive control altogether. Professional and patient rights organizations also have adopted detailed and restrictive guidelines for the therapeutic uses of aversive control.

10

Classical–Instrumental Interactions and the Associative Structure of Instrumental Conditioning

In Chapter 10 we consider in greater detail possible interactions between classical and instrumental conditioning and discuss issues related to the associative structure of instrumental conditioning. We will begin with a description of experiments concerning the possible role of instrumental reinforcement in classical conditioning procedures. We will then describe some of the extensive theoretical and empirical work on the role of classical conditioning in instrumental conditioning situations. Certain assumptions about the associative structure of instrumental conditioning are involved in that work. Those assumptions will be described in the last section, along with recent research on the associative structure of instrumental conditioning.

Classical and instrumental conditioning are clearly distinguishable conceptually and procedurally. As we saw in Chapters 3 and 4, classical conditioning is assumed to involve the learning of relations, or associations, between stimuli (usually the CS and the US), and classical conditioning procedures focus on when the stimuli occur in relation to each other independent of what the animal does. By contrast, as we noted in Chapters 5–7, instrumental conditioning is assumed to involve the learning or redistribution of the animal's responses, and instrumental conditioning procedures focus on the relation between occurrences of a specified (instrumental) response and delivery of the reinforcer. Despite these conceptual and procedural distinctions between classical and instrumental conditioning, in practice most conditioning procedures involve instrumental as well as classical components. Conditioning procedures typically involve both stimulus–stimulus and response–outcome relations. Furthermore, isolating the effects of these components is often difficult and sometimes impossible.

We already saw examples of the interaction of classical and instrumental conditioning processes in analyses of discrimination learning (Chapter 8) and avoidance behavior and punishment (Chapter 9). In the present chapter we will consider the interaction of classical and instrumental conditioning more generally. We will first describe the potential role of instrumental conditioning processes in classical conditioning experiments and ways in which investigators have tried to rule out instrumental conditioning. We will then describe the potential role of classical conditioning processes in instrumental learning. That research has provided information about the associative structure of instrumental conditioning, which is our last major topic.

The Role of Instrumental Reinforcement in Classical Conditioning Procedures

In classical conditioning procedures, a conditioned stimulus is periodically presented, followed by an unconditioned stimulus. With repetitions of such CS–US trials, the subject comes to make a conditioned response to the CS, but the occurrence of the conditioned response does not determine whether the US is presented. The US is presented irrespective of the conditioned response. In fact, this aspect of classical conditioning is one of the primary bases for distinguishing classical from instrumental training procedures. Nevertheless, investigators of conditioning mechanisms have long been concerned with the fact that an opportunity for instrumental reinforcement exists in many classical conditioning procedures—reinforcement that may be partly responsible for the ensuing learning (Coleman & Gormezano, 1979; Gormezano & Coleman, 1973).

The potential for instrumental reinforcement in classical conditioning is most obvious in situations in which the subject makes anticipatory conditioned responses. Anticipatory conditioned responses occur before presentation of the unconditioned stimulus on a given trial. This pairing of the CR with the US provides at least two possible opportunities for instrumental reinforcement. First, if the US is a positive reinforcer, such as food, its presentation shortly after the CR may result in unintended reinforcement of the CR. Second, the occurrence of the CR may somehow alter the unconditioned stimulus so as to make the US either more rewarding or more effective in conditioning (for example, Hebb, 1956; Perkins, 1955, 1968). The possibility that conditioned responses may make the US more effective or rewarding was first recognized by Schlosberg (1937). He proposed, for example,

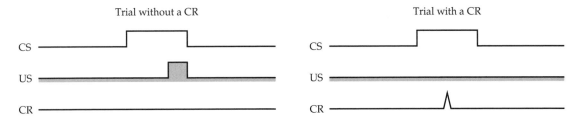

Figure 10.1   Diagram of the omission control procedure. On trials without a conditioned response (left), the CS is followed by the US in the usual manner. On trials with a conditioned response (right), the US is omitted.

that dogs may learn to salivate in a conditioning experiment using food as the US because anticipatory salivation makes it easier to dissolve and swallow dry food. Correspondingly, salivation may be learned in a classical conditioning situation with a drop of acid as the US because anticipatory salivation helps to dilute the aversive taste of the acid. Such instrumental modifications of the US can be postulated to occur in all classical conditioning experiments.

Two experimental strategies have been devised to evaluate the role of instrumental reinforcement in classical conditioning situations. One of these effectively eliminates the possibility of reinforcement of the conditioned response by presentation of the US. The other technique is designed to assess the role of modifications in the unconditioned stimulus caused by the occurrence of the CR by specifically arranging for such changes in the US. Experiments using both strategies have indicated that instrumental reinforcement is not necessary for the learning that takes place in classical conditioning procedures. Consequently, classical conditioning can be observed even if the situation does not permit the occurrence of instrumental reinforcement.

The Omission Control Procedure

As we noted above, if the US is a positive reinforcer, such as food, presentation of the US following the CR may result in unintended reinforcement of the CR. Investigators have attempted to rule out this kind of instrumental reinforcement by modifying the standard classical conditioning procedure. The modified technique, called the **omission control procedure,** is diagramed in Figure 10.1. In the omission control procedure, presentation of the US on a given trial depends on whether the conditioned response of interest occurs. If the subject fails to make the conditioned response on a particular trial, the CS is followed by the US in the usual manner. By contrast, if the subject performs the conditioned response, the US is omitted on that trial. The omission contingency ensures that the specified CR will not be followed by the US. This procedure is assumed to preclude instrumental reinforcement of the conditioned response.

The omission control procedure was introduced by Sheffield (1965) in the study of salivary conditioning in dogs. He tested dogs in conditioning with food and acid in the mouth as unconditioned stimuli. In both types of conditioning, omitting the US when a CR occurred did not prevent development of conditioned salivation. Acquisition of conditioned salivation was generally slower with the omission control procedure than with presentations of the US on all trials. Nevertheless, the omission procedure was remarkably effective. One dog, for example, continued to salivate on about 50% of trials after 800 trials on the omission control procedure.

Since its introduction by Sheffield, the omission control procedure has been tested in a variety of classical conditioning situations (for example, Gormezano & Hiller, 1972; Patten & Rudy, 1967). It has been perhaps most frequently used in studies of sign tracking. (For reviews, see Locurto, 1981; Tomie et al., 1989.) As we have noted, in sign tracking, animals come to approach and touch (peck, in the case of pigeons) stimuli that signal the delivery of a positive reinforcer, such as food. Investigations of omission control in sign tracking have provided inconsistent results (for example, Hursh, Navarick, & Fantino, 1974; Williams & Williams, 1969).

Peden, Browne, and Hearst (1977) provided one noteworthy demonstration of sign tracking in an omission control procedure. Pigeons were tested in an experimental chamber that had a food hopper built into one wall and a response key built into an adjacent wall 35 cm away. The key light was periodically illuminated for 8 seconds, followed by access to grain for 5 seconds. Approaching the key light was considered the conditioned response. In the first phase of the experiment (omission control), food delivery at the end of a trial was canceled if the pigeon approached within 20–25 cm of the key-light CS. In phase 2, food always followed illumination of the key light regardless of what the pigeons were doing. The investigators measured the percentage of trials on which the animals approached the light CS during each phase of the experiment.

The results are shown in Figure 10.2. The remarkable finding was that pigeons persisted in approaching the key-light CS during the first phase of the experiment even though such approach responses canceled the delivery of food. Fifty trials were conducted each day, and even after about 2,000 trials, the pigeons were observed to approach the CS approximately 40% of the time. This occurred even when subjects were not in the vicinity of the response key at the start of the trial. Other

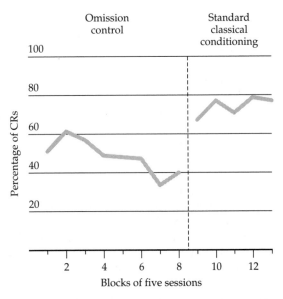

Figure 10.2 Percentage of trials on which a conditioned response (approach to the CS) was observed during blocks of five sessions. Each session consisted of 50 trials. During the first eight blocks of sessions (2,000 trials) an omission control procedure was in effect. During the remainder of the experiment a standard classical conditioning procedure was in effect. *(From "Persistent Approaches to a Signal for Food Despite Food Omission for Approaching" by B.F. Peden, M.P. Browne, and E. Hearst, 1977,* Journal of Experimental Psychology: Animal Behavior Processes, 3, *pp. 377–399. Copyright © 1977 by the American Psychological Association. Reprinted by permission.)*

research has shown that substantially fewer CS-approach responses occur if the CS and food are presented randomly so that the CS does not signal food (Peden et al., 1977, Experiment 2). Thus, as was true in Sheffield's (1965) experiment, an instrumental contingency was not necessary for the conditioned response to emerge.

As mentioned previously, in Sheffield's experiment with dogs acquisition of conditioned salivation was slower with the omission control procedure than with a standard classical conditioning procedure. Peden et al. obtained similar results in sign tracking. In the second phase of their experiment, when every trial ended in food delivery, approach responses increased (see Figure 10.2). A higher performance level with standard classical conditioning than with the omission control procedure is a common finding in studies of this kind (for example, Schwartz & Williams, 1972).

The difference between omission control and standard classical conditioning procedures in sign-tracking experiments has been the subject of considerable debate (Jenkins, 1977; Locurto, 1981). Why do omission control procedures lead to lower levels of responding than standard classical conditioning? One hypothesis emphasizes classical conditioning and explains the lower level of responding by pointing out that the US is not presented on every trial when occurrences of the CR are made to prevent US delivery in the omission control procedure. Classical conditioning generally leads to lower levels of performance if only some presentations of the CS end in delivery of the US. Other hypotheses emphasize instrumental conditioning. Omission control procedures may produce lower levels of responding because they punish the conditioned response by withholding an expected reward. They may also lower the probability of the CR by providing reinforcement for activities incompatible with the target CR (since only non-CR responses can be followed by reward in omission training). Yet another possibility is that unintended instrumental reinforcement of the CR during standard classical conditioning elevates the level of responding in standard classical conditioning above the level observed with omission training. The omission control experiment does not enable us to decide between these alternatives. However, the results obtained with omission control procedures permit the conclusion that some degree of classical conditioning can occur in the absence of instrumental reinforcement.

Conditioned Response Modifications of the US

A second experimental technique that has been used to evaluate the contribution of

instrumental reinforcement to the learning that occurs in classical conditioning procedures has focused on possible modifications of the US caused by the conditioned response. Consider, for example, a classical conditioning situation in which the US is an aversive stimulus. Perhaps in such cases the subject learns to make the conditioned response because this somehow reduces the aversiveness of the US. (Perhaps by making the CR, the subject "braces" itself against the US.) If this is true, then explicitly arranging for the intensity of the US to be reduced when the CR occurs should facilitate acquisition of the conditioned response.

The importance of CR modifications of the US was investigated in an experiment on the conditioning of the nictitating-membrane response in rabbits (Coleman, 1975). The CS was a tone and the US was a brief shock to the skin near one eye. Retraction of the nictitating membrane over the eyes was measured as the conditioned (and unconditioned) response. Four groups of rabbits were tested. All groups received a brief shock of 5.0 milliamperes (mA) after the CS on trials in which a conditioned response did not occur. For group 5-5, the shock was also 5.0 mA when the rabbits made a conditioned response. For the other groups, the shock intensity was decreased when a conditioned response occurred. For group 5-3, the shock was decreased to 3.3 mA on trials when the CR occurred. For group 5-1, the CR decreased the shock intensity to 1.7 mA, and for group 5-0, the CR prevented delivery of the shock altogether (essentially, group 5-0 received an omission control procedure). If shock reduction provides important instrumental reinforcement for the conditioned response in this type of classical conditioning, better learning should have occurred in groups 5-3, 5-1, and 5-0 than in group 5-5.

The results are shown in Figure 10.3. Contrary to the instrumental reinforcement prediction, the speed and level of conditioning were not increased by reducing the shock intensity whenever the conditioned response

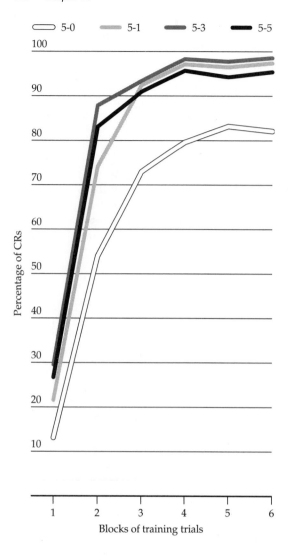

Figure 10.3 Percentage of conditioned responses in an experiment on nictitating-membrane conditioning with rabbits. The conditioned response resulted in reduction of the intensity of the shock US for groups 5-3 and 5-1 and omission of the US for group 5-0. By contrast, the conditioned response had no effect on the delivery of the US in group 5-5. *(From "Consequences of Response-Contingent Change in Unconditioned Stimulus Intensity Upon the Rabbit* (Oryctolagus cuniculus) *Nictitating Membrane Response" by S.R. Coleman, 1975,* Journal of Comparative and Physiological Psychology, 88, *pp. 591–595. Copyright © 1975 by the American Psychological Association. Reprinted by permission.)*

occurred. Groups 5-3, 5-1, and 5-0 did not learn the nictitating-membrane response faster than group 5-5. In fact, the only difference evident between the groups was that completely reducing the shock intensity to 0 mA whenever the conditioned response occurred (group 5-0) resulted in a lower level of conditioning than that exhibited by any of the other groups. This outcome probably reflects the fact that group 5-0 did not receive shock on every trial whereas the other groups did.

These results provide strong evidence that modifications of the US caused by the CR were not necessary for classical conditioning of the nictitating-membrane response and did not even facilitate learning. Thus, classical conditioning can occur in the absence of instrumental reinforcement. However, this does not preclude the role of instrumental reinforcement in all classical conditioning procedures. The contribution of instrumental reinforcement has to be evaluated separately in each case with the techniques we have described.

The Role of Classical Conditioning in Instrumental Conditioning Procedures

As we noted in Chapters 5 and 8, in an instrumental conditioning procedure the instrumental response occurs in the presence of certain distinctive stimuli and is followed by the reinforcer. In Figure 10.4, which reviews this sequence of events, S represents the stimuli that are present when the instrumental response is made, R represents the instrumental response, and O represents the reinforcer or response outcome. The wavy line between the response and the reinforcing stimulus signifies that the response causes the delivery of the reinforcer. This causal relation ensures that the reinforcer will be paired with the subject's exposure to stimuli S. The pairing of stimuli S with the reinforcer may result in classical conditioning, and an association may develop between stimuli S and the reinforcer.

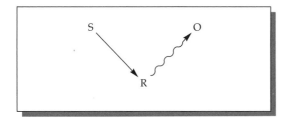

Figure 10.4 Relations that exist in instrumental conditioning. The instrumental response (R) occurs in the presence of distinctive stimuli (S) and results in delivery of the reinforcer outcome (O). The reinforcement of response R in the presence of stimuli S allows for the classical conditioning of S by the reinforcer.

In the preceding section we discussed ways in which instrumental reinforcement can be ruled out as a contributing factor in classical conditioning procedures. Unfortunately, analogous strategies do not exist for ruling out classical conditioning in instrumental procedures. To prevent classical conditioning, one cannot omit presenting the reinforcer after the animal's exposure to stimuli S because this would also result in nonreinforcement of the instrumental response.

Specification of an instrumental response ensures that the animal will always experience certain distinctive stimuli (S) in connection with making the response. These stimuli may involve the place where the response is to be performed, the texture of the object the subject is to manipulate, or distinctive olfactory or visual cues. Whatever they may be, reinforcement of the instrumental response will inevitably result in a pairing between stimuli S and the reinforcer. As we have stated, the only way to prevent this pairing is to omit the reinforcer. However, this would also prevent instrumental conditioning. We cannot assume, however, that pairings of stimuli S with the reinforcer will inevitably produce classical conditioning. As we noted in Chapters 3 and 4, the occurrence of classical conditioning depends on much more than just stimulus pairings. Nevertheless, pairings of stimuli S with the reinforcer provide the

potential for the occurrence of classical conditioning. Consequently, many important theories have been concerned with the role of classical conditioning in the control of instrumental behavior.

The r_g–s_g Mechanism

One of the earliest and most influential accounts of the role of classical conditioning in instrumental behavior was originally proposed by Clark Hull (1930, 1931) and was elaborated by Kenneth Spence (1956). Essentially, Hull and Spence added a classical conditioning component to the mechanism of instrumental behavior proposed by Thorndike (see Chapter 5). According to Thorndike, reinforcement of an instrumental response increases the future likelihood of the behavior by establishing an association between the response and the stimuli present at the time the response is made. Using the symbols in Figure 10.4, Thorndike's view assumes that reinforcement establishes an association between S and R. Therefore, the presence of S comes to trigger the occurrence of the instrumental response directly. This S–R association was assumed to be the basis for instrumental conditioning. Hull and Spence suggested that there is also a classical conditioning process that encourages or motivates the instrumental behavior. More specifically, they assumed that, during the course of instrumental conditioning, animals not only learn to make response R in the presence of stimuli S but also acquire an expectation that they will be rewarded. This reward expectancy is learned through classical conditioning and also motivates the instrumental response.

It seems intuitively reasonable that instrumental behavior occurs in part because organisms learn to expect reward. If you were to introspect about why you perform certain instrumental responses, the answer would probably be that you expect to be rewarded. You go to work because you expect to get paid; you study for a test because you expect that doing so will help you get a higher grade. As we will see, these informal ideas may be incorporated into a systematic theory of instrumental conditioning in several different ways. The first systematic proposal was the r_g–s_g mechanism.

Hull and Spence recognized that whenever the instrumental response R was followed by the reinforcer outcome O, the stimulus S present at the time of the response became paired with the reinforcer O. It was their belief that classical conditioning occurred by stimulus substitution. As we noted in Chapter 4, according to the stimulus-substitution hypothesis, the conditioned stimulus is assumed to acquire properties of the unconditioned stimulus to some extent. In the instrumental conditioning paradigm, S acts in the role of the CS, and the reinforcer acts in the role of the US. Therefore, Hull and Spence assumed that S will come to elicit some of the same responses that are elicited by the reinforcer. If the reinforcer is food, during the course of instrumental training, the animal will presumably come to salivate and perhaps make chewing movements when it experiences stimuli S. These classically conditioned responses are rarely as vigorous as the salivation and chewing elicited by the food itself, and they occur in anticipation of the food delivery. Therefore, they are called **fractional anticipatory goal responses.** The conventional symbol for such a response is r_g.

The fractional anticipatory goal response is assumed to be similar to other types of responses. As noted in Chapter 2, responses typically produce some sensory feedback. That is, the act of making a response usually creates distinctive bodily sensations. The sensory feedback produced by the fractional anticipatory goal response is represented by the symbol s_g.

The fractional anticipatory goal response, with its feedback stimulus, s_g, is assumed to constitute the expectancy of reward, r_g–s_g. Figure 10.5 illustrates the full sequence of events in the r_g–s_g mechanism. The fractional

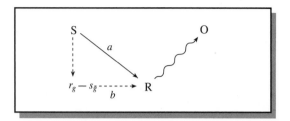

Figure 10.5   The r_g–s_g mechanism. During instrumental conditioning, the instrumental response R is followed by the reinforcer outcome O. Because this happens in the presence of distinctive situational cues S, an association is formed between S and R (arrow *a*). Delivery of the reinforcer following exposure to S results in the classical conditioning of S by the reinforcer. Therefore, S comes to elicit a classically conditioned fractional anticipatory goal response r_g with its feedback cues s_g. Because the instrumental response R is reinforced in the presence of s_g, an association also becomes established between s_g and R (arrow *b*).

anticipatory goal response r_g is elicited by S before the instrumental response occurs. Thus, the instrumental response is made in the presence of the sensory feedback s_g from r_g. Because the instrumental response is reinforced when it is made after experience with s_g, a connection becomes established between s_g and the response R. The outcome of these events is that as instrumental conditioning proceeds, the instrumental response comes to be stimulated by two factors. First, the presence of S comes to evoke the instrumental response directly by association with R. Second, the instrumental activity also comes to be made in response to the expectancy of reward (r_g–s_g) because of an association between s_g and R.

Functions of $\mathbf{r_g}$–$\mathbf{s_g}$.   The fractional anticipatory goal response mechanism (r_g–s_g) is assumed to have two important functions. First, it is assumed to contribute to the general level of motivation of the animal and thereby enhance instrumental behavior. Second, it directs behavior. Because of the association of the instrumental response (R) with the stimulus feedback (s_g) from the fractional anticipatory goal response (see arrow *b* in Figure 10.5), the instrumental response is predicted to occur whenever the fractional anticipatory goal response is elicited. Once the instrumental response has been conditioned to s_g, it will occur in the presence of any stimulus that elicits the fractional anticipatory goal response. As we will see, the general motivational properties of r_g–s_g have been abandoned in contemporary theorizing. However, the second function of r_g–s_g (directing behavior) continues to be recognized.

The r_g–s_g mechanism and positive instrumental reinforcement.

The r_g–s_g mechanism is consistent with numerous aspects of positively reinforced instrumental behavior. It predicts, for example, that classical conditioning procedures will influence the performance of positively reinforced instrumental behavior in certain ways. Consider, for example, a discrimination procedure in which rats are reinforced for pressing a response lever in the presence of a tone (S+) and not reinforced in the absence of the tone. How might this discriminated lever pressing be influenced by classical conditioning procedures involving the tone? The r_g–s_g mechanism predicts that performance of the lever-press response in the presence of the tone will be facilitated by initially conducting classical conditioning in which the tone is repeatedly paired with food. The response lever can be removed from the experimental chamber during this phase to avoid accidentally reinforcing lever presses. Classical conditioning of the S+ with food should condition the fractional anticipatory goal response to the tone S+. Elicitation of r_g by the tone should increase motivation for the instrumental behavior and thereby increase lever pressing during the tone. By contrast, once the discriminated lever-press response has been established, extinguishing the fractional anticipatory goal response should produce a decrement in the instrumental behavior. Such extinction can be accomplished by removing the response lever from the exper-

imental chamber and repeatedly presenting the S+ without food. Extinguishing the fractional anticipatory goal response is expected to reduce both its motivational and response-directing functions. Evidence consistent with these and similar predictions of the r_g–s_g mechanism has been obtained (for example, Trapold & Winokur, 1967).

Concurrent Measurement of Instrumental Behavior and Classically Conditioned Responses

The experiments reviewed in the preceding section involved somewhat indirect predictions from the r_g–s_g mechanism. One direct implication is that classically conditioned responses develop during instrumental conditioning. In addition, the r_g–s_g mechanism specifies how these classically conditioned responses should be related to the occurrence of the instrumental response. The r_g–s_g mechanism treats classically conditioned responses as reflections of a reward expectancy that motivates the instrumental response. Therefore, the classically conditioned responses are predicted to begin before the instrumental behavior on any trial (see Figure 10.5).

Perhaps the simplest and most direct approach to investigating the role of classical conditioning in instrumental learning is to measure classically and instrumentally conditioned responses at the same time. This is the approach taken by **concurrent-measurement experiments.** Numerous investigations of this type have been carried out in positive and negative reinforcement situations. (For reviews, see Black, 1971; Rescorla & Solomon, 1967.) All these experiments provide evidence that classically conditioned responses are learned during instrumental conditioning. However, the relation between the two types of conditioned responses varies from one situation to another. Furthermore, contrary to the r_g–s_g mechanism, classically conditioned responses do not invariably begin before the instrumental response.

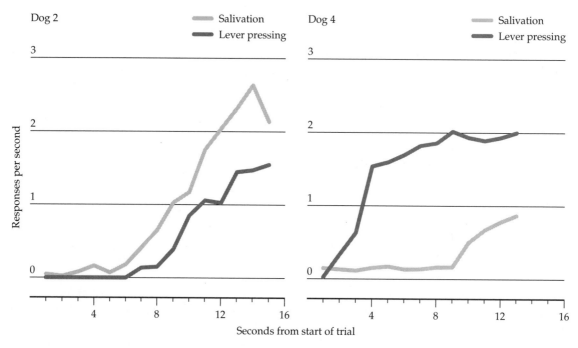

Figure 10.6 Rate of lever pressing and salivation observed with two dog subjects during successive 1-second periods leading up to the next delivery of food reinforcement. Dog 2 (left) was reinforced for lever pressing on a fixed-interval 16-second schedule of reinforcement. Dog 4 (right) was reinforced on a fixed-ratio 33 schedule of reinforcement. *(From "Classical Conditioning and Incentive Motivation" by D.R. Williams, in W.F. Prokasy (ed.), 1965, Classical Conditioning. Copyright © 1965 Prentice-Hall. Reprinted by permission.)*

Figure 10.6 provides two examples from a study of lever pressing in dog subjects (Williams, 1965). In addition to observing occurrences of the instrumental response, Williams also recorded conditioned salivation as a measure of classical conditioning. The rate of the lever-press and the salivary responses are graphed for two of the dogs. The graph on the left illustrates the results obtained with dog 2, which received extensive training on a fixed-interval 16-second schedule of food reinforcement. The first response that occurred 16 seconds or more after the last reinforcement was rewarded. As we noted in Chapter 6, a fixed-interval schedule typically produces a "scalloped" pattern of responding. The instrumental response occurs at a very low rate, if at all, at the beginning of the fixed interval. As the end of the interval (and the availability of the reinforcer) draws nearer, the rate of the instrumental response gradually

increases, which is precisely what happened with the lever-press response for dog 2. Interestingly, a similar pattern of behavior was observed on the FI schedule with the conditioned salivary response. In fact, the general pattern of increased responding toward the end of the fixed interval was nearly indistinguishable for the instrumental (lever-press) and classically conditioned (salivation) responses. This coincidence of salivation and instrumental responding on a fixed-interval schedule also has been observed by other investigators (Kintsch & Witte, 1962; Shapiro, 1960, 1961). Thus, contrary to the prediction of the r_g–s_g mechanism that classically conditioned responses precede instrumental behavior, in this situation the two types of responses occurred at the same time.

The results obtained with dog 4 are presented in the right-hand graph of Figure 10.6. This dog received extensive training on a fixed-ratio schedule of reinforcement. Food reinforcement was provided every time the dog completed 33 lever-press responses. As you may recall from Chapter 6, on a fixed-ratio schedule instrumental responding typically begins with a postreinforcement pause, which is followed by a high and steady rate. Consistent with that pattern, dog 4 showed a low rate of lever pressing during the first 3 seconds of the fixed-ratio cycle, followed by much higher rates during seconds 4–13. However, salivation did not appear until the 10th second of the cycle. Thus, classically conditioned salivary responding started only after instrumental responding was well under way, contrary to predictions of the r_g–s_g mechanism. (For other dramatic examples of the dissociation of instrumental and classically conditioned behavior, see Ellison & Konorski, 1964.)

These examples illustrate that concurrent measurement of instrumental and classically conditioned responses has failed to yield a consistent pattern of results. In different situations, classically conditioned responses have been observed to precede, coincide with, or follow instrumental behavior. Such results have stimulated alternative approaches to the interaction of classical and instrumental conditioning. One of the most influential of these alternative approaches has been modern two-process theory.

Modern Two-Process Theory

The model of the interrelation of classical and operant conditioning we will discuss in this section was brought into focus in 1967 by Rescorla and Solomon. However, it was developed from ideas entertained as early as the 1940s, especially in connection with theorizing about the mechanisms of avoidance learning (see Mowrer, 1960; Rescorla & Solomon, 1967). We term the model "modern two-process theory" to distinguish it from the two-process theory of avoidance learning discussed in Chapter 9. Modern two-process theory is similar to the r_g–s_g mechanism in that it assumes that classical conditioning is impor-

tant in motivating instrumental behavior. However, it adopts a different view of classical conditioning and a different view of the role of classical conditioning in motivation.

In contrast to the r_g–s_g mechanism, modern two-process theory does not regard classical conditioning as involving the learning of particular responses or as contributing to general motivation. Rather, it assumes that the primary outcome of classical conditioning is that a previously "neutral" stimulus comes to elicit a particular type of motivation, or **central emotional state.** The emotional state that comes to be elicited by a conditioned stimulus corresponds to the particular type of unconditioned stimulus that is used and is considered to be a characteristic of the central nervous system—a mood, if you will. Emotional states do not invariably lead to particular responses. On the contrary, they may be manifest in any one of a variety of actions. Anger, for example, may result in fighting, shouting, a frown, or refusal to acknowledge someone's presence, depending on the circumstances.

Because instrumental conditioning procedures allow for classical conditioning, modern two-process theory assumes that central emotional states are conditioned during ordinary instrumental training. These states become conditioned either to situational cues or to discriminative stimuli involved in the reinforcement procedure. Furthermore, the emotional states are assumed to motivate the instrumental behavior. The fact that classically conditioned emotional states are not always manifest in the same responses makes modern two-process theory much less precise than the r_g–s_g mechanism. It also makes the concurrent measurement of instrumental behavior and classically conditioned responses irrelevant to evaluation of the theory. Because modern two-process theory does not specify what responses a conditioned emotional state will lead to, it cannot be disproved by the type of evidence concurrent-measurement experiments provide.

If modern two-process theory cannot be

disproved by concurrent-measurement experiments, how can it be empirically tested? As it turns out, the theory makes one very important and unambiguous prediction about behavior—namely, that *the rate of an instrumental response will be modified by the presentation of a classically conditioned stimulus.* This prediction is based on the following considerations. During instrumental conditioning, a conditioned central emotional state is assumed to develop to motivate the instrumental response. Classically conditioned stimuli also are assumed to elicit central emotional states. Therefore, presentation of a classically conditioned stimulus to a subject while it is performing on an instrumental reinforcement schedule will alter the emotional state that was maintaining the instrumental response. This will be evident in a change in the rate of the instrumental behavior. We have already seen an example of this effect in the conditioned emotional response (CER) procedure, described in earlier chapters. You may recall that in the CER procedure animals are first trained to press a response lever for food reinforcement. A discrete stimulus, such as a light or a tone, is then repeatedly paired with shock. This classically conditioned fear stimulus is then presented to the animals while they are lever-pressing for food. Consistent with the prediction of modern two-process theory, presentation of the shock-conditioned CS produces a change in the rate of the lever-press response. The rate of lever pressing for food decreases.

Classically conditioned stimuli do not always suppress instrumental behavior, as in the CER procedure. According to two-process theory, the kind of changes that various kinds of classically conditioned stimuli will produce will depend on the emotional state created by these CSs and the emotional state created by the instrumental reinforcement schedule. If the classically conditioned stimulus produces emotions that are opposite to those that motivate the instrumental behavior, the rate of the instrumental response will de-

crease. This is presumably what happens in the CER procedure. The food-reinforcement schedule motivates lever pressing by way of a positive emotional state conditioned by food. This emotion is disrupted when the shock-conditioned CS is presented because the CS elicits an aversive emotional state. In other situations, the classically conditioned stimulus may evoke an emotion that is similar to the emotional state created by the instrumental reinforcement schedule. When this occurs, the two emotions will summate, and the rate of the instrumental behavior will increase.

Specific predictions of modern two-process theory. Specific predictions about how classically conditioned stimuli will influence instrumental behavior can be made by considering the types of emotions elicited by various types of CSs and by instrumental reinforcement schedules. Borrowing language introduced by Mowrer (1960), Table 10.1 provides metaphorical labels for the emotional states presumably elicited by some common types of classically conditioned stimuli. Let us first consider classical conditioning with a positive (appetitive) unconditioned stimulus, such as food or water. If the stimulus is a CS+, meaning that it becomes associated with the impending presentation of the US, we may refer to the emotional state created by the CS as **hope.** By contrast, if the stimulus is a CS−, meaning that it has become associated with the removal or the absence of the appetitive US, we may refer to the emotional state created as **disappointment.** In the case of a CS+ for the impending presentation of an aversive US, such as shock, the conditioned emotional state is called **fear.** Finally, if the conditioned stimulus is a CS− associated with the removal or absence of an aversive US, we may presume that **relief** is elicited by presentations of the CS. Using this same terminology, we may assume that instrumental behavior reinforced by the presentation of food (or other appetitive reinforcers) is motivated by "hope" and that instrumental behavior rein-

TABLE 10.1 *Emotional states elicited by the CS after various types of classical conditioning*

	Unconditioned Stimulus	
Conditioned Stimulus	*Appetitive (Such as Food)*	*Aversive (Such as Shock)*
CS +	Hope	Fear
CS −	Disappointment	Relief

forced by the avoidance or removal of shock (or other aversive events) is motivated by "fear." It is important to note that these labels are used for convenience only and do not imply that the Pavlovian CSs involved necessarily elicit the same emotions that people experience when they describe their feelings using the terms *hope, disappointment, fear,* and *relief.*

If presentation of a classically conditioned stimulus alters instrumental behavior solely by changing the emotions that motivate the instrumental response, what should we expect in various situations? Table 10.2 lists the predicted outcomes when classically conditioned stimuli eliciting hope, disappointment, fear, and relief are presented to animals responding either to obtain food (positive reinforcement) or to avoid shock (negative reinforcement). These predictions are based on the assumption that hope and relief are compatible (both being positive emotions) and

that fear and disappointment are compatible (both being negative emotions) (Goodman & Fowler, 1983). By contrast, hope and fear (and relief and disappointment) are assumed to be incompatible (Dickinson & Pearce, 1977).

Let us first consider predictions in the case of positive reinforcement (cells 1–4). The underlying emotional state created by positive reinforcement is hope. Hope is assumed to be incompatible with fear, and hence the rate of the instrumental response is expected to decline when a CS + for an aversive US is presented (cell 1). Hope and relief are assumed to be compatible emotions. Therefore, we predict an increase in the positively reinforced instrumental behavior when a CS − for an aversive US is presented (cell 2). The classically conditioned stimulus is also predicted to facilitate the instrumental behavior in cell 3 because here the CS elicits hope, which is the same type of emotion as the motivational state created by the instrumental procedure. By contrast, the instrumental behavior is predicted to decrease when a CS − for food is presented (cell 4) because the disappointment it elicits is incompatible with the hope that motivates the instrumental behavior.

Cells 5–8 state the predictions when the instrumental procedure involves negative reinforcement, such as shock avoidance. The underlying emotion that motivates the instrumental behavior in this case is fear. This fear is enhanced when a CS is presented that also

TABLE 10.2 *Effects of classically conditioned stimuli on the rate of instrumental behavior*

	Aversive US		Appetitive US	
Instrumental Schedule	*CS + (Fear)*	*CS − (Relief)*	*CS + (Hope)*	*CS − (Disappointment)*
Positive reinforcement (procurement of food) (*hope*)	1 Decrease	2 Increase	3 Increase	4 Decrease
Negative reinforcement (avoidance of shock) (*fear*)	5 Increase	6 Decrease	7 Decrease	8 Increase

elicits fear (cell 5). Hence, an increase in the rate of the instrumental response is predicted. The fear is reduced by presentation of a CS that has been associated with the removal or absence of an aversive US (cell 6). Instrumental responding therefore declines. Fear is presumably also reduced when the classically conditioned stimulus elicits hope (cell 7) because fear and hope are incompatible emotions. Finally, performance of the instrumental response is expected to increase when a CS− for an appetitive US is presented (cell 8) because disappointment and fear are both aversive emotional states.

Results consistent with modern two-process theory. We have already noted that the concurrent measurement of instrumental behavior and classically conditioned responses cannot be used to evaluate modern two-process theory. How, then, can the predictions in Table 10.2 be experimentally tested? The experiments that have been performed to evaluate modern two-process theory were modeled after the CER procedure and are called **transfer-of-control experiments.** Such experiments basically consist of three phases, as outlined in Table 10.3. Phase 1 involves instrumental conditioning of an operant response using some schedule of positive or negative reinforcement. In phase 2 the subjects are given classical conditioning in which an explicit CS is associated with either the presence or absence of an unconditioned stimulus. Phase 3 is the critical transfer phase. Here the animal is allowed to engage in the instrumental response, and the CS from phase 2 is periodically presented to observe its effect on the rate of the instrumental behavior. In some applications of the transfer-of-control design, the classical conditioning phase is conducted before instrumental conditioning. In some other experiments, phases 1 and 2 are conducted concurrently—that is, classical conditioning trials with the CS and US are periodically presented while the subject is being trained on the instrumental reinforce-

TABLE 10.3 *Outline of transfer-of-control experiments*

Phase 1	Phase 2	Phase 3
Instrumental conditioning of the baseline response	Classical conditioning of the CS	Transfer test: the CS is presented during performance of the baseline response

ment schedule. These variations in the basic design are often unimportant to the results observed in phase 3, the critical transfer phase.

Modern two-process theory has stimulated a great deal of research testing predictions of the type in Table 10.2 using the transfer-of-control design. Many of the results of these experiments have been consistent with the predictions. We cannot review all the evidence here, but we will cite some illustrative examples. Let us first consider the effects of classically conditioned stimuli on the performance of instrumental behavior maintained by positive reinforcement (cells 1–4 in Table 10.2). As we have already noted, cell 1 represents the conditioned emotional response procedure. The common finding is that a CS+ conditioned with an aversive US suppresses the rate of positively reinforced instrumental behavior. (For reviews, see Blackman, 1977; Davis, 1968; Lyon, 1968.) The effects of a signal for the absence of an aversive US (a CS−) on positively reinforced responding (cell 2) have not been as extensively investigated. However, the available data are again consistent with the prediction. Hammond (1966), for example, found that lever pressing in rats reinforced by food increased when a CS− for shock was presented (see also Davis & Shattuck, 1980). In certain situations, food-reinforced instrumental behavior is also increased by presentation of a CS+ for food, consistent with the prediction in cell 3 (for example, Estes, 1943, 1948; LoLordo, 1971; Lovibond, 1983). Research on the effects of a signal for the absence of an appetitive reinforcer (CS−) on positively reinforced responding (cell 4) has not been very extensively pursued. However, evidence consistent with two-process theory (a suppression of the instrumental response) has been observed in what studies there are (for example, Gutman & Maier, 1978; Hearst & Peterson, 1973).

Many experiments have been performed to determine how stimuli that signal an aversive US (CS+) or its absence (CS−) influence the rate of negatively reinforced instrumental behavior (cells 5 and 6). These studies generally support predictions of modern two-process theory. The rate of avoidance behavior is increased by the presentation of a CS+ for shock and decreased by the presentation of a CS− for shock (for example, Bull & Overmier, 1968; Desiderato, 1969; Rescorla & LoLordo, 1965; Weisman & Litner, 1969). Presentation of a signal for the presence of food (CS+) has also been noted to decrease the rate of instrumental avoidance behavior, as cell 7 predicts (for example, Bull, 1970; Davis & Kreuter, 1972; Grossen, Kostansek, & Bolles, 1969). The effects of a signal for the absence of food (CS−) on avoidance behavior (cell 8) have not been extensively investigated. One experiment that included a test of the prediction in cell 8 failed to find any effect on avoidance responding (Bull, 1970). However, in another study (Grossen et al., 1969), a classically conditioned CS− for food facilitated instrumental avoidance behavior, as predicted in cell 8.

Response Interactions in the Effects of Classically Conditioned Stimuli on Instrumental Behavior

The evidence reviewed in the preceding section provides many instances in which predictions of modern two-process theory have been confirmed. However, other studies have yielded results inconsistent with, and sometimes opposite to, these predictions. This has been particularly true with the effects of a CS+ for food on positively reinforced instrumental behavior (cell 3 of Table 10.2). Modern two-process theory predicts an increase in the instrumental behavior in this case. However, many investigators have found suppressions of behavior instead—a phenomenon sometimes called *positive conditioned suppression* (for example, Azrin & Hake, 1969; Konorski & Miller, 1930; Meltzer & Brahlek, 1970; Miczek & Grossman, 1971). These contradictory findings suggest that the interaction of central emotional states is not the only factor determining the outcome of transfer-of-control experiments; moreover, in certain situations it may not even have a critical role.

Classically conditioned stimuli elicit not only emotional states but also overt responses. Consequently, a classically conditioned stimulus may influence instrumental behavior through the overt responses it elicits. Consider, for example, a hypothetical situation in which the classically conditioned stimulus makes the animal remain still, and the instrumental response is shuttling back and forth in a shuttle box. In this case, presentation of the CS will decrease the instrumental response simply because the tendency to stop moving elicited by the CS will interfere with the shuttle behavior. An appeal to interaction between central emotional states elicited by the CS and the instrumental reinforcement schedule is not necessary to understand such an outcome. If the classically conditioned stimulus elicited overt responses that were similar to the instrumental behavior, presentation of the CS would increase responding because responses elicited by the CS would be added to the responses the animal was performing to receive instrumental reinforcement. Assumptions about central emotional states again would be unnecessary in explaining the results.

Investigators have been very concerned with the possibility that the results of transfer-of-control experiments are due to the fact that Pavlovian CSs elicit overt responses that either interfere with or facilitate the behavior required for instrumental reinforcement. This concern has given rise to a number of strategies to rule out this possibility. (For a review, see Overmier & Lawry, 1979.) These strategies generally have been successful in showing that many transfer-of-control effects are not produced by interactions between overt responses (see, for example, Grossen et al., 1969; Lovibond, 1983; Overmier, Bull, & Pack, 1971; Scobie, 1972). However, overt classically conditioned responses can have an important role in some transfer-of-control experiments.

Response interactions are especially important to consider in two types of situations. One of these involves transfer-of-control experiments in which classical conditioning is conducted with an appetitive stimulus, such as food or water, that subjects have to obtain in a particular location—from a cup placed in a corner of the experimental chamber, for example. If subjects have to go to a particular location to obtain the US, a CS+ may suppress instrumental responding because it elicits approach to the site of US delivery (for example, Karpicke, 1978).

Response interactions are also very important to consider when the classically conditioned stimulus is a discrete localized stimulus, such as a spot of light, because such CSs elicit sign tracking. As we noted earlier, when a localized stimulus becomes a CS+ for food, animals tend to approach it. By contrast, if the stimulus becomes a CS+ for shock, it comes to elicit withdrawal, or **negative sign tracking** (for example, Leclerc & Reberg, 1980). Positive and negative sign tracking elicited by classically conditioned stimuli may increase or decrease the performance of a baseline instrumental response, depending on whether the sign tracking is compatible or incompatible with the instrumental behavior (for example, LoLordo, McMillan, & Riley, 1974; Schwartz, 1976). This compatibility, in turn, often depends on the location of the classically conditioned stimulus relative to the location of the instrumental response (Karpicke, Christoph, Peterson, & Hearst, 1977).

Discriminative Stimulus Properties of Classically Conditioned States

We have described the results of many experiments showing that classically conditioned stimuli can influence the performance of instrumental behavior. In analyzing these effects we have emphasized two aspects of classically conditioned stimuli: the emotional state or particular type of motivation evoked by the stimuli and the overt responses these stimuli elicit. However, explanation of all the ways in which classically conditioned stimuli can influence instrumental behavior requires postulating a third variable as well. We must assume that classically conditioned stimuli evoke a theoretical state that not only has particular motivational and response-eliciting properties but stimulus characteristics as well. The idea is that the state of neural excitation in the brain created by classically conditioned stimuli leads to particular sensations in addition to eliciting particular types of motivation (emotions) and overt responses. These sensations can come to serve as discriminative stimuli for the instrumental behavior and thereby influence instrumental performance.

How might classically conditioned states acquire discriminative stimulus properties? Theoretically, the answer is rather straightforward. We know from Chapter 8 that a stimulus acquires discriminative control of behavior if responses in the presence of the stimulus are reinforced and responses in its absence are not reinforced. Therefore, stimulus features of a classically conditioned state should acquire discriminative control over instrumental behavior through differential reinforcement in the same manner. However, this is more easily postulated than proved experimentally. The experimental demonstration is complicated by the fact that we cannot directly manipulate the stimulus features of classically conditioned states; we cannot present and remove these stimuli at will the way we can turn a light or tone on and off.

One experimental approach to the study of

discriminative stimulus properties of classically conditioned states involves an instrumental discrimination procedure. Consider, for example, the procedure diagrammed in Figure 10.7. Subjects are placed in a two-way shuttle box and are reinforced with food for crossing from one side to the other when a clicker is sounded but are not reinforced in the absence of the clicker. Thus, the clicker becomes an appetitive S+. Because subjects receive food during the S+ (and not during its absence), the S+ also becomes classically conditioned by the food and presumably comes to elicit a classically conditioned state, denoted by the symbol T in the lower part of Figure 10.7. The classically conditioned state T presumably has stimulus features, denoted by s_T in Figure 10.7. These sensations (s_T) are present when the instrumental response is reinforced because the classically conditioned state (T) is elicited by the S+. However, the s_T sensations are not present on nonreinforced trials because the S− is not conditioned to elicit the classically conditioned state T. The presence of s_T on reinforced trials but not on nonreinforced trials may enable these stimuli to serve as discriminative cues for the instrumental response, as denoted by arrow *b* in the lower part of Figure 10.7.

According to the schema presented in Figure 10.7, it is plausible that the stimulus properties (s_T) of a classically conditioned state may acquire discriminative control over the instrumental behavior during discrimination training. However, according to the theoretical model, there are two means whereby the S+ can come to evoke the instrumental response. The S+ may evoke the instrumental response directly, as denoted by arrow *a* in the lower part of the figure, or it may evoke the response indirectly by way of the stimulus properties of the classically conditioned state (arrow *b*). Therefore, if we find that subjects make the shuttle response during the S+ and not during the S−, this does not tell us specifically that the stimulus properties s_T of the classically conditioned state have gained

PROCEDURE

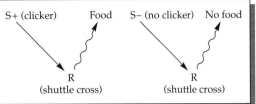

THEORETICAL MECHANISM

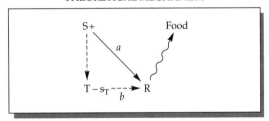

Figure 10.7   Procedure and theoretical mechanism for discrimination training of an instrumental shuttle response (R). Shuttle crossings are reinforced with food during a clicker (S+) and not reinforced in the absence of the clicker (S−). The S+ comes to elicit a classically conditioned state T with its stimulus properties s_T. The instrumental response can be evoked by the S+ either directly (arrow *a*) or by way of the discriminative stimulus properties of the classically conditioned state (arrow *b*).

discriminative control over the behavior. Behavior elicited by the S+ could just as well have occurred because of a direct connection between the S+ and the response.

To prove that s_T can evoke the instrumental response by itself, we would have to present s_T without the S+. In this case, any shuttling that we would observe would have to be attributed to s_T. But how can this be done, since we do not have direct control over s_T? One possibility is to condition some stimulus other than the S+ to also elicit the classically conditioned state T. Let us add a second phase to the experiment we have been considering. Following the discriminative shuttle-response training that we have conducted with the clicker as the S+, let us put the subjects in a distinctively different apparatus and conduct simple classical conditioning in which a pure tone (CS +) is paired with the presentation of food and a different pure tone (CS −) is presented without food. This procedure, together with the first phase of the experiment we have been considering, is summarized in Figure 10.8. Keep in mind that the second phase of the experiment involves only classical conditioning. The subject is not required to perform any particular instrumental response for the food to be delivered. Shuttle responses are not reinforced in this phase of the experiment. In fact, the conditioning is carried out in an apparatus where the subject cannot make shuttle crossings. Thus, in the second phase, the only thing that happens is that one tone becomes a CS + for food and another tone becomes a CS − for food.

Both phase 1 and phase 2 of the experiment shown in Figure 10.8 involve conditioning with food. Therefore, the pure tone CS + presumably comes to elicit the same classically conditioned state T in phase 2 that was conditioned to the S + in phase 1. We can assume that, after conditioning of the CS +, the CS + will elicit the classically conditioned state T, with its accompanying stimulus properties s_T. This brings us to the most important aspect of this complicated experiment. Recall that we are trying to prove that the stimulus properties s_T of the classically conditioned state came to serve as discriminative stimuli for the shuttle response in phase 1 of the experiment. If this is true, then any time the subjects experience s_T in the shuttle box, shuttle crossings should increase. Therefore, presentation of the food-conditioned CS + should evoke increased shuttle responding. Furthermore, this outcome would be expected even if the subject was not responding for positive reinforcement at the time.

The experiment that we have been describing was carried out by Overmier and his associates (see Overmier & Lawry, 1979). Dogs served as subjects. In describing the study, we omitted several aspects to simplify the presentation. Between phases 1 and 2 of the experiment, subjects received free-operant avoid-

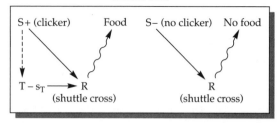

PHASE 1
(shuttle box)

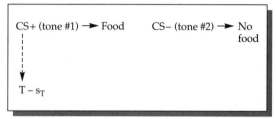

PHASE 2
(classical conditioning box)

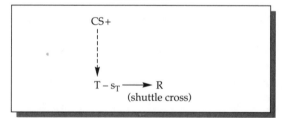

TRANSFER TEST
(shuttle box)

Figure 10.8 Outline of the experiment by Overmier and Lawry (1979). Instrumental discrimination training is conducted in a shuttle box in phase 1. Classical conditioning is then conducted in a separate apparatus that does not permit subjects to make the shuttle response. The CS + is then tested in the shuttle box to see whether it increases shuttle responding. (See the accompanying text for further details.)

ance training in the shuttle box in the presence of a bright light. (Each shuttle crossing here postponed the next scheduled shock by 30 seconds.) This free-operant avoidance schedule was in effect during the final phase of the experiment when the food-conditioned CS + was presented in the shuttle box. The point of interest was whether shuttle crossings would be increased by presentation of the CS +. The final transfer test also involved presentation of the food-conditioned CS−.

Figure 10.9 summarizes the results. The data are presented in terms of the percentage of change (increase or decrease) in shuttle responding caused by presentation of the food-conditioned CS+ and CS− stimuli. The free-operant avoidance schedule remained in effect for the shuttle behavior during these stimulus presentations. As indicated in Figure 10.9, presentation of the food-conditioned CS+ increased shuttle responding. This is a very significant finding because it cannot be explained by either the emotional properties of the state elicited by the CS+ or the responses elicited by the CS+. Since the CS+ was conditioned with food, the emotional state it evoked (hope) should have subtracted from the emotion (fear) maintaining the baseline avoidance behavior, and there should have been a decrease in shuttle responding. The responses conditioned to the CS+ cannot explain the increased shuttle behavior, because the CS+ was conditioned in a classical conditioning procedure and special precautions were taken to make sure that the shuttle response would not become conditioned to the CS+ in the second phase of the experiment. The increased responding evoked by the CS+ is best explained by the discriminative stimulus properties (s_T) of the classically conditioned state (T) elicited by the CS+. These cues presumably gained control over the shuttle response because of the training that subjects had received in phase 1 of the experiment.

Let us next consider what happened when the food-conditioned CS− was presented in the transfer test. This time a small decrease in shuttle crossings occurred. This is an important control observation because it shows that not all stimuli will produce increases in shuttling in this situation. Therefore, we can be sure that the effect observed with the CS+ was due to the specific conditioning history of that stimulus.

Overmier and his colleagues have conducted several experiments of the sort that we

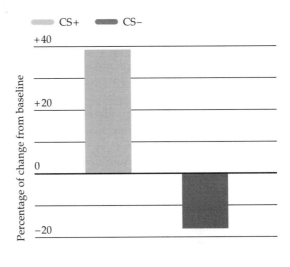

Figure 10.9 Percent change in shuttle shock-avoidance responding when a food-conditioned CS+ or CS− is presented. *(Adapted from J.B. Overmier and J.A. Lawry, 1979.)*

have described (see Overmier & Lawry, 1979). These studies provide strong support for the idea that classically conditioned states have stimulus properties that can acquire discriminative control over instrumental behavior. Furthermore, the discriminative properties of classically conditioned states can override the emotional properties of those states, as in the experiment just described.

It is interesting to note that the present theoretical analysis in terms of discriminative stimulus properties of classically conditioned states (see Figure 10.7) is very similar to the r_g–s_g mechanism discussed earlier (see Figure 10.5). As in the r_g–s_g mechanism, the stimuli present during instrumental conditioning (S+) are assumed to become classically conditioned, and the classically conditioned entity is assumed to have stimulus characteristics that come to serve as discriminative cues for the instrumental response. Thus, the present model has the same type of response-directing function that we previously discussed in connection with the fractional anticipatory goal response. However, the present account differs from the r_g–s_g mechanism in that a classically conditioned intervening state (T) is assumed to be acquired rather than a fractional anticipatory goal response (r_g). In addition, in the contemporary theoretical model, the classically conditioned entity elicited by the S+ is also assumed to have emotional properties that can add to or subtract from other elicited emotions, in accordance with the predictions of modern two-process theory.

Conditioned Central Emotional States or Reward-Specific Expectancies?

Modern two-process theory assumes that classical conditioning mediates instrumental behavior through the conditioning of central emotional states such as hope, disappointment, fear, and relief. However, a growing body of evidence indicates that in certain situations animals acquire specific reward expectancies instead of more general central emotional states during instrumental and classical conditioning (Peterson & Trapold, 1980). Baxter and Zamble (1982), for example, compared electrical stimulation of the brain (ESB) and food as rewards in transfer-of-control experiments with rats. Since both of these USs are positive reinforcers, they would be expected to condition the emotional state of hope. Baxter and Zamble found that a CS + for brain stimulation increased instrumental lever pressing reinforced with ESB and a CS + for food increased lever pressing reinforced with food. However, a CS + for ESB did not increase lever pressing conditioned with food reinforcement. Thus, a positive classically conditioned stimulus increased instrumental responding only if it signaled the same US that had been used to condition the instrumental response.

In another study, solid food pellets and a sugar solution were used as USs in classical and instrumental conditioning of rats (Kruse, Overmier, Konz, & Rokke, 1983). The results showed that a CS + for food had a much greater facilitory effect on instrumental responding reinforced with food than on instrumental behavior reinforced with the sugar

solution. Correspondingly, a CS + for sugar had a greater facilitory effect on instrumental behavior reinforced with sugar than on instrumental behavior reinforced with food pellets. Thus, as in the study by Baxter and Zamble (1982), expectancies for specific rewards rather than a more general central emotional state of hope determined the results (see also Hendersen, Patterson, & Jackson, 1980).

The studies we have just described clearly indicate that under some circumstances animals acquire reinforcer-specific expectancies rather than more general emotional states during instrumental and classical conditioning. Reinforcer-specific expectancy learning is a challenging alternative to modern two-process theory in explaining certain types of results. In particular, expectancy theory is more successful in explaining results of transfer-of-control experiments in which the USs used during classical and instrumental conditioning phases are of the same type— both aversive or both appetitive (cells 3, 4, 5, and 6 of Table 10.2). If the USs employed are identical in the two phases (classical and instrumental conditioning with the same type of food, for example), then predictions of expectancy and two-process theory are identical. If the USs are not identical but are of the same affective category (food pellets and sucrose, for example), the evidence we have described indicates that expectancy theory is more successful in explaining the results than two-process theory.

These considerations suggest that expectancy theory could replace modern two-process theory in explaining many findings. However, expectancy theory is not as successful as two-process theory in explaining effects of classical conditioning on instrumental performance when the USs used in the two types of conditioning are from opposite affective systems (food and shock, for example). (These instances are illustrated by cells 1, 2, 7, and 8 of Table 10.2.) For example, it is not clear on the basis of reinforcer-specific expectations why a CS − for food should facilitate shock-avoidance instrumental behavior (cell 8 of Table 10.2). The specific reinforcer expectancy elicited by a CS− for food is certainly not the same as the specific reinforcer expectancy presumably responsible for instrumental shock-avoidance behavior. However, the emotion elicited by a CS− for food (disappointment) is similar to the emotion presumably acquired during avoidance training (fear). Therefore, two-process theory is more successful in explaining such transfer results.

The Associative Structure of Instrumental Conditioning

The theoretical and empirical work we have been discussing was originally conceived as descriptive of the role of classical conditioning in the control of instrumental behavior. However, this research also may be thought of as descriptive of the nature of the associations that underlie instrumental conditioning, or the associative structure of instrumental conditioning.

As we noted in Chapter 5, the study of instrumental conditioning has two distinct intellectual traditions. One of these originated with Thorndike, who relied heavily on the concept of the reflex. Within the Thorndikian tradition, investigators typically have employed discrete-trial methods and have relied on theoretical analyses that are stated in terms of associations between stimuli and responses. The other intellectual tradition originated with Skinner. Within the Skinnerian tradition, investigators employ the free-operant method and rely on theoretical analyses that are stated in terms of feedback functions and contingencies of reinforcement. Explanations of instrumental behavior in terms of behavioral regulation, behavioral economics, and optimal foraging theory (see Chapter 7) represent contemporary work in the Skinnerian tradition. Explanations of instrumental behavior in terms of its underlying associative structure represent contemporary efforts in the Thorndikian tradition. Since the latter category of explanations evolved from studies of classical–instrumental interactions, we will describe those developments in the current chapter.

A Summary of Two-Process Approaches

The r_g–s_g mechanism and its various successors are, in a sense, different models of the types of associations involved in, and responsible for, instrumental conditioning. All of the two-process models discussed earlier in this chapter follow the Thorndikian tradition of explaining instrumental conditioning in terms of stimulus–response associations. The models assume that two such associations are learned. One is a direct association between external environmental stimuli S and the instrumental response R. This association is the same as the one Thorndike postulated as the mechanism of instrumental conditioning; it is represented by arrow *a* in Figures 10.5 and 10.7.

The second stimulus–response association—one that Thorndike did not think about—involves an association between classically conditioned internal events elicited by S and the response R. This association of R to internal cues is represented by arrow *b* in Figures 10.5 and 10.7. The classically conditioned internal event is characterized in different terms in the various models. In the r_g–s_g mechanism, it is feedback (s_g) from the fractional anticipatory goal response (r_g). In other models, it is a classically conditioned central emotional state or a reward-specific expectancy. Regardless of how the internal event is characterized, the common idea is that the instrumental response becomes conditioned to internal cues that arise through classical conditioning of the external stimuli S.

The response outcome (O), or reinforcer, is assumed to be involved in the machinery of instrumental conditioning in two ways. The first of these is the Thorndikian instrumental reinforcement process. Thorndike assumed that the reinforcer acts to strengthen associations between the instrumental response and the stimuli present when the response occurs. The reinforcer is not assumed to participate directly in an association with the response, but is assumed to "stamp in" or provide the "glue" for stimulus–response associations involving external and internal cues. The second way in which the reinforcer is assumed to be involved in the instrumental conditioning mechanism is in classical conditioning of the external cues (S) present in the instrumental conditioning situation. Because the reinforcer has these two different roles (instrumental conditioning of the response R, and classical conditioning of S), the models we have been considering are called two-process models.

Contemporary Approaches to the Associative Structure of Instrumental Conditioning

Two-process models of instrumental conditioning shared Thorndike's reliance on the concept of the reflex and incorporated knowledge of classical conditioning into the machinery presumed to be responsible for the performance of instrumental behavior. Contemporary approaches to the associative structure of instrumental conditioning follow in this tradition by applying research techniques and concepts that have been developed in recent studies of classical conditioning to the analysis of instrumental conditioning.

Much of the impetus for contemporary approaches to the associative structure of instrumental conditioning arose from two prominent developments in the study of classical conditioning. One of these was methodological; the other, conceptual. The methodological innovation was the use of reinforcer devaluation as a technique for studying the content of associations. We previously introduced this technique in discussions of the nature of associations learned in classical conditioning (see Chapter 4). The conceptual innovation was the exploration of conditional or hierarchical relations between stimuli. We encountered this topic earlier in

discussions of the stimulus control of behavior (see Chapter 8).

Possible associations in instrumental conditioning. Ignoring internal cues for the moment, the instrumental conditioning situation involves three terms—the instrumental response (R), the reinforcer delivered as an outcome of the response (O), and the stimuli present during instrumental conditioning (S). These three terms may be organized in various ways. Two-process models assume that S, R, and O are organized into two associations, S–R and S–O. Upon further reflection, however, this account may seem a bit odd for a couple of reasons (see Colwill & Rescorla, 1986).

First, notice that none of the presumed associations in two-process models involve a direct link between the response R and the reinforcer, or response outcome, O. All variants of two-process theory assume that the role of the reinforcer in strengthening the instrumental response is only to "stamp in" the S–R association. The response outcome O is not directly represented in the S–R association, or otherwise associated with the response. This is counterintuitive. If you asked someone why they were performing an instrumental response, the reply would most likely be that they expected the response to result in a reinforcer. You comb your hair because you expect that doing so will improve your appearance, you go to see a movie because you expect to enjoy it, and you open the refrigerator because you anticipate that doing so will get you something to eat. All these explanations are based on response–outcome associations. Although our informal explanations of instrumental behavior rely on R–O associations, such associations do not exist in two-process models.

Another peculiarity of the associative structure of instrumental conditioning assumed by two-process theories is that S is assumed to become associated directly with O on the assumption that the pairing of S with O is sufficient for the occurrence of classical conditioning. However, as we saw in Chapter 4, CS–US pairings are not sufficient for the development of Pavlovian associations. The CS also must provide information about the US, or in some way be "relevant" to the US.

In an instrumental conditioning situation, the stimuli present during reinforcement of the response are not predictive of reinforcement. The reinforcer O cannot be predicted from S alone. Rather O occurs if the subject makes response R in the presence of S. Thus, instrumental conditioning involves a conditional relation in which S is followed by O only if R occurs. This conditionality in the relation of S to O is ignored in two-process theories. We discussed this conditionality in Chapter 8 in the context of discrimination training. There, we noted that in a discrimination procedure reinforcement of the instrumental response is conditional upon the presence of the S+. These considerations suggest that the associative structure of instrumental conditioning is not adequately described by S–R and S–O associations. Rather, the associative structure might also include a conditional, or hierarchical, relation: S(R–O). Contemporary efforts to explore the associative structure of instrumental conditioning have concentrated on demonstrating R–O and conditional S(R–O) relations.

Evidence of R–O associations. A number of investigators have suggested that instrumental conditioning leads to the learning of response–outcome associations (for example, Bolles, 1972b; Mackintosh & Dickinson, 1979) and several different types of evidence have been obtained in support of this possibility. (For a review, see Colwill & Rescorla, 1986.) In one interesting demonstration, a reinforcer devaluation procedure was used to demonstrate R–O associations (Colwill & Rescorla, 1986).

Colwill and Rescorla first reinforced rats for pushing a vertical rod either to the right or the left. Responding in either direction was reinforced on a variable-interval 1-minute schedule of reinforcement. Both response alternatives were always available during training sessions. The only difference was that responses in one direction were reinforced with food pellets and responses in the opposite direction were always reinforced with a bit of sugar solution (sucrose). After both responses had become well established, the rod was removed and the reinforcer devaluation procedure was introduced. One of the reinforcers (either food pellets or sugar solution) was periodically presented in the experimental chamber, followed by an injection of lithium chloride to condition an aversion to that reinforcer. After an aversion to the selected reinforcer had been conditioned, the vertical rod was returned to the experimental chamber. The rats then received an extinction test during which they were free to push the rod either to the left or to the right.

The results of the extinction test are presented in Figure 10.10. The important finding was that during the extinction test subjects were less likely to make the response for which the reinforcer had been made aversive by pairings with lithium chloride. This finding cannot be explained easily in terms of the S–O or S–R associations that form the basis for two-process theory. The two responses, pushing the vertical rod left or right, were made in the same place and with the same manipulandum. Therefore, the two responses were reinforced in the presence of the same external stimuli S. If devaluation of one of the reinforcers had altered the properties of S, that should have changed the two responses equally. Instead, devaluation of a reinforcer selectively depressed the particular response that had been trained with that reinforcer. This outcome suggests that each response was associated separately with its own reinforcer. The subjects evidently had learned separate R–O associations.

Evidence of hierarchical S(R–O) relations. Skinner (1938) suggested many years ago that relations in instrumental conditioning between S, R, and O should be characterized as conditional S(R–O) relations. However, only

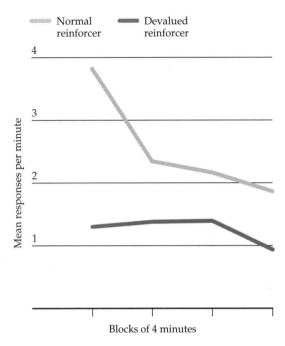

Figure 10.10 Effects of reinforcer devaluation on instrumental behavior. Devaluation of a reinforcer selectively reduces the response that was previously reinforced with that reinforcer. *(From "Associative Structures in Instrumental Learning" by R.M. Colwill and R.A. Rescorla, in G.H. Bower (Ed.), 1986, The Psychology of Learning and Motivation, Vol. 20, pp. 55–104. Copyright © 1986 Academic Press. Reprinted by permission.)*

TABLE 10.4   *Outline of procedures employed to demonstrate S(R–O) relations in instrumental conditioning (Rescorla, 1990a, Experiment 1.)*

Training

L : R1 → O1,   R2 → O2

N: R1 → O1,   R2 → O1

T : R1 → O2,   R2 → O2

Extinction

L : R1 → no O1,   R2 → no O2

Outcome

L : R1 → O1,   R2 → O2

Test

N: R1 → O1,   R2 → O1

T : R1 → O2,   R2 → O2

Prediction

N: R2 > R1

T : R1 > R2

NOTE: L, N, and T represent light, noise, and tone stimuli. R1 and R2 are different responses (lever press and chain pull) and O1 and O2 are different reinforcer outcomes (food pellets and sugar solution, respectively).

in the past few years has compelling evidence for such an associative structure been obtained. A variety of direct and indirect lines of evidence have been developed that suggest the learning of S(R–O) relations in instrumental conditioning (Colwill & Rescorla, 1990; Davidson et al., 1988; Holman & Mackintosh, 1981; Goodall & Mackintosh, 1987; Rescorla, 1990a, 1990b). Most of these studies have involved rather complicated discrimination training procedures. The design of one of the experiments (Rescorla, 1990a, Experiment 1) is presented in Table 10.4.

The experiment involved three discriminative stimuli: L, T, and N (a light, a tone, and a noise stimulus); two responses: R1 and R2 (pressing a lever and pulling a chain); and two

outcomes: O1 and O2 (food pellets and a sugar solution). During the training phase, subjects were trained on two R–O relations in the presence of each discriminative stimulus. During the light stimulus, R1 produced O1 and R2 produced O2; during the noise, each response produced O1 (R1–O1 and R2–O1); and during the tone, each response produced O2 (R1–O2 and R2–O2). The question addressed by the experiment was whether discrimination training produces only pairwise associations (S–O, S–R, and R–O) or also conditional S(R–O) relations. This question was answered by studying the effects of extinguishing both responses during the light in the second phase of the experiment and then looking to see how this extinction treatment influenced responding during the tone and noise stimuli. Extinguishing both responses during the light presumably disrupts the R1–O1 and the R2–O2 associations.

During the test session, the subjects were given a choice between the two responses, R1 and R2. To avoid any further conditioning, responses were not reinforced during the testing. What should we expect to happen during the noise and the tone in the test session? Since the noise and tone stimuli were not presented during the extinction phase, it would be reasonable to expect that they would still activate the R–O associations that the subjects presumably had learned in the presence of these cues during the training phase. These are listed in Table 10.4. Notice that one of the R–O associations for each auditory cue is the same as one of the R–O associations that was extinguished in phase 2. Thus, in the presence of the noise, the relation of R1 with its outcome (O1) was presumably disrupted as a result of extinction. By contrast, in the presence of the tone, the relation of R2 with its outcome (O2) was presumably disrupted as a result of extinction. These selective devaluations of the R–O associations should produce selective responding during the noise and tone stimuli. During the noise stimulus, subjects should prefer making R2 as compared to R1. By contrast, during the tone, they should prefer making R1 as compared to R2.

The results of the experiment are presented in Figure 10.11. Responding is shown for both the intertrial interval when neither the tone nor the noise stimulus was present, as well as for trials with these discriminative stimuli. Responding during the discriminative stimuli is presented separately for the response whose R–O association was extinguished in the extinction phase and for the response whose R–O association was not extinguished.

Several aspects of the results shown in Figure 10.11 are noteworthy. First, notice that more responding occurred during the noise

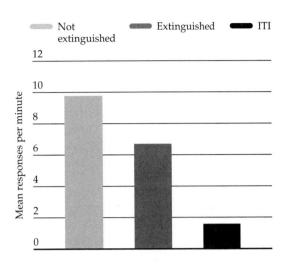

Figure 10.11 Responding during auditory discriminative stimuli presented separately for a response whose R–O association was extinguished in the presence of a visual discriminative stimulus and for a response whose R–O association was not extinguished during the light (see Table 10.4). *(From "Evidence for an Association Between the Discriminative Stimulus and the Response-Outcome Association in Instrumental Learning" by R.A. Rescorla, 1990,* Journal of Experimental Psychology: Animal Behavior Processes, *16, pp. 262–270. Copyright © 1990 by the American Psychological Association. Reprinted by permission.)*

and tone stimuli than during the intertrial interval (ITI). Thus, the noise and tone were effective discriminative stimuli. Second, as predicted, subjects were more likely to perform the response whose R–O association was not extinguished than the response whose R–O association had been extinguished during the second phase of the experiment. This selective effect of the extinction treatments on the two responses suggests the operation of an S(R–O) associative structure. The auditory stimuli presumably activated a unique R–O association involving each response. The subjects were more likely to perform the response whose R–O association had not been disrupted by prior extinction.

The differential effect of extinction on the two responses cannot be explained in terms of S–O associations because the two responses were reinforced by the same outcome in the presence of each auditory stimulus. The differential effect also cannot be explained in terms of S–R associations. The two responses underwent equivalent extinction in the extinction phase; therefore, S–R associations should have been equally weakened for both responses. The differential responding during the test session clearly indicates that each response was associated with its own unique outcome. Discriminative stimuli evidently stimulate behavior by activating these R–O associations, and the strength of the behavioral activation depends on the status of each R–O association.

As a final note, it is important to point out that R–O associations cannot act alone to produce instrumental behavior. As Mackintosh and Dickinson (1979) have pointed out, the fact that the response activates an expectancy of the reinforcer does not explain what causes the response in the first place. An additional factor is required to activate the R–O association. The S(R–O) structure provides this additional factor. The instrumental response presumably occurs because the R–O association is activated by the discriminative stimuli S.

Concluding Comments

Classical and instrumental conditioning procedures are clearly different from each other. However, instrumental reinforcement can be involved in classical conditioning procedures and classical conditioning processes can be involved in instrumental conditioning procedures. Experimental investigations have shown that classical conditioning can take place in the absence of the opportunity for instrumental reinforcement. However, comparable investigations cannot be conducted to show that instrumental conditioning is possible without the occurrence of classical conditioning.

All instrumental conditioning procedures allow for the occurrence of classical conditioning. Concurrent-measurement experiments have confirmed that classically conditioned responses in fact develop during instrumental conditioning procedures. However, the concurrent measurement of classically and instrumentally conditioned responses has not proved to be very helpful in elucidating the interrelation of these two processes. Another experimental technique, the transfer-of-control design, has provided much more enlightening information. In numerous instances, this type of experiment has confirmed the basic tenet of two-process theory—that classically conditioned stimuli can influence the performance of an independently established instrumental response. Research has shown that the transfer of control from Pavlovian conditioned stimuli to instrumental behavior is governed by several factors. One important factor is the nature of the central emotional state elicited by the Pavlovian CS in comparison with the central emotional state established by the baseline instrumental reinforcement schedule. (This factor has been emphasized by modern two-process theory.) A second important variable is the overt responses elicited by the Pavlovian CS and the extent to which these are compatible or incompatible with the instrumental behavior. A third factor in transfer-of-control experiments is the discriminative stimulus properties of the classically conditioned states. (This factor has been emphasized by theories similar to the r_g–s_g mechanism.) Finally, transfer-of-control experiments can also involve reinforcer-specific expectancies. Generally, particular transfer-of-control experiments have been designed to highlight the importance of a particular variable. Therefore, results of individual experiments often provide evidence consistent with one but not other perspectives on the interrelation of classical and instrumental conditioning. However, the totality of the evidence suggests that the interaction of classical and instrumental conditioning procedures is multiply determined.

In addition to elucidating the relation between classical and instrumental conditioning, two-process theories provide an account of the associative structure of instrumental conditioning. That account emphasizes stimulus–reinforcer (S–O) and stimulus–response (S–R) associations. External cues (S) in the instrumental conditioning situation are assumed to become classically conditioned by the reinforcer (O), producing the S–O association. In addition, the instrumental response is assumed to become associated both with external discriminative stimuli and with internal cues that are by-products of the S–O associations.

In addition to these S–R and S–O associations, contemporary views of the associative structure of instrumental conditioning assume the existence of associations between the instrumental response and the reinforcer (R–O associations). Furthermore, contemporary views assume that the three basic terms of instrumental conditioning (S, R, and O) are related not only in binary associations (S–R, S–O, and R–O), but also in a hierarchical fashion, S(R–O), whereby the discriminative stimuli S activate the R–O association.

11

Animal Cognition: Memory Mechanisms

In Chapter 11 we will begin a consideration of animal cognition — a relatively new and rapidly developing area of research relevant to the study of learning and behavior. After defining animal cognition and pointing out reasons for studying it, we will discuss one of the most important cognitive processes — memory. We will start by describing the relationship between learning and memory and the distinction between working memory and reference memory. We will then discuss several prominent working memory paradigms. In the next section, we will describe research relevant to three different stages of memory: acquisition, retention, and retrieval. We will then end the chapter with a discussion of different sources of forgetting.

As we noted in Chapter 1, interest in animal cognition dates back to the founding of the field of animal learning more than a century ago. Early experimental efforts to study animal cognition employed animal learning paradigms. However, studies of animal learning soon came to have a life of their own. Through much of the twentieth century, learning processes have been investigated in animals for what they told us about behavior rather than for what they told us about animal cognition or animal intelligence. However, the past 20 years have witnessed a return to broader questions about animal cognition and animal intelligence (for example, Griffin, 1976, 1982; Hulse, Fowler, & Honig, 1978; Kendrick, Rilling, & Denny, 1986; Roitblat, Bever, & Terrace, 1984; Weiskrantz, 1985).

The resurgence of interest in broader issues relevant to animal cognition is a part of the "cognitive revolution" that has swept over many areas of psychology in the past 25 years. These developments have stimulated considerable theoretical debate (for example, Amsel, 1989; Hintzman, 1991). Regardless of that debate, an important consequence of contemporary interest in animal cognition has been the extension of the study of animal learning to numerous new paradigms. These extensions have raised many new and interesting questions about behavior—questions that were not explored in conventional studies of classical and instrumental conditioning. We will describe some of these developments in this chapter and the next.

What Is Animal Cognition?

The word *cognition* comes from the Latin meaning "knowledge or thinking" and is commonly used in reference to thought processes. To most people, thought processes have two prominent characteristics. First, we tend to regard thinking as involving the voluntary, deliberate, and conscious consideration of some topic, usually with the use of language. Thus, thinking is informally considered to be a kind of "talking to oneself." The second prominent characteristic of thinking is that it can lead to actions that cannot be explained on the basis of external stimuli a person happens to experience when the thinking occurs. For example, on your way to work, you may remember that you did not lock up when you left home. This thought may make you return home and lock the door. Your returning cannot be explained by the external stimuli to which you were exposed as you went to work. You encounter these same stimuli every day, but usually they do not make you return home. Rather, your behavior is attributed to the thought of the unlocked door.

In the scientific study of animal behavior, *cognition* is used in a more restricted sense than in common language. It is not defined as voluntary or conscious reflection about a topic; thus, it does not refer to thinking in the ordinary sense. Although a clear consensus has not yet emerged concerning its definition, **animal cognition** refers to the use of *a neural representation, or model, of some past experience as a basis for action*. A neural representation ("mental" record or image, if you will) cannot be investigated directly by looking into the nervous system. Rather, it is inferred from behavior. Thus, an internal representation is a theoretical construct, in the same sense that gravity is a theoretical construct inferred from the behavior of, for example, falling objects. (For a more detailed discussion, see Roitblat, 1982.)

Internal representations may encode various types of information, such as particular features of stimuli or relations between previously experienced events. The concept of an internal representation is useful because it allows us to explain the occurrence of responses that are not entirely governed by external stimuli. Behavior can be guided by internal representations of events and relations rather than by concrete external stimuli. Consequently, cognitive mechanisms are often invoked when an animal's actions cannot be entirely explained in terms of the external stimuli the animal is exposed to at the time.

The assumption that animals possess cognitive processes should not be taken to mean that they also possess consciousness and self-awareness. As Terrace (1984) has commented, "The rationale for the study of cognitive processes in animals requires no reference to animal consciousness" (p. 8). Research on animal cognition is concerned with questions such as how representations are formed, what aspects of experience they encode, how the information is stored, and how it is used later to guide behavior. These questions are investigated with the same experimental rigor as any other research question that involves making theoretical inferences from observed behavior.

Cognition is clearly involved in memory, which we will discuss in this chapter. It is also involved in serial pattern learning, concept formation, reasoning, and language, which we will discuss in Chapter 12. However, cognition is also important in classical and instrumental conditioning. Much of our discussion of classical conditioning in Chapters 3 and 4 followed the strong cognitive orientation of contemporary research in this area. As we noted in Chapter 4, research on classical conditioning suggests that animals do not learn to make a particular response to the CS. Rather, they learn *an association between two stimuli, the CS and US (an S–S association).* The S–S approach assumes that the conditioned response is not elicited directly by the CS. Rather, the CS elicits or activates a representation ("mental image") of the US and the conditioned response is performed because of this representation. If the representation of the US is independently altered, the response elicited by the CS is thereby also altered (see "Modern approaches to stimulus substitution" in Chapter 4).

We have also discussed some cognitive mechanisms in instrumental conditioning. We noted in Chapter 10, for example, that according to two-process theories, the instrumental response becomes conditioned to external cues of the situation in which the response is reinforced as well as to internal cues that arise as by-products of the classical conditioning of these external stimuli. These internal cues, and associations involving the internal cues, may be regarded as cognitive mechanisms.

Animal Memory Paradigms

Memory is one of the most extensively investigated cognitive processes. Much of the research and theorizing dealing with memory has been concerned with the performance of human subjects. However, investigators of animal behavior have also become very much interested in the study of memory mechanisms over the past 20 years (for example, Honig & James, 1971; Kendrick, Rilling, & Denny, 1986; McGaugh & Herz, 1972; Medin, Roberts, & Davis, 1976; Spear, 1978; Spear & Miller, 1981). In the present chapter we will describe some of the prominent techniques used in the study of animal memory and also discuss a few of the major theoretical issues in the field.

The term **memory** is commonly used to refer to the ability to reproduce or recount information experienced at an earlier time. Thus, we are said to remember what happened in our childhood if we can tell stories of childhood experiences. We are said to remember a phone number if we can state it accurately, and we are said to remember someone's name if we call that person by the correct name. Unfortunately, similar tests of memory with animals are usually impractical. We cannot ask an animal to tell us what it did last week. Instead, we have to use the animal's overt responses as a clue to its memory. If your cat wanders far from home and finds its way back, you might conclude that it remembered where you live. If your dog has grown fond of you and eagerly greets you after a long vacation, you might conclude that it remembered you. These and similar cases illustrate that *the existence of memory in animals is identified by the fact that their current behavior can be predicted from some aspect of their earlier experiences.* Any time the animal's behavior is determined by past events, we can conclude that some type of memory mechanism is involved in the control of that behavior.

You may notice that our definition of memory is very similar to the definition of learning we proposed in Chapter 1. There, we characterized learning as an enduring change in responding to a particular situation as a result of prior experience with that type of situation. Thus, evidence of learning is also identified on the basis of changes in behavior that are due to earlier experiences. Indeed, learning is not possible without memory.

How, then, are studies of learning and memory to be distinguished? The differences between learning and memory experiments may be clarified by considering the components that are common to both types of experiments (see Table 11.1). The first thing that happens in both types of experiments is that subjects are exposed to certain kinds of stimuli or information. This phase is termed **acquisition.** The information that was acquired is then retained for some time, a period called the **retention interval.** At the end of the retention interval, subjects are tested for their memory of the original experience, which requires reactivation, or **retrieval,** of the information encountered during acquisition. Thus, studies of learning and studies of memory all involve basically three phases: acquisition, retention, and retrieval.

Consider, for example, riding a bicycle. Skilled bicyclists initially had to be trained to balance, pedal, and steer the bike (acquisition). They have to remember those training experiences (retention). And, when they get on a bicycle again, they have to reactivate their knowledge of bike riding (retrieval).

In studies of learning, the focus is on the acquisition phase. Learning experiments deal with the kind of information we acquire and

TABLE 11.1   *Comparison of learning and memory experiments*

Phase	Studies of Learning	Studies of Memory
Acquisition	Varied	Constant
Retention	Constant (long)	Varied (short and long)
Retrieval	Constant	Varied

the ways in which we acquire it. Thus, learning experiments all involve manipulations of the conditions of acquisition. The effects of different initial experiences on later performance are tested. The retention interval is always fairly long (a day or longer), because short-term changes in behavior are not considered to be instances of learning. Furthermore, the retention interval typically is not varied within the experiment. Because the emphasis is on the conditions of acquisition, the conditions of retrieval are also kept constant. All subjects in a given experiment are tested for their knowledge using the same test procedures.

In contrast to studies of learning, studies of memory focus on the retention interval and the retrieval phase of the experimental paradigm. Issues concerning acquisition are of interest only to the extent that they are relevant to retention and retrieval. The retention interval is often varied to determine how availability of the acquired information changes with time. Unlike studies of learning, which employ only long retention intervals, studies of memory can employ retention intervals of any duration. In fact, many studies of animal memory involve situations in which information is retained for only short periods of time. Evidence of remembering depends on the circumstances of retrieval. Consider, for example, taking a test of memory for technical terms in a college course. You may miss many items if the test consists of a series of fill-in-the-blanks and only the definitions are provided. You are likely to do much better if you are also provided with a list of the technical terms and are merely required to match up each term with its definition. These different forms of the test involve different conditions of retrieval. In this example, the conditions of acquisition and retention are not altered; evidence of retention depends on the conditions of retrieval.

Working and Reference Memory

Memory mechanisms have been classified in various ways depending on what is remembered (the contents of memory) and how long it is remembered (the retention interval). In research on animal learning, for example, a particularly useful classification has employed the distinction between working and reference memory. One of the earliest experimental investigations of animal memory was conducted by the American psychologist Walter S. Hunter (1913), who was interested in the ability of animals to retain a "mental" representation of a stimulus. Hunter tested rats, dogs, and raccoons in a simple memory task. The apparatus consisted of a start area from which the animals could enter any one of three goal compartments. Only one of the goal compartments was baited with a piece of food on each trial, and the baited compartment was marked by turning on a light above that compartment at the start of the trial. Which compartment was baited (and illuminated) was varied from trial to trial.

After the subjects had learned to choose the illuminated compartment on each trial, Hunter made the task a bit more difficult. Now the light marking the baited compartment remained on for only a short time. After the signal had been turned off, the subject was detained in the start area before being allowed to choose among the three compartments. Therefore, the animal had to somehow remember which compartment had been illuminated in order to find the food. The longer subjects were delayed before being allowed to

make a choice, the less likely they were to go to the correct compartment. The maximum delay rats could withstand was about 10 seconds. The performance of dogs did not deteriorate until the delay interval was extended to more than 5 minutes, and raccoons performed well as long as the delay was no more than 25 seconds. The species also differed in what they did during the delay interval. Rats and dogs were observed to maintain a postural orientation toward the correct compartment during the delay interval. No such postural orientations were observed in the raccoons. Since the raccoons did not maintain a postural orientation during the delay interval, their behavior required some type of neural memory mechanism.

With the delay procedure, the animals had to remember which compartment had been illuminated at the start of that trial. However, once the trial was finished, this information was no longer useful because the food was likely to be in a different compartment on the next trial. Thus, memory of which compartment had been recently illuminated was required only to complete the work during a given trial. This type of memory is called **working memory.**

Working memory is operative when information has to be retained only long enough to complete a particular task, after which the information is best discarded because it is not needed or (as in Hunter's experiment) because it may interfere with successful completion of the next task. If you have to go to several stores in a shopping mall, for example, it is useful to remember which stores you have already visited as you select which one to go to next. However, this information is useful only during that particular shopping trip. A mechanic changing the oil and lubricating a car has to remember which steps of the job already have been completed, but only as long as that particular car is being serviced. In cooking a good stew, you have to remember what spices you have already put in before adding others, but once the stew is finished, you can forget this information. All these illustrate instances of working memory.

Working memory is often short-lasting. In Hunter's experiment, the memory lasted for only 10 seconds in rats and for 25 seconds in raccoons. However, as we will see, in other situations working memory may last for several hours or days.

Examples of working memory illustrate the retention, for a limited duration, of recently acquired information. However, such information is useful only in the context of more enduring knowledge. In Hunter's experiment, for example, remembering which compartment had been illuminated at the start of a trial was not enough to obtain food. This information was useful only in the context of enduring knowledge that the light marked the baited compartment. In contrast to information in working memory that was disposed of after each trial, information about the relation between the light and food had to be remembered on all trials. Such memory is called **reference memory** (Honig, 1978).

Reference memory is long-term retention of information necessary for successful use of incoming and recently acquired information. To shop efficiently in a shopping mall, you have to remember not only what stores you have already been to but also general information about shopping malls. Similarly, information about what a mechanic has done recently is useless unless the mechanic generally knows how to lubricate a car and change the oil, and knowledge of what spices you have already added to a stew is useful only if you know which spices and how much of each to use. All successful uses of working memory require appropriate reference memories.

Since Hunter's research, increasingly sophisticated techniques have been developed for the study of working memory. In the balance of this section on animal memory paradigms, we will describe three situations that have provided important information about working memory. One of these, the delayed-matching-to-sample procedure, is a laboratory procedure that was developed without much regard for the innate behavioral predispositions of animals and can be adapted to the study of how animals remember any one of a variety of stimuli. The other techniques appear to be closely related to species-specific foraging strategies and illustrate some remarkable adaptive specializations in working memory for spatial stimuli.

Delayed Matching to Sample

The delayed-matching-to-sample procedure, one of the most versatile techniques for the study of working memory, is a substantial refinement of the technique that Hunter originally used. As in Hunter's procedure, the subject is exposed to a cue indicating the correct response on a particular trial. This stimulus is then removed before the animal is permitted to perform the designated behavior. In the typical experiment with pigeons, for example, the experimental chamber contains three response keys arranged in a row, as in Figure 11.1. The point of the study is to see whether the pigeons can remember a sample stimulus long enough to pick it out when they are later given a choice between the sample and some other stimulus. The center key is used to present the sample stimulus, and the two side keys are later used to present the choice cues. The test stimuli might consist of an array of horizontal or vertical lines projected on the response keys from the rear.

At the start of a trial, the center key is illuminated with a white light (see row A in Figure 11.1). After the pigeon pecks the white center key, one of the test stimuli—the horizontal array, for example—is projected on it (row B in Figure 11.1). This is the sample for that trial. Usually several pecks at the sample stimulus are required, after which the sample is turned off and the two side keys are lit up. One of the side keys is illuminated with the

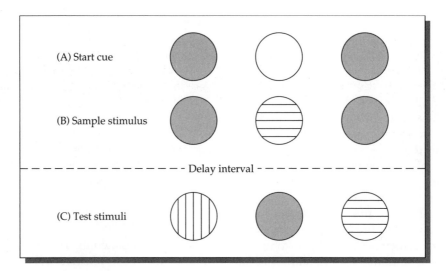

(A) Start cue

(B) Sample stimulus

— — — — — — — — — — — - Delay interval - — — — — — — — — — —

(C) Test stimuli

Figure 11.1   Diagram of the delayed-matching-to-sample procedure for pigeons. The experimental chamber has three response keys arranged in a row. At the start of a trial, the center key is illuminated with a white light (row A). After the pigeon pecks the white center key, the sample stimulus (horizontal) is projected on it (row B). This stimulus is then removed, and after a delay two choice stimuli (horizontal and vertical) are presented on the side keys (row C). Pecks at the choice stimulus that matches the sample are reinforced.

sample for that trial (horizontal), and the other key is illuminated with the alternative pattern (vertical) (row C in Figure 11.1). If the pigeon pecks at the pattern that matches the sample (in this case horizontal), the pigeon is reinforced. If it pecks the other pattern, no reward is provided. Thus, the reinforced response "matches" the sample. Which of the test stimuli serves as the sample is randomly varied from one trial to the next, and the matching stimulus is equally likely to be presented on the right or left key during the choice. Therefore, the pigeon can never predict which stimulus will be the sample on a given trial or where the matching stimulus will appear during the choice.

During the initial stages of matching-to-sample training, the sample stimulus remains visible until the subject has made the correct choice. Thus, in our example, the horizontal pattern on the center key would remain illuminated until the subject had correctly pecked the horizontal side key. Such a proce-

dure is called **simultaneous matching to sample.** It does not require memory processes because the cue for the correct response is visible when the response is made. Once subjects have mastered the simultaneous matching procedure, the sample stimulus can be presented only briefly and removed before the choice stimuli are provided. Introduction of a delay between exposure to the sample stimulus and availability of the choice cues changes the procedure to **delayed matching to sample.**

In most applications, as we mentioned, the matching stimulus is equally likely to appear on the left or the right choice key. Hence, subjects cannot make the correct choice by orienting to the right or left when the sample appears on the center key and holding this body posture until the choice stimuli are presented. Thus, in contrast to Hunter's procedure, simple postural orientations cannot be used to increase the likelihood of making the correct choice. Subjects are forced to use more sophisticated memory processes to obtain reinforcement in the delayed-matching procedure.

Procedural determinants of delayed matching to sample.

The delayed-matching-to-sample procedure has been used extensively with a variety of species, including monkeys, pigeons, dolphins, goldfish, rats, and human beings (Baron & Menich, 1985; Blough, 1959; D'Amato, 1973; D'Amato & Colombo, 1985; Forestell & Herman, 1988; Jarrad & Moise, 1971; Roberts & Grant, 1976; Steinert, Fallon, & Wallace, 1976; Wallace, Steinert, Scobie, & Spear, 1980). In addition, the procedure has been adapted to investigate how animals remember a variety of stimuli, including visual shapes, numbers of responses performed, presence or absence of reward, and the spatial location of stimuli (for example, D'Amato, 1973; Maki, Moe, & Bierley, 1977; Wilkie & Summers, 1982).

Three aspects of the matching-to-sample procedure are critical in determining the accuracy of performance. One of these is the nature of the stimulus that has to be remembered. Some stimuli are remembered better than others. Wilkie and Summers (1982), for example, tested the ability of pigeons to remember the spatial position of illuminated lights. Nine lights were arranged in an array of three columns and three rows. Three of the lights were illuminated on each trial. Memory for the position of the illuminated lights was much better when the three lights were in a straight line than when they formed a discontinuous pattern. (We will discuss the importance of patterns of stimulation further in Chapter 12.)

The two other factors that are important in determining the accuracy of delayed matching to sample are the delay interval and the duration of exposure to the sample stimulus at the start of the trial. In one experiment, for example, Grant (1976) tested pigeons in a standard three-key apparatus after they had received extensive training on delayed match-

ing to sample with visual stimuli. Two pairs of colors—red/green and blue/yellow—served as sample and comparison stimuli on alternate trials. At the start of each trial, the center key was illuminated with a white light. When the subject pecked the center key, the sample color for that trial was presented on the center key for 1, 4, 8, or 14 seconds. This was followed by delay intervals of 0, 20, 40, or 60 seconds, after which the two side keys were illuminated, one with the sample-matching color and the other with the paired alternate color. After the subject made its choice, all the keys were turned off for a 2-minute intertrial interval.

The results of the experiment are summarized in Figure 11.2. If subjects had pecked the choice keys randomly, they would have been correct 50% of the time. Higher scores indicate that subjects responded on the basis of their memory for the sample stimulus. For all the sample durations evaluated, the accuracy of matching decreased as longer delays were introduced between exposure to the sample and opportunity to make the choice response. In fact, if the sample was presented for only 1 second and the opportunity to make a choice was delayed 40 seconds or more, the pigeons responded at chance level. Performance improved if they were exposed to the sample for longer periods. When the sample was presented for 4, 8, or 14 seconds, the subjects performed above chance levels even when the delay interval was as long as 60 seconds. Thus, accuracy in the delayed-matching-to-sample procedure decreased as a function of the delay interval and increased as a function of the duration of exposure to the sample stimulus (see also Guttenberger & Wasserman, 1985).

Response strategies in matching to sample.

The matching-to-sample procedure is analogous to a discrimination problem in that the subject has to respond to a correct stimulus and refrain from responding to an incorrect

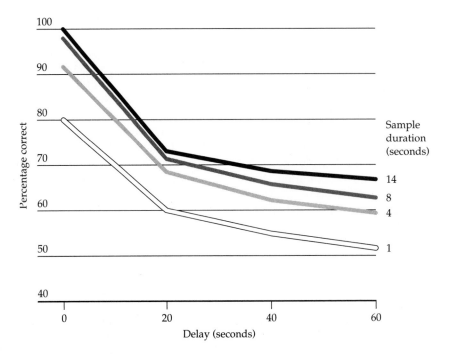

Figure 11.2 Percentage of correct responses in a delayed-matching-to-sample task as a function of duration of presentation of the sample stimulus (1–14 seconds) and delay between the sample and the choice stimuli (0–60 seconds). *(From "Effect of Sample Presentation Time on Long Delay Matching in the Pigeon" by D.S. Grant, 1976,* Learning and Motivation, 7, *pp. 580–590. Copyright © 1976 by Academic Press. Reprinted by permission.)*

one to get reinforced. As we noted in discussions of what is learned in discrimination training in Chapter 8, such a two-alternative task can be solved just by responding to the correct choice, just by inhibiting behavior to the incorrect choice, or by using both these response strategies. Discrimination learning (which may be considered to involve the establishment of a reference memory) appears to involve the combined response strategy. By contrast, subjects in matching to sample appear to focus only on the correct choice. One interesting experiment supporting this conclusion used a three-key apparatus for pigeons that was specially constructed so that the stimulus projected on a response key was visible only if the pigeon was standing directly in front of that key (Wright & Sands, 1981). This apparatus enabled the experimenters to

determine which response keys the pigeons looked at before making their choice responses in a matching-to-sample procedure. The results showed that the birds focused on the correct alternative. If they saw the matching stimulus, they pecked it without bothering to check what stimulus appeared on the other side (see also Roitblat, Penner, & Nachtigall, 1990; Wright, 1990; Zentall, Edwards, Moore, & Hogan, 1981).

General versus specific rule learning.   The evidence we have just reviewed indicates that animals focus on the correct choice in matching to sample. What leads them to identify a stimulus as correct? One possibility is that they learn a general rule involving a comparison between the sample and choice stimuli. The rule may be, for example, "Choose the same as the sample." Another possibility is that animals learn a series of specific rules or stimulus–response relations. In the experiment by Grant (1976), for example, pairs of colors were used — red/green and blue/yellow. The pigeons may have learned a series of specific stimulus–response relations: "Peck red after exposure to red," "Peck green after exposure to green," and so on. Most matching-to-sample procedures can be solved either by learning a general "same-as" rule or by learning a series of specific stimulus–response relations, and no clear consensus has developed on which of these types of learning predominates (for example, Roitblat, 1984; Zentall, Hogan, & Edwards, 1984).

Evidence in support of one or the other alternative has been provided by studies of transfer of training. One type of transfer experiment involves first conducting matching-to-sample training with one set of stimuli and then conducting the same kind of training with a new set of stimuli. The hypothesis of specific stimulus–response learning predicts little positive (or negative) transfer of matching behavior to new stimuli because the new task requires learning a new set of stimulus–response relations. By contrast, the hypothesis of general rule learning predicts considerable positive carryover because the second matching-to-sample task involves the same general "same-as" rule as the first one. Thus, in transfer of training from one matching-to-sample problem to another, the general-rule-learning hypothesis predicts better transfer performance than the specific-rule-learning hypothesis.

In a recent study (Oden, Thompson, & Premack, 1988), four infant chimpanzees were first trained on a matching-to-sample task with just one pair of stimulus objects, a stainless steel measuring cup and a brass bolt lock. One of the objects was presented to a subject at the start of the trial, followed by a choice of both objects. If the subject selected the matching object, it was reinforced with effusive praise, tickling, cuddling, or an edible

treat, depending on its preference. After the subjects had learned the task with the two training stimuli, they were tested with a variety of other stimulus objects. Remarkably, with most of the test objects, the transfer performance of the chimpanzees was better than 80% accurate. Thus, the chimps seemed to have learned a general "same-as" rule with just two training stimuli. This finding is remarkable because generalized matching-to-sample performance is not obtained after training with just two stimuli in pigeons. Such findings may encourage the conclusion that species differences in cognitive capacity determine whether subjects are apt to show evidence of generalized matching, indicating that they have acquired the "same-as" concept.

Although chimpanzees are more likely to show evidence of generalized matching than pigeons and other species, the preponderance of evidence suggests that both general rule learning and specific stimulus–response learning can occur as a result of matching-to-sample training in a variety of species. Which type of learning predominates appears to be related to the size of the stimulus set used in the matching-to-sample procedure. A study such as Grant's (1976) in which sample and comparison stimuli were selected from two pairs of colors is likely to favor the learning of specific stimulus–response relations. By contrast, procedures that employ a wide range of stimuli are more likely to favor the learning of a general rule. The extreme of a procedure of this type is the **trials-unique procedure.** In this procedure, a particular sample stimulus is used only once. A different stimulus serves as the sample on each trial and is paired with another stimulus during the choice test. Because a given sample stimulus is not presented more than once, accurate performance with a trials-unique procedure is possible only if the subject learns to respond on the basis of a general "same-as" rule. Successful learning of the same-as concept has been obtained with the trials-unique procedure with visual stimuli in pigeons and auditory stimuli in monkeys (Wright, Cook, Rivera, Sands, & Delius, 1988; Wright, Shyan, & Jitsumori, 1990).

Passive versus active memory processes. Another important issue in the analysis of delayed-matching-to-sample behavior concerns the type of memory involved. Results such as those shown in Figure 11.2 have encouraged an interpretation of short-term memory known as the **trace decay hypothesis** (Roberts & Grant, 1976). This hypothesis assumes that presentation of a stimulus produces changes in the nervous system that gradually decrease, or decay, after the stimulus has been removed. The initial strength of the stimulus trace is assumed to reflect the physical energy of the stimulus. Thus, longer or more intense stimuli are presumed to result in stronger stimulus traces. However, no matter what is the initial strength of the trace, it is assumed to decay at the same rate after the stimulus ends. The extent to which the memory of an event exerts control over the organism's actions depends on the strength of the stimulus trace at that moment. The stronger the trace, the stronger is the effect of the past stimulus on the subject's behavior. The trace decay model predicts results of exactly the sort summarized in Figure 11.2. Increasing the delay interval in the matching-to-sample procedure reduces the accuracy of performance presumably because the trace of the sample stimulus is weaker after longer intervals. By contrast, increasing the duration of exposure to the sample improves performance

Matching to Sample in Elderly People

BOX **11.1**

A matching-to-sample task can be solved by learning a matching rule ("same as") or by learning a set of stimulus–response associations. Which of these strategies is activated depends in part on the training procedures employed. As we have seen, trials-unique procedures encourage the learning of a matching rule. Which strategy is learned is also determined by subject characteristics. This is illustrated by a comparison of matching-to-sample learning in elderly people diagnosed to have Alzheimer-type dementia and normal elderly control subjects (Morris, 1987).

Both groups of subjects were about 79 years old. The matching-to-sample task required selecting a color chip that was the same as the sample stimulus on each trial. Training was conducted with red, white, and orange chips. Each trial started with one of these chips presented in the middle of a response panel. The sample chip was then removed and the subject was presented with two color chips on either side of the sample position. One of the comparisons was the same color as the sample; the other was one of the other colors. The subjects had to select the matching comparison stimulus. Correct responses were reinforced with a token hidden under the correct chip. The subjects were encouraged to try to obtain as many tokens as they could during each 24-trial session.

Each subject was trained with red, white, and orange chips until he or she responded correctly on 20 of the 24 trials of a session. At this point the original color chips were replaced with three new ones (yellow, green, and blue) and matching-to-sample training continued. If subjects had learned to respond on the basis of a general "same-as" rule, this learning should have transferred to the new color chips, and the subjects should have responded accurately when the new colors were introduced. By contrast, such positive transfer was not expected to occur if the subjects had learned a series of stimulus–response rules during the first phase of training.

The results obtained with some of the subjects are presented in Figure 11.3 by way of illustration. Notice that the Alzheimer's patients were as slow to learn the matching task in phase 2 of the experiment as in phase 1. Thus, having learned to match three colors in phase 1 did not facilitate learning to match a second set of three colors in phase 2. The results obtained with the normal elderly subjects were very different. They

presumably because longer exposures to the sample establish stronger stimulus traces.

The trace decay hypothesis emphasizes the physical characteristics of the sample stimulus and is a passive memory mechanism. After the stimulus has been terminated, the decay of its trace is assumed to proceed automatically. As the trace decays, information about the stimulus is assumed to become irretrievably lost.

Contrary to the trace decay hypothesis, various types of results suggest that working memory does not depend entirely on the physical features of the event to be remembered; rather, it involves active processes. For example, delayed-matching-to-sample performance improves with practice with the same types of stimuli. The learning history of a monkey named Roscoe provides a dramatic illus-

tration. After 4,500 training trials, Roscoe could not perform at above-chance level if a 20-second interval was introduced between the sample and choice stimuli. However, after 17,500 trials he correctly matched the sample stimulus nearly 80% of the time with a 2-minute sample-to-choice delay interval, and after approximately 30,000 trials his performance was better than chance with a 9-minute delay interval (D'Amato, 1973). Another important determinant of working memory is the extent to which the stimulus is surprising. Several lines of investigation have shown that surprising events are remembered better than expected events (Maki, 1979; Terry & Wagner, 1975). The existence of active memory processes in working memory is also implicated by studies showing that memory processes

learned the matching task much faster originally, responding with 100% accuracy by the third session. In addition, during phase 2 when three new stimuli were introduced, their performance remained perfectly accurate. These findings suggest that the Alzheimer's patients learned specific stimulus–response associations in the matching task whereas the normal elderly subjects learned to respond on the basis of a "same-as" rule.

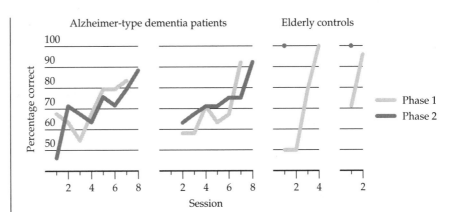

Figure 11.3 Accuracy in responding on a matching-to-sample task by two elderly Alzheimer's patients and two normal elderly control subjects during original training with three stimuli (phase 1) and a transfer training phase with three new stimuli (phase 2). *(From "Identity Matching and Oddity Learning in Patients with Moderate to Severe Alzheimer-Type Dementia" by R.G. Morris, 1987, Quarterly Journal of Experimental Psychology, 39B, pp. 215–227. Copyright © 1987 The Experimental Psychology Society. Reprinted by permission.)*

Figure 11.4 Rat foraging on a radial maze. *(Courtesy of Catherine Green, from Patricia Sharp Lab, Department of Psychology, Yale University.)*

can be brought under external stimulus control. (See discussion of "directed forgetting" later in this chapter.)

Spatial Memory in a Radial Maze

The matching-to-sample procedure can be adapted to investigate how animals remember a variety of stimuli. The next technique we will consider has more limited applicability but focuses on a very important type of memory — memory for places. To be able to move about their habitat efficiently, animals have to remember how their environment is laid out — where open spaces, sheltered areas, and potential food sources are located. In many environments, once food has been eaten at a location, it is not available there again for some time until it is replenished. Therefore, in foraging, animals have to remember where they last found food and avoid that location for awhile. Such foraging behavior has been nicely documented (Kamil, 1978) in a species of Hawaiian honeycreeper, the amakihi *(Loxops virens)*. These birds feed on the nectar of

mamane flowers. After feeding on a cluster of flowers, they avoid returning to the same flowers for about an hour. By delaying their return to clusters they have recently visited, the birds increase the chance that they will find nectar in the flowers they search. They appear to remember the spatial location of recently visited flower clusters.

Memory for locations in space — **spatial memory** — has been studied in the laboratory with the use of complex mazes (for example, Olton, 1979). A photograph of a rat in one such maze is presented in Figure 11.4. In an investigation by Olton and Samuelson (1976), rats were tested in a maze similar to that shown in Figure 11.5. The maze had eight arms radiating from a central choice area. During the first few days of the experiment, the rats were permitted to explore the maze without food pellets in the food cups. A pellet of food was then put at the end of each arm of the maze. For each test, the rat was placed in the center of the maze and was free to enter each arm to obtain the food there. Once a food pellet had been consumed, that arm of the

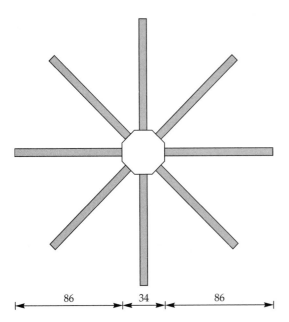

Figure 11.5 Top view of an eight-arm radial maze used in the study of spatial memory. Numbers indicate dimensions in centimeters. *(From "Remembrance of Places Passed: Spatial Memory in Rats" by D.S. Olton and R.J. Samuelson, 1976, Journal of Experimental Psychology: Animal Behavior Processes, 2, 97–116. Copyright © 1976 by the American Psychological Association. Reprinted by permission.)*

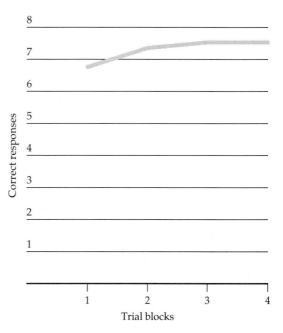

Figure 11.6 Mean number of correct responses rats made in the first eight choices during blocks of five test trials in the eight-arm radial maze. *(Adapted from D.S. Olton, 1978.)*

maze remained without food for the rest of the trial.

How should the rat have gone about finding food in this situation? It could have randomly selected which alley to enter each time. Thus, the rat might have entered an alley, eaten the food there, returned to the center area and then randomly selected another arm of the maze to enter next, and so on. However, this might have involved going down alleys from which the rat had already taken the food. A more efficient strategy would have been to enter only those arms of the maze that had not yet been visited on that trial. This is in fact what most of the animals learned to do. Entering an arm that had not been visited previously (and which therefore contained food) was considered to be a correct choice. Figure 11.6 summarizes the number of

correct choices subjects made during the first eight choices of successive tests. During the first five test runs after familiarization with the maze, the rats made a mean of nearly seven correct choices during each test. With continued practice, the mean number of correct choices was consistently above seven, indicating that the subjects rarely entered an arm they had previously chosen on that trial.

Figure 11.6 illustrates that the rats did not require much training to come to perform efficiently in the radial maze. The radial maze task appears to take advantage of the preexisting tendency of rats to explore a maze without returning to recently visited places. This tendency is, in fact, so strong that the failure of rats to return to a place where they recently have obtained food may not be related to having obtained food there (Gaffan & Davies, 1981). Several investigators have found that performance on a radial maze is equally accurate (in the sense of the rats not returning to recently visited arms of the maze) whether or not the maze arms are baited with food (FitzGerald, Isler, Rosenberg, Oettinger, & Bättig, 1985; Timberlake & White, 1990; see also Maki, 1987).

Regardless of why rats avoid returning to a recently visited arm of a maze, such behavior can be used as a test of working memory, provided that the animals are not basing their decisions on external cues or other strategies that do not require memory mechanisms. There are several mechanisms by which rats could choose to enter only previously unchosen arms of a maze without necessarily remembering which arms they had already visited. For example, they may be able to smell the food in unvisited arms at the entrance to those arms of the maze, or they may mark each arm they visit with something like a drop of urine, and then avoid maze arms that had this odor marker. Rats also may always select arms in a fixed sequence, such as entering successive arms in a clockwise order.

Numerous studies have been conducted to evaluate these nonmemory interpretations. Various procedures have convincingly ruled out use of food or other odor cues in the selection of maze arms (for example, Olton, Collison, & Werz, 1977; Olton & Samuelson, 1976; Zoladek & Roberts, 1978). The available evidence also indicates that rats in a radial maze experiment can perform efficiently without using response chains or entering maze arms in a fixed order from one trial to the next. As long as the central choice area is fairly small so that the rats can easily reach all the arms from anywhere in the central area, they do not choose arms in a fixed order (Olton & Samuelson, 1976; see also Olton et al., 1977). If the central area is made larger, the rats are more apt to select maze arms that are close by and enter adjacent arms on successive choices (Yoerg & Kamil, 1982). This response strategy serves to minimize their travel time for each pellet of food obtained and is predicted by optimal foraging theory.

The studies we have cited have been important in ruling out various potential cues for radial maze performance and suggest that spatial stimuli are critical. What are spatial cues and how are they identified? Spatial cues are stimuli that identify the location of an object in the environment. Rats appear to use such things as a window, door, corner of the room, or poster on the wall as landmarks of the experimental environment and to locate maze arms relative to these landmarks. Movement of these landmarks relative to the maze causes the rats to treat the maze arms as being in new locations (Suzuki, Augerinos, & Black, 1980). Thus, spatial location is identified relative to distal room cues, not to local stimuli inside the maze (see also Morris, 1981). The distal environmental cues seem to be perceived visually (Mazmanian & Roberts, 1983).

Because radial maze performance usually depends on memory for recently visited locations, the radial maze experiment has become a popular technique for the study of memory processes, both at the behavioral and physiological level. The memory capacity revealed by the technique is rather remarkable. For example, rats and gerbils have been observed to perform well in radial mazes with as many as 17 arms (Olton et al., 1977; Wilkie & Slobin, 1983), and this probably does not represent the limit of their spatial memory (Roberts, 1979). The duration and context specificity of spatial working memory are also remarkable.

In an important test of the limits of spatial memory, Beatty and Shavalia (1980b) allowed rats to make four choices in the eight-arm radial maze in the usual manner. The subjects were then detained in their home cages for various periods up to 24 hours. After the delay interval, they were returned to the maze and allowed to make choices 5–8. An entry into an alley they had not previously chosen was considered a correct choice, and an entry into a previously used alley was considered an error. Figure 11.7 shows the percentage of correct choices as a function of the delay

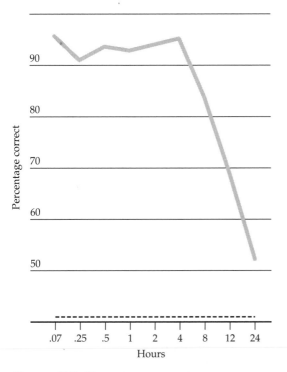

Figure 11.7 Percentage correct responses on choices 5–8 in an eight-arm radial maze. Between choices 4 and 5 the animals were returned to their home cages for varying intervals ranging from .07 to 24 hours. The dashed line indicates chance performance (41%). *(From "Rat Spatial Memory: Resistance to Retroactive Interference at Long Retention Intervals" by W.W. Beatty and D.A. Shavalia, 1980,* Animal Learning & Behavior, 8, *pp. 550–552. Copyright © 1980 by Academic Press. Reprinted by permission.)*

interval. A delay interval of up to 4 hours imposed after the first four choices did not disrupt performance. Longer periods of confinement in the home cage produced progressively poorer performance. In fact, only one rat out of five showed significant retention of the first four choices after a 24-hour period. These data show that spatial memory is not permanent, but that it can last for several hours (Maki, Beatty, Hoffman, Bierley, & Clouse, 1984; Strijkstra & Bolhuis, 1987).

Other research has shown that spatial working memory is context-specific and there-fore remarkably immune to disruption from other experiences. In one study (Beatty & Shavalia, 1980a), rats were trained on two identical eight-arm radial mazes located in different rooms. After completing four choices in one maze, they were taken to the other room and allowed to complete four choices in the other maze. Four hours after their choices in the first room, they were returned there to complete another four arm choices. The remarkable finding was that experiences in the second maze did not disrupt performance when the subjects were returned to the first maze, even though the two mazes were identical. The fact that the mazes were located in different rooms apparently served to segregate the memories of places visited in each room (see also, for example, Maki, Brokofsky, & Berg, 1979).

Techniques have been also developed for the study of spatial working memory in a variety of other species, including Siamese fighting fish *(Betta splendens),* monkeys, Clark's nutcrackers, and pigeons (Andrews, 1988; Balda & Kamil, 1988; Olson & Maki, 1983; Roberts & Veldhuizen, 1985; Roitblat, Tham, & Golub, 1982; Spetch, 1990; Spetch & Honig, 1988). Although early efforts suggested that spatial working memory is much less durable in pigeons than in rats, with some newly developed procedures, evidence of working memory on the order of 4 hours and longer has been obtained in some pigeons (Willson & Wilkie, 1991).

Spatial Memory in Food-Storing Birds

Animals in a radial maze experiment have to recover food items that were previously stored in various locations by the experimenter. This situation is a laboratory analogue of many natural situations in which animals have no control over the location of food items. Another interesting spatial memory problem involves the recovery of food items that were stored in various places by the animal itself. Under these circumstances, the location of the food items is under the subject's own control. A number of bird and mammalian species (including chipmunks and squirrels) hoard food in various locations during times of plenty and visit these caches later to recover the stored food items. (For a review, see Sherry, 1985.)

One remarkable example of cache recovery is provided by the Clark's nutcracker *(Nucifraga columbiana)* (Balda & Turek, 1984). These birds live in alpine areas of the western United States and harvest seeds from pine cones in late summer and early autumn. They hide the seeds in underground caches and recover them many months later in the winter and spring when other food sources are scarce. A Clark's nutcracker may store as many as 33,000 seeds in caches of four or five seeds each and recover several thousand of these during the next winter. Cache recovery also has been extensively investigated in the marsh tit *(Parus palustris)*, a small, lively bird found in England, and in its North American relative, the chickadee (Shettleworth, 1983b; Sherry, 1988). Marsh tits and chickadees store several hundred food items and recover them within a few days. Thus, these smaller birds do not use food storing to mitigate seasonal changes in the food supply.

What mechanisms might food-storing birds use to recover food they had previously placed in caches? One possibility is that they may remember where they stored each food item and subsequently return to the remembered cache locations. However, before one can accept a memory interpretation, other possibilities have to be ruled out. The possible alternatives to a memory interpretation are similar to those we considered in the analysis of spatial memory in a radial maze. One possibility is that birds may find caches by searching randomly among possible cache sites. Another possibility is that they may store food only in particular types of locations and then go around to these favored sites to recover the food items. They also may mark

food-storage sites somehow and then look for these marks when it comes time to recover the food. Yet another possibility is that they may be able to smell or see the stored food and identify caches in that way.

Ruling out nonmemory interpretations has required laboratory studies of the food-storing and retrieval behavior of birds (for example, Kamil & Balda, 1985, 1990; Sherry, 1984; Sherry, Krebs, & Cowie, 1981; Shettleworth & Krebs, 1986). In one such laboratory study, Shettleworth and Krebs (1982) tested marsh tits in a seminaturalistic environment consisting of tree branches distributed in an aviary (see Figure 11.8). The branches had about 100 small holes drilled in various locations, each just big enough to store a hemp seed. The holes were covered with small cloth flaps the birds had to lift in order to store a seed or look for one. In the first experiment, the birds were let into the aviary and permitted to store 12 seeds. They were then returned to a holding cage for 2–3 hours, after which they were let back into the aviary for a 12-minute recovery period. On average, the birds recovered 8 of the 12 seeds during this time and made few errors in their search. They were particularly accurate in finding their first 5 seeds, making only about one error per seed. If they had been searching for the seeds randomly, they would have made about eight errors for each seed they found. Other evidence indicated that the birds could not detect the location of the seeds by smell. They were very inefficient in finding seeds stored in various holes by the experimenters rather than those they had stored themselves.

In another experiment, Shettleworth and Krebs tested the possibility that the birds were simply returning to favorite locations rather than remembering where they had previously stored food. In this second experiment, two types of trials were involved. On one type of trial (hoard-recovery), the birds were first allowed to store 8 seeds and were then tested for recovery of these seeds 2.5 to 3 hours later. In the second type of trial (hoard-hoard-

Figure 11.8 Experimental environment for the study of spatial memory for hoarded food in marsh tits. Lines indicate flight paths and cache locations chosen by a marsh tit the second time it was permitted to hoard eight seeds. In choosing holes for the second batch of seeds (large circles with dots), it avoided the holes in which it had stored the first batch of seeds (large circles without dots). This indicates that it remembered the locations it had previously used to store seeds. *(From "Memory in Food-Hoarding Birds" by S.J. Shettleworth, 1983,* Scientific American, 248, *pp. 102–110. Copyright © 1983 by* Scientific American, Inc. *All rights reserved.)*

recovery), the first hoarding opportunity was followed 2.5 to 3 hours later by a second opportunity to hoard 8 more seeds. This was followed by a recovery test another 2.5 to 3 hours later. (The birds were induced to hoard by providing them with a bowl of seeds. They were induced to recover stored seeds by letting them explore the aviary with the seed bowl empty.) The hoard-hoard-recovery procedure was designed to test the specific-memory hypothesis. If the birds remembered the specific holes where they had previously stored food, they would stay away from these locations during the second hoarding opportunity because the holes were not big enough for two seeds. By contrast, if they always went to particularly favored holes, they would try to store seeds during the second hoarding opportunity in holes that already had seeds in them. The results clearly favored the specific-memory hypothesis (see Figure 11.8). The

birds stayed away from filled holes during the second hoarding opportunity but visited these locations during recovery tests. Thus, instead of just going to the same favored holes each time, they appeared to remember which holes were filled with previously stored seeds.

As these examples illustrate, laboratory studies have supported the conclusion that cache recovery in food-storing birds involves remembering the location of each cache. The memory processes are remarkable. As we noted earlier, field studies have indicated that these birds store hundreds of food items (thousands in the case of the Clark's nutcracker) and accurately recover them days (or months) later. Given these feats, it is tempting to entertain the possibility that food-storing birds have evolved unusual and specialized spatial memory skills (Sherry & Schacter, 1987). To determine the extent of this specialization, efforts are underway to directly compare the spatial memory skills of bird species that store food and those of bird species that do not store food. Such comparisons are difficult because they have to be conducted under conditions that are similar and at the same time equally appropriate for each species. Although some evidence in favor of a specialization hypothesis has been obtained, a definitive conclusion will require further research (see Hilton & Krebs, 1990; Balda & Kamil, 1988; Olson, 1991; Sherry, 1990).

Memory Mechanisms

In the preceding section, we described several prominent techniques for the study of memory processes in animals. Next, we turn to a discussion of factors that determine what we remember and how well we remember it. As we noted earlier, memory processes involve three phases: acquisition, retention, and retrieval (see Table 11.1). What we remember and how well we remember it depend on all three of these phases, often in combination with each other. In this part of the chapter, we will discuss animal research relevant to each of the three phases of memory processes.

Acquisition and the Problem of Stimulus Coding

Obviously, we cannot remember something (the winning goal in a championship game, for example) without having experienced the event in the first place. Memory depends on our having experienced an event and having made some kind of a record of that experience. However, even when our memory is excellent, it is not because we have retained a perfect and literal record of the earlier experience.

Experiences cannot be recorded in a literal sense, even by machines. A movie camera can do a remarkably good job in recording the sights and sounds of a goal in a championship game. The visual aspects of the event are recorded in terms of a series of stationary

images; the auditory aspects are recorded in terms of a pattern of magnetized particles on the film. Thus, the making of the goal is coded in terms of still photographs and magnetic patterns for the purposes of retention. However, the coded record (a strip of film with a soundtrack) bears little resemblance to the actual event. In a similar fashion, we do not have a literal record of a past experience in memory. Rather, the past experience is coded in the nervous system in some way for the purposes of retention. Our memory is based on how a past experience was coded and how that code is retrieved at a later time. Thus, stimulus coding is a critical feature of the acquisition phase of memory.

In studies of animal memory, investigators have been interested in several aspects of the problem of coding. Consider, for example, a rat foraging for food in a radial maze (see Figure 11.5). The subject has to enter the various arms of the maze to obtain the food located at the end of each arm. So as not to waste effort, the rat has to remember the arms it has already visited and select only new arms it has not yet tried that day. In what form does the rat retain information about previously visited arms? One possibility is that it makes a serial list of the maze arms it visits, adding an item to the list with each new arm visited. Given the excellent performance of rats on mazes with 17 arms or more (Olton et al., 1977; Roberts, 1979; Wilkie & Slobin, 1983), this would involve a rather long list. Such extensive list learning seems unlikely, since even humans have difficulty maintaining 17 items or more in working memory at one time. A more likely possibility is that animals form a spatial map of the maze and then use this mental map in deciding which arm of the maze to enter next (Roberts, 1984).

Investigators have been able to answer even more sophisticated questions about the nature of the memory code animals use to solve spatial problems. One may inquire, for example, whether the distances between points in a mental map correspond to the physical distances between corresponding points in the real world. Using multidimensional scaling and correlational analyses of errors in a spatial learning task, Wilkie (1989) was able to demonstrate that mental distances in a spatial map do in fact correspond to physical distances.

Research on spatial maps has provided information about the form of the memory code for spatial locations and has led to the conclusion that the memory code is like a map rather than like a serial list of alleys. However, such research does not tell us what aspect of this information (what aspect of the map) the animals keep in mind as they go about foraging in the radial maze. Perhaps the most obvious possibility is that the animals keep in mind where they have already been. This is called **retrospective memory,** or **retrospection.** However, an equally effective memory strategy would be for the animals to keep in mind which maze arms they still had to enter. This strategy is called **prospective memory,** or **prospection.** Investigators of animal memory processes have become very much interested in the distinction between retrospective and prospective memory (Honig & Thompson, 1982; Wasserman, 1986). Because all animal memory paradigms have a limited range of outcomes, they can all be solved successfully either by remembering what has happened (retrospection) or by remembering what will happen (prospection).

The notion of prospective memory may seem to be a contradiction in terms. How can we remember what will happen? After all, memory involves the retention of information based on a past event or experience. This apparent contradiction is resolved with the realization that retrospection and prospection are different forms of coding. Based on a given experience, we can form a code of that past event (retrospection) or form a code of a future response option (prospection). Although prospection involves information about a future course of action, it involves memory in that the plan of action must be kept

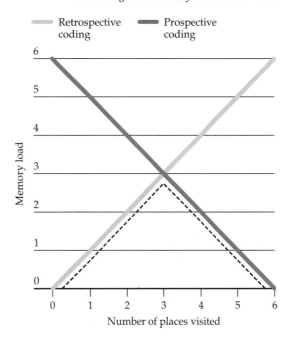

Figure 11.9 Memory load following different numbers of places visited, out of a possible total of six, given retrospective and prospective coding strategies. The dashed line represents memory load when the coding strategy is changed from retrospection to prospection halfway through the task.

in mind until it is time to execute it.

Consider going shopping at a mall. To complete your shopping, you have to visit six stores: a shoe store, a record store, a bookshop, a bakery, a clothing store, and a pharmacy. What memory strategy could you use as you did your shopping to make sure that you remembered to visit each of those six stores? One possibility would be to form a memory code for each store you had visited. (This would be a retrospective code.) You could then decide whether to enter the next store on the list based on whether or not you remembered already having been there. With such a retrospective strategy, the contents of your working memory would increase by one store with each store you visited. Thus, how much you had to remember (the memory load) would increase as you progressed through the task (see Figure 11.9).

The alternative would be to memorize all the stores you intended to visit before you started your trip. Such memory would involve prospection, because it would be memory for what you intended to do in the future. After finishing in a particular store, your prospective memory would be updated by removing that store from the list you had to remember. Thus, in this scheme, a visit to a store would be "recorded" by having that store deleted from the prospective memory. Because you would be keeping in mind only which stores remained, the memory load would decrease as you progressed through your shopping, as shown in Figure 11.9.

Numerous ingenious experiments have sought to establish the incidence of prospective versus retrospective coding. Many of these have involved variations of the matching-to-sample procedure with pigeon subjects. Some studies have provided clear evidence of prospective coding (for example, Roitblat, 1980; Santi & Roberts, 1985; Urcuioli, Zentall, Jackson-Smith, & Steirn, 1989). Other studies have provided clear evidence of retrospective coding (Urcuioli & Zentall, 1986). Of particular interest are experiments in which both types of coding were found, but under different conditions (Santi, Musgrave, & Bradford, 1988; Zentall, Jagielo, Jackson-Smith, & Urcuioli, 1987; Zentall, Urcuioli, Jagielo, & Jackson-Smith, 1989). Such experiments illustrate that coding strategies are flexible, with different strategies adopted in response to different task demands.

To illustrate how coding strategies might change as a function of task demands, let us return to the example of having to shop in six different stores in a mall. As we have noted, with a retrospective coding strategy the demands on working memory increase as you progress through the shopping trip, from having to remember the first store you visited to having to remember all six stores. Conversely, with a prospective coding strategy the demands on working memory decrease as you progress through the six stores, starting with having to remember all six stores to visit and ending with having to remember none. The question arises, How might you minimize the demands on your memory? Is there a way to keep the demands on working memory to three items or fewer throughout the shopping trip? As it turns out there is, if you change your memory strategy halfway through the task. Since the memory load is least for a retrospective strategy at the beginning of the trip, you should use a retrospective strategy to start with. Remembering where you have been works well for the first three stores you visit. After that, the memory load for retrospection begins to exceed the memory load for prospection (recall Figure 11.9). Therefore, after having visited three stores, you should switch to a prospective code and keep in mind only which stores remain to be visited. By switching coding strategies halfway through, you minimize how much you have to remember at any one time. If you use retrospection followed by prospection, memory load will at first increase and then decrease as you complete the task, as illustrated by the dashed line in Figure 11.9.

Do animals (and people) actually have such flexibility in coding strategies, and if so how could we prove it? Several experiments have been performed indicating that coding strategies change from retrospection to prospection as one goes through a list of places or items. Subjects remember what *has happened* early in the list and what *remains to happen* later in the list (Cook, Brown, & Riley, 1985; Zentall, Steirn, & Jackson-Smith, 1990; see also Brown, Wheeler, & Riley, 1989). In one study (Kesner & DeSpain, 1988), both rats and college students served as subjects. Evidence of a change in strategy from retrospection to prospection was obtained by estimating the memory load of the subjects. If subjects switch from retrospection to prospection in the course of remembering a series of places, memory load should first increase and then decrease. Memory load was estimated from the rate of errors the subjects made on a test that was conducted

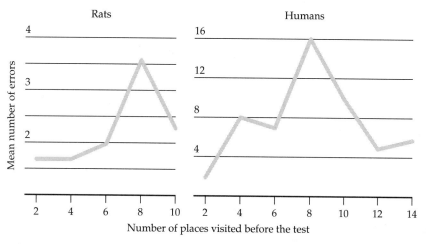

Figure 11.10 Error rate of rats (left) and college students (right) on spatial memory tasks requiring identification of a new place after a delay. The delay was imposed after the subjects had "visited" various numbers of locations. *(From "Correspondence Between Rats and Humans in the Utilization of Retrospective and Prospective Codes" by R.P. Kesner and M.J. DeSpain, 1988,* Animal Learning and Behavior, 16, pp. 299–302. Copyright © 1988 by the Psychonomic Society. Reprinted by permission.)

after the subjects had visited different numbers of places.

The rat subjects in Kesner and DeSpain's study were first trained to forage for food on a 12-arm radial maze in the standard manner. Once they had become proficient at obtaining food by going to each maze arm, a series of test trials was conducted. On each test trial, the rats were allowed to make a certain number of arm entries. They were then removed from the maze for 15 minutes. At the end of the delay, they were returned to the maze and allowed to enter either of two alleys. One of these was an alley they had entered earlier; the other one was new. Selecting the new alley was judged to be the correct response. The rate of errors the rats made during the test phase is presented in the left graph of Figure 11.10. As the number of visited locations before the test increased from 2 to 8 arms of the maze, the error rate increased. This finding is consistent with the hypothesis that the rats were using a retrospective coding strategy during the first eight arm entries. Interestingly, however, when the rats were tested

after having entered 10 arms, they made fewer errors. This improvement in memory performance after more alley entries is contrary to predictions of retrospective coding and suggests, instead, prospective coding.

The college students in the study were presented with a grid having 16 squares (corresponding to 16 places in a maze). During the course of a trial, the symbol X traveled from one square to another in a random order, simulating movement from one place to another in a maze. After the X had been at various numbers of locations, a delay of 5 seconds was introduced, followed by a test of two test locations. One test location was a place where an X had been; the other was a new square. The subjects had to identify which was the new square. Again, the rate of errors was used to estimate memory load. After the experiment was over, and the students were questioned about the memory strategies they had used during the test phase, half of the students described using a retrospective strategy first, followed by a prospective strategy. The rate of errors these students made is presented in the right graph of Figure 11.10 as a function of the number of places where the X had been before the test. The results were remarkably similar to the pattern of errors obtained with the rat subjects. The error rate initially increased as the number of places where the X had been increased, consistent with a retrospective coding strategy. After the X had been at eight places, however, the error rate decreased, consistent with a prospective coding strategy.

Results such as these illustrate that memory performance is a function of coding strategies and that coding strategies may vary as a function of task demands. Given alternative possible coding strategies, subjects will switch strategies so as to reduce memory load and thereby improve the accuracy of their responding.

Retention and the Problem of Rehearsal

The second phase of memory processes is retention. With working-memory tasks, the prominent issue in the context of retention is **rehearsal.** Rehearsal refers to keeping newly acquired information in an active state—a state in which the information is readily available for use. If someone tells you a phone number, you may rehearse the number by repeating it to yourself over and over again until you get to a phone. If someone is giving you directions for getting to the post office, you may try to create a mental image of the route and imagine yourself following the route a number of times. Such rehearsal strategies facilitate keeping newly acquired information readily at hand so that you can use it to guide your behavior.

Rehearsal processes were first investigated in animal memory as they relate to the learning or establishment of new associations. Models of learning and memory typically assume that associations are formed between two events (a conditioned and an unconditioned stimulus, for example) provided that the two events are rehearsed at the same time

(for example, Wagner, 1976, 1981). Given this assumption, learning is expected to be disrupted by manipulations that disrupt rehearsal. Early studies of rehearsal processes in animal memory focused on such manipulations and their effects on the learning of new associations (for example, Wagner, Rudy, & Whitlow, 1973). More recently, the focus of research on rehearsal processes in animals has been on the role of rehearsal in working-memory paradigms. The best evidence of rehearsal processes in working memory comes from studies of **directed forgetting.**

Much research has been done indicating that human memory performance can be modified by instructions stating that something will or will not be important to remember (for example, Bjork, 1972). This research has sparked interest in finding analogous directed-forgetting effects in research with animal subjects. Investigators reasoned that if maintenance of information in working memory involved some type of rehearsal process (Wagner, 1976), this process might be subject to stimulus control, permitting the demonstration of directed forgetting in animal working memory. Directed forgetting has been demonstrated in pigeons, rats, and squirrel monkeys (Grant, 1982b; Maki & Hegvik, 1980; Roberts, Mazmanian, & Kraemer, 1984). (For a review, see Rilling, Kendrick, & Stonebraker, 1984.)

In one experiment (Stonebraker & Rilling, 1981), a variation of the delayed-matching-to-sample procedure was used with pigeons. A circular pecking key was illuminated with either a red or a green light as the sample stimulus at the start of a trial. The first peck after 12 seconds terminated the sample and instituted a 4-second delay interval, after which the key light was again lit up either red or green. If the color after the delay interval matched the sample (red/red or green/green), pecks at the key were reinforced with food. If the color after the delay did not match the sample (red/green or green/red), pecks at the key did not end in reward. Thus, accurate performance required memory for the sample color with which each trial had begun. However, unlike the standard matching-to-sample procedure we discussed earlier, in this variation the matching and nonmatching comparison stimuli were not presented together at the end of the retention interval. This type of procedure is called **successive delayed matching to sample.**

Directed-forgetting training was instituted after subjects had learned to perform accurately on the delayed-matching-to-sample procedure. Arrays of black vertical and horizontal lines projected on the response key against a white background served as remember (R) and forget (F) cues. One or the other of these patterns was presented briefly (for 1/2 second) immediately after the sample red or green color on each trial. On R-cued trials, memory was tested in the usual manner at the end of the delay interval—the red or green color was presented, and responding was reinforced only if the matching color appeared. (To make sure that the pigeons would look at the response key when the test stimulus was presented, a tone was briefly sounded with the test stimulus.) On F-cued trials, memory was not tested at the end of the delay interval; the trial simply ended after the F cue was presented. The pigeons soon learned that the F cue always ended without the opportunity for reinforcement and turned away from the response key upon seeing the F cue.

The critical data of the experiment were obtained on special test trials at the end of the directed-forgetting training. Test trials were like training trials except that memory for the sample stimulus was tested even when exposure to the sample was followed by the forget cue. Thus, test trials measured the accuracy of memory following both R and F cues to see whether memory would be worse after exposure to the forget cue. Another factor of interest was the delay between presentation of the sample stimulus and presentation of the remember or forget cue. On some test trials, the R and F cues were presented immediately

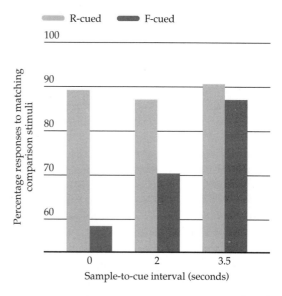

Figure 11.11 Percentage correct responses by pigeons in a successive-delayed-matching-to-sample procedure. On R-cued trials, a remember cue was presented 0–3.5 seconds after the sample stimulus. On F-cued trials, a forget cue was presented after the sample stimulus. *(From "Control of Delayed Matching-to-Sample Performance Using Directed Forgetting Techniques" by T.B. Stonebraker and M. Rilling, 1981,* Animal Learning & Behavior, 9, *pp. 196–201. Copyright © 1981 by Psychonomic Society. Reprinted by permission.)*

after the sample stimulus. On other trials the R and F cues were presented 2 or 3.5 seconds after the sample during the retention interval.

Figure 11.11 shows the results of the memory tests in terms of the percentage of the total number of pecks that were to the correct (matching) comparison stimulus during the memory tests. On remember-cued test trials, close to 90% of responses occurred to the correct stimulus regardless of when the remember cue was presented relative to the sample stimulus. Thus, the pigeons had learned to perform very well on the delayed-matching problem. Dramatically different results were obtained on forget-cued test trials. When the forget cue followed the sample stimulus immediately, performance on the memory test fell to below 60%. Thus, the forget cue produced a substantial decrement in performance on the memory test. Progressively less disruption occurred when the forget cue was presented 2 or 3.5 seconds after the sample stimulus.

Results such as those presented in Figure 11.11 are consistent with a directed-forgetting interpretation. Pigeons may have performed less accurately on forget-cued test trials than on remember-cued test trials because the F cue disrupted the rehearsal processes of working memory. Attractive as this interpretation may be, however, other alternatives also have to be evaluated. One important issue concerns the procedure that was used to train the forget cue. On forget-cued training trials, subjects were not tested for their memory of the sample stimulus and also could not earn reinforcement. The memory-disruption interpretation assumes that the absence of the memory test was critical. Several studies have shown that the absence of reinforcement on F-cued training trials is also important for directed-forgetting effects (Maki & Hegvik, 1980; Maki, Olson, & Rego, 1981). However, others have obtained directed-forgetting effects even when subjects were permitted to earn reinforcement on F-cued training trials (for example, Grant, 1982b; Grant & Barnet, 1991). (This was accomplished by permitting subjects to earn reinforcement on a substitute task that did not require memory.) Thus, directed-forgetting effects do not require that the forget cue become conditioned as a signal for the absence of reinforcement.

Another important question is whether F cues disrupt working memory specifically or produce a more general disruption of discriminative instrumental behavior. The possibility of a more general disruption was tested in pigeons by seeing whether an F cue would disrupt performance on a simultaneous discrimination task that did not require memory (Maki et al., 1981, Experiment 2). Stimuli consisting of displays of vertical and horizontal lines were simultaneously projected onto two pecking keys and pecking one of the patterns was reinforced. Presentation of a forget cue did not significantly disrupt the simultaneous discrimination performance. This outcome indicates that F cues do not have a general disruptive effect on the stimulus control of instrumental behavior.

Finally, it is important to consider what type of information-retention mechanism is being disrupted by forget cues. One possibility is that the memory is some type of central process located somewhere in the brain. Alternatively, the information might be maintained in the animal's overt behavior. People, for example, sometimes say a phone number over and over to themselves to remember it long enough to dial the number. Some instances of directed forgetting may involve disrupting such overt response mediation during the delay interval. This may have been the case in the study by Stonebraker and Rilling (1981). Results of their tests of memory following R and F cues were summarized in Figure 11.11. Stonebraker and Rilling also measured the number of times the pigeons pecked the stimulus key during the retention interval between presentation of the sample and comparison colors. Figure 11.12 shows the rate of this retention-interval pecking for their various test conditions. The remarkable finding was that presentation of the F cue not only disrupted accuracy of memory (Figure 11.11) but also disrupted delay-interval pecking (Figure 11.12). In fact, the effects on memory accuracy and delay-interval pecking were strikingly similar. This raises the strong possibility that the directed-forgetting effects were due to disruption of overt mediational behavior. Further research is required to determine how such overt mediational behavior is involved in this and other examples of directed forgetting.

Retrieval

In the third phase of memory processes, retrieval, stored information is recovered so that it can be used to guide behavior. Whereas

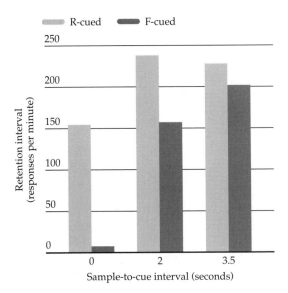

R-cued   F-cued

Figure 11.12 Rates of pecking by pigeons during the retention interval of a successive-delayed-matching-to-sample procedure. (For additional details, see Figure 11.11.) *(From "Control of Delayed Matching-to-Sample Performance Using Directed Forgetting Techniques" by T.B. Stonebraker and M. Rilling, 1981,* Animal Learning & Behavior, 9, *pp. 196–201. Copyright © 1981 by Psychonomic Society. Reprinted by permission.)*

problems of coding and rehearsal are primarily being investigated in working-memory paradigms, research on retrieval has focused on reference memory and, more specifically, on memory for learned associations. Retrieval processes are of special interest because instances of forgetting are often due to a deficit in recovering information from a memory store, or **retrieval failure.**

During the course of our daily lives, we acquire a wealth of information, all of which is somehow stored in the brain. Which aspect of our extensive knowledge we think of at a particular time depends on which pieces of information are retrieved from our long-term memory store. At any moment, we recall only a minute proportion of what we know. Retrieval processes are triggered by reminders, or **retrieval cues.** If you are discussing summer camp experiences with your friends, the

things they say will serve as retrieval cues to remind you of things you did at summer camp. Retrieval cues are effective in reminding you of a past experience because they are associated with the memory for that experience. A song may remind you of the concert you attended on your first date. Balancing on a bicycle will remind you of what you have to do to ride a bicycle. The sensations of sinking in a swimming pool will remind you of what you learned about swimming, and the voice of a friend you have not seen for a long time will stimulate retrieval of memories for the things you used to do together.

A variety of different types of stimuli that are present during acquisition of a memory can come to serve as retrieval cues for that memory. Borovsky and Rovee-Collier (1990), for example, investigated retrieval of the memory for instrumental conditioning in 6-month-old infants. The infants were trained in their own homes in playpens whose sides were covered with a cloth liner. Some of these liners were striped and others had a square pattern. Borovsky and Rovee-Collier investigated the role of the cloth liner as a retrieval cue for the instrumental response.

A mobile was mounted above the playpen. The infants were seated in the playpen in a reclining baby seat so that they could see the mobile. The instrumental response was kicking one of the legs and the reinforcer was movement of the mobile. One end of a satin ribbon was looped around the infant's ankle and the other end was attached to the stand that supported the mobile. With this arrangement, each time the infant kicked, it moved the mobile; the vigor of the movements of the mobile corresponded to the vigor of the infant's kicking. The kicking response first was conditioned in two short training sessions. The infants then received a test session 24 hours later. The cues present during the test session were varied for different groups of infants. Some of the babies were tested in a crib with the same cloth liner that had been present during the training sessions (group

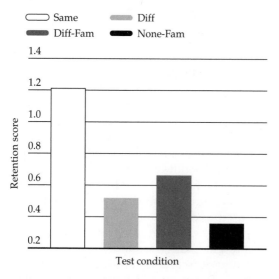

Same   Diff
Diff-Fam   None-Fam

Retention score

1.4
1.2
1.0
0.8
0.6
0.4
0.2

Test condition

Figure 11.13 Retention scores of 6-month-old infants in a test of instrumental conditioning. Group Same was tested in a playpen with the same cloth liner that had been present during conditioning. Group Diff was tested with a new cloth liner. Group Diff-Fam was tested with a familiar cloth liner that was different from the one that had been in the playpen during conditioning. Group None-Fam was tested without a cloth liner but in a familiar playpen in a familiar room. *(From "Contextual Constraints on Memory Retrieval at Six Months" by D. Borovsky and C. Rovee-Collier, 1990,* Child Development, *61, pp. 1569–1583. Copyright © 1990 by University of Chicago Press. Reprinted by permission.)*

Same). Others were tested with the alternate cloth liner that was new to them (group Diff). For a third group, the alternate cloth liner was familiar but it had not been present during the training trials (group Diff-Fam). Finally, a fourth group of babies was tested without a liner and could look around their familiar playroom (None-Fam).

The results of the experiment are summarized in Figure 11.13. The best retention performance was evident in the group that was tested with the same playpen liner that had been present during conditioning. Each of the other groups showed significantly poorer memory performance. The results obtained with group Diff-Fam are especially significant.

Subjects tested in a new situation may show poor memory performance because novelty somehow disrupts their behavior (Thomas & Empedocles, 1992). Thus, better performance in a familiar context than in one that is novel does not necessarily indicate that the context served as a retrieval cue. The poor performance of group Diff-Fam indicates that a change in liner from conditioning to testing for the infants resulted in poor performance even if the liner used during testing was familiar. The inferior performance of group Diff-Fam as compared to group Same provides strong evidence that the cloth liner served as a retrieval cue for the instrumental kicking behavior (see also Butler & Rovee-Collier, 1989; Hill, Borovsky, & Rovee-Collier, 1988; Rovee-Collier, Griesler, & Earley, 1985).

Contextual cues and the retrieval of conflicting memories. Changing the cloth pattern on the playpen liner changed the contextual cues of the playpen. Thus, the study by Borovsky and Rovee-Collier was a study of the role of contextual cues in memory retrieval. We previously encountered another example of contextual cues in memory retrieval in the discussion of contextual stimulus control in Chapter 8. In that chapter we described an experiment by Thomas, McKelvie, and Mah (1985) in which discrimination training was conducted with pigeons. In the first phase, the pigeons were reinforced for pecking when a vertical line (90°) was projected on the response key and were not reinforced when a horizontal (0°) line appeared. This initial discrimination training was provided in the presence of certain contextual cues. The contextual cues were then changed (by altering the sounds and lighting in the chamber) and the pigeons were trained on the reversal of the original discrimination. Now, the horizontal line was the cue for reinforcement of pecking and the vertical line was the cue for nonreinforcement.

Subsequent generalization tests in each context indicated that the subjects' responses to the vertical and horizontal lines depended on the context in which the lines were tested. In the original context, the pigeons responded in accord with the original discrimination contingencies; in the altered context, they responded in accord with the reversal discrimination contingencies (see Figure 8.15, p. 254). These results indicate that the contextual cues served as retrieval cues for the two discriminations. Which discrimination was retrieved (and which controlled the behavior of the birds) depended on which set of contextual cues the pigeons had experienced during the test. The study illustrates that subjects can retain memories of diametrically opposing response tendencies. Which of the conflicting memories controls behavior depends on which memory is retrieved at the time.

Training subjects on diametrically opposed tasks, as Thomas, McKelvie, and Mah did may seem a bit unusual. However, the principle illustrated by their study may have considerable generality. Contingencies of reinforcement rarely remain the same during an animal's lifetime. Although it may be rare for contingencies to become reversed, alterations in contingencies are fairly common. One such change in contingencies is extinction. Reinforced responses may undergo extinction as food supplies change, or the animal is forced into a new habitat by changes in the weather or by predators. The study by Thomas, McKelvie, and Mah suggests that organisms may not forget or unlearn things when extinction is introduced; rather, they may simply learn a new relationship. Whether the memory of original reinforcement or of extinction is reactivated will depend on the retrieval cues present in a test situation.

The role of retrieval processes in extinction has been investigated extensively by Bouton and his colleagues (Bouton, 1991; Bouton & Bolles, 1985; Bouton & Peck, 1989; see also Dekeyne & Deweer, 1990; Peck & Bouton, 1990). One important finding in this research has been that the effects of extinction are context-specific. If reinforced training is conducted in one context and extinction is conducted in another, returning the subjects to the context of reinforcement results in renewal of the conditioned responding. Thus, whether performance appropriate to reinforcement or performance appropriate to extinction is observed depends on whether contextual cues retrieve the memory of reinforcement or the memory of extinction.

If reinforced training and extinction are conducted in different contexts, a conflict between the opposed response tendencies created by the two procedures does not truly exist because only one or the other response tendency is retrieved in a given context. A more complicated situation arises if reinforced training and extinction are conducted in the same context. In this case, the contextual cues serve to retrieve the memory of both types of training. The more recently acquired memory (memory of extinction) typically will govern behavior. However, if the memory of reinforcement is reactivated by other kinds of reminder treatments following extinction (such as by presenting the unconditioned stimulus), the conditioned behavior can be reinstated (Bouton & King, 1983, 1986). Such results are contrary to the idea that extinction involves the unlearning of a conditioned response. Rather, extinction seems to involve new learning. Whether the subject's behavior is appropriate to extinction or to reinforcement is determined primarily by retrieval processes rather than by learning processes.

The generality of reminder treatments. Much has been learned about the facilitation of memory retrieval by reminder treatments (see Gordon, 1981; Spear, 1976, 1978, 1981). Various reminder procedures have been found to facilitate memory retrieval, including exposure to the unconditioned stimulus alone (Quartermain, McEwen, & Azmitia, 1970) and exposure to the conditioned stimulus alone (Gordon & Mowrer, 1980). Some treatments have successfully employed internal cues created by the injection of a sedative (Spear,

Smith, Bryan, Gordon, Timmons, & Chiszar, 1980) and exposure to the nonreinforced stimulus in a discrimination procedure (Campbell & Randall, 1976) as retrieval cues.

Another significant finding is that memories of a conditioned stimulus activated by a reminder treatment are in many ways similar to the effects of presenting the conditioned stimulus itself. For example, cue-retrieved memories of a CS last as long or longer than the memory of having the CS itself presented (Rovee-Collier, Sullivan, Enright, Lucas, & Fagen, 1980; Spear, Hamberg, & Bryan, 1980). In addition, properties of a cue-retrieved memory can be altered in much the same way as properties of a memory activated by the CS itself (Mactutus, Ferek, George, & Riccio, 1982; Misanin, Miller, & Lewis, 1968). In one study (Richardson, Riccio, & Smoller, 1987), for example, fear was conditioned to a black compartment by pairing exposure to this compartment with footshock. The memory of conditioned fear was then reactivated by giving the rats brief shock in a distinctively different chamber. For some rats, this reactivated memory of the CS was paired with sucrose to countercondition the fear that had been acquired to the CS. For control groups, counterconditioning was not conducted. Subsequent tests showed that the counterconditioning treatment was successful in reducing fear (see also Holland, 1981; Holland & Forbes, 1982). Such findings are remarkable because they demonstrate that subjects can learn about a stimulus even if they are not actually exposed to that stimulus. Reactivation of the memory of a CS is sufficient to permit learning something new about it.

Finally, reminder treatments can be used to reverse many instances of memory loss. (For a review, see Miller, Kasprow, & Schachtman, 1986.) For example, reminder treatments have been used to facilitate memory retrieval from short-term memory (Feldman & Gordon, 1979; Kasprow, 1987). They can remind older animals (and babies) of forgotten early-life experiences (for example, Campbell & Randall,

1976; Fagen & Rovee-Collier, 1983; Haroutunian & Riccio, 1979; Richardson, Riccio, & Jonke, 1983). Reminder treatments can counteract stimulus-generalization decrements that occur when learned behavior is tested in a new situation (Gordon, McCracken, Dess-Beech, & Mowrer, 1981; Mowrer & Gordon, 1983). Reminder treatments also have been observed to increase the low levels of conditioned responding that typically occur in latent inhibition, overshadowing, and blocking procedures (Kasprow, Cacheiro, Balaz, & Miller, 1982; Kasprow, Catterson, Schachtman, & Miller, 1984; Miller, Jagielo, & Spear, 1990; Schachtman, Gee, Kasprow, & Miller, 1983; see also Gordon, McGinnis, & Weaver, 1985).

Forgetting

As we have seen, memory mechanisms involve many different factors. Some of these concern coding and the acquisition of information. Others involve rehearsal and the retention of information. Still others involve processes of retrieval. Things can go wrong at any point along the way. Therefore, failures of memory, or **forgetting,** can occur for a variety of reasons.

When we fail to remember something, it could be because the information was never put into a memory store properly. This may have occurred for lack of a viable coding scheme or for lack of rehearsal necessary for moving information into a long-term store. Failures of memory also may be attributable to lack of necessary retrieval mechanisms. Retrieval failures can also occur if the retrieval processes do not fit the way in which the information was originally coded and stored. Consider, for example, trying to retrieve a book from the library. Libraries in the United States use either the Dewey decimal system or the Library of Congress system for coding and organizing their collections. If you had the Dewey decimal code for the book, but the library was organized according to the Library of Congress code, you would have a great deal of difficulty retrieving the book. For successful remembering, retrieval mechanisms must operate in accordance with how the information was originally coded.

In studies of animal memory, forgetting has been extensively investigated in the context of two types of phenomena—interference effects and retrograde amnesia. In the concluding sections of this chapter, we will consider these phenomena in turn.

Proactive and Retroactive Interference

The most common sources of memory disruption arise from exposure to prominent stimuli either before or after the event that one is trying to remember. Consider a party, for example. If the only ones at the party you do not know are a young couple, your new neighbors, chances are you will not have much trouble remembering who they are. However, if you are introduced to a number of new people before and/or after meeting your new neighbors, you may find it much harder to remember their names. There are numerous well-documented and analyzed situations in which memory is disrupted by exposure to a prominent stimulus prior to the event to be remembered. Because in these cases the interfering stimulus acts forward to disrupt the memory of a future target event, the disruption of memory is called **proactive interference.** In other instances memory is disrupted by exposure to a prominent stimulus after the event to be remembered. Because in these situations the interfering stimulus acts backward to disrupt the memory of a preceding target event, the disruption of memory is called **retroactive interference.**

The mechanisms of proactive and retroactive interference have been extensively investigated in human memory (Postman, 1971; Slamecka & Ceraso, 1960; Underwood, 1957). Proactive and retroactive interference also have been investigated in various animal

memory paradigms including delayed matching to sample (for example, Grant, 1975; Grant & Roberts, 1973, 1976) and spatial memory (for example, Gordon, Brennan, & Schlesinger, 1976; Gordon & Feldman, 1978; Hoffman & Maki, 1986; Maki et al., 1979; Roitblat & Harley, 1988). Proactive interference can be investigated in the delayed-matching-to-sample procedure by exposing subjects to an interfering stimulus just before presentation of the sample stimulus on each trial (see Grant, 1982a; Medin, 1980; Reynolds & Medin, 1981). Recall that in the standard matching-to-sample procedure, animals are given a sample (let us say S_1), followed by two choice stimuli (let us say S_1 and S_2), one of which (S_1) matches the sample. The subjects are reinforced only for responding to the matching stimulus. In one study of proactive interference with monkeys, illumination of stimulus panels with a red or a green light served as the S_1 and S_2 stimuli (Jarvik, Goldfarb, & Carley, 1969). The experimental chamber had three stimulus panels arranged in a row. The sample was always presented on the center panel. One second after presentation of the sample stimulus, the two side panels were illuminated with the choice stimuli. To investigate the effects of proactive interference, subjects were exposed to an interfering stimulus for 3 seconds at various intervals ranging from 1 to 18 seconds before presentation of the sample. The interfering cue was always the incorrect choice for that trial. If the sample on a given trial was the green color, the preceding interfering stimulus was exposure to the red color on the center key, and vice versa. Subjects also received control trials not preceded by exposure to an interfering stimulus.

The results are summarized in Figure 11.14. On control trials—that is, when no interfering cues were presented before exposure to the sample—the monkeys made the correct choice nearly 100% of the time. They responded less accurately when the sample stimulus was preceded by an interfering cue. Furthermore, greater disruptions of performance occurred

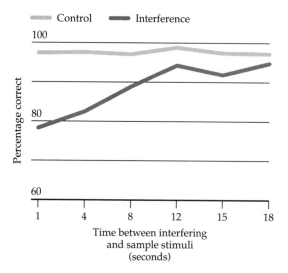

Figure 11.14 Percentage correct responses in a delayed-matching-to-sample task. On some trials a 3-second interfering stimulus was presented 1–18 seconds before the sample stimulus. *(From "Influence of Interference on Delayed Matching in Monkeys" by M.E. Jarvik, T.L. Goldfarb, and J.L. Carley, 1969, Journal of Experimental Psychology, 3, 81, pp. 1–6. Copyright © 1969 by the American Psychological Association. Reprinted by permission.)*

when the interfering stimulus more closely preceded the sample stimulus. No significant proactive interference occurred if the interfering stimulus was presented more than 8 seconds before the sample.

In the study just described, proactive interference was produced by introducing an explicit interfering stimulus before a regular matching-to-sample trial. Proactive interference in working-memory tasks can also arise from events experienced during the preceding regular trial, without there being an explicit interfering stimulus (for example, Edhouse & White, 1988a, 1988b; Jitsumori, Wright, & Shyan, 1989; Roitblat & Scopatz, 1983). Subjects can remember the stimuli and/or responses they made on the preceding trial, and this can disrupt their performance on the next trial. In at least one study (with monkey subjects), stimuli presented on one day were observed to cause proactive inter-

ference even with responding during the next day's session (Jitsumori, Wright, & Cook, 1988).

Most cases of proactive interference do not represent memory failure in the sense that subjects do not remember enough to respond accurately. Rather, the problem is that the subjects remember too much and end up basing their responses on irrelevant information. When it comes time to respond in a matching-to-sample procedure, the subjects may remember not only the correct response based on the sample stimulus of the current trial, but also the correct response based on the sample stimulus of the preceding trial. Errors occur because of confusion between what is appropriate to do on the current trial and what was appropriate to do on the last trial. Information concerning the current trial is not forgotten; it is just mixed up with other information acquired previously. Thus, proactive interference produces failures of memory by creating confusion, not by creating memory loss.

In contrast to the commonly observed proactive interference effects, retroactive interference effects are usually due to memory loss. The memory loss is due to disruption of rehearsal of needed information by introduction of interfering sources of stimulation. Retroactive interference can be studied in the delayed-matching-to-sample procedure by introducing an interfering stimulus between exposure to the sample and presentation of the choice stimuli. If the delayed-matching-to-sample task involves visual cues, memory is more likely to be disrupted by visual than by auditory cues presented during the delay interval (for example, Worsham & D'Amato, 1973; see also Thompson, Van Hemel, Winston, & Pappas, 1983). By contrast, if the sample is an auditory stimulus, memory is more likely to be disrupted by auditory than visual stimuli presented in the delay interval (Colombo & D'Amato, 1986).

Perhaps the simplest way to present interfering visual stimuli is to turn on a light so that

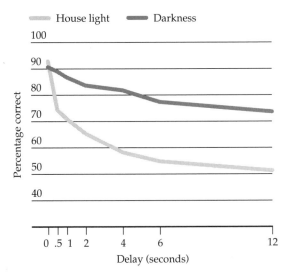

House light ▬▬▬ **Darkness**

Figure 11.15 Percentage of correct responses in a delayed-matching-to-sample task as a function of increasing delays (0–12 seconds) between the sample and the choice stimuli. On some trials the delay interval was spent in darkness. On other trials the house lights were on during the delay interval. *(From "An Analysis of Light-Induced Retroactive Inhibition in Pigeon Short-Term Memory" by W.A. Roberts and D.S. Grant, 1978,* Journal of Experimental Psychology: Animal Behavior Processes, 4, *pp. 219–236. Copyright © 1978 by the American Psychological Association. Reprinted by permission.)*

the animals can see various features of the experimental chamber. Several experiments have demonstrated that illumination of the experimental chamber during the delay interval impairs memory in a visual matching-to-sample task (for example, Grant & Roberts, 1976; Worsham & D'Amato, 1973). In one experiment, pigeons highly experienced in delayed matching to sample were tested with two visual cues as sample and choice stimuli (Roberts & Grant, 1978). The test cues, vertical or horizontal white stripes on a black background, were projected on circular response keys in the usual three-key experimental chamber. The choice stimuli were presented 0–12 seconds after exposure to the sample, and the experimental chamber was either illuminated or dark during the delay period. Figure 11.15 shows the results. Subjects cor-

rectly chose the matching stimulus over 90% of the time when there was no delay after the sample stimulus. Accuracy decreased as the interval between the sample and choice cues increased. However, this decrement in performance was much greater when the house lights were on during the delay interval. Thus, if subjects could see various features of the experimental chamber during the delay interval after exposure to the sample stimulus, their memory for the sample was impaired (see also Grant, 1988).

As we noted earlier, proactive interference seems to be caused by confusion between the interfering stimulus and the sample stimulus. By contrast, retroactive interference effects seem to reflect disruption of rehearsal and forgetting of the sample stimulus. One way to distinguish between these alternatives is to test the effects of similarity between the interfering stimulus and the sample stimulus. According to the confusion hypothesis, similarity between the interfering and sample stimuli should be important in determining the degree of interference because the more similar these two events are, the more likely they are to be confused. Research has confirmed the importance of stimulus similarity in studies of proactive interference (for example, Reynolds & Medin, 1981). By contrast, studies of retroactive interference have favored a forgetting interpretation (Cook, 1980; Roberts & Grant, 1978; Thompson et al., 1983). Disruptions of performance have been observed in retroactive interference studies even if the interfering stimulus could not cause confusion errors (Wright, Urcuioli, Sands, & Santiago, 1981).

Retrograde Amnesia

Severe head injury often causes loss of memory, which is technically called **amnesia**. For example, people in a car accident involving a blow to the head are likely to suffer memory loss. They are likely to forget events that took place just before the injury, but remember earlier events normally. They may forget how the injury occurred, where the accident took place, or who else was in the car at the time. However, they will continue to remember information acquired earlier, such as their name and address, where they grew up, and what they prefer for dessert.

The first extensive study of memory loss following brain injury in humans was conducted by Russell and Nathan (1946). They found that there is a temporal gradient of memory loss going back in time from the point of injury. The closer an episode is to the time of injury, the more likely the person is to forget that information. This phenomenon is called **retrograde amnesia.**

Retrograde amnesia has been extensively studied in animal laboratory experiments. The first studies of this sort used electroconvulsive shock (ECS) to induce amnesia. Electroconvulsive shock, introduced as a treatment for mental illness many years ago (Cerletti & Bini, 1938), is a brief electrical current passed through the brain between electrodes placed on each side of the head. It is not known exactly how ECS produces changes in disturbed patients. Investigators interested in memory started to study the effects of ECS because patients often reported amnesia after ECS treatment (for example, Mayer-Gross, 1943).

In the first laboratory investigation of the amnesic effects of ECS, Duncan (1949) trained rats to perform an instrumental response to avoid aversive stimulation. One conditioning trial was conducted on each of 18 days of training. All subjects except those in the control group received an electroconvulsive shock after each training trial. For independent groups of animals, the ECS was delivered at various times ranging from 20 seconds to 4 hours after the training trials. The question of interest was whether and to what extent ECS would disrupt learning of the task. The results are summarized in Figure 11.16. Subjects treated with electroconvulsive shock 1 hour or more after each training trial performed as

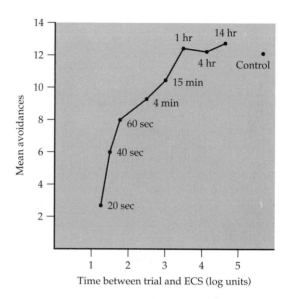

Figure 11.16 Mean number of avoidance responses for independent groups of rats given electroconvulsive shock (ECS) at various intervals after each avoidance trial. The control group was not given ECS. *(From "The Retroactive Effect of Electroshock on Learning" by C.P. Duncan, 1949,* Journal of Comparative and Physiological Psychology, 42, *pp. 32–44.)*

well on the avoidance task as the control group, which did not receive ECS. By contrast, the performance of the animals given ECS within 15 minutes of the training trials was disrupted. In fact, there was a gradient of interference: administration of ECS closer to the training trials resulted in poorer avoidance performance. This pattern of results is consistent with a retrograde-amnesia interpretation. Electroconvulsive shock is assumed to produce a gradient of amnesia such that events close to the ECS are not remembered as well as earlier events. Therefore, delivery of ECS shortly after a conditioning trial disrupts retention of that conditioning experience more than delivery of ECS that is delayed for a longer period following the trial.

Numerous studies have provided convincing evidence of experimentally induced retrograde amnesia in a wide variety of learning tasks. (For reviews, see McGaugh & Herz, 1972; Spear, 1978.) In addition, experiments have shown that retrograde amnesia can be produced by many treatments that affect the nervous system, including anesthesia (McGaugh & Petrinovich, 1965); temporary cooling of the body, or hypothermia (Riccio, Hodges, & Randall, 1968); and injection of drugs that inhibit protein synthesis (for example, Flexner, Flexner, & Stellar, 1963). Why do treatments such as these produce a graded loss of memory? One explanation of retrograde amnesia is the *memory-consolidation hypothesis* (see McGaugh & Herz, 1972). This hypothesis assumes that when an event is first experienced, it is in a short-term, or temporary, state. While in short-term memory, the information is vulnerable and can be lost because of presentation of interfering stimuli or other disruptive manipulations. However, if the proper conditions are met, the information gradually becomes consolidated into a relatively permanent form. **Memory consolidation** is assumed to be a physiological process by which information is gradually put into a long-term or permanent state. Neurophysiological disturbances such as electroconvulsive shock, anesthesia, body cooling, or inhibition of protein synthesis are assumed to interfere with the consolidation process and thereby disrupt the transfer of information to long-term memory. Disruption of consolidation produces amnesia only for information stored in short-term memory. Once information has been consolidated and transferred to long-term memory, it cannot be lost because of disruptions of consolidation. Amnesic agents presumably lead to loss of memory for recently experienced events but not earlier experiences because only the recent events are in short-term memory, and are thus susceptible to disruptions of consolidation.

Disruptions of performance caused by amnesic agents can also be explained in a very different way. According to this alternative account, amnesia results not from loss of the memory but from inability to retrieve information from the long-term storage system (Lewis, 1979; Miller & Springer, 1973; Riccio & Richardson, 1984; Spear, 1973). This explanation is called the *retrieval-failure hypothesis.* This hypothesis assumes that the amnesic agent alters the coding of new memories so as to make subsequent recovery of the information difficult. Thus, unlike the memory-consolidation view, the retrieval-failure hypothesis assumes that the information surrounding an amnesic episode is acquired and retained in memory. However, the information is retained in a form that makes it inaccessible.

What kinds of evidence would help decide between the memory-consolidation and retrieval-failure interpretations? If information is lost because of a failure of consolidation, it cannot be ever recovered. By contrast, the retrieval-failure view assumes that amnesia can be reversed if the proper procedure is found to remind subjects of the memory. Thus, to decide between the alternatives, we have to find techniques that can reverse the effects of amnesic agents. Several such procedures have been developed.

Numerous experiments have shown that memory for earlier conditioning trials can be reinstated by exposing subjects to some aspects of the stimuli that were present during the training trials. (For reviews, see Gordon, 1981; Spear, 1976, 1978.) In early investigations of this phenomenon, exposure to the reinforcer independent of behavior was often used as the reminder treatment. In one experiment, for example, memory loss produced by electroconvulsive shock was counteracted by reexposing subjects to the aversive unconditioned stimulus before the retention test (Quartermain et al., 1970). However, experiments in which the reminder episode involves the unconditioned stimulus have been criticized on the grounds that such procedures permit new learning to occur (for example, Gold, Haycock, Macri, & McGaugh, 1973; Schneider, Tyler, & Jinich, 1974). If the reminder treatment produces new learning, the improved performance of subjects given this treatment may be due to the new learning rather than the reinstatement or retrieval of an old memory.

It is always important to consider the possibility of new learning when evaluating the effects of reminder treatments. However, many aspects of research on the facilitation of memory retrieval are difficult to explain using the new-learning hypothesis. Perhaps the most convincing way to make sure that a reminder treatment does not produce new learning is to use an extinction trial to reinstate the old memory. Improved performance after an extinction trial clearly cannot be attributed to new learning that is compatible with the old memory.

Several experiments have demonstrated the facilitation of memory retrieval by an extinction trial. In one such study (Gordon & Mowrer, 1980), four groups of rats were conditioned to make a one-way avoidance response. The apparatus consisted of two compartments, one white and the other black. At the beginning of each trial, the subject was placed in the white compartment. Several seconds later the door to the black compartment was opened, simultaneously with the onset of a flashing light. If the subject crossed over to the black side within 5 seconds, it avoided shock. If it did not cross in time, the shock was presented until the rat entered the black compartment. Subjects received repeated conditioning trials until they had successfully avoided shock on three consecutive trials. Immediately after this training, two groups of rats were given electroconvulsive shock to induce amnesia.

Memory for the avoidance response was tested 72 hours after the end of training. During the retention test, subjects received five trials. These were conducted in the same manner as the conditioning trials, except now the shock was never turned on no matter how long the rats took to cross to the black side. The most important aspect of the experiment involved giving an extinction ("reminder")

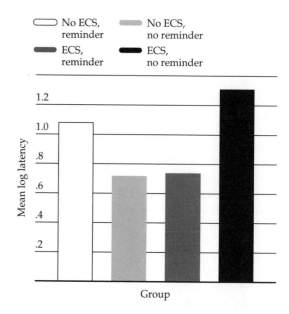

Figure 11.17 Latency of the avoidance response during a retention test for four groups of rats. Two of the groups were not given electroconvulsive shock (ECS) after training and were tested either after a reminder extinction trial or without the reminder trial. The other two groups were treated with ECS after training and were also tested either after a reminder extinction trial or without the reminder trial. *(Adapted from W.C. Gordon and R.R. Mowrer, 1980.)*

trial to some of the subjects 15 minutes before the beginning of the retention test. This reminder treatment consisted of placing the rats in the white compartment of the apparatus for 60 seconds with the flashing light turned on. No shock was delivered at the end of this stimulus exposure. Ordinarily we would expect such an extinction trial to decrease avoidance performance. The critical question was whether the extinction trial would also decrease the performance of rats made amnesic by electroconvulsive shock. If the extinction trial serves as a reminder treatment and facilitates retrieval of the memory of avoidance conditioning after ECS, it should facilitate avoidance behavior.

The results of the study are summarized in Figure 11.17. The data are presented in terms of the latency of avoidance responses during the retention test. Lower scores indicate that subjects performed the avoidance response faster. Higher scores indicate poorer performance. Let us first consider the two groups of rats that had not been given electroconvulsive shock. For these subjects, administration of the reminder extinction trial 15 minutes before the retention test resulted in slower avoidance behavior. This is the usual outcome of extinction. Let us next consider the results for subjects that had received ECS. Electroconvulsive shock in the absence of a reminder treatment (ECS, no reminder) resulted in the slowest avoidance responses. This outcome indicates that ECS produced amnesia for the prior avoidance training. However, if ECS-treated subjects were also given the extinction reminder trial before the retention test, their performance was much improved. In fact, the ECS rats given the reminder treatment responded as fast as subjects that had not received either ECS or the extinction trial. These results suggest that the reminder treatment fully restored the memory of the prior avoidance training. Thus, the amnesic effects of ECS were eliminated by exposing the subjects to the extinction trial. Since the extinction trial produced a decrement in performance in the absence of ECS, these results cannot be explained in terms of any new learning produced by the reminder treatment. (For a review of similar findings, see Riccio & Richardson, 1984.)

The fact that amnesia can be reversed by reminder treatments makes it difficult, if not impossible, to prove the memory-consolidation hypothesis. It is possible to argue that every instance of amnesia represents a failure of retrieval rather than a failure of consolidation (Miller & Springer, 1973). If one reminder treatment is found to be ineffective in reversing a particular case of amnesia, one cannot conclude that another reactivation treatment will also fail. Thus, one can never be sure that a memory is irretrievable, as is assumed by the consolidation-failure position.

Concluding Comments

The study of memory processes is central to the understanding of animal cognition. Memory processes involve acquisition and coding of information, rehearsal and retention, and retrieval. Difficulties in any of these phases or problems involving interactions among the phases can result in failures of memory, or forgetting. Several ingenious techniques for the study of memory processes in animals have been developed in the past 20 years. These techniques have told us much about the coding of information, rehearsal processes, and retrieval processes. This information has, in turn, allowed us to better understand failures of memory that occur in interference paradigms and in retrograde amnesia.

12 Complex Animal Cognition

Chapter 12 explores a diversity of contemporary research areas in animal cognition involving the processing of various types of information. We will start our discussion with time and number information, turning then to serial pattern learning, perceptual concept formation, and reasoning in nonhuman primates. In the concluding section, we will describe various language-training procedures used with chimpanzees and discuss some of the results of these language-training programs.

The various aspects of behavior we will discuss in this chapter—timing, counting, serial pattern learning, perceptual concept formation, reasoning, and language learning—have more apparent differences among them than similarities. They are not all reflections of a common underlying mechanism, nor are they all involved in the solution of a common behavioral problem or challenge to survival. However, they all involve contemporary areas of research in animal cognition that have stimulated a great deal of interest. This interest has come in part because until recently these cognitive processes were considered to be associated primarily with human behavior. The interest has also been stimulated by varying degrees of controversy that have surrounded each of these areas of research. The controversies have centered on whether complex cognitive processes had to be postulated to explain the various behaviors that were observed. Opponents of cognitive interpretations have argued that the phenomena of timing, counting, serial pattern learning, perceptual concept formation, reasoning, and language learning could be explained by traditional learning principles. By contrast, proponents of cognitive interpretations have argued that cognitive mechanisms provide simpler explanations for the phenomena and are more productive in stimulating new research. Work in animal cognition has amply borne out this latter justification. Without a cognitive perspective, much of the research we will describe in this chapter would never have been done and many of the phenomena would never have been discovered.

Timing and Counting

Interest in whether animals can tell time and count has a long history filled with entertaining anecdotes. However, only in the past 20 years has substantial progress been made toward understanding these cognitive processes in animals. (For reviews of timing, see Church, 1978; Maier & Church, 1991; Gibbon & Allan, 1984. For reviews of counting, see Davis & Pérusse, 1988; Davis & Memmott, 1982.) Meck and Church (1983) have suggested simple definitions of timing and counting. Animals are said to be timing if the duration of an event serves as a discriminative stimulus for them (a cue for responding one way rather than another). Correspondingly, animals are said to be counting if the number of events serves as a discriminative stimulus for them. (For a more precise definition of counting, see Davis & Pérusse, 1988.) Although these definitions are pretty straightforward, experimental applications of them can be difficult. A critical methodological requirement in research on both counting and timing is to make sure no other environmental events are correlated with duration (in the case of timing) or number (in the case of counting). The task for the subject has to be set up carefully to eliminate correlated stimuli that could inadvertently "tip off" the subject and permit it to respond correctly without the use of some sort of internal timing or counting process. Eliminating such correlated cues is easier to accomplish with timing than with counting. We will first describe research on timing and then describe a model that considers timing to be a variation of counting.

Techniques for the Measurement of Timing Behavior

Many aspects of animal behavior reflect sensitivity to time (Richelle & Lejeune, 1980). The study of timing is of particular interest because all of animal and human experience is embedded in a temporal context. Some things occur closely together in time; others are separated by longer intervals. In either case, the effects of stimuli are determined by their temporal distribution. We have already seen time-dependent behavioral phenomena in many of the previous chapters. Habituation, sensitization, and spontaneous recovery (Chapter 2) are all time-dependent effects. Pavlovian conditioning critically depends on the temporal relation between conditioned and unconditioned stimuli (Chapter 3), instrumental conditioning depends on the temporal relation between response and reinforcer (Chapter 5), and some schedules of reinforcement involve important temporal factors (Chapter 6). We have also encountered important time-dependent effects in our discussions of punishment (Chapter 9) and of memory (Chapter 11).

A variety of powerful techniques has been developed to investigate animal timing (for example, Chatlosh & Wasserman, 1987; Dreyfus, Fetterman, Smith, & Stubbs, 1988; Jasselette, Lejeune, & Wearden, 1990; McCarthy & Davison, 1986; Mellgren, Mays, & Haddad, 1983). Some tasks involve duration estimation. For example, rats may be presented with either a 5-second or an 8-second burst of white noise on a given trial and required to make a discriminative response based on the duration of the signal. Immediately after presentation of the short or long noise, two response levers may be inserted into the experimental chamber. If the short noise is presented, a response on the left lever will be rewarded with a pellet of food; if the long noise was presented, a response on the right lever will be rewarded. Rats can learn to perform accurately in such a task without too much difficulty (for example, Church, Getty, & Lerner, 1976; see also Wasserman, DeLong, & Larew, 1984).

Another very fruitful technique for the study of timing has involved duration production instead of duration estimation. This technique, called the **peak procedure**, involves a discrete-trial variation of a fixed-interval schedule. Each trial is defined by the presentation of a noise or light. A specified duration after the onset of the trial stimulus, a food pellet is set up, or primed. Once the food pellet has been set up, the subject can obtain it by pressing a lever. A study by Roberts (1981) nicely illustrates the technique. Rats were tested in standard lever-press chambers housed in sound-attenuating enclosures to minimize extraneous stimulation. On some trials a light stimulus was presented; on other trials, a noise was presented. In the presence of one of the trial stimuli, food was primed after 20 seconds; in the presence of the other stimulus, food was primed after 40 seconds. Most of the trials ended when the subject responded and obtained the food pellet. However, a small proportion of the trials continued for a variable duration of not less than 80 seconds and ended without food reward. These extra-long trials were included to see how the subject would behave after the usual time of reinforcement had passed.

Figure 12.1 presents the results of the experiment in terms of rates of responding at various points during a trial. The figure shows that during the 20-second signal, the highest rate of responding occurred around 20 seconds into the trial. By contrast, during the 40-second signal, the highest rate of responding occurred around 40 seconds into the trial. The incredible orderliness of the data and the correspondence of peak response rates to the times of food priming make this technique very useful in the analysis of animal timing. It should be noted, however, that these results were obtained only after extensive training. The data in Figure 12.1 were obtained during five daily 4-hour sessions after ten daily training sessions of 6 hours each. Behavior reflecting temporal discrimination developed slowly during the course of training. Early in training, animals did not show the distinctive peak responding. (For an example of more rapid adjustments to temporal variables, see Higa, Wynne, & Staddon, 1991.)

Results such as those presented in Figure 12.1 also have been obtained with human subjects (Wearden & McShane, 1988) and clearly indicate that behavior can be exquisitely tuned to the passage of time. How should such findings be conceptualized? One highly productive theoretical approach has been to

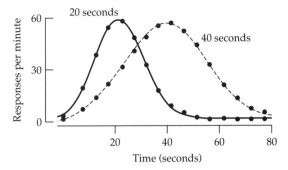

Figure 12.1 Rate of responding as a function of time during a signal in the presence of which food was primed after 20 seconds (solid line) and during a different signal in the presence of which food was primed after 40 seconds (dashed line). *(From "Isolation of an Internal Clock" by S. Roberts, 1981,* Journal of Experimental Psychology: Animal Behavior Processes, *7, pp. 242–268. Copyright © 1981 by the American Psychological Association. Reprinted by permission.)*

assume that animals (and people) use some kind of an internal clock and respond differentially based on the readings of this internal clock. Although the assumption of an internal clock may seem a bit fanciful at first glance, the suggestion is not that animals have something like a pocket watch that they can pull out and read now and then. Rather, the suggestion is that organisms have a timing mechanism localized somewhere in the nervous system that has clocklike properties.

Why should we entertain the possibility that organisms have an internal clock? The advantage of such a hypothesis is that it helps organize and stimulate research. As Church (1978) has pointed out, the concept of an internal clock may simplify explanation and discussion of instances of behavior under temporal control. Other alternatives are likely to be much more cumbersome to apply to a wide range of timing phenomena. Second, the concept of a clock is bound to stimulate questions about animal timing that we would not be likely to ask otherwise, as we will discuss shortly. Finally, an internal clock may be a physiological reality, which we are more

likely to find if we first postulate its existence and investigate its properties at a behavioral level (for example, Meck, 1988; Meck, Church, & Olton, 1984; Meck, Church, Wenk, & Olton, 1987).

Characteristics of the Internal Clock

If the concept of an internal clock is useful in explaining results in peak-response and other timing situations, we should be able to use the concept to generate interesting research questions. We may ask, for example, whether the clock can be temporarily stopped without loss of information about how much time has already elapsed. To answer this question, Roberts (1981) interrupted a 40-second time signal for 10 seconds on selected test trials (see also Roberts & Church, 1978). During intertrial intervals, the experimental chamber was dark. Each trial was marked by presentation of a light; on most trials, food was primed 40 seconds after the onset of the light. On special test trials without food reward, the light was turned off for 10 seconds starting 10 seconds after the start of the trial. Figure 12.2 shows the resulting distributions of response rates at various times during trials with and without this break. Introducing the 10-second break simply shifted the peak response rate by about 10 seconds (13.3 seconds, to be exact). These results suggest that, within a bit of error, the internal clock of rats stops timing when a break is introduced and resumes timing without resetting at the end of the break.

In other research on animal timing, results have shown that the internal clock of rats has many of the same properties as a stopwatch. Internal clocks measure how much time has elapsed (as does a stopwatch) rather than how much is left before the end of the interval (as does an oven timer). Rats seem to use the same internal clock to measure the duration of stimuli from different modalities (visual and auditory); they also use the same clock and clock speed to measure intervals of different durations (Meck & Church, 1982; Roberts,

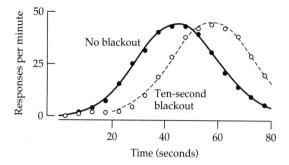

Figure 12.2 Rate of responding as a function of time during a signal in the presence of which food was primed after 40 seconds. On some trials, the signal was interrupted for a 10-second blackout period (dashed line). On other trials, no blackout occurred (solid line). *(From "Isolation of an Internal Clock" by S. Roberts, 1981,* Journal of Experimental Psychology: Animal Behavior Processes, 7, *pp. 242–268. Copyright © 1981 by the American Psychological Association. Reprinted by permission.)*

1981, 1982; Roberts & Church, 1978). (For a somewhat different pattern of results in pigeons, see Roberts, Cheng, & Cohen, 1989.)

Having documented these basic behavioral characteristics of timing, investigators have been able to begin studying what determines the speed and accuracy of the internal clock. Increases in the rate of food reinforcement appear to increase the speed of the internal clock (Fetterman & Killeen, 1991; MacEwen & Killeen, 1991). The speed of the clock is also altered by what animals eat just before a session (Meck & Church, 1987b) and by psychoactive drugs. For example, methamphetamine has been observed to increase the speed of the internal clock, whereas other drugs, such as haliperidol, have been noted to decrease clock speed (see Maricq, Roberts, & Church, 1981; Meck, 1983; Meck & Church, 1987a).

A Model of Timing

So far we have considered the notion of an internal clock somewhat loosely. What might be the details of a mechanism that permits animals (and people) to respond on the basis of temporal information? Gibbon and Church (1984) have proposed an information processing model of time estimation, which is diagramed in Figure 12.3 (see also Gibbon, Church, & Meck, 1984). The model assumes three independent processes: a clock process, a memory process, and a decision process. The clock process is activated by the start of the interval to be timed. Timing is assumed to be accomplished by having a pacemaker that generates impulses at a certain rate (something like a cardiac pacemaker). The pacemaker impulses are fed to a switch, which is turned on by the start of the interval to be timed. This allows the pacemaker impulses to go to an accumulator that counts the number that come through. When the interval to be timed ends, the switch closes, thereby blocking any further accumulations of pacemaker impulses. Thus, the accumulator accumulates information about elapsed time. This information is then fed to working memory, providing input about the current trial. The nervous system is also assumed to have information about the duration of similar stimuli in reference memory from past training. The contents of working and reference memory are compared in the decision process, and this comparison provides the basis for the animal's response. For example, in the peak-response procedure, if the time information in working memory matches the information in reference memory concerning availability of reward, the subject is encouraged to respond. If information in working and reference memory does not match closely enough, the animal is not encouraged to respond. This mechanism makes the peak rate close to the time of priming of the reward.

Spelling out the details of a hypothetical model of timing is helpful because it permits more detailed analyses of various types of error that animals may make in timing tasks (see Gibbon & Church, 1984). Such analyses permit explanations of more detailed aspects of timing behavior than would be possible otherwise. The model also suggests various

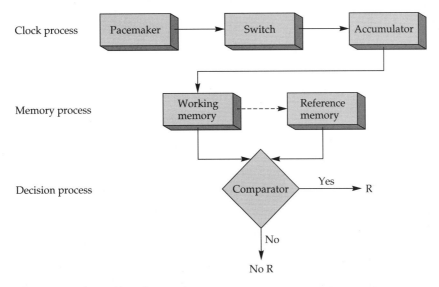

Figure 12.3 Diagram of an information processing model of timing. *(From "Sources of Variance in an Information Processing Theory of Timing" by J. Gibbon and R.M. Church, in H.L. Roitblat, T.G. Bever, & H.S. Terrace (Eds.), 1984,* Animal Cognition. *Copyright © 1984 Erlbaum. Reprinted by permission.)*

ways in which timing behavior can be altered. Evidence, for example, suggests that certain drugs alter timing behavior by changing the speed of the internal clock (altering the frequency of impulses generated by the pacemaker). By contrast, other drugs change timing behavior by altering the memory process, the remembered duration of past time intervals (Meck, 1983). These contrasting influences on timing behavior would be difficult to interpret without a model that distinguishes a clock process from a memory process.

All models of timing accept the idea of a clock process consisting of a pacemaker and an accumulator. However, some models do not assume that animals form mental representations of time and do not include the kind of memory and decision processes outlined in Figure 12.3. A prominent alternative to the Gibbon–Church model was offered by Killeen and Fetterman (1988) who characterized the timing process in more behavioral terms.

The behavioral theory of timing is built on the observation that situations in which the primary basis for deliveries of a reinforcer is the passage of time produce systematic time-related activities, called **adjunctive behaviors.** These activities are akin to the pacing or finger tapping that people engage in during periods of forced waiting. Those adjunctive behaviors that predominate early in the timed interval are known as *interim responses;* others *(terminal responses)* predominate later in the interval. You may recall that we previously described interim and terminal responses (see Chapter 5 under the heading "Reinterpretation of the superstition experiment").

In the behavioral theory of timing, a clock process is assumed to produce the adjunctive behaviors. Because different responses emerge at different intervals in a forced waiting period, these various responses can be used in a sense to tell time. Killeen and Fetterman proposed that in timing experiments animals come to use their adjunctive responses as discriminative stimuli for the experimentally required timing responses. Thus, instead of reading an internal clock, animals are assumed to "read" their adjunctive behavior to tell time. Such a behavioral theory of timing attempts to explain timing effects without the memory and decision processes assumed by the more cognitive Gibbon–Church model illustrated in Figure 12.3.

The behavioral theory of timing is a provocative proposal. So far, empirical efforts to decide between it and more cognitive models have been inconclusive (for example, Durlach & Dawson, 1991). The ultimate fate of the model will also depend on whether the kind of memory and decision processes assumed in the Gibbon–Church model turn out to be important for the understanding of adjunctive behavior.

The Relation Between Timing and Counting

The Gibbon–Church model of timing can be easily adapted for counting. Whether the system acts as a timer or a counter depends only on the operation of the switch that allows impulses to go from the pacemaker to the accumulator (see Figure 12.3). The contrasting modes of switch operation that result in timing and counting are displayed in Figure 12.4. In the timing mode, the switch stays open as long as a stimulus is on and is closed when the stimulus is turned off. With this arrangement, the number of impulses allowed to go to the accumulator provides information about how long the stimulus was on, irrespective of how many times it was turned on. In the counting mode, the switch is opened for a brief, fixed duration each time a stimulus is presented, irrespective of the duration of the stimulus. With this arrangement, the number of impulses allowed to go to the accumulator reflects the number of stimulus events—not their duration.

The preceding discussion raises the possibility that counting and timing are in many respects similar. This is an intriguing possibility that is attracting increasing research interest. The accumulating evidence suggests that the hypothesis may be correct. One way to assess similarity in timing and counting behavior is to compare the accuracy of rats in

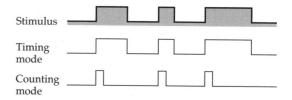

Figure 12.4 Contrasting modes of switch operation that result in timing or counting using the same pacemaker and accumulator. *(Adapted from W.H. Meck and R.M. Church, 1982.)*

making judgments about differences in time with their accuracy in making judgments about differences in number. Provided that the ratio of long to short durations is the same as the ratio of large to small numbers (8 seconds/2 seconds, compared with 8 events/2 events, for example), accuracy in time estimation is remarkably similar to accuracy in number estimation. Similarity in the mechanisms of timing and counting is also suggested by the fact that methamphetamine has very similar effects on the two types of behaviors (Meck & Church, 1983; see also Meck, Church, & Gibbon, 1985). (For other recent studies of counting in animals, see Capaldi & Miller, 1988a, 1988b; Davis & Albert, 1986; Rumbaugh, Savage-Rumbaugh, & Pate, 1988.)

Serial Pattern Learning

Time and number are ubiquitous characteristics of events in the environment. Another ubiquitous feature of the world is serial order. Stimuli rarely occur randomly and independently of each other. Rather, many aspects of the environment involve orderly sequences of stimulation. One thing leads to the next in a reliable fashion. Stimuli are arranged in orderly sequences as you walk from one end of a corridor to the other, as you work to open a package, as you eat your dinner from start to finish. Some of the major questions in contemporary studies of animal cognition have been whether animals recognize order in a series of stimuli, whether they can form a representa-

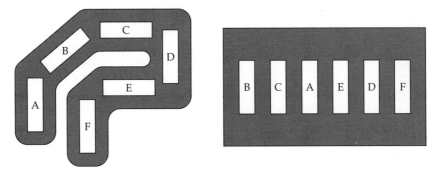

Figure 12.5 Two possible layouts of a six-hole miniature golf course: a sequential arrangement (left) and a simultaneous arrangement (right).

tion of the serial order of stimuli, and what mechanisms they use to respond correctly to a series of stimuli.

Possible Bases of Serial Pattern Behavior

There are several possible ways in which to respond to a series of stimuli. By way of analogy, consider playing through a six-hole miniature golf course, a schematic of which is shown to the left in Figure 12.5. Each hole involves a unique set of stimuli and may be represented by letters of the alphabet: A, B, C, D, E, and F. Each hole also requires a unique response—a unique way in which the ball must be hit to get it into the hole. Let's label the responses R1, R2, . . . , R6. In playing the course, you have to go in order from the first to the last hole, A → F. In addition, you have to make the correct response on each hole: R1 on hole A, R2 on B, and so on.

How might you learn to play the course successfully? The simplest way would be to learn which response goes with which stimulus. This would involve learning a set of associations: A–R1, B–R2, . . . , F–R6. If you learned such a set of associations, to play the course successfully you would simply start with A. In the presence of A, you would make R1, which would get you to B; in the presence of B, you would make R2, which would get you to C; and so on. If you learned the course

this way, you would have learned a **response chain.**

A response chain can result in responding appropriately to a series of stimuli. Interestingly, however, it does not require actually learning the stimulus sequence or forming a representation of the sequence. Response chains do not require cognitive mechanisms any more complex than the learning of a set of stimulus–response associations. The order in which the stimuli occur does not have to be learned.

A response-chain strategy works perfectly well on the usual miniature golf course, where the successive holes are laid out so that one is forced to go through them in the correct sequence, A → F. Now, let us consider a course with a different layout. The rules are the same in that you have to play in order from A to F, but this course is laid out in such a way that you are not forced to go in order. Imagine having the holes lined up next to each other in a random order on a large playing field, as shown to the right in Figure 12.5. After having played hole A, for example, your movement would not be restricted to hole B. It would be possible for you to go to any other hole. To earn points, however, you would still have to start with hole A, then play B, then C, and so forth. Learning a series of stimulus–response associations (A–R1, B–R2, and so on) would not be enough to succeed on such a course. If someone told you where to start (thus activating the A–R1 association), having played hole A would leave you at a loss as to where to go next.

What would you have to learn to respond correctly with a simultaneous stimulus array? This time, you would be forced to learn something about the order of the stimuli. You could get by with just knowing the order of successive pairs of stimuli. You could learn that A is followed by B, B is followed by C, and so forth. These would be a set of independent stimulus–stimulus associations (A–B, B–C, C–D, and so on). This type of mechanism is called **paired-associate learning.** Once you had learned the correct independent paired associates, having played hole A, you would know to go to B; having played B, you would know to go to C; and so on until you had completed the course.

Obviously, learning more than just the order of successive *pairs* of stimuli would also enable you to perform the task accurately. At the extreme, you might form a mental representation of the entire sequence: A-B-C-D-E-F. This alternative is called **serial representation learning.** A serial representation can be formed in different ways. One possibility is to string together a series of paired associates, such that A activates the representation of B, which in turn activates the representation of C, and so forth. Thus, a serial representation could consist of a chain of associations. Alternatively, you could learn that stimulus A is in position 1, B is in position 2, and so forth.

Returning to our simultaneous layout of the miniature golf course (Figure 12.5, to the right), consider being given a choice between holes C and E after having learned to respond successfully when the entire sequence, A → F, was presented. In a choice between C and E, which hole would you play first? If you had learned a representation of the entire stimulus sequence, you could respond without difficulty because you would know that C occurs before E in the sequence. Other possible mechanisms would create problems for vari-

ous reasons. For example, if you had learned some kind of a response chain in which one response led to the next, you would be in trouble because the response preceding C is not available in a choice of only C and E. You would also be in trouble if you had learned just the order of successive pairs of stimuli because C and E do not form a successive pair.

Serial Pattern Behavior with Simultaneous Stimulus Arrays

Numerous techniques have been developed to study the learning of serial representations in animals (for example, Hulse, 1978; Roitblat, Bever, Helweg, & Harley, 1991; Roitblat, Scopatz, Bever, 1987; Terrace, 1986a, 1986b). One particularly powerful technique involves testing subjects with subsets of stimuli after training with the entire sequence presented in a simultaneous array. This strategy was first employed by Straub and Terrace (1981) with pigeons in tests of learning a series of four stimulus elements, A → B → C → D (see also Terrace, 1987). The studies provided evidence that the pigeons had learned some features of the stimulus series. The birds were especially good at identifying which stimulus was first and which was last in the sequence. However, they had difficulty with the relative position of stimuli in the middle of the series. When they were tested with the interior pair of stimuli, B and C, they performed poorly.

D'Amato and Colombo (1988) adopted the simultaneous stimulus technique in a study with cebus monkeys *(Cebus apella)*. The monkeys were trained on a five-stimulus sequence, A → B → C → D → E. The stimuli were various visual patterns (dots, circles, and the like), which could be projected on any of five square panels. Which pattern appeared on which panel varied from one trial to the next, and all five stimuli were presented at the same time. The monkeys' task was to press the panels in a prescribed order, A → B → C → D → E. (Training started with just stimulus A. After the subjects had learned to press A, B was

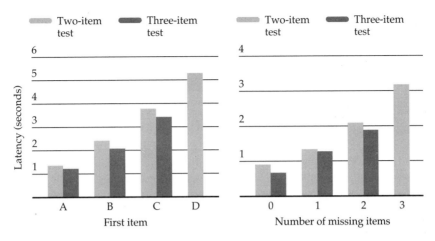

Figure 12.6 Latency of correct responses during tests of two- and three-item subsets of a five-item list with cebus monkeys. *Left:* Latency of responding to the first item of the subset as a function of the position of that item. *Right:* Latency of responding to the second item of the subset as a function of the number of items missing between the first and second item. *(From "Representation of Serial Order in Monkeys (Cebus apella)" by M.R. D'Amato and M. Colombo, 1988,* Journal of Experimental Psychology: Animal Behavior Processes, 14, *pp. 131–139. Copyright © 1988 by the American Psychological Association. Reprinted by permission.)*

added. After the subjects had learned the A → B sequence, C was added, and so forth.) After having learned the entire five-item sequence, the monkeys were tested with pairs and triples of the stimuli. They performed with above-chance accuracy on all these subsets—even subsets that included only stimuli in the middle of the series, BC, CD, and BCD. This indicates that the monkeys had learned quite a bit about the prescribed order of the stimuli.

D'Amato and Colombo also measured the latencies of the correct responses during the tests with subsets of the five-element series. These results are shown in Figure 12.6. The left-hand graph shows the latency of responding to the first item of subsets of stimuli. Some of these subsets started with A (as in the subset AC, for example); some started with B (as in the subset BC or BD); some started with C (as in CD); and one started with D (DE). When the first item of the subset was A, the subjects responded rapidly. When the first item was B, responding was slower. Responding was slower still when the first item was C or D.

Loosely speaking, these latencies suggest that at the start of a trial the monkeys started to walk through the sequence mentally. When they came to one of the stimuli presented on that trial, they responded to that stimulus. Since they encountered A first in this mental scan of the series, they responded to A quickest. Longer latencies occurred with items that came up later in their mental scan of the series. Such mental scanning would have been possible only if the subjects had formed a mental representation of the entire stimulus sequence. Thus, the latency data provide evidence of this mental representation.

Additional evidence for mental scanning of the stimulus sequence was provided by the latency of responding to the second item in the subset tests. Some of the subsets involved adjacent items in the list, such as subset BC. Others involved one missing item, such as subset BD or CE. Still others involved two missing items (BE) or three missing items (AE). If the subjects were walking through the list mentally as they performed the subset tests, how long they took to respond between the first and second item would be a function of the number of missing items. With more missing items between stimuli in a subset, the subject would take longer to respond to the second item. This is exactly what occurred (see Figure 12.6, right). These results provide additional evidence that the monkeys had formed a mental representation of the stimulus sequence. (For additional studies of the nature of that mental representation, see D'Amato and Colombo, 1989, 1990.)

Effects of the Structure of Serial Patterns

In the 1988 study by D'Amato and Colombo, evidence of serial pattern learning was obtained by looking at the accuracy of performance on subsets of stimuli and measuring the latency of responses. The structure or pattern of the list of items was not altered. All the monkeys were trained on the same type of A → B → C → D → E stimulus sequence. Another powerful approach to the study of whether animals form representations of a series of stimuli has involved seeing whether they recognize the pattern of the stimuli. Recognition of a pattern requires knowledge of the stimulus sequence, and hence is not likely to result from mechanisms that do not involve some form of representation of the serial order of the stimuli.

Behavior in response to serial patterns of stimuli has been extensively investigated in humans (for example, Jones, 1974; Restle & Brown, 1970; Simon & Kotovsky, 1963). Consider, for example, what you would do if you were asked to memorize the following list of numbers: 1234234534564567. You could learn the numbers by memorizing which number was in each of the 16 positions of the list. If you knew that 1 was in the first position, 2 in the second and fifth positions, 3 in the third, sixth, and ninth positions, and so on, you could recall the numbers in the correct order. However, this would be the hard way. A much simpler strategy would be to look for a pattern to the numbers. If you could figure out the pattern, you would have a rule that you could use to generate the sequence of numbers. The numbers used in our example were generated by a relatively simple rule, which might be stated as follows: Start counting with the number 1, but every four numbers subtract 2. Memorizing this rule is much easier than learning what number is located in each of the 16 positions of the list.

Abstracting a rule from a sequence of stimuli involves responding to the pattern of the stimuli. It is clear that humans respond on the basis of the patterns inherent in the stimuli they experience. Starting with the work of Hulse (1978), a great deal of evidence has been accumulated indicating that nonhuman animals, too, can respond on the basis of patterns of serially presented stimuli. Some of this evidence has been obtained from experiments designed to see if subjects can detect internal consistencies in a series of stimuli. Generally, recognizing internal consistencies in a series makes the series easier to learn. For example, the series of numbers 214325436547 is fairly difficult to learn because in this form the internal consistencies in the series are difficult to decipher. However, if the numbers are rewritten as 214 325 436 547, the list becomes a lot easier to learn. In this form, the internal structure of the series is more obvious. The series is made of four smaller units, each of which has the same internal structure (the second number in each subset is the first number minus 1 and the third number is the first number plus 2). Subdividing a series of items into subsets, each with its own internal structure, is called **chunking.**

In order to divide a list into smaller chunks, one must first recognize a pattern in the original list. Therefore, evidence that animals divide a list into chunks would constitute evidence of serial pattern learning. Chunking in animal learning has been observed using a variety of procedures with both rat and pigeon subjects (for example, Capaldi, in press; Capaldi, Nawrocki, Miller, & Verry, 1986; Capaldi, Miller, Alptekin, & Barry, 1990;

Dallal & Meck, 1990; Fountain, 1990; Fountain, Henne, & Hulse, 1984). In an extensive series of experiments, Terrace (1991a, 1991b, 1991c) investigated chunking in serial pattern learning in pigeons using a simultaneous stimulus array. We will now describe a part of one of these experiments (Terrace, 1991a, Experiment 1).

Terrace's pigeons faced a stimulus panel on which five stimuli were projected at the beginning of each trial. The stimuli could occur in any of eight different positions, and positions were varied between trials. Three of the stimuli were colors (red, green, and blue) and two were shapes (a horizontal line and a diamond). The pigeons had to peck the stimuli in a particular order for food reinforcement, which was delivered when they completed the series. In these respects, the experiment was similar to the study we previously described with cebus monkeys (D'Amato & Colombo, 1988). Unlike D'Amato and Colombo, however, Terrace varied the nature of the series the subjects had to learn.

For one group of pigeons, the three color stimuli and the two shapes were segregated in the series. The birds had to learn to go through the series of stimuli by first pecking the three colors and then the two shapes. The segregated series may be symbolized as $A \rightarrow B \rightarrow C \rightarrow D' \rightarrow E'$, where the primed letters designate the shapes and the nonprimed letters designate the color stimuli. A second group of pigeons had to learn to go through the series in a different way. For them, the shape stimuli were mixed in with the color stimuli. They had to learn the sequence $A \rightarrow B' \rightarrow C \rightarrow D' \rightarrow E$. In this sequence, the shapes appeared as the second and fourth items rather than as the fourth and fifth items.

The segregated sequence $A \rightarrow B \rightarrow C \rightarrow D' \rightarrow E'$ can be easily subdivided into two subsets or chunks. One chunk would consist of the three color stimuli, $A \rightarrow B \rightarrow C$; the other chunk would consist of the two shapes $D' \rightarrow E'$. By contrast, the mixed sequence $A \rightarrow B' \rightarrow C \rightarrow D' \rightarrow E$ does not have such

internal structure and cannot be so obviously divided into subsets. As we noted earlier, chunking a series makes it easier to learn. Therefore, if the pigeons had chunked the lists, we would expect that the segregated list would have been learned faster than the mixed list. This was indeed what happened. The birds took an average of 59 sessions to learn to respond correctly on the segregated list. They took more than twice as long (an average of 140 sessions) to learn the mixed list. They also differed in how they went through the lists once they had learned each type.

As we discussed in connection with the experiment by D'Amato and Colombo, the time it takes to respond can provide interesting insights into cognitive processes. Terrace also found this to be true. "Thinking" in the monkeys was evident in their latency to respond (see Figure 12.6). For the pigeons, "thinking" seemed to be better reflected in repeated responding to a particular stimulus. D'Amato and Colombo's monkeys hardly ever made repeat responses. By contrast, the pigeons sometimes perseverated (or dwelled) on a stimulus before moving on to the next one in the sequence. (As with taking extra time in playing a hole of golf, there was no penalty for this, provided the subject selected the next stimulus correctly.) How long the subject stayed with a particular stimulus is called the *dwell time*.

Figure 12.7 indicates the dwell times of the pigeons on each stimulus as a function of the position of that stimulus in the five-element sequence. (The first response to the fifth stimulus ended the trial; therefore, there is no data for dwelling on the fifth stimulus.) Pigeons that received the mixed order of stimuli ($A \rightarrow B' \rightarrow C \rightarrow D' \rightarrow E$) dwelled longest on stimulus A and picked up the pace as they went through the sequence. Importantly, they did not dwell on any of the interior elements of the series any longer than they took with stimulus A. For pigeons trained on the segregated pattern ($A \rightarrow B \rightarrow C \rightarrow D' \rightarrow E'$), the results were dramatically

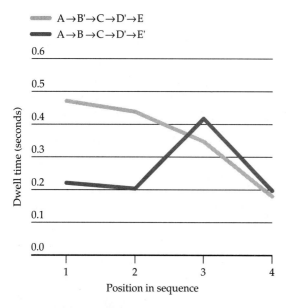

Figure 12.7 The dwell time of pigeons on each of the first four stimuli of a five-element series. One group was trained on a segregated series of stimuli ($A \rightarrow B \rightarrow C \rightarrow D' \rightarrow E'$). Another group was trained on a mixed series of stimuli ($A \rightarrow B' \rightarrow C \rightarrow D' \rightarrow E$). *(From "Chunking During Serial Learning by a Pigeon: I. Basic Evidence" by H.S. Terrace, 1991,* Journal of Experimental Psychology: Animal Behavior Processes, 17, *pp. 81–93. Copyright © 1991 by the American Psychological Association. Reprinted by permission.)*

different. These pigeons got off to a fast start, not dwelling very much on stimuli A and B, perhaps because the segregated series was easier to learn than the mixed series. However, they seemed to get stuck on stimulus C. The birds dwelled on stimulus C much longer than on the preceding or following stimuli. Stimulus C was the last of the color stimuli before the two shape cues. It was as if the pigeons had to take a bit of extra time thinking about what to do next as they moved from the color stimuli to the shape cues. This kind of increased dwell time at stimulus C is exactly what could be expected if the pigeons had chunked the series into two subsets. Increased processing time is expected to occur at boundaries of chunks. Therefore, the dwell time data

provide additional evidence that the pigeons were sensitive to the internal structure of the series of stimuli.

Perceptual Concept Learning

Organisms experience a great variety of stimuli during their lifetime. However, as we have seen, they often do not respond to these stimuli as independent and isolated events. We discussed one type of cognitive organization in the preceding section—responding to a series of stimuli on the basis of the structural pattern of the series. An even more basic form of cognitive organization of responses to stimuli involves perceptual concept learning. Consider, for example, seeing a chair. You may note some of its specific features: its color, shape, height, and firmness. You would also immediately identify it as a "chair." We can all agree on which things are chairs and which things are not chairs. "Chair" is an example of a **perceptual concept.**

Much of our interaction with the world is governed by perceptual concepts. We have perceptual concepts of physical objects, such as chairs, houses, trees, water, cats, and cars. We also have perceptual concepts of events, such as rain and wind or day and night. Perceptual concepts are important because they help us organize or categorize the wide variety of stimuli that we encounter during the course of normal experience. In the rough and tumble of the real world, nothing occurs exactly the same way twice. Even the same tree viewed from the same vantage point would appear slightly different to you each time you looked at it. The sun would be shining on it from a different angle, clouds would be casting a different pattern of shadows as the breeze moved the leaves, and so on. Perceptual concepts provide one means of navigating through the maze of ever-changing stimuli we encounter. Through perceptual concepts, certain variations among stimuli are ignored. You recognize your cat as the same animal, even though strictly speaking its image is different every time you see it. You also recognize various objects as chairs, even though they may differ in color, shape, and size. By contrast, other differences are emphasized. You distinguish between your cat and your neighbor's cat, or between your cat and your parakeet. You also distinguish between things that are called chairs and things that are called tables. Thus, perceptual concepts involve *generalization within a category* or set of stimuli *and discrimination between categories* or sets of stimuli.

A great deal of research has been done on the learning of perceptual concepts since the early work of Herrnstein and Loveland (1964) nearly 30 years ago (for example, Cerella, 1982; Commons, Herrnstein, Kosslyn, & Mumford, 1990; Herrnstein, 1984; Lea, 1984). In the tradition of Herrnstein and Loveland, much of the research has been done with pigeons responding to complex visual stimuli. A variety of visual concepts has been conditioned. Pigeons have learned to respond to the presence or absence of water in various forms (lakes, oceans, puddles, and so on) and to the presence or absence of a particular person (in various types of clothing, in various situations, and engaged in various activities) (Herrnstein, Loveland, & Cable, 1976). In other studies, pigeons have been conditioned to respond to the presence or absence of fish in underwater photographs (Herrnstein & deVilliers, 1980), to the presence of the letter *A* as opposed to other letters of the alphabet in various fonts (Morgan, Fitch, Holman, & Lea, 1976), and to various views of a particular location on campus (Honig & Stewart, 1988; Wilkie, Willson, & Kardal, 1989). Studies have also demonstrated perceptual concept learning in other modalities and species (for example, D'Amato & Van Sant, 1988; Kluender, Diehl, & Killeen, 1987; Roberts & Mazmanian, 1988; Schrier & Brady, 1987). In all of these cases, subjects learned to respond to stimuli belong-

ing to the category in question even though members of the category differed in numerous respects.

In one study with pigeons (Herrnstein et al., 1976), for example, color slides of various scenes were projected on one wall of the experimental chamber near a response key. If the scene included a tree or some part of a tree, the pigeons were reinforced with food for pecking the response key. If the picture did not include a tree or any part of one, pecking was not reinforced. Each experimental session consisted of 80 slide presentations, about 40 of which included a tree. During training, the stimuli for any given day were randomly selected from 500–700 pictures depicting various scenes from all four seasons of the year in New England. The same photographs were used more than once only occasionally. The reinforced stimuli included trees (or parts of trees) of all descriptions. However, the trees were not necessarily the main point of interest in the pictures. Some slides showed a tree far in the distance, others showed trees that were partly obstructed so that only some of the branches were visible, for example.

Generalization to Novel Exemplars

The pigeons tested by Herrnstein and his associates (1976) learned the requirements of the task without much difficulty. Soon they were pecking at a much higher rate in the presence of pictures that included a tree than in the presence of pictures without trees. What might have been responsible for the accuracy of their performance? One possibility is that the pigeons memorized what the reinforced and nonreinforced pictures looked like without paying particular attention to the presence or absence of trees. This is a distinct possibility. Pigeons have been found to be able to memorize several hundred pictures (Vaughan & Greene, 1984).

Herrnstein and his associates (1976) attempted to rule out picture memorization by

Figure 12.8 Photos illustrating the concept "person." A positive exemplar is shown on the right; a negative exemplar is shown on the left. *(Courtesy of Gail Meese, Meese Photo Research.)*

testing the subjects with a new set of pictures at the end of training. The pigeons performed nearly as accurately on the new pictures as on those used during training. Much higher rates of pecking occurred in the presence of new slides that included a tree (or part of one) than in the presence of new slides without trees. Such evidence of generalization to novel exemplars is most often used to support a concept-learning interpretation. However, several other interesting approaches also have been used.

Concept Training and Pseudoconcept Training Compared

All perceptual concept experiments involve presenting a series of stimuli, some of which exemplify the concept under investigation and some of which do not. Edwards and Honig (1987), for example, investigated the

learning of the concept "person" with a series of photographic slides. Half the slides depicted one or more people in various places. The remaining slides depicted the same scenes, but without the people (see Fig. 12.8). One group of pigeons (the concept group) was reinforced for pecking whenever a slide that included a person appeared and was not reinforced on trials that showed only the backgrounds. The pigeons quickly learned to respond more on trials depicting people than on trials without people.

Edwards and Honig were concerned with the possibility of picture memorization, just as Herrnstein, Loveland, and Cable had been in their (1976) experiment on concept learning. Edwards and Honig's birds might have simply memorized which slides were reinforced and which were not without categorizing the slides in terms of the presence or absence of a person. Here, too, this was a distinct possibil-

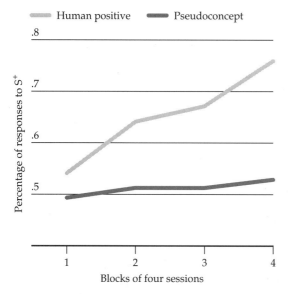

Human positive   Pseudoconcept

Figure 12.9 Percentage of total responses that were made to reinforced stimuli consisting of slide pictures. For the concept group, all reinforced stimuli included a person and nonreinforced stimuli showed only the backgrounds. For the pseudoconcept group, reinforced and nonreinforced stimuli consisted of mixtures of person and background-only slides. *(From "Memorization and 'Feature Selection' in the Acquisition of Natural Concepts in Pigeons" by C.A. Edwards and W.K. Honig, 1987,* Learning and Motivation, *18, pp. 235–260. Copyright © 1987 by Academic Press. Reprinted by permission.)*

ity because the experiment included only 40 slides with people and 40 without. If the pigeons had treated the slides as a series of arbitrary pictures, it should not have mattered which were in the reinforced set and which were in the nonreinforced set. To see if this was the case, Edwards and Honig trained another group of pigeons with the same 80 slides, but this time the slides were assigned to the reinforced and nonreinforced sets at random. This second group of pigeons was called the pseudoconcept group.

How the two groups of pigeons learned to discriminate between the reinforced and non-reinforced sets of pictures is summarized in Figure 12.9. The response measure presented is the percentage of all responses made that

occurred on reinforced trials. During the first block of trials, the subjects responded about equally to the reinforced and nonreinforced stimuli, making about 50% of their responses to the reinforced stimuli. As training progressed the concept group learned the discrimination, so that by the fourth block of trials 75% of its responses were made to the reinforced stimuli. By contrast, the pseudo-concept group continued to respond about equally to the reinforced and nonreinforced slides. It was evident, then, that the pigeons found it much easier to learn to distinguish the two sets of slides if one set included all the pictures with people and the other set included all the slides of only the backgrounds. If the people and background-only slides were intermixed as reinforced and nonreinforced slides, the birds did not learn the discrimination. This finding indicates that the subjects in the concept group were not treating the pictures as an arbitrary collection of reinforced and nonreinforced stimuli. Rather, they seemed to recognize that pictures with people had something in common.

Discrimination Between Perceptual Categories

In the studies of perceptual concept learning described so far, subjects had to discriminate between stimuli that contained an exemplar of the concept from stimuli that did not— pictures of a person versus pictures of just the background, for example. However, there was no unifying concept to the nonreinforced stimuli. The experiments demonstrated generalization within a category, but not discrimination between categories, which is a companion criterion for a perceptual concept.

How a concept discrimination is learned depends not only on the reinforced category but also on the nonreinforced stimuli. Roberts and Mazmanian (1988), for example, found that both pigeons and monkeys had difficulty learning to discriminate pictures of birds from pictures of other types of animals. However, the subjects could discriminate pictures of

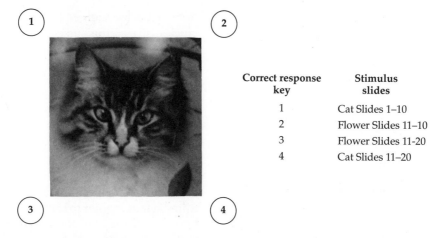

Correct response key	Stimulus slides
1	Cat Slides 1–10
2	Flower Slides 11–10
3	Flower Slides 11-20
4	Cat Slides 11–20

Figure 12.10 Outline of the experimental situation employed by Wasserman, Kiedinger, and Bhatt (1988). Slides were projected on a square screen that had a response key near each corner. Each response key was associated with a different set of 10 slides. One set of assignments is indicated. *(Photo courtesy of Merlin.)*

birds from pictures not containing animals. Other aspects of their study demonstrated that the failure to discriminate birds from other animals was not due to a general inability to distinguish between two categories. Rather, the difficulty was related to the level of abstractness of the concepts. The pigeons and monkeys easily learned to discriminate various views of a particular bird, the common kingfisher, from pictures of other types of birds. In other studies pigeons have been shown to be able to discriminate among four concrete perceptual categories simultaneously: cat, person, flower, and car or chair (Bhatt, Wasserman, Reynolds, & Knauss, 1988).

Development of Conceptual Errors

Training several concept discriminations at the same time provides an opportunity for direct observation of the development of generalization within categories and discrimination between them. As subjects learn to group together items in a perceptual category, they become more likely to generalize among those items and confuse them. This leads to

the counterintuitive outcome that perceptual concept learning can lead to an increase in confusion errors between members of the category. This effect can be observed if subjects are given a task that requires discriminating subsets of items within a category. We will now describe a study of this type.

Wasserman, Kiedinger, and Bhatt (1988) taught pigeons a discrimination involving two perceptual categories, cats and flowers, for example. Slides depicting cats and flowers of various sorts were projected onto a square viewing screen in the experimental chamber. Each corner of the viewing screen had a pecking key, as shown in Figure 12.10. There were 20 different slides of cats and 20 different slides of flowers. Each of these sets of 20 slides was arbitrarily divided into two subsets of 10 each, and each subset of 10 slides was assigned to one of the four response keys. One pattern of these assignments is shown in Figure 12.10. Here, responses on key 1 were reinforced whenever one of the cat slides 1–10 appeared, responses on key 4 were reinforced with cat slides 11–20, responses on key 2 were reinforced with flower slides 1–10, and responses on key 3 were reinforced with flower slides

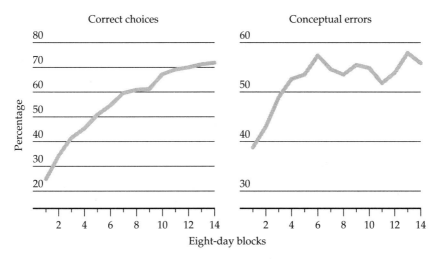

Figure 12.11   Rate of correct responses (left) and rate of conceptual errors (right) in the concept-discrimination experiment by Wasserman, Kiedinger, and Bhatt (1988). *(From "Conceptual Behavior in Pigeons: Categories, Subcategories, and Pseudocategories" by E.A. Wasserman, R.E. Kiedinger, and R.S. Bhatt, 1988,* Journal of Experimental Psychology: Animal Behavior Processes, 14, *pp. 235–246. Copyright © 1988 by the American Psychological Association. Reprinted by permission.)*

11–20. (Different pigeons were trained with the other possible response assignments.)

The pigeons in this task had to learn which of the four responses to make with each slide. Consider a trial in which cat slide 3 was presented. On this trial, response key 1 was correct, and keys 2, 3, and 4 were incorrect. Keys 2 and 3 were incorrect because they were associated with flower stimuli, and key 4 was incorrect because it was associated with a different set of cat slides. If the pigeons were unsure of the correct response to cat slide 3, what kinds of errors would they have made? If they had treated the slides as an arbitrary and independent collection of pictures, they would have distributed their errors equally among the three incorrect choices. They would have been just as likely to confuse cat slide 3 with other cat and flower slides they remembered. By contrast, if the pigeons were learning to group cat slides together as different from flower slides, they would have been more likely to confuse cat slide 3 with other cat slides than with flower slides. In that case, they would have been more likely to err by

pecking the wrong cat response key (key 4) than by pecking one of the flower response keys (keys 2 and 3). Such errors are called **conceptual errors** because they reflect confusions within a perceptual concept category.

The results of the experiment are presented in Figure 12.11. The left-hand graph shows that as training progressed, the pigeons made progressively more correct responses. A correct response in this task can be made by chance 25% of the time. By the end of training, the pigeons were selecting the correct response key over 70% of the time. Another way to think about the increase in accuracy with training is that the overall rate of errors declined. That is what we expect to happen in learning experiments. Interestingly, however, when the nature of the errors was analyzed more closely, it was found that the rate of conceptual errors increased with increased training. These data are presented in the right-hand graph. Although the number of mistakes decreased overall, the mistakes that remained tended to be conceptual errors. Of the three possible incorrect responses on each trial, one was a conceptual error and the other two were not (see the preceding description). Therefore, the rate of a conceptual error by chance was 33%. Figure 12.11 shows that the rate of conceptual errors started under 40% (near chance) and increased to about 55%. Furthermore, once the error rate had reached about 55%, it remained there for the remainder of the experiment (72 sessions). Further training was entirely ineffective in reducing the error rate.

Mechanisms of Perceptual Concept Learning

Evidence of generalization to novel exemplars, better learning of concept discriminations than pseudoconcept discriminations, and the development of conceptual errors with training provide diverse but converging evidence of perceptual concept learning in animals. Such evidence demonstrates that animals group stimuli into perceptual categories and generalize within those categories; however, it does not tell us how such perceptual categorization is accomplished. Although the various types of evidence of perceptual concepts suggest that members of a perceptual category are similar to each other in some way, what makes them similar, or in what sense they are similar, remains a puzzle. In animal research, investigators have focused on **feature analysis.** (Additional factors are involved with humans, whose concept learning involves experiences that are more complex than just having one stimulus set associated with food and another associated with no food [see Medin, 1989].)

The feature-analysis approach assumes that members of a perceptual category have certain stimulus features in common—features to which the instrumental response becomes conditioned. Investigators of perceptual concept formation have argued against a simple feature-analysis explanation because a feature common to all positive instances of natural perceptual concepts is often impossible to identify. In Herrnstein, Loveland, and Cable's

(1976) tree-concept experiment, for example, many of the trees shown had green coloration and were leafy, vertical, woody, and branching. However, the pigeons also responded to pictures of trees that did not have these characteristics. In addition, they failed to respond to pictures that did not have a tree but that did have some green, leafy, vertical, woody, and branching components. Thus, it is difficult to abstract a critical feature or combination of features. Similar difficulties are encountered with any natural perceptual category, such as a "chair," "person," "flower," or "cat." Possible variations in members of natural categories seem to extend beyond any efforts to identify critical stimulus features that could serve as membership criteria. Nevertheless, investigators have not abandoned the idea that common stimulus features might contribute to conceptual behavior. Empirical efforts to test a feature-analytic approach have been hampered by the richness and complexity of the kinds of photographs that are typically employed in studies of perceptual concept learning. A feature-analytic approach has been more successful with artificial stimuli, such as the letter *A* appearing in various fonts (Lea & Ryan, 1983). However, hints of the importance of stimulus features also have been seen in studies with photographs of real-world scenes.

In a study of the concept "human being" in rhesus monkeys, Schrier and Brady (1987) observed that accuracy of identifying slides of humans was related to how much of the slide consisted of images of people. The monkeys responded correctly 93% of the time to slides in which the people took up more than 50% of the picture. By contrast, they responded correctly only 66% of the time to slides in which the people constituted 25% or less of the picture. Evidently, the greater salience of people-related stimulus features in a slide made that slide easier to identify as belonging to the category "human."

D'Amato and Van Sant (1988) conducted a similar study of concept learning in cebus monkeys. The subjects showed significant transfer to new slides of people. However, they did very poorly when shown a black-and-white close-up view of a person's head and shoulders. The training slides had all been in color and none contained such a close-up view. D'Amato and Van Sant also observed an unusually large number of errors to a test stimulus that showed a piece of red watermelon but no people. As it turned out, about one-third of their training slides with people had included patches of red, usually in pieces of clothing. Apparently, the monkeys had learned to classify the stimuli in part on the basis of these red patches. Further analyses confirmed this hypothesis. The subjects were more likely to respond to nonperson slides that had some red in them than to nonperson slides without red. However, having some red in the slide was not the only relevant factor. Animal-like features were also important. The monkeys were most likely to respond to nonperson slides with red if the red was a part of an animal. Less responding occurred if the red was part of a flower, and even less occurred if the red was a part of an inanimate object.

As is illustrated by D'Amato and Van Sant's findings, the complexity and variability of stimuli in natural categories makes it unlikely that perceptual categorization is achieved on the basis of one or even a couple of stimulus features. The best working hypothesis is that perceptual categories are based on **polymorphic rules** (for example, Herrnstein, 1984; Lea & Harrison, 1978; von Fersen & Lea, 1990). According to a polymorphic rule, no one stimulus feature is necessary or sufficient for membership in a perceptual category. A variety of features are considered to be important, but no one feature alone or in combination with other features is critical for identifying an instance of a perceptual category. Rather, category membership is based on having a sufficient number of the relevant features. Thus, being woody, leafy, and vertical may all be important features of trees. Trees have a

certain number of treelike features, but none of these features by itself is necessary or sufficient to call something a tree.

Explanation of perceptual concepts as resulting from the application of polymorphic rules has retained feature analysis as an important aspect of concept learning. A related issue is thus raised: What makes something a feature of an object or an event? Are features inherent elemental properties of objects or are they "creations" of the perceiving organism? These questions are similar to the central issue of stimulus control we addressed in Chapter 8: What makes certain aspects of the environment gain control over instrumental behavior? Features arise from the way an animal sees an object or event. They are determined in part by perceptual predispositions and by contingencies of reinforcement. If responding to all four-legged creatures is reinforced and responding to all other creatures is not reinforced, a very broad concept is acquired. By contrast, reinforcement of responding to examples of collies but not to examples of German shepherds would lead to the acquisition of a more restricted concept. In a sense, then, concept discrimination procedures shape the formation of a perceptual concept by reinforcing some stimuli and not others.

Inferential and Analogical Reasoning

The present section on inferential and analogical reasoning and the section on language learning that follows discuss aspects of behavior that until recently have been considered to reflect uniquely human intellectual abilities. Both these aspects of intellectual functioning have been studied in chimpanzees. Research on language learning in chimpanzees has come up against much more controversy than research on inferential and analogical reasoning. However, both areas of research are fascinating and provide empirical evidence relevant to age-old beliefs about the special role of human beings in the animal kingdom.

Transitive Inferential Reasoning

In our discussion of serial pattern learning earlier in the chapter, we discussed how animals learn about the serial order of stimuli. In those experiments, subjects were trained directly to respond to a stimulus array in a particular order. In the present section, we will consider a related question: Can animals infer the order of a series of stimuli from experiences with only segments of the series? The ability to make such an inference can be an adaptive skill. Consider, for example, a social group of three monkeys, A, B, and C. Assume that monkeys A and B got into a fight, with the result that A defeated B. Monkeys B and C also got into a fight, and B defeated C. Should C, knowing the outcomes of these two fights, pick a fight with A? Since C has never fought A, on the basis of its direct experiences C would have no way of predicting the outcome. However, the knowledge that A can defeat B and that B can defeat C suggests that A would defeat C. Such reasoning involves making a transitive inference.

Transitive inference consists of inferring a serial order among stimuli based on experience with just adjacent pairs of stimuli. Evidence for such inferential reasoning can be obtained by asking subjects to judge the order of novel pairs of stimuli. In the preceding example, this logic formed the basis for trying to predict the outcome of a fight between monkeys A and C based on previous fights between monkeys A and B and monkeys B and C.

Transitive inference has been demonstrated in both pigeons and chimpanzees (Gillan, 1981, 1983; von Fersen, Wynne, Delius, & Staddon, 1991). Gillan (1981, 1983), for example, tested transitive inferential reasoning in three 5–6-year-old female chimpanzees, Jessie, Luvie, and Sadie. Although the subjects had been previously used in other

tests of animal cognition, they had not been taught a language system. Five food containers with different-colored lids (red, blue, orange, black, or white) were used in the experiment. The experimenter arranged the five containers, designated by letters A through E, in a serial order, A < B < C < D < E. However, on a given trial, only two adjacent pairs of containers were presented at a time: A < B, B < C, C < D, or D < E. Each time, the chimpanzees had to choose the container that was "greater than" its comparison in the monotonic series. Thus, B was correct in the choice A versus B, but B was incorrect in the choice between B and C. The correct choice was reinforced by a favored piece of food (candy, crackers, or pretzels) that had been placed in the correct container for that trial.

Training continued for about 2 months with 12–24 trials per session. Sadie performed most accurately at the end of training, responding correctly on 89% of the adjacent choices. Luvie's and Jessie's accuracy scores were only 72% and 69%, respectively. The critical test phase of the experiment involved presenting the chimpanzees with a choice between two stimuli they had not encountered together during training—B versus D. If training with adjacent pairs of stimuli had enabled the chimpanzees to infer the entire monotonic series, then they would have chosen D as being "greater than" B. Because this inference requires knowledge of the order of adjacent pairs of stimuli, performance on the choice of B versus D should be related to accuracy in responding to adjacent choices. The results generally supported these predictions. Sadie, who had been most accurate in choices between adjacent stimuli, correctly chose D over B on 12 out of 12 test trials. Luvie and Jessie performed less well, selecting D on only 5 and 7 out of 12 test trials, respectively.

After the first test session, Luvie was given additional training with adjacent stimulus pairs and then again tested on B versus D. This time her accuracy on the adjacent stimulus pairs improved to 88%; she correctly chose D over B on 10 out of 12 test trials. Thus, she also showed generalization of correct choice behavior to a nonadjacent stimulus pair.

The choice of stimulus D over B by Sadie and Luvie during the test sessions is difficult to explain without postulating some type of inferential reasoning (however, see von Fersen et al., 1991). Sadie and Luvie had not encountered a choice between D and B during training and therefore had not been conditioned to make a particular response in the presence of this combination of stimuli. In addition, stimuli B and D were equally often paired with reinforcement during training because each stimulus appeared both as the correct choice on some training trials (A versus B; C versus D) and as the incorrect choice on other trials (B versus C; D versus E). Therefore, the frequency of reinforcement (or nonreinforcement) of choices of B and D cannot explain the choice between them during testing.

In the study, choice between nonadjacent stimuli during testing (B versus D) was assumed to reflect the fact that the training sequence formed a linear sequence A → E. Sadie and Luvie presumably had inferred this sequence somehow. If this, indeed, was true, then the choice between nonadjacent stimuli during testing should have been disrupted by disrupting the linear order of the training stimuli. Gillan tested this prediction with additional training of Sadie. During the additional training, Sadie continued to receive trials of A < B, B < C, C < D, and D < E. Another element, F, was added to these comparisons, and subjects received trials in which F was reinforced in a choice with E (E < F). Thus, stimuli A through F were arranged in a linear order, A < B < C < D < E < F, and Sadie was reinforced for always choosing the "greater" stimulus in each pair of training stimuli. Sadie also received training with the pair of stimuli A versus F; given this pair, A was reinforced. Reinforcement of A in a choice between A and

F makes it impossible to infer a linear order among the stimuli. It is impossible to arrange stimuli A → F in a linear series given stimulus pairs A < B, B < C, C < D, D < E, E < F, and F < A.

Sadie took a long time to learn to make the correct choice with the new pairs of stimuli. In particular, she made a lot of mistakes on A versus F, selecting F instead of A. But finally she did reach 90% accuracy and was tested with novel nonadjacent stimulus pairs B versus D, B versus E, and C versus E. It is important to note that, during training, these stimuli (B through E) had occurred in pairs that could be arranged in a linear order (B < C < D < E). Only stimuli A and F were involved in a training pair that destroyed the linear sequence. Nevertheless, choices on nonadjacent stimuli B through E were severely disrupted. Disruption of the linear order by manipulating stimuli A and F reduced Sadie's performance on choices between stimuli B through E to chance. These results provide strong evidence that Sadie's choice behavior reflected an inference about the structure of the entire series of stimuli based on training experiences with adjacent stimulus pairs.

Analogical Reasoning

In the preceding studies, subjects were required to make an inference about the order of a series of stimuli. In **analogical reasoning** the task is to infer a relation between a sample pair of stimuli and apply this relation to a new pair of test stimuli. Assessments of human intellectual ability often include tests of analogical reasoning. For example, a test item may be *"Train* is to *track* as *car* is to _____ ." To answer the item correctly, one first has to infer the relation "rides on" from the sample stimuli *train* and *track*. Applying this relation to the test stimulus *car* provides the answer *road*. Gillan, Premack, and Woodruff (1981) demonstrated analogical reasoning in a 16-year-old chimpanzee, Sarah, who had previously received extensive training on various cognitive

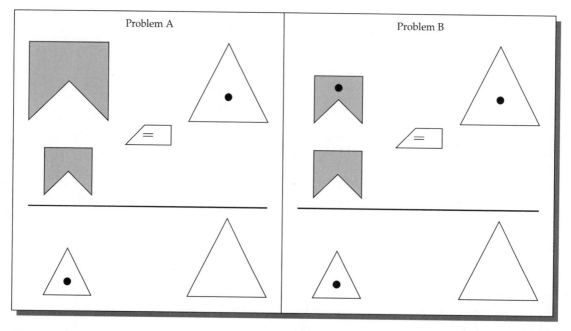

Figure 12.12 Geometric stimuli and structure of problems used by Gillan, Premack, and Woodruff (1981) in a test of analogical reasoning in the chimpanzee. Problems are presented above the horizontal line and possible answers are presented below the line. *(From "Reasoning in the Chimpanzee: I. Analogical Reasoning" by D.J. Gillan, D. Premack, and G. Woodruff, 1981,* Journal of Experimental Psychology: Animal Behavior Processes, 7, pp. 1–17.)

tasks (see also, Gillan, 1983). Sarah also had been taught a symbolic language, which we will describe in the next section.

In one set of experiments, Sarah was tested with a series of perceptual analogies. The stimuli were a series of geometric shapes cut from colored construction paper and glued onto cardboard. They varied in shape, color, size, and in the presence or absence of an easily noticed black dot. Figure 12.12 shows two examples of test problems. The stimuli were presented to Sarah on a stimulus tray, as they appear in the figure. The sample stimuli for a given trial were presented on the left-hand side. In problem A of Figure 12.12, these were a large and a small sawtooth. A symbol that Sarah had previously learned stood for "equal to" was placed next to the sample stimuli, and this was followed by one of the test stimuli. The bottom of the stimulus

tray contained two choice stimuli, one of which correctly completed the analogy. In problem A, the relation between the bottom and top sample stimuli was "smaller than." Because the test stimulus on the right was a large triangle with a dot, the correct stimulus for completing the analogy was a small triangle with a dot.

Problem B in Figure 12.12 used the same choice stimuli on the bottom of the stimulus tray as problem A. However, this time the top and bottom sample stimuli differed in that the bottom one lacked a dot. Therefore, the correct choice was the large triangle without the dot. Gillan and his colleagues used 26 pairs of problems like the pair shown in Figure 12.12. (The two problems of a pair were mixed in with all the other problems so that they did not appear in consecutive order.) The use of pairs of problems that had the same choice

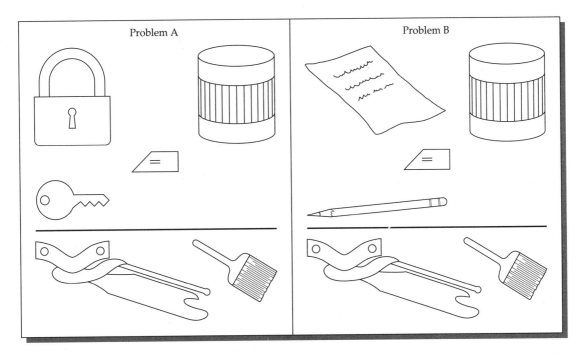

Figure 12.13 Objects used by Gillan, Premack, and Woodruff (1981) in a test of analogical reasoning in the chimpanzee. Problems are presented above the horizontal line and possible answers are presented below. *(From "Reasoning in the Chimpanzee: I. Analogical Reasoning" by D.J. Gillan, D. Premack, and G. Woodruff, 1981,* Journal of Experimental Psychology: Animal Behavior Processes, *7, pp. 1–17.)*

stimuli but different correct responses prevented Sarah from solving the analogies by always picking certain favored stimuli.

Sarah was remarkably adept at solving the perceptual analogies. On the first 52 different problems she was presented, she made the correct response 85% of the time. Sarah's performance was uniformly good in every session. During the first session with 12 problems, she was correct on 83% of them. Thus, her performance probably reflected past learning rather than learning during the course of the experiment.

The experiment we have just described required abstracting and applying perceptual relations ("smaller than," "lacking a dot," and the like). In a later study (Gillan et al., 1981) Sarah was tested on conceptual analogies. Here the physical appearance of the stimuli provided no clue to the relevant relation.

Rather, the relevant relation was based on the functions of the objects presented. Figure 12.13 shows a pair of problems of this type. The samples were again presented on the left of the stimulus tray, the test stimuli on the right, and the choice alternatives on the bottom. In problem A of Figure 12.13, the samples are a lock and a key. The functional relation between them is that the key opens the lock. The test stimulus is a can, and the choices are a can opener and a paintbrush. The correct choice is the can opener because it has the same functional relation to the can as the key has to the lock. In problem B the same choices are again used, but this time the relation being tested is "to mark or color," making the brush the correct choice.

Sarah was tested with 9 pairs of problems such as those shown in Figure 12.13. All the problems involved objects familiar to Sarah.

Again her performance was remarkably accurate. She made the correct choice on 83% of the 18 different problems.

The preceding demonstrations of inferential and analogical reasoning are important because they show that these intellectual skills are not uniquely human. The studies of inferential reasoning were conducted with chimpanzees that did not have prior language training. Therefore, we can conclude that inferential reasoning in chimpanzees is possible without language skills. Since Sarah did have extensive language training, further research is required to determine whether analogical reasoning is also possible without language.

Teaching Language to Chimpanzees

Perhaps the most complex cognitive skill is the use of language. In fact, many have assumed language use to be so complex and specialized as to be uniquely human. According to proponents of this view, the ability to use language depends on certain innate processes that have evolved only in our own species (for example, Chomsky, 1972; Lennenberg, 1967). By contrast, others have proposed that we use language because our species is especially intelligent and because we have had the necessary training—not because we are the only organisms with the required genetic background. This second view suggests that nonhuman animals may also acquire language, provided they are sufficiently intelligent and receive the proper training. Encouraged by this possibility, a number of people have tried to teach language skills to nonhuman animals. If we could teach language to animals, we might also be able to communicate with them and thereby gain unique insights into their lives. Talking to an animal would be something like talking to someone from outer space. We might see for the first time how the world looks through the experiences of nonhuman individuals. We

might also gain unique insights into ourselves. We would see for the first time how our own actions are viewed by an organism not biased by human experiences and ethnocentricity.

Most efforts to teach animals language have involved the chimpanzee because of all the primates, the chimpanzee is the most similar to human beings. Despite many similarities, however, chimpanzees do not learn to speak when they are given the same types of experiences that children have as they learn to speak. This became clear through observations of chimpanzees reared as children in people's homes. Nadezhda Kohts, of the Darwinian museum in Moscow, raised a chimpanzee in her home from 1913 to 1916 without once having it imitate the human voice or utter a word of Russian (see A. J. Premack, 1976). More detailed accounts of life with a chimpanzee are available from the experiences of Winthrop and Louise Kellogg, who raised a baby chimpanzee along with their baby boy in the 1930s (Kellogg, 1933). Their adopted charge also did not learn to speak in the normal manner. Undaunted by this evidence, Cathy and Keith Hayes raised a chimpanzee named Viki with the explicit intent of teaching her to talk (Hayes & Hayes, 1951). Despite several years of effort, Viki learned to say only three words: *mama, papa,* and *cup.*

The failure of the Hayeses to teach language to Viki despite their great efforts discouraged others from trying to teach chimpanzees to talk. However, people remained intrigued with the possibility that animals might acquire some language skills. The modern era in animal language-training research started with the innovative work of Allen and Beatrice Gardner and their students (Gardner & Gardner, 1969, 1975, 1978). Instead of trying to teach their chimpanzee Washoe to talk using vocal speech, they tried to teach her to communicate using American Sign Language. American Sign Language consists of manual gestures in place of words and is used by deaf people in North America. Chimpanzees are much more adept at making hand movements and gestures than at making the mouth, tongue, and lip movements required for the production of speech sounds. Washoe was a good learner. She learned to sign well over 100 words. Washoe's success suggests that earlier efforts to teach speech to chimpanzees may have failed not because of the inability of the chimpanzee to engage in language communication but because an inappropriate medium (vocalization) was used. Washoe held out the promise that, given the appropriate medium for language, meaningful communication might still be established between chimpanzees and human beings.

The success of the Gardners with Washoe encouraged other language-training efforts with chimpanzees, as well as with other species. These included a gorilla (Patterson, 1978); dolphins (Herman, 1987); sea lions (Schusterman & Gisiner, 1988); and an African Grey parrot (Pepperberg, 1990). Some investigators followed the approach of the Gardners in using American Sign Language to train chimpanzees (see Gardner, Gardner, & Van Cantfort, 1989, for a recent review) and gorillas (Patterson, 1978). Another approach has also avoided trying to teach chimpanzees vocalization. However, instead of adopting a human language in active use, such as sign language, this approach has employed artificial language. One artificial language, developed and used by David Premack and his associates, consists of plastic forms of various shapes in place of words (Premack, 1971b, 1976). Figure 12.14 shows examples of the plastic symbols. They have a metal backing and are placed on a magnetized board in a vertical order, as in Chinese, to create sentences. Another artificial language was developed by Duane Rumbaugh and his colleagues at the Language Research Center associated with Georgia State University and the Yerkes Regional Primate Research Center at Emory University (Rumbaugh, 1977; see also Savage-Rumbaugh, 1986). In this artificial language, geometric shapes of various colors represent words. These symbols, called **lexigrams,** are

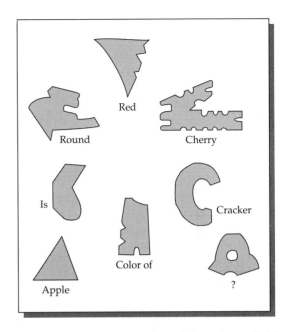

Figure 12.14 Examples of symbols in the artificial language developed by David Premack and his associates. *(Adapted from D. Premack, 1976.)*

presented on a board. The chimpanzee can select a word by pointing to or pressing the corresponding lexigram on the board.

When chimpanzees respond appropriately to signs made by a human trainer and also make signs in return, they are displaying both comprehension and production components of language. Comprehension and production components of language also have been taught to an African Grey parrot, Alex, who learned to recognize and speak about 40 words of the English language and who could then be questioned as to how many objects he was shown, whether two presented objects were the same or different, and what the shape or color of an object was (Pepperberg, 1990). Language training with dolphins and sea lions has concentrated on the comprehension side of human–animal communication (but see Richards, Wolz, & Herman, 1984). The dolphin and sea lion projects employed artificial languages in which various hand and arm gestures or computer-generated sounds represented words. The vocabulary consisted of about three dozen artificial words. Several words at a time were arranged as instructions the subjects had to carry out with objects in their tank to obtain food reinforcement. Given the sequence "Pipe Tail Touch," for example, the dolphin would have to touch a piece of pipe in the tank with its tail flukes.

Early language-training efforts attempted to determine whether nonhuman animals are capable of language. However, it has become evident that this is not an answerable question. Such a question is as difficult to answer as it is to determine at what point human infants have language. Language is not a unitary entity that one either does or does not have. Rather, it consists of component skills. A human infant's language abilities improve gradually as the infant acquires and integrates increasingly sophisticated language skills. In this developmental sequence, there is no one point at which the young child graduates from not having language to having it.

Based on such considerations, investigators have come to recognize that instead of trying to prove (or disprove) that nonhuman animals can learn language, a more productive approach to research is to investigate the acquisition of various components of language competence. There are two major issues in contemporary work on animal language training. One issue concerns documenting the nature of the language skills animals acquire through training. The second issue involves trying to identify the kinds of training procedures that are necessary for acquisition of the skills that are found.

Documenting acquired language skill is easier than determining the training procedures responsible for those skills. When an animal has presumably acquired a language skill, test procedures can be instituted that conclusively demonstrate the skill in question. Special test procedures are necessary because language training typically involves extensive interactions with the subject under conditions in which hints or prompts might be provided,

or conditions in which a trainer might give the subject "the benefit of the doubt" and credit that subject with more intelligent behavior than is warranted. Terrace and his colleagues (Terrace, 1979; Terrace, Petitto, Sanders, & Bever, 1979), for example, studied videotaped records of the sign-language behavior of their chimpanzee, Nim, and found that Nim often imitated signs previously made by the trainer. Signing that occurs in imitation of the trainer is prompted and is not good evidence of language skill.

Not only must test procedures be set up in a way that precludes inadvertent prompts, they must also be constructed to allow for objective measurement of behavior. In a test of sign-language vocabulary, for example, Gardner and Gardner (1984), presented pictures to Washoe for her to identify by signing. Two observers recorded the signs Washoe made. To minimize the possibility of prompting, neither observer could see the picture Washoe was trying to name. To ensure objective independent observations, the observers also could not see each other. With these elaborate procedures, Washoe could not be tipped off as to the correct sign. Since the observers did not know what the correct sign was on each trial, they also could not give her credit for incorrect responses. Despite these precautions, Washoe responded correctly about 80% of the time.

Washoe's vocabulary test was a test of word production. In subsequent studies with a bonobo chimpanzee, Kanzi, Savage-Rumbaugh and her colleagues found that Kanzi had learned the meaning of spoken English words. Kanzi, as other chimpanzees, could not produce the sounds of English words but he could understand what the words represented. In one test of this comprehension skill (Savage-Rumbaugh, McDonald, Sevcik, Hopkins, & Rubert, 1986), English words were "spoken" by a speech synthesizer to make sure Kanzi was not responding to the intonation of human speech. After each word, Kanzi was asked to select the lexical symbol for that word from a selection of three lexi-

Figure 12.15   The bonobo chimpanzee Kanzi participating in a test of English comprehension. Words were presented to him through the earphones, and he had to respond by pressing lexigrams on the panel in the background. *(Courtesy of the Georgia State University/Yerkes Language Research Center.)*

grams (see Figure 12.15). The experimenter did not see the possible choices, and thus could not inadvertently indicate which was correct. The choice alternatives were presented by a second experimenter who then did not observe Kanzi's choices, so that she also could not prompt the correct response. Each of 66 words was presented three times. Kanzi responded correctly each time 51 of the words was presented. In a similar test with spoken human speech, Kanzi only erred on one of the 66 words. Thus, synthesized speech was more difficult for Kanzi to comprehend, as it is for human listeners sometimes.

Interestingly, two other language-trained chimpanzees, Austin and Sherman, showed no evidence of comprehension of human spoken speech in similar tests after similar extensive experience with spoken English. Austin and Sherman are common chimpanzees of the same species as Washoe *(Pan troglodytes)*, whereas Kanzi is a bonobo chimpanzee *(Pan paniscus)*. Their differences in comprehension of spoken English may reflect species differences in this skill.

A Comparison of Training Procedures

As we noted earlier, it is easier to test for language skills than it is to determine which aspects of language-training procedures are responsible for the observed language competence. A variety of procedures have been employed to train language skills. For example, Pepperberg (1990), working with the African Grey parrot, Alex, employed an observational learning procedure known as the **model–rival** technique. In a three-way interaction between Alex and two human experimenters, one of the experimenters acts as a trainer and the other acts as a student who competes with Alex for the attention of the trainer. The trainer may present an object of interest to Alex and ask what color it is. The person acting as the student will then respond, sometimes correctly and sometimes incorrectly. An incorrect response results in a reprimand from the trainer and temporary removal of the object. A correct response results in praise and a chance to manipulate the object. Alex observes these interactions and attempts to gain the attention of the trainer (and obtain the object) by responding correctly before the human "student" does so.

In the dolphin and sea lion language-training projects, more conventional stimulus-discrimination procedures were used. Given a set of gestural "instructions," the correct response on the part of the marine mammal was reinforced with food; incorrect responses were not reinforced. Thus, the training procedures used with the African Grey parrot and the marine mammals differed in numerous respects, including opportunities for observational learning and the reinforcers employed. Observed differences between the language skills of the avian and mammalian subjects may have reflected species differences or any of the various differences in training procedures.

Specific aspects of language-training procedures that are responsible for the observed language competence seemingly would be easier to identify if the comparisons were made within a single species. Starting with the pioneering work of training sign language to Washoe, language training has been conducted with about a dozen chimpanzee subjects. Therefore, one might consider how different training procedures produce differences in language competence. However, comparisons between the chimpanzee subjects also must be regarded with caution.

One methodological problem arises from the complexity of the language-training procedures employed with chimpanzees. For example, sign-language training conducted by the Gardners and their associates was usually within the context of an established social relationship between the trainers and the chimpanzees. The chimpanzees lived in a rich homelike environment and were cared for by a small number of people throughout the day, each of whom was adept in sign language. Every effort was made to engage the chimpanzees in active conversation (through signing) during their waking hours. New signs were learned during games, in the course of getting dressed, or in going from place to place. The intent was to teach language to the chimpanzees in a naturalistic context—in the way that children presumably learn to talk during the normal course of interacting with parents and siblings.

In contrast to the efforts to create a naturalistic context for the training of sign language, early investigators using artificial languages conducted language training in a more confined laboratory setting with the use of explicit reinforcers (D. Premack, 1976; Rumbaugh, 1977). For example, in the initial efforts of Rumbaugh and his associates (Rumbaugh, 1977), the chimpanzee Lana was taught an artificial language consisting of lexigrams, each of which represented a different word. The lexigrams appeared on a modified keyboard hooked up to a computer. Lana could "talk" to the computer and make various requests. The computer, in turn, was programmed to reply with lexigrams presented on a display console. This procedure obviously was very different from that employed by the Gardners and their associates. Such differences in training procedures make it difficult to identify the specific component of a training procedure that is primarily responsible for differences in observed results.

A second difficulty is that although language training has been conducted with about a dozen chimpanzees altogether, any one procedure has been employed with just a few of these subjects (only one in some cases). Subjects of a single species (rats or pigeons, for example) can exhibit large individual differences in responding to a given complex learning task. There is no reason to assume that chimpanzees do not show similar individual differences. Therefore, differences observed across training procedures may reflect nonspecific individual differences between the subjects rather than differences in the efficacy of those procedures.

Finally, different training procedures have been used by different investigators in different laboratories. Therefore, unknown and unintended differences in laboratory procedures and personnel may lead to differences in the performance of the language-trained subjects. Terrace and his associates (Terrace et al., 1979), for example, attempted to teach sign language to their chimpanzee, Nim, at Columbia University using the same procedures that had been used by the Gardners to train Washoe at the University of Nevada. However, the Gardners have disputed that the Columbia University project managed to replicate the procedures of the Nevada project (for example, Gardner & Gardner, 1989).

Features of Language Competence in Chimpanzees

Although problematic, it is tempting to try to relate language competence to training method, especially in cases where striking differences in results are observed in the same laboratory. Several such opportunities have arisen at the Language Research Center associated with Georgia State University and the Yerkes Regional Primate Research Center at Emory University. Investigators at the center have varied their training regimes as new subjects entered the language training program.

The training procedure employed with their first subject, Lana, was described briefly in the previous section. Lana's training emphasized the naming of objects and the learning of short sequences of symbols. Two other chimpanzees, Austin and Sherman, entered the program after Lana (see Savage-Rumbaugh, 1986). In contrast to Lana, Austin and Sherman were reared with the kind of extensive human contact used by the Gardners and were taught language skills within

this context. However, the language they were trained on consisted of the same lexigrams that had been used in training Lana rather than American Sign Language. They interacted with caretakers and with each other by pointing to or pressing lexigrams on a stimulus board. Portable versions of the lexigram board were available to extend training to a variety of settings.

The learning of words. One of the undisputed results of language-training programs is that animals can learn to associate arbitrary symbols (be they manual signs or lexigrams) with objects. They can learn to correctly name a large number of different objects. To what extent does this skill represent having learned what we call *words* in human language? A word in human language is an abstract representation that can be used in a variety of ways. One can use the word as a label for its referent object (as in saying "tomato" when presented with an example of the vegetable). One can also identify the referent object in response to the word (as in picking out a tomato when asked "Which is the tomato?"). One can also use the word in relation to other words (as in saying "tomato" when asked to name examples of "vegetables").

In various types of tests of the use of lexigrams, Lana was found to be just as skillful as Austin and Sherman in labeling various objects and in sorting a set of objects into two categories, "food" and "tool," by putting the objects into separate piles (Savage-Rumbaugh, Rumbaugh, Smith, & Lawson, 1980). However, in contrast to Austin and Sherman, Lana was unable to generalize the labels "food" and "tool" to novel examples of foods and tools, even though she could sort these new objects accurately when required to put them into separate piles. Thus, Lana's knowledge of the words "food" and "tool" was much more restricted than Austin's and Sherman's.

In further training (see Savage-Rumbaugh et al., 1980), Austin and Sherman readily learned to label pictures of foods and tools and generalized this skill to novel photographs of exemplars of each category. In a final phase of the experiment, Austin and Sherman were trained to label lexigrams of various foods (beancake, orange, and bread) and tools (key, money, and stick) as "food" and "tool." They were then tested with a variety of symbols of new tools (magnet, sponge, lever, string, for example) and foods (M & M, banana, corn, for example). They had previously learned the lexigrams for each of these new tools and foods. However, they had not been explicitly trained to categorize or label these items in terms of their uses ("tool" and "food"). Nevertheless, Austin and Sherman performed with nearly perfect accuracy in categorizing these new lexigrams. Thus, they were able to use words to label and categorize other words.

This linguistic skill shows a level of abstractness similar to that with which words are used in human language. Other studies of animal language have failed to demonstrate such sophisticated usage of words. One is tempted to attribute the superior performance of Austin and Sherman as compared to Lana to the differences in how language training was conducted with the former chimpanzees. However, any such conclusion has to be tempered by the fact that the training procedures differed in numerous features. The critical difference cannot be identified with much confidence.

Evidence of "grammar" in language-trained chimpanzees.

Although it is agreed that nonhuman primates can learn a vocabulary, language is more than just a collection of words. In addition to a vocabulary, language involves arrangement of words in sequence according to certain rules set forth by the grammar of the language. Hence, a critical issue in teaching language to nonhuman primates is whether they can learn to construct word sequences on the basis of grammatical rules. There has been considerable debate about this. The smallest sequence of words possible is two words. However, the utterance of a pair of words does not prove that the subject is using grammar to create the sequence. One incident that has been the subject of controversy occurred when the chimp Washoe saw a swan in the water. She had never been exposed to a swan before. When asked "What is that?" she replied "Water bird." In this sequence was Washoe using "water" as an adjective to specify the kind of bird she saw? Perhaps she was. However, on the basis of just this much information, an equally plausible interpretation is that she signed "water" because she saw the water and "bird" because she saw a bird. That is, she may have signed "water bird" as two independent words rather than as an utterance of two words related to each other as adjective and noun (Terrace et al., 1979).

Difficulties of interpretation may also arise with words arranged in a sentence. Consider the following sentence that could have been made by Lana responding with lexigrams: "Please machine make music." If Lana had pressed the appropriate lexigrams in the correct order, the computer would have complied and made music. However, pressing the lexigrams in that order would not have proved that Lana could construct a sentence. She could have just memorized a sequence of symbols to get reinforced (Thompson & Church, 1980; see also Pate & Rumbaugh, 1983).

Early detailed studies of language production in the chimpanzee failed to provide convincing evidence of responding on the basis of some kind of grammar or set of rules for word combinations (Terrace, 1979; Terrace et al., 1979). The chimpanzee Nim, who was taught sign language by Terrace and his associates, performed sequences of signs, but these appeared to be imitations of the trainer and included meaningless repetitions. For example, Nim's most common four-sign combination was "eat-drink-eat-drink."

Convincing evidence of the development of grammatical word sequences has been obtained in studies of the language behavior

Figure 12.16 Kanzi working with a lexigram board. *(Courtesy of the Georgia State University/Yerkes Language Research Center.)*

of the bonobo chimpanzee Kanzi (Greenfield & Savage-Rumbaugh, 1990; see also Savage-Rumbaugh, Sevcik, Brakke, & Rumbaugh, 1990). As we noted earlier, Kanzi is rather remarkable in being able to comprehend spoken English words (Savage-Rumbaugh et al., 1986). Kanzi also has had a rather unusual language-training history. Prior to Kanzi, chimpanzees were first taught to produce language behavior (make signs in response to objects, for example) on the assumption that language comprehension would follow such language-production training. By contrast, Kanzi learned to understand spoken English words before he ever produced words by pointing to and pressing lexigram panels (see Figure 12.16). In this respect, Kanzi's language acquisition was similar to that of human infants, who also understand spoken words before they themselves are able to speak.

Kanzi's language acquisition was also unusual in comparison to previous language-training efforts with chimpanzees in that Kanzi did not receive formal language training. During the first 2½ years of his life he lived with his foster mother, Matata, who started language training at the Yerkes Language Research Center of Georgia State University when Kanzi was 6 months old. Matata was trained with standard procedures in which she had to indicate the lexigram names of food objects to obtain those foods. However, she progressed slowly and never attained the language competence of Austin and Sherman. For two years, Kanzi observed these training sessions but did not participate in them. Matata was then removed for a period for breeding purposes. During this separation Kanzi began to interact with the lexigram board spontaneously. The investigators took advantage of this spontaneous use of the lexigram board and allowed Kanzi to continue to use it in addition to communicating with manual gestures. They also allowed Kanzi to continue to learn language skills by listening to spoken English and observing humans communicating with gestures and lexigrams. However, Kanzi was never required to use the lexigrams to make requests or obtain things that he wanted.

TABLE 12.1 *Frequency of various two-element communications by Kanzi (lexigram responses are indicated by small capital letters)*

Word Order	Frequency	Example of Dominant Order
Action → Agent	119	CARRY → gesture to Phil, who agrees
Agent → Action	13	to carry Kanzi
Action → Object	39	KEEPAWAY BALLOON → wanting to tease
Object → Action	15	Bill with a balloon and start a fight
Goal → Action	46	COKE CHASE → researcher chases Kanzi
Action → Goal	10	to place in woods where Coke is kept

SOURCE: Adapted from P.M. Greenfield and E.S. Savage-Rumbaugh, 1990

Every effort was made to provide Kanzi with as rich and as natural an environment as possible. He was allowed to go on excursions on a 50-acre wooded area adjacent to his home quarters. The woods were provisioned with food stations at fixed locations. Excursions in the woods provided numerous opportunities for conversation concerning which food site to visit, what to take along, and so on.

Data for the analysis of the possible existence of grammatical structure in Kanzi's language production were obtained when Kanzi was 5½ years old (Greenfield & Savage-Rumbaugh, 1990). Over a 5-month period of observations, Kanzi communicated 13,691 "words." Of these, about 10% contained more than one element or "word." The analysis of word sequences was limited to spontaneous communications. Thus, responses to directed questions were excluded from the analyses, as were responses that Kanzi performed to obtain something that was otherwise withheld, or responses that involved some degree of imitation. Unlike Nim, Kanzi rarely repeated himself or combined words that did not make sense together. Analyses of the multiple-word communications revealed a structure indicative of rules for word order.

Kanzi's word combinations could be categorized according to the types of words that were involved. By way of example, Table 12.1 summarizes data from three different types of two-word combinations. The first type in-

volves a word for an action and a word for an agent. A total of 132 such action/agent combinations were observed. Of these, in 119 instances the word identifying the action preceded the word identifying the agent. In only 13 of the 132 cases did the word for the agent precede the word for the action. A similar bias in favor of a particular word order is evident with the other types of two-word combinations, action/object and goal/action. Notice that the "grammatical" rule is not a simple one. One of the words in all three of these types of two-word combinations involved an action. However, the action word did not come first predominantly in all three types of two-word combinations. When talking about an action and a goal, Kanzi tended to state the goal first.

Some of the rules for word order that were manifest in Kanzi's word combinations were probably learned by observing his human caretakers. However, other grammatical rules appeared to be Kanzi's original inventions. Perhaps the most prominent of these concerned word combinations that Kanzi made involving a lexigram and a hand gesture. In such cases, Kanzi nearly always performed the lexigram response first, followed by the gesture. For example, in requesting to be carried, Kanzi would press the lexigram for CARRY, followed by a gesture pointing to the caretaker. Kanzi did faithfully follow the rule of making the lexigram response before any manual gestures, but the caretakers usually performed such word sequences in the opposite order. Although he did not perform many three-word sequences, the ones that he did perform did not involve repetitions of the same words, as did Nim's. Furthermore, in Kanzi's three-word sequences the two-word combinations followed the rules for the order of two successive words.

Kanzi's performance provides the best evidence available so far that a nonhuman mammal not only can learn a substantial vocabulary but also can learn to form word combinations characterized by grammatical structure. One may be tempted to attribute Kanzi's linguistic sophistication to the special conditions of his language acquisition or to higher intelligence in bonobo chimpanzees than in common chimpanzees. However, for the methodological reasons that we noted earlier, such conclusions cannot be firmly substantiated.

The language sophistication of Kanzi proves that many complicated aspects of language are not uniquely human attributes. Thus, these findings vindicate Darwin's belief that seemingly unique human abilities and skills do not reflect a discontinuity in the animal kingdom.

Glossary

accidental reinforcement An instance in which the delivery of a reinforcer happens to coincide with a particular response even though that response was not responsible for the reinforcer presentation. Also called **adventitious reinforcement.**

acquired drive A source of motivation for instrumental behavior caused by the presentation of a stimulus that was previously conditioned with a primary, or unconditioned, reinforcer.

acquisition The initial stage of learning.

active avoidance An instrumental conditioning procedure in which the performance of a specific response prevents the delivery of an aversive stimulus.

adaptation Evolutionary change that increases the reproductive fitness of members of a species in a particular environmental niche.

adaptation level The level of sensitivity to stimuli that results from the average of the number and type of stimuli subjects encounter in a particular situation.

adjunctive behavior Systematic activities or responses related to the timing of reinforcers in schedules of reinforcement.

adventitious reinforcement Same as **accidental reinforcement.**

AESOP Acronym for Affective Extension of SOP. (see **SOP theory.**)

affective after-reaction Emotions experienced after the termination of a biologically significant event. The emotions experienced are typically the opposite of those experienced during the event.

afferent neuron A neuron that transmits messages from sense organs to the central nervous system. Also called a **sensory neuron.**

amnesia Loss of memory. (See also **retrograde amnesia.**)

analogical reasoning Responding to a pair of test stimuli on the basis of a relationship inferred from a pair of sample stimuli.

animal cognition Use of a neural representation, or code, as a basis for action.

appetitive stimulus A positive reinforcing stimulus.

"a" process Same as **primary process.**

association A connection between the representations of two events (two stimuli or a stimulus and a response) such that the occurrence of one of the events activates the representation of the other.

asymptote The limit of learning, when further training does not produce additional changes in behavior.

autoshaping Same as **sign tracking.**

aversive stimulus A noxious or unpleasant stimulus. Also called a **punisher.**

avoidance An instrumental conditioning procedure in which the subject's behavior prevents the delivery of an aversive stimulus.

avoidance trial A trial on which the occurrence of the avoidance response prevents the delivery of the aversive stimulus.

backward conditioning procedure A procedure in which the conditioned stimulus is presented after the unconditioned stimulus on each trial.

behavioral baseline The stable rate or pattern of operant behavior obtained after extensive exposure to a particular set of experimental conditions. The term is used mainly in connection with experiments that involve continuous recording of instrumental behavior.

behavioral bliss point The optimal distribution of activities in the absence of constraints or limitations imposed by an instrumental conditioning procedure.

behavioral homeostasis The balanced and stable distribution of a subject's activities. Deviations from this balanced state cause a redistribution of responses to reinstitute the stable state.

behavioral regulation A mechanism that determines the allocation or distribution of an animal's responses. It is assumed that animals work to maintain an optimal distribution of activities.

belongingness The theoretical idea, originally proposed by Thorndike, that the subject's evolutionary history causes certain responses to be more easily modified by certain reinforcers in instrumental conditioning than other responses.

bidirectional response system A response system in which both increases and decreases in responding may be observed.

biological homeostasis The state of the organism in which all physiological systems are in proper balance. Deviations from this state stimulate adjustments that return the subject to the balanced state. Also called **physiological homeostasis.**

blocking effect Interference with the conditioning of a novel stimulus because of the presence of a previously conditioned stimulus.

"b" process Same as **opponent process.**

central emotional state The general state of the nervous system assumed to be produced by the presentation of a classically conditioned stimulus.

CER Abbreviation for **conditioned emotional response.**

change-over delay A procedure used with concurrent schedules of reinforcement that prevents the delivery of the reinforcer for a short time after the subject switches from responding on one of the components of the concurrent schedule to responding on another component. This procedure prevents reinforcement of switching behavior per se.

chunking The subdivision of a series of items into subsets, each of which has its own internal structure.

classical conditioning Learning that results from presentation of a conditioned stimulus in conjunction with an unconditioned stimulus in-

dependent of the ongoing activities of the organism.

COD Abbreviation for **change-over delay.**

comparator hypothesis The idea that conditioned responding depends on a comparison between the associative strength of the conditioned stimulus (CS) and the associative strength of other cues present during training of the target CS.

compensatory response A response opposite in form to the reaction elicited by the unconditioned stimulus, and which therefore compensates for this reaction.

complementary commodities Commodities that are related so that increased use of one results in increased use of the other, as contrasted with substitutable commodities.

compound stimulus A stimulus consisting of two or more components or features.

compound-stimulus test A test procedure that identifies a stimulus as a conditioned inhibitor if that stimulus reduces the responding elicited by a conditioned excitatory stimulus. Also called a **summation test.**

conceptual error An error that results from failure to differentiate the subset of a category to which a stimulus belongs.

concurrent-chain schedule A complex reinforcement procedure in which the subject is permitted to choose which of several simple reinforcement schedules will be in effect. Once a choice has been made, the rejected alternatives become unavailable for a time.

concurrent-measurement experiment An experiment in which classically and instrumentally conditioned responses are measured at the same time.

concurrent schedule A complex reinforcement procedure in which the subject can choose any one of two or more simple reinforcement schedules that are available simultaneously. Concurrent schedules allow for the measurement of choice between simple schedule alternatives.

conditional relation Same as **hierarchical relation.**

conditional or *conditioned response* The response that comes to be made to the conditioned stimulus during classical conditioning.

conditional or *conditioned stimulus* A stimulus that does not elicit a particular response initially, but comes to do so as a result of becoming associated with an unconditioned stimulus.

conditioned compensatory response   A conditioned response opposite in form to the reaction elicited by the unconditioned stimulus, and which therefore compensates for this reaction.

conditioned emotional response   Suppression of positively reinforced instrumental behavior by the presentation of a stimulus conditioned with an aversive stimulus. Also called **conditioned suppression.**

conditioned excitation   A type of classical conditioning in which a conditioned stimulus becomes associated with the presentation of an unconditioned stimulus.

conditioned reinforcer   A stimulus that becomes an effective reinforcer because of its association with a primary, or unconditioned, reinforcer. Also called a **secondary reinforcer.**

conditioned suppression   Same as **conditioned emotional response.**

conditioning trial   A training episode involving presentation of a conditioned stimulus with (or without) an unconditioned stimulus.

configural-cue   An approach to the analysis of control by compound stimuli in which it is assumed that subjects respond to a compound stimulus as an integral whole, not divided into parts or elements. (Compare with **stimulus-element.**)

conservation of fear   The assumption that conditioned fear is maintained in a signaled avoidance procedure if subjects respond rapidly to turn off the CS because later segments of the CS are not experienced.

consummatory-response theory   A theory that assumes that species-typical consummatory responses (eating, drinking, and the like) are the critical feature of reinforcers.

contextual stimulus   A background stimulus in the presence of which more discrete stimuli may be presented.

contiguity   The simultaneous (or almost simultaneous) occurrence of two or more events. Also called **temporal contiguity.**

continuous reinforcement   A schedule of reinforcement in which every occurrence of the instrumental response produces the reinforcer.

counterconditioning   A conditioning procedure that reverses the organism's previous response to a stimulus. For example, an animal may be conditioned to approach a stimulus that initially elicited withdrawal reactions.

counting   A process presumed to cause responding to be controlled only by the frequency or number of stimuli or events that have occurred.

CR   Abbreviation for **conditioned response.**

CS   Abbreviation for **conditioned stimulus.**

CS-modification model   A model that explains differences in learning in terms of changes in the effectiveness of the conditioned stimulus.

CS-preexposure effect   Interference with conditioning produced by repeated exposures of the subject to the conditioned stimulus before the conditioning trials. Also called **latent-inhibition effect.**

CS–US interval   Same as **interstimulus interval.**

CS–US relevance   Same as **stimulus relevance.**

cumulative record   A graphical representation of the cumulative number of occurrences of a particular response as a function of the passage of time. The horizontal distance on the record represents the passage of time, the vertical distance represents the total number of responses that have occurred up to a particular moment, and the slope represents the rate of responding.

cumulative recorder   An automatic event recorder that records occurrences of a particular response cumulatively as a function of the passage of time.

delayed echolalia   Repetitious verbalization observed in some autistic children.

delayed matching to sample   A procedure in which subjects are reinforced for responding to a test stimulus that is the same as a previously presented sample stimulus.

demand curve   In consumer demand theory, the relation between how much of a commodity is purchased and the price of the commodity.

devaluation of a reinforcer   Reduction of the attractiveness of a reinforcer, usually achieved by aversion conditioning or satiation.

differential inhibition   A classical conditioning procedure in which one stimulus (the CS+) is paired with the unconditioned stimulus on some trials and another stimulus (the CS−) is presented without the unconditioned stimulus on other trials. As a result of this procedure, the CS+ comes to elicit a conditioned response and the CS− comes to inhibit this response. Also called the **stimulus-discrimination procedure** (in **classical conditioning**).

differential probability principle   A principle that assumes that reinforcement depends on how much more likely the subject is to perform the reinforcer response than the instrumental response.

differential reinforcement of high rates (DRH) A reinforcement schedule in which a response is reinforced only if it occurs *before* a specified amount of time has elapsed following the preceding response.

differential reinforcement of low rates (DRL) A reinforcement schedule in which a response is reinforced only if it occurs *after* a specified amount of time has elapsed following the preceding response.

differential reinforcement of other behavior (DRO) An instrumental conditioning procedure in which a positive reinforcer is periodically delivered only if the subject fails to perform a particular response.

directed forgetting Stimulus control of memory. Subjects are provided a cue indicating when they will, or will not, be required to remember something.

disappointment A hypothetical emotional state presumably elicited by classically conditioned stimuli that signal the absence or removal of a positive reinforcer, such as food.

discrete stimulus A stimulus that is presented for a relatively brief period, with a clear beginning and end.

discrete-trial method A method of instrumental conditioning in which the subject can perform the instrumental response only during specified periods, usually determined either by placement of the subject in an experimental chamber or by the presentation of a stimulus.

discriminated avoidance An avoidance conditioning procedure in which occurrences of the aversive stimulus are signaled by a conditioned stimulus. Responding during the conditioned stimulus terminates the CS and prevents the delivery of the aversive unconditioned stimulus. Also called **signaled avoidance.**

discrimination hypothesis An explanation of the partial reinforcement extinction effect according to which extinction is slower after partial reinforcement than continuous reinforcement because the onset of extinction is more difficult to detect following partial reinforcement.

discrimination training procedure See **differential inhibition** and **stimulus discrimination procedure** (in **instrumental conditioning**).

discriminative punishment A procedure in which responding is punished in the presence of a particular stimulus and not punished in the absence of that stimulus.

discriminative stimulus A stimulus that controls the performance of instrumental behavior because it signals the availability (or nonavailability) of reinforcement.

dishabituation Recovery of a habituated response as a result of a strong extraneous stimulus.

disinhibition Recovery of a partly extinguished conditioned response as a result of presentation of a novel stimulus.

drive-reduction theory A theory of reinforcement according to which reinforcers are effective because they reduce the subject's drive state and return the subject to homeostasis.

DRH Abbreviation for **differential reinforcement of high rates.**

DRL Abbreviation for **differential reinforcement of low rates.**

DRO Abbreviation for **differential reinforcement of other behavior.**

drug tolerance Reduction in the effectiveness of a drug as a result of repeated use of the drug.

dualism The view of behavior according to which actions can be separated into two categories: voluntary behavior controlled by the mind and involuntary behavior controlled by reflex mechanisms.

ECS Abbreviation for **electroconvulsive shock.**

efferent neuron A neuron that transmits impulses to muscles. Also called a **motor neuron.**

elasticity of demand In consumer demand theory, the degree to which price influences the consumption of a commodity. (See also **demand curve** and **substitutability.**)

electroconvulsive shock (ECS) Brief electric current passed through the brain between electrodes placed on either side of the head.

empiricism A philosophy according to which all ideas in the mind arise from experience.

equilibrium schedule Same as **nondepriving schedule.**

errorless discrimination procedure A procedure devised by H.S. Terrace in which subjects hardly ever respond to the S−. During initial phases of discrimination training, the S− is presented only briefly and at a low intensity, so that the subject does not respond to it. The duration and intensity of the S− are then gradually increased;

if this increase is conducted in small enough steps, subjects rarely, if ever, respond to the S−.

escape An instrumental conditioning procedure in which the instrumental response terminates an aversive stimulus. (See also **negative reinforcement.**)

escape trial A type of trial during avoidance training in which the required avoidance response is not made and the aversive unconditioned stimulus is presented. Performance of the instrumental response during the aversive stimulus results in termination of the aversive stimulus. Thus, the organism is able to escape from the aversive stimulus.

evolutionary adaptation See **adaptation.**

excitatory Pavlovian conditioning See **conditioned excitation.**

excitatory stimulus generalization gradient A gradient of responding that is observed when subjects are tested with the S+ from a discrimination procedure and with stimuli that increasingly differ from the S+. The highest level of responding occurs to stimuli similar to the S+; progressively less responding occurs to stimuli that increasingly differ from the S+. Thus, the gradient has an inverted-U shape.

experimental method A research technique in which an experimenter introduces or removes factors that are presumed to be responsible for certain behaviors. The effects of these manipulations are then measured.

explicitly unpaired control A procedure in which both conditioned and unconditioned stimuli are presented, but with sufficient time between them so that they do not become associated with each other.

exteroceptive stimulus A stimulus, such as a light or tone, that arises from events outside the organism. (Compare with **proprioceptive stimulus.**)

extinction Reduction of a learned response that occurs because the conditioned stimulus is no longer paired with the unconditioned stimulus (in classical conditioning) or because the response is no longer reinforced (in instrumental conditioning). Also, the procedure of repeatedly presenting a conditioned stimulus without the unconditioned stimulus, or of withdrawing reinforcement for a response.

facilitation A procedure in which one cue designates when another cue will be reinforced. Also called **occasion setting.**

fatigue A temporary decrease in behavior caused by repeated or excessive use of the muscles involved in the behavior.

fear A hypothetical emotional state presumably elicited when either an unconditioned aversive stimulus or a stimulus that was previously conditioned with an aversive event is presented.

feature analysis Analysis or identification of the particular aspect(s) of stimuli that have come to control responding.

feedback function The relation between rates of responding and rates of reinforcement allowed by a particular reinforcement schedule.

feedback stimulus A stimulus that results from the performance of a response.

FI Abbreviation for **fixed-interval schedule.**

fixed-interval scallop The gradually increasing rate of responding that occurs between successive reinforcements on a fixed-interval schedule.

fixed-interval schedule A reinforcement schedule in which reinforcement is delivered for the first response that occurs after a fixed amount of time following the last reinforcer.

fixed-ratio schedule A reinforcement schedule in which a fixed number of responses must occur in order for the next response to be reinforced.

flooding A procedure for extinguishing avoidance behavior in which the conditioned stimulus is presented while the subject is prevented from making the avoidance response. Also called **response prevention.**

foraging Activities involved in searching for and obtaining food.

forgetting A reduction of a learned response that occurs because of the passage of time, not because of particular experiences.

FR Abbreviation for **fixed-ratio schedule.**

fractional anticipatory goal response A theoretical entity or response that, according to the r_g-s_g mechanism, becomes classically conditioned to the stimuli experienced just before the performance of a reinforced instrumental response.

free-operant avoidance Same as **nondiscriminated avoidance.**

free-operant baseline Same as **operant level.**

free-operant level Same as **operant level.**

free-operant method A method of instrumental conditioning that permits repeated performance of the instrumental response without the subject being removed from the experimental chamber. (Compare with **discrete-trial method.**)

frustration An aversive emotional reaction that results from the unexpected absence of reinforcement.

frustration theory A theory of the partial reinforcement extinction effect, according to which extinction is retarded after partial reinforcement because the instrumental response becomes conditioned to the anticipation of frustrative nonreward.

generalization See **stimulus generalization.**

geotaxis Orientation movements in relation to gravity.

habituation effect A progressive decrease in the vigor of elicited behavior that may occur with repeated presentations of the eliciting stimulus.

habituation process A neural mechanism activated by repetitions of a stimulus that reduces the magnitude of responses elicited by the stimulus.

hedonism The philosophy proposed by Hobbes according to which the actions of organisms are determined entirely by the pursuit of pleasure and the avoidance of pain.

hierarchical relation A relation in which the significance of one type of stimulus or event depends on the status of another type of stimulus. Also called a **conditional relation.**

higher order conditioning A procedure in which a previously conditioned stimulus (CS_1) is used to condition a new stimulus (CS_2).

homeostasis See **behavioral homeostasis** and **biological homeostasis.**

hope A hypothetical emotional state presumably elicited by classically conditioned stimuli that signal the presentation of a positive reinforcer, such as food.

incentive motivation Motivation for instrumental behavior created by the sensory properties of a reinforcer.

inhibitory conditioning A type of classical conditioning in which the conditioned stimulus becomes a signal for the absence of the unconditioned stimulus.

inhibitory stimulus generalization gradient A gradient of responding observed when subjects are tested with the S− from a discrimination procedure and with stimuli that increasingly differ from the S−. The lowest level of responding occurs to stimuli similar to the S−; progressively more responding occurs to stimuli that increasingly differ from S−. Thus, the gradient has a U shape.

instinctive drift A gradual drift of instrumental behavior away from the responses required for reinforcement to species-typical or "instinctive" responses related to the reinforcer and to other stimuli in the experimental situation.

instrumental behavior An activity that occurs because it is effective in producing a particular consequence or reinforcer.

instrumental conditioning Conditioning that results from the relation between behavior and its consequences.

interim responses Responses that increase in frequency after the delivery of a reinforcer and then decline as the next reinforcer is due to be presented in a procedure that involves periodic presentations of the reinforcer.

intermittent reinforcement A schedule of reinforcement in which only some of the occurrences of the instrumental response are reinforced. The instrumental response is reinforced occasionally, or intermittently. Also called **partial reinforcement.**

internal clock A hypothetical process presumed to be involved in responding on the basis of the duration of stimuli or time.

interneuron A neuron in the spinal cord that transmits impulses from afferent (or sensory) to efferent (or motor) neurons.

interresponse time (IRT) The interval between successive responses.

interstimulus interval The amount of time that elapses between presentations of the conditioned stimulus (CS) and the unconditioned stimulus (US) during a classical conditioning trial. Also called the **CS–US interval.**

intertrial interval The amount of time that elapses between two successive trials.

interval schedule A reinforcement schedule in which a response is reinforced only if it occurs after a set amount of time following the last reinforcement.

intracranial self-stimulation Performance of an instrumental response that is reinforced by brief pulses of current passed through an electrode implanted in certain areas of the animal's brain.

intradimensional discrimination A discrimination between stimuli that differ in only one stimulus characteristic, such as color, brightness, or pitch.

irradiation of excitation A theoretical idea proposed by Pavlov according to which, when a CS is presented and paired with reinforcement, excitation occurs in the brain locus corresponding to the CS; this excitation radiates to adjacent brain locations, in much the same way that circular waves radiate from the point of contact when a pebble is tossed into a calm lake.

IRT   Abbreviation for **interresponse time.**

kinesis   An instance in which a stimulus produces a change in the speed of movement, irrespective of the direction of the movement.

labor supply curve   In economic theory, the relationship between how much work is performed at various wage rates and the total amount earned at those wage rates.

latency   The time elapsed between a stimulus (or the start of a trial) and the response that is made to the stimulus.

latent-inhibition effect   Same as **CS-preexposure effect.**

law of effect   A rule for instrumental behavior, proposed by Thorndike, which states that if a response in the presence of a stimulus is followed by a satisfying event, the association between the stimulus and the response will be strengthened; if the response is followed by an annoying event, the association will be weakened.

learned-helplessness effect   Interference with the learning of new instrumental responses as a result of exposure to inescapable and unavoidable aversive stimulation.

learned-helplessness hypothesis   A theoretical idea that assumes that during exposure to inescapable and unavoidable aversive stimulation subjects learn that their behavior does not control environmental events.

learned industriousness   A type of learning in which sensations involved in working hard become conditioned as secondary or conditioned reinforcers.

learning   An enduring change in the mechanisms of behavior involving specific stimuli and/or responses that results from prior experience with those stimuli and responses.

lexigram   A geometric shape or graphic design used to represent a word in an artificial language.

limited hold   A restriction on how long reinforcement remains available. In order for a response to be reinforced, it must occur during the limited-hold period.

long-delayed conditioning   A classical conditioning procedure in which the conditioned stimulus is presented long before the unconditioned stimulus on each conditioning trial.

long-term memory   A memory store that is presumed to be responsible for instances in which a particular experience has a long-lasting effect on the actions of the organism.

magazine training   A preliminary stage of instrumental conditioning in which a stimulus is repeatedly paired with the reinforcer to enable the subject to learn to go and get the reinforcer when it is presented. The sound of the food-delivery device, for example, may be repeatedly paired with food so that the animal will learn to go to the food cup when food is delivered.

magnitude of a response   A measure of the size, vigor, or extent of a response.

MAP   Abbreviation for **modal action pattern.**

matching law   A rule for instrumental behavior, proposed by R.J. Herrnstein, which states that the relative rate of responding on a particular response alternative equals the relative rate of reinforcement for that response alternative.

matching to sample   A procedure in which subjects are reinforced for selecting a stimulus that corresponds to the sample presented on that trial.

maturation   A change in behavior caused by physical or physiological development of the organism in the absence of experience with particular environmental events.

maximizing   The theoretical idea that subjects in a choice situation distribute their responses so as to receive the maximum reinforcement for the number of responses they perform.

melioration   A mechanism for achieving matching by responding so as to improve the local rates of reinforcement for response alternatives.

memory   A theoretical term used to characterize instances in which subjects' current behavior is determined by some aspect of their previous experience.

memory consolidation   The establishment of a memory in relatively permanent form, or the transfer of information from short-term to long-term memory.

memory retrieval   The recovery of information from a memory store.

minimum-deviation model   A model of instrumental behavior, according to which subjects respond to a response–reinforcer contingency in a manner that gets them as close as possible to their behavioral bliss point.

modal action pattern (MAP) A response pattern exhibited by most, if not all, members of a species in much the same way. Modal action patterns are often used as basic units of behavior in ethological investigations of behavior.

model–rival technique An observational learning procedure in which the subject observes a trainer teaching a student and tries to compete with that student for the trainer's attention.

molar theory A type of theory that assumes that instrumental behavior is determined by its consequences as calculated over the long term.

molecular theory A type of theory that assumes that instrumental behavior is determined by its consequences as calculated over a brief period following each response.

motor neuron Same as **efferent neuron.**

multiple schedule of reinforcement A procedure in which different reinforcement schedules are in effect in the presence of different stimuli presented in succession. Generally, each stimulus comes to evoke a pattern of responding that corresponds to whatever reinforcement schedule is in effect in the presence of that stimulus.

nativism A philosophy according to which human beings are born with innate ideas.

negative behavioral contrast Less responding for an unfavorable reinforcer following previous experience with a more desired reinforcer than in the absence of such prior experience.

negative reinforcement An instrumental conditioning procedure in which there is a negative contingency between the instrumental response and an aversive stimulus. If the instrumental response is performed, the aversive stimulus is terminated or prevented from occurring; if the instrumental response is not performed, the aversive stimulus is presented.

negative reinforcer An aversive stimulus, such as shock or loud noise. Also called a **punisher.**

negative sign tracking Movement away from a stimulus that signals an aversive event, such as a brief shock or the unavailability of positive reinforcers.

nervism The philosophical position adopted by Pavlov that all behavioral and physiological processes are regulated by the nervous system.

nondepriving schedule A schedule of reinforcement that allows the subject to maintain its behavioral bliss point without performing more or fewer of the instrumental or reinforcer responses overall than it performed during a free-operant baseline procedure. Also called an **equilibrium schedule.**

nondiscriminated avoidance An avoidance conditioning procedure in which occurrences of the aversive stimulus are not signaled by an external stimulus. In the absence of avoidance behavior, the aversive stimulus is presented periodically. Each occurrence of the avoidance response prevents delivery of aversive stimulation for a fixed period. Also called **free-operant avoidance;** originally called **Sidman avoidance.**

nonsense syllable A three-letter combination (two consonants separated by a vowel) that has no meaning.

O Abbreviation for the outcome of an instrumental response, or reinforcer.

object learning Learning associations between different stimulus elements of an object.

observational method A research technique in which behavior is observed without manipulations of the environment by the experimenter.

occasion setting Same as **facilitation.**

omission control procedure A procedure in which the unconditioned stimulus is presented after the conditioned stimulus (CS) only if the subject does not make the conditioned response during the CS. If the subject makes the conditioned response during the CS, the unconditioned stimulus is not presented on that trial.

omission training An instrumental conditioning procedure in which the instrumental response prevents the delivery of a reinforcing stimulus. (See also **differential reinforcement of other behavior.**)

one-way avoidance An avoidance conditioning procedure in which the required instrumental response is always to cross from one side of an experimental chamber to the other in the same direction.

operant level The rate of occurrence of an operant response before any experimental manipulation is introduced. Also called the **free-operant level** or **free-operant baseline.**

operant response A response that is defined by the effect it produces in the environment. Examples include pressing a lever and opening a door. Any sequence of movements that depresses the lever or opens the door constitutes an instance of that particular operant.

opponent process A compensatory mechanism that occurs in response to the primary process elicited by biologically significant events. The opponent process causes physiological and behavioral changes that are the opposite of those caused by the primary process. Sometimes referred to as the *b* process.

outcome Same as **reinforcer**.

overcorrection A procedure for discouraging behavior in which the subject is required to correct or rectify a mistake and extensively practice the correct response alternative.

overmatching Greater sensitivity to the relative rate of reinforcement than predicted by the matching law.

overshadowing Interference with the conditioning of a stimulus because of the simultaneous presence of another stimulus that is easier to condition.

paired-associate learning Learning associations between successive pairs of an ordered list of stimuli.

partial reinforcement Same as **intermittent reinforcement**.

partial-reinforcement extinction effect (PREE) A term used to describe greater persistence in instrumental responding in extinction after partial (intermittent) reinforcement training than after continuous reinforcement training.

passive avoidance A procedure in which the subject avoids an aversive stimulus by refraining from performing a particular response.

peak procedure A discrete-trial variation of a fixed-interval schedule used to study timing in animals.

peak-shift phenomenon A displacement of the highest rate of responding in a stimulus-generalization gradient away from the S+ in a direction opposite the S− after intradimensional discrimination training.

perceptual concept learning Learning to respond in a certain way to various objects (or views of an object) that belong to a set or category and in a different way to objects that do not belong to that category.

performance An organism's activities at a particular time.

perseverative behavior Repetitive responding, such as repeated manipulation of an object, observed in some children with autism.

phototaxis Orientation movements in relation to the source of light.

physiological homeostasis Same as **biological homeostasis**.

polymorphic rule A rule determining whether a stimulus belongs to a perceptual category, according to which categorization is determined by stimulus features. However, no one stimulus feature alone (or in combination with other features) is critical for membership in the category.

positive behavioral contrast Greater responding for a favorable reinforcer following previous experience with a less desired reinforcer than in the absence of such prior experience.

positive patterning A procedure in which two stimulus elements A and B are reinforced whenever they occur together (AB+) but are not reinforced whenever they occur individually (A−, B−).

positive reinforcement An instrumental conditioning procedure in which there is a positive contingency between the instrumental response and a reinforcing stimulus. If the subject performs the response, it receives the reinforcing stimulus; if the subject does not perform the response, it does not receive the reinforcing stimulus.

postreinforcement pause A pause in responding that typically occurs after the delivery of the reinforcer on fixed-ratio and fixed-interval schedules of reinforcement.

potentiation Enhanced conditioning of a CS caused by the presence of a more easily conditioned stimulus.

predatory imminence The perceived likelihood of being attacked by a predator. Different species-typical defense responses are assumed to be performed in the face of different degrees of predatory imminence.

PREE Abbreviation for **partial-reinforcement extinction effect**.

primary frustration An unconditioned stimulus or emotion produced by the encounter of a less-than-expected quantity or quality of reward.

primary motivation Motivation for instrumental behavior created by a drive state (either a biological drive or an acquired drive).

primary process The first process that is elicited by a biologically significant stimulus. Sometimes referred to as the *a* process.

principle of transsituationality The theoretical idea that if a stimulus is effective in strengthening (reinforcing) certain responses in one situation, it will also be effective in strengthening other kinds of responses in other situations.

proactive interference Disruption of memory by exposure to stimuli before the event to be remembered.

probability of a response The likelihood that a response will be made.

proprioceptive stimulus An internal response feedback stimulus that arises from the movement of muscles and/or joints. (Compare with **exteroceptive stimulus.**)

prospection Same as **prospective memory.**

prospective memory Memory of a plan for future action. Also called **prospection.**

pseudoconcept training A procedure in which reinforcement does not depend on whether or not the stimuli belong to a perceptual category.

pseudoconditioning Increased responding that may occur to a stimulus whose presentations are intermixed with presentations of an unconditioned stimulus (US) in the absence of the establishment of an association between the stimulus and the US.

psychic secretion The term originally used in Pavlov's laboratory to refer to the digestive secretions that occurred in dogs before the presentation of food.

punisher Same as **negative reinforcer** or **aversive stimulus.**

punishment An instrumental conditioning procedure in which there is a positive contingency between the instrumental response and an aversive stimulus. If the subject performs the instrumental response, it receives the aversive stimulus; if the subject does not perform the instrumental response, it does not receive the aversive stimulus.

puzzle box A type of experimental chamber used by Thorndike to study instrumental conditioning. The subject was put in the puzzle box and had to perform a specified behavior to be released.

radial maze A maze consisting of a central area from which alleys extend like spokes of a wheel.

random control procedure A procedure in which the conditioned and unconditioned stimuli are presented at random times with respect to each other.

ratio run The high and invariant rate of responding observed after the postreinforcement pause

on fixed-ratio reinforcement schedules. The ratio run ends when the necessary number of responses have been performed, and the subject is then reinforced.

ratio schedule A reinforcement schedule in which reinforcement depends only on the number of responses the subject performs, irrespective of when those responses occur.

ratio strain Disruption of responding that occurs when a fixed-ratio response requirement is increased too rapidly.

reference memory The retention of background information a subject has to have to respond successfully in a situation. (Compare with **working memory.**)

reflex A mechanism whereby a specific environmental event elicits a specific response.

reflex arc Neural structures, consisting of the efferent (sensory) neuron, interneuron, and afferent (motor) neuron, that enable a stimulus to elicit a reflex response.

rehearsal A theoretical process whereby some information is maintained in an active state, available to influence behavior and/or the processing of other information.

reinforcer A stimulus whose delivery shortly following a response increases the future probability of that response. (Also called **outcome.**)

relative rate of reinforcement The rate of reinforcement earned with one response alternative divided by the sum of the rates of reinforcement earned with all available response alternatives.

relative rate of response The rate of response on one response alternative divided by the sum of the response rates on all available response alternatives.

relative-waiting-time hypothesis The idea that conditioned responding depends on how long the subject has to wait for the unconditioned stimulus (US) in the presence of the conditioned stimulus (CS), as compared to how long the subject has to wait for the US in the experimental situation irrespective of the CS.

releasing stimulus Same as **sign stimulus.**

relief A hypothetical emotional state presumably elicited by classically conditioned stimuli that signal the absence or removal of an aversive stimulus, such as shock.

reminder treatment The presentation of a retrieval cue that reactivates a memory or facilitates memory retrieval.

response chain   A consecutively ordered series of responses in which each response produces the cue for the next response in the sequence.

response deprivation   Providing less opportunity to engage in a response than the subject made use of during a free-operant baseline period.

response-deprivation hypothesis   An explanation of reinforcement according to which response deprivation is sufficient to make the opportunity to perform a response an effective positive reinforcer.

response fatigue   See **fatigue.**

response prevention   Same as **flooding.**

response-rate schedule   A reinforcement schedule in which a response is reinforced depending on how soon that response is made after the previous occurrence of the behavior.

response–reinforcer contingency   The relation of a response to a reinforcer defined in terms of the probability of getting reinforced for making the response as compared to the probability of getting reinforced in the absence of the response.

retardation-of-acquisition test   A test procedure that identifies a stimulus as a conditioned inhibitor if that stimulus is slower to acquire excitatory properties than a comparison stimulus.

retention interval   The period of time between acquisition of information and a test of memory for that information.

retrieval   See **memory retrieval.**

retrieval cue   A stimulus related to an experience that facilitates the recall of other information related to that experience.

retrieval failure   A deficit in recovering information from a memory store.

retroactive interference   Disruption of memory by exposure to stimuli following the event to be remembered.

retrograde amnesia   A gradient of memory loss going back in time from the occurrence of a major injury or physiological disturbance. Amnesia is greatest for events that took place closest to the time of injury.

retrospection   Same as **retrospective memory.**

retrospective memory   Memory for a previously experienced event. Also called **retrospection.**

r_g Symbol for **fractional anticipatory goal response.**

R–S interval   The interval between the occurrence of an avoidance response and the next scheduled presentation of the aversive stimulus in a nondiscriminated avoidance procedure.

rule of thumb   A simple strategy or rule subjects may use in foraging. Such a rule does not involve precise calculations of optimality (maximum energy intake per unit time).

running speed   How fast (in feet per second, for example) subjects move in a runway.

running time   The amount of time subjects take to run from the start box to the goal box in a runway.

runway   An alley with a start box at one end and a goal box at the other. Animals are placed in the start box at the start of a trial and allowed to run to the goal box.

S+   A discriminative stimulus that evokes instrumental behavior because it signals that the instrumental response will be reinforced. Also called S^D.

S−   A discriminative stimulus that suppresses instrumental behavior because it signals that the instrumental response will not be reinforced. Also called S^Δ.

S^D Same as **S+.**

S^Δ Same as **S−.**

safe compartment   The compartment of a one-way avoidance apparatus in which shock is never delivered. Subjects have to enter this compartment to avoid or escape shock.

safety signal   A stimulus that signals the absence of an aversive event.

satiation   A procedure in which so much access to a reinforcer (such as food or water) is provided that the subject no longer seeks to contact or ingest it.

schedule of reinforcement   A program, or rule, that determines how and when the occurrence of a response will be followed by the delivery of the reinforcer.

secondary reinforcer   Same as **conditioned reinforcer.**

self-control   The foregoing of immediate gain for greater delayed benefits.

sensitization effect   An increase in the vigor of elicited behavior that may result from repeated presentations of the eliciting stimulus.

sensitization process   A neural mechanism that increases the magnitude of responses elicited by a stimulus.

sensory adaptation   A temporary reduction in the sensitivity of sense organs caused by repeated or excessive stimulation.

sensory neuron Same as **afferent neuron.**

sensory preconditioning A procedure in which one biologically weak stimulus (CS_2) is repeatedly paired with another biologically weak stimulus (CS_1). Then, CS_1 is conditioned with an unconditioned stimulus. In a later test trial, CS_2 also will elicit the conditioned response, even though CS_2 was never directly paired with the unconditioned stimulus.

sensory reinforcement Reinforcement provided by presentation of a stimulus unrelated to a biological need or drive.

sequential theory A theory of the partial reinforcement extinction effect according to which extinction is retarded after partial reinforcement because the instrumental response becomes conditioned to the memory of nonreward.

serial compound stimulus A compound stimulus consisting of two (or more) stimuli presented one after the other.

serial pattern behavior Responding on the basis of the pattern of a series of stimuli.

serial representation learning The formation of a mental representation of the order of an entire list of stimuli.

s_g Symbol for the response feedback stimuli produced by the fractional anticipatory goal response.

shaping Reinforcement of successive approximations to a desired instrumental response.

shock compartment The compartment of a one-way avoidance apparatus in which shock is delivered if the subject does not perform the avoidance response.

shock-frequency reduction A hypothesis according to which reduction in the frequency of shock serves to reinforce avoidance behavior.

short-delayed conditioning A classical conditioning procedure in which the conditioned stimulus is initiated shortly before the unconditioned stimulus on each conditioning trial.

short-term memory A memory store that is presumed to be responsible for instances in which a particular experience has only a short-lasting effect on the future actions of the organism.

shuttle avoidance A type of avoidance conditioning procedure in which the required instrumental response consists in going back and forth (shuttling) between two sides of an experimental apparatus.

Sidman avoidance Same as **nondiscriminated** or **free-operant avoidance.**

signaled avoidance Same as **discriminated avoidance.**

signal relation The extent to which the occurrence of one stimulus can be predicted from the prior occurrence of another stimulus.

sign stimulus A specific feature of an object or animal that elicits a modal action pattern in another organism. Also called a **releasing stimulus.**

sign tracking Movement toward and possibly contact with a stimulus that signals the availability of a positive reinforcer, such as food. (Also called **autoshaping.**) (See also **negative sign tracking.**)

simultaneous compound stimulus A compound stimulus consisting of two or more stimuli presented at the same time.

simultaneous conditioning A classical conditioning procedure in which the conditioned stimulus and the unconditioned stimulus are presented simultaneously on each conditioning trial.

simultaneous matching to sample A procedure in which subjects are reinforced for responding to a test stimulus that is the same as a sample stimulus. The sample and the test stimuli are presented at the same time.

Skinner box A small experimental chamber provided with a device that the subject can repeatedly manipulate, such as a response lever. Thus, the subject can repeatedly perform a particular response without being handled. The chamber usually also has a mechanism that can deliver a reinforcer, such as a pellet of food.

SOP theory The conditioning theory proposed by Wagner that makes certain assumptions about the Standard Operating Procedures of memory systems. Also called Sometimes Opponent Process theory.

spatial memory Memory of locations in space.

species-specific defense reactions (SSDRs) Species-typical responses animals perform in an aversive situation. The responses may involve freezing, fleeing, or fighting.

spontaneous recovery Recovery of a response produced by a period of rest after habituation or extinction.

S–R learning The learning of an association between a stimulus and a response, with the result that the stimulus comes to elicit the response.

S–R system The shortest neural pathway that connects the sense organs stimulated by an eliciting stimulus and the muscles involved in making the elicited response.

SSDR   Abbreviation for **species-specific defense reaction.**

S–S interval   The interval between successive presentations of the aversive stimulus in a nondiscriminated avoidance procedure when the avoidance response is not performed.

S–S learning   The learning of an association between two stimuli, with the result that exposure to one of the stimuli comes to activate a representation, or "mental image," of the other stimulus.

standard pattern of affective dynamics   As specified by the opponent-process theory of motivation, a pattern of emotional changes that is frequently observed when a novel, biologically significant event is presented.

startle response   A sudden jump or tensing of the muscles that may occur when an unexpected stimulus is presented.

state system   Neural structures that determine the general level of responsiveness, or readiness to respond, of the organism.

stereotypy   Repetitive aberrant behavior, such as hand waving, making noises, or rubbing objects, observed in some autistic children.

stimulus contiguity   The occurrence of two or more stimuli at the same time.

stimulus discrimination   Differential responding in the presence of two or more stimuli.

stimulus discrimination procedure (in classical conditioning)   Same procedure as **differential inhibition.**

stimulus-discrimination procedure (in instrumental conditioning)   A procedure in which reinforcement for responding is available whenever one stimulus (the S+, or S^D) is present and not available whenever another stimulus (the S−, or S$^\Delta$) is present.

stimulus-element   An approach to the analysis of control by compound stimuli in which it is assumed that subjects respond to a compound stimulus in terms of the elements that make up the compound. (Compare with **configural-cue.**)

stimulus generalization   The occurrence of behavior learned through habituation or conditioning in the presence of stimuli that are different from the stimuli used during training.

stimulus generalization gradient   A gradient of responding that may be observed if subjects are tested with stimuli that increasingly differ from the stimulus that was present during training. (See also **excitatory stimulus generalization gradient** and **inhibitory stimulus generalization gradient.**)

stimulus relevance   The observation that learning occurs much more rapidly with certain combinations of conditioned and unconditioned stimuli (such as tastes and sickness) than with other stimulus combinations (such as tastes and shock).

stimulus substitution   The theoretical idea that the outcome of classical conditioning is that organisms come to respond to the conditioned stimulus in much the same way that they respond to the unconditioned stimulus.

substitutability   In consumer demand theory, one of the factors that determines elasticity of demand. Two substances are said to be substitutable if increases in the price of one substance result in a shift in favor of purchasing more of the other substance.

successive delayed matching to sample   A matching-to-sample procedure in which the response alternatives are presented one at a time after the sample stimulus.

summation test   Same as **compound-stimulus test.**

supernormal stimulus   An artificially enlarged or exaggerated sign stimulus.

superstitious behavior   Behavior that increases in frequency because of accidental pairings of the delivery of a reinforcer with occurrences of the behavior.

tabula rasa   The concept proposed by Locke that the human mind is devoid of ideas at birth.

taxis   An orientation movement toward or away from an eliciting stimulus.

temporal contiguity   Same as **contiguity.**

temporal relation between the response and the reinforcer   When the reinforcer occurs relative to when the instrumental response occurs.

terminal responses   Responses that are much more likely to occur at the end of the interval between successive reinforcements than at other times in a procedure that involves periodic presentations of a reinforcer.

test trial   A trial in which the conditioned stimulus is presented without the unconditioned stimulus. This allows measurement of the conditioned response in the absence of the unconditioned response.

thermotaxis An orientation movement related to temperature.

T maze An alley constructed in the shape of a T, with the start box at the end of the longest stem of the maze and goal boxes at the ends of the other stems. After leaving the start box, the subject can choose to enter either the right or left goal box.

time out A period during which the opportunity to obtain reinforcement is removed. This may involve removal of the subject from the situation where reinforcers may be obtained.

timing A process presumed to be responsible for responding being controlled only by the duration of a stimulus or event.

tolerance See **drug tolerance.**

trace conditioning A classical conditioning procedure in which the unconditioned stimulus is presented after the conditioned stimulus has been terminated for a short period.

trace decay hypothesis The theoretical idea that exposure to a stimulus produces changes in the nervous system that gradually decrease after the stimulus has been terminated.

trace interval The interval between the end of the conditioned stimulus and the start of the unconditioned stimulus in trace-conditioning trials.

transfer-of-control experiment An experiment that assesses the effects of a classically conditioned stimulus (CS) on the performance of instrumental behavior. The CS and the instrumental behavior are first conditioned in independent phases of the experiment. The effects of the CS on instrumental behavior are then determined in a transfer phase.

transitive inference Inferring a serial order among stimuli on the basis of experience only with adjacent or successive pairs of stimuli.

transsituationality See **principle of transsituationality.**

triadic design An experimental design frequently used in studies of the learned-helplessness effect. It includes a group exposed to escapable shock, another group exposed to yoked inescapable shock, and a nonshocked control group. After these various treatments, each group is tested with a standard learning task.

trials-unique procedure A matching-to-sample procedure in which a different stimulus serves as the sample on each trial.

unconditional or *unconditioned response* A response that occurs to a stimulus without the necessity of prior training.

unconditional or *unconditioned stimulus* A stimulus that elicits a particular response without the necessity of prior training.

unconditioned reinforcer A stimulus that is an effective reinforcer without the necessity of prior training.

undermatching Less sensitivity to the relative rate of reinforcement than predicted by the matching law.

UR Abbreviation for **unconditioned response.**

US Abbreviation for **unconditioned stimulus.**

US devaluation See **devaluation of a reinforcer.**

US-modification model A model that explains differences in learning in terms of changes in effectiveness of the unconditioned stimulus.

US-preexposure effect Interference with conditioning produced by repeated exposures of the subject to the unconditioned stimulus before the conditioning trials.

US representation The hypothesized image or memory that organisms have of the unconditioned stimulus.

variable-interval schedule A reinforcement schedule in which reinforcement is provided for the first response that occurs after a variable amount of time from the last reinforcement.

variable-ratio schedule A reinforcement schedule in which the number of responses necessary to produce reinforcement varies from trial to trial. The value of the schedule refers to the average number of responses needed for reinforcement.

VI Abbreviation for **variable-interval schedule.**

vicious-circle behavior Maintenance by punishment of behavior that was originally conditioned with a negative reinforcement or escape procedure.

VR Abbreviation for **variable-ratio schedule.**

working memory The retention of information that is needed only to respond successfully for the task at hand, as contrasted with reference memory that involves background information that is also needed for future similar tasks.

References

Abramson, L. Y., Metalsky, G. I., & Alloy, L. B. (1989). Hopelessness depression: A theory-based subtype of depression. *Psychological Review, 96,* 358–372.

Adams, G. P. (1903). On the negative and positive phototropism of the earthworm *Allolobophora foetida* as determined by light of different intensities. *American Journal of Physiology, 9,* 26–34.

Ader, R. (1985). Conditioned taste aversions and immunopharmacology. *Annals of the New York Academy of Sciences.*

Ader, R., & Cohen, N. (1982). Behaviorally conditioned immunosuppression and murine systemic lupus erythematosus. *Science, 215,* 1534–1536.

Ader, R., Cohen, N., & Bovbjerg, D. (1982). Conditioned suppression of humoral immunity in the rat. *Journal of Comparative and Physiological Psychology, 96,* 517–521.

Albert, M., & Ayres, J. J. B. (1989). With number of preexposures constant latent inhibition increases with preexposure CS duration or total CS exposure. *Learning and Motivation, 20,* 278–294.

Allen, A. A. (1934). Sex rhythm in the ruffed grouse *(Bonasa umbellus)* and other birds. *Auk, 51,* 180–199.

Allison, J. (1983). *Behavioral economics.* New York: Praeger.

Allison, J. (1989). The nature of reinforcement. In S. B. Klein & R. R. Mowrer (Eds.), *Contemporary learning theories: Instrumental conditioning and the impact of biological constraints on learning* (pp. 13–39). Hillsdale, NJ: Erlbaum.

Allison, J., Buxton, A., & Moore, K. E. (1987). Bliss points, stop lines, and performance under schedule constraint. *Journal of Experimental Psychology: Animal Behavior Processes, 13,* 331–340.

Allison, J., & Moore, K. E. (1985). Lick-trading by rats: On the substitutability of dry, water, and saccharin tubes. *Journal of the Experimental Analysis of Behavior, 43,* 195–213.

Allison, J., Moore, K. E., Gawley, D. J., Mondloch, C. J., & Mondloch, M. V. (1986). The temporal patterns of unconstrained drinking: Rats' responses to inversion and identity constraints. *Journal of the Experimental Analysis of Behavior, 45,* 5–13.

Allison, J., & Timberlake, W. (1974). Instrumental and contingent saccharin-licking in rats: Response deprivation and reinforcement. *Learning and Motivation, 5,* 231–247.

Amsel, A. (1958). The role of frustrative nonreward in noncontinuous reward situations. *Psychological Bulletin, 55,* 102–119.

Amsel, A. (1962). Frustrative nonreward in partial reinforcement and discrimination learning. *Psychological Review, 69,* 306–328.

Amsel, A. (1967). Partial reinforcement effects on vigor and persistence. In K. W. Spence & J. T. Spence (Eds.), *The psychology of learning and motivation* (Vol. 1). New York: Academic Press.

Amsel, A. (1986). Developmental psychobiology and behavior theory: Reciprocating influences. *Canadian Journal of Psychology, 40,* 311–342.

Amsel, A. (1989). *Behaviorism, neobehaviorism, and cognitivism in learning theory.* Hillsdale, NJ: Erlbaum.

Amsel, A., & Rashotte, M. E. (1984). *Mechanisms of adaptive behavior: Clark L. Hull's theoretical papers, with commentary.* New York: Columbia University Press.

Anderson, D. C., Crowell, C. R., Cunningham, C. L., & Lupo, J. V. (1979). Behavior during shock exposure as a determinant of subsequent interference with shuttle box escape-avoidance learning in the rat. *Journal of Experimental Psychology: Animal Behavior Processes, 5,* 243–257.

Anderson, M. C., & Shettleworth, S. J. (1977). Behavioral adaptation to fixed-interval and fixed-time food delivery in golden hamsters. *Journal of the Experimental Analysis of Behavior, 25,* 33–49.

Andrews, M. W. (1988). Selection of food sites by *Callicebus moloch* and *Saimiri sciureus* under spatially and temporally varying food distribution. *Learning and Motivation, 19,* 254–268.

Anger, D. (1963). The role of temporal discrimination in

the reinforcement of Sidman avoidance behavior. *Journal of the Experimental Analysis of Behavior, 6,* 477–506.

Anisman, H., de Catanzaro, D., & Remington, G. (1978). Escape performance following exposure to inescapable shock: Deficits in motor response maintenance. *Journal of Experimental Psychology: Animal Behavior Processes, 4,* 197–218.

Anisman, H., Hamilton, M., & Zacharko, R. M. (1984). Cue and response-choice acquisition and reversal after exposure to uncontrollable shock: Induction of response perseveration. *Journal of Experimental Psychology: Animal Behavior Processes, 10,* 229–243.

Archer, T., & Sjoden, P.-O. (1982). Higher-order conditioning and sensory preconditioning of a taste aversion with an exteroceptive CS_1. *Quarterly Journal of Experimental Psychology, 34B,* 1–17.

Autor, S. M. (1969). The strength of conditioned reinforcers as a function of frequency and probability of reinforcement. In D. P. Hendry (Ed.), *Conditioned reinforcement* (pp. 127–162). Homewood, IL: Dorsey.

Ayres, J. J. B., Haddad, C., & Albert, M. (1987). One-trial excitatory backward conditioning as assessed by suppression of licking in rats: Concurrent observations of lick suppression and defensive behaviors. *Animal Learning & Behavior, 15,* 212–217.

Azorlosa, J. L., & Cicala, G. A. (1986). Blocking of conditioned suppression with 1 or 10 compound trials. *Animal Learning & Behavior, 14,* 163–167.

Azrin, N. H. (1956). Some effects of two intermittent schedules of immediate and non-immediate punishment. *Journal of Psychology, 42,* 3–21.

Azrin, N. H. (1958). Some effects of noise on human behavior. *Journal of the Experimental Analysis of Behavior, 1,* 183–200.

Azrin, N. H. (1959). Punishment and recovery during fixed ratio performance. *Journal of the Experimental Analysis of Behavior, 2,* 301–305.

Azrin, N. H. (1960). Effects of punishment intensity during variable-interval reinforcement. *Journal of the Experimental Analysis of Behavior, 3,* 123–142.

Azrin, N. H., & Hake, D. F. (1969). Positive conditioned suppression: Conditioned suppression using positive reinforcers as the unconditioned stimuli. *Journal of the Experimental Analysis of Behavior, 12,* 167–173.

Azrin, N. H., & Holz, W. C. (1961). Punishment during fixed-interval reinforcement. *Journal of the Experimental Analysis of Behavior, 4,* 343–347.

Azrin, N. H., & Holz, W. C. (1966). Punishment. In W. K. Honig (Ed.), *Operant behavior: Areas of research and application* (pp. 380–447). New York: Appleton-Century-Crofts.

Azrin, N. H., Holz, W. C., & Hake, D. F. (1963). Fixed-ratio punishment. *Journal of the Experimental Analysis of Behavior, 6,* 141–148.

Azrin, N. H., Hutchinson, R. R., & Hake, D. F. (1966).

Extinction-induced aggression. *Journal of the Experimental Analysis of Behavior, 9,* 191–204.

Babkin, B. P. (1949). *Pavlov: A biography.* Chicago: University of Chicago Press.

Baer, D. M., & Wolf, M. M. (1970). The entry into natural communities of reinforcement. In R. Ulrich, T. Stachnik, & J. Mabry (Eds.), *Control of human behavior* (Vol. 2, pp. 319–324). Glenview, IL: Scott Foresman.

Baerends, G. P. (1957). The ethological analysis of fish behavior. In M. E. Brown (Ed.), *The physiology of fishes.* New York: Academic Press.

Baerends, G. P. (1985). Do the dummy experiments with sticklebacks support the IRM-concept? *Behaviour, 93,* 258–277.

Baerends, G. P. (1988). Ethology. In R. C. Atkinson, R. J. Herrnstein, G. Lindzey, & R. D. Luce (Eds.), *Stevens' handbook of experimental psychology* (Vol. 1, pp. 765–830). New York: Wiley.

Baerends, G. P., & Drent, R. H. (Eds.). (1982). The herring gull and its egg. Part II. The responsiveness to egg features. *Behaviour, 82,* 1–417.

Baker, A. G., & Baker, P. A. (1985). Does inhibition differ from excitation? Proactive interference, contextual conditioning, and extinction. In R. R. Miller & N. E. Spear (Eds.), *Information processing in animals: Conditioned inhibition.* Hillsdale, NJ: Erlbaum.

Baker, A. G., & Mackintosh, N. J. (1977). Excitatory and inhibitory conditioning following uncorrelated presentations of CS and UCS. *Animal Learning & Behavior, 5,* 315–319.

Baker, A. G., & Mercier, P. (1982). Extinction of the context and latent inhibition. *Learning and Motivation, 13,* 391–416.

Baker, A. G., Singh, M., & Bindra, D. (1985). Some effects of contextual conditioning and US predictability on Pavlovian conditioning. In P. Balsam & A. Tomie (Eds.), *Context and learning.* Hillsdale, NJ: Erlbaum.

Baker, T. B., & Tiffany, S. T. (1985). Morphine tolerance as habituation. *Psychological Review, 92,* 78–108.

Balaz, M. A., Kasprow, W. J., & Miller, R. R. (1982). Blocking with a single compound trial. *Animal Learning & Behavior, 10,* 271–276.

Balda, R. P., & Kamil, A. C. (1988). The spatial memory of Clark's nutcrackers *(Nucifraga columbiana)* in an analogue of the radial arm maze. *Animal Learning & Behavior, 16,* 116–122.

Balda, R. P., & Turek, R. J. (1984). The cache-recovery system as an example of memory capabilities in Clark's nutcracker. In H. L. Roitblat, T. G. Bever, & H. S. Terrace (Eds.), *Animal cognition.* Hillsdale, NJ: Erlbaum.

Balsam, P. D. (1985). The functions of context in learning and performance. In P. D. Balsam & A. Tomie (Eds.), *Context and learning* (pp. 1–21). Hillsdale, NJ: Erlbaum.

Balsam, P. D. (1988). Selection, representation, and equivalence of controlling stimuli. In R. C. Atkinson, R. J. Herrnstein, G. Lindzey, & R. D. Luce (Eds.), *Stevens' handbook of experimental psychology: Vol. 2. Learning and cognition* (pp. 111–166). New York: Wiley.

Balsam, P. D., & Gibbon, J. (1988). Formation of tone-US associations does not interfere with the formation of context-US associations in pigeons. *Journal of Experimental Psychology: Animal Behavior Processes, 14,* 401–412.

Balsam, P. D., & Tomie, A. (Eds.). (1985). *Context and learning.* Hillsdale, NJ: Erlbaum.

Banks, R. K. (1976). Resistance to punishment as a function of intensity and frequency of prior punishment experience. *Learning and Motivation, 7,* 551–558.

Barker, L. M., Best, M. R., & Domjan, M. (Eds.). (1977). *Learning mechanisms in food selection.* Waco, TX: Baylor University Press.

Baron, A. (1965). Delayed punishment of a runway response. *Journal of Comparative and Physiological Psychology, 60,* 131–134.

Baron, A., & Menich, S. R. (1985). Reaction times of younger and older men: Effects of compound samples and a prechoice signal on delayed matching-to-sample performances. *Journal of the Experimental Analysis of Behavior, 44,* 1–14.

Barton, L. E., Brulle, A. R., & Repp, A. C. (1986). Maintenance of therapeutic change by momentary DRO. *Journal of Applied Behavior Analysis, 19,* 277–282.

Bashinski, H., Werner, J., & Rudy, J. (1985). Determinants of infant visual attention: Evidence for a two-process theory. *Journal of Experimental Child Psychology, 39,* 580–598.

Batsell, W. R., Jr., Ludvigson, H. W., & Kunko, P. M. (1990). Odor from rats tasting a signal of illness. *Journal of Experimental Psychology: Animal Behavior Processes, 16,* 193–199.

Baum, M. (1969). Extinction of avoidance response following response prevention: Some parametric investigations. *Canadian Journal of Psychology, 23,* 1–10.

Baum, M. (1970). Extinction of avoidance responding through response prevention (flooding). *Psychological Bulletin, 74,* 276–284.

Baum, W. M. (1974). On two types of deviation from the matching law: Bias and undermatching. *Journal of the Experimental Analysis of Behavior, 22,* 231–242.

Baum, W. M. (1975). Time allocation in human vigilance. *Journal of the Experimental Analysis of Behavior, 23,* 45–53.

Baum, W. M. (1979). Matching, undermatching, and overmatching in studies of choice. *Journal of the Experimental Analysis of Behavior, 32,* 269–281.

Baum, W. M. (1981). Optimization and the matching law as accounts of instrumental behavior. *Journal of the Experimental Analysis of Behavior, 36,* 387–403.

Baxter, D. J., & Zamble, E. (1982). Reinforcer and response specificity in appetitive transfer of control. *Animal Learning & Behavior, 10,* 201–210.

Beatty, W. W., & Shavalia, D. A. (1980a). Rat spatial memory: Resistance to retroactive interference at long

retention intervals. *Animal Learning & Behavior, 8,* 550–552.

Beatty, W. W., & Shavalia, D. A. (1980b). Spatial memory in rats: Time course of working memory and effects of anesthetics. *Behavioral and Neural Biology, 28,* 454–462.

Bechterev, V. M. (1913). *La psychologie objective.* Paris: Alcan.

Benedict, J. O., & Ayres, J. J. B. (1972). Factors affecting conditioning in the truly random control procedure in the rat. *Journal of Comparative and Physiological Psychology, 78,* 323–330.

Berlyne, D. E. (1969). The reward value of indifferent stimulation. In J. Tapp (Ed.), *Reinforcement and behavior.* New York: Academic Press.

Bernstein, D. J., & Ebbesen, E. B. (1978). Reinforcement and substitution in humans: A multiple response analysis. *Journal of the Experimental Analysis of Behavior, 30,* 243–253.

Bernstein, I. L. (1978). Learned taste aversions in children receiving chemotherapy. *Science, 200,* 1302–1303.

Bernstein, I. L., & Borson, S. (1986). Learned food aversion: A component of anorexia syndromes. *Psychological Review, 93,* 462–472.

Bernstein, I. L., & Webster, M. M. (1980). Learned taste aversions in humans. *Physiology and Behavior, 25,* 363–366.

Berridge, K. C., & Schulkin, J. (1989). Palatability shift of a salt-associated incentive during sodium depletion. *Quarterly Journal of Experimental Psychology, 41B,* 121–138.

Best, M. R., Batson, J. D., Meachum, C. L., Brown, E. R., & Ringer, M. (1985). Characteristics of taste-mediated environmental potentiation in rats. *Learning and Motivation, 16,* 190–209.

Best, M. R., Brown, E. R., & Sowell, M. K. (1984). Taste-mediated potentiation of noningestional stimuli in rats. *Learning and Motivation, 15,* 244–258.

Best, M. R., Dunn, D. P., Batson, J. D., Meachum, C. L., & Nash, S. M. (1985). Extinguishing conditioned inhibition in flavour-aversion learning: Effects of repeated testing and extinction of the excitatory element. *Quarterly Journal of Experimental Psychology, 37B,* 359–378.

Best, P. J., Best, M. R., & Henggeler, S. (1977). The contribution of environmental noningestive cues in conditioning with aversive internal consequences. In L. M. Barker, M. R. Best, & M. Domjan (Eds.), *Learning mechanisms in food selection* (pp. 371–393). Waco, TX: Baylor University Press.

Bhatt, R. S., & Wasserman, E. A. (1987). Choice behavior of pigeons on progressive and multiple schedules: A test of optimal foraging theory. *Journal of Experimental Psychology: Animal Behavior Processes, 13,* 40–51.

Bhatt, R. S., Wasserman, E. A., Reynolds, W. F., Jr., & Knauss, K. S. (1988). Conceptual behavior in pigeons: Categorization of both familiar and novel examples from four classes of natural and artificial stimuli. *Journal of Experimental Psychology: Animal Behavior Processes, 14,* 219–234.

Bickel, W. K., DeGrandpre, R. J., Hughes, J. R., & Higgins, S. T. (1991). Behavioral economics of drug self-administration. II. A unit-price analysis of cigarette smoking. *Journal of the Experimental Analysis of Behavior, 55,* 145–154.

Bitterman, M. E. (1964). Classical conditioning in the goldfish as a function of the CS-US interval. *Journal of Comparative and Physiological Psychology, 58,* 359–366.

Bitterman, M. E. (1975). The comparative analysis of learning. *Science, 188,* 699–709.

Bjork, R. A. (1972). The updating of human memory. In G. H. Bower (Ed.), *The psychology of learning and motivation* (Vol. 12). New York: Academic Press.

Black, A. H. (1971). Autonomic aversive conditioning in infrahuman subjects. In F. R. Brush (Ed.), *Aversive conditioning and learning.* New York: Academic Press.

Black, A. H. (1977). Comments on "Learned helplessness: Theory and evidence" by Maier and Seligman. *Journal of Experimental Psychology: General, 106,* 41–43.

Blackman, D. (1977). Conditioned suppression and the effects of classical conditioning on operant behavior. In W. K. Honig & J. E. R. Staddon (Eds.), *Handbook of operant behavior.* Englewood Cliffs, NJ: Prentice-Hall.

Blakely, E., & Schlinger, H. (1988). Determinants of pausing under variable-ratio schedules: Reinforcer magnitude, ratio size, and schedule configuration. *Journal of the Experimental Analysis of Behavior, 50,* 65–73.

Blakemore, C., & Cooper, G. F. (1970). Development of the brain depends on visual environment. *Science, 228,* 477–478.

Blass, E. M., Ganchrow, J. R., & Steiner, J. E. (1984). Classical conditioning in newborn humans 2–48 hours of age. *Infant Behavior and Development, 7,* 223–235.

Blough, D. S. (1959). Delayed matching in the pigeon. *Journal of the Experimental Analysis of Behavior, 2,* 151–160.

Boakes, R. A. (1979). Interactions between type I and type II processes involving positive reinforcement. In A. Dickinson & R. A. Boakes (Eds.), *Mechanisms of learning and motivation.* Hillsdale, NJ: Erlbaum.

Boakes, R. A. (1984). *From Darwin to behaviourism.* Cambridge: Cambridge University Press.

Boakes, R. A., & Halliday, M. S. (Eds.). (1972). *Inhibition and learning.* London: Academic Press.

Boice, R. (1973). Domestication. *Psychological Bulletin, 80,* 215–230.

Boice, R. (1977). Burrows of wild and albino rats: Effects of domestication, outdoor raising, age, experience, and maternal state. *Journal of Comparative and Physiological Psychology, 91,* 649–661.

Boice, R. (1981). Behavioral comparability of wild and domesticated rats. *Behavior Genetics, 11,* 545–553.

Boland, F. J., Mellor, C. S., & Revusky, S. (1978). Chemical aversion treatment of alcoholism: Lithium as the aversive agent. *Behaviour Research and Therapy, 16,* 401–409.

Bolles, R. C. (1969). Avoidance and escape learning: Simultaneous acquisition of different responses. *Journal of Comparative and Physiological Psychology, 68,* 355–358.

Bolles, R. C. (1970). Species-specific defense reactions and avoidance learning. *Psychological Review, 71,* 32–48.

Bolles, R. C. (1971). Species-specific defense reaction. In F. R. Brush (Ed.), *Aversive conditioning and learning.* New York: Academic Press.

Bolles, R. C. (1972a). The avoidance learning problem. In G. H. Bower (Ed.), *The psychology of learning and motivation* (Vol. 6). New York: Academic Press.

Bolles, R. C. (1972b). Reinforcement, expectancy, and learning. *Psychological Review, 79,* 394–409.

Bolles, R. C. (1975). *Theory of motivation* (2nd ed.). New York: Harper & Row.

Bolles, R. C., & Fanselow, M. S. (1980). A perceptual-defensive-recuperative model of fear and pain. *Behavioral and Brain Sciences, 3,* 291–323.

Bolles, R. C., & Grossen, N. E. (1969). Effects of an informational stimulus on the acquisition of avoidance behavior in rats. *Journal of Comparative and Physiological Psychology, 68,* 90–99.

Bolles, R. C., Holtz, R., Dunn, T., & Hill, W. (1980). Comparisons of stimulus learning and response learning in a punishment situation. *Learning and Motivation, 11,* 78–96.

Bolles, R. C., & Riley, A. L. (1973). Freezing as an avoidance response: Another look at the operant-respondent distinction. *Learning and Motivation, 4,* 268–275.

Bolles, R. C., Stokes, L. W., & Younger, M. S. (1966). Does CS termination reinforce avoidance behavior? *Journal of Comparative and Physiological Psychology, 62,* 201–207.

Bond, N. W. (Ed.). (1984). *Animal models in psychopathology.* Orlando, FL: Academic Press.

Borovsky, D., & Rovee-Collier, C. (1990). Contextual constraints on memory retrieval at six months. *Child Development, 61,* 1569–1583.

Borszcz, G. S., Cranney, J., & Leaton, R. N. (1989). Influence of long-term sensitization on long-term habituation of the acoustic startle response in rats: Central gray lesions, preexposure, and extinction. *Journal of Experimental Psychology: Animal Behavior Processes, 15,* 54–64.

Bouton, M. E. (1984). Differential control by context in the inflation and reinstatement paradigms. *Journal of Experimental Psychology: Animal Behavior Processes, 10,* 56–74.

Bouton, M. E. (1991). Context and retrieval in extinction and in other examples of interference in simple associative learning. In L. Dachowski & C. F. Flaherty

(Eds.), *Current topics in animal learning* (pp. 25–53). Hillsdale, NJ: Erlbaum.

Bouton, M. E., & Bolles, R. C. (1980). Conditioned fear assessed by freezing and by the suppression of three different baselines. *Animal Learning & Behavior, 8,* 429–434.

Bouton, M. E., & Bolles, R. C. (1985). Contexts, event-memories, and extinction. In P. Balsam & A. Tomie (Eds.), *Context and conditioning* (pp. 133–166). Hillsdale, NJ: Erlbaum.

Bouton, M. E., Dunlap, C. M., & Swartzentruber, D. (1987). Potentiation of taste by another taste during compound aversion learning. *Animal Learning & Behavior, 15,* 433–438.

Bouton, M. E., Jones, D. L., McPhillips, S. A., & Swartzentruber, D. (1986). Potentiation and overshadowing in odor-aversion learning: Role of method of odor presentation, the distal-proximal cue distinction, and the conditionability of odor. *Learning and Motivation, 17,* 115–138.

Bouton, M. E., & King, D. A. (1983). Contextual control of the extinction of conditioned fear: Tests for the associative value of the context. *Journal of Experimental Psychology: Animal Behavior Processes, 9,* 248–265.

Bouton, M. E., & King, D. A. (1986). Effect of context on performance to conditioned stimuli with mixed histories of reinforcement and nonreinforcement. *Journal of Experimental Psychology: Animal Behavior Processes, 12,* 4–15.

Bouton, M. E., & Peck, C. A. (1989). Context effects on conditioning, extinction, and reinstatement in an appetitive conditioning preparation. *Animal Learning & Behavior, 17,* 188–198.

Bouton, M. E., & Swartzentruber, D. (1986). Analysis of the associative and occasion-setting properties of contexts participating in a Pavlovian discrimination. *Journal of Experimental Psychology: Animal Behavior Processes, 12,* 333–350.

Bovbjerg, D., Ader, R., & Cohen, N. (1984). Acquisition and extinction of conditioned suppression of a graft-vs-host response in the rat. *Journal of Immunology, 132,* 111–113.

Bowe, C. A., Miller, J. D., & Green, L. (1987). Qualities and locations of stimuli and responses affecting discrimination learning of chinchillas *(Chinchilla laniger)* and pigeons *(Columbia livia). Journal of Comparative Psychology, 101,* 132–138.

Braveman, N. S., & Bronstein, P. (Eds.). (1985). *Annals of the New York Academy of Sciences: Vol. 443. Experimental assessments and clinical applications of conditioned food aversions.* New York: New York Academy of Sciences.

Breland, K., & Breland, M. (1961). The misbehavior of organisms. *American Psychologist, 16,* 681–684.

Brener, J., & Mitchell, S. (1989). Changes in energy expenditure and work during response acquisition in rats. *Journal of Experimental Psychology: Animal Behavior Processes, 15,* 166–175.

Brogden, W. J., Lipman, E. A., & Culler, E. (1938). The role of incentive in conditioning and extinction. *American Journal of Psychology, 51,* 109–117.

Brown, J. S. (1969). Factors affecting self-punitive behavior. In B. Campbell & R. M. Church (Eds.), *Punishment and aversive behavior.* New York: Appleton-Century-Crofts.

Brown, J. S., & Cunningham, C. L. (1981). The paradox of persisting self-punitive behavior. *Neuroscience & Biobehavioral Reviews, 5,* 343–354.

Brown, J. S., & Jacobs, A. (1949). The role of fear in the motivation and acquisition of responses. *Journal of Experimental Psychology, 39,* 747–759.

Brown, M. F., Wheeler, E. A., & Riley, D. A. (1989). Evidence for a shift in the choice criterion of rats in a 12-arm radial maze. *Animal Learning & Behavior, 17,* 12–20.

Brown, P. L., & Jenkins, H. M. (1968). Auto-shaping the pigeon's key peck. *Journal of the Experimental Analysis of Behavior, 11,* 1–8.

Brown-Su, A. M., Matzel, L. D., Gordon, E. L., & Miller, R. R. (1986). Malleability of conditioned associations: Path dependence. *Journal of Experimental Psychology: Animal Behavior Processes, 12,* 420–427.

Bull, J. A., III. (1970). An interaction between appetitive Pavlovian CS's and instrumental avoidance responding. *Learning and Motivation, 1,* 18–26.

Bull, J. A., III, & Overmier, J. B. (1968). Additive and subtractive properties of excitation and inhibition. *Journal of Comparative and Physiological Psychology, 66,* 511–514.

Burkhard, B., Rachlin, H., & Schrader, S. (1978). Reinforcement and punishment in a closed system. *Learning and Motivation, 9,* 392–410.

Burkhardt, P. E., & Ayres, J. J. B. (1978). CS and US duration effects in one-trial simultaneous conditioning as assessed by conditioned suppression of licking in rats. *Animal Learning and Behavior, 6,* 225–230.

Butler, J., & Rovee-Collier, C. (1989). Contextual gating of memory retrieval. *Developmental Psychobiology, 22,* 533–552.

Caggiula, A. R., & Hoebel, B. G. (1966). "Copulation-reward" site in the posterior hypothalamus. *Science, 153,* 1284–1285.

Camhi, J. M. (1984). *Neuroethology.* Sunderland, MA: Sinauer.

Camp, D. S., Raymond, G. A., & Church, R. M. (1967). Temporal relationship between response and punishment. *Journal of Experimental Psychology, 74,* 114–123.

Campbell, B. A., & Church, R. M. (Eds.). (1969). *Punishment and aversive behavior.* New York: Appleton-Century-Crofts.

Campbell, B. A., & Randall, P. K. (1976). The effect of reinstatement stimulus conditions on the maintenance of long-term memory. *Developmental Psychobiology, 9,* 325–333.

Cannon, D. S., & Baker, T. B. (1981). Emetic and electric

shock alcohol aversion therapy: Assessment of conditioning. *Journal of Consulting and Clinical Psychology, 49,* 20–33.

Cannon, D. S., Baker, T. B., Gino, A., & Nathan, P. E. (1986). Alcohol-aversion therapy: Relation between strength of aversion and abstinence. *Journal of Consulting and Clinical Psychology, 54,* 825–830.

Cannon, D. S., Best, M. R., Batson, J. D., & Feldman, M. (1983). Taste familiarity and apomorphine-induced taste aversions in humans. *Behaviour Research and Therapy, 21,* 669–673.

Capaldi, E. J. (1967). A sequential hypothesis of instrumental learning. In K. W. Spence & J. T. Spence (Eds.), *The psychology of learning and motivation* (Vol. 1, pp. 67–156). New York: Academic Press.

Capaldi, E. J. (1971). Memory and learning: A sequential viewpoint. In W. K. Honig & P. H. R. James (Eds.), *Animal memory* (pp. 115–154). New York: Academic Press.

Capaldi, E. J. (in press). Levels of organized behavior in rats. In W. K. Honig & J. G. Fetterman (Eds.), *Cognitive aspects of stimulus control.* Hillsdale, NJ: Erlbaum.

Capaldi, E. J., & Miller, D. J. (1988a). Counting in rats: Its functional significance and the independent cognitive processes that constitute it. *Journal of Experimental Psychology: Animal Behavior Processes, 14,* 3–17.

Capaldi, E. J., & Miller, D. J. (1988b). Number tags applied by rats to reinforcers are general and exert powerful control over responding. *Quarterly Journal of Experimental Psychology, 40B,* 279–297.

Capaldi, E. J., Miller, D. J., & Alptekin, S. (1989). Multiple-food-unit-incentive effect: Nonconservation of weight of food reward by rats. *Journal of Experimental Psychology: Animal Behavior Processes, 15,* 75–80.

Capaldi, E. J., Miller, D. J., & Alptekin, S., & Barry, K. (1990). Organized responding in instrumental learning: Chunks and superchunks. *Learning and Motivation, 21,* 415–433.

Capaldi, E. J., Nawrocki, T. M., Miller, D. J., & Verry, D. R. (1986). Grouping, chunking, memory, and learning. *Quarterly Journal of Experimental Psychology, 38B,* 53–80.

Capaldi, E. J., Nawrocki, T. M., & Verry, D. R. (1984). Stimulus control in instrumental discrimination learning and reinforcement schedule situations. *Journal of Experimental Psychology: Animal Behavior Processes, 10,* 46–55.

Carew, T. J., Hawkins, R. D., & Kandel, E. R. (1983). Differential classical conditioning of a defensive withdrawal reflex in *Aplysia californica. Science, 219,* 397–400.

Carr, W. J., Loeb, L. S., & Dissinger, M. E. (1965). Responses of rats to sex odors. *Journal of Comparative and Physiological Psychology, 59,* 370–377.

Carrell, L. E., Cannon, D. S., Best, M. R., & Stone, M. J. (1986). Nausea and radiation-induced taste aversions in cancer patients. *Appetite, 7,* 203–208.

Caspy, T., & Lubow, R. E. (1981). Generality of US preexposure effects: Transfer from food to shock or shock to food with and without the same response requirements. *Animal Learning & Behavior, 9,* 524–532.

Catania, A. C. (1963). Concurrent performances: A baseline for the study of reinforcement magnitude. *Journal of the Experimental Analysis of Behavior, 6,* 299–300.

Cerella, J. (1982). Mechanisms of concept formation in the pigeon. In D. J. Ingle, M. A. Goodale, & R. J. W. Mansfield (Eds.), *Analysis of visual behavior.* Cambridge, MA: M.I.T. Press.

Cerletti, U., & Bini, L. (1938). Electric shock treatment. *Bollettino ed atti della Accademia medica di Roma, 64,* 36.

Chance, W. T. (1980). Autoanalgesia: Opiate and non-opiate mechanisms. *Neuroscience and Biobehavioral Reviews, 4,* 55–67.

Channell, S., & Hall, G. (1983). Contextual effects in latent inhibition with an appetitive conditioning procedure. *Animal Learning & Behavior, 11,* 67–74.

Charlop, M. H., Kurtz, P. F., & Casey, F. G. (1990). Using aberrant behaviors as reinforcers for autistic children. *Journal of Applied Behavior Analysis, 23,* 163–181.

Chatlosh, D. L., & Wasserman, E. A. (1987). Delayed temporal discrimination in pigeons: A comparison of two procedures. *Journal of the Experimental Analysis of Behavior, 47,* 299–309.

Chomsky, N. (1972). *Language and mind.* New York: Harcourt Brace Jovanovich.

Chung, S.-H., & Herrnstein, R. J. (1967). Choice and delay of reinforcement. *Journal of the Experimental Analysis of Behavior, 10,* 67–74.

Church, R. M. (1963). The varied effects of punishment on behavior. *Psychological Review, 70,* 369–402.

Church, R. M. (1969). Response suppression. In B. A. Campbell & R. M. Church (Eds.), *Punishment and aversive behavior* (pp. 111–156). New York: Appleton-Century-Crofts.

Church, R. M. (1978). The internal clock. In S. H. Hulse, H. Fowler, & W. K. Honig (Eds.), *Cognitive processes in animal behavior.* Hillsdale, NJ: Erlbaum.

Church, R. M. (1989). Theories of timing. In S. B. Klein & R. R. Mowrer (Eds.), *Contemporary learning theories: Instrumental conditioning and the impact of biological constraints on learning* (pp. 41–71). Hillsdale, NJ: Erlbaum.

Church, R. M., Getty, D. J., & Lerner, N. D. (1976). Duration discrimination by rats. *Journal of Experimental Psychology: Animal Behavior Processes, 2,* 303–312.

Church, R. M., & Raymond, G. A. (1967). Influence of the schedule of positive reinforcement on punished behavior. *Journal of Comparative and Physiological Psychology, 63,* 329–332.

Cicala, G. A., & Owen, J. W. (1976). Warning signal termination and a feedback signal may not serve the same function. *Learning and Motivation, 7,* 356–367.

Cleland, G. G., & Davey, G. C. L. (1982). The effects of satiation and reinforcer devaluation on signal-centered behavior in the rat. *Learning and Motivation, 13,* 343–360.

Cleland, G. G., & Davey, G. C. L. (1983). Autoshaping in the rat: The effects of localizable visual and auditory signals for food. *Journal of the Experimental Analysis of Behavior, 40,* 47–56.

Cohen, L. B. (1988). An information processing view of infant cognitive development. In L. Weiskrantz (Ed.), *Thought without language* (pp. 211–228). Oxford: Oxford University Press.

Cohen, L. B., & Younger, B. A. (1984). Infant perception of angular relations. *Infant Behavior and Development, 7,* 37–47.

Coleman, S. R. (1975). Consequences of response-contingent change in unconditioned stimulus intensity upon the rabbit *(Oryctolagus cuniculus)* nictitating membrane response. *Journal of Comparative and Physiological Psychology, 88,* 591–595.

Coleman, S. R., & Gormezano, I. (1979). Classical conditioning and the "Law of Effect": Historical and empirical assessment. *Behaviorism, 7,* 1–33.

Collias, N. E. (1990). Statistical evidence for aggressive response to red by male three-spined sticklebacks. *Animal Behaviour, 39,* 401–403.

Colombo, M., & D'Amato, M. R. (1986). A comparison of visual and auditory short-term memory in monkeys *(Cebus apella). Quarterly Journal of Experimental Psychology, 38B,* 425–448.

Colwill, R. M., & Rescorla, R. A. (1986). Associative structures in instrumental learning. In G. H. Bower (Ed.), *The psychology of learning and motivation* (Vol. 20, pp. 55–104). Orlando, FL: Academic Press.

Colwill, R. M., & Rescorla, R. A. (1990). Evidence for the hierarchical structure of instrumental learning. *Animal Learning & Behavior, 18,* 71–82.

Commons, M. L., Herrnstein, R. J., Kosslyn, S. M., & Mumford, D. B. (Eds.). (1990). *Quantitative analyses of behavior: Vol. 8. Behavioral approaches to pattern recognition and concept formation.* Hillsdale, NJ: Erlbaum.

Commons, M. L., Herrnstein, R. J., & Rachlin, H. (Eds.). (1982). *Quantitative analyses of behavior: Vol. 2. Matching and maximizing accounts.* Cambridge, MA: Ballinger.

Commons, M. L., Kacelnik, A., & Shettleworth, S. J. (Eds.). (1987). *Quantitative analyses of behavior: Vol. 6. Foraging.* Hillsdale, NJ: Erlbaum.

Conger, R., & Killeen, P. (1974). Use of concurrent operants in small group research. *Pacific Sociological Review, 17,* 399–416.

Cook, M., & Mineka, S. (1990). Selective associations in the observational conditioning of fear in rhesus monkeys. *Journal of Experimental Psychology: Animal Behavior Processes, 16,* 372–389.

Cook, M., Mineka, S., & Trumble, D. (1987). The role of response-produced and exteroceptive feedback in the attenuation of fear over the course of avoidance learning. *Journal of Experimental Psychology: Animal Behavior Processes, 13,* 239–249.

Cook, R. G. (1980). Retroactive interference in pigeon short-term memory by a reduction in ambient illumination. *Journal of Experimental Psychology: Animal Behavior Processes, 6,* 326–338.

Cook, R. G., Brown, M. F., & Riley, D. A. (1985). Flexible memory processing by rats: Use of prospective and retrospective information in the radial maze. *Journal of Experimental Psychology: Animal Behavior Processes, 11,* 453–469.

Cooper, L. D., Aronson, L., Balsam, P. D., & Gibbon, J. (1990). Duration of signals for intertrial reinforcement and nonreinforcement in random control procedures. *Journal of Experimental Psychology: Animal Behavior Processes, 16,* 14–26.

Coulter, X., Riccio, D. C., & Page, H. A. (1969). Effects of blocking an instrumental avoidance response: Facilitated extinction but persistence of "fear." *Journal of Comparative and Physiological Psychology, 68,* 377–381.

Couvillon, P. A., & Bitterman, M. E. (1980). Some phenomena of associative learning in honeybees. *Journal of Comparative and Physiological Psychology, 94,* 878–885.

Couvillon, P. A., & Bitterman, M. E. (1982). Compound conditioning in honeybees. *Journal of Comparative and Physiological Psychology, 96,* 192–199.

Couvillon, P. A., & Bitterman, M. E. (1988). Compound-component and conditional discrimination of colors and odors by honeybees: Further tests of a continuity model. *Animal Learning & Behavior, 16,* 67–74.

Couvillon, P. A., & Bitterman, M. E. (1989). Reciprocal overshadowing in the discrimination of color-odor compounds by honeybees: Further tests of a continuity model. *Animal Learning & Behavior, 16,* 67–74.

Crespi, L. P. (1942). Quantitative variation in incentive and performance in the white rat. *American Journal of Psychology, 55,* 467–517.

Cronin, P. B. (1980). Reinstatement of postresponse stimuli prior to reward in delayed-reward discrimination learning by pigeons. *Animal Learning & Behavior, 8,* 352–358.

Crossman, E. K., Bonem, E. J., & Phelps, B. J. (1987). A comparison of response patterns on fixed-, variable-, and random-ratio schedules. *Journal of the Experimental Analysis of Behavior, 48,* 395–406.

Crozier, W. J., & Navez, A. E. (1930). The geotropic orientation of gastropods. *Journal of General Physiology, 3,* 3–37.

Culler, E. A. (1938). Recent advances in some concepts of conditioning. *Psychological Review, 45,* 134–153.

Cunningham, C. L. (1981). Association between the elements of a bivalent compound stimulus. *Journal of Experimental Psychology: Animal Behavior Processes, 7,* 425–436.

Dafters, R., Hetherington, M., & McCartney, H. (1983). Blocking and sensory preconditioning effects in morphine analgesic tolerance: Support for a Pavlovian conditioning model of drug tolerance. *Quarterly Journal of Experimental Psychology, 35B,* 1–11.

Dallal, N. L., & Meck, W. H. (1990). Hierarchical structures: Chunking by food type facilitates spatial memory.

Journal of Experimental Psychology: Animal Behavior Processes, 16, 69–84.

D'Amato, M. R. (1973). Delayed matching and short-term memory in monkeys. In G. H. Bower (Ed.), *The psychology of learning and motivation* (Vol. 7, pp. 227–269). New York: Academic Press.

D'Amato, M. R., & Colombo, M. (1985). Auditory matching-to-sample in monkeys *(Cebus apella). Animal Learning & Behavior, 13,* 375–382.

D'Amato, M. R., & Colombo, M. (1988). Representation of serial order in monkeys *(Cebus apella). Journal of Experimental Psychology: Animal Behavior Processes, 14,* 131–139.

D'Amato, M. R., & Colombo, M. (1989). Serial learning with wild card items by monkeys *(Cebus apella):* Implications for knowledge of ordinal position. *Journal of Comparative Psychology, 103,* 252–261.

D'Amato, M. R., & Colombo, M. (1990). The symbolic distance effect in monkeys *(Cebus apella). Animal Learning & Behavior, 18,* 133–140.

D'Amato, M. R., Fazzaro, J., & Etkin, M. (1968). Anticipatory responding and avoidance discrimination as factors in avoidance conditioning. *Journal of Comparative and Physiological Psychology, 77,* 41–47.

D'Amato, M. R., & Salmon, D. P. (1982). Tune discrimination in monkeys *(Cebus apella)* and in rats. *Animal Learning & Behavior, 10,* 126–134.

D'Amato, M. R., & Van Sant, P. (1988). The person concept in monkeys *(Cebus apella). Journal of Experimental Psychology: Animal Behavior Processes, 14,* 43–55.

Dardano, J. F., & Sauerbrunn, D. (1964). An aversive stimulus as a correlated block counter in FR performance. *Journal of the Experimental Analysis of Behavior, 7,* 37–43.

Darwin, C. (1897). *The descent of man and selection in relation to sex.* New York: Appleton-Century-Crofts.

Davey, G. C. L., & Cleland, G. G. (1982). Topography of signal-centered behavior in the rat: Effects of deprivation state and reinforcer type. *Journal of the Experimental Analysis of Behavior, 38,* 291–304.

Davey, G. C. L., Phillips, S., & Cleland, G. G. (1981). The topography of signal-centered behaviour in the rat: The effects of solid and liquid food reinforcers. *Behaviour Analysis Letters, 1,* 331–337.

Davidson, T. L., Aparicio, J., & Rescorla, R. A. (1988). Transfer between Pavlovian facilitators and instrumental discriminative stimuli. *Animal Learning & Behavior, 16,* 285–291.

Davis, E. R., & Platt, J. R. (1983). Contiguity and contingency in the acquisition and maintenance of an operant. *Learning and Motivation, 14,* 487–512.

Davis, H. (1968). Conditioned suppression: A survey of the literature. *Psychonomic Monograph Supplements, 2* (14, Whole No. 30), 283–291.

Davis, H., & Albert, M. (1986). Numerical discrimination by rats using sequential auditory stimuli. *Animal Learning & Behavior, 14,* 57–59.

Davis, H., & Kreuter, C. (1972). Conditioned suppression of an avoidance response by a stimulus paired with food. *Journal of the Experimental Analysis of Behavior, 17,* 277–285.

Davis, H., & Memmott, J. (1982). Counting behavior in animals: A critical evaluation. *Psychological Bulletin, 92,* 547–571.

Davis, H., & Pérusse, R. (1988). Numerical competence in animals: Definitional issues, current evidence, and a new research agenda. *Behavioral and Brain Sciences, 11,* 561–615. (Includes commentary.)

Davis, H., & Shattuck, D. (1980). Transfer of conditioned suppression and conditioned acceleration from instrumental to consummatory baselines. *Animal Learning & Behavior, 8,* 253–257.

Davis, M. (1970). Effects of interstimulus interval length and variability on startle-response habituation in the rat. *Journal of Comparative and Physiological Psychology, 72,* 177–192.

Davis, M. (1974). Sensitization of the rat startle response by noise. *Journal of Comparative and Physiological Psychology, 87,* 571–581.

Davis, M., & File, S. E. (1984). Intrinsic and extrinsic mechanisms of habituation and sensitization: Implications for the design and analysis of experiments. In H. V. S. Peeke & L. Petrinovich (Eds.), *Habituation, sensitization, and behavior.* New York: Academic Press.

Davis, M., Hitchcock, J. M., & Rosen, J. B. (1987). Anxiety and the amygdala: Pharmacological and anatomical analysis of the fear-potentiated startle paradigm. In G. H. Bower (Ed.), *The psychology of learning and motivation* (Vol. 21, pp. 263–304). Orlando, FL: Academic Press.

Davis, S. F., Best, M. R., & Grover, C. A. (1988). Toxicosis-mediated potentiation in a taste/taste compound: Evidence for within-compound associations. *Learning and Motivation, 19,* 183–205.

Davison, M. (1988). Concurrent schedules: Interaction of reinforcer frequency and reinforcer duration. *Journal of the Experimental Analysis of Behavior, 49,* 339–349.

Davison, M. (1991a). Choice, changeover, and travel: A quantitative model. *Journal of the Experimental Analysis of Behavior, 55,* 47–61.

Davison, M. (1991b). Concurrent schedules: Effects of time- and response-allocation constraints. *Journal of the Experimental Analysis of Behavior, 55,* 189–200.

Davison, M., & Kerr, A. (1989). Sensitivity of time allocation to an overall reinforcer rate feedback function in concurrent interval schedules. *Journal of the Experimental Analysis of Behavior, 51,* 215–231.

Davison, M., & McCarthy, D. (1988). *The matching law: A research review.* Hillsdale, NJ: Erlbaum.

Dawson, G. R., & Dickinson, A. (1990). Performance on ratio and interval schedules with matched reinforcement rates. *Quarterly Journal of Experimental Psychology, 42B,* 225–239.

Dean, S. J., & Pittman, C. M. (1991). Self-punitive behavior: A revised analysis. In M. R. Denny (Ed.), *Fear, avoidance and phobias* (pp. 259–284). Hillsdale, NJ: Erlbaum.

DeCarlo, L. T. (1985). Matching and maximizing with variable-time schedules. *Journal of the Experimental Analysis of Behavior, 43*, 75–81.

DeCola, J. P., & Rosellini, R. A. (1990). Unpredictable/uncontrollable stress proactively interferes with appetitive Pavlovian conditioning. *Learning and Motivation, 21*, 137–152.

DeCola, J. P., Rosellini, R. A., & Warren, D. A. (1988). A dissociation of the effects of control and prediction. *Learning and Motivation, 19*, 269–282.

Deich, J. D., Allan, R. W., & Zeigler, H. P. (1988). Conjunctive differentiation of gape during food-reinforced keypecking in the pigeon. *Animal Learning & Behavior, 16*, 268–276.

DeKeyne, A., & Deweer, B. (1990). Interaction between conflicting memories in the rat: Contextual pretest cuing reverses control of behavior by testing context. *Animal Learning & Behavior, 18*, 1–12.

Delamater, A. R., & Treit, D. (1988). Chlordiazepoxide attenuates shock-based and enhances LiCl-based fluid aversions. *Learning and Motivation, 19*, 221–238.

Delprato, D. J. (1969). Extinction of one-way avoidance and delayed warning signal termination. *Journal of Experimental Psychology, 80*, 192–193.

Delprato, D. J., & Rusiniak, K. W. (1991). Response patterns in shock avoidance and illness aversion. In M. R. Denny (Ed.), *Fear, avoidance and phobias* (pp. 285–315). Hillsdale, NJ: Erlbaum.

Desiderato, O. (1969). Generalization of excitation and inhibition in control of avoidance responding by Pavlovian CS's in dogs. *Journal of Comparative and Physiological Psychology, 68*, 611–616.

Dess, N. K., & Overmier, J. B. (1989). General learned irrelevance: Proactive effects on Pavlovian conditioning in dogs. *Learning and Motivation, 20*, 1–14.

Deutsch, R. (1974). Conditioned hypoglycemia: A mechanism for saccharin-induced sensitivity to insulin in the rat. *Journal of Comparative and Physiological Psychology, 86*, 350–358.

deVilliers, P. A. (1974). The law of effect and avoidance: A quantitative relationship between response rate and shock-frequency reduction. *Journal of the Experimental Analysis of Behavior, 21*, 223–235.

DeVito, P. L., & Fowler, H. (1987). Enhancement of conditioned inhibition via an extinction treatment. *Animal Learning & Behavior, 15*, 448–454.

Dickinson, A., & Dearing, M. F. (1979). Appetitive-aversive interactions and inhibitory processes. In A. Dickinson & R. A. Boakes (Eds.), *Mechanisms of learning and motivation* (pp. 203–231). Hillsdale, NJ: Erlbaum.

Dickinson, A., Nicholas, D. J., & Mackintosh, N. J. (1983). A re-examination of one-trial blocking in conditioned suppression. *Quarterly Journal of Experimental Psychology, 35*, 67–79.

Dickinson, A., & Pearce, J. M. (1977). Inhibitory interactions between appetitive and aversive stimuli. *Psychological Bulletin, 84*, 690–711.

Dinsmoor, J. A. (1952). A discrimination based on punishment. *Quarterly Journal of Experimental Psychology, 4*, 27–45.

Dinsmoor, J. A. (1954). Punishment: I. The avoidance hypothesis. *Psychological Review, 61*, 34–46.

Dinsmoor, J. A. (1962). Variable-interval escape from stimuli accompanied by shocks. *Journal of the Experimental Analysis of Behavior, 5*, 41–48.

Dinsmoor, J. A. (1977). Escape, avoidance, punishment: Where do we stand? *Journal of the Experimental Analysis of Behavior, 28*, 83–95.

Dinsmoor, J. A., & Sears, G. W. (1973). Control of avoidance by a response-produced stimulus. *Learning and Motivation, 4*, 284–293.

Dobrzecka, C., Szwejkowska, G., & Konorski, J. (1966). Qualitative versus directional cues in two forms of differentiation. *Science, 153*, 87–89.

Dolan, J. C., Shishimi, A., & Wagner, A. R. (1985). The effects of signaling the US in backward conditioning: A shift from excitatory to inhibitory learning. *Animal Learning & Behavior, 13*, 209–214.

Dollard, J., & Miller, N. E. (1950). *Personality and psychotherapy.* New York: McGraw-Hill.

Dollard, J., Miller, N. E., Doob, L. W., Mowrer, O. H., & Sears, R. R. (1939). *Frustration and aggression.* New Haven, CT: Yale University Press.

Domjan, M. (1976). Determinants of the enhancement of flavored-water intake by prior exposure. *Journal of Experimental Psychology: Animal Behavior Processes, 2*, 17–27.

Domjan, M. (1980). Ingestional aversion learning: Unique and general processes. In J. S. Rosenblatt, R. A. Hinde, C. Beer, & M. Busnel (Eds.), *Advances in the study of behavior* (Vol. 11). New York: Academic Press.

Domjan, M. (1983). Biological constraints on instrumental and classical conditioning: Implications for general process theory. In G. H. Bower (Ed.), *The psychology of learning and motivation* (Vol. 17). New York: Academic Press.

Domjan, M. (1987). Animal learning comes of age. *American Psychologist, 42*, 556–564.

Domjan, M. (1992). Adult learning and mate choice: Possibilities and experimental evidence. *American Zoologist, 32*, 48–61.

Domjan, M., & Best, M. R. (1980). Interference with ingestional aversion learning produced by preexposure to the unconditioned stimulus: Associative and nonassociative aspects. *Learning and Motivation, 11*, 522–537.

Domjan, M., Greene, P., & North, N. C. (1989). Contextual conditioning and the control of copulatory behavior by species-specific sign stimuli in male Japanese quail. *Journal of Experimental Psychology: Animal Behavior Processes, 15*, 147–153.

Domjan, M., Lyons, R., North, N. C., & Bruell, J. (1986). Sexual Pavlovian conditioned approach behavior in male Japanese quail *(Coturnix coturnix japonica). Journal of Comparative Psychology, 100,* 413–421.

Domjan, M., O'Vary, D., & Greene, P. (1988). Conditioning of appetitive and consummatory behavior in male Japanese quail. *Journal of the Experimental Analysis of Behavior, 50,* 505–519.

Domjan, M., & Ravert, R. D. (1991). Discriminating the sex of conspecifics by male Japanese quail *(Coturnix coturnix japonica). Journal of Comparative Psychology, 105,* 157–164.

Domjan, M., & Wilson, N. E. (1972). Specificity of cue to consequence in aversion learning in the rat. *Psychonomic Science, 26,* 143–145.

Doty, R. L., & Dunbar, I. (1974). Attraction of beagles to conspecific urine, vaginal and anal sac secretion odors. *Physiology and Behavior, 12,* 825–833.

Dougan, J. D., & McSweeney, F. K. (1985). Variation in Herrnstein's r_o as a function of alternative reinforcement rate. *Journal of the Experimental Analysis of Behavior, 43,* 215–223.

Dreyfus, L. R., Fetterman, J. G., Smith, L. D., & Stubbs, D. A. (1988). Discrimination of temporal relations by pigeons. *Journal of Experimental Psychology: Animal Behavior Processes, 14,* 349–367.

Duncan, C. P. (1949). The retroactive effect of electroshock on learning. *Journal of Comparative and Physiological Psychology, 42,* 32–44.

Dunham, P. J. (1971). Punishment: Method and theory. *Psychological Review, 78,* 58–70.

Dunham, P. J. (1972). Some effects of punishment on unpunished responding. *Journal of the Experimental Analysis of Behavior, 17,* 443–450.

Dunham, P. J. (1978). Changes in unpunished responding during response-contingent punishment. *Animal Learning & Behavior, 6,* 174–180.

Dunn, R., & Spetch, M. L. (1990). Choice with uncertain outcomes: Conditioned reinforcement effects. *Journal of the Experimental Analysis of Behavior, 53,* 201–218.

Durlach, P. J. (1983). Effect of signaling intertrial unconditioned stimuli in autoshaping. *Journal of Experimental Psychology: Animal Behavior Processes, 9,* 374–389.

Durlach, P. J. (1989). Role of signals for unconditioned stimulus absence in the sensitivity of autoshaping to contingency. *Journal of Experimental Psychology: Animal Behavior Processes, 15,* 202–211.

Durlach, P. J., & Dawson, G. R. (1991). Response specificity in animal timing. *Journal of the Experimental Analysis of Behavior, 55,* 11–20.

Durlach, P. J., & Rescorla, R. A. (1980). Potentiation rather than overshadowing in flavor-aversion learning: An analysis in terms of within-compound associations. *Journal of Experimental Psychology: Animal Behavior Processes, 6,* 175–187.

Dweck, C. S., & Wagner, A. R. (1970). Situational cues and correlation between conditioned stimulus and unconditioned stimulus as determinants of the conditioned emotional response. *Psychonomic Science, 18,* 145–147.

Edhouse, W. V., & White, K. G. (1988a). Cumulative proactive interference in animal memory. *Animal Learning & Behavior, 16,* 461–467.

Edhouse, W. V., & White, K. G. (1988b). Sources of proactive interference in animal memory. *Journal of Experimental Psychology: Animal Behavior Processes, 14,* 56–70.

Edwards, C. A., & Honig, W. K. (1987). Memorization and "feature selection" in the acquisition of natural concepts in pigeons. *Learning and Motivation, 18,* 235–260.

Egli, M., & Thompson, T. (1989). Effects of methadone on alternative fixed-ratio fixed-interval performance: Latent influences on schedule-controlled responding. *Journal of the Experimental Analysis of Behavior, 52,* 141–153.

Eibl-Eibesfeldt, I. (1970). *Ethology: The biology of behavior.* New York: Holt, Rinehart and Winston.

Eikelboom, R., & Stewart, J. (1982). Conditioning of drug-induced physiological responses. *Psychological Review, 89,* 507–528.

Eisenberger, R. (1992). Learned industriousness. *Psychological Review, 99,* 248–267.

Eisenberger, R., & Adornetto, M. (1986). Generalized self-control of delay and effort. *Journal of Personality and Social Psychology, 51,* 1020–1031.

Eisenberger, R., Karpman, M., & Trattner, J. (1967). What is the necessary and sufficient condition for reinforcement in the contingency situation? *Journal of Experimental Psychology, 74,* 342–350.

Eisenberger, R., & Masterson, F. A. (1983). Required high effort increases subsequent persistence and reduces cheating. *Journal of Personality and Social Psychology, 44,* 593–599.

Eisenberger, R., & Shank, D. M. (1985). Personal work ethic and effort training affect cheating. *Journal of Personality and Social Psychology, 49,* 520–528.

Elkins, R. L. (1975). Aversion therapy for alcoholism: Chemical, electrical, or verbal imaginary? *International Journal of the Addictions, 10,* 157–209.

Ellins, S. R., Cramer, R. E., & Martin, G. C. (1982). Discrimination reversal learning in newts. *Animal Learning & Behavior, 10,* 301–304.

Ellison, G. D. (1964). Differential salivary conditioning to traces. *Journal of Comparative and Physiological Psychology, 57,* 373–380.

Ellison, G. D., & Konorski, J. (1964). Separation of the salivary and motor responses in instrumental conditioning. *Science, 146,* 1071–1072.

Eslinger, P. J., & Ludvigson, H. W. (1980). Are there constraints on learned responses to odors from rewarded and nonrewarded rats? *Animal Learning & Behavior, 8,* 452–456.

Esplin, D. W., & Woodbury, D. M. (1961). Spinal reflexes

and seizure patterns in the two-toed sloth. *Science, 133,* 1426–1427.

Estes, W. K. (1943). Discriminative conditioning: I. A discriminative property of conditioned anticipation. *Journal of Experimental Psychology, 32,* 150–155.

Estes, W. K. (1944). An experimental study of punishment. *Psychological Monographs, 57* (3, Whole No. 263).

Estes, W. K. (1948). Discriminative conditioning: II. Effects of a Pavlovian conditioned stimulus upon a subsequently established operant response. *Journal of Experimental Psychology, 38,* 173–177.

Estes, W. K. (1969). Outline of a theory of punishment. In B. A. Campbell & R. M. Church (Eds.), *Punishment and aversive behavior* (pp. 57–82). New York: Appleton-Century-Crofts.

Estes, W. K., & Skinner, B. F. (1941). Some quantitative properties of anxiety. *Journal of Experimental Psychology, 29,* 390–400.

Ettinger, R. H., Reid, A. K., & Staddon, J. E. R. (1987). Sensitivity to molar feedback functions: A test of molar optimality theory. *Journal of Experimental Psychology: Animal Behavior Processes, 13,* 366–375.

Fagen, J. W., & Rovee-Collier, C. (1983). Memory retrieval: A time-locked process in infancy. *Science, 222,* 1349–1351.

Falls, W. A., & Kelsey, J. E. (1989). Procedures that produce context-specific tolerance to morphine in rats also produce context-specific withdrawal. *Behavioral Neuroscience, 103,* 842–849.

Fanselow, M. S. (1989). The adaptive function of conditioned defensive behavior: An ecological approach to Pavlovian stimulus-substitution theory. In R. J. Blanchard, P. F. Brain, D. C. Blanchard, & S. Parmigiani (Eds.), *Ethoexperimental approaches to the study of behavior* (NATO ASI Series D, Vol. 48, pp. 151–166). Boston: Kluver Academic Publishers.

Fanselow, M. S. (1991). Analgesia as a response to aversive Pavlovian conditioned stimuli: cognitive and emotional mediators. In M. R. Denny (Ed.), *Fear, avoidance and phobias* (pp. 61–86). Hillsdale, NJ: Erlbaum.

Fanselow, M. S., & Baackes, M. P. (1982). Conditioned fear-induced opiate analgesia on the formalin test: Evidence for two aversive motivational systems. *Learning and Motivation, 13,* 200–221.

Fanselow, M. S., & Lester, L. S. (1988). A functional behavioristic approach to aversively motivated behavior: Predatory imminence as a determinant of the topography of defensive behavior. In R. C. Bolles & M. D. Beecher (Eds.), *Evolution and learning* (pp. 185–212). Hillsdale, NJ: Erlbaum.

Fanselow, M. S., Lester, L. S., & Helmstetter, F. J. (1988). Changes in feeding and foraging patterns as an antipredator defensive strategy: A laboratory simulation using aversive stimulation in a closed economy. *Journal of the Experimental Analysis of Behavior, 50,* 361–374.

Fantino, E., & Abarca, N. (1985). Choice, optimal foraging, and the delay-reduction hypothesis. *Behavioral & Brain Sciences, 8,* 315–330.

Fantino, E., Freed, D., Preston, R. A., & Williams, W. A. (1991). Choice and conditioned reinforcement. *Journal of the Experimental Analysis of Behavior, 55,* 177–188.

Fantino, E., & Preston, R. A. (1988). Choice and foraging: Effects of accessibility on acceptability. *Journal of the Experimental Analysis of Behavior, 50,* 395–403.

Farley, J., & Alkon, D. L. (1980). Neural organization predicts stimulus specificity for a retained associative behavioral change. *Science, 210,* 1373–1375.

Feldman, D. T., & Gordon, W. C. (1979). The alleviation of short-term retention decrements with reactivation. *Learning and Motivation, 10,* 198–210.

Felton, M., & Lyon, D. O. (1966). The post-reinforcement pause. *Journal of the Experimental Analysis of Behavior, 9,* 131–134.

Ferster, C. B., & Skinner, B. F. (1957). *Schedules of Reinforcement.* New York: Appleton-Century-Crofts.

Fetterman, J. G., Dreyfus, L. R., & Stubbs, D. A. (1989). Discrimination of duration ratios. *Journal of Experimental Psychology: Animal Behavior Processes, 15,* 253–263.

Fetterman, J. G., & Killeen, P. R. (1991). Adjusting the pacemaker. *Learning and Motivation, 22,* 226–252.

FitzGerald, R. E., Isler, R., Rosenberg, E., Oettinger, R., & Bättig, K. (1985). Maze patrolling by rats with and without food reward. *Animal Learning & Behavior, 13,* 451–462.

Flaherty, C. F. (1982). Incentive contrast: A review of behavioral changes following shifts in reward. *Animal Learning & Behavior, 10,* 409–440.

Flaherty, C. F. (1991). Incentive contrast and selected animal models of anxiety. In L. Dachowski & C. F. Flaherty (Eds.), *Current topics in animal learning* (pp. 207–243). Hillsdale, NJ: Erlbaum.

Flaherty, C. F., & Rowan, G. A. (1986). Successive, simultaneous, and anticipatory contrast in the consumption of saccharin solutions. *Journal of Experimental Psychology: Animal Behavior Processes, 12,* 381–393.

Flexner, J. B., Flexner, L. B., & Stellar, E. (1963). Memory in mice as affected by intracerebral puromycin. *Science, 141,* 57–59.

Foree, D. D., & LoLordo, V. M. (1973). Attention in the pigeon: The differential effects of food-getting vs. shock avoidance procedures. *Journal of Comparative and Physiological Psychology, 85,* 551–558.

Forestell, P. H., & Herman, L. M. (1988). Delayed matching of visual materials by a bottlenosed dolphin aided by auditory symbols. *Animal Learning & Behavior, 16,* 137–146.

Fountain, S. B. (1990). Rule abstraction, item memory, and chunking in rat serial-pattern tracking. *Journal of Experimental Psychology: Animal Behavior Processes, 16,* 96–105.

Fountain, S. B., Henne, D. R., & Hulse, S. H. (1984). Phrasing cues and hierarchical organization in serial pattern learning by rats. *Journal of Experimental Psychology: Animal Behavior Processes, 10,* 30–45.

Fowler, H., Kleiman, M., & Lysle, D. (1985). Factors controlling the acquisition and extinction of conditioned inhibition suggest a "slave" process. In R. R. Miller & N. E. Spear (Eds.), *Information processing in animals: Conditioned inhibition.* Hillsdale, NJ: Erlbaum.

Fowler, H., Lysle, D. T., & DeVito, P. L. (1991). Conditioned excitation and conditioned inhibition of fear: Asymmetrical processes as evident in extinction. In M. R. Denny (Ed.), *Fear, avoidance and phobias* (pp. 317–362). Hillsdale, NJ: Erlbaum.

Foxx, R. M., & Azrin, N. H. (1973). The elimination of autistic self-stimulatory behavior by overcorrection. *Journal of Applied Behavioral Analysis, 6,* 1–14.

Fraenkel, G. S., & Gunn, D. L. (1961). *The orientation of animals* (2nd ed.). New York: Dover.

France, K. G., & Hudson, S. M. (1990). Behavior management of infant sleep disturbance. *Journal of Applied Behavior Analysis, 23,* 91–98.

Frankel, F. D. (1975). The role of response-punishment contingency in the suppression of a positively-reinforced operant. *Learning and Motivation, 6,* 385–403.

Gaffan, E. A., & Davies, J. (1981). The role of exploration in win-shift and win-stay performance on a radial maze. *Learning and Motivation, 12,* 282–299.

Galbicka, G. (1988). Differentiating the behavior of organisms. *Journal of the Experimental Analysis of Behavior, 50,* 343–354.

Galef, B. G., Jr., & Osborne, B. (1978). Novel taste facilitation of the association of visual cues with toxicosis in rats. *Journal of Comparative and Physiological Psychology, 92,* 907–916.

Gallup, G. G., Jr., & Suarez, S. D. (1985). Alternatives to the use of animals in psychological research. *American Psychologist, 40,* 1104–1111.

Gamzu, E., Vincent, G., & Boff, E. (1985). A pharmacological perspective on drugs used in establishing conditioned food aversions. *Annals of the New York Academy of Sciences, 443,* 231–249.

Gamzu, E. R., & Williams, D. R. (1971). Classical conditioning of a complex skeletal act. *Science, 171,* 923–925.

Gamzu, E. R., & Williams, D. R. (1973). Associative factors underlying the pigeon's key pecking in autoshaping procedures. *Journal of the Experimental Analysis of Behavior, 19,* 225–232.

Gantt, W. H. (1966). Conditional or conditioned, reflex or response? *Conditioned Reflex, 1,* 69–74.

Garb, J. J., & Stunkard, A. J. (1974). Taste aversions in man. *American Journal of Psychiatry, 131,* 1204–1207.

Garber, J., & Seligman, M. E. P. (Eds.). (1980). *Human helplessness: Theory and application.* New York: Academic Press.

Garcia, J., Ervin, F. R., & Koelling, R. A. (1966). Learning with prolonged delay of reinforcement. *Psychonomic Science, 5,* 121–122.

Garcia, J., & Koelling, R. A. (1966). Relation of cue to consequence in avoidance learning. *Psychonomic Science, 4,* 123–124.

Gardner, E. T., & Lewis, P. (1976). Negative reinforcement with shock-frequency increase. *Journal of the Experimental Analysis of Behavior, 25,* 3–14.

Gardner, R. A., & Gardner, B. T. (1969). Teaching sign language to a chimpanzee. *Science, 165,* 664–672.

Gardner, R. A., & Gardner, B. T. (1975). Early signs of language in child and chimpanzee. *Science, 187,* 752–753.

Gardner, R. A., & Gardner, B. T. (1978). Comparative psychology and language acquisition. *Annals of the New York Academy of Science, 309,* 37–76.

Gardner, R. A., & Gardner, B. T. (1984). A vocabulary test for chimpanzees *(Pan troglodytes). Journal of Comparative Psychology, 98,* 381–404.

Gardner, R. A., & Gardner, B. T. (1989). A cross-fostering laboratory. In R. A. Gardner, B. T. Gardner, & T. E. Van Cantfort (Eds.), *Teaching sign language to chimpanzees* (pp. 1–28). Albany: State University of New York Press.

Gardner, R. A., Gardner, B. T., & Van Cantfort, T. E. (Eds.). (1989). *Teaching sign language to chimpanzees.* Albany: State University of New York Press.

Gawley, D. J., Timberlake, W., & Lucas, G. A. (1987). System-specific differences in behavior regulation: Overrunning and underdrinking in molar nondepriving schedules. *Journal of Experimental Psychology: Animal Behavior Processes, 13,* 354–365.

Gemberling, G. A., & Domjan, M. (1982). Selective association in one-day-old rats: Taste-toxicosis and texture-shock aversion learning. *Journal of Comparative and Physiological Psychology, 96,* 105–113.

George, J. T., & Hopkins, B. L. (1989). Multiple effects of performance-contingent pay for waitpersons. *Journal of Applied Behavior Analysis, 22,* 131–141.

Gibbon, J., & Allan, L. (Eds.). (1984). *Annals of the New York Academy of Sciences: Vol. 423. Time and time perception.* New York: New York Academy of Sciences.

Gibbon, J., & Balsam, P. (1981). Spreading association in time. In C. M. Locurto, H. S. Terrace, & J. Gibbon (Eds.), *Autoshaping and conditioning theory* (pp. 219–253). New York: Academic Press.

Gibbon, J., & Church, R. M. (1984). Sources of variance in an information processing theory of timing. In H. L. Roitblat, T. G. Bever, & H. S. Terrace (Eds.), *Animal cognition.* Hillsdale, NJ: Erlbaum.

Gibbon, J., Church, R. M., Fairhurst, S., & Kacelnik, A. (1988). Scalar expectancy theory and choice between delayed rewards. *Psychological Review, 95,* 102–114.

Gibbon, J., Church, R. M., & Meck, W. H. (1984). Scalar timing in memory. *Annals of the New York Academy of Sciences, 423,* 52–77.

Gillan, D. J. (1981). Reasoning in the chimpanzee: II. Transitive inference. *Journal of Experimental Psychology: Animal Behavior Processes, 7,* 150–164.

Gillan, D. J. (1983). Inferences and the acquisition of knowledge by chimpanzees. In M. L. Commons, R. J.

Herrnstein, & A. R. Wagner (Eds.), *Quantitative analyses of behavior. Vol. 4: Discrimination processes.* Cambridge, MA: Ballinger.

Gillan, D. J., & Domjan, M. (1977). Taste-aversion conditioning with expected versus unexpected drug treatment. *Journal of Experimental Psychology: Animal Behavior Processes, 3,* 297–309.

Gillan, D. J., Premack, D., & Woodruff, G. (1981). Reasoning in the chimpanzee: I. Analogical reasoning. *Journal of Experimental Psychology: Animal Behavior Processes, 7,* 1–17.

Gillette, K., Martin, G. M., & Bellingham, W. P. (1980). Differential use of food and water cues in the formation of conditioned aversions by domestic chicks *(Gallus gallus). Journal of Experimental Psychology: Animal Behavior Processes, 6,* 99–111.

Glickman, S. E., & Schiff, B. B. (1967). A biological theory of reinforcement. *Psychological Review, 74,* 81–109.

Goddard, M. J., & Jenkins, H. M. (1987). Effect of signaling extra unconditioned stimuli on autoshaping. *Animal Learning & Behavior, 15,* 40–46.

Gold, P. E., Haycock, J. W., Macri, J., & McGaugh, J. L. (1973). Retrograde amnesia and the "reminder effect": An alternative interpretation. *Science, 180,* 1199–1201.

Goodall, G. (1984). Learning due to the response-shock contingency in signalled punishment. *Quarterly Journal of Experimental Psychology, 36B,* 259–279.

Goodall, G., & Mackintosh, N. J. (1987). Analysis of the Pavlovian properties of signals for punishment. *Quarterly Journal of Experimental Psychology, 39B,* 1–21.

Goodman, J. H., & Fowler, H. (1983). Blocking and enhancement of fear conditioning by appetitive CSs. *Animal Learning & Behavior, 11,* 75–82.

Gordon, W. C. (1981). Mechanisms for cue-induced retention enhancement. In N. E. Spear & R. R. Miller (Eds.), *Information processing in animals: Memory mechanisms.* Hillsdale, NJ: Erlbaum.

Gordon, W. C., Brennan, M. J., & Schlesinger, J. L. (1976). The interaction of memories in the rat: Effects on short-term retention performance. *Learning and Motivation, 7,* 406–417.

Gordon, W. C., & Feldman, D. T. (1978). Reactivation-induced interference in a short-term retention paradigm. *Learning and Motivation, 9,* 164–178.

Gordon, W. C., McCracken, K. M., Dess-Beech, N., & Mowrer, R. R. (1981). Mechanisms for the cueing phenomenon: The addition of the cueing context to the training memory. *Learning and Motivation, 12,* 196–211.

Gordon, W. C., McGinnis, C. M., & Weaver, M. S. (1985). The effect of cuing after backward conditioning trials. *Learning and Motivation, 16,* 444–463.

Gordon, W. C., & Mowrer, R. R. (1980). An extinction trial as a reminder treatment following electroconvulsive shock. *Animal Learning & Behavior, 8,* 363–367.

Gormezano, I. (1966). Classical conditioning. In J. B. Sidowski (Ed.), *Experimental methods and instrumentation in psychology.* New York: McGraw-Hill.

Gormezano, I., & Coleman, S. R. (1973). The law of effect and CR contingent modification of the UCS. *Conditioned Reflex, 8,* 41–56.

Gormezano, I., & Hiller, G. W. (1972). Omission training of the jaw-movement response of the rabbit to a water US. *Psychonomic Science, 29,* 276–278.

Gormezano, I., & Kehoe, E. J. (1981). Classical conditioning and the law of contiguity. In P. Harzem & M. D. Zeiler (Eds.), *Predictability, correlation, and contiguity.* Chichester, England: Wiley.

Gormezano, I., Kehoe, E. J., & Marshall, B. S. (1983). Twenty years of classical conditioning research with the rabbit. In J. M. Prague & A. N. Epstein (Eds.), *Progress in psychobiology and physiological psychology* (Vol. 10). New York: Academic Press.

Graham, J. M., & Desjardins, C. (1980). Classical conditioning: Induction of luteinizing hormone and testosterone secretion in anticipation of sexual activity. *Science, 210,* 1039–1041.

Grant, D. S. (1975). Proactive interference in pigeon short-term memory. *Journal of Experimental Psychology: Animal Behavior Processes, 1,* 207–220.

Grant, D. S. (1976). Effect of sample presentation time on long-delay matching in the pigeon. *Learning and Motivation, 7,* 580–590.

Grant, D. S. (1982a). Intratrial proactive interference in pigeon short-term memory: Manipulation of stimulus dimension and dimensional similarity. *Learning and Motivation, 13,* 417–433.

Grant, D. S. (1982b). Stimulus control of information processing in rat short-term memory. *Journal of Experimental Psychology: Animal Behavior Processes, 8,* 154–164.

Grant, D. S. (1988). Sources of visual interference in delayed matching-to-sample with pigeons. *Journal of Experimental Psychology: Animal Behavior Processes, 14,* 368–375.

Grant, D. S., & Barnet, R. C. (1991). Irrelevance of sample stimuli and directed forgetting in pigeons. *Journal of the Experimental Analysis of Behavior, 55,* 97–108.

Grant, D. S., & Roberts, W. A. (1973). Trace interaction in pigeon short-term memory. *Journal of Experimental Psychology, 101,* 21–29.

Grant, D. S., & Roberts, W. A. (1976). Sources of retroactive inhibition in pigeon short-term memory. *Journal of Experimental Psychology: Animal Behavior Processes, 2,* 1–16.

Greeley, J., Lé, D. A., Poulos, C. X., & Cappell, H. (1984). Alcohol is an effective cue in the conditioned control of tolerance to alcohol. *Psychopharmacology, 83,* 159–162.

Green, L., Kagel, J. H., & Battalio, R. C. (1987). Consumption-leisure tradeoffs in pigeons: Effects of changing marginal wage rates by varying amount of reinforcement. *Journal of the Experimental Analysis of Behavior, 47,* 17–28.

Green, L., & Rachlin, H. (1991). Economic substitutability of electrical brain stimulation, food, and water. *Journal of the Experimental Analysis of Behavior, 55,* 133–143.

Greenfield, P. M., & Savage-Rumbaugh, E. S. (1990). Grammatical combination in *Pan paniscus:* Processes of learning and invention in the evolution and development of language. In S. T. Parker & K. R. Gibson (Eds.), *"Language" and intelligence in monkeys and apes* (pp. 540–578). Cambridge: Cambridge University Press.

Grice, G. R. (1948). The relation of secondary reinforcement to delayed reward in visual discrimination learning. *Journal of Experimental Psychology, 38,* 1–16.

Griffin, D. R. (1976). *The question of animal awareness.* New York: Rockefeller University Press.

Griffin, D. R. (Ed.). (1982). *Animal mind—human mind.* Berlin: Springer-Verlag.

Griffiths, R. R., & Thompson, T. (1973). The postreinforcement pause: A misnomer. *Psychological Record, 23,* 229–235.

Grossen, N. E., & Kelley, M. J. (1972). Species-specific behavior and acquisition of avoidance behavior in rats. *Journal of Comparative and Physiological Psychology, 81,* 307–310.

Grossen, N. E., Kostansek, D. J., & Bolles, R. C. (1969). Effects of appetitive discriminative stimuli on avoidance behavior. *Journal of Experimental Psychology, 81,* 340–343.

Groves, P. M., Lee, D., & Thompson, R. F. (1969). Effects of stimulus frequency and intensity on habituation and sensitization in acute spinal cat. *Physiology and Behavior, 4,* 383–388.

Groves, P. M., & Thompson, R. F. (1970). Habituation: A dual-process theory. *Psychological Review, 77,* 419–450.

Guha, D., Dutta, S. N., & Pradhan, S. N. (1974). Conditioning of gastric secretion by epinephrine in rats. *Proceedings of the Society for Experimental Biology and Medicine, 147,* 817–819.

Gunther, M. (1961). Infant behavior at the breast. In B. Foss (Ed.), *Determinants of infant behavior.* London: Wiley.

Gutman, A., & Maier, S. F. (1978). Operant and Pavlovian factors in cross-response transfer of inhibitory stimulus control. *Learning and Motivation, 9,* 231–254.

Guttenberger, V. T., & Wasserman, E. A. (1985). Effects of sample duration, retention interval, and passage of time in the test on pigeons' matching-to-sample performance. *Animal Learning & Behavior, 13,* 121–128.

Guttman, N., & Kalish, H. I. (1956). Discriminability and stimulus generalization. *Journal of Experimental Psychology, 51,* 79–88.

Hailman, J. P. (1967). The ontogeny of an instinct. *Behaviour Supplements, 15,* 1–159.

Hake, D. F., & Azrin, N. H. (1965). Conditioned punishment. *Journal of the Experimental Analysis of Behavior, 8,* 279–293.

Hall, G., & Honey, R. C. (1989). Contextual effects in conditioning, latent inhibition, and habituation: Associative and retrieval functions of contextual cues. *Journal of Experimental Psychology: Animal Behavior Processes, 15,* 232–241.

Hall, G., Kaye, H., & Pearce, J. M. (1985). Attention and conditioned inhibition. In R. R. Miller & N. E. Spear (Eds.), *Information processing in animals: Conditioned inhibition.* Hillsdale, NJ: Erlbaum.

Hall, R. V., Axelrod, S., Foundopoulos, M., Shellman, J., Campbell, R. A., & Cranston, S. S. (1971). The effective use of punishment to modify behavior in the classroom. *Educational Technology, 11(4),* 24–26.

Hall, S. M., Hall, R. G., & Ginsberg, D. (1990). Pharmacological and behavioral treatment for cigarette smoking. In M. Hersen, R. M. Eisler, & P. M. Miller (Eds.), *Progress in behavior modification* (Vol. 25, pp. 86–118). Newbury Park, CA: Sage.

Hallam, S. C., Matzel, L. D., Sloat, J. S., & Miller, R. R. (1990). Excitation and inhibition as a function of posttraining extinction of the excitatory cue used in Pavlovian inhibition training. *Learning and Motivation, 21,* 59–84.

Hamm, S. L., & Shettleworth, S. J. (1987). Risk aversion in pigeons. *Journal of Experimental Psychology: Animal Behavior Processes, 13,* 376–383.

Hammond, L. J. (1966). Increased responding to CS− in differential CER. *Psychonomic Science, 5,* 337–338.

Hammond, L. J. (1968). Retardation of fear acquisition by a previously inhibitory CS. *Journal of Comparative and Physiological Psychology, 66,* 756–759.

Hankins, W. G., Rusiniak, K. W., & Garcia, J. (1976). Dissociation of odor and taste in shock-avoidance learning. *Behavioral Biology, 18,* 345–358.

Hanson, H. M. (1959). Effects of discrimination training on stimulus generalization. *Journal of Experimental Psychology, 58,* 321–333.

Hanson, J., & Green, L. (1986). Time and response matching with topographically different responses. *Animal Learning & Behavior, 14,* 435–442.

Hanson, S. J., & Timberlake, W. (1983). Regulation during challenge: A general model of learned performance under schedule constraint. *Psychological Review, 90,* 261–282.

Harlow, H. F. (1969). Age-mate or peer affectional system. In D. S. Lehrman, R. H. Hinde, & E. Shaw (Eds.), *Advances in the study of behavior* (Vol. 2). New York: Academic Press.

Haroutunian, V., & Riccio, D. C. (1979). Drug-induced "arousal" and the effectiveness of CS exposure in the reinstatement of memory. *Behavioral and Neural Biology, 26,* 115–120.

Hart, B. L. (1973). Reflexive behavior. In G. Bermant (Ed.),

Perspectives in animal behavior. Glenview, IL: Scott, Foresman.

Hastjarjo, T., Silberberg, A., & Hursh, S. R. (1990a). Quinine pellets as an inferior good and a Giffen good in rats. *Journal of the Experimental Analysis of Behavior, 53,* 263–271.

Hastjarjo, T., Silberberg, A., & Hursh, S. R. (1990b). Risky choice as a function of amount and variance in food supply. *Journal of the Experimental Analysis of Behavior, 53,* 155–161.

Hayashi, S., & Kimura, T. (1974). Sex attractant emitted by female mice. *Physiology and Behavior, 13,* 563–567.

Hayes, K. J., & Hayes, C. (1951). The intellectual development of a home-raised chimpanzee. *Proceedings of the American Philosophical Society, 95,* 105–109.

Hearst, E. (1968). Discrimination learning as the summation of excitation and inhibition. *Science, 162,* 1303–1306.

Hearst, E. (1969). Excitation, inhibition, and discrimination learning. In N. J. Mackintosh & W. K. Honig (Eds.), *Fundamental issues in associative learning.* Halifax: Dalhousie University Press.

Hearst, E. (1975). Pavlovian conditioning and directed movements. In G. Bower (Ed.), *The psychology of learning and motivation* (Vol. 9). New York: Academic Press.

Hearst, E. (1989). Backward associations: Differential learning about stimuli that follow the presence versus the absence of food in pigeons. *Animal Learning & Behavior, 17,* 280–290.

Hearst, E., & Franklin, S. R. (1977). Positive and negative relations between a signal and food: Approach-withdrawal behavior to the signal. *Journal of Experimental Psychology: Animal Behavior Processes, 3,* 37–52.

Hearst, E., & Jenkins, H. M. (1974). *Sign-tracking: The stimulus-reinforcer relation and directed action.* Austin, TX: Psychonomic Society.

Hearst, E., & Peterson, G. B. (1973). Transfer of conditioned excitation and inhibition from one operant response to another. *Journal of Experimental Psychology, 99,* 360–368.

Hebb, D. O. (1956). The distinction between "classical" and "instrumental." *Canadian Journal of Psychology, 10,* 165–166.

Heiligenberg, W. (1974). Processes governing behavioral states of readiness. In D. S. Lehrman, J. S. Rosenblatt, R. Hinde, & E. Shaw (Eds.), *Advances in the study of behavior* (Vol. 5, pp. 173–200). New York: Academic Press.

Hendersen, R. W., Patterson, J. M., & Jackson, R. L. (1980). Acquisition and retention of control of instrumental behavior by a cue signaling airblast: How specific are conditioned anticipations? *Learning and Motivation, 11,* 407–426.

Herberg, L. J. (1963). Seminal ejaculation following positively reinforcing electrical stimulation of the rat hypothalamus. *Journal of Comparative and Physiological Psychology, 56,* 679–685.

Herman, L. M. (1987). Receptive competencies of language-trained animals. In J. S. Rosenblatt, C. Beer, M.-C. Busnel, & P. J. B. Slater (Eds.), *Advances in the study of behavior* (Vol. 17, pp. 1–60). Orlando, FL: Academic Press.

Herman, R. L., & Azrin, N. H. (1964). Punishment by noise in an alternative response situation. *Journal of the Experimental Analysis of Behavior, 7,* 185–188.

Herrnstein, R. J. (1961). Relative and absolute strength of response as a function of frequency of reinforcement. *Journal of the Experimental Analysis of Behavior, 4,* 267–272.

Herrnstein, R. J. (1969). Method and theory in the study of avoidance. *Psychological Review, 76,* 49–69.

Herrnstein, R. J. (1970). On the law of effect. *Journal of the Experimental Analysis of Behavior, 13,* 243–266.

Herrnstein, R. J. (1984). Objects, categories, and discriminative stimuli. In H. L. Roitblat, T. G. Bever, & H. S. Terrace (Eds.), *Animal cognition.* Hillsdale, NJ: Erlbaum.

Herrnstein, R. J., & deVilliers, P. A. (1980). Fish as a natural category for people and pigeons. In G. H. Bower (Ed.), *The psychology of learning and motivation* (Vol. 14, pp. 60–97). New York: Academic Press.

Herrnstein, R. J., & Heyman, G. M. (1979). Is matching compatible with reinforcement maximization on concurrent variable interval, variable ratio? *Journal of the Experimental Analysis of Behavior, 31,* 209–223.

Herrnstein, R. J., & Hineline, P. N. (1966). Negative reinforcement as shock-frequency reduction. *Journal of the Experimental Analysis of Behavior, 9,* 421–430.

Herrnstein, R. J., & Loveland, D. H. (1964). Complex visual concept in the pigeon. *Science, 146,* 549–551.

Herrnstein, R. J., Loveland, D. H., & Cable, C. (1976). Natural concepts in pigeons. *Journal of Experimental Psychology: Animal Behavior Processes, 2,* 285–301.

Herrnstein, R. J., & Vaughan, W., Jr. (1980). Melioration and behavioral allocation. In J. E. R. Staddon (Ed.), *Limits to action.* New York: Academic Press.

Herzog, H. A., Jr. (1988). The moral status of mice. *American Psychologist, 43,* 473–474.

Heth, C. D. (1976). Simultaneous and backward fear conditioning as a function of number of CS-UCS pairings. *Journal of Experimental Psychology: Animal Behavior Processes, 2,* 117–129.

Heth, C. D., & Rescorla, R. A. (1973). Simultaneous and backward fear conditioning in the rat. *Journal of Comparative and Physiological Psychology, 82,* 434–443.

Heyman, G. M. (1983). Optimization theory: Close but no cigar. *Behaviour Analysis Letters, 3,* 17–26.

Heyman, G. M., & Herrnstein, R. J. (1986). More on concurrent interval-ratio schedules: A replication and review. *Journal of the Experimental Analysis of Behavior, 46,* 331–351.

Heyman, G. M., & Monaghan, M. M. (1987). Effects of

changes in response requirement and deprivation on the parameters of the matching law equation: New data and review. *Journal of Experimental Psychology: Animal Behavior Processes, 13,* 384–394.

Higa, J. J., Wynne, C. D. L., & Staddon, J. E. R. (1991). Dynamics of temporal discrimination. *Journal of Experimental Psychology: Animal Behavior Processes, 17,* 281–291.

Hilgard, E. R. (1936). The nature of the conditioned response: I. The case for and against stimulus substitution. *Psychological Review, 43,* 366–385.

Hill, W. L., Borovsky, D., & Rovee-Collier, C. (1988). Continuities in infant memory development. *Developmental Psychobiology, 21,* 43–62.

Hilton, S. C., & Krebs, J. K. (1990). Spatial memory of four species of *Parus:* Performance in an open-field analogue of a radial maze. *Quarterly Journal of Experimental Psychology, 42B,* 345–368.

Hineline, P. N. (1976). Negative reinforcement without shock reduction. *Journal of the Experimental Analysis of Behavior, 14,* 259–268.

Hineline, P. N. (1977). Negative reinforcement and avoidance. In W. K. Honig & J. E. R. Staddon (Eds.), *Handbook of operant behavior.* Englewood Cliffs, NJ: Prentice-Hall.

Hineline, P. N. (1981). The several roles of stimuli in negative reinforcement. In P. Harzem & M. D. Zeiler (Eds.), *Predictability, correlation, and contiguity.* Chichester, England: Wiley.

Hinson, J. M., & Lockhead, G. R. (1986). Range effects in successive discrimination. *Journal of Experimental Psychology: Animal Behavior Processes, 12,* 270–276.

Hinson, J. M., & Staddon, J. E. R. (1983a). Hill-climbing by pigeons. *Journal of the Experimental Analysis of Behavior, 39,* 25–47.

Hinson, J. M., & Staddon, J. E. R. (1983b). Matching, maximizing, and hill-climbing. *Journal of the Experimental Analysis of Behavior, 40,* 321–331.

Hinson, R. E. (1982). Effects of UCS preexposure on excitatory and inhibitory rabbit eyelid conditioning: An associative effect of conditioned contextual stimuli. *Journal of Experimental Psychology: Animal Behavior Processes, 8,* 49–61.

Hinson, R. E., Poulos, C. X., & Cappell, H. (1982). Effects of pentobarbital and cocaine in rats expecting pentobarbital. *Pharmacology, Biochemistry and Behavior, 16,* 661–666.

Hinson, R. E., & Siegel, S. (1980). Trace conditioning as an inhibitory procedure. *Animal Learning & Behavior, 8,* 60–66.

Hinson, R. E., & Siegel, S. (1986). Pavlovian inhibitory conditioning and tolerance to pentobarbital-induced hypothermia in rats. *Journal of Experimental Psychology: Animal Behavior Processes, 12,* 363–370.

Hintzman, D. L. (1991). Twenty-five years of learning and memory: Was the cognitive revolution a mistake? In D.

E. Meyer & S. Kornblum (Eds.), *Attention and performance XIVP.* Hillsdale, NJ: Erlbaum.

Hittesdorf, M., & Richards, R. W. (1982). Aversive second-order conditioning in the pigeon: Elimination of conditioning to CS1 and effects on established second-order conditioning. *Canadian Journal of Psychology, 36,* 462–477.

Hoebel, B. G., & Teitelbaum, P. (1962). Hypothalamic control of feeding and self-stimulation. *Science, 135,* 375–377.

Hoffman, H. S. (1966). The analysis of discriminated avoidance. In W. K. Honig (Ed.), *Operant behavior: Areas of research and application.* New York: Appleton-Century-Crofts.

Hoffman, H. S., & Fleshler, M. (1964). An apparatus for the measurement of the startle-response in the rat. *American Journal of Psychology, 77,* 307–308.

Hoffman, H. S., & Solomon, R. L. (1974). An opponent-process theory of motivation: III. Some affective dynamics in imprinting. *Learning and Motivation, 5,* 149–164.

Hoffman, N., & Maki, W. S. (1986). Two sources of proactive interference in spatial working memory: Multiple effects of repeated trials on radial maze performance by rats. *Animal Learning & Behavior, 14,* 65–72.

Hogan, J. A. (1974). Responses in Pavlovian conditioning studies. *Science, 186,* 156–157.

Holland, P. C. (1977). Conditioned stimulus as a determinant of the form of the Pavlovian conditioned response. *Journal of Experimental Psychology: Animal Behavior Processes, 3,* 77–104.

Holland, P. C. (1980). Influence of visual conditioned stimulus characteristics on the form of Pavlovian appetitive conditioned responding in rats. *Journal of Experimental Psychology: Animal Behavior Processes, 6,* 81–97.

Holland, P. C. (1981). Acquisition of representation-mediated conditioned food aversions. *Learning and Motivation, 12,* 1–18.

Holland, P. C. (1984). Origins of behavior in Pavlovian conditioning. In G. H. Bower (Ed.), *The psychology of learning and motivation* (Vol. 18, pp. 129–174). Orlando, FL: Academic Press.

Holland, P. C. (1985). The nature of conditioned inhibition in serial and simultaneous feature negative discriminations. In R. R. Miller & N. E. Spear (Eds.), *Information processing in animals: Conditioned inhibition.* Hillsdale, NJ: Erlbaum.

Holland, P. C. (1986). Temporal determinants of occasion setting in feature-positive discriminations. *Animal Learning & Behavior, 14,* 111–120.

Holland, P. C. (1989a). Feature extinction enhances transfer of occasion setting. *Animal Learning & Behavior, 17,* 269–279.

Holland, P. C. (1989b). Occasion setting with simultaneous compounds in rats. *Journal of Experimental Psychology: Animal Behavior Processes, 15,* 183–193.

Holland, P. C. (1989c). Transfer of negative occasion setting and conditioned inhibition across conditioned and unconditioned stimuli. *Journal of Experimental Psychology: Animal Behavior Processes, 15,* 311–328.

Holland, P. C., & Forbes, D. T. (1982). Representation-mediated extinction of conditioned flavor aversions. *Learning and Motivation, 13,* 454–471.

Holland, P. C., & Rescorla, R. A. (1975a). The effect of two ways of devaluing the unconditioned stimulus after first- and second-order appetitive conditioning. *Journal of Experimental Psychology: Animal Behavior Processes, 1,* 355–363.

Holland, P. C., & Rescorla, R. A. (1975b). Second-order conditioning with food unconditioned stimulus. *Journal of Comparative and Physiological Psychology, 88,* 459–467.

Holland, P. C., & Straub, J. J. (1979). Differential effect of two ways of devaluing the unconditioned stimulus after Pavlovian appetitive conditioning. *Journal of Experimental Psychology: Animal Behavior Processes, 5,* 65–78.

Holliday, M., & Hirsch, J. (1986). Excitatory conditioning of individual *Drosophila melanogaster. Journal of Experimental Psychology: Animal Behavior Processes, 12,* 131–142.

Hollis, K. L. (1982). Pavlovian conditioning of signal-centered action patterns and autonomic behavior: A biological analysis of function. *Advances in the Study of Behavior, 12,* 1–64.

Hollis, K. L. (1984a). The biological function of Pavlovian conditioning: The best defense is a good offense. *Journal of Experimental Psychology: Animal Learning and Behavior, 10,* 413–425.

Hollis, K. L. (1984b). Cause and function of animal learning processes. In P. Marler & H. S. Terrace (Eds.), *The biology of learning.* New York: Springer-Verlag.

Hollis, K. L., Cadieux, E. L., & Colbert, M. M. (1989). The biological function of Pavlovian conditioning: A mechanism for mating success in the blue gourami *(Trichogaster trichopterus). Journal of Comparative Psychology, 103,* 115–121.

Holman, J. G., & Mackintosh, N. J. (1981). The control of appetitive instrumental responding does not depend on classical conditioning to the discriminative stimulus. *Quarterly Journal of Experimental Psychology, 33B,* 21–31.

Holz, W. C., & Azrin, N. H. (1961). Discriminative properties of punishment. *Journal of the Experimental Analysis of Behavior, 4,* 225–232.

Honey, R. C., Willis, A., & Hall, G. (1990). Context specificity in pigeon autoshaping. *Learning and Motivation, 21,* 125–136.

Honig, W. K. (1978). Studies of working memory in the pigeon. In S. H. Hulse, H. Fowler, & W. K. Honig (Eds.), *Cognitive processes in animal behavior.* Hillsdale, NJ: Erlbaum.

Honig, W. K. (1991). Discrimination by pigeons of mixtures and uniformity in arrays of stimulus elements. *Journal of Experimental Psychology: Animal Behavior Processes, 17,* 68–80.

Honig, W. K., Boneau, C. A., Burstein, K. R., & Pennypacker, H. S. (1963). Positive and negative generalization gradients obtained under equivalent training conditions. *Journal of Comparative and Physiological Psychology, 56,* 111–116.

Honig, W. K., & James, P. H. R. (Eds.). (1971). *Animal memory.* New York: Academic Press.

Honig, W. K., & Stewart, K. E. (1988). Pigeons can discriminate locations presented in pictures. *Journal of the Experimental Analysis of Behavior, 50,* 541–551.

Honig, W. K., & Thompson, R. K. R. (1982). Retrospective and prospective processing in animal working memory. In G. H. Bower (Ed.), *The psychology of learning and motivation* (Vol. 16, pp. 239–283). Orlando, FL: Academic Press.

Honig, W. K., & Urcuioli, P. J. (1981). The legacy of Guttman and Kalish (1956): 25 years of research on stimulus generalization. *Journal of the Experimental Analysis of Behavior, 36,* 405–445.

Hull, C. L. (1930). Knowledge and purpose as habit mechanisms. *Psychological Review, 30,* 511–525.

Hull, C. L. (1931). Goal attraction and directing ideas conceived as habit phenomena. *Psychological Review, 38,* 487–506.

Hulse, S. H. (1978). Cognitive structure and serial pattern learning by animals. In S. H. Hulse, H. Fowler, & W. K. Honig (Eds.), *Cognitive processes in animal behavior.* Hillsdale, NJ: Erlbaum.

Hulse, S. H., Fowler, H., & Honig, W. K. (Eds.). (1978). *Cognitive processes in animal behavior.* Hillsdale, NJ: Erlbaum.

Hunter, W. S. (1913). The delayed reaction in animals and children. *Behavior Monographs, 2,* serial #6.

Hursh, S. R. (1980). Economic concepts for the analysis of behavior. *Journal of the Experimental Analysis of Behavior, 34,* 219–238.

Hursh, S. R. (1984). Behavioral economics. *Journal of the Experimental Analysis of Behavior, 42,* 435–452.

Hursh, S. R., Navarick, D. J., & Fantino, E. (1974). "Automaintenance": The role of reinforcement. *Journal of the Experimental Analysis of Behavior, 21,* 117–124.

Hursh, S. R., Raslear, T. G., Shurtleff, D., Bauman, R., & Simmons, L. (1988). A cost-benefit analysis of demand for food. *Journal of the Experimental Analysis of Behavior, 50,* 419–440.

Hutt, P. J. (1954). Rate of bar pressing as a function of quality and quantity of food reward. *Journal of Comparative and Physiological Psychology, 47,* 235–239.

Imada, H., & Imada, S. (1983). Thorndike's (1898) puzzle-box experiments revisited. *Kwansei Gakuin University Annual Studies, 32,* 167–184.

Innis, N. K., Reberg, D., Mann, B., Jacobson, J., & Turton, D. (1983). Schedule-induced behavior for food and water: Effects of interval duration. *Behaviour Analysis Letters, 3,* 191–200.

Innis, N. K., Simmelhag-Grant, V. L., & Staddon, J. E. R. (1983). Behavior induced by periodic food delivery: The effects of interfood interval. *Journal of the Experimental Analysis of Behavior, 39,* 309–322.

Irwin, J., Suissa, A., & Anisman, H. (1980). Differential effects of inescapable shock on escape performance and discrimination learning in a water escape task. *Journal of Experimental Psychology: Animal Behavior Processes, 6,* 21–40.

Israel, A. C., Devine, V. T., O'Dea, M. A., & Hamdi, M. E. (1974). Effect of delayed conditioned stimulus termination on extinction of an avoidance response following differential termination conditions during acquisition. *Journal of Experimental Psychology, 103,* 360–362.

Ito, M., & Fantino, E. (1986). Choice, foraging, and reinforcer duration. *Journal of the Experimental Analysis of Behavior, 46,* 93–103.

Jackson, R. L., Alexander, J. H., & Maier, S. F. (1980). Learned helplessness, inactivity, and associative deficits: Effects of inescapable shock on response choice escape learning. *Journal of Experimental Psychology: Animal Behavior Processes, 6,* 1–20.

Jackson, R. L., & Fritsche, M. B. (1989). Potentiation and overshadowing in pigeons. *Learning and Motivation, 20,* 15–35.

Jackson, R. L., & Minor, T. R. (1988). Effects of signaling inescapable shock on subsequent escape learning: Implications for theories of coping and "learned helplessness." *Journal of Experimental Psychology: Animal Behavior Processes, 14,* 390–400.

Jarrard, L. E., & Moise, S. L. (1971). Short-term memory in the monkey. In L. E. Jarrard (Ed.), *Cognitive processes of nonhuman primates.* New York: Academic Press.

Jarvik, M. E., Goldfarb, T. L., & Carley, J. L. (1969). Influence of interference on delayed matching in monkeys. *Journal of Experimental Psychology, 81,* 1–6.

Jasselette, P., Lejeune, H., & Wearden, J. H. (1990). The perching response and the laws of animal timing. *Journal of Experimental Psychology: Animal Behavior Processes, 16,* 150–161.

Jenkins, H. M. (1962). Resistance to extinction when partial reinforcement is followed by regular reinforcement. *Journal of Experimental Psychology, 64,* 441–450.

Jenkins, H. M. (1977). Sensitivity of different response systems to stimulus-reinforcer and response-reinforcer relations. In H. Davis & H. M. B. Hurwitz (Eds.), *Operant-Pavlovian interactions* (pp. 47–62). Hillsdale, NJ: Erlbaum.

Jenkins, H. M., Barnes, R. A., & Barrera, F. J. (1981). Why autoshaping depends on trial spacing. In C. M.

Locurto, H. S. Terrace, & J. Gibbon (Eds.), *Autoshaping and conditioning theory* (pp. 255–284). New York: Academic Press.

Jenkins, H. M., Barrera, F. J., Ireland, C., & Woodside, B. (1978). Signal-centered action patterns of dogs in appetitive classical conditioning. *Learning and Motivation, 9,* 272–296.

Jenkins, H. M., & Harrison, R. H. (1960). Effects of discrimination training on auditory generalization. *Journal of Experimental Psychology, 59,* 246–253.

Jenkins, H. M., & Harrison, R. H. (1962). Generalization gradients of inhibition following auditory discrimination learning. *Journal of the Experimental Analysis of Behavior, 5,* 435–441.

Jenkins, H. M., & Moore, B. R. (1973). The form of the autoshaped response with food or water reinforcers. *Journal of the Experimental Analysis of Behavior, 20,* 163–181.

Jitsumori, M., Wright, A. A., & Cook, R. G. (1988). Long-term proactive interference and novelty enhancement effects in monkey list memory. *Journal of Experimental Psychology: Animal Behavior Processes, 14,* 146–154.

Jitsumori, M., Wright, A. A., & Shyan, M. R. (1989). Buildup and release from proactive interference in a rhesus monkey. *Journal of Experimental Psychology: Animal Behavior Processes, 15,* 329–337.

Job, R. F. S. (1987). Learned helplessness in an appetitive discrete-trial T-maze discrimination test. *Animal Learning & Behavior, 15,* 342–346.

Job, R. F. S. (1989). A test of proposed mechanisms underlying the interference effect produced by non-contingent food presentations. *Learning and Motivation, 20,* 153–177.

Jones, F. R. H. (1955). Photo-kinesis in the ammocoete larva of the brook lamprey. *Journal of Experimental Biology, 32,* 492–503.

Jones, M. R. (1974). Cognitive representations of serial patterns. In B. Kantowitz (Ed.), *Human information processing: Tutorials in performance and cognition.* Hillsdale, NJ: Erlbaum.

Kagel, J. H., Rachlin, H., Green, L., Battalio, R. C., Basmann, R. L., & Klemm, W. R. (1975). Experimental studies of consumer demand behavior using laboratory animals. *Economic Inquiry, 13,* 22–38.

Kalat, J. W. (1974). Taste salience depends on novelty, not concentration, in taste-aversion learning in the rat. *Journal of Comparative and Physiological Psychology, 86,* 47–50.

Kamil, A. C. (1978). Systematic foraging by a nectar-feeding bird, the amakihi *(Loxops virens). Journal of Comparative and Physiological Psychology, 92,* 388–396.

Kamil, A. C., & Balda, R. P. (1985). Cache recovery and spatial memory in Clark's nutcrackers *(Nucifraga columbiana). Journal of Experimental Psychology: Animal Behavior Processes, 11,* 95–111.

Kamil, A. C., & Balda, R. P. (1990). Differential memory for different cache sites by Clark's nutcrackers *(Nucifraga columbiana). Journal of Experimental Psychology: Animal Behavior Processes, 16,* 162–168.

Kamil, A. C., & Clements, K. C. (1990). Learning, memory, and foraging behavior. In D. A. Dewsbury (Ed.), *Contemporary issues in comparative psychology* (pp. 7–30). Sunderland, MA: Sinauer.

Kamil, A. C., Krebs, J. R., & Pulliam, H. R. (Eds.). (1987). *Foraging behavior.* New York: Plenum.

Kamil, A. C., & Sargent, T. D. (Eds.). (1981). *Foraging behavior.* New York: Garland STPM.

Kamil, A. C., Yoerg, S. I., & Clements, K. C. (1988). Rules to leave by: Patch departure in foraging blue jays. *Animal Behaviour, 36,* 843–853.

Kamin, L. J. (1956). The effects of termination of the CS and avoidance of the US on avoidance learning. *Journal of Comparative and Physiological Psychology, 49,* 420–424.

Kamin, L. J. (1965). Temporal and intensity characteristics of the conditioned stimulus. In W. F. Prokasy (Ed.), *Classical conditioning.* New York: Appleton-Century-Crofts.

Kamin, L. J. (1968). "Attention-like" processes in classical conditioning. In M. R. Jones (Ed.), *Miami Symposium on the Prediction of Behavior: Aversive stimulation* (pp. 9–31). Miami: University of Miami Press.

Kamin, L. J. (1969). Predictability, surprise, attention, and conditioning. In B. A. Campbell & R. M. Church (Eds.), *Punishment and aversive behavior* (pp. 279–296). New York: Appleton-Century-Crofts.

Kamin, L. J., & Brimer, C. J. (1963). The effects of intensity of conditioned and unconditioned stimuli on a conditioned emotional response. *Canadian Journal of Psychology, 17,* 194–198.

Kamin, L. J., Brimer, C. J., & Black, A. H. (1963). Conditioned suppression as a monitor of fear of the CS in the course of avoidance training. *Journal of Comparative and Physiological Psychology, 56,* 497–501.

Kamin, L. J., & Schaub, R. E. (1963). Effects of conditioned stimulus intensity on the conditioned emotional response. *Journal of Comparative and Physiological Psychology, 56,* 502–507.

Kandel, E. R., Schwartz, J. H., & Jessell, T. M. (Eds.). (1991). *Principles of neural science.* New York: Elsevier.

Kaplan, P. S. (1984). The importance of relative temporal parameters in trace autoshaping: From excitation to inhibition. *Journal of Experimental Psychology: Animal Behavior Processes, 10,* 113–126.

Kaplan, P. S., & Hearst, E. (1982). Bridging temporal gaps between CS and US in autoshaping: Insertion of other stimuli before, during, and after the CS. *Journal of Experimental Psychology: Animal Behavior Processes, 8,* 187–203.

Kaplan, P. S., Werner, J. S., & Rudy, J. W. (1990). Habituation, sensitization, and infant visual attention. In C. Rovee-Collier & L. P. Lipsitt (Eds.), *Advances in infancy research* (Vol. 6, pp. 61–109). Norwood, NJ: Ablex.

Karpicke, J. (1978). Directed approach responses and positive conditioned suppression in the rat. *Animal Learning & Behavior, 6,* 216–224.

Karpicke, J., Christoph, G., Peterson, G., & Hearst, E. (1977). Signal location and positive versus negative conditioned suppression in the rat. *Journal of Experimental Psychology: Animal Behavior Processes, 3,* 105–118.

Kasprow, W. J. (1987). Enhancement of short-term retention by appetitive-reinforcer reminder treatment. *Animal Learning & Behavior, 15,* 412–416.

Kasprow, W. J., Cacheiro, H., Balaz, M. A., & Miller, R. R. (1982). Reminder-induced recovery of associations to an overshadowed stimulus. *Learning and Motivation, 13,* 155–166.

Kasprow, W. J., Catterson, D., Schachtman, T. R., & Miller, R. R. (1984). Attenuation of latent inhibition by post-acquisition reminder. *Quarterly Journal of Experimental Psychology, 36B,* 53–63.

Kasprow, W. J., Schachtman, T. R., & Miller, R. R. (1987). The comparator hypothesis of conditioned response generation: Manifest conditioned excitation and inhibition as a function of relative excitatory strengths of CS and conditioning context at the time of testing. *Journal of Experimental Psychology: Animal Behavior Processes, 13,* 395–406.

Katzev, R. D. (1967). Extinguishing avoidance responses as a function of delayed warning signal termination. *Journal of Experimental Psychology, 75,* 339–344.

Katzev, R. D. (1972). What is both necessary and sufficient to maintain avoidance responding in the shuttle box? *Quarterly Journal of Experimental Psychology, 24,* 310–317.

Katzev, R. D., & Berman, J. S. (1974). Effect of exposure to conditioned stimulus and control of its termination in the extinction of avoidance behavior. *Journal of Comparative and Physiological Psychology, 87,* 347–353.

Kaufman, L. W., & Collier, G. (1983). Cost and meal pattern in wild-caught rats. *Physiology and Behavior, 30,* 445–449.

Keehn, J. D. (Ed.). (1986). *Animal models for psychiatry.* London: Routledge & Kagan Paul.

Keehn, J. D., & Nakkash, S. (1959). Effect of a signal contingent upon an avoidance response. *Nature, 184,* 566–568.

Kehoe, E. J. (1986). Summation and configuration in conditioning of the rabbit's nictitating membrane response to compound stimuli. *Journal of Experimental Psychology: Animal Behavior Processes, 12,* 186–195.

Kehoe, E. J., & Graham, P. (1988). Summation and configuration: Stimulus compounding and negative patterning in the rabbit. *Journal of Experimental Psychology: Animal Behavior Processes, 14,* 320–333.

Kelley, M. J. (1986). Selective attention and stimulus-reinforcer interactions in the pigeon. *Quarterly Journal of Experimental Psychology, 38B,* 97–110.

Kellogg, W. N. (1933). *The ape and the child.* New York: McGraw-Hill.

Kelsey, J. E., & Allison, J. (1976). Fixed-ratio lever pressing by VMH rats: Work vs. accessibility of sucrose reward. *Physiology & Behavior, 17,* 749–754.

Kempe, R. S., & Kempe, C. H. (1978). *Child abuse: The developing child.* Cambridge, MA: Harvard University Press.

Kendrick, D. F., Rilling, M. E., & Denny, M. R. (Eds.). (1986). *Theories of animal memory.* Hillsdale, NJ: Erlbaum.

Kesner, R. P., & DeSpain, M. J. (1988). Correspondence between rats and humans in the utilization of retrospective and prospective codes. *Animal Learning & Behavior, 16,* 299–302.

Killeen, P. R. (1981). Learning as causal inference. In M. L. Commons & J. A. Nevin (Eds.), *Quantitative analyses of behavior: Vol. 1. Discriminative properties of reinforcement schedules.* Cambridge, MA: Ballinger.

Killeen, P. R., & Fetterman, J. G. (1988). A behavioral theory of timing. *Psychological Review, 95,* 274–295.

Killeen, P. R., & Smith, J. P. (1984). Perception of contingency in conditioning: Scalar timing, response, bias, and erasure of memory by reinforcement. *Journal of Experimental Psychology: Animal Behavior Processes, 10,* 333–345.

King, D. A., Bouton, M. E., & Musty, R. E. (1987). Associative control of tolerance to the sedative effects of a short-acting benzodiazepine. *Behavioral Neuroscience, 101,* 104–114.

King, G. R., & Logue, A. W. (1987). Choice in a self-control paradigm with human subjects: Effects of changeover delay duration. *Learning and Motivation, 18,* 421–438.

Kintsch, W., & Witte, R. S. (1962). Concurrent conditioning of bar press and salivation responses. *Journal of Comparative and Physiological Psychology, 52,* 963–968.

Klein, M., & Rilling, M. (1974). Generalization of freeoperant avoidance behavior in pigeons. *Journal of the Experimental Analysis of Behavior, 21,* 75–88.

Klosterhalfen, S., & Klosterhalfen, W. (1990). Conditioned cyclosporine effects but not conditioned taste aversion in immunized rats. *Behavioral Neuroscience, 104,* 716–724.

Kluender, K. R., Diehl, R. L., & Killeen, P. R. (1987). Japanese quail can learn phonetic categories. *Science, 237,* 1195–1197.

Köhler, W. (1939). Simple structural functions in the chimpanzee and in the chicken. In W. D. Ellis (Ed.), *A source book of Gestalt psychology* (pp. 217–227). New York: Harcourt Brace Jovanovich.

Konorski, J., & Miller, S. (1930). Méthode d'examen de l'analysateur moteur par les réactions salivomotrices. *Compte et Mémoires de la Société de Biologie, 104,* 907–910.

Konorski, J., & Szwejkowska, G. (1950). Chronic extinction and restoration of conditioned reflexes: I. Extinction against the excitatory background. *Acta Biologiae Experimentalis, 15,* 155–170.

Konorski, J., & Szwejkowska, G. (1952). Chronic extinction and restoration of conditioned reflexes: IV. The dependence of the course of extinction and restoration of conditioned reflexes on the "history" of the conditioned stimulus (The principle of the primacy of first training). *Acta Biologiae Experimentalis, 16,* 95–113.

Korol, B., Sletten, I. W., & Brown, M. I. (1966). Conditioned physiological adaptation to anticholinergic drugs. *American Journal of Physiology, 211,* 911–914.

Koshland, D. E., Jr. (1989). Animal rights and animal wrongs. *Science, 243,* 1253.

Kraemer, P. J., & Roberts, W. A. (1985). Short-term memory for simultaneously presented visual and auditory signals in the pigeon. *Journal of Experimental Psychology: Animal Behavior Processes, 11,* 13–39.

Krane, R. V., & Wagner, A. R. (1975). Taste aversion learning with a delayed shock US: Implications for the "generality of the laws of learning." *Journal of Comparative and Physiological Psychology, 88,* 882–889.

Krank, M. D. (1987). Conditioned hyperalgesia depends on the pain sensitivity measure. *Behavioral Neuroscience, 101,* 854–857.

Krank, M. D., & MacQueen, G. (1988). Conditioned compensatory responses elicited by environmental signals for cyclophosphamide-induced suppression of the immune system. *Psychobiology, 16,* 229–235.

Krebs, J. R., & McCleery, R. H. (1984). Optimization in behavioural ecology. In J. R. Krebs & N. B. Davies (Eds.), *Behavioural ecology* (2nd ed.). Sunderland, MA: Sinauer.

Kremer, E. F. (1978). The Rescorla-Wagner model: Losses in associative strength in compound conditioned stimuli. *Journal of Experimental Psychology: Animal Behavior Processes, 4,* 22–36.

Kruse, J. M., Overmier, J. B., Konz, W. A., & Rokke, E. (1983). Pavlovian conditioned stimulus effects upon instrumental choice behavior are reinforcer specific. *Learning and Motivation, 14,* 165–181.

Lamarre, J., & Holland, P. C. (1987). Transfer of inhibition after serial feature negative discrimination training. *Learning and Motivation, 18,* 319–342.

Lang, W. J., Brown, M. L., Gershon, S., & Korol, B. (1966). Classical and physiologic adaptive conditioned responses to anticholinergic drugs in conscious dogs. *International Journal of Neuropharmacology, 5,* 311–315.

Lashley, K. S., & Wade, M. (1946). The Pavlovian theory of generalization. *Psychological Review, 53,* 72–87.

Lattal, K. A., & Gleeson, S. (1990). Response acquisition with delayed reinforcement. *Journal of Experimental Psychology: Animal Behavior Processes, 16,* 27–39.

Lavin, M. J. (1976). The establishment of flavor-flavor

associations using a sensory preconditioning training procedure. *Learning and Motivation, 7,* 173–183.

Lea, S. E. G. (1978). The psychology and economics of demand. *Psychological Bulletin, 85,* 441–466.

Lea, S. E. G. (1984). In what sense do pigeons learn concepts? In H. L. Roitblat, T. G. Bever, & H. S. Terrace (Eds.), *Animal cognition* (pp. 263–276). Hillsdale, NJ: Erlbaum.

Lea, S. E. G., & Harrison, S. N. (1978). Discrimination of polymorphous stimulus sets by pigeons. *Quarterly Journal of Experimental Psychology, 30,* 521–537.

Lea, S. E. G., & Roper, T. J. (1977). Demand for food on fixed-ratio schedules as a function of the quality of concurrently available reinforcement. *Journal of the Experimental Analysis of Behavior, 27,* 371–380.

Lea, S. E. G., & Ryan, C. M. E. (1983). Feature analysis of pigeon's acquisition of concept discrimination. In M. L. Commons, R. J. Herrnstein, & A. R. Wagner (Eds.), *Quantitative analyses of behavior: Vol. 4. Discrimination processes.* Cambridge, MA: Ballinger.

Leaton, R. N. (1976). Long-term retention of the habituation of lick suppression and startle response produced by a single auditory stimulus. *Journal of Experimental Psychology: Animal Behavior Processes, 2,* 248–259.

Leclerc, R., Reberg, D. (1980). Sign-tracking in aversive conditioning. *Learning and Motivation, 11,* 302–317.

Lee, R. K. K., & Maier, S. F. (1988). Inescapable shock and attention to internal versus external cues in a water discrimination escape task. *Journal of Experimental Psychology: Animal Behavior Processes, 14,* 302–310.

Lemere, F., & Voegtlin, W. L. (1950). An evaluation of the aversion treatment of alcoholism. *Quarterly Journal of Studies on Alcohol, 11,* 199–204.

Lennenberg, E. H. (1967). *Biological foundations of language.* New York: Wiley.

Lett, B. T. (1980). Taste potentiates color-sickness associations in pigeons and quail. *Animal Learning & Behavior, 8,* 193–198.

Lett, B. T. (1982). Taste potentiation in poison avoidance learning. In M. L. Commons, R. J. Herrnstein, & A. R. Wagner (Eds.), *Quantitative analyses of behavior: Vol. 3. Acquisition.* Cambridge, MA: Ballinger.

Levine, F. M., & Sandeen, E. (1985). *Conceptualization in psychotherapy: The models approach.* Hillsdale, NJ: Erlbaum.

Levis, D. J. (1976). Learned helplessness: A reply and alternative S-R interpretation. *Journal of Experimental Psychology: General, 105,* 47–65.

Levis, D. J. (1981). Extrapolation of two-factor learning theory of infrahuman avoidance behavior to psychopathology, *Neuroscience & Biobehavioral Reviews, 5,* 355–370.

Levis, D. J. (1989). The case for a return to a two-factor theory of avoidance: The failure of non-fear interpretations. In S. B. Klein & R. R. Mowrer (Eds.), *Contemporary learning theories: Pavlovian conditioning and the status of learning theory* (pp. 227–277). Hillsdale, NJ: Erlbaum.

Levis, D. J. (1991). A clinician's plea for a return to the development of nonhuman models of psychopathology: New clinical observations in need of laboratory study. In M. R. Denny (Ed.), *Fear, avoidance and phobias* (pp. 395–427). Hillsdale, NJ: Erlbaum.

Lewis, D. J. (1979). Psychobiology of active and inactive memory. *Psychological Bulletin, 86,* 1054–1083.

Leyland, C. M. (1977). Higher order autoshaping. *Quarterly Journal of Experimental Psychology, 29,* 607–619.

Lieberman, D. A., Davidson, F. H., & Thomas, G. V. (1985). Marking in pigeons: The role of memory in delayed reinforcement. *Journal of Experimental Psychology: Animal Behavior Processes, 11,* 611–624.

Lieberman, D. A., McIntosh, D. C., & Thomas, G. V. (1979). Learning when reward is delayed: A marking hypothesis. *Journal of Experimental Psychology: Animal Behavior Processes, 5,* 224–242.

Lieberman, D. A., & Thomas, G. V. (1986). Marking, memory and superstition in the pigeon. *Quarterly Journal of Experimental Psychology, 38B,* 449–459.

Linscheid, T. R., & Cunningham, C. E. (1977). A controlled demonstration of the effectiveness of electric shock in the elimination of chronic infant rumination. *Journal of Applied Behavior Analysis, 10,* 500.

Little, A. H., Lipsitt, L. P., & Rovee-Collier, C. (1984). Classical conditioning and retention of the infant's eyelid response: Effects of age and interstimulus interval. *Journal of Experimental Child Psychology, 37,* 512–524.

Lockard, R. B. (1968). The albino rat: A defensible choice or a bad habit? *American Psychologist, 23,* 734–742.

Locurto, C. M. (1981). Contributions of autoshaping to the partitioning of conditioned behavior. In C. M. Locurto, H. S. Terrace, & J. Gibbon (Eds.), *Autoshaping and conditioning theory.* New York: Academic Press.

Locurto, C. M., Terrace, H. S., & Gibbon, J. (Eds.). (1981). *Autoshaping and conditioning theory.* New York: Academic Press.

Loeb, J. (1900). *Comparative physiology of the brain and comparative psychology.* New York: G. P. Putman.

Logue, A. W. (1982). Expecting shock. *Behavioral and Brain Sciences, 5,* 680–681.

Logue, A. W. (1985). Conditioned food aversion learning in humans. *Annals of the New York Academy of Sciences.*

Logue, A. W. (1988a). A comparison of taste aversion learning in humans and other vertebrates: Evolutionary pressures in common. In R. C. Bolles & M. D. Beecher (Eds.), *Evolution and learning* (pp. 97–116). Hillsdale, NJ: Erlbaum.

Logue, A. W. (1988b). Research on self-control: An integrating framework. *Behavioral and Brain Sciences, 11,* 665–709.

Logue, A. W., & Chavarro, A. (1987). Effect on choice of absolute and relative values of reinforcer delay, amount, and frequency. *Journal of Experimental Psychology: Animal Behavior Processes, 13,* 280–291.

Logue, A. W., King, G. R., Chavarro, A., & Volpe, J. S. (1990). Matching and maximizing in a self-control paradigm using human subjects. *Learning and Motivation, 21,* 340–368.

Logue, A. W., Ophir, I., & Strauss, K. E. (1981). The acquisition of taste aversions in humans. *Behaviour Research and Therapy, 19,* 319–333.

Logue, A. W., Peña-Correal, T. E., Rodriguez, M. L., & Kabela, E. (1986). Self-control in adult humans: Variation in positive reinforcer amount and delay. *Journal of the Experimental Analysis of Behavior, 46,* 159–173.

Logue, A. W., Rodriguez, M. L., Peña-Correal, T. E., & Mauro, B. C. (1984). Choice in a self-control paradigm: Quantification of experience-based differences. *Journal of the Experimental Analysis of Behavior, 41,* 53–67.

LoLordo, V. M. (1971). Facilitation of food-reinforced responding by a signal for response-independent food. *Journal of the Experimental Analysis of Behavior, 15,* 49–55.

LoLordo, V. M. (1979). Selective associations. In A. Dickinson & R. A. Boakes (Eds.), *Mechanisms of learning and motivation* (pp. 367–398). Hillsdale, NJ: Erlbaum.

LoLordo, V. M., & Fairless, J. L. (1985). Pavlovian conditioned inhibition: The literature since 1969. In R. R. Miller & N. E. Spear (Eds.), *Information processing in animals: Conditioned inhibition.* Hillsdale, NJ: Erlbaum.

LoLordo, V. M., Jacobs, W. J., & Foree, D. D. (1982). Failure to block control by a relevant stimulus. *Animal Learning & Behavior, 10,* 183–193.

LoLordo, V. M., McMillan, J. C., & Riley, A. L. (1974). The effects upon food-reinforced pecking and treadle-pressing of auditory and visual signals for response-independent food. *Learning and Motivation, 5,* 24–41.

Lorenz, K., & Tinbergen, N. (1939). Taxis und Instinkthandlung in der Eirollbewegung der Graugans: I. *Zeitschrift für Tierpsychologie, 3,* 1–29.

Lovibond, P. F. (1983). Facilitation of instrumental behavior by a Pavlovian appetitive conditioned stimulus. *Journal of Experimental Psychology: Animal Behavior Processes, 9,* 225–247.

Lubow, R. E. (1989). *Latent inhibition and conditioned attention theory.* Cambridge, England: Cambridge University Press.

Lucas, G. A., Timberlake, W., & Gawley, D. J. (1988). Adjunctive behavior of the rat under periodic food delivery in a 24-hour environment. *Animal Learning & Behavior, 16,* 19–30.

Lyon, D. O. (1968). Conditioned suppression: Operant variables and aversive control. *Psychological Record, 18,* 317–338.

Lysle, D. T., & Fowler, H. (1985). Inhibition as a "slave" process: Deactivation of conditioned inhibition through extinction of conditioned excitation. *Journal of*

Experimental Psychology: Animal Behavior Processes, 11, 71–94.

MacEwen, D., & Killeen, P. (1991). The effects of rate and amount of reinforcement on the speed of the pacemaker in pigeons' timing behavior. *Animal Learning & Behavior, 19,* 164–170.

Machado, A. (1989). Operant conditioning of behavioral variability using a percentile reinforcement schedule. *Journal of the Experimental Analysis of Behavior, 52,* 155–166.

Mackintosh, N. J. (1975). A theory of attention: Variations in the associability of stimuli with reinforcement. *Psychological Review, 82,* 276–298.

Mackintosh, N. J., Bygrave, D. J., & Picton, B. M. B. (1977). Locus of the effect of a surprising reinforcer in the attenuation of blocking. *Quarterly Journal of Experimental Psychology, 29,* 327–336.

Mackintosh, N. J., & Dickinson, A. (1979). Instrumental (Type II) conditioning. In A. Dickinson & R. A. Boakes (Eds.), *Mechanisms of learning and motivation* (pp. 143–169). Hillsdale, NJ: Erlbaum.

MacLennan, A. J., Jackson, R. L., & Maier, S. F. (1980). Conditioned analgesia in the rat. *Bulletin of the Psychonomic Society, 15,* 387–390.

MacQueen, G. M., & Siegel, S. (1989). Conditioned immunomodulation following training with cyclophosphamide. *Behavioral Neuroscience, 103,* 638–647.

MacQueen, G. M., Siegel, S., & Landry, J. O. (1990). Acquisition and extinction of conditional immunoenhancement following training with cyclophosphamide. *Psychobiology, 18,* 287–292.

MacRae, J. R., & Siegel, S. (1987). Extinction of tolerance to the analgesic effect of morphine: Intracerebroventricular administration and effects of stress. *Behavioral Neuroscience, 101,* 790–796.

Mactutus, C. F., Ferek, J. M., George, C. A., & Riccio, D. C. (1982). Hypothermia-induced amnesia for newly acquired and old reactivated memories: Commonalities and distinctions. *Physiological Psychology, 10,* 79–95.

Mahoney, W. J., & Ayres, J. J. B. (1976). One-trial simultaneous and backward conditioning as reflected in conditioned suppression of licking in rats. *Animal Learning & Behavior, 4,* 357–362.

Maier, S. F. (1990). Role of fear in mediating shuttle escape learning deficit produced by inescapable shock. *Journal of Experimental Psychology: Animal Behavior Processes, 16,* 137–149.

Maier, S. F., & Church, R. M. (1991). *Special issue on animal timing. Learning and Motivation, 22,* 1–252.

Maier, S. F., & Jackson, R. L. (1979). Learned helplessness: All of us were right (and wrong): Inescapable shock has multiple effects. In G. H. Bower (Ed.), *The psychology of learning and motivation* (Vol. 13). New York: Academic Press.

Maier, S. F., Jackson, R. L., & Tomie, A. (1987). Potentiation, overshadowing, and prior exposure to inescapable shock. *Journal of Experimental Psychology: Animal Behavior Processes, 13,* 260–270.

Maier, S. F., Rapaport, P., & Wheatley, K. L. (1976). Conditioned inhibition and the UCS-CS interval. *Animal Learning and Behavior, 4,* 217–220.

Maier, S. F., & Seligman, M. E. P. (1976). Learned helplessness: Theory and evidence. *Journal of Experimental Psychology: General, 105,* 3–46.

Maier, S. F., Seligman, M. E. P., & Solomon, R. L. (1969). Pavlovian fear conditioning and learned helplessness. In B. A. Campbell & R. M. Church (Eds.), *Punishment and aversive behavior.* New York: Appleton-Century-Crofts.

Maier, S. F., & Warren, D. A. (1988). Controllability and safety signals exert dissimilar proactive effects on nociception and escape performance. *Journal of Experimental Psychology: Animal Behavior Processes, 14,* 18–25.

Maki, W. S. (1979). Pigeon's short-term memories for surprising vs. expected reinforcement and nonreinforcement. *Animal Learning & Behavior, 7,* 31–37.

Maki, W. S. (1987). On the nonassociative nature of working memory. *Learning and Motivation, 18,* 99–117.

Maki, W. S., Beatty, W. W., Hoffman, N., Bierley, R. A., & Clouse, B. A. (1984). Spatial memory over long retention intervals: Nonmemorial factors are not necessary for accurate performance on the radial arm maze by rats. *Behavioral and Neural Biology, 41,* 1–6.

Maki, W. S., Brokofsky, S., & Berg, B. (1979). Spatial memory in rats: Resistance to retroactive interference. *Animal Learning & Behavior, 7,* 25–30.

Maki, W. S., & Hegvik, D. K. (1980). Directed forgetting in pigeons. *Animal Learning & Behavior, 8,* 567–574.

Maki, W. S., Moe, J. C., & Bierley, C. M. (1977). Short-term memory for stimuli, responses, and reinforcers. *Journal of Experimental Psychology: Animal Behavior Processes, 3,* 156–177.

Maki, W. S., Olson, D., & Rego, S. (1981). Directed forgetting in pigeons: Analysis of cue functions. *Animal Learning & Behavior, 9,* 189–195.

Marchant, H. G., III, Mis, F. W., & Moore, J. W. (1972). Conditioned inhibition of the rabbit's nictitating membrane response. *Journal of Experimental Psychology, 95,* 408–411.

Margules, D. L., & Olds, J. (1962). Identical "feeding" and "rewarding" systems in the lateral hypothalamus of rats. *Science, 135,* 374–375.

Maricq, A. V., Roberts, S., & Church, R. M. (1981). Methamphetamine and time estimation. *Journal of Experimental Psychology: Animal Behavior Processes, 7,* 18–30.

Marlin, N. A. (1981). Contextual associations in trace conditioning. *Animal Learning & Behavior, 9,* 519–523.

Marsh, G. (1972). Prediction of the peak shift in pigeons from gradients of excitation and inhibition. *Journal of Comparative and Physiological Psychology, 81,* 262–266.

Martens, B. K., Lochner, D. G., & Kelly, S. Q. (1992). The effects of variable-interval reinforcement on academic

engagement: A demonstration of matching theory. *Journal of Applied Behavior Analysis, 25,* 143–151.

Maser, J. D., & Seligman, M. E. P. (Eds.). (1977). *Psychopathology: Experimental models.* New York: W. H. Freeman.

Masserman, J. H. (1946). *Principles of dynamic psychiatry.* Philadelphia: Saunders.

Mast, M., Blanchard, R. J., & Blanchard, D. C. (1982). The relationship of freezing and response suppression in a CER situation. *Psychological Record, 32,* 151–167.

Matthews, T. J., Bordi, F., & Depollo, D. (1990). Schedule-induced kinesic and taxic behavioral stereotypy in the pigeon. *Journal of Experimental Psychology: Animal Behavior Processes, 16,* 335–344.

Matzel, L. D., Brown, A. M., & Miller, R. R. (1987). Associative effects of US preexposure: Modulation of conditioned responding by an excitatory training context. *Journal of Experimental Psychology: Animal Behavior Processes, 13,* 65–72.

Matzel, L. D., Gladstein, L., & Miller, R. R. (1988). Conditioned excitation and conditioned inhibition are not mutually exclusive. *Learning and Motivation, 19,* 99–121.

Matzel, L. D., Held, F. P., & Miller, R. R. (1988). Information and expression of simultaneous and backward associations: Implications for contiguity theory. *Learning and Motivation, 19,* 317–344.

Matzel, L. D., Schachtman, T. R., & Miller, R. R. (1988). Learned irrelevance exceeds the sum of CS-preexposure and US-preexposure deficits. *Journal of Experimental Psychology: Animal Behavior Processes, 14,* 311–319.

Matzel, L. D., Shuster, K., & Miller, R. R. (1987). Covariation in conditioned response strength between stimuli trained in compound. *Animal Learning & Behavior, 15,* 439–447.

Mayer-Gross, W. (1943). Retrograde amnesia. *Lancet, 2,* 603–605.

Mazmanian, D. S., & Roberts, W. A. (1983). Spatial memory in rats under restricted viewing conditions. *Learning and Motivation, 14,* 123–139.

Mazur, J. E. (1988). Choice between small certain and large uncertain reinforcers. *Animal Learning & Behavior, 16,* 199–205.

Mazur, J. E., & Logue, A. W. (1978). Choice in a "self-control" paradigm: Effects of a fading procedure. *Journal of the Experimental Analysis of Behavior, 30,* 11–17.

Mazur, J. E., & Vaughan, W., Jr. (1987). Molar optimization versus delayed reinforcement as explanations of choice between fixed-ratio and progressive-ratio schedules. *Journal of the Experimental Analysis of Behavior, 48,* 251–261.

McAllister, D. E., & McAllister, W. R. (1991). Fear theory and aversively motivated behavior: Some controversial issues. In M. R. Denny (Ed.), *Fear, avoidance and phobias* (pp. 135–163). Hillsdale, NJ: Erlbaum.

McAllister, W. R., & McAllister, D. E. (1971). Behavioral

measurement of fear. In F. R. Brush (Ed.), *Aversive conditioning and learning.* New York: Academic Press.

McAllister, W. R., McAllister, D. E., & Benton, M. M. (1983). Measurement of fear of the conditioned stimulus and of situational cues at several stages of two-way avoidance learning. *Learning and Motivation, 14,* 92–106.

McCarthy, D., & Davison, M. (1986). On the discriminability of fixed- from variable-stimulus durations. *Journal of Experimental Psychology: Animal Behavior Processes, 12,* 48–58.

McDowell, J. J. (1981). On the validity and utility of Herrnstein's hyperbola in applied behavioral analysis. In C. M. Bradshaw, E. Szabadi, & C. F. Lowe (Eds.), *Quantification of steady-state operant behaviour.* Amsterdam: Elsevier/North-Holland.

McDowell, J. J. (1982). The importance of Herrnstein's mathematical statement of the law of effect for behavior therapy. *American Psychologist, 37,* 771–779.

McDowell, J. J., & Wixted, J. T. (1988). The linear system theory's account of behavior maintained by variable-ratio schedules. *Journal of the Experimental Analysis of Behavior, 49,* 143–169.

McDowell, J. J., & Wood, H. M. (1985). Confirmation of linear system theory prediction: Rate of change of Herrnstein's *k* as a function of response-force requirement. *Journal of the Experimental Analysis of Behavior, 43,* 61–73.

McGaugh, J. L., & Herz, M. J. (1972). *Memory consolidation.* San Francisco: Albion.

McGaugh, J. L., & Petrinovich, L. F. (1965). Effects of drugs on learning and memory. *International Review of Neurobiology, 8,* 139–196.

McGee, G. G., Krantz, P. J., & McClannahan, L. E. (1986). An extension of incidental teaching procedures to reading instruction for autistic children. *Journal of Applied Behavior Analysis, 19,* 147–157.

McSweeney, F. K., Melville, C. L., Buck, M. A., & Whipple, J. E. (1983). Local rates of responding and reinforcement during concurrent schedules. *Journal of the Experimental Analysis of Behavior, 40,* 79–98.

Meachum, C. L., & Bernstein, I. L. (1990). Conditioned responses to a taste conditioned stimulus paired with lithium-chloride administration. *Behavioral Neuroscience, 104,* 711–715.

Meck, W. H. (1983). Selective adjustment of the speed of internal clock and memory processes. *Journal of Experimental Psychology: Animal Behavior Processes, 9,* 171–201.

Meck, W. H. (1988). Hippocampal function is required for feedback control of an internal clock's criterion. *Behavioral Neuroscience, 102,* 54–60.

Meck, W. H., & Church, R. M. (1982). Abstraction of temporal attributes. *Journal of Experimental Psychology: Animal Behavior Processes, 8,* 226–243.

Meck, W. H., & Church, R. M. (1983). A mode control model of counting and timing processes. *Journal of*

Experimental Psychology: Animal Behavior Processes, 9, 320–334.

Meck, W. H., & Church, R. M. (1987a). Cholinergic modulation of the content of temporal memory. *Behavioral Neuroscience, 101,* 457–464.

Meck, W. H., & Church, R. M. (1987b). Nutrients that modify the speed of internal clock and memory storage processes. *Behavioral Neuroscience, 101,* 465–475.

Meck, W. H., Church, R. M., & Gibbon, J. (1985). Temporal integration in duration and number discrimination. *Journal of Experimental Psychology: Animal Behavior Processes, 11,* 591–597.

Meck, W. H., Church, R. M., & Olton, D. S. (1984). Hippocampus, time, and memory. *Behavioral Neuroscience, 98,* 3–22.

Meck, W. H., Church, R. M., Wenk, G. L., & Olton, D. S. (1987). Nucleus basalis magnocellularis and medial septal area lesions differentially impair temporal memory. *Journal of Neuroscience, 7,* 3505–3511.

Medin, D. L. (1980). Proactive interference in monkeys: Delay and intersample interval effects are noncomparable. *Animal Learning & Behavior, 8,* 553–560.

Medin, D. L. (1989). Concepts and conceptual structure. *American Psychologist, 44,* 1469–1481.

Medin, D. L., Roberts, W. A., & Davis, R. T. (1976). *Processes of animal memory.* Hillsdale, NJ: Erlbaum.

Meehl, P. E. (1950). On the circularity of the law of effect. *Psychological Bulletin, 47,* 52–75.

Mehrabian, A. (1970). A semantic space for nonverbal behavior. *Journal of Consulting and Clinical Psychology, 35,* 248–257.

Mehrabian, A., & Weiner, M. (1966). Decoding of inconsistent communications. *Journal of Personality and Social Psychology, 6,* 109–114.

Mellgren, R. L. (1972). Positive and negative contrast effects using delayed reinforcement. *Learning and Motivation, 3,* 185–193.

Mellgren, R. L. (1982). Foraging in simulated natural environments: There's a rat loose in the lab. *Journal of the Experimental Analysis of Behavior, 38,* 93–100.

Mellgren, R. L., Mays, M. Z., & Haddad, N. F. (1983). Discrimination and generalization by rats of temporal stimuli lasting for minutes. *Learning and Motivation, 14,* 75–91.

Meltzer, D., & Brahlek, J. A. (1970). Conditioned suppression and conditioned enhancement with the same positive UCS: An effect of CS duration. *Journal of the Experimental Analysis of Behavior, 13,* 67–73.

Melvin, K. B. (1971). Vicious circle behavior. In H. D. Kimmel (Ed.), *Experimental psychopathology.* New York: Academic Press.

Melvin, K. B., & Ervey, D. H. (1973). Facilitative and suppressive effects of punishment of species-typical aggressive display in *Betta splendens. Journal of Comparative and Physiological Psychology, 83,* 451–457.

Mendelson, J. (1967). Lateral hypothalamic stimulation in

satiated rats: The rewarding effects of self-induced drinking. *Science, 157,* 1077–1079.

Menzel, R. (1983). Neurobiology of learning and memory: The honeybee as a model system. *Naturwissenschaften, 70,* 504–511.

Miczek, K. A., & Grossman, S. (1971). Positive conditioned suppression: Effects of CS duration. *Journal of the Experimental Analysis of Behavior, 15,* 243–247.

Midgley, M., Lea, S. E. G., & Kirby, R. M. (1989). Algorithmic shaping and misbehavior in the acquisition of token deposit by rats. *Journal of the Experimental Analysis of Behavior, 52,* 27–40.

Miller, H. L. (1976). Matching-based hedonic scaling in the pigeon. *Journal of the Experimental Analysis of Behavior, 26,* 335–347.

Miller, J. S., Jagielo, J. A., & Spear, N. E. (1990). Changes in the retrievability of associations to elements of the compound CS determine the expression of overshadowing. *Animal Learning & Behavior, 18,* 157–161.

Miller, J. S., McCoy, D. F., Kelly, K. S., & Bardo, M. T. (1986). A within-event analysis of taste-potentiated odor and contextual aversions. *Animal Learning & Behavior, 14,* 15–21.

Miller, N. E. (1948). Studies of fear as an acquirable drive: I. Fear as motivation and fear-reduction as reinforcement in the learning of new responses. *Journal of Experimental Psychology, 38,* 89–101.

Miller, N. E. (1951). Learnable drives and rewards. In S. S. Stevens (Ed.), *Handbook of experimental psychology.* New York: Wiley.

Miller, N. E. (1960). Learning resistance to pain and fear: Effects of overlearning, exposure, and rewarded exposure in context. *Journal of Experimental Psychology, 60,* 137–145.

Miller, N. E. (1985). The value of behavioral research on animals. *American Psychologist, 40,* 423–440.

Miller, N. E., & Dollard, J. (1941). *Social learning and imitation.* New Haven, CT: Yale University Press.

Miller, N. E., & Kessen, M. L. (1952). Reward effect of food via stomach fistula compared with those of food via mouth. *Journal of Comparative and Physiological Psychology, 45,* 555–564.

Miller, R. R., Kasprow, W. J., & Schachtman, T. R. (1986). Retrieval variability: Sources and consequences. *American Journal of Psychology, 99,* 145–218.

Miller, R. R., & Matzel, L. D. (1988). The comparator hypothesis: A response rule for the expression of associations. In G. H. Bower (Ed.), *The psychology of learning and motivation* (pp. 51–92). Orlando, FL: Academic Press.

Miller, R. R., & Matzel, L. D. (1989). Contingency and relative associative strength. In S. B. Klein and R. R. Mowrer (Eds.), *Contemporary learning theories: Pavlovian conditioning and the status of learning theory* (pp. 61–84). Hillsdale, NJ: Erlbaum.

Miller, R. R., & Spear, N. E. (Eds.). (1985). *Information processing in animals: Conditioned inhibition.* Hillsdale, NJ: Erlbaum.

Miller, R. R., & Springer, A. D. (1973). Amnesia, consolidation, and retrieval. *Psychological Review, 80,* 69–79.

Miller, V., & Domjan, M. (1981). Selective sensitization induced by lithium malaise and footshock in rats. *Behavioral and Neural Biology, 31,* 42–55.

Mineka, S. (1979). The role of fear in theories of avoidance learning, flooding, and extinction. *Psychological Bulletin, 86,* 985–1010.

Mineka, S., & Cook, M. (1988). Social learning and the acquisition of snake fear in monkeys. In T. Zentall and B. G. Galef, Jr. (Eds.), *Social learning* (pp. 51–73). Hillsdale, NJ: Erlbaum.

Mineka, S., & Gino, A. (1979). Dissociative effects of different types and amounts of nonreinforced CS exposure on avoidance extinction and the CER. *Learning and Motivation, 10,* 141–160.

Mineka, S., & Gino, A. (1980). Dissociation between conditioned emotional response and extended avoidance performance. *Learning and Motivation, 11,* 476–502.

Mineka, S., Miller, S., Gino, A., & Giencke, L. (1981). Dissociative effects of flooding on a multivariate assessment of fear reduction and on jump-up avoidance extinction. *Learning and Motivation, 12,* 435–461.

Mineka, S., Suomi, S. J., & DeLizio, R. (1981). Multiple separations in adolescent monkeys: An opponent-process interpretation. *Journal of Experimental Psychology: General, 110,* 56–85.

Minor, T. R., Dess, N. K., & Overmier, J. B. (1991). Inverting the traditional view of "learned helplessness." In M. R. Denny (Ed.), *Fear, avoidance and phobias* (pp. 87–133). Hillsdale, NJ: Erlbaum.

Minor, T. R., Trauner, M. A., Lee, C.-Y., & Dess, N. K. (1990). Modeling signal features of escape response: Effects of cessation conditioning in "learned helplessness" paradigm. *Journal of Experimental Psychology: Animal Behavior Processes, 16,* 123–136.

Misanin, J. R., Miller, R. R., & Lewis, D. J. (1968). Retrograde amnesia produced by electroconvulsive shock after reactivation of a consolidated memory trace. *Science, 160,* 554–555.

Mitchell, S. H., & Brener, J. (1991). Energetic and motor responses to increasing food requirements. *Journal of Experimental Psychology: Animal Behavior Processes, 17,* 174–185.

Mogenson, G. J., & Cioe, J. (1977). Central reinforcement: A bridge between brain function and behavior. In W. K. Honig & J. E. R. Staddon (Eds.), *Handbook of operant behavior.* Englewood Cliffs, NJ: Prentice-Hall.

Mogenson, G. J., & Huang, Y. H. (1973). The neurobiology of motivated behavior. In G. A. Kerkut & J. W. Phillis (Eds.), *Progress in neurobiology* (Vol. 1). Oxford: Pergamon.

Mogenson, G. J., & Kaplinsky, M. (1970). Brain self-stimulation and mechanisms of reinforcement. *Learning and Motivation, 1,* 186–198.

Mogenson, G. J., & Morgan, C. W. (1967). Effects of induced drinking on self-stimulation of the lateral hypothalamus. *Experimental Brain Research, 3,* 111–116.

Mogenson, G. J., & Stevenson, J. A. F. (1966). Drinking and self-stimulation with electrical stimulation of the lateral hypothalamus. *Physiology and Behavior, 1,* 251–254.

Morgan, C. L. (1903). *Introduction to comparative psychology* (rev ed.). New York: Scribner.

Morgan, L., & Neuringer, A. (1990). Behavioral variability as a function of response topography and reinforcement contingency. *Animal Learning & Behavior, 18,* 257–263.

Morgan, M. J., Fitch, M. D., Holman, J. G., & Lea, S. E. G. (1976). Pigeons learn the concept of an "A." *Perception, 5,* 57–66.

Morris, C. J. (1987). The operant conditioning of response variability: Free-operant versus discrete-response procedures. *Journal of the Experimental Analysis of Behavior, 47,* 273–277.

Morris, R. G. (1987). Identity matching and oddity learning in patients with moderate to severe Alzheimer-type dementia. *Quarterly Journal of Experimental Psychology, 39B,* 215–227.

Morris, R. G. M. (1974). Pavlovian conditioned inhibition of fear during shuttlebox avoidance behavior. *Learning and Motivation, 5,* 424–447.

Morris, R. G. M. (1975). Preconditioning of reinforcing properties to an exteroceptive feedback stimulus. *Learning and Motivation, 6,* 289–298.

Morris, R. G. M. (1981). Spatial localization does not require the presence of local cues. *Learning and Motivation, 12,* 239–260.

Mowrer, O. H. (1947). On the dual nature of learning: A reinterpretation of "conditioning" and "problem-solving." *Harvard Educational Review, 17,* 102–150.

Mowrer, O. H. (1960). *Learning theory and behavior.* New York: Wiley.

Mowrer, O. H., & Lamoreaux, R. R. (1942). Avoidance conditioning and signal duration: A study of secondary motivation and reward. *Psychological Monographs, 54* (Whole No. 247).

Mowrer, R. R., & Gordon, W. C. (1983). Effects of cuing in an "irrelevant" context. *Animal Learning & Behavior, 11,* 401–406.

Moye, T. B., & Thomas, D. R. (1982). Effects of memory reactivation treatments on postdiscrimination generalization performance in pigeons. *Animal Learning & Behavior, 10,* 159–166.

Murphy, B. T., & Levine, F. M. (1982). *Nonverbal behavior in peer-victimized children.* Paper presented at meeting of the Association for the Advancement of Behavior Therapy.

Myerson, J., & Hale, S. (1988). Choice in transition: A comparison of melioration and the kinetic model.

Journal of the Experimental Analysis of Behavior, 49, 291–302.

Nairne, J. S., & Rescorla, R. A. (1981). Second-order conditioning with diffuse auditory reinforcers in the pigeon. *Learning and Motivation, 12,* 65–91.

Nash, S., & Domjan, M. (1991). Learning to discriminate the sex of conspecifics in male Japanese quail *(Coturnix coturnix japonica):* Tests of "biological constraints." *Journal of Experimental Psychology: Animal Behavior Processes, 17,* 342–353.

Nash, S., Domjan, M., & Askins, M. (1989). Sexual-discrimination learning in male Japanese quail *(Coturnix coturnix japonica). Journal of Comparative Psychology, 103,* 347–358.

Nation, J. R., & Cooney, J. B. (1982). The time course of extinction-induced aggressive behavior in humans: Evidence for a stage model of extinction. *Learning and Motivation, 13,* 95–112.

Neill, J. C., & Harrison, J. M. (1987). Auditory discrimination: The Konorski quality-location effect. *Journal of the Experimental Analysis of Behavior, 48,* 81–95.

Neuenschwander, N., Fabrigoule, C., & Mackintosh, N. J. (1987). Fear of the warning signal during overtraining of avoidance. *Quarterly Journal of Experimental Psychology, 39B,* 23–33.

Neuringer, A. (1991). Operant variability and repetition as functions of interresponse time. *Journal of Experimental Psychology: Animal Behavior Processes, 17,* 3–12.

Nevin, J. A. (1969). Interval reinforcement of choice behavior in discrete trials. *Journal of the Experimental Analysis of Behavior, 12,* 875–885.

Nevin, J. A. (1979). Overall matching versus momentary maximizing: Nevin (1969) revisited. *Journal of Experimental Psychology: Animal Behavior Processes, 5,* 300–306.

Nicoll, C. S., & Russell, S. M. (1990). Analysis of animal rights literature reveals the underlying motives of the movement: Ammunition for counter offensive by scientists. *Endocrinology, 127,* 985–989.

Noble, G. K., & Vogt, W. (1935). An experimental study of sex recognition in birds. *Auk, 52,* 278–286.

Obál, F. (1966). The fundamentals of the central nervous system of vegetative homeostasis. *Acta Physiologica Academiae Scientiarum Hungaricae, 30,* 15–29.

Oden, D. L., Thompson, R. K. R., & Premack, D. (1988). Spontaneous transfer of matching by infant chimpanzees *(Pan troglodytes). Journal of Experimental Psychology: Animal Behavior Processes, 14,* 140–145.

Olds, J. (1958). Effects of hunger and male sex hormone on self-stimulation of the brain. *Journal of Comparative and Physiological Psychology, 51,* 320–324.

Olds, J., & Milner, P. (1954). Positive reinforcement produced by electrical stimulation of septal area and other regions of the rat brain. *Journal of Comparative and Physiological Psychology, 47,* 419–427.

Oliverio, A., & Castellano, C. (1982). Classical conditioning of stress-induced analgesia. *Physiology and Behavior, 25,* 171–172.

Olson, D. J. (1991). Species differences in spatial memory among Clark's nutcrackers, scrub jays, and pigeons. *Journal of Experimental Psychology: Animal Behavior Processes, 17,* 363–376.

Olson, D. J., & Maki, W. S. (1983). Characteristics of spatial memory in pigeons. *Journal of Experimental Psychology: Animal Behavior Processes, 9,* 266–280.

Olton, D. S. (1978). Characteristics of spatial memory. In S. H. Hulse, H. Fowler, & W. K. Honig (Eds.), *Cognitive processes in animal behavior* (pp. 341–374). Hillsdale, NJ: Erlbaum.

Olton, D. S. (1979). Mazes, maps, and memory. *American Psychologist, 34,* 583–596.

Olton, D. S., Collison, C., & Werz, M. A. (1977). Spatial memory and radial arm maze performance of rats. *Learning and Motivation, 8,* 289–314.

Olton, D. S., & Samuelson, R. J. (1976). Remembrance of places passed: Spatial memory in rats. *Journal of Experimental Psychology: Animal Behavior Processes, 2,* 97–116.

Ost, J. W. P., & Lauer, D. W. (1965). Some investigations of salivary conditioning in the dog. In W. F. Prokasy (Ed.), *Classical conditioning.* New York: Appleton-Century-Crofts.

Overmier, J. B., Bull, J. A., & Pack, K. (1971). On instrumental response interaction as explaining the influences of Pavlovian CSs upon avoidance behavior. *Learning and Motivation, 2,* 103–112.

Overmier, J. B., & Lawry, J. A. (1979). Pavlovian conditioning and the mediation of behavior. In G. H. Bower (Ed.), *The psychology of learning and motivation* (Vol. 13). New York: Academic Press.

Overmier, J. B., & Seligman, M. E. P. (1967). Effects of inescapable shock upon subsequent escape and avoidance learning. *Journal of Comparative and Physiological Psychology, 63,* 23–33.

Owen, J. W., Cicala, G. A., & Herdegen, R. T. (1978). Fear inhibition and species specific defense reaction termination may contribute independently to avoidance learning. *Learning and Motivation, 9,* 297–313.

Page, S., & Neuringer, A. (1985). Variability as an operant. *Journal of Experimental Psychology: Animal Behavior Processes, 11,* 429–452.

Paletta, M. S., & Wagner, A. R. (1986). Development of context-specific tolerance to morphine: Support for a dual-process interpretation. *Behavioral Neuroscience, 100,* 611–623.

Papini, M. R., & Bitterman, M. E. (1990). The role of contingency in classical conditioning. *Psychological Review, 97,* 396–403.

Parker, L. A. (1988). Positively reinforcing drugs may produce a different kind of CTA than drugs which are not positively reinforcing. *Learning and Motivation, 19,* 207–220.

Pate, J. L., & Rumbaugh, D. M. (1983). The language-like behavior of Lana chimpanzee: Is it merely discrimination and paired-associate learning? *Animal Learning & Behavior, 11,* 134–138.

Patten, R. L., & Rudy, J. W. (1967). The Sheffield omission of training procedure applied to the conditioning of the licking response in rats. *Psychonomic Science, 8,* 463–464.

Patterson, F. G. (1978). The gestures of a gorilla: Language acquisition in another pongid. *Brain and Language, 5,* 56–71.

Pavlov, I. P. (1927). *Conditioned reflexes* (G. V. Anrep, trans.). London: Oxford University Press.

Pear, J. J., & Legris, J. A. (1987). Shaping by automated tracking of an arbitrary operant response. *Journal of the Experimental Analysis of Behavior, 47,* 241–247.

Pearce, J. M. (1987). A model for stimulus generalization in Pavlovian conditioning. *Psychological Review, 94,* 61–73.

Pearce, J. M., & Dickinson, A. (1975). Pavlovian counterconditioning: Changing the suppressive properties of shock by association with food. *Journal of Experimental Psychology: Animal Behavior Processes, 1,* 170–177.

Pearce, J. M., & Hall, G. (1980). A model for Pavlovian learning: Variations in the effectiveness of conditioned but not of unconditioned stimuli. *Psychological Review, 87,* 532–552.

Pearce, J. M., & Wilson, P. N. (1990a). Configural associations in discrimination learning. *Journal of Experimental Psychology: Animal Behavior Processes, 16,* 250–261.

Pearce, J. M., & Wilson, P. N. (1990b). Feature-positive discrimination learning. *Journal of Experimental Psychology: Animal Behavior Processes, 16,* 315–325.

Peck, C. A., & Bouton, M. E. (1990). Context and performance in aversive-to-appetitive and appetitive-to-aversive transfer. *Learning and Motivation, 21,* 1–31.

Peden, B. F., Browne, M. P., & Hearst, E. (1977). Persistent approaches to a signal for food despite food omission for approaching. *Journal of Experimental Psychology: Animal Behavior Processes, 3,* 377–399.

Peeke, H. V. S., & Petrinovich, L. (Eds.). (1984). *Habituation, sensitization, and behavior.* New York: Academic Press.

Peele, D. B., Casey, J., & Silberberg, A. (1984). Primacy of interresponse-time reinforcement in accounting for rate differences under variable-ratio and variable-interval schedules. *Journal of Experimental Psychology: Animal Behavior Processes, 10,* 149–167.

Pelchat, M. L., Grill, H. J., Rozin, P., & Jacobs, J. (1983). Quality of acquired responses to tastes by *Rattus norvegicus* depends on type of associated discomfort. *Journal of Comparative Psychology, 97,* 140–153.

Pelchat, M. L., & Rozin, P. (1982). The special role of nausea in the acquisition of food dislikes by humans. *Appetite, 3,* 341–351.

Pepperberg, I. M. (1990). Some cognitive capacities of an African grey parrot *(Psittacus erithacus).* In P. J. B. Slater,

J. S. Rosenblatt, & C. Beer (Eds.), *Advances in the study of behavior* (Vol. 19, pp. 357–409). San Diego: Academic Press.

Perkins, C. C., Jr. (1955). The stimulus conditions which follow learned responses. *Psychological Review, 62,* 341–348.

Perkins, C. C., Jr. (1968). An analysis of the concept of reinforcement. *Psychological Review, 75,* 155–172.

Perry, D. G., & Parke, R. D. (1975). Punishment and alternative response training as determinants of response inhibition in children. *Genetic Psychology Monographs, 91,* 257–279.

Peterson, C., & Seligman, M. E. P. (1984). Causal explanations as a risk factor for depression: Theory and evidence. *Psychological Review, 91,* 347–374.

Peterson, G. B., Ackil, J. E., Frommer, G. P., & Hearst, E. S. (1972). Conditioned approach and contact behavior toward signals for food and brain-stimulation reinforcement. *Science, 177,* 1009–1011.

Peterson, G. B., & Trapold, M. A. (1980). Effects of altering outcome expectancies on pigeons' delayed conditional discrimination performance. *Learning and Motivation, 11,* 267–288.

Phillips, A. G., & Mogenson, G. J. (1968). Effects of taste on self-stimulation and induced drinking. *Journal of Comparative and Physiological Psychology, 66,* 654–660.

Pickens, R., & Dougherty, J. (1971). Conditioning the activity effects of drugs. In T. Thompson & C. Schuster (Eds.), *Stimulus properties of drugs.* New York: Appleton-Century-Crofts.

Pisacreta, R. (1982). Some factors that influence the acquisition of complex, stereotyped, response sequences in pigeons. *Journal of the Experimental Analysis of Behavior, 37,* 359–369.

Pisacreta, R., Gough, D., Redwood, E., & Goodfellow, L. (1986). Auditory word discrimination in the pigeon. *Journal of the Experimental Analysis of Behavior, 45,* 269–282.

Platt, J. R. (1973). Percentile reinforcement: Paradigms for experimental analysis of response shaping. In G. H. Bower (Ed.), *The psychology of learning and motivation* (Vol. 7, pp. 271–296). Orlando, FL: Academic Press.

Platt, S. A., Holliday, M., & Drudge, O. W. (1980). Discrimination learning of an instrumental response in individual *Drosophila melanogaster. Journal of Experimental Psychology: Animal Behavior Processes, 6,* 301–311.

Plotkin, H. C., & Odling-Smee, F. J. (1979). Learning, change, and evolution: An enquiry into the teleonomy of learning. In J. S. Rosenblatt, R. A. Hinde, C. Beer, & M.-C. Busnel (Eds.), *Advances in the study of behavior* (Vol. 10). New York: Academic Press.

Plous, S. (1991). An attitude survey of animal rights activists. *Psychological Science, 2,* 194–196.

Poling, A., Nickel, M., & Alling, K. (1990). Free birds aren't fat: Weight gain in captured wild pigeons maintained under laboratory conditions. *Journal of the Experimental Analysis of Behavior, 53,* 423–424.

Porter, D., & Neuringer, A. (1984). Music discrimination by pigeons. *Journal of Experimental Psychology: Animal Behavior Processes, 10,* 138–148.

Postman, L. (1971). Transfer, interference, and forgetting. In J. W. Kling & L. A. Riggs (Eds.), *Woodworth and Schlosberg's experimental psychology* (3rd ed.). New York: Holt, Rinehart and Winston.

Poulos, C. X., Hinson, R. E., & Siegel, S. (1981). The role of Pavlovian processes in drug tolerance and dependence: Implications for treatment. *Addictive Behaviors, 6,* 205–211.

Premack, A. J. (1976). *Why chimps can read.* New York: Harper & Row.

Premack, D. (1962). Reversibility of the reinforcement relation. *Science, 136,* 255–257.

Premack, D. (1965). Reinforcement theory. In D. Levine (Ed.), *Nebraska Symposium on Motivation* (Vol. 13, pp. 123–180). Lincoln: University of Nebraska Press.

Premack, D. (1971a). Catching up with common sense, or two sides of a generalization: Reinforcement and punishment. In R. Glaser (Ed.), *The nature of reinforcement.* New York: Academic Press.

Premack, D. (1971b). Language in chimpanzee? *Science, 172,* 808–822.

Premack, D. (1976). *Intelligence in ape and man.* Hillsdale, NJ: Erlbaum.

Preston, R. A., & Fantino, E. (1991). Conditioned reinforcement value and choice. *Journal of the Experimental Analysis of Behavior, 55,* 155–175.

Puente, G. P., Cannon, D. S., Bet, M. R., & Carrell, L. E. (1988). Occasion setting of fluid ingestion by contextual cues. *Learning and Motivation, 19,* 239–253.

Quartermain, D., McEwen, B. S., & Azmitia, E. C., Jr. (1970). Amnesia produced by electroconvulsive shock or cycloheximide: Conditions for recovery. *Science, 169,* 683–686.

Rachlin, H. C. (1978). A molar theory of reinforcement schedules. *Journal of the Experimental Analysis of Behavior, 30,* 345–360.

Rachlin, H. C., Battalio, R., Kagel, J., & Green, L. (1981). Maximization theory in behavioral psychology. *Behavioral and Brain Sciences, 4,* 371–417.

Rachlin, H. C., & Burkhard, B. (1978). The temporal triangle: Response substitution in instrumental conditioning. *Psychological Review, 85,* 22–47.

Rachlin, H. C., & Green, L. (1972). Commitment, choice, and self-control. *Journal of the Experimental Analysis of Behavior, 17,* 15–22.

Rachlin, H. C., Green, L., Kagel, J. H., & Battalio, R. C. (1976). Economic demand theory and studies of choice. In G. H. Bower (Ed.), *The psychology of learning and motivation* (Vol. 10). New York: Academic Press.

Rachlin, H., Green, L., & Tormey, B. (1988). Is there a

decisive test between matching and maximizing? *Journal of the Experimental Analysis of Behavior, 50,* 113–123.

Rachlin, H. C., & Herrnstein, R. L. (1969). Hedonism revisited: On the negative law of effect. In B. A. Campbell & R. M. Church (Eds.), *Punishment and aversive behavior.* New York: Appleton-Century-Crofts.

Randich, A. (1981). The US preexposure phenomenon in the conditioned suppression paradigm: A role for conditioned situational stimuli. *Learning and Motivation, 12,* 321–341.

Randich, A., & LoLordo, V. M. (1979). Associative and non-associative theories of the UCS preexposure phenomenon: Implications for Pavlovian conditioning. *Psychological Bulletin, 86,* 523–548.

Randich, A., & Ross, R. T. (1984). Mechanisms of blocking by contextual stimuli. *Learning and Motivation, 15,* 106–117.

Randich, A., & Ross, R. T. (1985). The role of contextual stimuli in mediating the effects of pre- and postexposure to the unconditioned stimulus alone on acquisition and retention of conditioned suppression. In P. Balsam & A. Tomie (Eds.), *Context and learning.* Hillsdale, NJ: Erlbaum.

Rashotte, M. E., Griffin, R. W., & Sisk, C. L. (1977). Second-order conditioning of the pigeon's keypeck. *Animal Learning & Behavior, 5,* 25–38.

Rashotte, M. E., & Henderson, D. (1988). Coping with rising food costs in a closed economy: Feeding behavior and nocturnal hypothermia in pigeons. *Journal of the Experimental Analysis of Behavior, 50,* 441–456.

Reberg, D. (1972). Compound tests for excitation in early acquisition and after prolonged extinction of conditioned suppression. *Learning and Motivation, 3,* 246–258.

Reberg, D., & Black, A. H. (1969). Compound testing of individually conditioned stimuli as an index of excitatory and inhibitory properties. *Psychonomic Science, 17,* 30–31.

Reberg, D., Innis, N. K., Mann, B., & Eizenga, C. (1978). "Superstitious" behavior resulting from periodic response-independent presentations of food or water. *Animal Behaviour, 26,* 506–519.

Redhead, E., & Tyler, P. A. (1988). An experimental analysis of optimal foraging behaviour in patchy environments. *Quarterly Journal of Experimental Psychology, 40B,* 83–102.

Reed, P. (1991). Multiple determinants of the effects of reinforcement magnitude on free-operant response rates. *Journal of the Experimental Analysis of Behavior, 55,* 109–123.

Reed, P., & Wright, J. E. (1989). Effects of magnitude of food reinforcement on free-operant response rates. *Journal of the Experimental Analysis of Behavior, 49,* 75–85.

Repp, A. C., & Singh, N. N. (Eds.). (1990). *Perspectives on the use of nonaversive and aversive interventions for persons with developmental disabilities.* Sycamore, IL: Sycamore.

Rescorla, R. A. (1967a). Inhibition of delay in Pavlovian fear conditioning. *Journal of Comparative and Physiological Psychology, 64,* 114–120.

Rescorla, R. A. (1967b). Pavlovian conditioning and its proper control procedures. *Psychological Review, 74,* 71–80.

Rescorla, R. A. (1968a). Pavlovian conditioned fear in Sidman avoidance learning. *Journal of Comparative and Physiological Psychology, 65,* 55–60.

Rescorla, R. A. (1968b). Probability of shock in the presence and absence of CS in fear conditioning. *Journal of Comparative and Physiological Psychology, 66,* 1–5.

Rescorla, R. A. (1969a). Conditioned inhibition of fear resulting from negative CS-US contingencies. *Journal of Comparative and Physiological Psychology, 67,* 504–509.

Rescorla, R. A. (1969b). Pavlovian conditioned inhibition. *Psychological Bulletin, 72,* 77–94.

Rescorla, R. A. (1973). Effect of US habituation following conditioning. *Journal of Comparative and Physiological Psychology, 82,* 137–143.

Rescorla, R. A. (1974). Effect of inflation on the unconditioned stimulus value following conditioning. *Journal of Comparative and Physiological Psychology, 86,* 101–106.

Rescorla, R. A. (1979). Aspects of the reinforcer learned in second-order Pavlovian conditioning. *Journal of Experimental Psychology: Animal Behavior Processes, 5,* 79–95.

Rescorla, R. A. (1980a). *Pavlovian second-order conditioning.* Hillsdale, NJ: Erlbaum.

Rescorla, R. A. (1980b). Simultaneous and successive associations in sensory preconditioning. *Journal of Experimental Psychology: Animal Behavior Processes, 6,* 207–216.

Rescorla, R. A. (1981). Within-signal learning in autoshaping. *Animal Learning & Behavior, 9,* 245–252.

Rescorla, R. A. (1982a). Effect of a stimulus intervening between CS and US in autoshaping. *Journal of Experimental Psychology: Animal Behavior Processes, 8,* 131–141.

Rescorla, R. A. (1982b). Simultaneous second-order conditioning produces S-S learning in conditioned suppression. *Journal of Experimental Psychology: Animal Behavior Processes, 8,* 23–32.

Rescorla, R. A. (1982c). Some consequences of associations between the excitor and the inhibitor in a conditioned inhibition paradigm. *Journal of Experimental Psychology: Animal Behavior Processes, 8,* 288–298.

Rescorla, R. A. (1983). Effect of separate presentation of the elements on within-compound learning in autoshaping. *Animal Learning & Behavior, 11,* 439–446.

Rescorla, R. A. (1985). Conditioned inhibition and facilitation. In R. R. Miller & N. E. Spear (Eds.), *Information processing in animals: Conditioned inhibition.* Hillsdale, NJ: Erlbaum.

Rescorla, R. A. (1986). Extinction of facilitation. *Journal of Experimental Psychology: Animal Behavior Processes, 12,* 16–24.

Rescorla, R. A. (1987). Facilitation and inhibition. *Journal of Experimental Psychology: Animal Behavior Processes, 13,* 250–259.

Rescorla, R. A. (1988a). Facilitation based on inhibition. *Animal Learning & Behavior, 16,* 169–176.

Rescorla, R. A. (1988b). Pavlovian conditioning: It's not what you think it is. *American Psychologist, 43,* 151–160.

Rescorla, R. A. (1990a). Evidence for an association between the discriminative stimulus and the response-outcome association in instrumental learning. *Journal of Experimental Psychology: Animal Behavior Processes, 16,* 326–334.

Rescorla, R. A. (1990b). The role of information about the response-outcome relation in instrumental discrimination learning. *Journal of Experimental Psychology: Animal Behavior Processes, 16,* 262–270.

Rescorla, R. A., & Cunningham, C. L. (1977). The erasure of reinstatement. *Animal Learning & Behavior, 5,* 386–394.

Rescorla, R. A., & Cunningham, C. L. (1979). Spatial contiguity facilitates Pavlovian second-order conditioning. *Journal of Experimental Psychology: Animal Behavior Processes, 5,* 152–161.

Rescorla, R. A., & Durlach, P. J. (1981). Within-event learning in Pavlovian conditioning. In N. E. Spear & R. R. Miller (Eds.), *Information processing in animals: Memory mechanisms* (pp. 81–112). Hillsdale, NJ: Erlbaum.

Rescorla, R. A., Durlach, P. J., & Grau, J. W. (1985). Contextual learning in Pavlovian conditioning. In P. Balsam & A. Tomie (Eds.), *Context and learning* (pp. 23–56). Hillsdale, NJ: Erlbaum.

Rescorla, R. A., & Furrow, D. R. (1977). Stimulus similarity as a determinant of Pavlovian conditioning. *Journal of Experimental Psychology: Animal Behavior Processes, 3,* 203–215.

Rescorla, R. A., & Gillan, D. J. (1980). An analysis of the facilitative effect of similarity on second-order conditioning. *Journal of Experimental Psychology: Animal Behavior Processes, 6,* 339–351.

Rescorla, R. A., Grau, J. W., & Durlach, P. J. (1985). Analysis of the unique cue in configural discriminations. *Journal of Experimental Psychology: Animal Behavior Processes, 11,* 356–366.

Rescorla, R. A., & Heth, D. C. (1975). Reinstatement of fear to an extinguished conditioned stimulus. *Journal of Experimental Psychology: Animal Behavior Processes, 1,* 88–96.

Rescorla, R. A., & LoLordo, V. M. (1965). Inhibition of avoidance behavior. *Journal of Comparative and Physiological Psychology, 59,* 406–412.

Rescorla, R. A., & Solomon, R. L. (1967). Two-process learning theory: Relationships between Pavlovian conditioning and instrumental learning. *Psychological Review, 74,* 151–182.

Rescorla, R. A., & Wagner, A. R. (1972). A theory of Pavlovian conditioning: Variations in the effectiveness of reinforcement and nonreinforcement. In A. H. Black & W. F. Prokasy (Eds.), *Classical conditioning II: Current research and theory* (pp. 64–99). New York: Appleton-Century-Crofts.

Restle, F., & Brown, E. (1970). Organization of serial pattern learning. In G. H. Bower & J. T. Spence (Eds.), *The psychology of learning and motivation* (Vol. 4). New York: Academic Press.

Revusky, S. H., & Garcia, J. (1970). Learned associations over long delays. In G. H. Bower & J. T. Spence (Eds.), *The psychology of learning and motivation* (Vol. 4). New York: Academic Press.

Reynolds, G. S. (1961). Attention in the pigeon. *Journal of the Experimental Analysis of Behavior, 4,* 203–208.

Reynolds, G. S. (1975). *A primer of operant conditioning.* Glenview, IL: Scott, Foresman.

Reynolds, T. J., & Medin, D. L. (1981). Stimulus interaction and between-trials proactive interference in monkeys. *Journal of Experimental Psychology: Animal Behavior Processes, 7,* 334–347.

Riccio, D. C., Hodges, L. A., & Randall, P. R. (1968). Retrograde amnesia produced by hypothermia in rats. *Journal of Comparative and Physiological Psychology, 3,* 618–622.

Riccio, D. C., & Richardson, R. (1984). The status of memory following experimentally induced amnesias: Gone, but not forgotten. *Physiological Psychology, 12,* 59–72.

Richards, D. G., Wolz, J. P., & Herman, L. M. (1984). Mimicry of computer-generated sounds and vocal labeling of objects by a bottlenosed dolphin. *Journal of Comparative Psychology, 98,* 10–28.

Richardson, R., Riccio, D. C., & Jonke, T. (1983). Alleviation of infantile amnesia in rats by means of a pharmacological contextual state. *Developmental Psychobiology, 16,* 511–518.

Richardson, R., Riccio, D. C., & Smoller, D. (1987). Counterconditioning of memory in rats. *Animal Learning & Behavior, 15,* 321–326.

Richelle, M., & Lejeune, H. (1980). *Time in animal behavior.* New York: Pergamon.

Richter, C. P. (1953). Experimentally produced behavior reactions to food poisoning in wild and domesticated rats. *Annals of the New York Academy of Sciences, 56,* 225–239.

Riegert, P. W. (1959). Humidity reactions of *Melanoplus birittatus* (Say) and *Camnula pellucida* (Scudd.) (Orthoptera, Acrididae): Reactions of normal grasshoppers. *Canadian Entomologist, 91,* 35–40.

Riley, A. L., & Tuck, D. L. (1985). Conditioned food aversions: A bibliography. *Annals of the New York Academy of Sciences.*

Rilling, M. (1977). Stimulus control and inhibitory processes. In W. K. Honig & J. E. R. Staddon (Eds.), *Handbook of operant behavior*. Englewood Cliffs, NJ: Prentice-Hall.

Rilling, M., Kendrick, D. F., & Stonebraker, T. B. (1984). Directed forgetting in context. In G. H. Bower (Ed.), *The psychology of learning and motivation* (Vol. 18). New York: Academic Press.

Rizley, R. C., & Rescorla, R. A. (1972). Associations in second-order conditioning and sensory preconditioning. *Journal of Comparative and Physiological Psychology, 81*, 1–11.

Robbins, S. J. (1990). Mechanisms underlying spontaneous recovery in autoshaping. *Journal of Experimental Psychology: Animal Behavior Processes, 16*, 235–249.

Roberts, S. (1981). Isolation of an internal clock. *Journal of Experimental Psychology: Animal Behavior Processes, 7*, 242–268.

Roberts, S. (1982). Cross-modal use of an internal clock. *Journal of Experimental Psychology: Animal Behavior Processes, 8*, 2–22.

Roberts, S., & Church, R. M. (1978). Control of an internal clock. *Journal of Experimental Psychology: Animal Behavior Processes, 4*, 318–337.

Roberts, W. A. (1979). Spatial memory in the rat on a hierarchical maze: *Learning and Motivation, 10*, 117–140.

Roberts, W. A. (1984). Some issues in animal spatial memory. In H. L. Roitblat, T. G. Bever, & H. S. Terrace (Eds.), *Animal cognition*. Hillsdale, NJ: Erlbaum.

Roberts, W. A., Cheng, K., & Cohen, J. S. (1989). Timing light and tone signals in pigeons. *Journal of Experimental Psychology: Animal Behavior Processes, 15*, 23–35.

Roberts, W. A., & Grant, D. S. (1976). Studies of short-term memory in the pigeon using the delayed matching to sample procedure. In D. L. Medin, W. A. Roberts, & R. T. Davis (Eds.), *Processes of animal memory*. Hillsdale, NJ: Erlbaum.

Roberts, W. A., & Grant, D. S. (1978). An analysis of light-induced retroactive inhibition in pigeon short-term memory. *Journal of Experimental Psychology: Animal Behavior Processes, 4*, 219–236.

Roberts, W. A., & Mazmanian, D. S. (1988). Concept learning at different levels of abstraction by pigeons, monkeys, and people. *Journal of Experimental Psychology: Animal Behavior Processes, 14*, 247–260.

Roberts, W. A., Mazmanian, D. S., & Kraemer, P. J. (1984). Directed forgetting in monkeys. *Animal Learning & Behavior, 12*, 29–40.

Roberts, W. A., & Veldhuizen, N. V. (1985). Spatial memory in pigeons on the radial maze. *Journal of Experimental Psychology: Animal Behavior Processes, 11*, 241–260.

Rochford, J., & Stewart, J. (1987). Morphine attenuation of conditioned autoanalgesia: Implications for theories of situation-specific tolerance to morphine analgesia. *Behavioral Neuroscience, 101*, 690–700.

Roitblat, H. L. (1980). Codes and coding processes in pigeon short-term memory. *Animal Learning & Behavior, 8*, 341–351.

Roitblat, H. L. (1982). The meaning of representation in animal memory. *Behavioral and Brain Sciences, 5*, 353–406.

Roitblat, H. L. (1984). Representations in pigeon working memory. In H. L. Roitblat, T. G. Bever, & H. S. Terrace (Eds.), *Animal cognition*. Hillsdale, NJ: Erlbaum.

Roitblat, H. L., Bever, T. G., Helweg, D. A., & Harley, H. E. (1991). On-line choice and the representation of serially structured stimuli. *Journal of Experimental Psychology: Animal Behavior Processes, 17*, 55–67.

Roitblat, H. L., Bever, T. G., & Terrace, H. S. (Eds.). (1984). *Animal cognition*. Hillsdale, NJ: Erlbaum.

Roitblat, H. L., & Harley, H. E. (1988). Spatial delayed matching-to-sample performance by rats: Learning, memory, and proactive interference. *Journal of Experimental Psychology: Animal Behavior Processes, 14*, 71–82.

Roitblat, H. L., Penner, R. H., & Nachtigall, P. E. (1990). Matching-to-sample by an echolocating dolphin *(Tursiops truncatus)*. *Journal of Experimental Psychology: Animal Behavior Processes, 16*, 85–95.

Roitblat, H. L., & Scopatz, R. A. (1983). Sequential effects in pigeon delayed matching-to-sample performance. *Journal of Experimental Psychology: Animal Behavior Processes, 9*, 202–221.

Roitblat, H. L., Scopatz, R. A., & Bever, T. G. (1987). The hierarchical representation of three-item sequences. *Animal Learning & Behavior, 15*, 179–192.

Roitblat, H. L., Tham, W., & Golub, L. (1982). Performance of *Betta splendens* in a radial arm maze. *Animal Learning & Behavior, 10*, 108–114.

Romanes, G. J. (1884). *Animal intelligence*. New York: Appleton.

Rosellini, R. A., & DeCola, J. P. (1981). Inescapable shock interferes with the acquisition of a low-activity response in an appetitive context. *Animal Learning & Behavior, 9*, 487–490.

Rosellini, R. A., DeCola, J. P., Plonsky, M., Warren, D. A., & Stilman, A. J. (1984). Uncontrollable shock proactively increases sensitivity to response-reinforcer independence in rats. *Journal of Experimental Psychology: Animal Behavior Processes, 10*, 346–359.

Rosellini, R. A., DeCola, J. P., & Shapiro, N. R. (1982). Cross-motivational effects of inescapable shock are associative in nature. *Journal of Experimental Psychology: Animal Behavior Processes, 8*, 376–388.

Rosellini, R. A., Warren, D. A., & DeCola, J. P. (1987). Predictability and controllability: Differential effects upon contextual fear. *Learning and Motivation, 18*, 392–420.

Ross, R. T. (1983). Relationships between the determinants of performance in serial feature-positive discriminations. *Journal of Experimental Psychology: Animal Behavior Processes, 9*, 349–373.

Ross, R. T., & Holland, P. C. (1981). Conditioning of simultaneous and serial feature-positive discriminations. *Animal Learning & Behavior, 9,* 293–303.

Rovee, C. K., & Rovee, D. T. (1969). Conjugate reinforcement of infant exploratory behavior. *Journal of Experimental Child Psychology, 8,* 33–39.

Rovee-Collier, C. K., Griesler, P. C., & Earley, L. A. (1985). Contextual determinants of retrieval in three-month-old infants. *Learning and Memory, 16,* 139–157.

Rovee-Collier, C. K., Sullivan, M. W., Enright, M., Lucas, D., & Fagen, J. W. (1980). Reactivation of infant memory. *Science, 208,* 1159–1161.

Rowland, W. J. (1982). The effects of male nuptial coloration on stickleback aggression: A reexamination. *Behaviour, 80,* 118–126.

Rowland, W. J., & Sevenster, P. (1985). Sign stimuli in the threespine stickleback *(Gasterosteus aculeatus)*: A reexamination and extension of some classic experiments. *Behaviour, 93,* 241–257.

Rozin, P., & Kalat, J. W. (1971). Specific hungers and poison avoidance as adaptive specializations of learning. *Psychological Review, 78,* 459–486.

Rozin, P., & Zellner, D. (1985). The role of Pavlovian conditioning in the acquisition of food likes and dislikes. *Annals of the New York Academy of Sciences, 443,* 189–202.

Rudolph, R. L., Honig, W. K., & Gerry, J. E. (1969). Effects of monochromatic rearing on the acquisition of stimulus control. *Journal of Comparative and Physiological Psychology, 67,* 50–58.

Rudolph, R. L., & Van Houten, R. (1977). Auditory stimulus control in pigeons: Jenkins and Harrison (1960) revisited. *Journal of the Experimental Analysis of Behavior, 27,* 327–330.

Rumbaugh, D. M. (Ed.). (1977). *Language learning by a chimpanzee: The Lana project.* New York: Academic Press.

Rumbaugh, D. M., Savage-Rumbaugh, E. S., & Pate, J. L. (1988). Addendum to "Summation in the chimpanzee *(Pan troglodytes).* Journal of Experimental Psychology: Animal Behavior Processes, 14,* 118–120.

Rusiniak, K. W., Palmerino, C. C., & Garcia, J. (1982). Potentiation of odor by taste in rats: Tests of some nonassociative factors. *Journal of Comparative and Physiological Psychology, 96,* 775–780.

Rusiniak, K. W., Palmerino, C. C., Rice, A. G., Forthman, D. L., & Garcia, J. (1982). Flavor-illness aversions: Potentiation of odor by taste with toxin but not shock in rats. *Journal of Comparative and Physiological Psychology, 96,* 527–539.

Russell, W. R., & Nathan, P. W. (1946). Traumatic amnesia. *Brain, 69,* 280–300.

Rzoska, J. (1953). Bait shyness, a study in rat behaviour. *British Journal of Animal Behaviour, 1,* 128–135.

Sahley, C., Rudy, J. W., & Gelperin, A. (1981). An analysis of associative learning in a terrestrial mollusc: I.

Higher-order conditioning, blocking, and a transient US-pre-exposure effect. *Journal of Comparative Physiology–A, 144,* 1–8.

Sajwaj, T., Libet, J., & Agras, S. (1974). Lemon-juice therapy: The control of life-threatening rumination in a six-month-old infant. *Journal of Applied Behavior Analysis, 7,* 557–563.

Saladin, M. E., & Tait, R. W. (1986). US preexposures retard excitatory and facilitate inhibitory conditioning of the rabbit's nictitating membrane response. *Animal Learning & Behavior, 14,* 121–132.

Saladin, M. E., ten Have, W. N., Saper, Z. L., Labinsky, J. S., & Tait, R. W. (1989). Retardation of rabbit nictitating membrane conditioning following US preexposures depends on the distribution and numbers of US presentations. *Animal Learning & Behavior, 17,* 179–187.

Santi, A., Musgrave, S., & Bradford, S. A. (1988). Utilization of cues signaling different test stimulus dimensions in delayed matching to sample by pigeons. *Learning and Motivation, 19,* 87–98.

Santi, A., & Roberts, W. A. (1985). Prospective representation: The effects of varied mapping of sample stimuli to comparison stimuli and differential trial outcomes on pigeons' working memory. *Animal Learning & Behavior, 13,* 103–108.

Savage-Rumbaugh, E. S. (1986). *Ape language.* New York: Columbia University Press.

Savage-Rumbaugh, E. S., McDonald, K., Sevcik, R. A., Hopkins, W. D., & Rubert, E. (1986). Spontaneous symbol acquisition and communicative use by pigmy chimpanzees *(Pan paniscus). Journal of Experimental Psychology: General, 115,* 211–235.

Savage-Rumbaugh, E. S., Rumbaugh, D. M., Smith, S. T., & Lawson, J. (1980). Reference: The linguistic essential. *Science, 210,* 922–925.

Savage-Rumbaugh, E. S., Sevcik, R. A., Brakke, K. E., & Rumbaugh, D. M. (1990). Symbols: Their communicative use, comprehension, and combination by bonobos *(Pan paniscus).* In C. Rovee-Collier & L. P. Lipsitt (Eds.), *Advances in infancy research* (Vol. 6, pp. 221–278). Norwood, NJ: Ablex.

Scavio, M. J., Jr., & Gormezano, I. (1974). CS intensity effects on rabbit nictitating membrane conditioning, extinction and generalization. *Pavlovian Journal of Biological Science, 9,* 25–34.

Schachtman, T. R., Brown, A. M., Gordon, E. L., Catterson, D. A., & Miller, R. R. (1987). Mechanisms underlying retarded emergence of conditioned responding following inhibitory training: Evidence for the comparator hypothesis. *Journal of Experimental Psychology: Animal Behavior Processes, 13,* 310–322.

Schachtman, T. R., Gee, J.-L., Kasprow, W. J., & Miller, R. R. (1983). Reminder-induced recovery from blocking as a function of the number of compound trials. *Learning and Motivation, 14,* 154–164.

Schiff, R., Smith, N., & Prochaska, J. (1972). Extinction of avoidance in rats as a function of duration and number of blocked trials. *Journal of Comparative and Physiological Psychology, 81*, 356–359.

Schindler, C. W., & Weiss, S. J. (1982). The influence of positive and negative reinforcement on selective attention in the rat. *Learning and Motivation, 13*, 304–323.

Schlinger, H., Blakely, E., & Kaczor, T. (1990). Pausing under variable-ratio schedules: Interaction of reinforcer magnitude, variable-ratio size, and lowest ratio. *Journal of the Experimental Analysis of Behavior, 53*, 133–139.

Schlosberg, H. (1934). Conditioned responses in the white rat. *Journal of Genetic Psychology, 45*, 303–335.

Schlosberg, H. (1936). Conditioned responses in the white rat: II. Conditioned responses based upon shock to the foreleg. *Journal of Genetic Psychology, 49*, 107–138.

Schlosberg, H. (1937). The relationship between success and the laws of conditioning. *Psychological Review, 44*, 379–394.

Schneider, A. M., Tyler, J., & Jinich, D. (1974). Recovery from retrograde amnesia: A learning process. *Science, 184*, 87–88.

Schneiderman, N., Fuentes, I., & Gormezano, I. (1962). Acquisition and extinction of the classically conditioned eyelid response in the albino rabbit. *Science, 136*, 650–652.

Schneiderman, N., & Gormezano, I. (1964). Conditioning of the nictitating membrane of the rabbit as a function of CS-US interval. *Journal of Comparative and Physiological Psychology, 57*, 188–195.

Schnur, P., & Martinez, R. A. (1989). Environmental control of morphine tolerance in the hamster. *Animal Learning & Behavior, 17*, 322–327.

Schreibman, L., Koegel, R. L., Charlop, M. H., & Egel, A. L. (1990). Infantile autism. In A. S. Bellack, M. Hersen, & A. E. Kazdin (Eds.), *International handbook of behavior modification and therapy* (pp. 763–789). New York: Plenum.

Schrier, A. M., & Brady, P. M. (1987). Categorization of natural stimuli by monkeys *(Macaca mulatta)*: Effects of stimulus set size and modification of exemplars. *Journal of Experimental Psychology: Animal Behavior Processes, 13*, 136–143.

Schull, J. (1979). A conditioned opponent theory of Pavlovian conditioning and habituation. In G. H. Bower (Ed.), *The psychology of learning and motivation* (Vol. 13). New York: Academic Press.

Schuster, R. H., & Rachlin, H. (1968). Indifference between punishment and free shock: Evidence for the negative law of effect. *Journal of the Experimental Analysis of Behavior, 11*, 777–786.

Schusterman, R. J., & Gisiner, R. (1988). Artificial language comprehension in dolphins and sea lions: The essential cognitive skills. *Psychological Record, 38*, 311–348.

Schwartz, B. (1976). Positive and negative conditioned suppression in the pigeon: Effects of the locus and modality of the CS. *Learning and Motivation, 7*, 86–100.

Schwartz, B. (1980). Development of complex, stereotyped behavior in pigeons. *Journal of the Experimental Analysis of Behavior, 33*, 153–166.

Schwartz, B. (1981). Reinforcement creates behavioral units. *Behavioural Analysis Letters, 1*, 33–41.

Schwartz, B. (1982). Interval and ratio reinforcement of a complex sequential operant in pigeons. *Journal of the Experimental Analysis of Behavior, 37*, 349–357.

Schwartz, B. (1985). On the organization of stereotyped response sequences. *Animal Learning & Behavior, 13*, 261–268.

Schwartz, B. (1986). Allocation of complex, sequential operants on multiple and concurrent schedules of reinforcement. *Journal of the Experimental Analysis of Behavior, 45*, 283–295.

Schwartz, B. (1988). The experimental synthesis of behavior: Reinforcement, behavioral stereotypy, and problem solving. In G. H. Bower (Ed.), *The psychology of learning and motivation* (Vol. 22, pp. 93–138). Orlando, FL: Academic Press.

Schwartz, B., & Williams, D. R. (1972). The role of the response-reinforcer contingency in negative automaintenance. *Journal of the Experimental Analysis of Behavior, 17*, 351–357.

Schweitzer, J. B., & Sulzer-Azaroff, B. (1988). Self-control: Teaching tolerance for delay in impulsive children. *Journal of the Experimental Analysis of Behavior, 50*, 173–186.

Scobie, S. R. (1972). Interaction of an aversive Pavlovian conditioned stimulus with aversively and appetitively motivated operants in rats. *Journal of Comparative and Physiological Psychology, 79*, 171–188.

Seligman, M. E. P. (1975). *Helplessness: On depression, development and death*. San Francisco: W. H. Freeman.

Seligman, M. E. P., & Maier, S. F. (1967). Failure to escape traumatic shock. *Journal of Experimental Psychology, 74*, 1–9.

Seligman, M. E. P., & Weiss, J. (1980). Coping behavior: Learned helplessness, physiological activity, and learned inactivity. *Behaviour Research and Therapy, 18*, 459–512.

Serban, G., & Kling, A. (Eds.). (1976). *Animal models in psychobiology*. New York: Plenum.

Sevenster, P. (1973). Incompatibility of response and reward. In R. A. Hinde & J. Stevenson-Hinde (Eds.), *Constraints on learning*. London: Academic Press.

Shapiro, A. P., & Nathan, P. E. (1986). Human tolerance to alcohol: The role of Pavlovian conditioning processes. *Psychopharmacology, 88*, 90–95.

Shapiro, K. L., Jacobs, W. J., & LoLordo, V. M. (1980). Stimulus-reinforcer interactions in Pavlovian conditioning of pigeons: Implications for selective associations. *Animal Learning & Behavior, 8*, 586–594.

Shapiro, K. L., & LoLordo, V. M. (1982). Constraints on

Pavlovian conditioning of the pigeon: Relative conditioned reinforcing effects of red-light and tone CSs paired with food. *Learning and Motivation, 13,* 68–80.

Shapiro, M. M. (1960). Respondent salivary conditioning during operant lever pressing in dogs. *Science, 132,* 619–620.

Shapiro, M. M. (1961). Salivary conditioning in dogs during fixed-interval reinforcement contingent upon lever pressing. *Journal of the Experimental Analysis of Behavior, 4,* 361–364.

Sheffield, F. D. (1948). Avoidance training and the contiguity principle. *Journal of Comparative and Physiological Psychology, 41,* 165–177.

Sheffield, F. D. (1965). Relation between classical conditioning and instrumental learning. In W. F. Prokasy (Ed.), *Classical conditioning.* New York: Appleton-Century-Crofts.

Sheffield, F. D., Roby, T. B., & Campbell, B. A. (1954). Drive reduction versus consummatory behavior as determinants of reinforcement. *Journal of Comparative and Physiological Psychology, 47,* 349–354.

Sheffield, F. D., Wulff, J. J., & Backer, R. (1951). Reward value of copulation without sex drive reduction. *Journal of Comparative and Physiological Psychology, 44,* 3–8.

Sherry, D. F. (1984). Food storage by black-capped chickadees: Memory for the location and contents of caches. *Animal Behaviour, 32,* 451–464.

Sherry, D. F. (1985). Food storage by birds and mammals. *Advances in the study of behavior, 15,* 153–188.

Sherry, D. F. (1988). Learning and adaptation in food-storing birds. In R. C. Bolles & M. D. Beecher (Eds.), *Evolution and learning* (pp. 79–95). Hillsdale, NJ: Erlbaum.

Sherry, D. F. (1990). Evolutionary modification of memory and the hippocampus. In L. R. Squire & E. Lindenlaub (Eds.), *The biology of memory* (Symposia Medica Hoechst 23, 1990) (pp. 401–421). Stuttgart, Germany: F. K. Schattauer Verlag.

Sherry, D. F., Krebs, J. R., & Cowie, R. J. (1981). Memory for the location of stored food in marsh tits. *Animal Behaviour, 29,* 1260–1266.

Sherry, D. F., & Schacter, D. L. (1987). The evolution of multiple memory systems. *Psychological Review, 94,* 439–454.

Shettleworth, S. J. (1975). Reinforcement and the organization of behavior in golden hamsters: Hunger, environment, and food reinforcement. *Journal of Experimental Psychology: Animal Behavior Processes, 1,* 56–87.

Shettleworth, S. J. (1978). Reinforcement and the organization of behavior in golden hamsters: Punishment of three action patterns. *Learning and Motivation, 9,* 99–123.

Shettleworth, S. J. (1981). Reinforcement and the organization of behavior in golden hamsters: Differential overshadowing of a CS by different responses.

Quarterly Journal of Experimental Psychology, 33B, 241–255.

Shettleworth, S. J. (1983a). Function and mechanism in learning. In M. D. Zeiler & P. Harzem (Eds.), *Advances in analysis of behaviour* (Vol. 3). Chichester, England: Wiley.

Shettleworth, S. J. (1983b). Memory in food-hoarding birds. *Scientific American, 248,* 102–110.

Shettleworth, S. J. (1988). Foraging as operant behavior and operant behavior as foraging: What have we learned? In G. H. Bower (Ed.), *The psychology of learning and motivation* (Vol. 22, pp. 1–49). Orlando, FL: Academic Press.

Shettleworth, S. J. (1989). Animals foraging in the lab: Problems and promises. *Journal of Experimental Psychology: Animal Behavior Processes, 15,* 81–87.

Shettleworth, S. J., & Krebs, J. R. (1982). How marsh tits find their hoards: The roles of site preference and spatial memory. *Journal of Experimental Psychology: Animal Behavior Processes, 8,* 354–375.

Shettleworth, S. J., & Krebs, J. R. (1986). Stored and encountered seeds: A comparison of two spatial memory tasks in marsh tits and chickadees. *Journal of Experimental Psychology: Animal Behavior Processes, 12,* 248–257.

Shimp, C. P. (1966). Probabilistically reinforced choice behavior in pigeons. *Journal of the Experimental Analysis of Behavior, 9,* 443–455.

Shimp, C. P. (1969). Optimum behavior in free-operant experiments. *Psychological Review, 76,* 97–112.

Shurtleff, D., & Ayres, J. J. B. (1981). One-trial backward excitatory fear conditioning in rats: Acquisition, retention, extinction, and spontaneous recovery. *Animal Learning & Behavior, 9,* 65–74.

Sidman, M. (1953a). Avoidance conditioning with brief shock and no exteroceptive warning signal. *Science, 118,* 157–158.

Sidman, M. (1953b). Two temporal parameters of the maintenance of avoidance behavior by the white rat. *Journal of Comparative and Physiological Psychology, 46,* 253–261.

Sidman, M. (1960). *Tactics of scientific research.* New York: Basic Books.

Sidman, M. (1962). Reduction of shock frequency as reinforcement for avoidance behavior. *Journal of the Experimental Analysis of Behavior, 5,* 247–257.

Sidman, M. (1966). Avoidance behavior. In W. K. Honig (Ed.), *Operant behavior.* New York: Appleton-Century-Crofts.

Siegel, S. (1975). Conditioning insulin effects. *Journal of Comparative and Physiological Psychology, 89,* 189–199.

Siegel, S. (1977). A Pavlovian conditioning analysis of morphine tolerance (and opiate dependence). In N. A. Krasnegor (Ed.), *Behavioral tolerance: Research and treatment implications.* National Institute for Drug Abuse, Monograph No. 18. Government Printing Office Stock

No. 017-024-00699-8. Washington, DC: Government Printing Office.

Siegel, S. (1983). Classical conditioning, drug tolerance, and drug dependence. In Y. Israel, F. B. Glaser, H. Kalant, R. E. Popham, W. Schmidt, & R. G. Smart (Eds.), *Research advances in alcohol and drug problems* (Vol. 7). New York: Plenum.

Siegel, S. (1984). Pavlovian conditioning and heroin overdose: Reports by overdose victims. *Bulletin of the Psychonomic Society, 22,* 428–430.

Siegel, S. (1989). Pharmacological conditioning and drug effects. In A. J. Goudie & M. W. Emmett-Oglesby (Eds.), *Psychoactive drugs: Tolerance and sensitization* (pp. 115–180). Clifton, NJ: Humana Press.

Siegel, S., & Domjan, M. (1971). Backward conditioning as an inhibitory procedure. *Learning and Motivation, 2,* 1–11.

Siegel, S., Hinson, R. E., Krank, M. D., & McCully, J. (1982). Heroin "overdose" death: Contribution of drug-associated environmental cues. *Science, 216,* 436–437.

Sigmundi, R. A., & Bolles, R. C. (1983). CS modality, context conditioning, and conditioned freezing. *Animal Learning & Behavior, 11,* 205–212.

Silberberg, A., Warren-Boulton, F. R., & Asano, T. (1987). Inferior-good and Giffen-good effects in monkey choice behavior. *Journal of Experimental Psychology: Animal Behavior Processes, 13,* 292–301.

Simon, H. A., & Kotovsky, K. (1963). Human acquisition of concepts for sequential patterns. *Psychological Review, 70,* 534–546.

Singh, N. N., & Solman, R. T. (1990). A stimulus control analysis of the picture-word problem in children who are mentally retarded: The blocking effect. *Journal of Applied Behavior Analysis, 23,* 525–532.

Skinner, B. F. (1938). *The behavior of organisms.* New York: Appleton-Century-Crofts.

Skinner, B. F. (1948). "Superstition" in the pigeon. *Journal of Experimental Psychology, 38,* 168–172.

Skinner, B. F. (1953). *Science and human behavior.* New York: Macmillan.

Slamecka, N. J., & Ceraso, J. (1960). Retroactive and proactive inhibition of verbal learning. *Psychological Bulletin, 57,* 449–475.

Small, W. S. (1899). An experimental study of the mental processes of the rat: I. *American Journal of Psychology, 11,* 133–164.

Small, W. S. (1900). An experimental study of the mental processes of the rat: II. *American Journal of Psychology, 12,* 206–239.

Smith, J. C., & Roll, D. L. (1967). Trace conditioning with X-rays as an aversive stimulus. *Psychonomic Science, 9,* 11–12.

Smith, M. C., Coleman, S. R., & Gormezano, I. (1969). Classical conditioning of the rabbit's nictitating membrane response at backward, simultaneous, and for-ward CS-US intervals. *Journal of Comparative and Physiological Psychology, 69,* 226–231.

Solomon, R. L. (1964). Punishment. *American Psychologist, 19,* 239–253.

Solomon, R. L. (1977). An opponent-process theory of acquired motivation: The affective dynamics of addiction. In J. D. Maser & M. E. P. Seligman (Eds.), *Psychopathology: Experimental models* (pp. 66–103). San Francisco: W. H. Freeman.

Solomon, R. L., & Corbit, J. D. (1973). An opponent-process theory of motivation: II. Cigarette addiction. *Journal of Abnormal Psychology, 81,* 158–171.

Solomon, R. L., & Corbit, J. D. (1974). An opponent-process theory of motivation: I. The temporal dynamics of affect. *Psychological Review, 81,* 119–145.

Solomon, R. L., Kamin, L. J., & Wynne, L. C. (1953). Traumatic avoidance learning: The outcomes of several extinction procedures with dogs. *Journal of Abnormal and Social Psychology, 48,* 291–302.

Solomon, R. L., & Wynne, L. C. (1953). Traumatic avoidance learning: Acquisition in normal dogs. *Psychological Monographs, 67* (Whole No. 354).

Soltysik, S. S., Wolfe, G. E., Nicholas, T., Wilson, W. J., & Garcia-Sanchez, L. (1983). Blocking of inhibitory conditioning within a serial conditioned stimulus-conditioned inhibitor compound: Maintenance of acquired behavior without an unconditioned stimulus. *Learning and Motivation, 14,* 1–29.

Sonuga-Barke, E. J. S., Lea, S. E. G., & Webley, P. (1989a). An account of human "impulsivity" on self-control tasks. *Quarterly Journal of Experimental Psychology, 41B,* 161–179.

Sonuga-Barke, E. J. S., Lea, S. E. G., & Webley, P. (1989b). The development of adaptive choice in a self-control paradigm. *Journal of the Experimental Analysis of Behavior, 51,* 77–85.

Spear, N. E. (1973). Retrieval of memory in animals. *Psychological Review, 80,* 163–194.

Spear, N. E. (1976). Retrieval of memories: A psychobiological approach. In W. K. Estes (Ed.), *Handbook of learning and cognitive processes* (Vol. 4). Hillsdale, NJ: Erlbaum.

Spear, N. E. (1978). *The processing of memories: Forgetting and retention.* Hillsdale, NJ: Erlbaum.

Spear, N. E. (1981). Extending the domain of memory retrieval. In N. E. Spear & R. R. Miller (Eds.), *Information processing in animals: Memory mechanisms.* Hillsdale, NJ: Erlbaum.

Spear, N. E., Hamberg, J. M., & Bryan, R. (1980). Forgetting of recently acquired or recently reactivated memories. *Learning and Motivation, 11,* 456–475.

Spear, N. E., & Miller, R. R. (Eds.). (1981). *Information processing in animals: Memory mechanisms.* Hillsdale, NJ: Erlbaum.

Spear, N. E., Smith, G. J., Bryan, R. G., Gordon, W. C.,

Timmons, R., & Chiszar, D. A. (1980). Contextual influences on the interaction between conflicting memories in the rat. *Animal Learning & Behavior, 8,* 273–281.

Speers, M. A., Gillan, D. J., & Rescorla, R. A. (1980). Within-compound associations in a variety of compound conditioning procedures. *Learning and Motivation, 11,* 135–149.

Spence, K. W. (1936). The nature of discrimination learning in animals. *Psychological Review, 43,* 427–449.

Spence, K. W. (1937). The differential response in animals to stimuli varying within a single dimension. *Psychological Review, 44,* 430–444.

Spence, K. W. (1956). *Behavior theory and conditioning.* New Haven, CT: Yale University Press.

Spetch, M. L. (1990). Further studies of pigeons' spatial working memory in the open-field task. *Animal Learning & Behavior, 18,* 332–340.

Spetch, M. L., & Honig, W. K. (1988). Characteristics of pigeons' spatial working memory in an open-field task. *Animal Learning & Behavior, 16,* 123–131.

Spetch, M. L., & Wilkie, D. M. (1981). Duration discrimination is better with food access as the signal than with light as the signal. *Learning and Motivation, 12,* 40–64.

Spetch, M. L., Wilkie, D. M., & Pinel, J. P. J. (1981). Backward conditioning: A reevaluation of the empirical evidence. *Psychological Bulletin, 89,* 163–175.

Spetch, M. L., Wilkie, D. M., & Skelton, R. W. (1981). Control of pigeons' keypecking topography by a schedule of alternating food and water reward. *Animal Learning & Behavior, 9,* 223–229.

Staddon, J. E. R. (1979). Operant behavior as adaptation to constraint. *Journal of Experimental Psychology: General, 108,* 48–67.

Staddon, J. E. R. (1980). Optimality analyses of operant behavior and their relation to optimal foraging. In J. E. R. Staddon (Ed.), *Limits to action.* New York: Academic Press.

Staddon, J. E. R. (1983). *Adaptive behavior and learning.* Cambridge: Cambridge University Press.

Staddon, J. E. R. (1988). Quasi-dynamic choice models: Melioration and ratio invariance. *Journal of the Experimental Analysis of Behavior, 49,* 303–320.

Staddon, J. E. R., & Simmelhag, V. L. (1971). The "superstition" experiment: A reexamination of its implications for the principles of adaptive behavior. *Psychological Review, 78,* 3–43.

Starr, M. D. (1978). An opponent-process theory of motivation: VI. Time and intensity variables in the development of separation-induced distress calling in ducklings. *Journal of Experimental Psychology: Animal Behavior Processes, 4,* 338–355.

Starr, M. D., & Mineka, S. (1977). Determinants of fear over the course of avoidance learning. *Learning and Motivation, 8,* 332–350.

Steinert, P., Fallon, D., & Wallace, J. (1976). Matching to sample in goldfish *(Carassuis auratus). Bulletin of the Psychonomic Society, 8,* 265.

Stephens, D. W., & Krebs, J. R. (1986). *Foraging theory.* Princeton, NJ: Princeton University Press.

Stephenson, D., & Siddle, D. (1983). Theories of habituation. In D. Siddle (Ed.), *Orienting and habituation: Perspectives in human research.* Chichester, England: Wiley.

Stevens, S. S. (1951). Mathematics, measurement and psychophysics. In S. S. Stevens (Ed.), *Handbook of experimental psychology* (pp. 1–49). New York: Wiley.

Stewart, J., & Eikelboom, R. (1987). Conditioned drug effects. In L. L. Iversen, S. D. Iversen, & S. H. Snyder (Eds.), *Handbook of psychopharmacology* (Vol. 19, pp. 1–57). New York: Plenum.

Stiers, M., & Silberberg, A. (1974). Lever-contact responses in rats: Automaintenance with and without a negative response-reinforcer dependency. *Journal of the Experimental Analysis of Behavior, 22,* 497–506.

Stokes, P. D., & Balsam, P. D. (1991). Effects of reinforcing preselected approximations on the topography of the rat's bar press. *Journal of the Experimental Analysis of Behavior, 55,* 213–231.

Stokes, T. F., & Baer, D. M. (1977). An implicit technology of generalization. *Journal of Applied Behavior Analysis, 10,* 349–367.

Stonebraker, T. B., & Rilling, M. (1981). Control of delayed matching-to-sample performance using directed forgetting techniques. *Animal Learning & Behavior, 9,* 196–201.

Straub, R. O., & Terrace, H. S. (1981). Generalization of serial learning in the pigeon. *Animal Learning & Behavior, 9,* 454–468.

Strijkstra, A. M., & Bolhuis, J. J. (1987). Memory persistence of rats in a radial maze varies with training procedure. *Behavioral and Neural Biology, 47,* 158–166.

Suarez, S. D., & Gallup, G. G. (1981). An ethological analysis of open-field behavior in rats and mice. *Learning and Motivation, 12,* 342–363.

Suomi, S. J., Mineka, S., & Harlow, H. F. (1983). Social separation in monkeys as viewed from several motivational perspectives. In E. Satinoff & P. Teitelbaum (Eds.), *Handbook of neurobiology: Vol. 6. Motivation.* New York: Plenum.

Susswein, A. J., & Schwarz, M. (1983). A learned change of response to inedible food in *Aplysia. Behavioral and Neural Biology, 39,* 1–6.

Sutherland, N. S., & Mackintosh, M. J. (1971). *Mechanisms of animal discrimination learning.* New York: Academic Press.

Suzuki, S., Augerinos, G., & Black, A. H. (1980). Stimulus control of spatial behavior on the eight-arm maze in rats. *Learning and Motivation, 11,* 1–18.

Tait, R. W., & Saladin, M. E. (1986). Concurrent development of excitatory and inhibitory associations during backward conditioning. *Animal Learning & Behavior, 14,* 133–137.

ter Pelkwijk, J. J., & Tinbergen, N. (1937). Eine reizbiologische Analyse einiger Verhaltensweisen von *G. aculeatus. Zeitschrift für Tierpsychologie, 1,* 193–204.

Terrace, H. S. (1964). Wavelength generalization after discrimination learning with and without errors. *Science, 144,* 78–80.

Terrace, H. S. (1966). Stimulus control. In W. K. Honig (Ed.), *Operant behavior: Areas of research and application.* New York: Appleton-Century-Crofts.

Terrace, H. S. (1972). By-products of discrimination learning. In G. H. Bower (Ed.), *The psychology of learning and motivation* (Vol. 5). New York: Academic Press.

Terrace, H. S. (1979). *Nim.* New York: Knopf.

Terrace, H. S. (1984). Animal cognition. In H. L. Roitblat, T. G. Bever, & H. S. Terrace (Eds.), *Animal cognition.* Hillsdale, NJ: Erlbaum.

Terrace, H. S. (1986a). A nonverbal organism's knowledge of ordinal position in a serial learning task. *Journal of Experimental Psychology: Animal Behavior Processes, 12,* 203–214.

Terrace, H. S. (1986b). Positive transfer from sequence production to sequence discrimination in a nonverbal organism. *Journal of Experimental Psychology: Animal Behavior Processes, 12,* 215–234.

Terrace, H. S. (1987). Chunking by a pigeon in a serial learning task. *Nature, 325,* 149–151.

Terrace, H. S. (1991a). Chunking during serial learning by a pigeon: I. Basic evidence. *Journal of Experimental Psychology: Animal Behavior Processes, 17,* 81–93.

Terrace, H. S. (1991b). Chunking during serial learning by a pigeon: II. Integrity of a chunk on a new list. *Journal of Experimental Psychology: Animal Behavior Processes, 17,* 94–106.

Terrace, H. S. (1991c). Chunking during serial learning by a pigeon: III. What are the necessary conditions for establishing a chunk? *Journal of Experimental Psychology: Animal Behavior Processes, 17,* 107–118.

Terrace, H. S., Petitto, L. A., Sanders, R. J., & Bever, T. G. (1979). Can an ape create a sentence? *Science, 206,* 891–1201.

Terry, W. S., & Wagner, A. R. (1975). Short-term memory for "surprising" versus "expected" unconditioned stimuli in Pavlovian conditioning. *Journal of Experimental Psychology: Animal Behavior Processes, 1,* 122–133.

Testa, T. J. (1974). Causal relationships and the acquisition of avoidance responses. *Psychological Review, 81,* 491–505.

Theios, J. (1962). The partial reinforcement effect sustained through blocks of continuous reinforcement. *Journal of Experimental Psychology, 64,* 1–6.

Thomas, D. R., Cook, S. C., & Terrones, J. P. (1990). Conditional discrimination learning by pigeons: The role of simultaneous versus successive stimulus presentations. *Journal of Experimental Psychology: Animal Behavior Processes, 16,* 390–401.

Thomas, D. R., Curran, P. J., & Russell, R. J. (1988). Factors affecting conditional discrimination learning by pigeons: II. Physical and temporal characteristics of stimuli. *Animal Learning & Behavior, 16,* 468–476.

Thomas, D. R., & Empedocles, S. (1992). Novelty vs. retrieval cue value in the study of long-term memory in pigeons. *Journal of Experimental Psychology: Animal Behavior Processes, 18,* 22–23.

Thomas, D. R., Mariner, R. W., & Sherry, G. (1969). Role of preexperimental experience in the development of stimulus control. *Journal of Experimental Psychology, 79,* 375–376.

Thomas, D. R., McKelvie, A. R., & Mah, W. L. (1985). Context as a conditional cue in operant discrimination reversal learning. *Journal of Experimental Psychology: Animal Behavior Processes, 11,* 317–330.

Thomas, D. R., Mood, K., Morrison, S., & Wiertelak, E. (1991). Peak shift revisited: A test of alternative interpretations. *Journal of Experimental Psychology: Animal Behavior Processes, 17,* 130–140.

Thomas, G. V., & Lieberman, D. A. (1990). Commentary: Determinants of success and failure in experiments on marking. *Learning and Motivation, 21,* 110–124.

Thomas, G. V., Robertson, D., & Lieberman, D. A. (1990). The effects of relative intensity of cue and marker on marked trace conditioning in pigeons. *Quarterly Journal of Experimental Psychology, 42B,* 267–287.

Thomas, J. R. (1968). Fixed ratio punishment by timeout of concurrent variable-interval behavior. *Journal of the Experimental Analysis of Behavior, 11,* 609–616.

Thompson, C. R., & Church, R. M. (1980). An explanation of the language of a chimpanzee. *Science, 208,* 313–314.

Thompson, R. F., Donegan, N. H., & Lavond, D. G. (1988). The psychobiology of learning and memory. In R. C. Atkinson, R. J. Herrnstein, G. Lindzey, & R. D. Luce (Eds.), *Stevens' handbook of experimental psychology: Vol. 2. Learning and cognition* (pp. 245–347). New York: Wiley.

Thompson, R. F., Groves, P. M., Teyler, T. J., & Roemer, R. A. (1973). A dual-process theory of habituation: Theory and behavior. In H. V. S. Peeke & M. J. Herz (Eds.), *Habituation.* New York: Academic Press.

Thompson, R. F., & Spencer, W. A. (1966). Habituation: A model phenomenon for the study of neuronal substrates of behavior. *Psychological Review, 73,* 16–43.

Thompson, R. K. R., Van Hemel, P. E., Winston, K. M., & Pappas, N. (1983). Modality-specific interference with overt mediation by pigeons in a delayed discrimination task. *Learning and Motivation, 14,* 271–303.

Thorndike, E. L. (1898). Animal intelligence: An experimental study of the association processes in animals. *Psychological Review Monograph, 2* (Whole No. 8).

Thorndike, E. L. (1911). *Animal intelligence: Experimental studies.* New York: Macmillan.

Thorndike, E. L. (1932). *The fundamentals of learning.* New York: Teachers College, Columbia University.

Tierney, K. J., Smith, H. V., & Gannon, K. N. (1987). Some tests of molar models of instrumental performance. *Journal of Experimental Psychology: Animal Behavior Processes, 13,* 341–353.

Tiffany, S. T., & Maude-Griffin, P. M. (1988). Tolerance to morphine in the rat: Associative and nonassociative effects. *Behavioral Neuroscience, 102,* 534–543.

Tiffany, S. T., Petrie, E. C., Baker, T. B., & Dahl, J. L. (1983). Conditioned morphine tolerance in the rat: Absence of a compensatory response and cross-tolerance with stress. *Behavioral Neuroscience, 97,* 335–353.

Timberlake, W. (1980). A molar equilibrium theory of learned performance. In G. H. Bower (Ed.), *The psychology of learning and motivation* (Vol. 14). New York: Academic Press.

Timberlake, W. (1983a). The functional organization of appetitive behavior: Behavior systems and learning. In M. D. Zeiler & P. Harzem (Eds.), *Advances in analysis of behavior: Vol. 3. Biological factors in learning* (pp. 177–221). Chichester, England: Wiley.

Timberlake, W. (1983b). Rats' responses to a moving object related to food or water: A behavior-systems analysis. *Animal Learning & Behavior, 11,* 309–320.

Timberlake, W. (1984). Behavior regulation and learned performance: Some misapprehensions and disagreements. *Journal of the Experimental Analysis of Behavior, 41,* 355–375.

Timberlake, W., & Allison, J. (1974). Response deprivation: An empirical approach to instrumental performance. *Psychological Review, 81,* 146–164.

Timberlake, W., & Farmer-Dougan, V. A. (1991). Reinforcement in applied settings: Figuring out ahead of time what will work. *Psychological Bulletin, 110,* 379–391.

Timberlake, W., Gawley, D. J., & Lucas, G. A. (1987). Time horizons in rats foraging for food in temporally separated patches. *Journal of Experimental Psychology: Animal Behavior Processes, 13,* 302–309.

Timberlake, W., Gawley, D. J., & Lucas, G. A. (1988). Time horizons in rats: The effects of operant control of access to future food. *Journal of the Experimental Analysis of Behavior, 50,* 405–417.

Timberlake, W., & Grant, D. S. (1975). Auto-shaping in rats to the presentation of another rat predicting food. *Science, 190,* 690–692.

Timberlake, W., & Lucas, G. A. (1985). The basis of superstitious behavior: Chance contingency, stimulus substitution, or appetitive behavior? *Journal of the Experimental Analysis of Behavior, 44,* 279–299.

Timberlake, W., & Lucas, G. A. (1989). Behavior systems and learning: From misbehavior to general principles. In S. B. Klein & R. R. Mowrer (Eds.), *Contemporary learning theories: Instrumental conditioning and the impact of biological constraints on learning* (pp. 237–275). Hillsdale, NJ: Erlbaum.

Timberlake, W., Wahl, G., & King, D. (1982). Stimulus and response contingencies in the misbehavior of rats. *Journal of Experimental Psychology: Animal Behavior Processes, 8,* 62–85.

Timberlake, W., & Washburne, D. L. (1989). Feeding ecology and laboratory predatory behavior toward live and artificial moving prey in seven rodent species. *Animal Learning & Behavior, 17,* 2–11.

Timberlake, W., & White, W. (1990). Winning isn't everything: Rats need only food deprivation and not food reward to efficiently traverse a radial arm maze. *Learning and Motivation, 21,* 153–163.

Tinbergen, N. (1951). *The study of instinct.* Oxford: Clarendon Press.

Tinbergen, N., & Perdeck, A. C. (1950). On the stimulus situation releasing the begging response in the newly hatched herring gull chick *(Larus argentatus argentatus Pont.). Behaviour, 3,* 1–39.

Tolman, E. C. (1938). The determiners of behavior at a choice point. *Psychological Review, 45,* 1–41.

Tomie, A., Brooks, W., & Zito, B. (1989). Sign-tracking: The search for reward. In S. B. Klein & R. R. Mowrer (Eds.), *Contemporary learning theories: Pavlovian conditioning and the status of learning theory* (pp. 191–223). Hillsdale, NJ: Erlbaum.

Trapold, M. A., & Winokur, S. (1967). Transfer from classical conditioning to acquisition, extinction, and stimulus generalization of a positively reinforced instrumental response. *Journal of Experimental Psychology, 73,* 517–525.

Trenholme, I. A., & Baron, A. (1975). Immediate and delayed punishment of human behavior by loss of reinforcement. *Learning and Motivation, 6,* 62–79.

Turkkan, J. S. (1989). Classical conditioning: The new hegemony. *The Behavioral and Brain Sciences, 12,* 121–179.

Twitmyer, E. B. (1974). A study of the knee jerk. *Journal of Experimental Psychology, 103,* 1047–1066.

Underwood, B. J. (1957). Interference and forgetting. *Psychological Review, 64,* 49–60.

Urcuioli, P. J., & Kasprow, W. J. (1988). Long-delay learning in the T-maze: Effects of marking and delay-interval location. *Learning and Motivation, 19,* 66–86.

Urcuioli, P. J., & Zentall, T. R. (1986). Retrospective coding in pigeons' delayed matching-to-sample. *Journal of Experimental Psychology: Animal Behavior Processes, 12,* 69–77.

Urcuioli, P. J., Zentall, T. R., Jackson-Smith, P., & Steirn, J. N. (1989). Evidence for common coding in many-to-one matching: Retention, intertrial, interference, and transfer. *Journal of Experimental Psychology: Animal Behavior Processes, 15,* 264–273.

Vaccarino, F. J., Schiff, B. B., & Glickman, S. E. (1989).

Biological view of reinforcement. In S. B. Klein & R. R. Mowrer (Eds.), *Contemporary learning theories: Instrumental conditioning and the impact of biological constraints on learning* (pp. 111–142). Hillsdale, NJ: Erlbaum.

Vaughan, W., Jr. (1981). Melioration, matching, and maximizing. *Journal of the Experimental Analysis of Behavior, 36,* 141–149.

Vaughan, W., Jr. (1985). Choice: A local analysis. *Journal of the Experimental Analysis of Behavior, 43,* 383–405.

Vaughan, W., Jr., & Greene, S. L. (1984). Pigeon visual memory capacity. *Journal of Experimental Psychology: Animal Behavior Processes, 10,* 256–271.

von Fersen, L., & Lea, S. E. G. (1990). Category discrimination by pigeons using five polymorphous features. *Journal of the Experimental Analysis of Behavior, 54,* 69–84.

von Fersen, L., Wynne, C. D. L., Delius, J. D., & Staddon, J. E. R. (1991). Transitive inference formation in pigeons. *Journal of Experimental Psychology: Animal Behavior Processes, 17,* 334–341.

Wagner, A. R. (1976). Priming in STM: An information processing mechanism for self-generated or retrieval-generated depression in performance. In T. J. Tighe & R. N. Leaton (Eds.), *Habituation: Perspectives from child development, animal behavior, and neurophysiology.* Hillsdale, NJ: Erlbaum.

Wagner, A. R. (1981). SOP: A model of automatic memory processing in animal behavior. In N. E. Spear & R. R. Miller (Eds.), *Information processing in animals: Memory mechanisms* (pp. 5–47). Hillsdale, NJ: Erlbaum.

Wagner, A. R., & Brandon, S. E. (1989). Evolution of a structured connectionist model of Pavlovian conditioning (AESOP). In S. B. Klein & R. R. Mowrer (Eds.), *Contemporary learning theories: Pavlovian conditioning and the status of learning theory* (pp. 149–189). Hillsdale, NJ: Erlbaum.

Wagner, A. R., & Larew, M. B. (1985). Opponent processes and Pavlovian inhibition. In R. R. Miller & N. E. Spear (Eds.), *Information processing in animals: Conditioned inhibition.* Hillsdale, NJ: Erlbaum.

Wagner, A. R., Logan, F. A., Haberlandt, K., & Price, T. (1968). Stimulus selection in animal discrimination learning. *Journal of Experimental Psychology, 76,* 171–180.

Wagner, A. R., & Rescorla, R. A. (1972). Inhibition in Pavlovian conditioning: Application of a theory. In R. A. Boakes & M. S. Halliday (Eds.), *Inhibition and learning.* London: Academic Press.

Wagner, A. R., Rudy, J. W., & Whitlow, J. W. (1973). Rehearsal in animal conditioning. *Journal of Experimental Psychology, 97,* 407–426.

Wallace, J., Steinert, P. A., Scobie, S. R., & Spear, N. E. (1980). Stimulus modality and short-term memory in rats. *Animal Learning & Behavior, 8,* 10–16.

Walter, H. E. (1907). The reaction of planarians to light. *Journal of Experimental Zoology, 5,* 35–162.

Walters, G. C., & Glazer, R. D. (1971). Punishment

of instinctive behavior in the Mongolian gerbil. *Journal of Comparative and Physiological Psychology, 75,* 331–340.

Walters, G. C., & Grusec, J. F. (1977). *Punishment.* San Francisco: W. H. Freeman.

Wanchisen, B. A., Tatham, T. A., & Hineline, P. N. (1988). Pigeons' choices in situations of diminishing returns: Fixed- versus progressive-ratio schedules. *Journal of the Experimental Analysis of Behavior, 50,* 375–394.

Warren-Boulton, F. R., Silberberg, A., Gray, M., & Ollom, R. (1985). Reanalysis of the equation for simple action. *Journal of the Experimental Analysis of Behavior, 43,* 265–277.

Wasserman, E. A. (1973). Pavlovian conditioning with heat reinforcement produces stimulus-directed pecking in chicks. *Science, 181,* 875–877.

Wasserman, E. A. (1974). Responses in Pavlovian conditioning studies (reply to Hogan). *Science, 186,* 157.

Wasserman, E. A. (1981). Response evocation in autoshaping: Contributions of cognitive and comparative-evolutionary analyses to an understanding of directed action. In C. M. Locurto, H. S. Terrace, & J. Gibbon (Eds.), *Autoshaping and conditioning theory.* New York: Academic Press.

Wasserman, E. A. (1986). Prospection and retrospection as processes of animal short-term memory. In D. F. Kendrick, M. E. Rilling, & M. R. Denny (Eds.), *Theories of animal memory* (pp. 53–75). Hillsdale, NJ: Erlbaum.

Wasserman, E. A., DeLong, R. E., & Larew, M. B. (1984). Temporal order and duration: Their discrimination and retention by pigeons. *Annals of the New York Academy of Sciences, 423,* 103–115.

Wasserman, E. A., Franklin, S. R., & Hearst, E. (1974). Pavlovian appetitive contingencies and approach versus withdrawal to conditioned stimuli in pigeons. *Journal of Comparative and Physiological Psychology, 86,* 616–627.

Wasserman, E. A., Kiedinger, R. E., & Bhatt, R. S. (1988). Conceptual behavior in pigeons: Categories, subcategories, and pseudocategories. *Journal of Experimental Psychology: Animal Behavior Processes, 14,* 235–246.

Wearden, J. H., & Burgess, I. S. (1982). Matching since Baum (1979). *Journal of the Experimental Analysis of Behavior, 38,* 339–348.

Wearden, J. H., & Clark, R. B. (1988). Interresponse-time reinforcement and behavior under aperiodic reinforcement schedules: A case study using computer modeling. *Journal of Experimental Psychology: Animal Behavior Processes, 14,* 200–211.

Wearden, J. H., & McShane, B. (1988). Interval production as an analogue of the peak procedure: Evidence for similarity of human and animal timing processes. *Quarterly Journal of Experimental Psychology, 40B,* 363–375.

Weinberger, N. (1965). Effect of detainment on extinction

of avoidance responses. *Journal of Comparative and Physiological Psychology, 60,* 135–138.

Weiskrantz, L. (Ed.). (1985). *Animal intelligence.* London: Oxford University Press.

Weisman, R. G., & Litner, J. S. (1969). The course of Pavlovian excitation and inhibition of fear in rats. *Journal of Comparative and Physiological Psychology, 69,* 667–672.

Weisman, R. G., & Litner, J. S. (1972). The role of Pavlovian events in avoidance training. In R. A. Boakes & M. S. Halliday (Eds.), *Inhibition and learning.* London: Academic Press.

Weisman, R. G., & Premack, D. (1966). *Reinforcement and punishment produced by the same response depending upon the probability relation between the instrumental and contingent responses.* Paper presented at the meeting of the Psychonomic Society, St. Louis.

Weiss, S. J., & Schindler, C. W. (1981). Generalization peak shift in rats under conditions of positive reinforcement and avoidance. *Journal of the Experimental Analysis of Behavior, 35,* 175–185.

Weiss-Fogh, T. (1949). An aerodynamic sense organ stimulating and regulating flight in locusts. *Nature, 164,* 873–874.

Welsh, J. H. (1933). Light intensity and the extent of activity of locomotor muscles as opposed to cilia. *Biological Bulletin, 65,* 168–174.

Wesierska, M., & Zielinski, K. (1980). Enhancement of bar-pressing rate in rats by the conditioned inhibitor of the CER. *Acta Neurobiologica Experimentalis, 40,* 945–963.

Westbrook, R. F., Greeley, J. D., Nabke, C. P., & Swinbourne, A. L. (1991). Aversive conditioning in the rat: Effect of benzodiazepine and of an opioid agonist and antagonist on conditioned hypoalgesia and fear. *Journal of Experimental Psychology: Animal Behavior Processes, 17,* 219–230.

Westbrook, R. F., Harvey, A., & Swinbourne, A. (1988). Potentiation by a novel flavour of conditioned place aversions based on both toxicosis and shock. *Quarterly Journal of Experimental Psychology, 40B,* 305–319.

Westbrook, R. F., Smith, F. J., & Charnock, D. J. (1985). The extinction of an aversion: Role of the interval between nonreinforced presentations of the averted stimulus. *Quarterly Journal of Experimental Psychology, 37B,* 255–273.

Whitlow, J. W., Jr., & Wagner, A. R. (1984). Memory and habituation. In H. V. S. Peeke & L. Petrinovich (Eds.), *Habituation, sensitization, and behavior.* New York: Academic Press.

Wiens, A. N., & Menustik, C. E. (1983). Treatment outcome and patient characteristics in an aversion therapy program for alcoholism. *American Psychologist, 38,* 1089–1096.

Wigglesworth, V. B., & Gillett, J. D. (1934). The function of

the antennae of *Rhodnius prolixus* (Hemiptera) and the mechanisms of orientation to the host. *Journal of Experimental Biology, 11,* 120–139.

Wilkie, D. M. (1989). Evidence that pigeons represent Euclidian properties of space. *Journal of Experimental Psychology: Animal Behavior Processes, 15,* 114–123.

Wilkie, D. M., & Masson, M. E. (1976). Attention in the pigeon: A reevaluation. *Journal of the Experimental Analysis of Behavior, 26,* 207–212.

Wilkie, D. M., & Slobin, P. (1983). Gerbils in space: Performance on the 17-arm radial maze. *Journal of the Experimental Analysis of Behavior, 40,* 301–312.

Wilkie, D. M., & Summers, R. J. (1982). Pigeons' spatial memory: Factors affecting delayed matching of key location. *Journal of the Experimental Analysis of Behavior, 37,* 45–56.

Wilkie, D. M., Willson, R. J., & Kardal, S. (1989). Pigeons discriminate pictures of a geographic location. *Animal Learning & Behavior, 17,* 163–171.

Willer, J. C., Dehen, H., & Cambier, J. (1981). Stress-induced analgesia in humans: Endogenous opioids and naloxone-reversible depression of pain reflexes. *Science, 212,* 689–691.

Williams, B. A. (1983). Another look at contrast in multiple schedules. *Journal of the Experimental Analysis of Behavior, 39,* 345–384.

Williams, B. A. (1988). Reinforcement, choice, and response strength. In R. C. Atkinson, R. J. Herrnstein, G. Lindzey, & R. D. Luce (Eds.), *Stevens' handbook of experimental psychology: Vol. 2. Learning and cognition* (pp. 167–244). New York: Wiley.

Williams, B. A., & Dunn, R. (1991). Preference for conditioned reinforcement. *Journal of the Experimental Analysis of Behavior, 55,* 37–46.

Williams, D. A., Butler, M. M., & Overmier, J. B. (1990). Expectancies of reinforcer location and quality as cues for a conditional discrimination in pigeons. *Journal of Experimental Psychology: Animal Behavior Processes, 16,* 3–13.

Williams, D. A., & Overmier, J. B. (1988a). Backward inhibitory conditioning with signaled and unsignaled unconditioned stimuli: Distribution of trials across days and intertrial interval. *Journal of Experimental Psychology: Animal Behavior Processes, 14,* 26–35.

Williams, D. A., & Overmier, J. B. (1988b). Some types of conditioned inhibitors carry collateral excitatory associations. *Learning and Motivation, 19,* 345–368.

Williams, D. A., Travis, G. M., & Overmier, J. B. (1986). Within-compound associations modulate the relative effectiveness of differential and Pavlovian conditioned inhibition procedures. *Journal of Experimental Psychology: Animal Behavior Processes, 12,* 351–362.

Williams, D. R. (1965). Classical conditioning and incentive motivation. In W. F. Prokasy (Ed.), *Classical conditioning.* New York: Appleton-Century-Crofts.

Williams, D. R., & Williams, H. (1969). Automaintenance in

the pigeon: Sustained pecking despite contingent non-reinforcement. *Journal of the Experimental Analysis of Behavior, 12,* 511–520.

Willson, R. J., & Wilkie, D. M. (1991). Discrimination training facilitates pigeons' performance on one-trial-per-day delayed matching of key locations. *Journal of the Experimental Analysis of Behavior, 55,* 201–212.

Wilson, M. I., & Bermant, G. (1972). An analysis of social interaction in Japanese quail *(Coturnix coturnix japonica). Animal Behaviour, 20,* 252–258.

Wilson, P. N., & Pearce, J. M. (1990). Selective transfer of responding in conditional discriminations. *Quarterly Journal of Experimental Psychology, 42B,* 41–58.

Winter, J., & Perkins, C. C. (1982). Immediate reinforcement in delayed reward learning in pigeons. *Journal of the Experimental Analysis of Behavior, 38,* 169–179.

Wolfe, J. B. (1934). The effect of delayed reward upon learning in the white rat. *Journal of Comparative and Physiological Psychology, 17,* 1–21.

Wolpe, J. (1990). *The practice of behavior therapy.* (4th ed.). New York: Pergamon.

Woods, S. C. (1991). The eating paradox: How we tolerate food. *Psychological Review, 98,* 488–505.

Woodworth, R. S., & Schlosberg, H. (1954). *Experimental psychology.* New York: Holt, Rinehart and Winston.

Worsham, R. W., & D'Amato, M. R. (1973). Ambient light, white noise, and monkey vocalization as sources of interference in visual short-term memory of monkeys. *Journal of Experimental Psychology, 99,* 99–105.

Wright, A. A. (1990). Markov choice processes in simultaneous matching-to-sample at different levels of discriminability. *Animal Learning & Behavior, 18,* 277–286.

Wright, A. A., Cook, R. G., Rivera, J. J., Sands, S. F., & Delius, J. D. (1988). Concept learning by pigeons: Matching-to-sample with trial-unique video picture stimuli. *Animal Learning & Behavior, 16,* 436–444.

Wright, A. A., & Sands, S. F. (1981). A model of detection and decision processes during matching to sample by pigeons: Performance with 88 different wavelengths in delayed and simultaneous matching tasks. *Journal of Experimental Psychology: Animal Behavior Processes, 7,* 191–216.

Wright, A. A., Shyan, M. R., & Jitsumori, M. (1990). Auditory *same/different* concept learning by monkeys. *Animal Learning & Behavior, 18,* 287–294.

Wright, A. A., Urcuioli, P. J., Sands, S. F., & Santiago, H. C. (1981). Interference of delayed matching to sample in pigeons: Effects of interpolation at different periods

within a trial and stimulus similarity. *Animal Learning & Behavior, 9,* 595–603.

Yerkes, R. M., & Morgulis, S. (1909). The method of Pavlov in animal psychology. *Psychological Bulletin, 6,* 257–273.

Yoerg, S. I., & Kamil, A. C. (1982). Response strategies in the radial arm maze: Running around in circles. *Animal Learning & Behavior, 10,* 530–534.

Zalaquett, C. P., & Parker, L. A. (1989). Further evidence that CTAs produced by lithium and amphetamine are qualitatively different. *Learning and Motivation, 20,* 413–427.

Zamble, E., Hadad, G. M., Mitchell, J. B., & Cutmore, T. R. H. (1985). Pavlovian conditioning of sexual arousal: First- and second-order effects. *Journal of Experimental Psychology: Animal Behavior Processes, 11,* 598–610.

Zeiler, M. D. (1987). On optimal choice strategies. *Journal of Experimental Psychology: Animal Behavior Processes, 13,* 31–39.

Zener, K. (1937). The significance of behavior accompanying conditioned salivary secretion for theories of the conditioned response. *American Journal of Psychology, 50,* 384–403.

Zentall, T. R., Edwards, C. A., Moore, B. S., & Hogan, D. E. (1981). Identity: The basis for both matching and oddity learning in pigeons. *Journal of Experimental Psychology: Animal Behavior Processes, 7,* 70–86.

Zentall, T. R., Hogan, D. E., & Edwards, C. A. (1984). Cognitive factors in conditional learning by pigeons. In H. L. Roitblat, T. G. Bever, & H. S. Terrace (Eds.), *Animal cognition.* Hillsdale, NJ: Erlbaum.

Zentall, T. R., Jagielo, J. A., Jackson-Smith, P. & Urcuioli, P. J. (1987). Memory codes in pigeon short-term memory: Effects of varying the number of sample and comparison stimuli. *Learning and Motivation, 18,* 21–33.

Zentall, T. R., Steirn, J. N., & Jackson-Smith, P. (1990). Memory strategies in pigeons' performance of a radial-arm-maze analog task. *Journal of Experimental Psychology: Animal Behavior Processes, 16,* 358–371.

Zentall, T. R., Urcuioli, P. J., Jagielo, J. A., & Jackson-Smith, P. (1989). Interaction of sample dimension and sample-comparison mapping on pigeons' performance of delayed conditional discriminations. *Animal Learning & Behavior, 17,* 172–178.

Zimmer-Hart, C. L., & Rescorla, R. A. (1974). Extinction of Pavlovian conditioned inhibition. *Journal of Comparative and Physiological Psychology, 86,* 837–845.

Zoladek, L., & Roberts, W. A. (1978). The sensory basis of spatial memory in the rat. *Animal Learning & Behavior, 6,* 77–81.

Name Index

Subject Index